For Loren, whose elegant likeness appears on the upper front cover, and Pat, whose portrait on the lower right is a travesty.

Fondly

Dan

14/011/26

The End of Serfdom

Russian Research Center Studies, 75

The End of Serfdom

Nobility and Bureaucracy in Russia, 1855-1861

Daniel Field

Harvard University Press,
Cambridge, Massachusetts
London, England
1976

Library of Congress Cataloging in Publication Data
Field, Daniel, 1938-
   The end of serfdom.
   (Russian Research Center studies; 75)
   Bibliography: p.
   Includes index.
   1. Land tenure—Russia. I. Title. II. Series:
Harvard University. Russian Research Center. Stud-
ies; 75.
HD715.F47   1976   333.1'0947   75-23191
ISBN 0-674-25240-3

To the memory of
Caroline Crosby Field
and
Margaret Swain Beecher,
who encouraged me

Acknowledgments

In working for more than a decade on the abolition of serfdom, I have accumulated great and numerous debts of gratitude. I want first of all to thank the various institutions that supported my research and writing. I have had fellowships from the Foreign Area Fellowship Program, the Fulbright-Hays Program, the Inter-University Committee on Travel Grants (now known as the International Research and Exchanges Board); research fellowships at the History Faculty of Moscow State University and the Russian Research Center, Harvard University; a senior fellowship from the Russian Institute, Columbia University; and a grant-in-aid from the American Council of Learned Societies. Most recently, Barnard College, Columbia University, has joined in sponsoring this book, for which I am grateful to the college's Committee on Travel and Research and to its chairman, Dean LeRoy Breunig.

I am beholden most of all to the Russian Research Center, which has lavished financial support upon me over the years. No less important, it has given me moral support from the very beginning of my career as a historian. It has housed me, in my working capacity, by providing the commodious office in which I wrote most of this book. It has fed me in its justly famous lunchroom. Now it stands sponsor to this book. I could not list all the members of the center who have favored me with encouragement, advice, and affection, but I would like to single out a few who have made a special contribution to this unique scholarly environment: the successive directors, the late Merle Fainsod, Abram Bergson, Richard Pipes, and Adam Ulam; the present deputy director, Edward L. Keenan; Mary Towle, Helen Parsons, Rose DiBenedetto, Susan Gardos, Curlie May Black, Leonard Kirsch, Mark Pinson, and Sanford Lieberman.

I also want to pay tribute to the zealous assistance I had from librarians and archivists in the institutions where I did my research: the Harvard College Library, the Harvard Law School Library, the Library of the Russian Research Center, the Library of Congress, the Butler Library of Columbia University, the New York Public Library, the Lenin Library in Moscow, the Gor'kii Library of Moscow University, the Library of the Academy of Sciences and the Saltykov-Shchedrin Library in Leningrad, the Central State Archive of the October Revolution and Socialist Construction in Moscow, and the Central State Archive and Pushkin House in Leningrad. Special thanks are also due to E. Willis Brooks and Robert C. Williams for providing me with material.

A number of friends and colleagues have been kind enough to read part or all of one or more versions of this text. Richard Pipes first encouraged me to become a historian and joined with Alexander Gerschenkron in giving a *nihil obstat* to the dissertation from which this book derives. I also want to thank Harriet Beecher Field, Jonathan Beecher, Abbott Gleason, Leopold Haimson, Marc Raeff, Loren Graham, S. Frederick Starr, Arcadius Kahan, and Richard Wortman for their comments and suggestions. They are due much of the credit for this book's merits.

I am also grateful to Judith Burton, Brenda Sens, Mary Towle, Gwendolyn Andrews, Rose DiBenedetto, Helen Constantine, Elizabeth Mead, and Susan Dimitris for turning a succession of manuscripts into handsome typescript.

Last, and most important, I want to pay tribute here to Professor Petr Andreevich Zaionchkovskii of Moscow University. I am sure there is much in these pages of which he will not approve and little that he could not make better, yet it is beyond doubt that his help and guidance to a young and stumbling scholar made this book possible. He is renowned as the greatest authority on the political history of nineteenth-century Russia, and especially on the abolition of serfdom. I can testify that his erudition is more than matched by his enthusiasm, his wisdom, and his generosity of spirit. At Moscow University he served as my *rukovoditel'*, which literally means "guide." If every young historian could have such a guide, and be worthy of him, we would understand the past much better than we do.

Barnard, Vermont   Daniel Field

Contents

A Note on Translation, Transliteration, and Transcription

The subject matter of this book presents problems to anyone who deals with it in English, because the most important terms have no counterparts in our experience or in our language. The group that I call "the nobility" here is usually called "the gentry" in English. I followed this usage for some years, but have now abandoned it for a combination of substantive and practical reasons. "Gentry" suggests an informal category of men enjoying esteem and local power. The Russian *dvorianstvo* was a legal category established by the state, and many of its members were bereft of esteem, power, and wealth. Russians who spoke French called the dvorianstvo "la noblesse," emphasizing that it was first of all a hereditary caste. Furthermore, I must use an English equivalent for dvorianstvo and its derivatives thousands of times in this book, and "gentry" is nonproductive; it does not yield a convenient adjective or a noun designating individual members.

Other words present problems of their own. *Obrok* and *barshchina* are usually rendered in English as "quitrent" and "corvée," but I believe these two words have the wrong connotations for the American ear and have used transliterated forms instead. By unfortunate coincidence, "estate" is the English for two distinct words in Russian, *imenie* (i.e., manor) and *soslovie* (as in the expression, "estate of the realm"). I have resolved these problems by consistently leaving a few terms in transliterated Russian and by uniformly using the same English words for certain others. A list of these equivalents with their Russian or English counterparts follows this note.

I adhere to the system of transliteration used in the publications of the Russian Research Center, except for the omission of the soft sign in the names of provinces and provincial capitals as they occur in the text. If a family name is variously spelled, I use one form in the text and follow the original in the footnotes and bibliography.

American scholarly practice requires a strict observance of the orthographic peculiarities of the original. Soviet scholars usually render everything in modern orthography, denying the upper case to God himself (but not to Perun'). I have transliterated everything as if the original were in modern orthography, but follow the peculiarities of the original as regards capitalization and spelling. In quotations, all italicized portions are italicized or otherwise emphasized in the original, and all words and phrases emphasized in the original are italicized here. Apart from one or two exceptions indicated in the footnotes, the only exception is *vysochaishii* and other adjectives referring to the tsar, which were routinely emphasized in the documents of the Imperial bureaucracy.

Glossary

Translated terms

allotment	*nadel*
amelioration of the way of life	*uluchshenie byta*
arbiter of the peace	*mirovoi posrednik*
cartage	*podvoz*
Civil Division (of the Ministry of Internal Affairs)	*Zemskii otdel*
cut-outs	*otrezki*
district	*uezd*
dues	*povinnost', povinnosti*
Editorial Commission	*Redaktsionnye komissii*
estate (of the realm)	*soslovie*
household serfs	*dvorovye liudi*
marshal (of the nobility)	*predvoditel' (dvorianstva)*
nobility	*dvorianstvo*
noble(s), nobleman, -men	*dvorianin*, pl. *dvoriane*
plot, household plot	*usad'ba*
proprietary	*pomeshchich'i*
province	*guberniia*
provincial board	*gubernskoe prisutstvie*
rank	*chin*
serfdom	*krepostnoe pravo*

Transliterated terms

barshchina	dues rendered in labor
desiatina	2.7 acres
muzhik	peasant, often a pejorative
obrok	dues in cash or kind
pereobrochka	redetermination of dues
pomeshchik	owner of an estate with serfs
reviziia	census, for taxation
sanovnik	dignitary, high official
tiaglo	a unit of two or three adults, used for the allocation of land and obligations

The End of Serfdom

Introduction

I have called this book *The End of Serfdom* to draw attention to the particular contribution it makes. In it I seek to explain how a centuries-old system of bondage, pervading every aspect of Russian life, met its end. Other historians have examined most of the political and social events with which I deal. Yet they have treated the abolition of serfdom not as an end, but as a beginning. They have searched the events of 1855-1861 for an understanding of later tendencies: the agrarian crisis of the 1890s, the rise of heavy industry, political movements around the turn of the century, and so on. Before 1917, political considerations prompted this search. Most historians of the reform era saw the abolition of serfdom as Imperial Russia's greatest accomplishment. They sought to encourage the regime to new feats of reform by showing that this accomplishment was the fruit of collaboration among enlightened bureaucrats, public men, and journalists, at least implying that this collaboration should be renewed. The spirit that prevailed is clear in *The Great Reform*, a six-volume collection of articles published on the fiftieth anniversary of the promulgation of the reform. Some of the contributors to the collection were critical or even caustic about particular reformers or aspects of the reform. Yet the purpose of the collection, as both tone and format indicated, was celebration. The contributors were seeking objects of emulation and heroes. They were increasingly prone to disagree about who should be admitted to the pantheon of reform, but not about the importance of building and maintaining the pantheon itself.

After the October Revolution, and to some extent even before, historians ceased celebrating the reform, but they continued to face forward from the vantage point of 1861. In his *Abolition of Serfdom in Russia*, Zaionchkovskii, the greatest authority on the subject, devotes only one chapter to the preparation of the reform. Robinson and Gerschenkron both proceed from the Statutes of 1861 and follow out their consequences over the ensuing fifty-six years. This emphasis upon consequences made the best of sense. The very language of some articles of the statutes was more important for the Russia of 1900 than most of the disputes discussed in this book. Yet to emphasize the implementation of the reform is to turn from the reform process itself and to maintain, in a very different spirit, the perspective of prerevolutionary historians.

Furthermore, to seek embryos of future developments in the reform era has entailed concentrating on the winners. Historians have neglected those who vacillated, equivocated, and lost. This neglect has been all the easier because, once the abolition of serfdom was safely enacted, the losers were reticent about their recent activities. Yet there is abundant material about these activities, and this material must be a part of any comprehensive rendering of the reform process. Consider, for example, the Secret Committee (later called the Main Committee) on the Peasant Question, which figures prominently in Chapters 2, 4, and 8 of this book. This committee of influential ministers, courtiers, and generals, serving directly under the tsar, was formally in charge of the reform from early 1857 through the promulgation of the Statutes of February 19, 1861. Its journal was published in an excellent edition in 1915, and its archive is well preserved. The committee was a consistent loser. It opposed the initial commitment to the reform of serfdom and the subsequent reformulation of policy that produced the principles underlying the eventual legislation. The responsibility for drafting this legislation was wrested from the committee, and when the complete draft finally came before it, it was able to impose few changes. Whenever an issue was squarely joined, the committee capitulated. Yet it is important to investigate these acts of capitulation, as well as the committee's ephemeral triumphs and instances of its collaboration with the reformers, in order to understand the legislative process. Furthermore, the committee and its potential influence were powerful considerations in the minds of the authors of the reform legislation. To focus solely upon these authors is to produce tableaux in which the protagonists are brightly lit while their antagonists are in deep shadow. Indeed, by setting up these tableaux, as also by emphasizing the implementation and consequences of the reform, historians have turned away from the first question they must answer.

The first question about the abolition of serfdom is, How did *this*

reform emerge from *that* regime? How did a cautious and
traditionalist regime find the courage and the means to destroy the
fundamental institution of Russian life, and to do so in despite of
the nobility, the acknowledged first bastion of the Russian throne?
Historians facing forward in time from the vantage point of 1861
are not well prepared to answer this question. They have tended,
indeed, to explain it away by minimizing the distance between the
terms of the reform and the disposition of the regime and of
educated society. Initially, they exaggerated the force of
abolitionist sentiment and the influence of reformers, with more or
less emphasis on the zeal of the tsar-liberator himself. More
recently, and more wisely, they have emphasized the affinities
between the reform legislation and the ways of serfdom, showing
that the legislation "plundered" the peasantry and maintained the
sway of bureaucrats and landowners. Yet in 1855-1857, no one
who exercised authority or hoped for influence suggested anything
so thoroughgoing as the legislation promulgated in 1861, for the
distance between the principles of the reform and the values of the
regime, prior to 1861 and even afterwards, was very great. One
measure of this distance is the situation of the reformers
themselves; they occupied secondary and tenuous positions during
the reform era, and their detractors enjoyed high office.

While the reformers' influence within the administration was
limited, their influence upon historians has been excessive. It suited
the reformers both to minimize the extent of the landed nobility's
opposition to their views and to exaggerate the vigor, determination and number of the opponents they did acknowledge. To
demonstrate their own loyal service, they represented these opponents, bureaucrats and landowners alike, as conspirators who
sought to thwart the tsar's true will and encroach upon his autocratic authority. The reformers' canards and their oblique praise
of themselves have passed into scholarly literature without much
modification, so that historians still represent the controversy
over the reform as a struggle between "liberals" and "*krepostniki*,"
or adherents of serfdom. Yet if these terms are used with precision
and consistency, it is nearly impossible to find an unequivocal
liberal or krepostnik even marginally involved in the legislative
process.

In this book, I follow the progress of the reform of serfdom and
the reverberations of that progress in Russian society. I approach
the abolition of serfdom not as the beginning of a new era, but as
the end of an old era. To understand what men did, and why, I look
to the particular controversies in which they were engaged and also
to the period just preceding. To understand motives, it is more
useful to face backward than forward. Indeed, an explanation of the

end of serfdom necessarily draws attention to some of the distinctive and important traits of serfdom in its last phase.

Three of these cardinal traits will be particularly important throughout this book. One is the political culture of nineteenth-century Russian autocracy. Some historians emphasize the views and character of the autocrat himself; others treat the administration as an emanation of social and economic forces. Neither approach is much use in understanding how serfdom came to be abolished. It is more important to appreciate the distinctive patterns of political behavior, within the bureaucracy and in educated society, that derived from the way in which sovereign power was held and exercised. These patterns flourished, like autocracy itself, in association with serfdom; like autocracy, they persisted while serfdom was being abolished.

The nobility's attitude to the autocracy was one part of a second cardinal trait, a complex of attitudes that together made up the mentality of the nineteenth-century Russian serfholder. Russian nobles, naturally enough, tried to protect and promote their interests during the reform era. To understand their behavior, it is important to see how serfdom determined their understanding of where their interests lay by shaping their conceptions of the marketplace, the regime, the peasantry, and the nobility itself.

The mentality of the serfholders was the product of their experience of serfdom. Yet even those nobles who were most imbued with it were subject to a tension between attitudes drawn from experience and their own cultural values. Herzen described how this tension gripped young Russians of his generation—which was, by and large, the generation of the authors of the reform legislation and of their opponents.

What gave them pause was the complete contradiction between the words they were taught and life as it was lived around them. Teachers, books, the university said one thing, and to this the mind and heart responded. Parents, relatives and their whole milieu said something else, to which the mind and heart did not assent—but the powers-that-be and financial advantage did assent to this latter.

And Herzen went on to insist that the contradiction between *vospitanie* and *nravy*—that is, between inculcated values and the ways of daily life, or what the French call *l'education* and *les moeurs*—was greater in servile Russia than anywhere else.[1] This contradiction was another cardinal trait of servile Russia and, like the others, persisted into the reform era. It affected all educated Russians, for abolitionists had no monopoly of minds and hearts or even books, and they, too, had to reckon with complacent relatives and the powers-that-be. I will show that this contradiction played a major role in the government's initial commitment to a reform of serfdom. This commitment did not narrow the gap between *vospitanie* and *nravy*, but it turned the "contradiction" into an open conflict, to be waged on intermediate terrain. The exponents of practical experience had to articulate and adapt their views, while those who cherished abstract, cosmopolitan values had to bring them down to earth. Serfdom had not provided much preparation for either task.

To understand the abolition of serfdom, then, it is important to appreciate long-standing habits and attitudes formed under serfdom. Yet that is not enough. The actions of institutions, groups, and individuals were also shaped by immediate events, which entail a very different level of inquiry. To return to the question, How did *this* reform emerge from *that* regime? the best short answer would be, "In stages." It is essential to identify these stages in order to comprehend the astonishing reversals of course that are characteristic of both nobility and bureaucracy in this period. For example, the rapid acquiescence of the nobility to the loss of privileges is an astonishing phenomenon. Close scrutiny shows that the nobility was not, in fact, as compliant as historians have supposed, but it was more compliant than we would expect or the regime did expect. This compliance had its roots in the nobility's experience of serfdom and can be understood in terms of the cardinal traits of the servile era. Yet it also constituted a series of responses to particular events. The nobility never did assent to the reform enacted in 1861 nor even, by and large, to the very different reform program of 1857. Many nobles did assent—more exactly, they did not protest when officials held that they had assented— to an amalgam of the program of 1857 and their own mis-apprehensions, with many of the latter foisted upon them by these same officials. To understand the act of assent we have to understand not only the forces for compliance but also the object of assent. More generally, it is important to establish the particular circumstances to which a group or institution was responding. It was not the system enacted in 1861 that provided the agenda for the controversies of 1858-1860 in the press and among the nobility, it was the government's nebulous and moderate program of 1857. This program and its distance from the legislation of 1861 must be kept in mind; it was the manifest inadequacy of this program, coupled with a formal, public commitment to a reform of serfdom, that impelled the regime to adopt a far more venturesome program in 1858 and to enact it, with substantial modifications, in 1861.

My analysis, then, proceeds with one eye on long-standing attitudes and the other on immediate circumstances. As a result, my answers to various questions are different from those that other historians have offered, and they are usually more complex. There is always a temptation to abandon complexities in favor of simple and forceful explanations, as a distinguished historian of Russia has observed with feeling.

What historian . . . faced with the contradictory quality of most historical evidence (and Russia, one should remember, is the classic country of contradictions), has not had to face the temptation to improve the coherence and persuasiveness of his account by ignoring or softening the contradictory nature of the material he has before him?[2]

I have resisted this temptation as best I can by maintaining a consistent skepticism. I avoid making inferences from abstractions, such as the spirit of the age or the prevailing socioeconomic formation. I believe that I understand that spirit and that formation reasonably well. This understanding can illuminate the motives and actions of particular individuals and institutions, but it cannot explain them. Explanation must come from the sources.

The sources on which this book rests are to be found, in large part, in Soviet archives; in still larger part, they are printed sources that are scarcely more accessible or familiar than manuscripts. Yet the important questions concerning the abolition of serfdom cannot be answered simply by the presentation of new or neglected sources. Primary sources, as Marc Bloch observes, do not speak to us at all unless they are properly questioned. The bulk of this study consists of the persistent cross-questioning of sources.

I expect that most historians will accept the details of the interpretation that emerges from this interrogation of sources, but they may be disturbed, as I am, by the over-all picture. What is disquieting is not the interpretation of particular episodes, but the components that seem to be missing from the whole. Soviet historians speak with confidence of the "feudal formation" and the "ruling class" in nineteenth-century Russia. American historians tend to avoid these terms, but they speak with no less confidence of "bureaucracy," "ideology," and "modernization." Underlying these differences of vocabulary, however, are common expectations which historians of all schools and nations share and which these terms evoke. We are not prepared for a modern society that lacked any significant quantity of power outside the administrative hierarchy. We know that any ongoing sociopolitical system must have what Mannheim called an ideology. It is disturbing to find that basic elements we expect are insignificant or missing, as they were in mid-century Imperial Russia. Latter-day serfdom, for all its tenacity, lacked the support of an ideology; indeed, the ideology of serfdom was most fully articulated in the debates about what should succeed it. Russia's nobles, as they appear in this book, display more truculence than is usually attributed to them, but also less cohesion and less political capacity. Their behavior was very far indeed from what might be expected from an established and acknowledged elite caste. It turns out that the senior bureaucrats involved in the reform did not possess and could not command the skills we properly call "bureaucratic." Lower-level officials and rank outsiders were able to play a decisive role in drawing up the reform, largely because of their mastery of these same skills. And, in the interests of the reform, they were devious, dissembling, and conniving; they made effective use of the manipulative arts we would expect from entrenched officials hostile to reform. The muted conflict between the reformers and the senior officials is a long tale of cunning doves and innocent serpents.

Again and again in the history of Imperial Russia, conventional expectations are confounded, plausible assumptions collapse, and stereotypes turn inside out. Therein lie many difficulties and much fascination for the historian. These anomalies should not be explained away. They should be mastered, through patient research and careful analysis, as I have tried to do in this book.

Servile Russia

1

This chapter provides a background for the narrative and analysis that make up the balance of the book. Since the book is a mixture of social and political history, the first section of this chapter gives a composite portrait of the nobility, and the last outlines the government's practices and policies concerning serfdom. The middle section, devoted to manorial agriculture, should make the debates of 1855-1861 and the attitudes they reflected more intelligible. In all three sections, the discussion sometimes anticipates aspects of these debates, but it is primarily intended to provide a general understanding of the structure of serfdom in the reign of Nicholas I (1825-1855), to outline the distinctive polity associated with serfdom, and to indicate the peculiarities of the servile economy.

The Nobility

The Russian nobility, or *dvorianstvo*, was the first estate of the realm; in ceremonial terminology, it was the *blagorodnoe soslovie*, meaning that it was indeed "noble"—honorable and generous as well as privileged. Alternatively, in Speranskii's definition, the nobility was "a handful of idlers who, God knows why and to what end, have grabbed all the rights and advantages."[1] Speranskii later discovered a rationale for the nobility's rights, but he was certainly correct about its monopoly of advantages. According to V. P. Botkin, these rights and advantages, and first of all the right to hold serfs, had fatally corrupted the nobility. Noble landowners were "parasites," equally remote from civic responsibility and the life of the common people. Yet Botkin had to concde that "Russian poetry and literature and, in general, that measure of civilization which has made it possible for us to emerge on the European path of history emerged from that same [noble] estate."[2] Indeed, in the last century of serfdom, almost every Russian who achieved any literary or political celebrity was of noble origin. For the few who were not, like Botkin and Speranskii, their social origin was a crucial biographical fact.

The hereditary nobles who exercised this sway numbered some 300,000 males in 1858. The nobility of all kinds, including "personal nobles" who could not hold serfs and a large number of squires in the western provinces who were ennobled as a by-product of the partitions of Poland, comprised about one and one-half percent of the population of the empire. In the thirty-six Great Russian and Ukrainian provinces, there were roughly 100,000 noblemen, who made up less than half of one percent of the male population.[3]

Hereditary nobility was a formal legal status, transmitted patrilineally to both males and females. Noble status could, however, be acquired automatically by gaining a specified rank in the civil and military services.[4] Many nobles resented this open access to their ranks, and their spokesmen complained about it. Karamzin, for example, wanted to reverse the practice, reserving certain offices for the nobility and eliminating ennoblement through office-holding.[5] The state responded to this resentment by raising the requirements for the acquisition of noble status, thereby reducing the instances for ennoblement but maintaining the principle involved.

The state did not inquire into the antibureaucratic sentiment that underlay the nobility's resentment. This animosity to *chinovniki*, or functionaries, found wide expression in the century preceding the abolition of serfdom and represents, on the face of things, a paradox. All nobles enjoyed privileged status because their ancestors or they themselves had served the state; the overwhelming majority of them still devoted at least part of their lives to state service. And the regime and its officials could scarcely have been more accommodating to the serfholding nobility. This paradox is worth dwelling on because of its significance for the behavior and attitudes of the nobility once the regime decided to move against serfdom.

Antibureaucratic sentiment is, in some measure, a by-product of bureaucracy itself, and the experience of modern American society suggests that those who get special benefits from the bureaucracy are still prone to complain about bureaucrats. Furthermore, while Russian nobles enjoyed patronage in their role as a serfholders, they suffered frustration and exasperation along with other Russians in

the law courts and bureaus. The lower reaches of the administration were underfunded and understaffed,[6] but "undergovernment"
was nonetheless perceived as maladministration and malfeasance
and blamed on the functionaries. Yet the nobility's hostility to the
bureaucracy derived its cutting edge and wide spread from considerations of status. The hereditary noble railed against the
functionary, even though the nobility and the upper bureaucracy
were largely coextensive and never in conflict, because by "functionary" he meant upstart, or *homo novus*.[7] This kind of fulmination
is as old as settled elites and is, perhaps, a natural emanation of
elite status. In servile Russia, where the middle class was weak
and quiescent, the functionary was the only plausible target. The
nobility's antibureaucratic sentiment did not derive from the
conflicts on fundamental social and economic issues and, unless it
and its exponents underwent a transformation, it could not serve
to galvanize the nobility into concerted political action. For
throughout the servile era, antibureaucratic sentiment and
deference to governmental authority went hand in hand.
Karamzin, who gave classic expression to this sentiment, yielded to
no one in his devotion to the autocrat and to the principle of
autocracy. And in his dictum that what Russia needed was fifty
good governors, he singled out the official who was the cynosure of
the provincial nobility. However much contempt squires might
show for subordinate officials, they made much of the governor,
showing him the flattery and deference due to an autocrat in
miniature. The nobility's antibureaucratic sentiment, then, was
enduring and widespread but was nonetheless superficial.

Nobles enjoyed immunity from direct taxation and corporal
punishment and the privilege, unique to themselves, of holding and
acquiring serfs. Many of them, however, could not avail themselves
of this privilege.[8] Indeed, in the decades before the abolition of
serfdom, a considerable number of nobles decided or were obliged
to give up their serfs; in Riazan Province, for example, some 1700
nobles (or their descendants) ceased to hold serfs between 1833 and
1857.[9] Nonetheless, when contemporaries spoke of "the nobility"
they usually meant the serfholders, ignoring the legal demarcation
of the estate. Nobles without serfs were not thought to have a
common interest with the rest of the nobility, and were excluded by
law from participating in the corporate institutions of their estate.
An eighteenth-century nobleman had declared that "nobiliary
dignity is regarded in our country as something holy, which
distinguishes a man from his fellows, for it gives to him and his
descendents the right to hold full sway over their own kind."[10] The
nineteenth century did not produce any real alternative to this
definition of "nobiliary dignity."

Some nobles were dismayed that their estate, derived from government service and delimited by bondage, lacked the qualities of a true aristocracy. Admiral Chichagov wrote, for example, that

"noble" or "gentry" . . . do not have any definite significance in Russia, first of all because the real nobility of feeling which is essential to them is incompatible with slavery; then, too, because in Russia there is no concept of authentic social hierarchies. . . . The only distinguishing privilege of the [noble] class consists in the right granted to it to buy and sell its own kind. To engage in this repulsive trade, it is enough to have the rank of major, which is most commonly attained through intrigues and self-abasement. Valets, cooks, and footmen have been known to have been elevated to nobiliary dignity in this way. . . . There is a foul seat of slavery to be found in the so-called Russian nobility. My poor country has no constitution except serfdom, because it is the only condition which accords with the natural inclinations of the nation.[11]

Chicagov and those like him who found the nobility insufficiently aristocratic had an idealized notion of nobility, derived from English examples, a notion of dignity and independent authority that is common even today. They were not aware of the extent to which the nobility in other continental countries derived from service to the state and depended upon official salaries.[12]

Whatever its aristocratic qualities, the Russian nobility was defined by serfdom. Consequently, when, in 1857-1858, the government undertook to abolish serfdom, that commitment presented a threat to the status as well as the revenues of the nobility. This threat was especially disorienting because it came from the state, which had fostered the serfholders for generations. Because the state was the sponsor and patron of serfdom, and the nobility was defined and delimited by serfdom, state and nobility were bound together. But which party was in bondage? The tsar's counsellors generally argued that the state must rely upon the nobility, which was, as Semen Vorontsov put it,

the direct mediator between the sovereign and the people. It helps to keep the people under restraint and serves as the only support for the throne. It is necessary to inspire the people with a profound respect for the nobility. . . . It was only through the humiliation and destruction of the nobility that the Girondists and Jacobins managed to overthrow the monarchy in France.[13]

Many subsequent commentators reiterated this notion of the state's dependence upon the nobility. Alexander Herzen, however, construed the relationship differently. In the first publication of his

Free Russian Press he argued, in terms surprisingly reminiscent of Chichagov, that by its acceptance of serfdom the nobility was enslaved to the state. He called upon Russia's nobles to undertake emancipation, not only to avert a dreadful peasant insurrection, but also to recover their own independence and dignity.

Could not the tsar say, "You want to be free? What's the point? Take *obrok* from your peasants, take their labor, take their children as servants, cut back their land, sell them, buy, resettle, beat, whip them, and if you get tired, send them to me at the police station, I will gladly whip them for you. Isn't that enough for you? You want to know honor? Our predecessors yielded you a part of our autocracy; by binding free men to you, they cut off the hem of their purple robe and threw it over the poverty of your fathers. You did not renounce it, you, too, are covered by it and live under it—so how can you and I talk of freedom? Stay bound to the tsar, so long as orthodox Christians are bound to you."[14]

There is more than satire in this imaginary speech; it expressed the tacit compact by which government and society functioned. The principal elements of the compact were autocracy and serfdom, which affected every part of the body politic. However, while nobles were loath to take a self-reliant stance in relation to the state, as Chichagov and Herzen complained, the relationship was not so one-sided as they represented it to be. The government dominated and patronized the nobility, but the nobility permeated and dominated the government. In the first half of the nineteenth century, the government and the nobility were distinct conceptually, but not in practice. Their relationship was not so much an embodiment as a parody of the Marxist representation of the ruling class and its executive committee.

The Russian nobility, however, was a legal estate, not a class in the Marxist sense. When Marx himself used the concept in political analysis, he held that a class must have a certain degree of cohesion and sense of common purpose. His discussion of the French small-holding peasantry on this count is, paradoxically, applicable to the Russian nobility under serfdom.

Insofar as millions of families live under economic conditions of existence that separate their mode of life, their interests and their culture from those of the other classes, and put them in hostile opposition to that latter, they form a class. Insofar as there is merely a local interconnection among these small-holding peasants, and the identity of their interests begets no community, no national bond and no political organization among them, they do not form a class. They are consequently incapable of enforcing their class interests in their own name. . . . They cannot represent themselves, they must be represented. Their representative must at the same time appear as their master, as an authority over them, as an unlimited governmental power that protects them against the other classes and sends them rain and sunshine from above. The political influence of the small-holding peasants, therefore, finds its final expression in the executive power subordinating society to itself.[15]

Even in its simplest Marxist usage, "class" denotes a common relationship to the means of production, and this relationship varied widely within the nobility. Many nobles were salaried officials, others were agricultural entrepreneurs, still others were rentiers of the purest type. Finally, there were a great many nobles—significant   numerically,   but   insignificant   in influence—who worked the fields and lived a common life with their few serfs. These petty proprietors were despised by their better-favored brethren, and the government made some attempt to eliminate them by acquiring their serfs. Their status as serfholding nobles counted for almost nothing because they were at one, in their culture and poverty, with the peasantry; their plight is yet another sign of the nobility's lack of cohesion and solidarity. The nobility was a coherent whole only in that almost every nobleman benefited, or believed that he benefited, from the exploitation of servile labor.

This labor force in 1858 amounted to 11,338,042 male serfs and a slightly larger total of females, constituting almost 40 percent of the population of the empire, a large but dwindling proportion. Somewhat more than half the serfs inhabited the Great Russian heartland, and many more lived in the Ukrainian and Belorussian lands acquired through the partitions of Poland. The proportion of serfs was lower in the outlying regions, and in Siberia there were scarcely any.[16] Still more uneven than their territorial distribution was their distribution among the serfholders, for four-fifths of them lived on estates of 100 or more "souls" (the tax collectors' term for males). Owners of estates with fewer than 100 souls, comprising about three-quarters of the serf-holding nobility, held less than 20 percent of the serf population; conversely, some 3500 magnates, comprising less than one-twentieth of the serfholding nobles, held more than 40 percent of all serfs.[17] These figures, as regards both the concentration of serfs in a few hands and the size of the average estate, suggest an unhealthy swollen condition that may have been a major infirmity of the servile order.

Russian serfdom, as it was systematized by Peter the Great, was an institution to compel peasants to provide revenues for the state and support for military officers and civil officials, whose service was compulsory, perpetual, and hereditary. Serfdom, then, was one aspect of the hierarchy of estates; in theory, the status of every Russian was defined according to the needs of the state, and status entailed a prescribed vocation and ascription to a particular place. The theory was very much vitiated in the last century of serfdom; as the legal and economic rigors of serfdom increased, the obligations of the serfholders were largely abolished and their privileges were augmented. Yet the rationale of serfdom was surprisingly durable; though the individual nobleman was no longer obligated to serve, nobles continued to assume their traditional role of officials supported, in cash or kind, by serfs. Some were very lavishly supported, to be sure, while others relied mainly on their salaries and on bribes, but serfdom provided vital sustenance for the upper ranks of the civil and military services.

The powers of the nobleman (in his capacity as owner of an estate with serfs he was called a *pomeshchik*) were extensive. A serf could not marry, take holy orders, enter government service, or leave the area of the estate without his master's permission, nor could he take part in civil legal actions or acquire property; on most criminal matters, he was subject to his master's manorial jurisdiction, and the master could require state officials to carry out his sentence. The serf could be sent into the army out of turn or exiled to Siberia on his master's authority, and his master would then be compensated for the loss of a laborer. A pomeshchik could freely transfer a serf to another of his villages or to service in his household. Finally, in most parts of the empire, the serf could be bought, sold, mortgaged, exchanged, given away, or inherited. Russians discussed their property rights in fellow Christians with appropriate diffidence, but Speranskii, for example, asserted that in Russian legal practice serfs were "moveable property," that is, on the same footing as horses.[18]

The laws did differentiate between serfs and horses by imposing various restrictions on the serfholder, which became more numerous and specific in the thirty years before emancipation. The serfholder could not subject serfs to excessive corporal punishment or to economic "ruin." He was responsible for their capitation tax and had to provide for them in the event of famine or disaster. He could not acquire serfs unless he had land to which they could be ascribed, nor could he, according to a variously construed act of 1827, carry out a transaction in land that would leave his serfs with less than four and a half *desiatiny* of land per male soul.[19] According to a still more ambiguous *ukaz* of 1797, he should not compel his serfs to work more than three days a week on the demesne land.[20]

The restrictions on the pomeshchik's authority were rarely enforced, and it would seem that custom and common sense protected the serfs better than the laws did. The ineffectiveness of the restrictions derived not so much from their vagueness as from the lack of the will and the machinery to enforce them. An attempt at regular enforcement was thought to undermine the pomeshchik's manorial authority and thus the authority of the state, for the pomeshchik was, in effect, an agent of the state; resistance to his authority was treason.[21] As a panegyrist put it in 1828,

I conceive a pomeshchik to be a hereditary functionary, to whom the sovereign power has given land [and] entrusted stewardship over the people there settled. He is the natural protector of these people, their local judge, their intercessor, and the guardian of the poor and orphaned; he inculcates the good and maintains order and morality.[22]

Or, as Nicholas I put it to the nobility of St. Petersburg Province in 1848, "I have no police, gentlemen; I don't like them; you are my police. Each of you is my steward."[23]

The steward was virtually autonomous, for the state had no direct relations with the serfs. Only when the pomeshchik invoked the governmental machinery or when the serfs became felons did the state acknowledge them as its own. The state counted them as tax-paying units and received them into the army, but the pomeshchik collected the soul tax and chose the recruits. Serfs did not even swear allegiance to the tsar on his accession. Most important, serfs were forbidden by law to lay their grievances before government officials. It was a crime for serfs to make a formal complaint against their master (except to charge that they were illegally enserfed). This crime was frequently committed and severely punished, although officials sometimes found it prudent to act upon serfs' complaints.[24] If the prohibition on complaints was not enough to vitiate most of the laws affecting serfdom, the circle was closed by the nobility's collective authority: most of the administrative and judicial officials charged with supervising the nobles' treatment of serfs were elected by the local nobility.

Other free estates had corporate organizations and a role in local affairs, but the nobility's organization was the most developed and its ambit was the widest. This provincial corporate organization had three components: the assembly, the district deputies, and the marshals of the nobility.

The assemblies convened every three years in the provincial capitals. They reviewed the work of the corporate officials, appropriated money, and passed resolutions. They had the unique right of petitioning the tsar about the nobility's local needs and the malfeasance of local officials. This right was not often exercised and rarely produced any result; Nicholas I, at least, consistently refused to receive deputations sent by assemblies of the nobility. The assemblies were also ceremonial and social occasions, which culminated in a ball, and it seems that the social aspect was the most important to the participants.[25] Finally, the deputies and marshals as well as certain officials of local government were elected at the assemblies.

The deputies' functions were originally limited to the verification and attestation of the status of those who became nobles by birth or through service. They did not, however, have the right to reject any would-be nobleman who met the legal requirements. In time, they acquired certain other functions in the allocation of local taxes and so on, but the office was a minor one.

The provincial marshal of the nobility was second only to the provincial governor, according to official protocol, while the district marshal was first in the district. Both provincial and district marshals were elected at the triennial provincial assembly. They were first of all corporate officials who saw to the nobility's business between assemblies; they oversaw the nobility's educational institutions and noble orphans in the province, for example. It was in their capacity as corporate officials that they were charged with enforcing the legal restrictions on the pomeshchik's authority.

Almost from the first, however, the marshals were given governmental functions as well. By the latter part of Nicholas's reign, the provincial marshal found himself sitting ex officio on a great number of provincial commissions responsible for roads, recruiting, grain reserves, and similar public concerns. On the eve of the emancipation, the marshal was a component part of the provincial bureaucracy, duly subordinated to the Minister of Internal Affairs and with an appropriate rank in the civil service. Yet he remained the elected leader of the nobility. This double role scarcely ever put much strain on the provincial marshal, however, for the administration was accommodating to the needs and point of view of his serfholding electorate, while the electorate was rarely importunate on matters of public policy.

The nobility also elected local judges and police officials from among their number. In the reign of Nicholas I, the role of the nobles was increased in the judiciary and diminished in the police, though their officials were consulted on an irregular basis about the appointment of constables. This electoral authority was under bureaucratic control, for both the corporate and the public officials elected by the nobility had to be confirmed in office by the governor or appropriate ministry. State officials were repeatedly enjoined from interfering in the elections; the governor and the provincial procurator were barred by law from the assemblies. However, the governor's superiors held him responsible for the outcome of the elections, and he could usually be trusted to produce the right results.

The power of confirmation and the governor's interference might have been sources of discord, but nobles did not show much resentment of this kind of bureaucratic control. After all, they were or had been government officials themselves. It was not their pretensions but their indifference that made for friction. The government constantly complained that they put inferior or incompetent men in both corporate and public office, and these complaints are confirmed by historians sympathetic to the nobility. In many cases the nobles did not avail themselves of their privilege, being unable to find anyone willing to assume the lower offices. An ukaz of 1832 complained that "the best nobles refuse to serve or acquiesce indifferently to the election of men who lack the qualities required. Hence judicial officials prove uninformed about the law, while abuses have come to light in police matters." Many nobles did not bother to appear at the assemblies. Another ukaz complained:

The Sovereign Emperor, upon discovering from the reports of the heads of provinces that sometimes nobles blatantly abstain from participation in the general provincial assemblies of the nobility and in elections, has been pleased to issue an Imperial Order to those concerned, in all places, strictly reaffirming precise and unfailing execution of the statutory rules; the marshals of the nobility will be called to account for any deviation from these rules.[26]

As this ukaz suggests, the work of the assemblies and of the officials they elected was compulsory service to the state.[27] The nobleman's obligation to serve the state had, of course, been abolished in 1762, and this emancipation had been ceremonially reaffirmed in the Charter of the Nobility of 1785. The individual nobleman was, indeed, almost entirely emancipated, for he was required only to participate in the assembly, provided he could meet the franchise requirements; the penalties for neglecting this obligation were mild, the most stringent sanction being exclusion from future assemblies. As an estate, however, the nobility of each province was obliged to fill various government offices, while its corporate officials had to carry out the orders of the provincial governor and the central government. The members of the assembly were, in effect, drafted into state service for the duration of the elections; they were required to wear special uniforms while they participated.

The nobility's lack of enthusiasm for elective office has been attributed to this compulsory element, but the mixed character of the office was probably more to blame. Elected officials, even the provincial marshals, were subordinate to functionaries of the state, provoking the question,

Who wants to serve when an *ispravnik*, who by law is the head of the district, the censor of morals, the guardian of morality and order, is nowadays ordered around by governors and even by their clerks, and according to their whim races like a whippet from one province to another . . . ?[28]

This combination of the woes of elective and appointive office was not appealing to a rich and well-educated nobleman, settled in the provinces in deliberate rejection of a traditional career in state service. For those ambitious nobles who sought official careers, the regular bureaucracy promised greater perquisites, more prestige, and more power. Since elective offices did not offer much scope for advancement, they fell to pensioned army officers and petty proprietors who needed the salaries to make ends meet, or else stood vacant, to be filled by government appointment. This tradition of indifference to elections and elective office would stand the nobility in bad stead when, in 1857, the government invited it to elect provincial committees to discuss the reform of serfdom.

Nobiliary institutions were also weakened by the gap between rich and poor nobles and the divergent roles the two groups played. Magnates dominated the electoral assemblies but filled elective offices with their clients among the petty squires. This long-standing tendency was augmented, paradoxically, by the law of December 6, 1831, which attempted to enhance the prestige of elective office by establishing a new franchise for assemblies of the nobility. Broadly speaking, the law stiffened the requirements for voting and lowered them for office holding, much enlarging the number of nobles who could not vote for the offices they held. To vote, a nobleman had to have won a rank in government service and to hold more than a hundred male serfs.[29] Nobles with more than five serfs and fewer than a hundred could band together to form a group holding more than a hundred and cast a single vote. The government hoped that by turning the assemblies over to a relatively few rich pomeshchiki, the rich would be prompted to invest the nobiliary institutions with their superior qualities. The nobility did not protest this purge of its ranks; indeed, assemblies expressed gratitude for this clarification of their procedure.[30]

The law of December 5 spoke the language of popular cynicism, not official rhetoric. Real noble status was not a matter of gentle birth or past services to the fatherland, it was a function of rank and serfholding. Those who held many serfs and had at least been blooded in the service of the state were full-fledged noblemen, those who held a modest number of serfs were equivocally noble, while the unfortunates who had few serfs or none, even though heroes of 1812 or descendants of Riurik, were effectively excluded from the noble estate. The law did not strive for cynicism, it simply reflected Nicholas I's conviction that nobles ought to serve the state, one form of service being the administration of serfs. Cynical or not, the law failed to revive the nobiliary institutions.

To summarize the traditional explanations, the institutions of the nobility languished because they offered almost nothing but responsibility—little money, prestige, power, or room for initiative. These explanations are persuasive, but, being embedded in the context of the times, they are essentially circular. To say that nobles shunned elective office because of a lack of prestige is a tautology, since prestige does not subsist in institutions but in the view of the beholder. Then, too, the traditional explanations apply largely to individuals, not to the nobility as a whole, and do not explain why the noble estate allowed offices affecting its members' immediate interests to be filled by incompetents. A vital and coherent interest-group does not neglect opportunities for exercising power and can always find the personnel for onerous but necessary functions.

The Russian nobility, as events surrounding the emancipation would show, was lacking in both coherence and vitality. Whether considered as a legally defined status or, more realistically, in terms of the franchise law, it was divided within itself; the very style of life of a nobleman would differ radically according to his career in government service and the number of serfs he held. Yet even these divisions within the nobility were ultimately a product of the lack of corporate vitality, since they might have been overcome if there had been the will and the necessity. There was simply no spur of necessity to mobilize the nobility.

For a social stratum, as distinct from its individual members, the principal goal of political action is control of men and goods. The cohesion and political energies of the nobility atrophied, or failed to develop, because nineteenth-century serfdom provided the nobility with a virtual monopoly of this kind of control. Few nobles were rich and fewer still had large cash incomes, but there was little private wealth in other hands, and the other estates had almost no influence on the regime. The coercive authority of the state stood squarely behind the nobles' authority over their serfs, and the state's economic policies consistently favored their interests.[31] The nobility dominated the bureaucracy and the army and, more important, almost every bureaucrat could be counted on to favor the nobility in the event of conflict. Ministers and department heads served at the pleasure of the autocrat, but they could not have been more zealous in the nobility's behalf if the nobles had selected them. It is doubtful that the nobility could have secured more for itself through the effective use of political power than it attained passively, in what seemed the nature of things. And yet, as Treitschke observed, a nonpolitical nobility is no nobility at all.[32]

Alexander Herzen argued in 1856 that the nobility was so bureaucratized and politically passive that there was no need for the government to consult its wishes about emancipation.

If the obdurate pomeshchiki and muscovite boyars are opposed, their opposition will necessarily be limited to grumbling. Why not let them babble about their discontent? To be sure, they have preached to us about unconditional submission to the Imperial power so much that it would be just to demand that they set an example. And what are their rights? They have possessed *muzhiki* and ruined them by the tsar's favor; by the tsar's disfavor they would cease to ruin them. These people have no party, their power is imaginary.[33]

Herzen's prophecy would be fulfilled within a few years. The same analysis was advanced, though very rarely, in the highest government circles. Fifty years earlier, Pavel Stroganov, reflecting on the humiliation of the nobility under Paul I, declared in the "Unofficial Committee" of Alexander I,

What is this nobility which [the other members] seem to fear? . . . The nobility in our country is made of a number of persons who have become gentlemen only by virtue of government service, who have not received any education, and who in all their thinking are not inclined to look any further than the Emperor's authority. Neither rights nor justice nor anything else can generate the mere idea of resistance in them! . . . One part lives in the country and is in a state of gross ignorance, the other, on government service, is animated by a spirit which is not dangerous; the great proprietors are not to be feared. . . . What was not done in the reign just past against justice, against the rights of these people, and against their personal security! [But] all the repressive measures were carried out with astonishing promptness, and it was the nobleman who carried out these measures, directed against his own kind and contrary to the interests and the honor of his corporate estate.[34]

Here Stroganov showed perception and the capacity to rise above the assumption, as common in Russia as elsewhere, that the elite of a nation necessarily enjoy preponderant power. If the nobility was unable to mobilize and act in despite of the regime, if, in fact, there was no significant reserve of political power outside the administrative chain of command, then it would be very much easier for the regime to move against the institution of serfdom. Stroganov did not, however, follow up on his insight. Instead, like the other counsellors to Alexander I, Nicholas I, and the newly enthroned Alexander II, he condemned serfdom in principle but could not bring himself to recommend decisive action.

The Manorial Economy

Although the institution of serfdom was much the same throughout the empire, the manorial enterprise took various forms. The organization and operation of estates varied according to the natural conditions of the area, the size of the estate itself, access to markets, and the proprietor's place of residence.[35] Rich magnates set up bureaucratic administrations in imitation of the government,[36] petty proprietors worked the land along with their serfs. The negligence of the pomeshchiki, great and small, was proverbial; they were not sedulous in the role of *homo economicus*, as one of them remarked with complacent self-mockery in his diary:

A visit to [my] steppe village for a day and a half does not deserve an eleaborate account. My reception by the peasants on their knees, hand kissing by my father's old servants and their children, the distribution of cash prizes and of the presents I brought, the satisfaction of requests, a tour of the fields, a bad dinner and a good sleep—that is the whole story of a day's visit by a lax pomeshchik in his natural state.[37]

The author of these lines was Count Kiselev; though he labored to rationalize and reorganize the administration of the state peasantry, he was willing to let his own estate run itself.

To say that the pomeshchiki were negligent does not mean that they were indulgent. Kiseleve's own serfs found the exactions of their lax pomeshchik too much to bear and made formal protest.[38] The point is that most pomeshchiki were no more than exacting; they insisted repeatedly that their peasants fulfill all their obligations, but their own efforts to secure or improve their revenues rarely went beyond making threats and imposing punishments.[39] They did not direct or instruct the peasants in the cultivation of the land. At most, they supervised the peasants' work closely, believing—with some justice—that this was the surest means of increasing income from an estate.

Because the nobility made its exactions within the framework of custom, the serf village remained, in Confino's phrase, *"propriété seigneuriale, mais domaine paysan."*[40] Peasant custom determined the configuration of the village and the fields and the phases of the cycle of cultivation; it dictated the choice of crops and of tools, for the plows, sickles, carts, and horses all belonged to the peasants. The most important characteristic of the estate was the insignificance of the proprietor's imprint on the pattern of life and work.

In this respect, as in others, the estates of Russian serfholders made a striking contrast to the slave plantations of the American South. The plantation was a commercial operation, especially in the lower South; occasionally so much land was given over to the cash crop that some of the slaves' food was purchased. Estates in servile Russia were not so oriented to commodity production, and could not have been, given the difficulty of transporting the crop to market. Most of the serfs' output went to their pomeshchik's household or to their own, and never left the estate; the emphasis was on consumption, not the market.[41] More important, however, was the character of the whole unit. American slaves might exercise responsibility and even establish a sphere of autonomy and security on the plantation, but it was a little world created by their master. The Russian village was no one's deliberate creation, but it was a peasant world; the pomeshchik was an outsider even on his ancestral estate. There was no effective limitation on his authority, and on any particular issue he was no less bound to prevail than his American counterpart. Yet his capacity to determine the pattern of life and of agriculture was comparatively small. Unless he had unusual determination and skill, he was obliged to implement his will through traditional techniques and traditional institutions. Even if the communal village institutions (which were almost universal in Great Russia), were revived by the state and perpetuated by the nobles for their own purposes, there was no need for anything similar on the plantation.

Despite his extensive powers, conferred by statute and sanctioned by usage, the pomeshchik was enmeshed in a network of traditional institutions, refractory human beings, and the exigencies of agricultural biology. It was easy to play the despot, but difficult for him to realize upon his power in a creative way, as Tolstoi's Nekliudov found to his chagrin.[42] It is for this reason that the modernization of manorial agriculture was so much discussed and so rarely attempted. The eighteenth-century agronomist

Bolotov held out the promise that a radical alteration of techniques and crops "permits [us] easily to obtain great freedom of action, to do and to undertake all that we would like, especially since we will deliver ourselves at one fell swoop from numerous annoying impediments and deficiencies."[43] On the face of things, who enjoyed more freedom of action than the pomeshchik on his estate? Yet for Bolotov, and perhaps for later pomeshchiki, the ideal of modernization represented a dream of power and freedom.

The better-educated pomeshchiki, inspired by the propaganda of western agronomists, gave much thought to the introduction of new crops and new techniques, but systematic attempts to modernize the manorial economy were rare and often abortive.[44] It was easy enough to buy a piece of agricultural machinery from the celebrated firm of Butentop; it could stand in the squire's yard in testimony to his superior culture. To alter the rotation of crops and make the concomitant improvements in the soil and livestock, however, entailed great expense and great difficulties. The initial outlay on more powerful draft animals and more sophisticated tools would entail a still larger outlay for the peasants' subsistence during the transition from the three-field cultivation of rye and oats to a more complex rotation and more demanding crops. To meet the standards of advanced agronomists, the pomeshchik would also have to reconstitute the village completely, enclosing the fields, expelling some peasants and relocating the rest in isolated farmsteads.

The peasants mounted a passive but stubborn and largely successful resistance to this kind of modernization, and understandably so. Their distrust of the pomeshchik and remoteness from him made them doubt that commercial agriculture would sustain them as well as the essentially subsistence agriculture they practiced. They could not welcome the destruction of the very pattern of village life, which the creation of farmsteads would entail. And apart from other dangers, new crops and new tools necessarily required greater effort on their part, with the benefit from this increased exploitation going to the pomeshchik.

The pomeshchik was free, to be sure, to make almost any disposition he liked on his estate. Yet he was reluctant to invoke his plenitude of power in the face of peasant resistance to innovation. He could argue that he lacked the capital to make the transition or that commercial agriculture was too risky, but these excuses were more or less specious, at least for the magnates. The most important impediment to innovation, as Confino maintains, was the "social mentality" of the nobility; the pomeshchik was constrained by the inertia and attachment to tradition for which he was quick to reproach the peasant. Like the peasant, he would blame a poor harvest on the climate or the weather, not on his own efforts and methods. Like the peasant, he would make "an appeal to experience and to the wisdom of his ancestors, who 'obtained bountiful harvests' using the procedures that some men now wanted to abolish."[45]

Among these procedures, more important than the cultivation of rye and the use of flails, was serfdom itself. Indeed, the experience of serfdom shaped the nobility's outlook on agriculture and on life. Worthy savants might argue that hired labor is superior to servile labor, but the pomeshchik knew that the labor, draft animals, and implements of his serfs cost him nothing, and he could rarely bring himself to pay out money for such things. He had little capacity to think as a venturesome investor, or, indeed, to peer over the horizon of experience. Experience taught that the way to increase revenues was to use existing structures to put more pressure on his serfs,[46] And so he left these structures—the commune, the crops and their cycle, the pattern of land use, the tools, and his own arbitrary authority—much as he found them. Serfdom was the major impediment to the modernization of Russian agriculture because of the cast of mind it imparted to the nobility.

Despite these unsuspected affinities of outlook and attitude, nobles and serfs were culturally remote, and his remoteness increased the pomeshchik's isolation and lack of influence on his own estate. Outside of the former Polish territories, nobles and serfs had a common faith and language and essentially the same ethnic make-up; there was no racial basis to serfdom as there was to American slavery. Both slaveowners and serfholders, to be sure, maintained that their authority was necessary because of the distinctive laziness and irresponsibility of the subject population; in both countries the proprietors were themselves accused of laziness and heedlessness, as if these imputations derive from bondage itself.

Yet the cultural difference between lord and serf was as deep as that between black slaves and their white masters. A century after Peter the Great, the nobility was completely westernized, except at the very bottom rung; the nobles' intellectual and social life, the details of their dress, deportment, food, and furniture were European. Technology and literary genres, forms of administration and the very language of government—all were borrowed from the West. As a whole, the nobility was as westernized as it could be while exercising power over human beings of a kind no longer known beyond the Vistula. However, the subjugation of the serfs had advanced parallel to the process of westernization, so that their exposure to cultural change was comparatively limited. Their westernization took superficial forms, such as the use of tobacco and machine-made cloth, which left their way of life and way of thinking intact.

The estate, then, was essentially a peasant village, occupied with production for consumption by traditional methods, in which the pomeshchik was a suspect, extrinsic figure vested with arbitrary power.[47] This general pattern prevailed, whatever the form of the peasants' dues. More than half the Great Russian serfs rendered *barshchina*, or dues in labor, while somewhat more than one-third paid *obrok*, or money dues.[48] On those obrok estates where there was no cultivated demesne and all the land was in peasant hands, the plowland was divided into three field, with the pasture and the hayfields usually worked in common. The peasant commune (*mir*) would divide each of the three fields into strips, scaled according to the quality of the land, and each household (*dvor*) would be allotted an appropriate number of strips in each field. The household would plow, sow, tend, and harvest its strips, each operation being timed according to custom as formulated by the mir. After setting apart enough for seed, fodder, and food, it would take the balance of the harvest to market.

This pattern also obtained on most barshchina estates, since the peasant allotments and the demesne land were divided, allotted, and cultivated in the same way;[49] the peasants were supposed to spend half their time working the demesne and in practice spent somewhat more. On some barshchina estates, labor on the demesne was determined by tasks, rather than days, but it appears that this system did not alter the customary allocation and cultivation of the land.[50] Under both barshchina and obrok, the productive unit was a peasant household working a number of scattered strips in each of the three fields.

Barshchina provided more occasions than obrok for the pomeshchik to intervene. He could impose tasks or factory labor; he could, and commonly did, reserve the best days for harvesting for work on his demesne, and he could determine the allocation of the barshchina obligation within each household. If he had the determination and the means, he could introduce new techniques and crops into the demesne or even into the peasant allotments. Barshchina was more onerous because of this arbitrary power, and was held over defaulting obrok peasants as a threat.

Obrok, like barshchina, subsumed a range of variants. Obrok peasants could turn from agriculture to crafts, trade, or wage labor to get the money for their dues, and these possibilities widened if the pomeshchik gave permission, as he generally did when asked, to leaves the estate on a passport. Hence some obrok peasants went out on *otkhod* and worked as stevedores, bargemen, factory workers, village hucksters, and seasonal agricultural laborers. The diverse activities of this group obscure the fact that most obrok serfs, like those on barshchina, met their obligations through agriculture in their home villages.[51]

The great difference between barshchina and obrok lay not so much in the pattern of agriculture as in the relationship to the market. Under barshchina, the gain (or loss) from the fluctuations of the grain market accrued to the lord, not the peasant. This was an especially important consideration because regional and seasonal fluctuations of prices were enormous. Peasants generally marketed their grain relatively close to home and in the autumn, to pay their taxes and obrok. The pomeshchik could withold his grain until the price rose, or ship it to a distant market where the price was better; the cost of transport might make this operation uneconomical, but any loss was absorbed by his serfs, because cartage was either part of their barshchina or a supplementary obligation.[52]

Consequently, in making his choice between obrok and barshchina, the pomeshchik was influenced first of all by the possibility of producing a profitable surplus of grain. Where the land was poor or inadequate to the number of his serfs, where the possibilities for nonagricultural employment were greater, where the supervision of barshchina was expensive or unwieldy, the pomeshchik opted for obrok. It was relatively common in the North. In the extreme South, where labor was expensive and where grain was produced for export, obrok was almost unknown. It was also rare in Little Russia (the Left-Bank Ukraine), where petty proprietors were numberous.

Because of the lord's plenitude of power, barshchina and obrok were not the only forms of dues. Official figures indicate that about 15 percent of the serfs rendered mixed dues, but there were few peasants who both performed labor and paid cash in significant amounts.[53] Squires introduced mixed dues to get a return from the serfs' wintertime crafts, or to get free labor at harvest time from peasants who sent most of the year on obrok. If the estate had lucrative agricultural land but not enough to provide an adequate return from all the households settled on it, some peasants would be turned onto obrok. In the main, mixed-dues estates adhered to the form of dues prevailing in the area, and the mixing was a further extension of the widespread practice of supplementary collections and exactions—fruit, meat, construction work, watchman service.[54]

It was within the pomeshchik's power to carry barshchina to the extreme of *mesiachina*, which meant that he took the whole estate into the demesne and provided the peasants with a monthly ration of food; the resemblance to plantation methods is misleading, for mesiachina was not a means of expanding commodity production but the desperate resort of a few petty proprietors.[55] It was more common, but still rare, to carry otkhod to its extreme and convert an obrok serf to a "household serf"; he could then be stripped of his allotment and sent out on a passport to pay obrok through wage labor. Most household serfs (*dvorovye*), however, were attached to the manor or to their lord's person and worked either as domestic servants or as craftsmen within the manorial economy—black-smiths, carpenters, and so on. They comprised less than 10 percent of the serf population on the eve of emancipation.

Serfdom had a political economy of its own. For example, there were no significant economies of scale, since the productive unit remained the peasant household, however many households there might be on the estate; a large estate was simply a large total of household units. Indeed, since the per capita cost of administration and supervision was greater on the biggest estates,[56] and since the smaller proprietors were more exacting than their greater brethren were able—or willing—to be, there was a diseconomy of scale.

While the bookkeeping of even the greatest magnates was haphazard, serfdom made it difficult to keep accounts. Most nobles assessed the performance of their estates only by the year-to-year fluctuations of income.[57] It was possible to assign a paper value to the land and treat obrok as rent; the allotments of the serfs on barshchina could be regarded as wages for agricultural labor, and thus the return on landed capital determined. This kind of reckoning entailed too many fictions to be useful, for the land was inseparable from the peasants on it and could not be put to any other use. Even if there had been buyers and renters of agricultural land in sufficient numbers, it was illegal to manumit entire villages without land. Besides, obrok was in fact not rent, but a levy on peasant incomes; the components of barshchina (the proportion of allotment land and demesne and the labor expended on each) did not have the character of wages and wage labor, since they were determined according to a rough estimate of the pomeshchik's requirements and the serfs' subsistence.

Similarly, the pomeshchik did not reckon his "costs of production"[58] because, on most estates, they did not exist. It was necessary to make an outlay for supervision—the salary of the steward (if any), and the concealed outlay entailed in excusing the village officials from dues. On the typical barshchina or obrok estate, however, the pomeshchik did not make any regular outlay for production. He was liable for sporadic grants to maintain household that suffered calamities, loss of livestock, or shortage of food.[59] This liability was contingent on the weather and other chance factors, but was greater if the pomeshchik was more exacting. In this sense the grants did represent an irregular "cost of production," but, properly understood, they were analogous to the paper loss represented by arrears of obrok. Like the grants, these arrears were a fluctuating but regular element in the pomeshchik's reckoning, dependent in part on the weather and in part of the level of exactions. However, arrears of obrok were so universal that the assessment (*obrochnoi oklad*) was a conventional fiction; it was the obrok proprietor's form of wishful thinking, the counterpart of the barshchina proprietor's exhortation to his serfs to work zealously on his behalf, and its quantitative form did not give it any more force than the exhortation.

The prevalence of arrears further diminished the difference between barshchina and agricultural obrok.[60] Barshchina was generally regarded as more profitable for the proprietor, but obrok was supposed to increase the serf's incentive, because he could keep whatever was left after he had paid his dues and taxes. On most obrok estates, however, any surplus for a particular year would simply be absorbed by the accumulated arrears; obrok peasants, then, rarely stood to gain by earning or producing more. Pomeshchiki sometimes wrote off arrears in the hope of increased productivity and more punctual payment, but arrears generally began accumulating again. Perhaps they were the obrok serf's counterpart to the notorious malingering of peasants doing barshchina, and represented a form of day-to-day resistance to bondage. At any rate, motivation and productivity were not much greater under agricultural obrok than under barshchina.

Considering the manorial economy in a national perspective, historians can find some unequivocal tendencies. Regional specialization, which had a long tradition in Russia, was stronger than ever.[61] Broadly speaking, the far South produced grain for export through the Black Sea ports, the West for export through the Baltic, while the central black-soil region made good the deficit in food production of the more diverse economy of the North. Manorial factories, many of which had been set up in the first three decades of the century, had not been able to compete with factories operated with hired laborers (often obrok serfs).[62] The manorial factories that survived were most often distilleries, sugar beet refineries, or other enterprises directly connected to agriculture. There was a significant decline in the number of estates, mostly because the smaller pomeshchiki were being squeezed out. On the other hand, the number of estates of a thousand souls and more was holding steady, which indicates that nobles were forming new large units, since estates were generally divided among the heirs at the death of the owner.[63] Furthermore, the total land owned by the nobility showed a slight increase in the last two decades of serfdom.[64]

Soviet historians have asserted the existence of a crisis in the system of serfdom, an assertion that seems to derive from the notion that a system must undergo a crisis before it is abolished. Recently, however, I. D. Koval'chenko has produced figures that do indicate a real malady in the serf economy.[65] He has shown, by collating the figures in the annual reports of provincial governors, that in the last twenty years of serfdom there was a significant decline in yield and in the harvest per capita on the pomeshchik estates, and a slight decline in the sowing of demesne land. This decline was greater in the grain-producing areas where barshchina dominated; the estates in Moscow Province and the provinces surrounding it to the north held their own. Koval'chenko has also shown, with data drawn from the records of large estates in various Great Russian provinces, that there was a marked decline in the prosperity of serfs, as measured by the number of draft animals per household. A growing number of serfs were no longer able to work their allotments and their share of the demesne. Koval'chenko finds that the intensity of exploitation by the pomeshchiki was primarily responsible for the decline in the serfs' well-being and, in particular, for the decline in the serf population.[66] Koval'chenko's data and methods require careful scrutiny, for—as he is the first to point out—his sources are deficient. The tendencies he elicits from these sources, however, are consistent and persuasive, even if his figures are far off the mark in absolute terms.

The decline in productivity of the manorial unit and the impoverishment of the serfs were due in part to the backwardness of Russian agricultural techniques. Down into the nineteenth century, it had been possible to compensate for shortcomings such as lack of fertilizer and the depletion of the soil by expanding the sown area. In time, there was no longer much suitable land in reserve, and it became necessary to plow up pastures and hayfields. As the availability of new plowland became more and more limited, and methods of cultivation remained the same, a decline in yield was inevitable.[67] Furthermore, engrossing pasture and hayfields into three-field cultivation precluded any advance so long as that rotation was maintained; by diminishing fodder and forage, it augmented the major infirmities of three-field agriculture: lack of manure for fertilizer and lack of powerful draft animals. It became hard for serfs to support the cattle they had previously held, and all the harder if the pomeshchik sought to maintain his revenues by expanding his demesne at the expense of peasant allotments.[68]

The situation on obrok estates was somewhat different. Koval'chenko has refuted the view that there was no real increase in obrok in the last eighty years of serfdom by showing a pronounced rise, whether calculated in silver rubles, the equivalent in rye, or as a proportion of peasant income.[69] Here, too, he finds a decline in peasant well-being as measured in the number of cattle per household. Indeed, he reports that the average obrok peasant in the four provinces of his special study was running at a deficit of seven to fourteen silver rubles a year, or from 18 to 53 percent of the peasant's income.[70] If Koval'chenko's data and his econometric model were better, this deficit would probably fall into the range where it would correspond to the level of arrears typical of an obrok household. It does seem that the obrok serfs, like those on barshchina, were squeezed to very near the limit, for the general level of obrok assessments—to say nothing of obrok actually collected—reached a plateau twenty or thirty years before the abolition of serfdom. Obrok rose the most in the nineteenth century in those districts where it had been lowest around the year 1800 and where a significant part of it derived from wage labor rather than agriculture; in the black-soil districts where the obrok rates had been highest, they declined in absolute terms in the last half-century of serfdom.[71]

Contemporaries were only dimly aware of these indices of decline, for it is the sophisticated computations of historians that have brought them clearly to light. An official might note the relative and absolute decline of the serf population, because the tax collectors made a periodic count of serf souls. A pomeshchik might notice that his own serfs had fewer horses and cows than thirty years before. Each might bemoan the times, but neither could make any certain inference about the manorial economy in the absence of comprehensive data. In judging the performance of the manorial economy, contemporaries looked first of all to revenues and debts.

The nobility's mortgage debt was staggering. On the eve of emancipation, the government was, so to speak, the majority shareholder in the enterprise of serfdom, for in 1856, 61.7 percent of all serfs were mortgaged to it, and nobles had considerable debts to private borrowers as well.[72] Mortgages were the resort of the larger serfholders; the proportion of mortgaged serfs was almost twice as high as the proportion of mortgaged estates, and great magnates regarded loans from the state as a regular item of their annual income.[73]

The state was an indulgent creditor. Mortgages could usually be renewed easily and, while default was common, foreclosure and sale were rare.[74] The temptation to mortgage serfs was hard to resist. The high proportion of mortgaged serfs cannot serve as evidence that nobles were acquiring capital to modernize their estates, as Struve suggests, nor yet that the estates were economically unsound and declining, as Koval'chenko maintains. They pertain first of all to consumption, not production, and the only certain inference from them is that many nobles were not satisfied with the revenues they drew from their estates. In particular, there is no necessary relationship between the nobility's debts to the state and the abolition of serfdom. Pushkin and others believed that these mortgage loans were a major impediment to emancipation, since the state would not dare to move against serfdom for fear of a massive default. Foreclosure is a practical resort only when the creditor can expect to sell the mortgaged property for the amount of the loan, and where in Russia could the state find buyers for all the mortgaged estates? On the other hand, the government acquired the leverage on the nobility that any creditor has on his debtor. It was able to exert this leverage in 1858, however, only because its debtors were disorganized and timid.

Extrapolation of the available data on the impoverishment of the serfs and the rise in mortgages suggests that the last proprietary estate would have passed to the treasury by foreclosure shortly before the utter ruin of the last serf. However, there is no reason to assume that the tendencies of the forties and fifties would have continued indefinitely had serfdom not been abolished. Furthermore, serfdom as a system did exhibit a degree of slack, despite the strain indicated by the rise of debt and the decline of yields and cattle. For example, arrears of obrok could be reduced by diligent administration and draconian remedies.[75] The reliance on the household as the productive unit and the *tiaglo** as the unit for the assessment of dues meant that part of the serf population was underexploited.[76] Dues were relatively light on many large estates, where a large portion of the serfs was concentrated.[77] Finally, while it is often remarked that the Russian peasant required much more land for his subsistence than his counterparts in Western Europe, the number of serfs required to maintain a noble family is more striking still. There were a hundred male serfs for every serfholder. Ia. A. Solov'ev estimated that it took a hundred serfs to maintain a nobleman the year round on an estate in Smolensk Province, and five hundred to support an absentee proprietor in suitable

*The *tiaglo* was the unit of two or three able-bodied workers according to which taxes, dues, and lands were allocated within the commune; a household might include one or several *tiagla*.

fashion.[78] Nationwide, one serfholder in five held more than a hundred male serfs; in the antebellum South, one slaveowner in two hundred had more than a hundred slaves of both sexes. Even though many serfs were barely able to sustain their households and meet their obligations to the pomeshchik and the state, the very size of the economic units in use indicates that there were underexploited resources in the manorial economy.

Russian nobles, however, did not assess the performance of their estates by making comparisons with French villages or American plantations; they looked to the revenues their estates produced. Neither nostalgia for the good old days of docile peasants and bountiful harvests nor admiration for agronomists elsewhere would alter the pomeshchik's behavior so long as his revenues held up. Unfortunately, the available data on revenues are fragmentary. Manorial accounting was so haphazard that, even when the records have survived, it is difficult to elicit meaningful results. Koval'chenko does provide data on the revenues from four barshchina estates, all belonging to one proprietor, for the period 1802-1860. These figures show a considerable, although fluctuating, increase in the revenues of all four, despite the decline of these estates according to physical indices. The revenues do not stand in a direct relationship to the size of the harvest. It was possible to turn a good profit on demesne production in those years when prices were high because the peasants—including the lord's own serfs—were forced to buy grain.[79] "All the pomeshchiki who turned little holdings into great," according to Prince Cherkasskii, did so by withholding their grain until the peasants entered the market as buyers; they made it a rule "not to sell grain in a year of good harvest and not to buy it in a bad year."[80]

If high profits depended upon high prices rather than high output, then they were achieved at the expense of peasant consumers, including the pomeshchik's own serfs, and therefore at the expense of the manorial enterprise. When a serf sold a horse in the spring to buy bread grains, he was putting money in the pocket of a pomeshchik, perhaps his own pomeshchik; but he was also depriving the estate he lived on of part of its livestock, in which it was probably deficient anyway. There is an anlogy between this kind of profit making and the pomeshchik's attempts to increase his production by expanding his demesne at the expense of the peasants' allotments and pasture. In both instances, the pomeshchik met immediate needs by devouring the productive capacity of his estate. In a figurative but very significant sense, both output and revenues were increased by an unwitting cannibalism.

Whatever the tendency of manorial revenues, Russians did not complain of a decline, and their silence is eloquent. Most nobles and officials in the 1850s believed that serfdom, and barshchina in particular, was an acceptable basis for Russian agriculture. Critics of serfdom framed their arguments a priori or by invoking the experience of other countries. Few sources show a realization that the nobility's economic position was declining, and apart from those who advocated emancipation for extraeconomic reasons, scarcely anyone suggested that a nobleman could expect material gain from a radical alteration of his relationship with the peasantry. In short, there is little contemporary testimony on the crisis that is supposed to have preceded, if not dictated, the decision to abolish serfdom. This silence does not mean that the tendencies outlined by Koval'chenko and others did not exist. Economic thinking in mid-century Russia was static rather than dynamic in its concepts, and economic policy was discussed primarily in terms of morality and security rather than development.[81] In this context, and in the prevailing structure of society, no perceived tendency in the manorial economy was powerful enough to generate the reform of serfdom.

It is on this rock (if silence can serve as a metaphorical rock) that Petr Struve erected his analysis of the serf economy.[82] He also made pointed reference to the persistence of quasi-servile relations well after the emancipation—an embarrassment to the latter-day historians who are most persuaded of the crisis of the servile system.[83] Struve concluded that barshchina was a viable and developing basis for commodity production and that a new class of enterprising pomeschiki was making effective use of it. The real impediment to the further development of barshchina agriculture, he found, was Russia's primitive transportation system, which made it difficult to market the crop.

Struve encountered difficulties when he tried to find evidence that barshchina agriculture was burgeoning. He suggested that pomeschiki invested their mortgage loans in agricultural improvements and that debts were a sign of entrepreneurial vigor, but ingenuously observed that the sources indicate that most of the money borrowed went for consumption, not production. Struve also lost sight of important considerations, such as the advantages that accrued to barshchina proprietors of the central black-soil area from regional and seasonal fluctuations in grain prices and the difficulty of achieving economies of scale on large estates. He seems to have imputed to barshchina agriculture aspects of the plantation system that were rarely to be found in Russia. His model cannot be accepted, but it has two cardinal merits: it takes into account the apparent satisfaction of the government and the nobility with serfdom as an economic system, and it deals with the serf economy as a whole.

Those who represent barshchina as stagnant in its productive capacity and in the proportion of serfs who rendered it leave the South and Southeast out of account and concentrate on the central black-soil region.[84] Yet in the last eighty years of serfdom there was a pronounced territorial expansion of barshchina to the South and Southeast, though the serfs there constituted only a small part of the serf population of the empire. Since many proprietors in the new land were absentees, there was a flow of barshchina revenues back into the center. Then, too, there was an indeterminate flow of capital back to the estates of the central regions from the sale of serfs for resettlement in the new lands; since the traffic in serfs has been studied even less than manorial revenues,[85] this is still a matter for speculation.

The available information is too scanty to answer many important questions about the quantitative development of the manorial economy. But development is more than quantitative. Social transformations are not achieved simply by the multiplication (or diminution) of goods, they entail the development of people, of society as a whole. In this perspective, the manorial economy can be seen to have impaired the development of alternatives. Progress within the obrok sector developed the skills of the peasants as producers and entrepreneurs, but it made the proprietor more of a parasite than ever; not only did he lack a positive function, he became more and more of a rentier in regard to people, as their enterprise rather than his land became a greater component of his income. The barshchina sector offered the pomeshchik the possibility of a positive directing and entrepreneurial role, but the more effective he was in this role, the more he reduced the initiative of his peasants. Progressive barshchina made serfdom almost indistinguishable from plantation slavery. To be an improving squire meant to impose on the peasants a minute direction of the agricultural cycle on the demesne while cutting the allotment land to the minimum,[86] reducing the peasants to producers of bare subsistence on their land and to the status of working capital in the lord's fields. Finally, the parallel development of the free economy may have undermined the serf system at certain points, but it subsidized the serfowners, either in their capacity as owners of part of the labor force or as producers of raw materials consumed within the free economy. Both forms of serfdom collected their tribute from the free economy.

In sum, there was a crisis of the servile economy in the middle of the nineteenth century, but not a crisis of attitudes. Agricultural production was sustained, and the low productivity of serf labor and the exhaustion of the soil by the three-field system were overcome, through a variety of essentially short-term resorts. The nobility's revenues were maintained or even increased by devices of even shorter term: intensified supervision and exploitation of the serfs, manipulation of fluctuations in the grain market, expansion of the demesne at the expense of pasture or allotment land. These devices all undermine the viability and productive capacity of peasant households and thus the long-term prospects of the estate. And these devices taken together did not generate enough income to satisfy the pomeshchik. To maintain an appropriate style of life, he needed subvention: direct subvention from the state, in the form of mortgage loans, and indirect subvention from the free economy, extracted from the wages of obrok serfs.

Yet the servile economy had all the force of an ongoing economic system. The pomeshchiki did not regard themselves as the legatees of a dying system, still less as the selfless supporters of an uneconomic system maintained in the interests of social order. They read with interest and even enthusiasm of the productivity of wage labor and the marvellous benefits of new crops and complex systems of cultivation. Many of them believed the promises of the agronomists and economists, but they stuck by the tried and true. In part, they shrank before the effort and investment that the transformation of their estates would entail; in part, they were of two minds, believing in the benefits of modernization in principle and rejecting modernization on the ground of practicality. On both counts, their attitude towards the economics of serfdom paralleled the regime's attitudes towards serfdom as a social system.

Government Policy

Under Nicholas I, the government consistently supported the institution of serfdom. There were, to be sure, contrary tendencies within the government hostile to serfdom or to some of its aspects. In the inner councils of the government, arguments against reform were framed in terms of practicality and prudence, for serfdom as such had few articulate defenders in the upper bureaucracy. Certain acts of legislation enacted uner Nicholas were implicitly hostile to serfdom. These acts, however, generally included an explicit repudiation of "false declarations regarding the supposed emancipation of the peasants" and an exhortation to the serfs to maintain "unwavering submission to the lawful authority of their pomeshchiki."[87] Moreover, in the day-to-day actions of its administrative agencies, the government acted consistently in

behalf of the nobility and serfdom. The contrary tendency within
the government was barely perceptible to the ordinary Russian,
who inferred the government's intentions from public statements
and the public activities of police, fiscal, and other agencies.

The police power of the state stood squarely behind the
pomeschik's authority. If the insubordination of his peasants was
too much for civil officials to handle, they would have troops
brought in and quartered in the refractory village until the peasants
submitted. This was done 381 times in the second quarter of the
nineteenth century; the insignificance of the pretext in most
instances is clear from the fact that only on eight occasions was
there armed conflict between serfs and soldiers, and only twice did
the serfs attack the soldiers sent to their village.[88] The government
upheld the pomeshchik's authority, but it did not side with him
blindly. Sometimes officials put covert pressure on him to make
some concessions to his serfs. Then, too, provincial and central
officials were more prone to take action against a pomeshchik who
abused his power than were the local officials, elected by the
nobility. If a pomeshchik subjected his serfs to excessive physical
punishment or reduced them to ruin, the corporate organization of
the nobility was supposed to sequester his estates; in practice,
nobles were unwilling to take action against their brethren even in
flagrant instances, and, when estates were sequestered, the
initiative usually came from governmental agencies.[89] Most
important, all the authorities, central and local (and including the
ecclesiastical), conceived their first task to be the restoration of
order, which meant restoration of the pomeshchik's power over the
serfs. The government did not suppose that many pomeshchiki
came close to the ideal of Christian stewardship, but it feared that
even a minor instance of insubordination could blossom into
servile war like the Pugachev revolt in the 1770s.

The government supported serfdom with money as well as force;
it was a lavishly subsidized institution. The principal form of
subsidy was mortgage loans. The state accepted serfs as security
for loans, and the loans could be had easily and on generous terms;
they were more often extended or renegotiated than repaid.[90] The
sum of outstanding loans increased sixfold in the reign of Nicholas,
reaching the sum of 398 million silver rubles in 1856. The state
made no attempt to see to it that the loans were put to productive
use, and only serfs were accepted as security for these loans. The
modernization of manorial agriculture required enormous outlays,
but costly capital goods, improved plowland, and the use of hired
labor were of no account with the governmental credit institutions.
Consequently, the mortgage system promoted the most backward
and the specifically servile aspects of the economy.[91]

The state even indirectly subsidized excessive exploitation of serfs through its rising expenditures for famine relief.[92] If the pomeshchik could not meet his obligation to feed his serfs in years of bad harvest, he could get aid from the state. Yet the need often arose, particularly in the best grain-producing regions, because the pomeshchik had taken too much of the crop in past years.

These forms of support were natural or even necessary for the state so long as serfdom was in force, and did not signify a positive attitude to the institution. In a society dominated by serfdom, the ordinary functions of government inevitably served, effectively or not, to bolster it. Aspects of policy far removed from agriculture and the nobility were affected or even determined by serfdom, which permeated government no less than society. The army was a striking example, not so much for the advantages given to nobles entering the officer corps, as in the recruitment of the lower ranks. The government thought it inconceivable to return an ex-soldier to serf status and imprudent to send him back to the village as a free man, and so the term of service for drafted recruits was set at twenty-five years—in effect, for life.[93] The long term of service made it difficult to modify the size of the army as needed; indeed, the considerable cost of maintaining a swollen army in peacetime constituted a further, though indirect, subsidy to serfdom. The pomeshchik could turn a direct profit on the draft system. It followed from his manorial authority that he should be able to choose which of his serfs went into the army; using this power, he could sell exemption from a recruitment levy, sometimes at a very high price, to his more prosperous serfs. And, despite laws designed to prevent the practice, he could often sell one of his serfs to another peasant community, to be sent into the army in fulfillment of that community's quota.

In education, as in fiscal and military matters, the state favored the nobility and restricted the serfs. Nobles were favored primarily in their capacity as potential civil servants, but the regime also maintained the prestige of serfholders by providing for the education of poor nobles. As for the serfs, they were not condemned to illiteracy by statute, as slaves were in the antebellum South, but, to avoid "a contradiction between a person's civil status and the education of his intellect," they were barred from secondary schools and could get training only in the practical skills appropriate to their station.[94] Nicholas I believed, with Herzen and others, that educated serfs were inevitably discontented, and he was convinced that they would transmit this discontent in dangerous forms to other serfs.

Finally, serfdom and the privileges of the nobility, like other institutions of state, were under the protection of the censorship.

Censors were instructed to ban "works in which regret is expressed about the position of serfs, the abuses of the pomeshchiki are described, or it is argued that a change in the formers' relation to the latter would be beneficial."[95] Thus the pomeshchik's authority could not be questioned in print. Perfection was as unattainable in this sphere as in others, and certain aspects of serfdom were treated in fiction and in technical discussions of agriculture and economics. Nonetheless, the public press was virtually silent about the fundamental institution of society.[96]

These and other measures in behalf of serfdom were only natural, since serfdom was not an excrescence or anomaly, but the very foundation of society. So long as the government was unwilling to reconstruct the foundation, it was obliged to maintain it, lest the whole edifice of society be destroyed. Whatever their private views of serfdom or their long-range goals, officials had to give serfdom almost undiscriminating support.

The serfholding nobility, then, was the beneficiary of systematic government aid and subvention, which nobles happily accepted as their due. Neither they nor responsible officials suspected that this unstinting patronage would facilitate the abolition of serfdom, as the experience of 1857-1861 suggests that it did. The nobility had no need to develop cohesion and cultivate political skills. The pursuit of the monarch's favor promised more with no output of effort. When the government first declared its intention to reform serfdom, the nobility was beset by alarm, bewilderment, and disorganization; in time, it more or less quietly acquiesced. The atrophy that was generally recognized to have pervaded the corporate organization of the nobility turned out to extend far beyond this institutional framework. The government, quite unwittingly, had stifled the nobility's collective energies, actual and potential, with largesse.

A brief comparison with American slavery in its final stage brings the governmental component of serfdom into sharp relief. In the statute books, the slaveowner's powers were even broader than the pomeshchik's but he was less dependent on public bodies to uphold these powers; when he needed help in imposing submission, he turned to his neighbors. Seventy years after emancipation, ex-slaves retained vivid and painful memories of the "paterrollers";[97] it was not Washington or its agents that mounted these patrols. Furthermore, since the slaveowner lived in a republic instead of an autocracy, he and his fellows had to strive for hegemony within the white population. It was not through privilege or by royal favor but by their own deliberate efforts that they were politically dominant in the South and even in the nation. Serfholders did not have to be so self-reliant.

Both slaveowners and serfholders piled up debts; it seems inherent in servile systems that the dominant class should live beyond its means.[98] In the American South, indebtedness to private lenders created pressure for intensified commodity production. In Russia, the state lent money without commercial purpose and so relieved the pressure for developing the manorial economy.

Finally, in contrast to the slaveowners, Russian nobles were not schooled in polemics and debates. The censorship prevented the public expression of the arguments against serfdom but also impeded, to almost the same degree, the development of arguments for serfdom. The government-sponsored doctrine of "official nationality" was implicitly favorable to serfdom since it vindicated the status quo and since devotion to tradition and authority was among the traits of national character that the regime of Nicholas I propagated and honored. The first exponent of official nationality, Count Uvarov, was privately convinced that serfdom and autocracy were necessarily and inseparably intertwined.[99] The regime did not, however, sponsor or even tolerate a full-scale defense of serfdom as such. Defense would suggest that serfdom was a matter for debate, and a public debate on the merits of serfdom was out of the question. Ukaz and homily exhorted the serfs to be obedient and dutiful and their masters to be just, and there the matter was made to rest. Thus the censorship contributed to the tranquility of pomeshchiki, but contributed also to a significant anomaly: compared with other sociopolitical formations of modern times, serfdom strikingly lacked an articulate ideology.

To be sure, the satisfied pomeshchik was not simply mute. In the face of tacit criticism, he could say, like Maradii Apollonych in *A Sportsman's Sketches*, "I'm a simple man, and I go about things in the old-fashioned way. As I see it, the squire is the squire, the *muzhik* is the *muzhik*, and that's that."[100] This "clear and convincing argument," as Turgenev's narrator characterized it, was more than shamefaced silence, but a good deal less than the books, articles, speeches, and sermons produced in behalf of slavery in the American South. The writings of Fitzhugh, DeBow, and their kind may not be so rich in insight as some commentators now maintain, but this literature had no counterpart at all in Russia.[101] Serfdom was, of course, discussed in private conversation and in official committees; with the dissemination of the ideas of the Enlightenment, at the very latest, educated Russians could not blithely take serfdom for granted, but neither the most ardent Voltairian nor the most cynical Hobbesian could discuss his views in any public forum. When, in 1858, the government briefly allowed the press to discuss the abolition of serfdom, it turned out that the serfholding nobility had no writer or journalist of any competence to articulate its fears and defend its interests. The pomeshchiki in the provinces, and many in the capitals as well, had never had to marshal their thoughts and defend their privileges before any audience more critical than the squires of the neighborhood.

There were, of course, a multitude of differences between American slaveowners and Russian serfholders, and almost as many reasons for them. The comparison does indicate, however, how significant the government's role was in maintaining a system of bondage in nineteenth-century Russia. And it suggests that the nobility was inept, disorganized, and submissive in the crisis of 1857-1861 because of the habits that government patronage had instilled in it.

The Russian government was a patron with misgivings, however. While executive agencies continued to support the nobility, the government's inclinations for change found a quiet forum in a series of secret committees dealing with serfdom. The general public could guess the government's misgivings about serfdom only from the few equivocal laws that emerged from these committees. Indeed, secrecy was perhaps the most important aspect of the committees; in the absence of any public commitment to action, the temptation to yield to the problems that inevitably arise in the legislative process was very great. The work of the committees took various courses; in some instances, the tsar developed last-minute doubts; in others, he decided to yield to the weight of the opinion of his advisors. Only one draft, introduced with Nicholas's preliminary endorsement, passed intact through all the stages; this law, which would permit serfs to buy their village if it was put up for auction, was repealed within a year as a concession to the protests of officials and nobles in the provinces. The continuity in membership from committee to committee suggests that their inaction did not cause great anguish to the tsar or the senior officials.[102]

Of the eight secret committees, the most important were the Committee of December 6 (1826-1831) and a euphemistically named Committee on Dues in Treasury Estates in the Western Provinces (1839-1842). The Committee of December 6 was in effect a Royal Commission on the Decembrist movement, but its frame of reference on substantive issues was surprisingly archaic. It treated serfdom merely as one aspect of the official hierarchy of estates and proposed its modest reforms as part of a general reform of the estate system. This approach provided the committee with a pretext for making concessions to the nobles while somewhat limiting their power over their serfs. The committee would satisfy a long-standing aspiration by abolishing the automatic grant of noble status through government service, and would also accommodate those who favored entail as a means of making a true aristocracy out of the nobility.[103] For the benefit of serfs, the committee would ban the transfer of peasants to the status of household serfs and the sale of serfs apart from land. The proposals concerning serfdom were passed in the Council of State, after heated debate, but rejected by Nicholas I despite his earlier encouragement.

The second major secret committee was convened to review the rarely used law on "free agriculturists" of 1803, which permitted pomeshchiki to manumit entire serf villages with land. The committee was informed that

it is presently the government's fixed intention to ameliorate the peasants' life and to bring them gradually out of serf status, without weakening the importance of the property of the nobility, which consists exclusively of land. To this end, the transition to a better order and to prosperity is to be facilitated through the publication of regulations which will unobtrusively avert all disorders arising from false rumors and ideas of a misleading tendency.[104]

It may be that no undertaking begun with so many explicit doubts could accomplish much. Nonetheless, the committee's point of departure was a sweeping program, drafted by P. D. Kiselev, Minister of State Properties, and favored with the endorsement of the tsar. Kiselev proposed a system of voluntary contracts between lord and peasant which would much enlarge the peasants' liberty but, in contrast to the law of 1803, would not deprive the pomeshchik of his title to the peasant allotments. If the pomeshchik and peasants did not come to agreement, a schedule of dues and land allotments would be imposed by the government. This second element of the plan, an adaptation of the inventories on estates in the western provinces, was clearly the more important, because it would be compulsory.[105] However, Kiseleve abandoned the compulsory inventories, under intense fire from the other members of the committee. Their victory was sealed when the chairman announced:

In the past His Majesty did not at any time consider giving the proposed amendment to the ukaz of 1803 the force of positive law, and he is not pleased to consider the idea now; consequently, it is the desire of His Imperial Majesty that the pomeshchik's own desire to release his peasants should be taken as the basis of the amendment under consideration.[106]

This amendment was drawn up accordingly and enacted as the law on "obligated peasants" of 1842. As Kiselev had originally proposed, the law provided for the determination of dues and allotments, if the pomeshchik wished, by an agreement freely contracted with his serfs and subject to government approval. The allotment land would be held in communal tenure, but the pomeshchik retained his property right to the land, and could sell or mortgage it so long as the contract was observed. He also retained his manorial jurisdiction over the peasants, but "obligated peasants," unlike serfs, could bring abuse of manorial authority and violation of the contract before the courts. This system proved even less practicable than the law of 1803. Under its provisions, a total of three noble families converted 24,708 serfs into obligated peasants.

To be sure, the government was careful not to interfere with the experiment by putting pressure on the nobility. When the marshal of the nobility of Skvira District wrote to the Minister of Finance, urging him to set an example to the nobility by making a contract with his serfs in the district, the Minister of Internal Affairs reprimanded the marshal for the "illegality and utter inappropriateness" of his appeal.[107] While nobles were reluctant to avail themselves of the law, this reluctance was not, as skeptics had predicted, the only difficulty. In some instances, peasants would not consent to a contract, because they thought it was a ruse to deny them the more generous settlement they expected from the tsar. If the peasants agreed to onerous terms, the government refused to confirm the contract, for it hoped that the contracts could serve as models for prescriptive legislation at some time in the future. Indeed, nobles suspected this purpose, which made them still more reluctant to enter into contracts.[108]

The discussions preceding the law of 1842 were more important than the law itself. Until this time, the government officials who, like Speranskii, had thought seriously about the final form of emancipation had assumed that eventually the peasants would be emancipated without land; those serfs who had not been able to purchase land during a lengthy transitional period would become renters, sharecroppers, or hired laborers. The models most frequently offered for emulation were England and, later, the Baltic provinces of Russia,[109] where peasants had been emancipated without land beginning in 1804. Kiselev managed to reverse the terms of debate, adducing the Baltic provinces as an example of what must be avoided. Arguing first of all in terms of state security and state revenues, for he believed that the state's interests were superior to those of any class, Kiselev maintained that landless emancipation would be a disaster for the peasants and for Russia. He won the tsar Nicholas entirely over to his view. Thereafter when the tsar's counsellors deliberated on the reform of serfdom, it was axiomatic that when the Russian serfs were finally emancipated, they must be provided with allotments of land.[110] References to the deplorable plight of the Baltic peasants became commonplace in the upper bureaucracy.

Kiselev's victory was in the sphere of theory only. Indeed, the Baltic reform had had few whole-hearted admirers in the central government; the merits of the Baltic system were advanced by those who would prefer no reform at all, and no influential statesman actually proposed that it be extended to Great Russia. Prince A. S. Menshikov, for example, argued against Kiselev on the ground that the Baltic reform represented the "only just means" of emancipating serfs, "that is, so that the land remains the property of the pomeshchik and the peasants have the right of personal freedom."[111] When Kiselev was defeated by the elimination of the compulsory element of the law on obligated peasants, Menshikov lost interest in the Baltic system.

Semevskii correctly emphasizes the importance of Kiselev's victory in principle: recognition of the necessity of landed emancipation advanced the debate on serfdom to a higher stage. This was, however, advancement into a blind alley, for Kiselev and Nicholas, like the most stubborn opponents of reform, firmly believed in the sanctity of the nobles' property right to their land. This right, solemnly proclaimed by Catherine II and reaffirmed by her successors, was advanced by Nicholas as the principal argument against prescriptive legislation. Kiselev put the matter more broadly in criticizing the land settlement attendant on emancipation in Prussia.

First of all, the property rights of the nobility were destroyed; secondly, the independence of the first estate of the realm was weakened, and this destroyed the crucial moral force through which the sovereign power had reached the common people; thirdly, the masses were drawn into participation in vital matters of state administration by virtue of their property right to the land.[112]

Emancipation with land being no more acceptable than landless emancipation, it was possible to consider only schemes for government regulation of the kind advanced and rejected in the various secret committees. The rejection of landless emancipation under Nicholas I was sound statesmanship, but it scarcely brought the abolition of serfdom any nearer.

Discussion of the other secret committees under Nicholas can be limited to a brief mention of the committees of 1840 and 1844 on household serfs. The debate was begun and concluded in the context of the government's long-range commitment to the emancipation of serfs with land. It was taken for granted that allotting land to the ex-serfs would also be a means of binding them to their native villages and so preventing vagabondage and disorder;[113] this concept persisted and was incorporated into the reform legislation of 1861. Household serfs presented a special obstacle to this eventual goal because they did not have any land to which they could be attached. They were also worthy of immediate attention because their situation was closest to full slavery and because they were thought to be particularly discontented. Then, too, the morality of domestic servants was conceived to be distinctly lower than that of ordinary peasants, although neither committee went on to inquire why daily contact with the noble estate should impair a peasant's morality.

The committees were specially charged by Nicholas to limit the number of household serfs who held passports and lived apart from their masters as craftsmen or hired laborers. The tsar was reminded that this was a useful and productive category of serfs whose status was as far as possible from slavery; there was only a formal affinity between butler and footmen and these industrious craftsmen. However, Nicholas (and the committee, following his lead) persisted in this dilettantish preoccupation; they looked to the character of domestic servants, with whom they were familiar, and to the mobility of craftsmen, with whom they had no personal contact, and were disturbed by the largely imaginary combination of qualities. However, with the household serfs as with their brethren in the field, action was eventually judged to be more dangerous and disruptive than inaction; as Baron Korf argued, any legislative expression of concern for this segment of the serf population would make the rest more resentful of their bondage. The goal of the government's policy on the serf question, as Nicholas told the Committee of 1844, was to "change the status of the serfs around us," but any restriction on the pomeschik's right to turn peasants into household serfs would be "absolutely impossible for a long time."[114] Therefore the committee did no more than permit pomeshchiki to manumit household serfs under contractual conditions and to free some household serfs living on mortgaged estates.

Although the legislative output of the secret committees was meager, some of the concerns they expressed were reflected in laws subsequently issued under Nicholas. The ban on sales apart from land proposed by the Committee of December 6 was not enacted, but is related to the laws forbidding the purchase of serfs by nobles who owned no land and the sale of a serf apart from his family. Then, too, compulsory inventories, recommended by Kiselev for estates throughout the empire, were imposed in the western provinces. Only in the three southwestern provinces, where the governor-general was sympathetic to the reform, was a serious attempt made to implement and enforce the law. Inventories, or written statements of the serfs' obligations and allotments, had long existed by custom in western territories taken from Poland. Since they were drawn up by the pomeshchik or his steward, they did not have any contractual element, nor did they acquire any through the law, which, within very broad limits, simply consecrated the existing inventories, with some adjustment in the pomeshchik's favor.[115] The result, then, was simply to stabilize the peasants' obligations and allotments and deprive the pomeshchik of his arbitrary power to demand extra labor or take away land. However, he retained most of his manorial authority, and the attempt to combine this power with government intervention on behalf of the serfs proved very awkward in practice.[116]

Even if the secret committees are credited with all the legislation on serfdom issued under Nicholas, the gap between their stated goals and their accomplishments was wide. However, the premises of the goals and the accomplishments were much the same and should be identified, since they carried over into the reign of Alexander II. First of all, the interests of the state must be put uppermost in formulating—or at least, in justifying—policy on the peasant question, and the state's primary interest was internal security. It is here that serf discontent was most significant, not in its actual scope but in its supposed potential to develop into a peasant rebellion. The ghost of Pugachev was a familiar figure in the chancelleries of St. Petersburg, but the ghost, like the original, was an unwitting force against reform. Serfs frequently expressed the belief, despite the evidence to the contrary, that they, not the nobles, were the true objects of the tsar's favor;[117] even modest reforms, officials argued, would encourage this naive monarchism to the point where the serfs would turn on their lords and launch a new *pugachevshchina*, a revolt undertaken in the tsar's name. This danger could best be averted by maintaining every authority, beginning with the pomeshchik.

A second premise of these discussions was disapproval of serfdom on humanitarian grounds; as Nicholas I explained to a group of nobles, a serf "cannot be considered property, still less can he be considered a thing."[118] It was in this spirit that the government considered restrictions on the purchase and sale of serfs and imposed a few. It also undertook to buy up the estates of petty proprietors on the assumption that the poorest pomeshchiki were the most oppressive.[119] Compulsory inventories were not intended to abolish serfdom, but to regulate it, so that the peasants would be protected from the arbitrary exercise of manorial authority. It was the abuse of arbitrary power, or *proizvol*, that generally aroused humanitarian objections to serfdom. Proizvol, in its legal and illegal manifestations, was much discussed, but the secret committees did not raise objections to serfdom as an economic system or to its pattern of hegemony and subordination. Unfortunately, proizvol was inseparable from the aspect of serfdom that the government most cherished, the pomeshchik's direct control of the peasants on his estate. Across the spectrum of Nicholas's advisors, no one doubted that manorial authority was beneficial for lord and serf and necessary for the state. Indeed, for more than a year after Nicholas's successor made a public commitment to emancipation, government policy attempted to square the circle by abolishing serfdom while maintaining the pomeshchik's manorial authority.

Through the discussions in Nicholas's secret committees, as in similar committees convened by Nicholas's predecessor, the government discovered how tightly it was entangled with the pomeshchiki; it was at once patron and client to the nobility, dependent upon it and supportive of it. Under Nicholas I, no reform plan was pushed far enough to show which aspect of the relationship was paramount. For, as the tsar told the Council of State in explaining his opposition to any legal regulation of serf dues,

Of course, I am an autocrat, accountable to no one, but I will never venture to undertake such a measure, just as I will never order the pomeshchiki to conclude contracts; this must be a matter of their good will, and only experience will show the extent to which it will be possible to pass from the voluntary to the compulsory.[120]

And so, as a further premise of its policies on serfdom, Nicholas's government relied on good will rather than compulsion—that is, it attempted by legislation to promote favorable developments within the servile system and to encourage nobles to take the initiative in moving away from serfdom. It may have been utopian, as Kizevetter suggests,[121] to hope that serfdom and its beneficiaries could generate alternatives that would be acceptable to the government, but this hope was a major premise of policy, especially in the 1840s. It lies behind the law on obligated peasants and also the law permitting serfs to acquire landed property with their pomeshchik's permission.

The same reliance on good will prompted the government to make overtures to two groups of nobles in 1847. The more important of these overtures was the tsar's private appeal to a delegation from Smolensk Province. Speaking to them as "the first nobleman in the state," the tsar said he was disappointed with the nobility's failure to avail itself of the law on obligated peasants and asked for help on this matter. The delegation undertook to confer with the nobles of Smolensk. Nicholas's initiative was vitiated when the Minister of Internal Affairs urged the delegation to proceed with extreme caution, but semiofficial discussions were nonetheless held in Smolensk Province. The discussions revealed that, under no more pressure than the government had applied, even the most hidebound squires would accept reforms of the kind the government had considered and rejected. The weight of opinion, to be sure, was highly unfavorable; of the district marshals of nobility in the province, all but one opposed reform, and this mild dissident was reproved by his colleagues: "Think of it, you are a nobleman, yet you are acting against the rights of your own kind."[122] Yet the nobility's opposition to the proposed reforms was limited to this kind of grumbling and recrimination.

The other negotiations began when the government resurrected a scheme of manumission that a group of pomeshchiki from Tula Province had offered in 1844.[123] The nobility of Tula responded with a proposal that all the nobles of the province elect an official committee to consider plans for reform. When this idea was rejected by the government, some of those responsible for the 1844 plan offered a new variant, applicable to their own estates only, whereby individual serfs could redeem themselves and a desiatina of land for a hundred rubles.

The Tula group did not demonstrate reckless philanthropy in its proposals, both of which were probably too one-sided for the government to endorse. And the Tula nobility as a whole did not yield to other provinces in the tenacity of its attachment to serfdom. At the assembly of the nobility two years later, when the marshal proposed a toast, "to all who work for the common weal," the nobles were offended that he did not mention anyone in the hall by name. "They even said," a police agent reported, "Besides, that word 'common' he used somehow resembles communism."[124]

Nonetheless, the actions of these pomeshchiki show that there was a small segment of the nobility eager for major change. This is apparent in the confrontation between their spokesman Miasnov and L. A. Perovskii, the same minister who had urged caution on the nobles of Smolensk. Perovskii maintained that peasants understand freedom to mean "anarchy and insubordination." He had told Nicholas that the nobles

fear the consequences of freedom, *for they know how unmanageable the common people are, once they have departed in any way from their customary status and from the bounds of subordination*; but the proprietors no longer have any fear of a loss of income from giving freedom to their people. The pomeshchiki themselves are beginning to understand that the peasants are a great burden and that it would be desirable to alter their mutually unprofitable relations [but they] *are frightened by the consequences of great change, as any sensible man who knows the people and their ideas and inclinations ought to be.*[125]

Miasnov agreed with Perovskii that the peasants must be kept under strict control, but he asserted, as few if any officials then did, that "the prevailing tumultuous expectancy produces much more disruption from the dissemination of harmful rumors" than would result if the government announced its intention to reform; the peasants would be grateful and, accordingly, obedient to authority. Thus a marshal of the nobility attacked one of the major arguments against reform.[126]

Before the deliberations of the nobles at Tula and Smolensk could develop very far, they became academic. Both groups were informed in a brusque letter that "the Sovereign Emperor has no intention whatsoever of changing the present relationship of proprietary peasants to the serfholders." Hence the nobles' proposals were sent back with instructions to pass this letter on to "all those who suppose the government to have such intentions."[127] This letter produced a full stop, among the nobility and within the government. In the last eight years of Nicholas's reign, there were no attempts at reform and no secret discussions of emancipation.

Revolutionary events in Western Europe distracted the regime from the issue of serfdom, and anxieties provoked by the revolutions of 1848 shut off all consideration of reform in Russia. It was, in a sense, appropriate that discussions should end in this way, for currents from the West had animated and informed the discussion. It was the experiments and achievements of western agronomists that called into question the procedures of Russian servile agriculture. Domestic needs had produced incremental changes over the years, but the existence of a wholly different model created pressures for a transformation of the estate into an enterprise in which there was no place for the simple tools, feeble animals, traditional crops, and lackadaisical labor of serfs. Similarly, Russians did not need foreign examples to be moved to indignation when bondsmen were mistreated, but concepts from the West did stimulate educated Russians to object in principle to the bondage of serfs and the arbitrary power of their masters.

Against these currents, there were powerful native and nativist countercurrents. The cultivation of clover and the rule of law were fine things in their way, but they were alien and bookish. Practical experience and prudence spoke powerfully in behalf of the three-field system, barshchina, and manorial authority. It was difficult, in agronomy and on the statute books, to alter any part of the prevailing system without bringing down the whole. And serfdom was the system that worked; servile Russia was a mighty European power. In this countercurrent against reform, indolence and caution were reinforced by pride and complacency. When one of Nicholas's secret committees observed, "So long as Russia does not lose her unity and her might, other powers cannot serve her as examples,"[128] it was articulating a commonplace of the official world. Many educated Russians were equally satisfied with the polity and the social order. When Prince N. B. Iusupov's steward proposed introducing German peasants to set an example for the prince's serfs, Iusupov (writing from Paris) rebuked him fiercely.

That is against common sense; the Russian peasant is more intelligent than the rabble overseas; in Russia we have happiness, while they are dying from hunger abroad. . . . We Russians subsist solely on the firm foundations of faith in God and love for the tsar and the fatherland, but abroad they love only money and let dogs into church.[129]

Since Russia was mighty, happy, patriotic, and pious, any reform must be considered and introduced with the greatest circumspection, for the object of reform must be, as the tsar himself explained, to keep Russia what it was.[130] Russia was permeated by serfdom, so that a reform of serfdom was nearly a contradiction in terms.

Historians often maintain that the government of Nicholas I prepared the way for the abolition of serfdom under his successor.[131] The issues that Alexander II and his ministers had to confront were discussed under Nicholas I in a more sophisticated and through way than ever before. Yet these discussions were nonetheless circular, repetitious, and inconclusive. The contradictions that had long beset statemen who reflected on the abolition of serfdom had been refined and enlarged; their resolution had been made to seem more difficult, and, given the solid virtues of the social order and Russia's international power, less necessary. The new tsar did not inherit this complacency in full measure, of course, but apart from a few items of palliative legislation, his legacy from his father's deliberations on serfdom was frustration and failure.

The Commitment to Reform

2

In late 1857, the Russian government publicly undertook to reform serfdom and, in effect, made an irreversible pledge to emancipate the serfs. It is necessary to appreciate how, and in what terms, the regime made that commitment in order to understand the controversies to which the balance of this book is devoted. Moreover, an analysis of that commitment is the best way of determining the immediate causes of the abolition of serfdom.

Disingenuous official sources presented the emancipation of the serfs as the result of the spontaneous desire of the nobility. This explanation, which was briefly revived by certain Marxist scholars,[1] can be set aside for the moment. However, simply to ridicule this grotesque representation of the noble estate (or "ruling class") begs an important question, for none of the standard explanations of the emancipation provides an adequate model of the relationship between the nobility and the state.

The emancipation has been more plausibly explained by the government's desire to allay peasant discontent and avert a major peasant rebellion. Academician Druzhinin now takes this view,[2] and few historians refrain from quoting the remark of Nicholas's Chief of Gendarmes that serfdom was a "powder keg" under the government.[3] The metaphor is particularly apt: it is dangerous to live over a powder keg and more dangerous still to move it. Both before and after the commitment to reform, most officials believed that serfdom was potentially explosive and that disillusionment and insurrection were the most likely consequences of the abolition of serfdom.[4] Given the choice between the devil they knew and the devil they didn't, they could be expected to agree with Baron Korf, to whom a member of one of Nicholas' secret committees complained:

Here is our misfortune. They think it is impossible to touch a part without convulsing the whole, but they refuse to touch the whole because they say it is dangerous to lay hands on twenty-five millions of people. Where is the way out?

Korf replied, "It's very simple: don't touch either the part or the whole and we may, perhaps, live a little longer."[5] Alexander II himself shared Korf's point of view; even in the celebrated speech in which he stated that it was better to abolish serfdom from above than have it abolished from below, he disclaimed the intention of taking immediate action. Abolitionists advanced the danger of peasant discontent as an argument for reform, but in the inner councils of government, it was a major argument for temporizing.

An explanation of the commitment to reform which emphasizes the danger of serf discontent, or the "peasant movement," presents a further difficulty: the nobles, the immediate targets of discontent, were willing to take their chances. An individual pomeshchik who had survived a dangerous encounter with his serfs might be induced to consider emancipation,[6] but there is no evidence that any considerable part of the nobility was apprehensive enough to desire a major reform. The individual proprietor was not concerned about the possibility of mass violence but about the day-to-day insubordination and recalcitrance of his own serfs.[7] To be sure, the government of Alexander II, like that of Nicholas I, had a very low tolerance for disruptions of order, and no state can tolerate a permanent threat to order simply because the potential victims prefer to run the risk. More important, the army was the apple of the tsar's eye, and there is no doubt that the war effort had been disrupted in 1855 by serf discontent.

The fear of peasant unrest was to play its role in the further evolution of the government's policy, but it cannot be shown to have been decisive in the decision to emancipate. The data most often adduced to show this—the official statistics on peasant discontent—in fact suggest the opposite. The recorded instances of peasant discontent increase greatly *after* the decision to emancipate. This increase is largely due to a new system in the collection of data, introduced because the government expected trouble as a result of the reform.[8]

Many historians prefer to explain the abolition of serfdom in economic terms, emphasizing the "crisis of the servile economy." This crisis is represented in two aspects, a restless burgeoning of the nonservile sector of the economy and a decay of manorial agriculture; some advocates of this view stress the elements of growth and their incompatibility with serfdom, other the dwindling viability of the servile sector. Yet it is certain, as Gerschenkron points out, that economic development did not call to life any social group that exerted political pressure in behalf of emancipation; state and society alike were dominated by serfholders, for whom the greater productivity of free labor would not outweigh the cheapness of serf labor.[9] Serfholders could respond to a deterioration of their fortunes with readjustments within the servile framework, such as a shift to barshchina cultivation and reliance on mixed dues or, more broadly, with a more aggressive defense of their privileges.[10] More important, it cannot be shown that they were aware of any significant deterioration; it has taken years of sophisticated research to lay bare the crisis in the servile economy. If the serfholders had perceived or sensed that serfdom was economically in jeopardy, the regime could have chosen to weather this crisis as it had others. Governments usually pay more attention to the state of the treasury than to the economy as a whole, and fiscal experts, to whom the Russian government was inclined to defer, gave no comfort to the abolitionist cause.[11] To find a direct relationship between the state of the economy and the commitment to reform requires a massive inference from the commitment itself, an inference based on a metaphysical faith in "materialist" explanations.[12] The discrepancy of scale is otherwise insurmountable: there was no perceived phenomenon or tendency in the prereform economy comparable in magnitude to the decision to reconstruct the socioeconomic system.

The economic explanation of the reform has much in common with the explanation in terms of security. There was a vague but widespread belief that, in the very long run, the abolition of serfdom would make Russia more stable and secure, and also more prosperous and powerful. Yet in practice a concern for security or the economy stifled the impulse to reform; statesmen and squires alike feared peasant rebellion and economic disruption as consequences of abolition. So it was that the regime in 1857, in setting forth its reform program, specified that the major economic components of serfdom—the ascription of the peasantry, the rendering of barshchina and obrok, and the pomeschik's manorial power—should be retained. Serfdom was to be abolished, not the servile economy.

Several historians now reject a narrowly economic explanation of the emancipation and represent Russia's defeat in the Crimean War as the crucial consideration. Gerschenkron, for example, argues that Russia's statesmen realized that a servile society and economy could not compete on an equal military footing with the powers of Western Europe.[13] This explanation has the merit of emphasizing military power and prestige, to which the regime attached much more importance than it did to economic development as such. And it does not have the paradoxical defect, as other explanations do, of fastening upon a prevailing argument against the abolition of serfdom and offering it as the prime cause of abolition.

A military explanation does, however, present difficulties. Primary sources do not provide much more basis for this than for rival theories.[14] Some abolitionists did hope that defeat would move the government to reform. But if anyone in a position of responsibility became convinced by Russia's defeat that serfdom must now be abolished, no record of his conversion has survived.[15] Also, the more significance is attached to military considerations, the more the nobility's acquiescence demands explanation. Analogies between the Crimean War and the Battle of Jena, which precipitated the abolition of serfdom in Prussia, are misleading, for the Crimean defeat was not so much a national catastrophe as a governmental disgrace. The government had linked its prestige firmly to Russia's armed might, and it was the government that was discredited by this limited military campaign. Educated society reacted with recriminations against the bureaucracy for its corruption, ineptitude, and myopia.[16] Shaken by military defeat and by the attendant financial difficulty and domestic criticism, the regime, understandably enough, undertook to reform its own apparatus. But was this the moment for the regime to take the offensive to the nobility and carry out a reform against the expressed interests of its acknowledged first bastion? The Crimean defeat may have "discredited" the old social system as well as the administration, but it is difficult to see how, as Rieber goes on to maintain, it "opened up a broader range of options for the new tsar."[17] As the governor-general of Moscow put it in response to rumors that emancipation was impending, "Can one imagine that after the inglorious Peace of Paris, Alexander II has decided to do what Alexander I did not venture after the glorious capture of Paris?"[18] An explanation in military terms, for all its merit, has a failing in common with the others. They all take the political impotence and submissiveness of the nobility as premises of the reform, when these qualities were revealed to contemporaries only as a result of the decision to reform. In the best of times, the regime could not be sure that it could ride out the opposition, social disruption, and economic dislocation that the abolition of serfdom must, it was convinced, entail.

The period after the Crimean War was far from the best of times, and particularly hard for officials eager for reform. The very forces that, from the point of view of a thoughtful citizen, made reform imperative, made it almost impracticable from an administrative point of view. The Grand Duke Konstantin Nikolaevich, the most ardent and least steadfast reformer among the tsar's ministers, experienced this dilemma as head of the Naval Ministry. He was able to implement various procedural reforms in the post-Crimean period; but even though Russia's outmoded navy had proved painfully inadequate in the war, the Grand Duke was obliged to set an example in cutting back expenditures. With the state as a whole in his purview, the dilemma was more painful still, as he explained in a letter to Prince Bariatinskii:

The state of our finances, which is embarrassed to the highest degree, requires a curtailment, without delay and in all departments, of all expenditures . . . and a sacrifice of many bright hopes for the future, in order to escape from the present situation. This situation becomes graver still by virtue of other vital problems of our internal administration, which now present themselves with new force and demand the speediest resolution.

Among these problems Konstantin Nikolaevich listed serfdom, religious dissidents, and the reform of the courts, police, and administration. And it was no less imperative to bring Russia's economic power up to the level of more advanced nations, for "we cannot deceive ourselves any longer; we must say that we are both weaker and poorer than the first-class powers, and furthermore poorer not only in material but also in mental resources, especially in matters of administration."[19] Russia's other bureaucratic reformers could trace this vicious circle for themselves. They were impelled to reform by Russia's backwardness, fiscal weakness, inadequate administration, and recent humiliation, but these forces impaired their ability to act, and especially to act in despite of the dominant social class. From an administrative point of view, perhaps, the time is never ripe for major reform, but the Crimean defeat did not dislodge the administrative point of view from the direction of Russian policy.

Jerome Blum has reviewed these and other standard

explanations of the abolition of serfdom and, finding them all inadequate, has settled on the personal desire of the tsar as the crucial factor.[20] Alexander's desire was, indeed, a necessary condition of the reform. He had, however, inherited this desire from his father, and with it the misgivings and anxieties that had induced Nicholas to leave serfdom much as he had found it.[21] Alexander did not share Nicholas's energy and capacity to inspire awe, but he retained his ideals of statesmanship and even his statesmen. The change of reign did help to alter the climate of opinion, but brought only minimal change in the atmosphere of the Winter Palace. Alexander's periodic interventions in the legislative process would prove important for the progress of the reform, and so would the hopes and fears that officials and others invested in him. Any explanation of the reform that relies heavily on the personality of the new tsar, however, founders on the strong continuity of values and methods between the two reigns.

All of these explanations seek for a single or primary cause. The best Soviet historians, however, now resist that temptation. A recent survey of Soviet writing on the causes of the reform finds that its particular merit is "reckoning with a variety of factors." Similarly, Zaionchkovskii offers a judicious summary of causal factors without assigning primacy to any one.[22] A complex and extended explanation may not be as gratifying as a simplistic one, but it is better able to withstand critical scrutiny. Yet, once multiple causes are admitted, there is almost no restraint on their further multiplication. The authors of the survey just mentioned proceed to expand the list of causal factors further still, coming to the verge of offering an abstract representation of prereform Russia as an explanation of the reform. As explanations of causation become more sophisticated, they tend to lose the character of explanations.

A narrower perspective may offer a way out. The abolition of serfdom was a watershed of momentous significance, yet it was also an act of legislation. The causes of an act of legislation, at least in the short run, are the motives of the men who undertake it. It ought to be possible to ascertain the proximate causes of the reform by analyzing the legislative prehistory, the origins of the rescript of November 20, 1857, by which the regime commited itself to reform. In the exalted, if constricted, arena of high politics the question becomes, Why was serfdom finally denied another stay of execution?

The Prudence of Statesmen

In the decades prior to 1857, the government had refrained from any serious encroachment on serfdom. The great constraint was wisdom—the conventional wisdom of the dignitaries (sanovniki) who surrounded the tsars, headed the ministries, and sat on the committees. Their holding action scarcely deserves the term "opposition," for the necessity of emancipation, in principle, at some time in the future, was rarely denied. The sanovniki did not claim to represent the interests of the nobility; they were the spokesmen of prudence, experience, and statesmanship. They prevailed for a century. Emancipation simply was not a political issue for the nobility at large, and could not be, until this handful of nobles was converted, circumvented, or overcome.

The prevailing official attitude towards the question of serfdom during the two decades before the emancipation is succinctly set forth in a speech by Nicholas I to the Council of State.[23] The occasion was the discussion of the proposed law on "obligated peasants," which provided pomeshchiki with the option of determining the serfs' obligations by mutual agreement. Nicholas flatly condemned serfdom as an "evil, palpable and obvious to all"; the condemnation was in moral terms, for he sought to retain the principal economic elements of serfdom. Apart from its moral evil, serfdom had become a source of "disorders, which are becoming more and more frequent of late." The peasant discontent causing these disorders arose because serfs had been acquiring an education incompatible with their station and because "certain serfholders— thanks be to God, a very small number of them—forget their noble duty and abuse their authority." But

at the *present* time any thought of [emancipation] would be neither more nor less than a criminal infringement on domestic tranquility and the welfare of the state. The Pugachev rebellion showed what the turbulence of the mob can produce.

In other words, serfdom was a security problem but reform would be more dangerous still.

Although Nicholas feared a *jacquerie* as a consequence of emancipation, he did not mention the possibility of a *Fronde*. Both Nicholas I and Alexander II preferred to represent their relations with the nobility in terms of positive affinity.[24] Despite the assassination of his father and grandfather over lesser issues, it may indeed be that Nicholas was not constrained by any apprehensions about the reaction of the nobles, but their compliance or even active support was essential to emancipation simply to get the work of government done. Russia's bureaucratic machine, despite the continual tinkering that marked Nicholas's reign, was manifestly inadequate for the administration of the country. Nicholas showed his low regard for the bureaucracy by pursuing cherished projects outside the regular apparatus and by entrusting the most important posts to military men. Yet emancipation would effectively double the population for which the regular administration was responsible, since the serfs were administered by pomeshchiki or stewards.[25] Furthermore, the administration was dominated, at least in its upper reaches, by serfholders.[26] A merely passive hostility to the reform on the part of the nobility could threaten the reform and the state itself.

Apart from the natural affinity of monarchs for landowners and officials, therefore, there were practical reasons for Nicholas's solicitude for the nobility. Disclaiming any thought of legislative encroachment on serfdom, he observed that the proposed law on "obligated peasants" would simply amplify, in the nobles' interest, the law on "free agriculturalists" of 1803. A nobleman might choose to avail himself of the new law, but he would not be impelled to do so by any agency more imperious than "the promptings of his own heart." More important, the preservation of the nobles' property right to their land was a "holy obligation for myself and for those who will follow me." Indeed, the proposed law would help imbue serfs with the idea that "the land is not the property of the peasants who are settled on it."

The conflict of two concepts of landed property, to which Nicholas here referred, was the greatest single obstacle to emancipation. Eighteenth-century legislation and the westernization of Russian legal thinking gave the pomeshchik the same absolute property right to his land that prevailed in France or the United States.[27] This right was sanctioned and protected by the full force of state law, and most educated Russians believed, like their western contemporaries, that the sanctity of private property was the basis of the political and social order. But the Russian peasantry was oblivious to the Western (ultimately Roman) concept of property in land. Ignoring the transactions in land that went on with the obvious sanction of the state, serfs professed to believe that land belonged to the tiller, that is, to themselves; forests, pastures, and so on belonged to the tsar, to God, or to no one at all, but certainly not to a private individual. Even when they submitted to bondage, they were intransigent about the land. Serfs reportedly often said to their squire, "We are yours, but the land is ours."[28]

The two ardently held concepts of property could coexist because the peasants stood outside the conceptual world of the upper classes and the state, and because there was no frontal challenge to the peasant concept so long as the peasants and their land were both under the pomeshchik's control.[29] Under Nicholas I, deliberations over serfdom established, as a rigid rule of statecraft, that a general emancipation statute could not separate the peasant from the land. This principle, largely derived from positive and negative examples in the West,[30] appeared to favor the peasantry, yet it blocked even the first step towards emancipation. Landless emancipation was unthinkable, but the massive expropriation (as it would be in terms of state law) of the nobility's lands was equally unthinkable. The land, as Nicholas put it in his speech to the Council of State, must remain "forever inviolate in the hands of the nobility (an idea which I hold unswervingly)."

Nicholas located the way out of this impasse in the remote future, the present task being "to prepare paths to a *gradual transition* to another order of things." Eventually, "questions . . . which now seem vexing will doubtless be untangled through experience"; that is, accumulated examples of agreements between serfs and their lords "will form the basis of a complete and prescriptive legislative act." This appears to mean that the settlements to which certain proprietors agreed would then be imposed on the rest, in the form of a massive expropriation of the property whose protection was "a holy obligation." However, Nicholas was not conscious of any self-contradiction, any more than Catherine II was playing at paradoxes when she hoped for an emancipation imperceptible to the peasants themselves.[31] Each in his own way was expressing the intensity of the dilemma. Similarly, the appeals of statesmen for an emancipation process extending over generations are not to be understood as programs for action. They were meant to testify to a devotion to emancipation in principle, coupled with a sober perception of the insoluble conflicts of principles and interests that emancipation must entail in practice. At the death of Nicholas I, the sum of official wisdom on the question of serfdom was a hope that some day the problems would be magically resolved.

The accession of Alexander II did not augment the sum of that wisdom, although it did increase the longing for a resolution. For the educated elite, including officials, Russia's backwardness was more painful than ever before. In a letter to the venerable A. M. Turgenev, one of them represented Russia as a dear mother lying ill and unattended in a squalid hut. "It is with a mournful feeling," he confessed, "that a traveller now returns to his beloved motherland from countries where, it seems, he has seen order, the rule of law, and a prosperous citizenry." Since serfdom was the crux of Russia's ills, "talk of emancipation becomes more serious and substantial with every passing day; not only babblers, but men of authority, worthy of belief, assert that a beginning will be made soon." But this talk had not advanced the resolution of long-standing problems, for the returned traveller was moved to pray, "Oh Lord, give us men! That is the prayer that Russia should make to God in this critical era, when everyone talks about great reforms but few know—it may be that no one knows—how to undertake them."[32] Here, indeed, from the official point of view, was the dilemma. The need for reform was acknowledged even more readily than in the past. But Russia had no reformers and no plan of reform; it had to pray for "men" and an understanding of "how" to emancipate. A half-century or more of official deliberations and private speculation had yielded nothing at all.

In this anguished point of view, it is easy enough to find, in the light of hindsight, an obtuse lack of perception. Carefully crafted plans of emancipation were circulating in manuscript. The experience of the reform era would show that society and the government's own agencies were well enough endowed with reformers—men with ready answers to the question, "How?" To see solid value in these plans and to see the reformers as statesmen, however, was beyond the capacity of the sanovniki. That perception required a shock from without or an access of determination far greater than the Crimean defeat and the death of Nicholas I seemed to provide.

Alexander inherited his father's outlook along with his throne, and his actions upon accession did not advance the abolitionist cause. His first public speech was an emotional expression of solidarity with the nobility, although, since he was almost incapable of unambiguous statement, even these words could subsequently be construed as an appeal for cooperation in the work of reform.[33] The trend of his ministerial appointments, however, was unequibocal. D. G. Bibikov, the sponsor of the inventory reforms, was replaced as Minister of Internal Affairs by S. S. Lanskoi, who inaugurated his term by reaffirming the inviolability of the rights and privileges of the nobility.[34] M. N. Murav'ev took over the Ministry of State Properties from Kiselev, Nicholas's "chief of staff on the peasant question." While Kiselev's reforming zeal had cooled by the mid-fifties, Murav'ev was a zealous counterreformer; he proposed reorganizing the state domains in imitation of the appanage estates—in other words, restoring the elements of serfdom Kiselev had eliminated. When one of Kiselev's protégés complained, Alexander replied, "I must say that I have heard and continue to hear a multitude of complaints about the administration of state properties."[35] This remark indicates who had the new tsar's ear, for a favorite technique of the opponents of emancipation, as the subsequent debate would show, was a counterattack on the Ministry of State Properties and Kiselev's reforms.

Proponents of emancipation could only be dismayed by Alexander's choice of advisors. They were encouraged, however, by the end of the Crimean War and the manifesto announcing the Peace of Paris. The manifesto expressed the hope that "every man, under the shelter of laws equally just for all and equally protective of all, may enjoy in peace the fruits of innocent labor."[36] Abolitionists took heart, not in response to official actions but to a shift in the climate of opinion. The death of Nicholas and the ending of the war imparted to educated society a sense of relief and a feeling, which some did not find pleasant, that new possibilities were opening up. The onset of hope and enthusiasm in the late 1850s has often been exaggerated in retrospect. Yet the period between the death of Nicholas and the outbreak of the Polish Rebellion, while not an easy time for a reformer, was positively unsettling for the *bien-pensant*. At no other time in the nineteenth century did Russians find it harder to discern the perimeter of the feasible and the appropriate. These years were characterized, as Eidel'man puts it, by "a feeble and changing boundary between 'it's all right' and 'it's forbidden', between publicity and secrecy, between . . . fear of expanding the permissible and thinking of taking advantage of that expansion."[37] A venerable pomeshchik like General Grabbe, who had spent his mature years in devoted service to Nicholas I, could now condemn serfdom as a noxious swamp and give a respectful hearing to ideas that had recently been forbidden. But one night Grabbe was visited by the reproachful ghost of Nicholas himself, who complained, "How is it, during this general rebellion against me and everything I created, that even you are against me!"[38]

In this atmosphere, abolitionists began to compose and circulate proposals for the reform of serfdom. They sought to foster a shift in public opinion,[39] but they also forwarded their writings to high officials. Elements of these proposals would eventually be incorporated into the emancipation legislation. Their main common characteristic, however, is extreme caution. The authors—Kavelin, Chicherin, Koshelev, Cherkasskii, Samarin, and even Pozen—were subsequently to advocate a genuine and far-reaching reform, but in composing these plans they assessed the political climate of 1855-1856 and found it unfavorable. Kavelin, who was exposed to the society of dignitaries and courtiers for the first time in this period, wrote to Pogodin,

Visit the kitchen where state policies and laws are prepared and you will be seized with terror. No, better a peasant from behind the plow, better a huckster from the bazaar than these————, who are good for nothing but petty intrigue.[40]

When Kavelin became better acquainted with the government's thinking on the peasant question and was initiated into the outer circle of its deliberations, he moderated his proposals still further.[41] Like the other abolitionists, he was willing to pay a very high price, in the form of prolonged delays or concessions to the nobility, in order to rescue the principle of emancipation from the realm of wishful thinking to which official wisdom had consigned it.

The government ook an initiative on the peasant question for the first time in March 1856, but the initiative was most ambiguous. Count Zakrevskii, governor-general of Moscow, was disturbed because, as he wrote to a friend, "rumors about freedom are circulating among the people, rumors that freedom will be proclaimed on coronation day, and although this is nonsense, it must be attended to. . . .There's no joking about transformations like that." Although such rumors were commonplace among the peasantry in advance of coronations, royal birthdays, and similar occasions, Zakrevskii asked Alexander to reassure the nobility. This is the laconic speech Alexander delivered to the marshals of the nobility of Moscow Province:

It is rumored that I want to give liberty to the peasants; this rumor is unjust, and you can say this to everyone, on all sides. But a hostile feeling between peasants and their pomeshchiki does, unfortunately, exist, and this has already led to several instances of insubordination to pomeshchiki. I am convinced, that sooner or later we must come to this. I think that you agree with me, consequently, it is better that this come from above, than from below.

Since this text was corrected by Alexander himself, the ambiguity (such as the lack of any reference for the "this" to which we must come sooner or later) must be deliberate. The tsar did emphatically disclaim any intention of emancipating the serfs, yet there was no precedent for even a semipublic statement from the throne that emancipation must come some day. Almost a century earlier, Catherine II had expressed the same sentiments—but in a private letter.[42] In effect, then, the speech was a guarded appeal to the nobility to advance plans for emancipation, an appeal which was more forthright in a corrupt but widely circulated text of this speech.[43]

An appeal to the nobility was the sum and substance of the government's peasant policy for most of 1856. This appeal was pushed forward in talks conducted at the coronation by A. I. Levshin, Deputy Minister of Internal Affairs. The same purpose is clear in the turn given to the Grand Duchess Elena Pavlovna's plan for a reform on her estate in Poltava Province; the government wanted Elena Pavlovna to develop the plan in consultation with local nobles, so that it would not be merely an act of royal munificence. For, as Alexander wrote to her late in 1856,

rather than hastening to outline general statutes for a new disposition of the most numerous estate in the realm, I am waiting, so that the right-thinking [pomeshchiki] themselves will speak out and indicate the extent to which they conceive it possible to improve the lot of their peasants, on principles which will be humanitarian and not onerous for either side.[44]

The policy of appealing to the nobility was not promising. It had been tried in a small way and found wanting a decade earlier. It also tended to vitiate the government's commitment to emancipation with land; the greater the pressure on the nobles, the more they would be tempted to diminish peasant landholding. One pomeshchik responded to rumors that emancipation was impending by giving the following instruction:

I strongly urge you to try to release as many people as possible from the Sergievskoe estate at the guardians rate.* The more people we set free, the more land we will receive when the peasants are emancipated, and you know yourself that we have little land. . . . Every peasant set free now, even at a loss for me, preserves three or four desiatiny of land for me in the future.[45]

Other nobles reached the same conclusion and, so long as their powers as serfholders were intact, they had ample means to act upon it. They could increase the demense at the expense of the peasants' allotments, transfer peasants to the status of household serfs, and manumit them. In response to the government's tentative overtures and rumors about more determined action,

---

*Za opekunskuiu tsenu, indicating that the estate in question was mortgaged. For each serf he set free, the owner of a mortgaged estate had to remit a fixed sum to the Council of Guardians, the agency that held the government-sponsored mortgages.

many nobles did increase their demesne landholdings by these means.[46] Peasants would have lost a great deal of land by the time the deliberations of the noble estate, without further stimulus, could have borne fruit.

Most important, the policy was defective in its essence. The impulse behind the appeal was not simply a desire to forestall resistance by accommodating the nobility's desires. The government appealed to the nobility from the depths of its own bafflement.[47] When it overcame this bafflement, it would regret the appeal, for seeking the opinion of the public on cardinal principles was contrary to its traditional legislative practices. It still had no inkling of a program of its own, however, and the hope that the nobles' "experience" could overcome obstacles it had found insuperable was vain and even pathetic.

The nobility was quick to appreciate the government's quandry, and there is an element of smug insolence in the response of the provincial marshals to Levshin, who sounded them out at the time of the coronation. Like the tsar's ministers, they found it easy to commit themselves to emancipation in principle. But they argued, anticipating a point many spokesmen for the nobility would make in the years ahead, that no mandate could permit them to make any disposition of the rights and property of their electorate. And, as Levshin reported to the tsar, "they did not know the basic principles on which the government proposes to accomplish this change, and without this knowledge they could not themselves come to any decision."[48]

The coronation discussions did have consequences. Because the marshals from the Northwest seemed more accommodating than the rest, it was decided to instruct the governor-general of Vilna, Grodno, and Kovno provinces to cajole or coerce the local nobility into taking an initiative. This effort was eventually to provide the pretext for the formal and public decision to emancipate the serfs. In the meantime, however, the government dropped the policy of appealing to the nobility,[49] to take a different, more familiar, but no more promising course.

The Secret Committee

The establishment of the Secret Committee on the Peasant Question marked the turn to a new course and, incidentally, a rebuff to the Ministry of Internal Affairs.[50] In December 1856, Lanskoi reported to the tsar that appeals to the nobility had been fruitless and that it was impossible to proceed further without a program. It was therefore necessary to set up a small committee to produce one, assisted by temporary "technical" committees.[51] The compiler of the report, Levshin, ingenuously admitted in his memoirs that he expected to be the intermediary between the two committees and thus arbiter of the reform; this would not be the last time that ordinary ambition would intrude into the "holy cause." The tsar, however, gave the proposal an unexpected turn. He rejected the proposal for technical committees and with it the idea of relying on the "well-intentioned" elements of the nobility. As for the committee of officials, Lanskoi had proposed that its members be

convinced of the necessity of passing without a minute's delay to a new order, but at the same time prepared to enter into all objections and contradictions, without shrinking before them, so as to avert all the bad consequences of half-baked proposals.

As chosen by the tsar, the committee was much better qualified on the second count than on the first; indeed, four of its members had accumulated experience in entering into objections and contradictions as members of committees identical to Alexander's new one.[52] The committee's activities began with a review of the proposals on the peasant question advanced in Nicholas's reign. Alexander was lowering buckets into exhausted wells.

The Secret Committee, like its predecessors, did not indulge in contradiction. The tsar, in his opening speech, declared that serfdom "has almost outlived its time," and the committee dutifully rejoined that serfdom "is in and of itself an evil, requiring correction," and that pomeshchiki and serfs alike were in "a certain state of expectancy." Rather than challenging the tsar on a principle to which almost every statesman of the last half-century had given lip-service, the committee resorted to what Russians call "deaf" opposition: procrastination, semantic evasions, and facility in seeing difficulties. In its first session, with the tsar in the chair, the committee agreed to undertake "a detailed review" of legislation and proposals for reform in order to determine

the principles on which it can be possible to proceed to the emancipation of the serfs among us . . . without abrupt or sharp overturns, but rather according to a plan assiduously and maturely considered in all its details.[53]

In its second session, meeting without the tsar, the committee quietly added an element to the formula; it pronounced in favor of emancipation "without abrupt or sharp overturns and without coercive measures."[54] In other words, the committee tactily redefined its goal, "emancipation," as meaning "voluntary manumission" rather than a general act of prescriptive legislation. To renounce coercion meant abandoning abolition.

In this session, the committee also delegated the onerous labor of reviewing legislation and proposals on the peasant question to a subcommittee of three, since the other members were burdened with ministerial and departmental duties. In the subcommittee, the most resolute opponent of landed emancipation on the Secret Committee, Prince Pavel Gagarin, was balanced by Baron Modest Korf and General Rostovtsev, both of whom sought to be excused on the grounds, quite legitimate, of ignorance; they knew nothing of peasant life and did not own any serfs. To this Count Orlov, chairman of the Secret Committee, replied that the other members, although serfowners, were no better prepared, but what was wanted was "a statesmanlike point of view"; besides, their appointment had already been approved by the tsar.[55] So the problem of serfdom was delivered over to this unlikely trio.

There remained only the question of the excitement and expectancy in the country at large, on which the committee had remarked in its first session. The majority now decided that the serfs were not excited after all, but their masters were, and that they should be reassured so that agriculture could pursue its regular course. This cherished purpose could be achieved only with some sacrifice of a cherished principle, secrecy, and a conflict ensued. The majority held that "to calm the pomeshchiki it is necessary that they know that the Government has no designs at all on their rights and property," and that it would move gradually, taking the inoffensive laws of 1803 and 1842 as its point of departure. Gagarin countered with the observation that these laws were virtually worthless, as the committee itself had acknowledged; therefore it would be better to keep the secrecy of the deliberations inviolate, at least "for a few weeks," until the government had a clearer idea of its own intentions.

The tsar's resolution on the journal* of this second session was ambiguous. He approved the journal and thereby accepted the limited goals the committee had set for itself in his absence. Yet, since he agreed with Gagarin that these goals and the government's deliberations over them should not be made public, he rejected a curious "reassuring ukaz" offered by the majority. The ukaz would yet again exhort the peasants to submission and assure their masters that there would be no emancipation except through the

---

*A *zhurnal* was a committee's report to the tsar on its deliberations and conclusions at one or more sessions and bore the date of his acceptance or rejection of the conclusions.

existing laws on manumission, as they might be amended and improved.[56]

The tsar's resolution had the effect of expressing mild dissatisfaction with the conclusions he was explicitly endorsing and mild encouragement to Gagarin's premise that the government must introduce certain "main principles" into its peasant policy. It remained to be seen whether the tsar could accept the principle that Gagarin himself had in mind, which was to permit manumission on a large scale without land. It was axiomatic that the serfs could not be set free without land, but this axiom, once established, impeded any further action, as the newest secret committee was showing once more. At best, Alexander's rejection of the "reassuring ukaz'" was a frail straw in the wind; it is not likely that Orlov and the other members, as they dispersed while the subcommittee did its work, shared the agitation that was supposed to be rife among the *hobereaux*.

The subcommittee labored on into the spring and determined that none of the proposals and memoranda submitted to the government offered "a complete and feasible plan, according to which it would be possible to undertake a general change in the relations between pomeshchiki and serfs."[57] Furthermore, the three members could not agree among themselves and had to offer three separate memoranda, which triangulated the government's dilemma.

General Rostovtsev, the novice, submitted the first and longest memorandum.[58] He had taken literally the injunction to study the proceedings of Nicholas's secret committees, and, as Zaionchkovskii observes, he borrowed even his supporting arguments from them. He found serfdom morally intolerable. "No thinking and enlightened person who loves his country can be against the emancipation of the serfs. A man should not belong to another man. A man should not be a thing." Furthermore, abolition would bring "great benefit to the state." But in his few months of study Rostovtsev had penetrated to the dead center of the cluster of obstacles to emancipation: emancipation of the peasants with little or no land was impossible, uncompensated expropation of peasant lands would ruin the nobility, and the government did not have the means for simultaneous and immediate compensation. If it should redeem the peasant lands in one part of the empire only (as Kavelin and others were suggesting), the peasants awaiting emancipation elsewhere would be provoked to rebellion. Then, too, the serfs were unprepared: "It is impossible and undesirable to transfer half-educated men abruptly from complete slavery to complete liberty."

So Rostovtsev, like the previous secret committees, postponed "complete liberty" to the remote future through a three-stage plan. In the first stage, serfdom would be moderated—that is, the legislation against the abuses of manorial power would be extended, providing evidence to the serfs of the government's concern. In the second state, the serfs would gradually become "obligated peasants" or "free agriculturists" on the basis of the laws of 1803 and 1842; the reluctance of their masters would be overcome by the lure of easy credit.[59] The third stage, complete liberty, would be the work of Alexander's successors; Rostovtsev did not offer a more precise timetable, but Alexander was young and healthy. "This whole transformation," Rostovtsev wrote, "will be accomplished imperceptibly, gradually and soundly, though not quickly." Along with the dream of imperceptible emancipation, Rostovtsev acquired from the traditional wisdom an equal dread of action and of inaction. He conceded,

The objection will be made that the people will not wait, the people will demand freedom and emancipate themselves. A popular revolution can indeed break out, if the government is going to continue to vex men's minds without making any fundamental change. Who would venture to answer for the future? But if this revolution might actually take place in the course of time, what are the immediate and, so to speak, mathematically precise means by which it can be averted? And what if the government, fearing the anticipated revolution, should itself evoke revolution deliberately so to speak, through a bold, abrupt and (*unfortunately for Russia*) *ill-considered* measure?

The "mathematically precise means" with which Rostovtsev would embellish the traditional compromise between action and inaction was his "reassuring ukaz," which had been rejected earlier.

Rostovtsev's colleagues on the subcommittee were less anxious about peasant rebellion, but were not on that account any more venturesome, since they, too, proposed remedies that had already been rejected. Gagarin[60] took as his point of departure, as many nobles would do in the debate to come, the importance of the nobility in the economic and political life of Russia and also the "legal rights" and "long-standing enactments" that underlay their privileges. He hinted at the danger of a Fronde. The implementation of any reform of serfdom.

should be left to the unconstrained initiative of the nobility; the pomeshchiki, as owners of landed property, constitute a firm basis for the throne and the state; consequently, any impairment of their interests and proprietary rights cannot pass without influence on the life of the empire.

Furthermore, Gagarin did not perceive any crisis in the economy. The very merit of his system was that it "does not change the economic life of either [peasants] or pomeshchiki" and would facilitate "the retention of that bond between plowman and landowner from which the might of Russia is derived."

So far, Gagarin was articulating concepts (the sanctity of private property, in particular) that his colleagues shared but did not express so boldly. Gagarin did not, however, find the situation hopeless, because he rejected the axiom that emancipation without land was unthinkable. He dismissed the government's fear of a proletariat by saying that a rural proletariat was impossible in principle, especially in a country as rich in land as Russia. This reasoning, supported by "a proper view of the historical rights of peasants and pomeshchiki," led Gagarin to conclude "that in our autocratic empire, liberty can only be given to the peasants personally,* without rights to the land, and should consist in their personal protection from oppression by the landowner." Peasants would acquire this protection by gaining the right of appeal to the district marshal of the nobility "as an agent of the government"; otherwise the manorial power of the pomeshchiki would be left virtually intact. The essence of Gagarin's memorandum, then, was his disquisition on the word "proletariat," by which he hoped to allay fears of a solution to which his colleagues were otherwise inclined.

Baron Korf did not offer any solution and did not believe that bureaucrats could produce one. He warned that if the Secret Committee clung to bureaucratic methods, it would go the way of its eight predecessors, despite "our unanimous conviction" that serfdom was an obstacle to progress and an affront to humanity. Resolution of the dilemmas could come only from "the experience and benign inclinations" of provincial nobles, who should be invited to submit reform plans. The guidelines he proposed were at once so vague and so unattainable that the essence of his proposal was to offer the nobility a carte blanche.[61] Korf argued that such an appeal to the nobility would not, as Rostovtsev and others feared, evoke peasant violence.

Since the peasants are convinced that the government desires their emancipation and that only the pomeshchiki resist it, they will see from the publication of the circular [Korf's proposed appeal] that the pomeshchiki are also facilitating emancipation—or at least, that the government has set this before them as an obligation.

---

*It is not clear whether "personally" (*lichno*) meant "without land" or "by manumission."

Korf's primary consideration, however, was not fear of either a Fronde or a jacquerie. Like the government in the previous year, he would appeal to the nobility not simply for support, but for solutions to basic problems.

Korf's proposal was disingenuous, Liashchenko has suggested, for he must have assumed that the nobility's response would be so hostile as to postpone emancipation indefinitely.[62] It is more probable that he was trying, by proposing a course that had been found wanting in the previous year, to push the question of serfdom back on the dead center where it had reposed so long. It is wise, however, to be careful in imputing motives to men like Korf and Orlov, and to be skeptical of anecdotes about them.[63] They had spent their lives serving a state that was permeated by serfdom and was dedicated, in practice, to its preservation. In this service they assimilated certain loyalties and policies, but also absorbed basic attitudes about subordination, economics, morality, and human nature itself. A bureaucrat can alter policies and redirect loyalties more easily than most men, but it is no easier for him than for anyone else to overcome his basic attitudes. These attitudes had to be overcome if proffered solutions to major questions—such as those that would gradually be accepted over the next two years—were to be recognized as solutions. Korf was confessing, in the oblique manner of an experienced bureaucrat, that he was unable to resolve the problem his sovereign had put to him; a confession of incapacity deserves some credit.

Prince Orlov's comment[64] on these three memoranda consisted largely of an attack on Korf's plan to appeal to the nobility, which he found dangerous and futile. Since the appeal could not be kept secret (indeed, Korf had not suggested that it should), it would only make the serfs impatient for freedom.

Their expectation, however, can scarcely be realized in the near future. Therefore, the measure Baron Korf proposed will arouse a new nationwide tumult in men's minds, perhaps a stronger and more dangerous one than there was before.

Apart from this danger, the principles of the reform must be imposed upon the nobility, not elicited from them, for,

If the basic principles of the future relations of peasants to pomeshchiki are not clearly and positively indicated, if they are not adopted and confirmed by the government in advance, then surely the nobles of each province will persistently strive to one and the same goal—to preserve their rights and their present relationship to the peasants.

Orlov did not venture to suggest what these "basic principles" might be. Noncommittal on questions of substance, he sought to maintain the Secret Committee's commanding position and the principle of secrecy itself.

Alexander's reply to Orlov's epitome of conventional wisdom expressed a certain impatience:

I have read all these papers with great interest. . . . I am more than ever convinced how *difficult* and *complex* this question is, but all the same I *desire* and *demand* that your committee produce a *general conclusion as to how it is to be undertaken, instead of burying it in the files under various pretexts.*[65]

Orlov did not attach much importance to this august reproof. He circulated the three memoranda among the committee members and put to them eight questions derived from the memoranda. Some of the members found it embarassing that the government had no plan of action, but none would undertake any general legislation for the present. And Korf, reassured by the other members' commitment to "partial and transitional measures," concluded that it was not necessary to appeal to the nobility after all.[66]

After the speculative adventures of the spring, the Secret Committee was driving hard for the haven of its January position. It was not diverted by a further expression of mild dismay from the tsar.[67] Along the way, it unceremoniously rejected a plan produced in the Ministry of Internal Affairs, which had most of the elements of the reform program that would be adopted in November.

To understand the ministry's position, it is necessary to return for a moment to the origins of the Secret Committee. It was the misbegotten issue of a proposal designed to overcome the disadvantages of secrecy. Lanskoi and his deputy, Levshin, were dismayed by their ignorance of agricultural practices in various regions, for they believed that the reform must be tailored to each region. Once the secrecy of the government's deliberations was broken and knowledgeable subordinates could be consulted, ignorance would not seem such a problem and the central organs would become as confident as ever of their ability to cope with local peculiarities. So long as secrecy was observed, Lanskoi and Levshin were thrown back on their own modest resources. Hence they proposed the creation of a small committee of emancipators that would mediate between the government and "technical committees of compilers of plans for the emancipation of the peasants, well-intentioned pomeshchiki and a few representatives of the nobility."[68] The government would gain access to their knowledge and experience without arousing the nobility at large—and the issue of serfdom would remain the special preserve of the Ministry of Internal Affairs.

In the event, the technical committees were forgotten and the ministry unexpectedly found itself in thrall to a powerful and independent committee in which Lanskoi could have little influence. The ministry promptly (even before the Secret Committee's first meeting) began evolving a scheme to ransom itself. The main element of this scheme was a compromise between purely bureaucratic methods and reliance on initiative from the nobility. The nobility could not, argued Levshin, be counted on to volunteer a reform plan or to respond even to explicit appeals for one. If, however, the government indicated the main principles of the reform in advance, the nobility, sitting in provincial committees; could flesh out these principles to suit the peculiarities of each region.[69]

Through Levshin's compromise, the obstacles to emancipation were eventually to be overcome or evaded. It is nonetheless clear that the impulse behind this compromise was the ministry's plight in relation to the Secret Committee, for Lanskoi was pleased with the procedure Levshin outlined but discerned a difficulty—the ministry had no idea what "main principles" the government should impose. Pressed by his chief, Levshin produced the rudiments of what was to become the government's initial plan of emancipation. He proposed that the peasants were to be personally free and provided with their present household plots, which they would redeem in the course of time. The ex-serfs could be counted on to purchase the plowland they needed gradually.[70]

Memoranda setting forth Levshin's ideas were turned over to the Secret Committee, apparently with the same standing as the unsolicited proposals the government had received. Levshin's memoranda were ignored, and deserved to be. Whatever the merits of the provincial committees might be, the principles offered to guide them were manifestly inadequate. Levshin had papered over the land question with a compromise uncomfortably close to Gagarin's plan and he had no proposals to offer concerning village administration.[71]

The ministry continued, however, to press along the lines indicated by Levshin. In May, Lanskoi revived the idea of committees guided by unspecified "general principles" to be imposed by the government.[72] When Lanskoi was asked to comment on the three memoranda produced by the subcommittee of the Secret Committee, he construed Korf's plan for an appeal to the nobility along the lines of Levshin's earlier proposal, and, in pronouncing Korf's plan "sound and reliable," gave the rationale for committees of the nobility.

An appeal of this kind, addressed to the nobility will *reassure* it by indicating the extent of the sacrifices for which it should prepare; *flatter* it by showing that the Sovereign trustingly invites it to participation in the great cause; *puts a seal of silence* on those who would wish to grumble or express dissatisfaction; finally, if the peasants should by some means find out that the government is actively occupied with improving their lot, then the thought that the nobility will help the government in this matter will soften, if not destroy, *their unfavorable suspicions about the pomeshchiki.*

Lanskoi's diffidence in treating the three memoranda indicates that he felt his position was weak. For example, he graciously credited Gagarin with perceiving how important the land question was, but he did not indicate his own ministry's opinion on this or any other point of substance.[73]

By the end of July, perhaps in reaction to Alexander's expressed impatience with the Secret Committee, the ministry asserted itself more vigorously in two memoranda for the committee. One was an analysis of the failure of the laws of 1803 and 1842, which the committee was using as its point of departure. The laws had served only to put rigid limits on the nobles' emancipatory impulses, but any plan that would rely on their initiative must fail.

Has the government any basis for supposing that a majority of the nobles (to say nothing of the overall mass of them) would desire to renounce willingly the advantages they derive from serfdom and exchange the certain present for a doubtful future? Exceptions do not make a general rule. . . . Very many benevolent pomeshchiki who are ready to begin to release their own serfs have declared to me that they do not desire to set an example for their fellows, and do not believe they have the right to do so, especially since examples of this kind can be utterly ruinous for their neighbors.[74]

The memorandum did not indicate how the proposed provincial committees would induce pomeschiki to accept a "doubtful future," but the accompanying memorandum[75] showed how much ingenuity had already been expended to make their future more certain. For example, the ministry attacked the problem of the pomeshchiki who had little land of value and derived their income from obrok, and produced a solution that would, in a more sophisticated form, become part of the eventual settlement. It would have the peasants redeem their houses and household plots:

where the land was less valuable, the price would be inflated to the point where the lord would be compensated for the lost obrok. In principle, however, serfs would not be obliged to redeem themselves, because this would not be necessary in areas where nobles could get an adequate income from landownership alone.

The ministry was no less ingenious in dealing with the sacred right of property. "How," it asked, "can property rights be preserved intact without jeopardizing the general tranquility?" The lord would retain his title to the land, but, apart from the plots, the peasants would get an unspecified amount of land in "conditional usufruct" (*uslovnoe pol'zovanie*), for which they would remit obrok or barshchina. They would be encouraged to purchase this land from the pomeshchik, but the time limit to their right of tenure would not be announced. The ministry expected, in other words, to restore the pomeshchik's property rights in full at some time in the future, when it had the courage and the means; this supposition is borne out by the ministry's favorable references to the emancipation settlement in the Baltic provinces. Finally, the gradualism demanded by the tsar would be territorial; the reform would begin in the Northwest, where the Baltic system was near at hand and familiar, and move east.

The ministry's plan was as vague on administrative matters in July as it had been in December, but in other respects the new version was more inventive and more complete; certainly, the ministry's arguments against the Secret Committee's intention of resurrecting the laws of 1803 and 1842 were persuasive. However, the committee rejected the plan with no more ceremony than before. Lanskoi was not wholly convinced of the merits of the memoranda presented in his name, or else he sought to make the best of defeat, for he joined the rest of the Secret Committee in signing the Journal of August 18.

The Journal of August 18 is of great importance for an understanding of the genesis of the abolition of serfdom. Historians have assumed that, by the summer of 1857, the pressures for reform were overwhelming. Yet the tsar's senior advisors showed not one whit more sensitivity to these pressures than they had twenty years before. Their considered, conclusive statement of policy makes them look foolish in retrospect, and examples of folly in high office are instructive. But their statement should also teach historians to be cautious in using such words as "ineluctable" and "inevitable."

In the Journal of August 18, the committee informed the tsar that

after assiduous and detailed discussion . . . the Committee has become positively convinced that it is not presently possible to undertake the general emancipation of the serfs among us, that they are not at all prepared to receive liberty suddenly and abruptly; that if they were freed by a general proclamation, their age-old relations to the pomeshchiki would be disrupted and the peace and order of theState might be shaken. . . . At the present time, not only the peasants and pomeshchiki but even the Government itself are not prepared for a general emancipation of the servile estate.

Lest this last conclusion be construed as a criticism of the regime and the sanovniki themselves, the committee pointedly reminded the tsar of his own repeated appeals for caution and discretion.

Accordingly, the committee offered a three-stage plan that differed from Rostovtsev's only in detail; there was less explicit reliance on the laws of 1803 and 1842, and all serfs were to be granted certain civil rights "gradually, step by step," in the second stage instead of the third. In the first stage, which was of most immediate interest, the government was to "alleviate and mollify" the serfs' status in ways to be determined later, but without weakening the pomeshchik's manorial authority. This was an absurdity, since any meaningful state intervention between lord and serf would weaken the lord's authority. Nobles would be encouraged to manumit their serfs by mutual agreement without being restricted by the terms of the laws of 1803 and 1842. Instead, these agreements would be subject to conditions that would have the same effect, since the manumitted peasants would have to have the means of subsistence, rent, and taxes.

This renewed commitment to the principle of landed emancipation was reinforced by the committee's rejection of Gagarin's familiar proposal that pomeshchiki should be allowed to release their serfs without mutual agreement and without any land except household plots. Finally, during the first stage, the Minister of Internal Affairs should remedy the "absolute lack of data and facts" by various means, including soliciting information and opinion from governors, marshals, and "experienced pomeshchiki"; this proposal was a remnant of the policy of appealing to the nobility. It would be premature even to suggest substantive measures for the second and third stages until the material solicited had been assimilated. The duration of the first stage was not indicated.

The Secret Committee, then, paid ritual tribute to the necessity of emancipating the serfs and then gave serfdom yet another reprieve. This was scarcely the decisive action Alexander had demanded, but he accepted the committee's program. Indeed, he favored the committee with a rare expression of positive approval; in his resolution on the Journal of August 18 he re-echoed the note of caution the committee had sounded to justify itself and hoped for its members' continued "help and active participation in all matters relevant to this vital question."[76]

The tsar could express satisfaction with the committee's work because he and its members were in the same quandary. Like the late tsar Nicholas and his counsellors, they perceived that it was desirable to abolish serfdom but they conceived that it was impracticable to do so. For Alexander, the quandary was particularly painful because the ultimate responsibility for action or inaction was his. Each course had its influential advocates. The dilemma even pursued the tsar on his summer tour of western Europe. Baron von Haxthausen, fresh from a conference with a group of Russian abolitionists, waylaid Alexander as he arrived at the spa of Kissingen. Haxthausen made a strong case for emancipation with land and offered the tsar various practical proposals to that end. There was nothing strikingly novel about the substance of Haxthausen's proposals, which had much in common with the reform plans circulating in manuscript through Russian society and the chancelleries, but their exponent was no mere functionary or man of letters. Haxthausen was a conservative savant of European standing, who had devoted much of his life to the study of peasant communities and had enjoyed the patronage of Nicholas I himself. Familiar arguments took on new force, coming from a man who represented the European lobe of Russia's conscience.[77]

If Alexander was moved, he was not moved to action. Kiselev records his saying at this time,

The problem of the peasants continues to bother me. . . . More than ever, I am full of determination [but] I have no one to help me on this important matter. You know how I like Orlov, but you are also familiar with his ways, and especially his laziness.

It was true that the tsar had no one to help him, in that appeals to the nobility and to the bureaucratic apparatus brought equally meager results. Yet Orlov presided over the Secret Committee by the tsar's appointment. What was required was the determination to break through the conventional wisdom or circumvent Orlov and its other exponents. Kiselev gave full credit to the tsar's "determination," by which he meant nearly the opposite—a mere desire to see the serfs free. For he predicted that the autocrat would be overcome by the "obstacles and various difficulties which are arising from all quarters." One quarter was Kiselev himself, who two weeks later presented the tsar with yet another memoran-

dum reciting the standard obstacles to emancipation and concluding that "to give *full liberty* to twenty-two million serfs of both
sexes is *undesirable* and *impossible*."[78] Kiselev, the most celebrated
reformer of the senior officials, who had occupied himself with
the peasant question for twenty years, had come around to the
position of Orlov. Little wonder that K. D. Kavelin, the leading
abolitionist at the imperial court in the summer of 1857, concluded that the political climate was too unfavorable for any
progress towards emancipation.[79]

The Journal of August 18 was the upshot of the conflict between
Haxthausen's encouragement and Kiselev's caution. Upon
returning from his summer tour of western Europe, the tsar had
appointed his brother Konstantin Nikolaevich to the Secret
Committee. The Grand Duke was "the chief of the liberal
bureaucrats," according to Zaionchkovskii, and "the tsar set [him]
the task of animating the work of the committee and beginning the
preparation of the reform."[80] Even earlier, Nikolai Miliutin had
proposed that Konstantin Nikolaevich should spearhead the
abolitionist forces, for only his combination of youthful energy and
royal prestige could prevail over the difficulties and opposition the
reform would generate.[81] Yet it was he, according to an intimate
subordinate, who sponsored the Journal of August 18.[82] Perhaps,
being a novice in these matters, Konstantin Nikolaevich attached
real significance to the journal's recognition of emancipation as an
eventual goal. Perhaps he supposed, quite erroneously, that once
the sanovniki had pronounced against emancipation, they would be
discredited and excluded from subsequent deliberations on the
peasant question. His maneuver, if such it was, gained nothing.[83]
The Journal of August 18 was a reaffirmation, even in its details, of
the temporizing policy the regime had pursued for more than a
generation.[84] The conventional wisdom of the sanovniki had
triumphed again.

Light out of the Northwest

Interred along with the idea of emancipation was the idea of
seeking the collaboration of the nobility. Indeed, overtures from
nobles in St. Petersburg Province were rebuffed. Presumably
responding to rumors about the Secret Committee, the assemblies
of the nobility of Iamburg and Peterhof districts and a group of
district marshals and deputies had submitted reform proposals to
the government in April. Orlov's report to the tsar was adverse. "In
these proposals there is nothing resembling emancipation, but only
a more or less precise indication of the dues which peasants are

obliged to render to the pomeshchiki under serfdom."[85] Orlov was probably right in his suspicion that the proponents hoped to "compel the government to give up its concern for the emancipation of the serfs and confine itself to confirming their proposals."

Lanskoi tried to find an affinity between the St. Petersburg proposals and his own ministry's evolving program. It was important not to "chill" the nobility's good intentions, lest "the government be deprived of the convenient means offered to it to inaugurate this arduous business at the initiative of the pomeshchiki themselves." Even Lanskoi demurred on such points at the Iamburg nobility's insistence what, while barshchina would ostensibly become a form of rent, the peasants would be obliged to perform it whether or not they got any land.[86] For the majority of the committee, however, the principal obstacle was procedural; a favorable response would end the committee's monopoly of the peasant question. Gagarin approved of the substance of the three proposals because they reaffirmed the pomeshchik's title to all his land, but he found that "to confirm them would constitute a premature decision of the question which has, according to the Imperial will, been put before the Special [i.e., Secret] Committee."[87] While the government made no formal response to the St. Petersburg nobles, the Secret Committee had their proposals in hand and ignored them in producing the Journal of August 18.

The committee also ignored the so-called inventory committees, which were set up as part of the earlier policy of appealing to the nobility for a reform plan. These committees were ostensibly involved in the government's twenty-year struggle to impose inventories, or binding schedules of dues and allotments, on the Polish nobles of three northwestern provinces: Vilna, Grodno, and Kovno. In fact, they had been reconstituted in the hope that, as Levshin reported to the tsar,

in their desire to cooperate with Your Imperial Highness in his good intentions, they will conceive proposals which can facilitate a new and solid arrangement for the peasants, without any palpable losses for the pomeshchiki.[88]

This means was chosen because Levshin; in his conversations at the coronation, had detected among some of the marshals of the Northwest "a readiness . . . to undertake a review of the relations of pomeshchiki and peasants, a review inclined towards the emancipation of the latter." The governor-general of the three provinces, V. I. Nazimov, expressed his confidence that he could persuade the nobility to offer a reform plan.[89] In informing Nazimov of the tsar's approval of this course, Lanskoi expressed his confidence that

under his [Nazimov's] wise and cautious leadership and through the directions and oral exhortations which he . . . thinks necessary to give the marshals of the nobility, the important commission imparted to them by the special confidence of the government will be carried out in the most satisfactory way.[90]

But in fact the nobles were not to be given anything so explicit as a "commission."

There is no necessity, when the inventory rules are returned, of saying *directly* why this is being done. One may hope that the marshals themselves will understand the purpose of this action, while Governor-General Nazimov can give them more explicit directions and permission orally and with due caution.[91]

In other words, Nazimov would attempt to secure consent to emancipation by threats and promises, but orally and semiofficially, so that the government could not be badly compromised if he failed. The nobility would, it was hoped, "be the first to pronounce the word *emancipation*," by a kind of ventriloquism.

Nazimov did proceed with "due caution." He devoted six months to "clear and frank" discussions before ordering the formation of the new committees. He reported that he had not met any opposition, but nonetheless the committees were organized to be compliant; they were appointed by the provincial marshals, who themselves were under close bureaucratic supervision in this former Polish territory.[92]

Nazimov's efforts were rewarded; the committees did "pronounce the word emancipation," but in a thick German accent. The committees in Grodno and Kovno provinces opted for emancipation without land, on the Baltic model; the ex-serfs were to contract for land with proprietors, without any government interference. This was no more than the Grodno inventory committee had volunteered in 1854.[93] One member of the Kovno Committee proposed that pomeshchiki should be obliged to rent the peasant allotments to their present occupants; this proposal, akin to the formula the government was later to impose, was defeated thirty-three to two.[94] The Vilna Committee was divided. One faction was in general accord with the Grodno and Kovno committees; the other, headed by Provincial Marshal Domeiko, proposed waiting until the next assembly of the Vilna nobility. This faction did not, according to the Third Section, reject emancipation of the serfs, but it disputed the committee's "right to make any resolution on so important a subject without securing the assent of all the proprietors."[95]

Domeiko appears to have attached some significance to the government's theoretical commitment to landed emancipation than his colleagues in Kovno and Grodno did; he had been to St. Petersburg in 1855 to battle for the Vilna nobles' right to dispose of their land freely.[96] A committee of the nobility could simply be overruled on this cardinal point. However, action might be forestalled by putting the question before the Vilna assembly of the nobility, and he proposed in the meantime to carry out a survey (*liustratsiia*) of estates with serfs. This survey would facilitate a timely increase of demesne land, so that when and if landed emancipation was imposed, the peasant allotments would be appropriately reduced.[97]

Nonetheless, a majority of the nobility of the Northwest, as represented in the three hand-picked committees, had been induced to take a formal stand for emancipation. In part, they were amenable because, as Levshin pointed out several times, the Northwest bordered on areas where the peasants were already free. Hence the pomeshchiki could see that their property and local power need not suffer, while their peasants would understand that emancipation did not mean freedom from all obligations. Simple familiarity with nonservile agriculture did make the pomeshchiki more amenable to reform. Some nobles in Kovno Province even believed that emancipation would increase their revenues,[98] an idea with very little currency in Great Russia in 1857.

The threat of the inventories was more important, however. The nobility of the Northwest had carried on a more or less successful holding action against the inventories for a generation; the concessions their representatives had recently exacted, with the aid of Count Chernyshev, provided a model of political action based on corporate solidarity. But the nobles did not need Nazimov's "oral exhortations" to tell them that government intervention could not be postponed forever, for they did not enjoy the same favor in St. Petersburg as did their Russian counterparts. The inventory rules had been introduced only where the nobility was prdominantly Polish, and introduced with more vigor where the Polish component was bigger.[99] The government could deny them control of two-thirds of their land simply by enforcing existing laws. Hence many nobles in the Northwest, eager to preclude systematic government intervention between themselves and the peasantry, were amenable to an abolition of serfdom that would give them clear title to all their land.

Nazimov had accomplished his task in a year, but in the meantime the Secret Committee had been established and a new formulation of policy had received the tsar's sanction on August 18. Nonetheless, the Ministry of Internal Affairs decided to use the pretext Nazimov provided to try to overturn the formulation of August 18 and revive the ministry's plan for provincial committees. This attempt required some dissimulation.

First of all, the proposals of the northwestern nobility were subjected to cosmetic surgery. They were, Levshin recalled,

evasive, and expressed much less desire to undertake this business than we had hoped, . . . but I thought it my duty to make use of their amenability, weak though it was, in order to escape from the closed circle drawn by the Secret Committee in the Journal of August 18.[100]

Nazimov, having failed to overcome the dissent in the Vilna Committee minimized it in his report of September 25 to the ministry.[101] The ministry, reporting to the tsar, did not mention it at all:

The committees' replies are vague, but a majority of them express one very important fact, to wit: the nobility of these provinces has acknowledged that the time has come to put an end to serfdom, that it is necessary to replace it with free agreements betweeen the pomeshchiki and the peasants, and that until this radical change takes place it is better to leave the existing inventories alone. The committees do not outline the means of attaining this important goal, and indeed they could not, without knowing the extent to which the government will permit them to follow this new path; they simply make reference to the adjacent Baltic provinces, Courland in particular.[102]

The shortcomings of the proposals were explained away or, on the land question, barely hinted at; the assent of the committees to the bare principle of emancipation was offered as a pretext for the election of committees of the nobility in the three northwestern provinces, which would, applying principles to be laid down by the Secret Committee, draft "complete and definitive statutes" of emancipation.

Lanskoi was careful to express appropriate respect for the Secret

Committee, and the formation of these provincial committees was justified with a reference to the Journal of August 18, which instructed the minister to collect information. He also reiterated the idea of territorial gradualism first expressed in his July report: emancipation would begin in the Northwest and spread south and east.

Nazimov, Lanskoi, and Levshin were guilty of hypocrisy, not deceit, and guilty because they were unsure of their position. The tsar and the Secret Committee knew from other sources what the northwestern nobility had proposed and how the Vilna Committee had been divided.[103] And no deference to the Secret Committee and its Journal of August 18 could hide the fact that Lanskoi was renewing a proposal that had been rejected with the tsar's sanction. Lanskoi's and Nazimov's misrepresentation was not intended to deceive, but to minimize the initiative they were taking in the event that it failed, for they were offering the tsar a meager pretext for reversing the policy he had formally approved two months before. This reversal would embrace the whole empire; despite his territorial gradualism Lanskoi proposed, in response to the questionable initiative from the Northwest, to convene committees of the nobility "in all provinces."

The gamble worked. Two weeks after Lanskoi submitted the report, the tsar turned it over to the Secret Committee with his endorsement.[104] For the first time, the tsar had provided the committee with his opinion on a point of substance, instead of simply passing on its journal. Innocuous in form, his action was the first step forward on the circuitous road to the promulgation of emancipation in 1861. The sources offer no hint about his motives in taking this step, nor any evidence that he believed it to be a fateful one.[105]

The tsar's action left the dignitaries of the Secret Committee the options of backing off from their position of August 18 or resigning. As Levshin observed, Russian statesmen surrender their principles instead of their offices. The committee accepted the fiction that Lanskoi's report was simply an application of its program, any discrepancies being due to the peculiarities of the inventory system.

The committee empowered Lanskoi and M. N. Murav'ev, the Minister of State Properties, to confer with Nazimov and draw up rules of procedure for the committees of the Northwest and to outline the main principles to which they should adhere. This would seem a simple task, requiring only a reformulation of the ministry's vindicated July program in the form of a rescript to Nazimov. However, Levshin, the compiler of that program and, by his own modest account, the great champion of emancipation within his ministry, developed unexpected misgivings: the responsibility was too great, the Secret Committee had never approved the July program, a document that would decide Russia's future could not be compiled in the three days allotted.[106] However, Lanskoi prevailed upon him, and a "Survey of Basic Premises" was produced on time by Levshin in collaboration with two assistants and the two ministers.[107] Lanskoi and Murav'ev reworked the survey into a statement of "General Principles" and supplemented it with three memoranda on procedure.[108] The recommendations of Lanskoi and Murav'ev were accepted by the Secret Committee, but it was decided to make a distinction between binding principles and mere recommendations to the provincial committees. The former would go into a rescript to Nazimov, which would be published, the latter into a directive (*otnoshenie*), which would not. The tsar accepted the Secret Committee's drafts of the rescript and the directive of November 20, eighteen days after he had turned over Lanskoi's report.

The Rescripts and Directives

The rescript of November 20[109] authorized the nobles of the three provinces of the Northwest to elect committees to draft a statute which would provide "a systematic amelioration of the way of life on the proprietary peasants" (*ustroistvo i uluchshenie byta pomeshchich'ikh krest'ian*)[110] The rescript made no mention of emancipation or the abolition of serfdom except indirectly, by stating that the statute was to be drafted "in accord with the initiative taken by the nobility's own representatives" that summer. However, the first of the government's "main premises," which would be binding on the committees, simply ignored the nobility's proposal for emancipation without land. It held:

The pomeshchiki retain their property right to all the land, but the peasants are to remain settled on their household plots,[111] which they are to acquire as property by means of redemption within a definite period; furthermore, the peasants are to be provided with the use of a quantity of land which will be adequate, according to local circumstances, for their subsistence [*obezpechenie byta*] and for the fulfillment of their obligations to the Government and the pomeshchik; for this land they are either to pay obrok or to perform labor for the pomeshchik.

This was the government's answer to the main dilemma of the reform, the conflict between the pomeshchik's property right and the peasants' need for land.[112] Instead of resolving the conflict, the rescript embraced it, in one breath proclaiming the sanctity of private property and infringing it with the provisions on household plots and plowland.

The accompanying directive, which bluntly used the words "abolition" and "emancipation," only augmented this conflict.[113] It seemed to interpret the rescript as providing for *bauerland*: "The land set aside for the use of the peasants cannot be added to the lord's fields, but must remain constantly at the disposal of the peasantry as a whole." On the other hand, the directive empowered the provincial committees to determine the size of the allotments, without any suggestion that they must adhere to the present allotments as indicated in the inventories; it also suggested that peasants could be deprived of their allotments after a transitional period of not more than twelve years, or sooner if they fell into arrears. Taken together, the rescript and directive imply that the government intended, as Levshin had earlier suggested, to uphold the peasants' right to their allotments only until it would be prudent to abolish it. This reservation cannot, however, be found in the documents themselves, which simply provide for a public combat between opposed principles, the pomeshchik's property right and the peasants' tenure.

While the central problem of the reform was left up in the air, others were simply resolved in the nobility's interest. The reform was to be gradual, "so as not to disrupt the economic arrangement presently existing on proprietary estates"; the peasants were to remain submissive to their masters, whose powers would be intact until the new statute was confirmed, and were to ignore malicious rumors. These were commonplaces, but the rescript also imparted significant authority to the nobility on two counts, in the administration of villages and in the competence of the provincial committees.

According to the second of the "main premises," the peasants were to form village societies, retaining the commune where it existed, but the pomeshchik was endowed with "manorial police authority." The meaning of this phrase, *votchinnaia politsiia*, was not clear; it had no previous currency in Great Russia.[114] It seemed to offer the pomeshchik much the same manorial authority he presently enjoyed, to be exercised under the supervision of a board of local nobles. The only specific limitation on the pomeshchik's own authority.

The competence of the provincial committees, as set forth in the rescript and directive, was narrow but far-reaching. They were bound by the three main premises—the two covering land and administration, and a third providing that the reform must not impede the flow of tax revenue. They were obliged to reconsider any of their decisions with which the governor-general expressed disagreement and to explain any divergence from the "considerations" set forth in the directive. If a committee ventured to discuss subjects outside its competence, the governor-general was to close it. Yet within their sphere, the provincial committees were granted real legislative authority; they were not to submit mere proposals, but a draft statute, which the Minister of Internal Affairs would turn over to the tsar for his review. The rescript did not provide for any intermediate legislative authority between the committees and the tsar. Their competence went much further than that of the earlier inventory committees or the advisory councils attached to certain ministries, and constituted a major constitutional innovation for Russia.

Because of the peculiarities of the inventory system and the nationality of the northwestern nobility, it was not immediately clear whether the reform should be extended to the interior provinces. In the report that set these events in motion, Lanskoi had been ambiguous; he had called for the formation of committees in all provinces but had reiterated the principle of territorial gradualism. It remained to be seen which of these ideas would prevail.

On November 22, Lanskoi asked the tsar's permission to circulate the directive of November 21 to the provincial governors and marshals. The rescript was so terse that the more detailed directive would be useful "for the consideration and in certain instances for the guidance of the local governors, and also as an added reassurance to the nobility." He would, of course, bring the matter before the Secret Committee, but he thought it his duty to secure the tsar's approval first. The next day Orlov weighed in with an almost identical note, urging the circulation of the rescript and directive in order to "avert the dissemination of harmful comments and rumors"; he was making the request directly instead of incorporating it into a journal of the Secret Committee "in order to gain time."[115]

Lanskoi and Orlov were trying a time-honored ruse, most recently exploited by Lanskoi with his report of October 18: each was seeking to win the tsar's endorsement in advance and present the rest of the committee with this accomplished fact. But why should they run this little race when their proposals were identical and innocuous? Secrecy was not the issue, for the tsar had already approved the Secret Committee's proposal to publish the rescript in the official section of the *Journal of the Ministry of Internal Affairs* "in order to reassure the nobility of the interior provinces, which is alarmed by various groundless rumors."[116] The point at issue, then, was not the distribution of the documents but the accompanying circular to the governors and marshals. Orlov would send a disclaimer of immediate action by acquainting these officials with the principles laid down for the western provinces "which, in the course of time, may be applied, to a greater or lesser extent, to the other provinces of Russia as well."[117] Lanskoi, on the other hand, wanted to instruct the governors and marshals to cajole or coerce the nobility to petition for the formation of their own provincial committees. The matter actually in dispute was the extension of the reform machinery to the interior.

The tsar gave formal approval to both Lanskoi's and Orlov's notes, but the circular that was sent to the marshals and governors on November 24 reflected Lanskoi's views. It informed them that the government, in response to the inventory committees' finding that emancipation was necessary, had instructed the nobility of the Northwest to elect committees to "draw up the appropriate plans." The circular concluded,

I have the honor, esteemed sir, to provide Your Excellency with copies of [the rescript and directive] for your information and consideration in the event that the Nobility of the province entrusted to you should express a similar desire.[118]

Since the circular put implicit pressure on the governors and marshals to elicit an expression of "a similar desire," it inaugurated the process of abolishing serfdom in Great Russia.

It was a fateful step. Partly because the muted infighting that lay behind it was not generally known, and partly because these maneuvers did not seem adequate to the great occasion, the circular generated a dynasty of anecdotes. As the anecdotal tradition developed, the opposition of the sanovniki was represented in increasingly garish tones, making a striking contrast to the calm resolution of the tsar-liberator. These anecdotes were plausible enough so that reformist officials incorporated them, with all their improbabilities and inconsistencies, into their memoirs, and they passed from there into respectable secondary literature.[119] The anecdotes are innocuous, but they obscure the character of the upper bureaucracy and the kind of problem serfdom presented to it. Senior officials could still struggle over a grave matter through formulaic niceties and slide into a great enterprise on a covering letter.

The circular of November 24 thrust the reform process into

Great Russia, but it did not indicate whether the terms of the rescript to Nazimov would be applied elsewhere. Again there was disagreement and again the majority of the Secret Committee was defeated. The most it could salvage for the Orthodox, Russian-speaking nobles was a few semantic or ephemeral concessions. On November 23, the committee took up—six months after they were submitted—the three petitions from the nobility of St. Petersburg Province. The committee remarked, Orlov reported, that the petitions did not call for emancipation, and it wondered if "partial and palliative measures" would be adequate, for it would be "impossible and even harmful, given the present ferment in men's minds, to take measures which might weaken the authority and significance of the pomeshchiki." The committee favored reforms that would reduce the number of household serfs, encourage serfs to acquire property and to make contractual arrangements with their masters, but "would not change existing relations" between lord and serf.[120]

Two days later, the circular of November 24 having been issued in the interim, the committee retreated to a less definite position: the principles embodied in the rescript and directive to Nazimov *were* applicable to St. Petersburg Province and Great Russia, but "not in their entirety." Accordingly, Lanskoi and Murav'ev were delegated once again to draft suitable variants, in consultation with the governor-general of St. Petersburg, P.N. Ignat'ev.[121] While the drafts were under study, the tsar offered another expression of his impatience.[122] With no more apparent embarrassment than before, the committee reversed itself. On December 4, it acknowledged that "the principles set forth in the rescript . . . of November 20, since they are essential and unalterable and equally applicable to all the provinces of Russia, should be prescribed as the basis of the work of the St. Petersburg Committee."[123] Hence the rescript to Ignat'ev was virtually identical to the one sent to Nazimov. The structure and procedure of the committee was somewhat changed, since only a single province was involved; to avoid overstraining the public's credulity, the initial reference to the high-minded initiative of the nobility was muted.[124] The main premises on land and administration were left as before.

The accompanying directive to Ignat'ev, on the other hand, was significantly different from its predecessor; at least, the differences were meant to be significant.[125] All references to "abolition" and "emancipation" were erased and nothing was substituted, which produced some curious expressions; instead of redeeming "the rights of free status," the serfs were bidden to redeem "the rights of status." The new directive also diminished the governor's supervisory authority over the provincial committee and dropped the threat of dissolution if the committee should raise inappropriate questions; instead, it was instructed to stick to business. These changes simply reflect a fonder attitude to the Great Russian pomeshchiki than to their counterparts in the Northwest.

Changes were also made in the points of substance that the committee was to "take into consideration." The degree of mobility that peasants might enjoy, once they had redeemed "the rights of status," would be determined subsequently by the government. There was no provision for depriving a peasant of his allotment if he fell into arrears; instead, the committee was to produce detailed rules to ensure that there would be no arrears. In contrast to the earlier directive, a pomeshchik could incorporate peasant land into the demesne, but only if he could get the assent of the commune and the permission of a "District Board." The most important difference concerned the character of dues and redemption payments; in the Northwest, they were supposed to correspond to the value of the land the peasants received. The directive to Ignat'ev held that the redemption payments for household plots and dues for allotments were to "be determined not merely by an assessment of the land and the buildings on the plot, but also by an assessment of the nonagricultural resources and advantages of the area." In other words, they would not have the character of rent or purchase, but would be set according to the committee's judgment of what the peasants could pay. They would be distinct from the dues of serfs only in being determined by a committee of pomeshchiki instead of the individual proprietor.

None of these recommendations was binding, though the St. Petersburg Committee was obliged, like the committees of the Northwest, to justify any departure from them. In sum, the changes made the peasants' tenure more certain but facilitated encroachment on their allotments by the pomeshchik; their potential mobility was restricted and their dues would have an element of "extraeconomic constraint." It is difficult to say whether the government's program, as revised for the Great Russian provinces, was more or less favorable to the nobles' interest than the directive to Nazimov, but it was a long step closer to serfdom.

It would be seemly to pause at this point and mark the first victim of the November triumph. This was not Orlov or Zakrevskii but Levshin, the principal architect of the government's program. His misgivings about the rescript of November 20 swelled to outright opposition when the process was extended to Great Russia. He regretted that his chief had unexpectedly become "a persecutor of the nobility" and regretted still more his own plight, stigmatized by some for composing the government's program and by others for opposing it. His objections were grounded in a fear that the government's rash commitment to reform would provoke a rebellion of disillusioned peasants. He continued nominally to occupy his post for some months more, but he was not involved in the reform of serfdom after November.[126]

Levshin's fall was the first instance of the general disruption within educated society (to say nothing of the village) produced by the government's public commitment to reform. There would be more self-styled abolitionists, in the capitals and in the provinces, who would unexpectedly find that their loyalties to the squires were stronger than their desire for emancipation, or that their desire was weaker than their fear of the consequences. November 1857 is more important in this connection than February 1861. Levshin was simply the first to feel the ground shift beneath his feet.

Implications of the Program

Contradiction and confusion are the striking characteristics of the rescripts and directives. The government was to profess its fidelity to these documents until the promulgation of emancipation. In its particulars, however, as in its spirit and design, the legislation of 1861 had little in common with the program of 1857. In 1857 the regime made a commitment to certain terms of reform; this commitment set in motion the forces that produced the quite different terms of the eventual legislation. That is the extent of the relationship between the legislation and the initial program. The program of 1857 did contain language, such as "amelioration of the peasants' way of life," that would be used to justify quite different principles in the statutes. The rescripts may have mollified the serfs and did reassure their masters, although not in the sense that Alexander II and Orlov had in mind: they served to divert the nobility's attention from questions of substance, which the government undertook to work out for itself, to questions of procedure. These incidental functions do not derive from any Machiavellian cunning in the upper bureaucracy, for the documents were the product of conflict, improvisation, and dilettantism. Moreover, these functions should not obscure the great distinction between the program to which the regime committed itself in 1857 and the provisions of the legislation enacted in 1861.

The terms of the rescripts and directives were less important than the publicity given them. The directive to Nazimov, which forthrightly used the words "abolition" and "emancipation," was withheld from the press, but the two rescripts and the directive to Ignat'ev were published. This publication constituted a promise, made from the height of the throne. Even if peasant revolt had not been a matter of anxiety, this time the problem of serfdom could not be quietly recommitted to the files. As Dmitri Miliutin explained upon reading the rescript for the first time,

However weakly the government's views are set forth in this document, all the same this measure must be considered a most important step towards the fulfillment of a task about which heretofore debates and deliberations have been conducted almost without hope of success.[127]

Since the government's deliberations on the peasant question were no longer a secret, the conditions of combat were fundamentally changed.

The government entered this new combat lightly armed. On the central question of land and property rights, the tsar's counsellors had not overcome their bafflement but displayed it to the world. They rebaptized the dragon of manorial authority instead of slaying it. They forgot to make any provision for the one and a half million serfs who were classified as "household people" and held no land.[128]

The provision for "manorial police power" is an instructive example of the kind of improvisation that went into the program of 1857, and indicated how little accrued to the regime from the years of discussion that had gone before. The peasants had long been regarded as "unprepared" for real freedom; this was an insuperable obstacle in the eys of Kiselev, Rostovtsev, and other participants in the debate leading up the Journal of August 18. "Unprepared" was a conventional euphemism. Peasants were thought capable of settling disputes among themselves, dividing the land, and so on. Peasant justice might be rough, but this was not cause for great concern so long as only peasants were affected. However, the peasants were thought to be "unprepared" (more plainly, unwilling) to pay taxes, deliver recruits, repair roads, and render dues to the pomeshchik without direct external coercion.

The Ministry of Internal Affairs did not have any formula for bringing this coercion to bear, but a formula had to be produced under the pressure of events in November. The provision for "manorial police power" may exprss some affinity for the Baltic system, but the inspiration was M. N. Murav'ev's. Some time before, he had submitted a memorandum to the tsar in which he accepted, in principle, the necessity of emancipation. Unfortunately, Murav'ev observed, there was no authority in the countryside except the pomeshchik's, and

if it is abolished, there will be complete anarchy; hence it should not be subjected to any abrupt shock until it can be replaced with another authority of equal force; rather, it should be placed within sensible limits by reducing all its unsuitable arbitrary aspects.[129]

This was not a particularly sophisticated proposal; it was probably advanced with a view to postponing decisive action.[130] But Murav'ev, in contrast to Lanskoi and Levshin, was armed with the knowledge of what he wanted, and so he prevailed when the "Survey of Basic Premises" was drawn up.[131] An argument against immediate reform became part of the government's reform program.

Still, few hard questions are solved in laws, fewer still in the preliminary versions of laws. If the program of 1857 contributed to the security of the regime, that might be achievement enough. No jacquerie or Fronde took place, but the rescripts and directives cannot therefore be said to have forestalled these calamities. If these documents are read with the statutes of 1861 in mind, they seem to be a statesmanlike advance towards the government's goal—securing landed emancipation while preserving the political structure. If, however, they are taken literally, as Russians had to take them in 1857 and 1858, they seem only to augment the dangers they were supposed to avert.

The danger of a massive peasant rebellion, a *pugachevshchina*, was advanced as an argument for and against emancipation. If there was real danger, it did not lie in the individual acts of peasant violence that were so much emphasized in the police reports.[132] It lay in collective expressions of peasant protest, often relatively passive, which might get out of control and snowball until the regime itself was threatened. The necessity of containing any collective expression of peasant discontent was clear to every constable and district marshal.

The program of 1857 was a weak remedy against the possibility of rebellion because it would perpetuate the situations that tended to produce collective protest. It would limit the pomeshchik's power over persons and retain his power over resources—land and labor. He would no longer be able to prevent peasants from acquiring property, marrying at pleasure, serving in the Senate, and doing other things the authors of the program enjoyed doing. However, this arbitrary power over persons did not pose great danger to the state because it evoked individual revenge, not collective protest. It was hard to mobilize a village in behalf of an affronted fiancé and relatively easy to arouse it against a shift from obrok to barshchina.

If enacted, the program would probably have reduced the occasions for assault and murder of pomeshchiki and stewards. It would also have eliminated some occasions for collective protest, such as the transfer of entire villages to remote provinces. It offered no remedy for situations such as the flight of thousands of peasants from their villages during the Crimean War; by and large, they had not fled from the abuses the program would eliminate but from the authority it would perpetuate. Insofar as peasant rebellions were a threat to the regime, the program did not meet that threat. It would simply abolish the aspects of serfdom that most affronted the consciences of westernized bureaucrats.

The rescripts and directives also jeopardized the political structure of the state. The generous procedural concessions to the provincial committees undermined two of the basic principles of the Russian state, autocracy and centralization. The rescripts introduced a principle that the public (or at least the nobility) could play a direct role in the legislative process if the interests at stake were sufficiently important; and furthermore, that each province would legislate for itself. These are the constitutional innovations held out by the rescripts, if taken literally. The significance of these innovations is uncertain, since the government reneged on them; it imposed a common emancipation statute, with some regional variants, on the whole empire, and it excluded the provincial committees from any real legislative role. There is no evidence, however, that the government always planned to renege, or even that it gave much consideration to the constitutional implications of the committees. The merits of these committees were debated within the Secret Committee and elsewhere, but no one seems to have given serious thought to the limits of their authority, despite the government's traditional jealousy of its prerogatives.[133] The commitment to reform was achieved only with great strain and deep misgivings; the effort threw the government off balance.

When the government recovered its equilibrium, it discovered that the concessions had been made to little purpose. It wanted two things from the nobility: formal assent to the reform and information on the economic peculiarities of each region and area. Both of these could be had, as it turned out, without any action by the provincial committees. Assent took the form of a petition for the formation of a provincial committee "on the amelioration of peasant life"; the committee itself, formed as a result of the petition, could not enhance that assent and might seek to qualify it. Nor was the committee a necessary or useful source of information. Once discussion of emancipation was brought into the open by the publication of the rescripts, the government could draw freely on its own resources, the press, and the public at large. The provincial committees would be but one stream in the flood of information, and a muddy stream at that. They proved almost incapable of presenting the special features of a province, be they water meadows, truck farms, or hempyards, except as part of a scheme of self-aggrandizement. It would rarely be useful or possible to separate the kernel of information from the husk of special pleading.

By and large, then, the program of November 1857 evaded the major problems of reform. However, the adoption of the rescript and directive of November 20-21 and their extension to the Great Russian provinces in the next few weeks did signify that the opposition of the sanovniki, the nobility's first line of defense, had been overcome. It was not certain what its second line of defense was, since the first line had not been penetrated before.

November and December of 1857 mark a divide in Russian political history. Until that time, the arguments for action on the peasant question had been overborne by practical considerations advanced by the tsar's senior advisors. In November, these practical considerations, as reformulated in the Journal of August 18, were implicitly rejected by the tsar. Defeated in regard to the Northwest, the exponents of the conventional wisdom regrouped to take a stand on St. Petersburg Province; they employed the traditional tactics again, and again were defeated. They had always relied on a manipulation of the tsar's anxieties, and had only one string to their bow, the tsar's confidence in themselves.

Yet their defeat was not total because, oddly enough, they retained the tsar's confidence. Orlov, Dolgorukov, and the others had offered the sovereign their considered judgment on the great question of Russian life. The tsar had rejected their judgment, but he was no more disposed to make an issue of principle than they were. They did not feel they should resign, he did not ask them to, and this mutual accommodation produced an anomaly that would be of crucial political importance. The government was undertaking to reconstruct the foundations of Russian society. Despite a sincere or even desperate desire for continuity and a minimum of change, this undertaking disrupted the whole edifice and set almost every element in motion, for the government had publicly renounced the principle on which the sociopolitical structure reposed. Throughout the structure, well before the aboliton of serfdom was made law, traditional relationships would weaken or fall away. Yet the pinnacle did not respond. The ministerial portfolios and the tsar's confidence remained the preserve of the old order—bureaucrats and generals who had spent their lives in the service of the servile system and showed, as D. A. Obolenskii put it, "no apparent inclination to reform their views, their habits or their methods in conformity with . . . the new reforms."[134] This circumstance would convince many that fundamental change might indeed be averted, that the old tactics and the old politics were still valid. The continuity in office of the sanovniki did limit the scope of the emancipation legislation somewhat. The chief result, however, was to provide false encouragement to the opponents of the government's program, including the opponents with ministerial portfolios, so that their opposition would be belated or misdirected.

With programs, as with personnel, some superior cunning seems to have been at work. The defects and anomalies in the government's 1857 program were eventually turned to account for the benefit of the reform, as the chapters to follow will show. The shortcomings that could not be turned to account could, as it turned out, be sloughed off without much embarrassment. The government's continued professions of fidelity to that program provided reassurance to those anxious nobles who thought the initial program went far enough, or too far. It is tempting to impute a strategic design to the autocrat and, more broadly, to infer from the enactment of reforms that Alexander had the special personal qualities of a reformer.

The veteran statesman Kiselev knew what a reformer must be; in the summer of 1857, spelling out for the empress the reforms that would define the new phase which Russia was entering, he explained that

the work ahead is as enormous as it is difficult; that it is necessary to undertake it courageously, prepared to encounter many unexpected obstacles, which it will take all the constancy and energy of a reformer to overcome; that it is important not to lose heart but, treading carefully, to ascend to that high role which Providence has foreordained for her August Husband; and it is especially necessary, I added, to avoid vacillating now in one direction, now in the other, for that will undermine confidence in the government.[135]

Prince Obolenskii agreed that "firm convictions" and "will" were of the essence, and despaired because Alexander lacked them, and even lacked "the upbringing and education to understand the issues".[136] Obolenskii, however, saw Alexander at a remove and was acquainted only with his public face. To appraise his gifts and grasp his design, it is necessary to penetrate through the ceremonial platitudes and hypocrisy of his official statements. Unfortunately, to penetrate through Alexander's official hypocrisy is to come out on the other side of him; if he was endowed with superior cunning, he buried it so deep as to leave no trace for posterity. For example, Gerasimova has culled Alexander's diary and private correspondence and found nothing, except for disparaging remarks about journalists and Poles, that would be inappropriate in a coronation manifesto.[137] Rieber discovered and published Alexander's letters to his boyhood friend Bariatinskii, but it turns out that the tsar wrote to his boyhood friend as if filling in a form.[138] His marginal comments on government documents reveal an intense interest in personalities, but almost no ideas except the idea of autocracy. While he would later take pride in his role in abolishing serfdom, he did not condescend to master the details of the contending programs. His remarks on the subject, both before and after the commitment to reform, were laconic, ambiguous, and inconsistent one with another; he was strangely out of touch.

It is hard to find in Alexander the reformer's breadth of vision and harder still to find strength of will. The public supposed he was timid and malleable, those who knew him well were convinced of it. The history of the Secret Committee is full of the kinds of vacillation against which Kiselev warned. The tsar convened a committee of officials lukewarm or hostile to reform, goaded it into taking action, accepted its temporizing recommendations, and then elicited from it a half-baked program very like one it had previously rejected. It can be argued that the byplay with the committee was a maneuver within a broader strategy, but what object was served? Guile without an object is fooling around.

Alexander lacked salient traits of a reformer, but these traits were not needed to initiate the abolition of serfdom. What was decisive was not the personality of the autocrat but the institution of autocracy. Alexander was reared to play this institutional role and he adapted deftly to it.[139] He vacillated and hesitated, but he never floundered. His autocratic will did not manifest itself in bold strokes, but in a passive tenacity. Three times his intervention was decisive for the commitment to reform, and each time he intervened in response to someone else's initiative. That proved to be enough to inaugurate the reform process; to see it through to enactment would be another matter.

Serfdom had only a single survival mechanism, which was enmeshed in autocracy. The tsar's couosellors would periodically report that the abolition of serfdom was untimely on prudential grounds, the autocrat would defer to the counsel of prudence, and serfdom would receive a new lease on life. This mechanism had been so effective over the years that no reserve mechanism had developed. The prereform polity was rich in devices for the enforcement and support of serfdom, but not for its defense. The autocrat had only once to refuse to play out his part, to deny the customary reprieve, and serfdom was condemned. This refusal required courage, but no great force of will or understanding of intricate issues. It did require an attachment to the autocrat's prerogatives, which had sustained serfdom so long, and an affinity for "emancipation." These Alexander had. There is no evidence that he had worked out in his own mind what "emancipation" meant or scrutizined his own motives for seeking it.

Alexander's amorphous motives were another trait he shared with the sanovniki. The issue least discussed in the debates of 1856-1857 was *why* emancipation was necessary. In his speech at Moscow in 1856, Alexander referred to a "hostile feeling" between lord and serf, and later he told the Secret Committee that serfdom had "almost outlived its time." Korf advanced the "unanimous conviction" of the Secret Committee as an argument for reform, and he and Rostovtsev referred in vague terms to the benefits that would accrue to the state. Advocacy of reform was often associated with invidious comparisons between Russia and the prosperous and well-ordered societies of western Europe, but high officials did not say that Russia should abolish serfdom to emulate the West.

The motive most usually advanced during the debates was the moral one; Nicholas I's declaration that serfdom was an "obvious and palpable evil" was echoed in Rostovtsev's memorandum and in several journals of the Secret Committee. The moral argument was sometimes expressed with a variant of Alexander's dictum that "serfdom has almost outlived its time"; provincial nobles were to favor this oblique form. Most aspects of serfdom, such as the subordination of the peasantry, were not thought to be immoral as such. The ostensible target of the moral argument was the abuses of serfdom by those squires who, in Nicholas's phrase, "forget their noble duty." It was against abuses, legal and illegal, that the program of 1857 was primarily directed, though only a few pomeshchiki were thought guilty of them. Perhaps, then, the moral arguments for reform were reiterated so often because they contained a kind of self-reproach, an expression of the conflict between rejecting serfdom in principle and accepting it in practice.

These moral considerations do not provide any explanation of the actual commitment to reform. The immorality of serfdom did not significantly increase between August and November of 1857. Furthermore, neither the moral nor the other arguments for emancipation were advanced with any force, in an attempt to persuade an opponent. They were offered casually, as a matter of routine, for in the upper bureaucracy there were no avowed opponents of emancipation in principle. Well before the accession of Alexander, the question of principle had been transformed into a question of timing, and it was on this issue that the discussion was ostensibly conducted. The rescript of November 20 constituted a complete reversal of the policy adopted in the Journal of August 18, but everyone chose to pretend that the rescript was only the implementation of the journal, and so to avoid discussing the principles behind the change. In this milieu no prudent man took a stand on principle; Orlov put his signature to the program of November 20-21, just as Lanskoi had signed the Journal of August 18.

The necessity for emancipation, then, was taken for granted and did not, among the tsar's close advisors, have to be justified. Serfdom was discredited in the minds of its crucial defenders. This commitment to the principle of emancipation was formal, if not hypocritical, since it lacked practical application. Because it had always been accompanied by reservations about immediate action, it was empty of content. "Emancipation" could remain an abstract concept that at some happy future time would bring Russia into accord with the norms of civilized nations. In 1857, the concept was hastily and haphazardly provided with content from various sources, of which the least important was the ostensible one. The result was the deformed product of effort, hopes, and misgivings.

The longstanding formal commitment to the principle of emancipation did not impart any substance to the government program, but it did disarm opposition to it. On the Secret Committee there were few converts, men who decided of themselves that circumstances had at last made emancipation timely, or at least worth the risk. However, when the tsar and one or two others unexpectedly resolved that the time for action had come, the rest could only convey their misgivings in certain details of the rescript and directive. They had no ground for resistance because of their longstanding commitment in principle. The westernization of Russia's elite finally claimed its due.

Difficulties remain, but the process is clear enough. The commitment to the reform of serfdom came about because the device that had perpetuated serfdom failed to work. In the language of the Marxists, serfdom was abolished because it lost—or lacked—the elements of superstructure that a viable formation requires. It might be prudent to adopt this language in order to make a narrowly cultural explanation of this political process seem more impressive. If it is essential to substitute a single causal factor for those rejected earlier, it would have to be a cultural factor. That kind of explanation is unfashionable and may seem inadequate to so great an undertaking. It is, however, the only explanation that finds solid support in the sources bearing on the commitment to reform, and it is congruent with the milieu in which the commitment was made.

The Russian nobleman, according to Herzen, had one foot in the bureaucracy and the other on the *pomest'e*. The sanovnik, to pursue the metaphor, had his feet on Russian ground and his head in Western Europe. He derived his income from the dues of serfs and spent his career administering and upholding the servile system, but his education and upbringing did not provide him with any positive arguments for that system.[140] Indeed, what was there in Russian life that he could look at directly and say, "That is good"? For Russia's elite, the long struggle between what Miliukov calls the "critical" and the "national" tendencies had culminated in the triumph of cosmopolitan values.[141] Praise of things Russian, if it was not hypocrisy for the benefit of foreigners, was diffident and defensive, entailing a tacit or explicit comparison with Western Europe. In this cultural context, serfdom was an embarrassment to educated Russians, as a comparison of two classic texts will suggest. Catherine II's "Instruction" to the Cofidication Commission of 1767 served as a kind of charter for generations of reforming bureaucrats. A comparable expression of hostility to reform was Karamzin's "Memoir" of 1811, which forcefully set forth the sentiments of complacent pomeshchiki. Apart from reaffirmation of the necessity of autocracy, the two texts agree on very little. When they turn to the subject of serfdom, however, both of these lucid and self-confident authors become contradictory and evasive; both were obviously eager to move on to other subjects. Their aversion to the very subject of serfdom constituted an oblique but telling tribute to a common system of values that had no place for Russia's fundamental institution.[142]

It was because the sway of cosmopolitan values was so complete that some Russians sought, in the reign of Nicholas I, to construct doctrines that would nourish the national feeling of educated Russians. Neither the regime's propaganda of "official nationality" not the slavophilism of the Moscow salons was an effusion of devotion to the native. Each was deliberately mounted to reverse a cultural current that had been flowing for generations. Each failed.

Official nationality, particularly in its blandly affirmative expressions, was discredited by the careerism of its exponents and the insipidity of their productions.[143] Slavophilism attracted some of Russia's most sophisticated intellects, but it had few followers. Both doctrines necessarily incorporated many "critical" elements. Official nationality, being linked to the bureaucracy, was also linked to the ideal of bureaucratic rationality and even to the Petrine ideal of social engineering by the state. Slavophilism, by virtue of its aversion to bureaucracy, was explicitly hostile to many aspects of Imperial Russia and at least implicitly libertarian. Each had to reckon with the prevailing cosmopolitan values and to incorporate many of them. And neither provided any ideological basis for serfdom. Indeed, in the reign of Alexander II, both Pogodin, the most respected spokesman for official nationality, and the second generation of slavophiles became eager abolitionists.

As of 1855, then, "Westernism," in the broadest sense of the word, was strongly entrenched, and the factitious and contradictory character and lack of following of doctrines of national affirmation were further evidence that what Netting calls "liberalism" had triumphed in the minds of educated Russians. Netting identifies the main components of this "liberalism" as humanitarianism, individualism, and faith in progress. Each of these components was obviously hostile to serfdom. Yet the dominant cast of mind was only a cast of mind; it was, as Netting emphasizes, abstract rather than pragmatic. It discredited serfdom but it did not (in the reign of Nicholas I) generate abolitionists or even practical plans for the reform of serfdom. Serfdom stood condemned, but it was left to the state to find the most expedient way to put serfdom out of its misery.[144]

There the matter might rest for the editors, writers, and educators who, insofar as the censorship permitted, continued to disseminate humanitarianism and individualism. The sanovnik, however, was left with the dilemma. He could not shake free of the concepts that condemned serfdom. Yet he knew that the abolition of serfdom was, for reasons of state, untimely. Abolition would be intolerably disruptive—socially, politically, and economically. Serfdom was an embarrassment, but the practical problems abolition presented had not been resolved. Serfdom made no appeal to the mind or heart but, with the inertial power of an ongoing system that seems to work, it had a powerful hold on the pit of the stomach—the organ in which prudence and anxiety have their seat. So the sanovnik temporized, prevaricated, and indulged in wishful thinking. He could not tell the tsar that serfdom was a positive good or that it ought to be made better, but only that its abolition or radical reform was untimely. The tsar, who by and large shared the sanovnik's world view and his practical misgivings, would defer to the counsel of prudence.

In the fall of 1857, the counsel of prudence was finally called into question. The sanovnik had no other resources to throw into the breach. He could not, at what unexpectedly proved to be the eleventh hour, reverse the tendency of a century and declare that serfdom was a positive good. To do so would discredit himself and very likely exclude him from participation in the reform settlement; it was by no means clear how far the regime would move from serfdom, or in what direction, so that there would still be ample occasion to draw upon the sanovnik's reserves of prudence. No sanovnik protested against the commitment to reform once it was made, for serfdom had ceased to be a binary, yes-or-no issue of principle. Nor did any sanovnik invoke the legions of squires and officials who were satisfied with serfdom as a practical expedient and terrified of any alternative. The most hidebound sanovnik, no less than the most ardent reforming bureaucrat, was wedded to bureaucratic instruments. Nothing in his experience taught him to appeal to the public on matters of state. The "public" to which he might have appealed had no more experience in responding, galvanizing itself, and putting pressure on the regime. Even in 1859-1860, when the regime offered unique institutional forms that seemed to encourage the public to bring pressure, the sanovnik and their lesser brethren would prove to be tentative and maladroit in using these forms. They lacked the experience and even the disposition to engage in extrabureaucratic politics.

Nineteenth-century Russian serfdom lacked supporting ideological and political structures. Consequently, its time-tested defense mechanism failed in 1857. It is easy to conjure up reasons why serfdom might have been abolished. Only by fixing on these considerations—ultimately, on what Herzen called the contradiction between vospitanie and nravy in Russia's elite—is it possible to understand how the regime made its initial, fateful commitment to reform.

With this commitment and its cultural roots in mind, other factors can be restored to conditional citizenship in the explanatory scheme. The sources show that they did not precipitate the political process of reform because they were not the motives of the participants in that process. Positive economic arguments for the emancipation of the serfs appear only, and without great emphasis, in some of the plans for reform reviewed and dismissed by the subcommittee of the Secret Committee; there is no evidence that the compilers of the government program perceived that the

servile economy was in a state of crisis, while the very terms of that
program show that they feared an economic decline as a result of
reform. Similarly, they were anxious about the tension and
antagonism that bondage generated, but more anxious still about
the disruption and loss of control that must ensue when the bonds
were loosened. And for them, the first lesson of the Crimean defeat
was not the infirmity of the socioeconomic system but the
incapacity of the bureaucratic regime over which they presided. In
the regime's commitment to the abolition of serfdom, the
conventional causal factors functioned as countervailing forces.

These factors did, however, impinge obliquely on the political
process, operating diffusely, at a remove from causation. They
stimulated abolitionists, who did not share the sanovnik's
bureaucratic perspective; mature and prosperous men were moved
to present considered plans of emancipation. The sanovniki
dismissed these plans, but exposure to them undercut the
confidence with which they expounded the conventional wisdom.
They believed that emancipation would bring social and economic
disruption, but in their daily round they heard the commonplace
complaints that serfs were getting lazier and more recalcitrant. In
these diffuse forms, social tensions and economic problems could
intrude into the government's deliberations, not prevailing over
the conventional wisdom but moderating the vigor of its
spokesmen. Similarly, defeat in the Crimean War was not a direct
cause of the commitment to reform, but it did figure in the spirit in
which the reform was undertaken. The bureaucracy had waged and
lost the war, the bureaucracy initiated the reform. It did so
apprehensively, displaying very little confidence that Russia was
taking an affirmative step towards a better future. It wanted the
credit and the benefit which, beyond doubt, must follow from the
great feat of emancipation, but it did not want to part with the
pattern of subordination or the constraints on market forces that
were essential parts of serfdom. To put the matter fancifully, the
regime undertook the abolition of serfdom as penance for its sins,
now revealed to all by the Crimean fiasco.

The Engineering of Assent

3

In the six months following the publication of the rescript to Ignat'ev, the nobility of every province expressed its consent to the reform of serfdom. The nobles had their misgivings and misapprehensions; they maneuvered in various ways and would continue to do so. Only in the spring of 1858, however, did they have a chance to say yes or no about the institution that sustained and defined them. They said, or were made to seem to say, no. This reply shattered the adamantine peasant question, reducing it to a series of particular questions concerning land, labor, money, and authority. The government's initiative found its complement in the nobility's assent, and the fate of serfdom as such was settled.

The nobility's response is more remarkable than the government's action. There were, of course, abolitionist noblemen, but most pomeshchiki had shown no disposition at all to part with their privileges. Yet no other elite in modern times renounced bondage so readily. To be sure, it took an extensive and largely covert campaign to procure their assent. Most of this chapter deals with that campaign, which prefigured the subsequent interaction of the nobility and the administration; techniques that were developed for this campaign would be used again in the three years to follow. Then, too, a scrutiny of the ordinary nobles, as opposed to the few outspoken reformers, offers insight into the character of serfdom in its last years. Even if formal assent was a foregone conclusion, as most historians have maintained, the nobles' response tells a great deal about their view of themselves and their serfs. Indeed, the very act of assent was a legacy of serfdom, for it was the product of the leadership and attitude to authority that serfdom had imparted to the Russian nobility.

The rescripts to Nazimov and Ignat'ev took the public by surprise. Although there had been rumors and speculation about the government's intentions, scarcely anyone expected a far-reaching commitment to reform so soon. Among the provincial nobility, shock was mixed with dismay. In response to a secret circular inquiring "what impression these dispositions have produced in various provinces," governors and marshals of the nobility reported that, in the words of Governor-General Zakrevskii of Moscow, the rescripts and the directive to Ignat'ev "made a very unfavorable impression on the greater part of the nobility." Iakov Solov'ev, whose task it was to collate these reports, recalled that no Great Russian Province reported "full and unconditional sympathy" for the provisions of the rescripts. The replies, he found, were written

partly under the influence of a genuine fear and partly with the intention of arousing fear in the government and so halting the further development of measures for the emancipation of the peasants. Justice compels me to say that at first it was [genuine] fear that predominated.

Solov'ev's belief that the nobility was more prone to panic than to cunning was presumably derived from his years in provincial agencies, which left him convinced that the Great Russian nobility was "a dark mass, into which the light of civilized life had only fitfully and very recently begun to penetrate."[1]

It was widely reported that the rescripts, despite the previous circulation of rumors about the Secret Committee, found provincial nobles unprepared. The news, Zakrevskii continued, "alarmed the pomeshchiki, who were not mentally prepared for the great change." Other governors more sympathetic to the reform reported in similar terms. A. N. Murav'ev, governor of the first heartland province to petition for the formation of a committee, reported that "the question was so new, no one expected action so soon, and therefore they could not assimilate it immediately." Another Murav'ev, governor of Pskov Province, wrote to Lanskoi that "the question of emancipating the peasants was entirely new for a majority [of the nobility] and, frankly speaking, incomprehensible for some."[2]

There was more to these reports than official caution. Prince S. V. Volkonskii was himself ready with proposals of his own, but he maintained that the nobility as a whole had more to fear from its own bewilderment than from governmental constraint. This bewilderment embraced even the prosperous and educated segment of the nobility; as Sergei Aksakov wrote to Ivan Turgenev, "the crisis caught us utterly unawares."[3]

To be sure, there were adherents of emancipation, especially in the two capitals, who believed that the rescripts inaugurated a glad new era, not a crisis. They were elated both by the commitment to reform and by the role assigned to the nobility in the legislative process. On December 28, 1857, they held a triumphal banquet in Moscow and drank enthusiastic toasts to the tsar. The merchant and liquor dealer V. A. Kokorev offered a vast sum to help compensate the nobility for the losses the abolition of serfdom would entail. And K. D. Kavelin, one of the sponsors of the banquet, observed with pleasure that "the most enlightened estate, which stands above the others and whose interests are vitally involved . . . has been granted a most active role." Kavelin organized a still grander banquet for February 19, 1858, the anniversary of the tsar's accession. The government, however, had misgivings. Zakrevskii complained,

What is needed at the present time is soundly and maturely considered proposals and plans, which are necessary for the edification and persuasion of the nobility, not western "meetings," which develop democratic ideas, not the after-dinner speeches of a vain merchant [Kokorev], . . . the advocate of the serf estate, which is near to him by blood.

The tsar agreed, and the proposed banquet in his honor was banned.[4]

In forbidding a celebration of its action, the government indicated its continuing uncertainty about the significance of its pronouncements. Because of this uncertainty, the public was bewildered as well as shocked. The rescripts and the directive to Ignat'ev were ambiguous, and no authoritative statement gave any aid in interpreting them. The responses of Russians abroad, who had only the texts to go on, show what diverse interpretations could be placed upon them. The euphemism "amelioration of the peasants' way of life" fooled no one. Herzen's The Bell hailed the rescripts with the banner headline "EMANCIPATION OF THE PEASANTS!" but noted in the body of the article that it was necessary to wait, "without opposition," until the government clarified its position on the land question. Other commentators were not so cautious. The ex-Decembrist N. I. Turgenev explained that the rescripts obliged the pomeshchik to turn over half his estate to the serfs and that "manorial police power" did not entail the right to judge or punish. N. A. Bezobrazov sent a pamphlet to a select circle in Russia explaining that the problem, "mistakenly called emancipation," was largely imaginary, being derived from a semantic confusion between "serf" and "title deed." Any further difficulties could be resolved by taking existing legislation as both inspiration and point of departure.[5] Each of these three commentators interpreted the rescripts and directive in the light of his own hopes, as Russians at home would also do. None of the three, however, had anything to gain from deliberately misrepresenting them, and they were untrammeled by censorship. Taken together, their comments indicate that the documents did not yield any certain meaning.

Russians close to the scene, who could draw on a rich store of rumor and speculation, also construed the rescripts and directive in diverse ways. V. P. Orlov-Davydov, who had recently exploited his connections at court to acquire the title Count, was no more deceived by the euphemism than Herzen; it was the "termination of status of serf" that was at issue, and the reform was welcome.

If there is any consolation to be found when one recalls that our compatriots and coreligionists have spent 260 years in cruel dependency and have suffered oppression and indignity beyond reckoning during that time, the only consolation is the thought that we shall soon be witnesses and accessories to the emancipation of the peasants.[6]

The reform was especially welcome since it would produce a flow of freed peasants into the rich and underpopulated lands of the East and Southeast—where, as luck would have it, the newly fledged count had enormous estates.[7] Orlov-Davydov did remark that the rescripts' provision for the redemption of household plots was beneath criticism, especially since the avowed goal of this measure, the reduction of vagabondage, could be better achieved by other means. If all the state lands were turned over to nobles, an equilibrium between land and labor would be achieved that would eliminate the need for ascription or any other constraints on peasant mobility; this measure would be especially appropriate since the nobles' powers under serfdom, properly regarded, were simply compensation for the unnatural retention of so much populated land in the hands of the state. As an afterthought, Orlov-Davydov turned his attention to the plight of the nobles with infertile, obrok estates who could expect, once equilibrium between land and labor was restored, to be abandoned by many of their peasants. In a scheme of breathtaking simplicity, he suggested that these peasants should continue to pay their obrok, diminished by the actual rental value of the inferior land they had abandoned. This scheme was recommended in the name of "justice" alone; the count acknowledged that it would not be easy to get a free peasant in Saratov Province to make annual payments to his old master in Novgorod.[8]

Like Orlov-Davydov, S. V. Volkonskii was a black-soil pomeshchik, though not so rich, so well connected, or so sweeping in his vision. He had acquired a modest reputation as an abolitionist in his home province of Riazan and greeted the rescripts with enthusiasm. He emphasized that the noble's property right was especially sacred in Riazan, where the land was valuable. Since there was no guarantee that peasants would pay their dues in the absence of serfdom, the pomeshchik must be given broad powers to expel them from their household plots and allotments. Like Orlov-Davydov, he made a casual provision for the unfortunate proprietors of the crowded and infertile estates of the North.[9] The nobility of the North was inventive on its own behalf, however. A. M. Unkovskii, marshal of Tver Province, responded to the rescripts by offering a substitute for the proposed redemption of household plots by the peasants. Unkovskii would have the whole nation redeem the plots, the allotment land, and the serfs themselves, since they too were property; only thus, he argued, could the ex-serfs be truly free and independent of the nobles, who would presumably be placated for the loss of all prerogatives by receiving a large capital sum. Unkovskii's memorandum was unusual for its forthright attack on the rescripts, which he found offered freedom "only on paper," and more unusual still for his vigorous optimism about the economic and political advantages of emancipation.[10] Another northern pomeshchik offered the government a more modest redemption scheme in more guarded language: serfs were to redeem themselves and a desiatina of land apiece by paying twenty-two rubles per tiaglo for thirty-seven years, after which they would be delivered into the jurisdiction of an "administrator" elected by the local pomeshchiki.[11]

These early commentators all interpreted the rescripts as a mere pledge to reform, with the content of the reform still to be determined. Orlov-Davydov did observe that the rescripts imposed certain "fixed conditions" on the provincial committees, but he assumed that a committee could be excused from any particularly unpalatable condition.[12] The assumption that no hard line had been laid down was general among officials and nobles in the provinces. Many of them wrote to the Minister of Internal Affairs offering their comments on the rescripts, and while few challenged the substance of the rescripts, fewer still attempted to conform to it.[13] Almost no one conceived that the rescripts contained, as the government would subsequently insist they did, "imperiallyproclaimed principles," binding and unalterable. The nobility, in its shock and confusion, was beset by a fundamental misapprehension: it believed the government program, as set forth in the rescripts, was flexible as well as ambiguous. This misapprehension would be most useful in the campaign to secure the nobility's consent to the reform, and the government did not try to dispel it.

The nobility's initial bewilderment was colored with fear. The conventional wisdom, which held that serfs would be aroused to revolt by any official action in their favor, was as pervasive in the provinces as among the sanovniki of St. Petersburg. The pomeshchiki, Zakrevskii reported, "fear not only for their property but for their persons." Here again. A. N. Murav'ev agreed, observing that "trivial disorders can have serious consequences now that the transformation of the proprietary peasants' way of life is foreordained." The governors of Kazan and other provinces wrote to Lanskoi of the nobility's fear of "disorders," but they were moderate in their language compared to the pomeshchiki themselves. As soon as he learned of the rescripts, N. A. Ushakov appealed to Lanskoi through the governor of Novgorod Province, urging him to push ahead with the reform but offering detailed recommendations on the placement of troops necessary to avert a general rebellion.[14] A pomeshchik in Simbirsk Province wrote to a friend,

The peasants here are beginning to carry on loudly about the favor of the tsar-*batiushka* and are drinking to his good health. For the time being, everything is quiet, but for how long? How will the Christian people take the declaration that all the land belongs to the pomeshchik, to whom they must be forever in bondage? Will they really believe that the tsar wills it so? It will be no wonder if, while the committees deliberate and decide, the village commune gets tired of waiting so long and takes up the pike.[15]

These apprehensions, if they were not impervious to experience, should have died down in the course of 1858. Some serfs did "carry on loudly," like Saltykov-Shchedrin's Feklushka, a lady's maid who proclaimed ceremonially in a general convocation of all the serving girls that soon she, Feklushka, would be sitting at the same table with the mistress, and that it was still an open question whether she would comb Praskov'ia Pavlovna's pigtails at bedtime, or Praskov'ia Pavlovna would comb hers.[16]

According to Iakushkin, peasants reasoned that "household people won't get land, since household people don't know how to plow the land, but after all, the nobles don't know how either, so why should they get land?"[17] But in 1858 the peasants maintained an attitude of watchful waiting, even though the tsar had publicly renounced the principle under which they were kept in bondage.

Local officials did not assimilate this renunciation as quickly as Feklushka had; a sheriff wrote from the Don to the Minister of Justice, assuring him that peasants circulating "false rumors about their supposed freedom" would be strictly punished. In Penza Province, too, according to a major of gendarmes, some "muzhiki [are] excited by rumors about freedom, as if it were near at hand." It took about a year for police officials to change the time-honored rubric and acknowledge that there was some basis for the rumors. These rumors, however, were no more troublesome for the authorities than they had been when they were indeed false.

The rescripts may have affected the economic operation of some estates. The governor of Smolensk Province reported about a group of peasants inspired by "perverted interpretations regarding the amelioration" of their way of life, who turned out in the fields only when they pleased and worked so lazily that their master was obliged to complain to the authorities, "by whom this disobedience was brought to a timely end." A pomeshchik in Vladimir Province, writing to a friend in Moscow at harvest time, went further and declared that the nobles' estates were "already economically ruined," since it was impossible to coerce the peasants in the old way, and no new system had been set up.[18] The sum of these and similar incidents, however, was very far from the dreaded jacquerie. Three government agencies made special studies of serf insubordination and all three agreed that the disruption produced by the rescripts had been insignificant.[19]

Once provincial nobles had recovered from their initial shock, they fastened upon the proposed land settlement and found it ominous. Some, like A. S. Taneev, complained that it challenged "one of the most important rights of the nobility—the inviolability of landed property." He recalled that when serfdom had been abolished in the Baltic provinces, "all the rights of the nobility were upheld and all the land remains the property of the pomeshchiki. This favor is all the more to be expected for the nobility of the Russian heartland."[20]

Nikolai Bezobrazov, S. V. Volkonskii, and other spokesmen for the nobility also defended the sanctity of private property, but others made the same point in more practical terms. A. A. Chicherin sent Lanskoi a letter in which he praised the tsar's emancipatory impulse but mildly observed that the folly of having the serfs redeem their household plots must be blamed on the impracticality of career bureaucrats like Lanskoi; Chicherin argued for a landless emancipation, after which peasants could rent plots and plowland for five- or ten-year periods, which would be sufficient to "restore the Patriarchal relationship between Lord and Peasant." A. V. Staritskii, a self-made man, as he proudly observed, who had accumulated eight hundred souls in Little Russia, wrote to the tsar proposing that all serfs born after 1850 be proclaimed free from their masters and from their land. Thus, the peasants would gradually come to appreciate the exigencies of freedom. Staritskii conceded that, under his plan, emancipation would not come "with the haste that some suppose possible," but the desire for haste—in Little Russia, at least—was born of "inappropriate philanthropy" or "disloyalty," for Russia could not slavishly follow the example of countries "where civilization is infinitely more developed than it is here."[21]

Pomeshchiki objected first of all to the rescript's provision for compulsory redemption of household plots, rather than to the compulsory allotment of plowland. They appear to have been satisfied with the customary division of estates into demesne and peasant allotments, so long as they could determine who occupied the cottages and plots.[22] Peasants owning their plots were conceived to have a bargaining power that pomeshchiki found distasteful. Thus both Orlov-Davydov and Unkovskii attacked the redemption plan, though from different points of view. Proprietors of rich land like Orlov-Davydov objected that it did not provide the lord with enough freedom of contract; proprietors outside the black-soil area found it provided the peasant with too much freedom of contract. Most of the northern proprietors, however, still preferred some quasi-servile form of ascription to the redemption of both plot and plowland advocated by Unkovskii. For example, a self-styled "Patriot-agronomist," proceeding from the unarguable truth that "a landowner should have settlers proportional to the quantity of his land," proposed a scheme of compulsory sharecropping coupled with ascription.[23]

However, some nobles were amenable in principle to the provision for redemption and allotment. Proprietors in underpopulated areas on the periphery, where labor was expensive and land was cheap, did not follow Orlov-Davydov in cherishing freedom of contract; like the owners of relatively barren estates in the North, they preferred some variety of ascription that would let them keep their labor force on terms favorable to themselves. A group of pomeshchiki in Ekaterinoslav Province was willing to have the peasants redeem their plots provided the plots were resold to the pomeshchik if the peasant moved away, but insisted on "retaining their property right in the peasant's person" until the peasant had amortized his purchase price. Since these peasants had been purchased and transported south in good faith and with the sanction of the laws, their abrupt emancipation would weaken public confidence in paper money and in the government itself.[24]

Some spokesmen for the nobility reminded the government of their services, as individuals or as an estate, to the throne and the fatherland, implying that these services were badly requited by the rescripts. They also recalled, in what would become a kind of incantation in the next few years, that demesne production fed the cities, the army, the navy, and the export market. Almost all concrete objections, however, were put in economic terms—the pomeshchik was presented as a landowner, the peasantry as a labor force.

The nobility was correspondingly quick to disclaim the arbitrary power over persons that so troubled the conscience of the bureaucracy. For example, Colonel I. V. Likhachev (ret.) found that the idea of emancipation was "originally inspired by foreigners from the West," since the bond between lord and serf was Russia's strength and an ideal form of administration for the inherently anarchic peasantry. He would retain the essential bond through economic interdependence—the lord would provide the land and the peasant the labor. This division would be strictly observed; the lord would no longer have any obligations to his peasants, but he would retain his powers of "tutelage" and acquire the administrative prerogatives of the Baltic barons. Yet even Likhachev conceded that the traffic in serfs was unnatural and that peasants should have personal and property rights.[25] He might even have agreed with State Councillor Kishkin, who wrote from Maloiaroslavets to tell Lanskoi that slavery was anathema. Unfortunately, he continued, his experience in running his estates had taught him that agricultural work was so unpleasant that it had to be compulsory. Kishkin was as rich in ingenuity as in experience, and produced a plan to keep the peasants in the fields and protect Russia from the evils of a proletariat. Each tiaglo would be provided with at least five desiatiny of plowland as inalienable property, and the proprietor would be paid seventy rubles by the government. The government would recover this sum by collecting three rubles a year from the peasants. (Kishkin observed that the government might want to continue to collect payments after the debt had been paid.) The peasant would also incur the obligation of working a section of demesne land half again as big as his allotment, or almost twice as much as he had worked as a serf on barshchina. He would, however, have the satisfaction of being a property owner, a satisfaction vitiated only by his inability to dispose of his property or move from it without the permission of the lord, who also retained his manorial authority, or responsibility for "morality and tranquility."[26]

Very few articulate nobles would go so far as Likhachev or even Kishkin in defending serfdom in the abstract. Once they had recovered from the initial shock of the rescripts, nobles conceded that serfdom was immoral and that their plenitude of arbitrary power was unseemly in the nineteenth century. However, almost all of them rejected, from diverse points of view, the basic economic provisions of the rescript and directive to Ignat'ev. Their dismay at the idea of reform was reinforced by a fear of the disruption and danger that, they believed, any significant reform must entail. Yet the publication of the rescripts and the circular with which it was distributed to the provinces put pressure upon them to acquiesce. More broadly, opposition held the threat that the bureaucracy would impose a solution without consulting them and the danger that they would be stigmatized in the eyes of their peasants for opposing the tsar's wishes.

In this dilemma, the nobility temporized. Zakrevskii represented the nobility of Moscow as "on the one hand having an imperial appeal to assist the government in the amelioration of peasant life, while on the other hand fearing to arouse the hatred of the lower orders against themselves because of their inaction." Zakrevskii found, however, that "right-thinking people" agreed that

it would be useful to wait without hastening and see how the difficult business undertaken by the government, the abolition of servile dependency, will be resolved in those provinces where the committees have alrady opened for this purpose, in order to have more data and greater facility for deciding so important a question of state on a firmer basis, satisfactorily for both pomeshchiki and peasants, and without disruption.[27]

It turned out that the provinces were full of right-thinking people. The district assembly of the nobility in Poltava, for example, passed a unanimous resolution stating that "there is not at the present time any possibility that we follow the example" of the three northwestern provinces. The resolution went on to indicate most persuasively the ways in which Poltava differed from the Northwest and concluded with the hope that

not only time, but also the experience of those provinces where it has been acknowledged to be possible to undertake this business will show clearly the principles, at least, which we should follow in order to avert dire consequences for ourselves.[28]

The nobles of Kazan, Samara, Tambov, Pskov, and other provinces reacted among similar lines.[29] The response was so uniform in diverse parts of the empire as to demonstrate yet again the sublime regularity of the historical process. Each province turned out to have natural and institutional peculiarities that made it appropriate to await the results of the experiment elsewhere. The ball was back in the government's court.

Eliciting Assent

For each province, the nobility's expression of assent took the form of a petition (adres) to the tsar for permission to elect a provincial committee "on the amelioration of the way of life of the proprietary peasants." Most historians have assumed that the submission of these petitions was a matter of course. Those who have given the matter any thought usually allude to the bureaucratization of the nobility and its institutions; thus Liashchenko speaks of a "vespodanneishaia konkurentsiia," or competition in loyalty, among the provinces. Kornilov, on the other hand, maintains that any province that did not submit the petition would have suffered a peasant rebellion.[30] Neither interpretation is implausible; indeed, both were advanced by contemporaries.[31] And in combination they are persuasive; thus Herzen wrote,

The rotten, self-seeking, savage, selfish opposition of the incorrigible pomeshchiki, their wolf-yelps—these are not dangerous. How can they retaliate with authority and freedom against them?[32]

While these interpretations find support in contemporary testimony, the regime strove to conceal from contemporaries the means by which it procured the nobility's assent. If the public at large had learned of these means, then formal expressions of assent would have been of no use in mollifying the nobility or calming the peasants.

Among historians, only Zaionchkovskii preceives how much effort the regime expended. He cites the report of the Third Section for 1858, in which Dolgorukov informed the tsar that it was "only the insistence of the local authorities and the cooperation of a few chosen pomeshchiki that induced the nobles . . . to request the establishment of provincial committees."[33] The "insistence of the local authorities" was indeed the basic mechanism, but it was variously applied and variously reinforced by covert pressure from the central government.

Although most nobles were inclined to "wait without hastening," one province did respond favorably and fairly promptly—although, if all the details had been generally known, the precedent was not auspicious. On December 17, the Nizhnii Novgorod Provincial Assembly of the Nobility, which happened to be in session at the time, passed a resolution acknowledging "with deep and reverential gratitude . . . the lofty confidence in the nobility which the Sovereign Emperor had been pleased to manifest" and testifying to "absolute readiness to execute His holy will, according to such fundamental principles as His Majesty may be pleased to indicate."[34] The credit for this prompt and unequivocal action belonged to the provincial governor, A. N. Murav'ev.[35] Murav'ev absented himself from the assembly, as the law required, but he sent this account to Lanskoi:

Some [nobles] clearly recognized the necessity of subscribing forthrightly to the government's views, but others hoped to avoid this under some kind of pretext, being unable to comprehend any relationship between a pomeshchik and peasants except an arbitrary one. Little by little, however, . . . benevolent and rational ideas prevailed, and when Your Excellency's circular of December 8 [suggesting that other provinces might solicit a rescript and directive like those sent to Ignat'ev] was read to the assembly of the nobility, the whole assembly resounded with three cheers, which served as a unanimous and, of course, absolutely irreversible expression of the general opinion.[36]

Murav'ev spared his minister certain details to enhance the dramatic effect of his report. Well before the assembly opened, the provincial marshal of the nobility circulated the rescript and directive to Nazimov among the pomeshchiki of the province. Some of them did set about to mobilize support for the government's stand, but the overall reaction was not particularly favorable.[37] Indeed, when Murav'ev asked the marshal to turn over the material he had collected on the nobility's reaction, the marshal begged off, arguing that the opinions of individual nobles were no longer of interest since the nobility as a whole had *already* expressed its willingness to carry out the tsar's will. The marshal's reply to Murav'ev is dated December 16, the day before the resolution was voted, which suggests that the patriotic spectacle described in Murav'ev's report was carefully prepared.[38]

Nor was Murav'ev confident that three cheers constituted an "absolutely irreversible" commitment. He sent a clerk off to Moscow at three in the morning to telegraph the good news to St. Petersburg and sped the resolution itself to the capital in the custody of a special courier. And so, when the assembly of the nobility repented of its decision, as it did the next day, the resolution could not simply be quashed. The assembly therefore chose a deputation, consisting of Count S. V. Sheremetev and Prince A. I. Potemkin, to overtake the unfortunate resolution. The deputation was the embodiment of wealth and influence,[39] but it was speed that was really wanted. The count and the prince did not manage to catch up with the courier, who presented the resolution to Lanskoi within two days of his departure from Nizhnii.[40] Lanskoi gave credit where credit was due, and a broad hint to the governors of other provinces, by awarding the Order of St. Anne to Murav'ev.[41]

Sheremetev and Potemkin had to return to Nizhnii with a rescript and directive identical to those sent to Ignat'ev and the tsar's special thanks to the Nizhnii nobles for "setting the first example of readiness to undertake this important matter." The Secret Committee on the Peasant Question directed that the resolution of the Nizhnii nobility and the names of the signers be published "so that this praiseworthy action of the Nobility will receive appropriate publicity."[42]

The praiseworthy action was a step forward but it was accompanied by a step backward in the sphere of policy. At the same session of the Secret Committee where the rescript to Nizhnii was approved, Lanskoi presented an inquiry from Governor-General Ignat'ev of St. Petersburg. In essence, Ignat'ev was seeking to determine, on behalf of the St. Petersburg nobility, how broad the competence of the provincial committee would be. Lanskoi's draft reply to the questions of substance raised made it clear that the committee's competence was as narrow as was consistent with the original rescript and directive.[43] The Secret Committee overruled Lanskoi and drew up a new reply (in Lanskoi's name), which explained that the provincial committee had been set up to answer just the kind of questions Ignat'ev had raised, that is, to make an "appropriate application" of the main principles of the rescript "to the peculiarities and special circumstances of the area." The nobles of St. Petersburg could be expected to read "the pomeshchik's requirements" for "peculiarities and special circumstances." In case anyone missed the point, the reply reiterated that the original directive to Ignat'ev was merely "a form of assistance" for the provincial committee, and if the committee should find any of its provisions "inconvenient," it had only to explain why.[44] In other words, the Secret Committee had pared the government's position back to the bare bones of the rescript and, in so doing, reinforced the general belief that the provisions of the rescript itself were flexible.

Lanskoi, understandably enough, did not circulate this new directive to Ignat'ev to the other provincial governors. However, the general pattern of the next six months had been established: the more success Lanskoi and his subordinates had in securing the nobility's assent to reform, the more the Secret Committee retreated from the perimeter of policy established in November and December of 1857.

The tsar was especially anxious that Moscow, the second capital, should solicit a rescript. The precedent of Nizhnii Novgorod increased the pressure on Moscow; indeed, General Rostovtsev had told the tsar that all the provinces would fall like a row of toy soldiers when one gave way.[45] Then, too, the broad patent issued to the St. Petersburg Committee may have diminished the misgivings of the Moscow nobility as reported, and obviously shared,[46] by Governor-General Zakrevskii. Two weeks after the Secret Committee's action on Nizhnii and St. Petersburg, the marshals and deputies of Moscow Province requested permission to set up a provincial committee. These minor officials were not ordinarily authorized to speak for the nobility on important matters, and presumably they were acting under Zakrevskii's instructions. Zakrevskii, for his part, reported that the nobility's "alarm" had now passed, thanks to the "benevolent and enlightened tendency of government policy." He expressed confidence that "the important matter of amelioration . . . will be resolved by the Moscow nobility in a satisfactory manner, insofar as possible." The limits of the possible were suggested in an accompanying petition, which asked permission for the committee to extend its deliberations beyond the six-month limit and to "discuss freely the basic principles to be used in compiling the draft."

The second petition reflected the widespread assumption that the terms of the rescripts could be modified to suit pomeshchiki elsewhere. This petition had to be rejected for, as the tsar noted on the original, "the basic principles as confirmed by Me are not subject to discussion." The rejection of the second petition, however, did not prevent acceding to the first, in which the nobles of Moscow Province expressed their zeal for reform. Accordingly, the Secret Committee sent the now-familiar rescript and directive to Zakrevskii. They were to be published "in all newspapers and journals," along with the resolution of the Moscow deputies and marshals and the names of all the Moscow pomeshchiki who had testified to their assent. Zakrevskii also received a second, secret directive, flatly rejecting the petition for free discussion and an extended term.[47]

This second directive complemented the reply sent three weeks before to Ignat'ev by indicating that the government would not on any account cut into the rescript itself. However, it was obvious that the belief that the rescript represented a flexible position lay behind Moscow's request to form a committee. Zakrevskii himself had encourage this assumption; when some of the marshals and deputies had refused to sign an unconditional petition, he had pronounced their motives "well-grounded and worthy of respect"; the marshals and deputies then reconvened to compose a second petition with conditions.[48] Since this kind of misapprehension on the part of provincial governors would be helpful in securing assent elsewhere, the government did not dispel it. Any governor or marshal who explicitly asked if the rescript could be modified was duly informed that it could not, but no attempt was made to eliminate the misunderstanding once and for all by circulating the second directive to Zakrevskii. Indeed, the Secret Committee held that it "cannot and should not become common knowledge."[49]

The other provinces did not fall over according to Rostovtsev's toy-soldier analogy. The difficulty may have been Lanskoi's failure to circulate the Secret Committee's reply to Ignat'ev. It would have been quite natural if Lanskoi had not wanted to broadcast a document at odds with his own views, but if the omission was a ruse, it was misguided. On February 17, he was obliged to issue a new directive reiterating more emphatically than before that his original directives to Nazimov and Ignat'ev constituted no more than advice. The directive explained,

There is no detailed program for the committee's deliberations to be found in my previous directives or in this present one. My ideas and proposals should not be considered as decisive in any question that may arise. . . . The Nobility itself is empowered by the Imperial rescript to develop these issues and adapt them to local conditions without being constrained by the advice, so to speak, which is set forth in my directives.[50]

Lanskoi went on to indicate certain ways in which the principles of the rescript, "unalterable in their essence," could be developed and adapted to local conditions. In its form, the directive of February 17 was a directive to Governor-General Ignat'ev, like the reply to his December inquiry. However, in case Lanskoi should imagine that this new version was not appropriate for "common knowledge," he was instructed that, by the tsar's wish, it should be published "in all newspapers and magazines."[51] Rumor had it that the new directive was drawn up in the Secret Committee and imposed on Lanskoi by his overbearing colleagues, who wanted to humiliate the minister and to accommodate the prejudices of the provincial nobles.[52] Be that as it may, Lanskoi was able to turn the directive of February 17 to account in the campaign to collect petitions on the formation of provincial committees.

About three weeks after the clarification of February 17, the petitions began to pour in. The nobles of Orel Province, whose amiable ways are described in Turgenev's *Sportsman's Sketches*, responded in early March. This response testified to their rapid recovery from the shock and dismay with which they had greeted the rescripts. Indeed, one district marshal of the nobility committed political suttee. "This worthy gentleman's reason," a friend wrote, "was troubled by the question of the emancipation of the peasants to the point where he decided to destroy himself."[53] The other district marshals, however, gradually set about eliciting a petition from the local nobles. The district marshal in Elets, encountering intense opposition, threatened to resign his post, warning his constituents, "then it would be frightful for you to live in your villages."[54] V. A. Elagin also thought that the resistance of his pomeshchik neighbors in Volkhov District was dangerous as well as deplorable, for they were "loudly cursing" the government's initiative. In time, however, "the herd of pigs followed the stable boys"—so Elagin's wife described the Volkhov nobles' assent, under the suasions of the district marshal and a local magnate, to the formation of a provincial committee.[55]

The acquiescence of the nobility of Orel was largely the accomplishment of the provincial marshal, V. V. Apraksin. With more than twenty thousand souls, he was the greatest magnate of the province, while his ancient family gave him a better claim than most to aristocratic dignity. He was on easy terms with the tsar and on equal terms with his ministers. As soon as he received the rescripts to Nazimov and Ignat'ev, he gathered the district marshals and asked them to circulate the rescripts to the Orel nobility and elicit such "opinions and remarks" as might be "provoked by the requirements of the area." It was still too soon for the nobility to commit itself, Apraksin wrote to Lanskoi on January 7, but he could already detect sympathy "for the Government's benevolent desire to make it possible for the pomeshchiki to define their relations with their peasants accurately and fairly."[56] At this point, then, Apraksin was not trying to penetrate the euphemism "amelioration of the way of life of the proprietary peasants."

Lanskoi had requested the governors and provincial marshals to report the nobility's reaction to the rescripts and directives "very frankly, in private letters to be delivered to me personally."

In order [continued Lanskoi] to be dispassionate witnesses and observers of the course of this matter, you should not use any insistence or persuasion, except as specifically indicated to you by me.[57]

Apraksin did not hesitate to use insistence and persuasion, and he proudly reported to Lanskoi what he had done. Apart from working on his own nobility, he had written to the marshals of five neighboring provinces, urging them to persuade their constituents to submit petitions. He considered it his "holy obligation to incline every noble to cooperate with the government's views, if not out of conviction, then from a feeling of personal self-preservation." If nobles did not respond of their own accord, the government would impose a bureaucratic solution; if they did respond, Apraksin was confident that the government would moderate the terms of the rescript in their favor. The governor of Orel, Safonovich, reporting to Lanskoi on Apraksin's success in securing the cooperation of the nobility, expressed the same confidence: surely the rescript's onerous land settlement would not be applied to Orel.[58] Lanskoi did not at this point disabuse Safonovich or Apraksin of their idea that the "government's views" could be modified as they supposed.

Six weeks later, Safonovich wrote to Lanskoi that the nobility of Orel, though it had initially been wholly unprepared for reform, was now more or less favorable. Credit was due to the explanations of Apraksin and the soothing effect of Lanskoi's directive of February 17. A few days later, Safonovich reported complete success and sent Lanskoi a resolution, signed by all but three of the district marshals and district deputies, offering thanks for the government's expression of confidence in the nobility and asking permission to set up a provincial committee. Attached to the resolution was a list of 970 "nobles and pomeshchiki of Orel province who had submitted testimonials declaring their willingness to consolidate their peasants' way of life."[59]

Unlike their counterparts in Moscow, the marshals and deputies of Orel did not attach any conditions to their assent. Indeed, with such a champion as Apraksin, they must have imagined that a conditional petition would have been bad tactics. For Apraksin had sent a circular letter to the district marshals, enclosing drafts of two resolutions, one expressing conditional assent, the other unconditional, and strongly urging the adoption of the latter.[60] The nobility's bargaining position, he reasoned, would be improved once they had demonstrated their willingness to cooperate with the government. The reasoning of a dignitary with Apraksin's influence and sources of information was good enough for many of the Orel nobles. Those who were not swayed were overborne by Apraksin's authority as marshal. Some districts began attaching conditions to their assent,[61] but he refused to acknowledge these conditional resolutions unless they carried the district conference unanimously.[62]

The bargain Apraksin had in mind is indicated in his "Supplementary Report" to Lanskoi, bearing the same date as the resolution of unconditional assent. Apraksin solicited "favor" for the nobility of Orel: the right to full and free discussion in the provincial committee, a waiver of the compulsory redemption of household plots, and the right, presently enjoyed by the Baltic nobility, to determine its own membership.[63]

Lanskoi received these documents ten days later and made his report to the Secret Committee, which now blazoned its existence as "The Main Committee on the Peasant Question." He gave the committee the resolution of the deputies and marshals and the accompanying list of names, stating that "the Orel Nobility requests the opening of a Nobles' Committee unconditionally." He proposed that a committee should be set up in Orel "on the same general principles as have been proclaimed for other provinces." The Main Committee agreed, voted a tribute to the Orel nobility for its unconditional petition, and responded with the usual rescript and directive.[64] Three weeks later, Lanskoi got around to writing to Apraksin rejecting his "Supplementary Report" and explaining (as Apraksin would already have learned from the rescript and directive) that Orel could not be excused from any part of the rescript.[65]

In his private views, Apraksin was not so hostile to serfdom as Murav'ev, nor so devoted to it as Zakrevskii. Unlike them, he was an elected official, but he embraced the government's new policy as dutifully as if he had been a regular functionary. And the nobles of Orel, like those of Nizhnii Novgorod and Moscow, were used to deferring to provincial marshals and governors, who in turn were generally accommodating to the interest of serfholders. This habit of deference was so strong that it could be turned against the institution that had fostered it.

Along with the petition from Orel, the Main Committee considered petitions from four other provinces—Simbirsk, Saratov, Samara, and Tver. Apart from Simbirsk, which petitioned without conditions, these provinces unwittingly followed the pattern set by Moscow and Orel: the petitions were variously accompanied by conditions, reservations, and pleas for special terms, forwarded with the endorsement of the provincial officials who had secured the petitions. These quibbles were ignored or explained away by Lanskoi in his presentation to the Main Committee, and the committee disregarded them.[66]

The petition from Tver is of particular interest. The twelve districts of the province split three ways, none of them subscribing to the terms of the rescript. Four districts adhered to the program of Provincial Marshal Unkovskii, calling for the redemption of the serfs' allotment land and of the serfs themselves. Of the other districts, four would not have the peasants redeem any land at all and four would have them redeem themselves and their household plots while holding their allotments in usufruct. The committee split the difference by sending the usual rescript and directive. It took no notice of the proposed redemption of allotments, which would be the cornerstone of the legislation of 1861. Nor did it condemn the idea that the serfs should purchase themselves, or "redeem their personal dependency," as it was delicately expressed, although this idea would soon be proclaimed a rank heresy, incompatible with the rescripts.[67]

Three weeks later, on March 29, the Main Committee considered five petitions from five more provinces. Of these, the petition from Riazan is of special interest because the *otzyvy*, or responses from individual nobles on which the petition was ostensibly based, have survived. In his December report on the initial reaction to the rescripts, the Riazan marshal, A. S. Selivanov, had given the conventional gloomy assessment: the measures were unexpected, the nobility was unprepared and apprehensive of peasant disorders. He had pointedly remarked that there were only two battalions of soldiers stationed in the province and warned against the promiscuous use of the word "freedom." The provincial governor had reported in similar terms. Since then, however, the district marshals had labored to elicit a favorable response. At first, they had not been able to get a significant number of pomeshchiki to commit themselves at all; by mid-March, they had formal responses from only one-tenth of the local nobility, and many of these responses were evasive. One pomeshchik was not satisfied with the rescript's reaffirmation of his property rights.

Reverently undertaking to fulfill the Imperial will, I request a petition for the retention, through the Monarch's favor, of the many lands I possess, which became my property by dint of much sacrifice, deprivation, and the assumption of personal debts; I express my assent, if this will not entail deprivation or a detriment to my property.[68]

Another, more bluntly, gave his assent "provided that I am not deprived of the income I receive, by which I maintain my family of seven children."

One respondent angrily punctured the euphemism "amelioration."

I do not consider it necessary to request permission to undertake amelioration of our peasants' way of life, because every one of us has been constantly concerned to ameliorate his peasants and there is no necessity of soliciting the government's permission for that. Such a solicitiation seems to me a kind of arbitrary accusation against the nobility, grievous for its honor; besides, it is not the amelioration of the peasants' way of life that is now at issue, but, properly speaking, the abolition of serfdom; why avoid calling things by their names?

But others seized upon the euphemism.

Despite my very limited means and a limited amount of land, I have always been concerned about the amelioration of my peasants' way of life. The means I have employed to ameliorate their life are so clearly manifest on the face of things that, while several of those that I purchased originally proved to be of unsatisfactory morality, at the present time, thanks to my paternal concern for them, they have been put in good condition.

He continued, "As to the alteration of their way of life, I leave that to the discretion of the higher authorities." Another pointed out that he had taught his serfs literacy, "useful trades," and "the fear of God."

From a different point of view, it was not the peasants' morality, but their immorality, that impeded reform.

Our peasants are so underdeveloped in respect to morality that at the present time the system currently prevailing is best for them, because, like children, they need a guardian, and that guardian is the pomeshchik.

This respondent went on to dismiss any analogy between serfdom, which was rooted in brotherly love and community of interest, and slavery; he trailed off with dark reminders of the French Revolution. Yet even he found that it would be better to "liberate the peasants absolutely" (presumably without land) than to adopt the half measures set forth in the rescripts. In the end he would probably have agreed with his neighbor who wrote that "the alteration of the proprietary peasants' way of life is the fixed desire of the Sovereign Emperor, so I suppress my own desires, unconditionally accepting His Imperial Will."

On March 15, the district deputies and marshals of Riazan judged that the responses so far received constituted an adequate authority for an unconditional petition. The petition was accompanied by a letter from Selivanov asking that Riazan be excused from the compulsory redemption of household plots, which would entail "many inconveniences." Lanskoi and the Secret Committee found that since 717 nobles had formally given their unconditional assent (this was the total of responses received) and since Riazan did not present any significant peculiarities, there was no "adequate cause to deviate from general principles."[69]

In Kazan Province, whose petition was accepted along with Riazan's, the role that the provincial marshals had played in Orel and Riazan fell to the governor. He had written to Lanskoi that the local nobles wanted "to avail themselves of the examples of other Great Russian provinces in this matter" before proceeding, "as they fear disorders when the new rules are introduced." Lanskoi had replied that "disorders are rather to be expected because of [their] present attempt to preserve the former organization of the peasant estate." The tsar was giving them time for reflection; "nonetheless, the nobles should not languish in passivity."[70]

The governor took this broad hint and responded with a proposal that he convene an extraordinary assembly of the nobility. In Lanskoi's view, this was almost as bad as passivity; he denied permission for the assembly, noting that a meeting of the district marshals and deputies had been adequate elsewhere. The governor interpreted Lanskoi's letter as permission to use "insistence and persuasion." Six weeks later he was able to report that the nobility of Kazan was now "entirely prepared" for the reform and that the district marshals and deputies, "with some assistance on my part," had voted the necessary petition.[71]

Lanskoi did not always have to resort to pressure, as he had with Kazan, or deception, has he had with Orel. His handling of Kostroma Province should have satisfied his deputy Levshin, who lamented that Lanskoi had become a persecutor of the nobility. Levshin admitted, "I do not have a very high opinion of my fellow nobles." Yet he argued for "indulgence and patience," for "so long as [the nobility] has not lost the habit of submission to the autocratic power, one can lead it forward with a kind word and a smile, taking it amiably by the hand."[72] A kind word did prove almost enough for Kostroma.

The Kostroma nobility, Marshal Mironov reported, had been alarmed by the rescripts. "This alarm does not derive from a spirit of opposition," he continued, but from "the peculiarities of our area," which he proceeded to list. The essential peculiarity was the prevalence of obrok estates; the peasants worked at various trades and the land itself was so poor that, after the transitional period, estates would not yield enough to cover the mortgage payments.[73] He therefore requested eight deviations from the government's program, as he understood it. The gist of his request was that the ex-serfs, apart from certain restrictions on their mobility and their assumption of part of the mortgage debt, must continue to rent their allotments. Since a woodcutter or factory hand might resent having to rent a piece of barren plowland, the police must exact rents on a parity with taxes.

The ministry's point-by-point reply was encouraging. Mironov was informed that the government was re-examining police procedures on private debts and was also mindful of two other problems Mironov raised, household serfs and petty pomeshchiki; the considered opinion of the provincial committee was specially desired on problems of this kind. This reply did not produce the desired result; some weeks later, Lanskoi added flattery to encouragement. He informed Mironov that he had reviewed his report and his eight-point program.

Your remarks [he wrote], based on a diligent study of the peculiarities of the area, will be taken into account in good time. Meanwhile, it is my pleasure to reiterate my belief that the Nobility of Kostroma Province will find you, good sir, a well-informed and benevolent leader in the impending matter of the abolition of servile dependency.

Lanskoi added a postscript in his own hand. "At the present time the only pressing necessity is that the Nobility should ask permission to open a Committee according to the example of St. Petersburg and Nizhnii Novgorod Provinces, that is, unconditionally."[74]

Mironov did his best, and the resolution that arrived a few weeks later (and was considered with those from Riazan and Kazan) did not carry any conditions on matters of substance. Unfortunately, it carried the signatures of only nine of the twenty-four district marshals and deputies. The other fifteen objected that only 320 nobles, or about ten percent of the total, had signified their assent, and that two districts had not been polled at all. They wanted to solicit more opinions lest they "invoke the reproaches of the nobles" by precipitate action. Since assent was "not open to question," they proposed to submit a petition enhanced with more signatures by June 1.

The governor of Kostroma held that if the "general assent is not open to question," no more pomeshchiki need be polled; besides, delay was undesirable because the serfs were becoming impatient and even insubordinate. The provincial marshal supported the same position on narrower grounds: since the total of "responses" received (he did not say they were all favorable) considerably surpassed the number of nobles participating in the most recent provincial election, the resolution had adequate authority. The Main Committee agreed and issued the usual rescript and directive.[75]

This was the only occasion on which a potentially embarrassing question was brought before the Main Committee: the authority of the marshals and the deputies jointly to act for the nobility of a province. Lanskoi, it is clear from his letter to the governor of Kazan, had no doubts about their authority; he positively preferred this small and manageable body to a crowded assembly of nobles. However, the district marshals and especially the deputies were mere corporate functionaries; they did not even have the right to make minor levies upon the nobility. It was as if the district attorneys and probate judges of Massachusetts were abruptly convened as a constitutional convention.

The marshals and deputies made up for their meager status and authority with a statesmanlike capacity to suppress their own views. In Voronezh Province, this capacity reached heroic proportions. In January, the marshals and deputies of Voronezh responded to the rescripts with a paean to serfdom, which they represented as a "burden" selflessly borne by the nobility, and a warning that anarchy and ruin would unfailingly follow upon its abolition. Nonetheless,

if the sovereign emperor, in his power and wisdom (which are not, of course, drawn from any human source), has decided to undertake these transformations of institutions of state now . . . then the provincial and district marshals of the nobility and deputies of the nobility consider themselves proud . . . to attest that the nobility which elected them has always been inspired by the same idea.

They did request permission to verify their constituents' inspiration, but three months later they submitted an unconditional petition and were vouchsafed the usual rescript and directive.[76]

Although they were elected by the nobility, the marshals and deputies functioned as part of the bureaucracy and were accordingly susceptible to pressure from above. As more and more provinces signified their assent, pressure on the remaining provinces increased. In March, *The Russian Herald* pointedly listed the provinces that had not yet expressed their "patriotic desire" to accede to the reform.[77] Official sources and the press publicized the assent of each province in turn, and there was no way that laggard provinces could readily learn how the central government pared off the conditions from petitions of assent. In the rescripts sent in reply, the tsar's thanks were expressed in one of three forms according to the character of the petition—conditional, unconditional, or accompanied by explicit reservations.[78] At first, however, only initiates could grasp the distinction being made. It was not until May or June that most provincial officials realized the futility of attaching conditions to a petition, and their ignorance made it easier for them to secure the assent of the nobles under their jurisdiction.

Then, too, provincial officials pruned off as many excrescences as they could before submitting the petitions. This process can be illustrated with the examples of Penza and Poltava; petitions from these two provinces were considered a few days after those from Kazan and Kostroma. When word of the coming reform reached Penza, the governor and provincial marshal informed Lanskoi flatly that the local nobility would not petition for the formation of committee, and that the chief present concern was to stop false rumors circulating among the peasants. Lanskoi or a subordinate noted on the governor's report, "He must be brought to his senses and persuaded that at this point there is no turning back and that the nobility are *obligated* to execute the will of the Sovereign, who summons them to cooperate in the amelioration of peasant life." Lanskoi's reply contained no threats, but made his expectations clear and emphasized the nobility's obligation. Three weeks later, the governor had the pleasure of reporting that the nobles would indeed meet their obligation, but only under certain conditions. An official hand noted cryptically "not likely," a sentiment that was presumably communicated to Penza. The marshals and deputies acted accordingly and petitioned without conditions. There was only one blot on Penza's otherwise immaculate petition; Collegial Assessor Popov insisted on writing the tsar to explain that he did not want any reform on *his* estate.[79]

Poltava was a harder case. When the rescript and directive to Nazimov were issued, the provincial marshal urged the nobility of Poltava to agree to reform on the same terms. However, the resolutions drawn up by the Poltava nobles at district conferences were, the governor reported, "far from meeting the government's views and desires," and some rejected the reform outright. The nobles of Poltava District argued that their serfs were at once less prepared for reform and more prosperous than their counterparts in the Northwest. At the same time, since the Poltava nobles desired "amelioration" no less than the government did, they undertook to eliminate the remotest possibility of abuse of manorial authority. Anything more would be impossible, all their estates, "with a very few exceptions," being mortgaged to the state. The application of the rescript and directive to Poltava would compel them to default on their mortgages and "we and our families would be left without shelter and without the very means of subsistence, sacrifices which no one demands of us." Of course, they would make this sacrifice if the tsar did demand it, but

our monarch, as an autocratic sovereign, cannot in any situation be constrained in the expression of his will, which it is our sacred and unequivocal duty to fulfill; but since his will has not been expressed, this means that H.I.M. has been pleased to put the question before us for discussion . . . and we, gratefully accepting this new evidence of the monarch's favor for us, permit ourselves to express our conviction that the establishment of committees for the immediate emancipation of the peasants would not bring them any significant benefit, while it would destroy the proprietary estates at their very foundation.

These pomeshchiki were defending their interests with a deaf ear, but the apprehensions they expressed were not to be overborne in several consultations between the provincial and district marshals.

The governor of Poltava, A. P. Volkov, reminded Lanskoi that he had no right to interfere, but when some marshals turned to him for advice, "I could not," he reported, "deny them my assistance as a human being, unofficially." His assistance converted some waverers, but not enough. Volkov thereupon convened a group of officials and other "respected nobles" of Poltava to serve as "dispassionate arbitrators." He reported,

In this general assembly, the opinions of the districts were fairly and dispassionately reviewed; the obstacles they advanced were modestly and persuasively turned aside, [but] significant and substantial difficulties were culled from all the district resolutions.[80]

To this ad hoc assembly, Volkov invited M. P. Pozen. Pozen owned one of the biggest and most successful estates in the province, and no one could match his combination of prestige in

Poltava and influence in St. Petersburg. Although he was of Jewish origin and had been eased out of the army on suspicion of corruption, he was known to have the ear of the tsar and the confidence of the tsar's friend General Rostovtsev. His reform plan was put before the Secret Committee at its first session. He was to play a role at every subsequent stage of the debate over emancipation—in Poltava, as Rostovtsev's advisor, as a member of the Editorial Commission, and as a deputy before that commission. By and large, these would be inglorious roles, and he became notorious as a retrograde intriguer; his protestations have been ignored, and his reputation has not improved with the passage of time. It is important, therefore, to appreciate that in early 1858 he still enjoyed a reputation as an abolitionist. Ivan Aksakov, who met him in 1856, was impressed (although he was bored by Pozen's interminable refutations of the allegations of corruption); he proposed to hold a conference of emancipators at Pozen's house. Pozen's Poltava neighbors were less enthusiastic; one found him a glib manipulator, while the abolitionist G. P. Galagan was suspicious of Pozen's reform plan because of its author's questionable character and his excessive exploitation of his own serfs. Certainly Pozen was notorious for cupidity, if not corruption, and as early as April of 1857 he had to warn State Secretary Butkov of the intriguers arrayed against him. Nonetheless, it was as an influential abolitionist that Pozen was invited to the Poltava assembly—an abolitionist, moreover, who was not disposed to make much of formalities; he had recently advised the tsar to convene the provincial committees without bothering about petitions from the nobility.[81]

Pozen's influence on the Poltava assembly, according to his later account, was decisive; he urged the other "dispassionate arbitrators"

to sign the petition at once and without conditions, but to draw up a memorandum about the difficulties forseen [in the district conferences] which derive from local peculiarities, and present it to the Minister of Internal Affairs.[82]

This is what the assembly did.

The major "difficulty," according to this memorandum, was intermingled holdings (*chrespolosnost'*). A village in Poltava Province might be a jumble of the demesne land of several petty squires, scattered amidst allotments of varying sizes held by their serfs, and interspersed with small lots owned by these serfs or by third parties. This kind of confusion would make it difficult to implement the rescript's land settlement, several district conferences had argued, and Governor Volkov agreed that here was an authentic local peculiarity, deserving of special consideration. He implied that since he had managed to wear down many greater objections, the Poltava nobles were entitled to concessions on this point.[83]

The Ministry of Internal Affairs did undertake to study chrespolosnost' and to call in consultants from Poltava. While this review was going on, however, the government ruled that the peculiarities of land tenure in the Ukraine did not warrant any deviation from the principles set forth in the rescript to Nazimov. Accordingly, the Main Committee ordered that the serfs of Poltava should be granted their present holdings, insofar as possible, pending a general survey and consolidation of landholdings. The committee went on to consider the ad hoc conference's suggestion that serfs who owned no cattle should not be alloted plowland and ruled that all serfs should receive allotments at the time of emancipation, whether or not they presently held them. Instead of limiting the peasants' right to an allotment, as the Poltava pomeshchiki had hoped when they submitted their petition, the committee extended it further than they had feared.[84]

More petitions arrived in April and May. Most came without conditions, but some were accompanied by memoranda that had the same purpose as explicit conditions and met the same fate. With the passage of time, provincial governors took on a more active role in eliciting consent, as Volkov had done. Governor V. N. Murav'ev of Pskov had to tour the districts himself when the efforts of the marshals proved unsuccessful. Finding the nobles fearful of peasant disorders, he played upon their fears, just as Lanskoi was doing with wavering provincial marshals and governors. Many Pskov pomeshchiki came to see, Murav'ev informed Lanskoi, that their "indecisiveness will give the peasants a pretext for various absurd notions and interpretations."[85]

Iaroslav Province was also slow to respond. Here Lanskoi overplayed his hand, perhaps because the first reaction from Iaroslav was so favorable. On December 8, 1857, the district marshals had passed a resolution stating that the relationship between pomeshchik and serf, though not so bad as outsiders might think, was unnatural and outmoded; serfdom had endured only because the right alternative had not been found, as it now must be. However, six weeks later, in joint session with the district deputies, the marshals decided simply to ascertain the local nobility's opinion about the reform, and asked for "the right to a free discussion of basic principles . . . without being constrained by the rules and time limit issued to other provinces."

Lanskoi's response was harsh.

The assembly of the Iaroslav marshals and deputies has arrogated a right it does not have. The government has no need whatever of the assent or dissent of the nobility of this or that province concerning the arrangement of peasant life; it expects only that they should express their desire to take up this matter, and nothing more. . . . The basic principles confirmed by His Majesty are not subject to discussion.

The marshals and deputies did not take Lanskoi's letter to heart. A month after he wrote, they reassembled and decided on further delay, since it would be unseemly to present a petition to the tsar from which the names of the biggest proprietors, who were absentees, were missing. The governor hastened to assure Lanskoi that in six weeks, when the roads would again be passable, the nobility would surely produce the required petition "thanks to my constant and tireless efforts." He complained that the local pomeshchiki were "heedless" and "reckless" and found it "hard to grasp" the necessity for reform: it required "constant consultation and instruction" to move the provincial marshal to appropriate action. Lanskoi responded coldly to these apologies, finding that "it would be unseemly to delay any further in making this appeal to the sovereign, as it does not require any special consideration, especially now that responses have been received from the nobility resident in the province." When they were able to reconvene, the marshals and deputies agreed with this reasoning and voted for an unconditional petition.[86]

The contours of the process emerge clearly enough from these instances, although the experience of each province was slightly different. In some provinces, it was the governor that elicited assent to reform; in others, it was the provincial marshal, with more or less assistance from the district marshals and "dispassionate arbitrators." Some local officials took the initiative in applying pressure; others did not, and found themselves under pressure from the center, which they transmitted to the nobility at large. In either event, they often deceived the nobility about the character of the rescripts, but the deception was unwitting. They also carefully ignored questions of competence; the authority of some nobles to speak for the rest and the right of corporate officials to act for the noble estate had to be taken for granted. The central government played a quiet role, badgering local officials and turning back conditions attached to the nobility's petitions. It is clear enough, at any rate, that neither fear nor the habit of submission was enough, in and of itself, to procure the nobility's assent. And it is clearer still that very few rank-and-file nobles had any desire for a reform of serfdom.

Perhaps only in Vladimir Province did local nobles take the lead in securing assent, for here the provincial marshal, S. N. Bogdanov, did not respond to "consultation and instruction" from the administration. One of his constituents caustically observed,

All his quasi-liberalism has disappeared; he says the most terrible things—about age-old rights, blood, wounds, patriotism, the graves of our fathers, and so on; he has utterly surrendered to the planters and is leading others astray.

Hence Vladimir was among the last provinces to solicit a rescript. Initially, the district marshals and deputies had made a favorable response, but they withdrew it the following day.[87] Formal assent was the work of a group of local nobles, who produced a petition bearing the signatures of 2937 Vladimir pomeshchiki. This was an impressive figure, far surpassing the total collected in any other province. Indeed, it considerably surpassed the number of nobles owning serfs in the province, as one journalist noted, adding, "Given such a reassuring fact, why look for a misprint?"[88]

In other provinces, the nobles who signed similar petitions corresponded to somewhat more than one-fifth of the total of serfholders (see Table 1) and much less than one-fifth of the membership of the noble estate. It cannot be determined how many serfless nobles assented to the reform of an institution in which they had no personal stake, but the restrictive franchise in use at the assemblies of the nobility was not imposed: any noble, without regard to rank, sex, or property holding, was allowed to sign the petition. At any rate, not many pomeshchiki responded to direct solicitation and assented to the reform of serfdom.

It might be expected that nobles in government service would take the lead in supporting the government's initiative, but a check of the 502 original signers of the Moscow petition indicates the opposite.[89] About twenty held honorific positions at the tsar's court, on the Council of State, and in the Moscow departments of the Senate. Only six or seven, including Zakrevskii and his deputy, were employed in the Moscow provincial administration, and no more than five or six served elsewhere in the civil, military, and diplomatic services. The Ministers of Internal Affairs and of Justice did not sign, although they were qualified to do so as owners of estates in Moscow Province. On the other hand, almost all the officials of the corporate organization of the nobility signed, and so did a good many district officials, most of whom were local

Table 1. Signatures on petition soliciting a rescript.

Province (in order of receipt of rescript)	Number of signatures[a]	Serfholders in province[b]	Percentage of serfholders signing	Date rescript issued to province[c]
Nizhnii Novgorod	138	1411	9.8	24/XII/57
Moscow	514[d]	2439	21.1	/I/58
Saratov	223	2592	8.6	9/III
Orel	970	3823	25.4	16/III
Novgorod	419	4261	9.8	I/IV
Riazan	799	5215	15.3	I/IV
Kostroma	320	3264	9.8	I/IV
Tambov	651	3265	19.9	5/IV
Ekaterinoslav	341	2448	13.9	5/IV
Penza	498	2029	24.5	5/IV
Kursk	1471	5475	26.8	20/IV
Iaroslav	716	2810	25.5	3/V
Tula	1339	3864	34.8	3/V
Vologda	193	1264	15.3	3/V
Pskov	637	1952	32.6	3/V
Mogilev	286	2165	13.2	3/V
Kherson	653	2688	24.3	10/V
Chernigov	1443	4445	32.5	18/V
Smolensk	773	5308	14.6	28/V
Vladimir	2937	2659	110.5	8/VI
Kaluga	1319	2440	54.0	24/VI
For 21 provinces	16,640[e]	65,817	23.3	
For 20 provinces (excluding Vladimir)	13,703	63,158	21.7	

[a]Data from *Zhurnal Ministerstva vnutrennikh del*, kn. 2-8 for 1858, except Nizhnii Novgorod (*TsGIAL, f.* 1180, *op.* XV, *d.* 10, *l.* 212), Saratov (*TsGIAL, f.* 1291, *op.* 1, *d.* 8, *l.* 3), and Tula (*ZhSGK*, p. 152). Other sources give slightly smaller totals for Orel, Novgorod, Riazan, and Pskov.

[b]Data from A. Troinitskii, *Krepostnoe naselenie*, p. 45. These figures are presented as "total of *vladel'tsy*," or serfholders, but in fact they probably represent estates, as the *reviziia* materials from which Troinitskii worked did not reckon proprietors as such. Hence the owner of three estates will figure as three "*vladel'tsy*" and the joint owners of a single estate will figure as one. Since each of these co-owners might sign the petition, the pool of potential signers was probably considerably larger, and the percentage of signers correspondingly lower, than indicated in this table.

[c]Data from *SbPR*, pp. 253-245.

[d]Including twelve signatures on supplementary list.

[e]According to Lanskoi, a total of 18,548 nobles signed petitions requesting that the imperial rescript be extended to their province. This total includes some 250 owners of estates in outlying provinces with few serfs and no corporate organization of the nobility; the balance of the discrepancy should be allocated to the provinces, such as Kharkov and Tauride, for which there is no available information on the petition or the number of signers. See S. S. Lanskoi, "Vzgliad na polozhenie krest'ianskogo voprosa v nastoiashchee vremia," in N. Semenov, *Osvobozhdenie*, vol. I, appendix, p. 827.

pomeshchiki elected to their posts by the nobility. More than thirty signers were associated with state-supported philanthropic or cultural institutions in Moscow. But altogether, about three-quarters of the male signers held no kind of public office, although almost all had earned a rank (*chin*) in the service at one time.[90] More than a quarter of the signers were women, who were entitled to own estates but were ordinarily denied a direct role in the corporate affairs of the nobility. As regards holdings of serfs, the signers of the Moscow petition present a similar picture. Eleven or 12 of the 36 magnates in the province, owners of 1000 or more serfs apiece, signed the petition (many were also holders of honorific offices). Between one-tenth and one-fifth of those who had more than 100 serfs and fewer than 1000 signed. The great bulk of the signers, however, do not appear on the register of owners of estates with more than 100 serfs and must have been lesser pomeshchiki (if they owned any serfs at all).[91] Most of the signers then, were retired petty officials with small holdings—the very element of the nobility that contemporaries supposed was most firmly opposed to the abolition of serfdom.[92]

To be sure, the signatures did not have an essential function, except possibly in Kaluga and Vladimir provinces. The individual pomeshchik was not constrained by the alternative of having a bureaucratic settlement imposed because of his refusal to acquiesce. In ten provinces, the marshals and deputies simply petitioned on their own authority. Local officials elsewhere submitted lists of names as proof of their zeal. Hence the totals represent something near the upper limit, as these officials conceived it, of the nobility's acquiescence to the rescript and directive, as they might or might not be modified to suit "local peculiarities." The totals are impressive, considering the nobility's supposed devotion to serfdom; considering the scale of the interests and prejudices involved, they are not so impressive. Most important, apart from the tentative stand taken by the marshals and deputies of Kostroma, no one objected that the totals were inadequate. Almost any document emanating from a laggard province was acceptable as a petition and evoked the usual rescript. Once the rescript had been issued, the nobility of each province tried to make the best of the new situation. No spokesman for the nobility would jeopardize his standing with the government by raising a procedural quibble about the validity of his province's assent.

Authority and Leadership

The Russian nobility acquiesced to the abolition of serfdom, but it did so slowly and with unseemly reluctance. Despite its strong tradition of service to the state, the nobility showed that it was imperfectly bureaucratized. However, the bureaucratization of the bureaucracy proved nearly perfect. Left to their own devices, the provincial governors and marshals of the nobility would not take any initiative towards the abolition of serfdom or volunteer plans for its reform, as the government had informally invited them to do as recently as 1856. But when abolition was put on an official footing, they responded admirably. They had rarely if ever faced a major conflict between the sentiments of the local nobility and the demands of St. Petersburg; when the choice was squarely put, most of them inclined to St. Petersburg. They acted under pressure from above, but they acted in good faith: no provincial governor or marshal deceived the nobles by encouraging them to submit a conditional petition with the foreknowledge that the conditions would be ignored.

Officials in the central administration maintained, in retrospect, that there was no problem in securing the assent of the nobility once Moscow Province had submitted,[93] but the task did not seem so easy to those who had to carry it out. At each level, officials struck a different balance between the demands of their superiors and the apprehensions of their neighbors. District marshals were more accommodating to their electors than were provincial marshals, who in turn were less exacting than the governors. Each official pared seemingly unreasonable reservations from the nobility's response and passed the remnant further up the hierarchy. Even the governors, appointed from the center, were responsive to local sentiment and passed along what they conceived to be the irreducible minimum of objections and special circumstances appropriate to the province in their charge. In St. Petersburg, where local sentiment was absent and standards correspondingly rigid, the last excrescences were peeled off and another pearl of assent was added to the string.

The nobles themselves cooperated in this process, sometimes presenting their views in expurgated form. In Tambov, where the assembly of the nobility initially decided to postpone action on the rescript, the squires found themselves, with heavy heart, calling on the governor and proclaiming their willingness to sacrifice for the great cause. They also gathered at the house of N. A. Nikitorov to bewail their impending ruin and extinction; here they applauded the retrograde views of the Blank brothers and circulated proposals lacking, according to a friendly observer, "any sense whatever."[94]

The nobles assented under pressure from local officials, and many applied this pressure in the manner of Saltykov-Shchedrin's district marshal Sergeev. Convening his pomeshchik neighbors, Sergeev began diffidently: "Speaking frankly, it would be very agreeable if for our part . . . to offer our services . . . in a word, something of that kind. I hope, gentlemen, that you understand me?" One pomeshchik understood very well, remarking, "If we don't take an initiative now, then tomorrow or next week we will all the same be obliged to do so." Sergeev agreed, continuing,

Arguments, contradictions, representations and so on are good and appropriate only when the need for them is felt by those who . . . in a word, by those who have, so to speak, a confidential authorization for this. In the present instance, this need is not felt.

However, these oblique explanations did not move the group to action, at which Sergeev became more exacting. "I am a liberal not only in words but in deeds," he confessed. "I seek freedom everywhere—nothing but freedom." Consequently, "I shall not tolerate any objections in a retrograde sense. In this instance I shall be firm and unswerving." After further deliberations, Sergeev's neighbors took the expected "initiative," since, as one of them observed, "it is necessary first of all to observe the forms, so that everything will look seemly and smooth." "And then," another explained, "leave everything as it was before."[95]

Frequently, local officials found allies within the nobility, whose zeal helped overcome the recalcitrance of the majority. So long as serfdom enjoyed the patronage and support of the state, the provincial nobles who desired its abolition rarely took overt action, and the routine of provincial life often wore down their abolitionist beliefs. But when the state offered them a form and focus for action, they emerged from among the mass of pomeshchiki who were at least satisfied with serfdom.[96]

It is the behavior of this mass of pomeshchiki that requires explanation. Why did they respond so docilely to pressure, example, and chicanery? The answer lies partly in their attitude to serfdom and the serfs, and partly in the character of their leadership.

The provincial pomeshchik appears to have regarded serfdom as nothing more than a matter of land, labor, and money; at least, there was nothing else in serfdom that he cherished—no affective or sentimental element. Contemporaries believed that the nobles had long opposed any reform because they prized their patriarchal authority, their *barstvo*, as Nikitenko called it.[97] The Decembrist S.

P. Trubetskoi, observing the unwillingness of the nobles of Kiev Province to assent to reform, also found that barstvo was the psychological foundation of serfdom:

Long-standing command and the habit of possessing one's own kind have inculcated in [the nobility] the idea that the right of holding serfs does not in the least contradict the laws of nature; that it is necessary for the welfare of the state, the power, might and order of which are based upon the noble estate, which serves as the faithful and reliable bastion of the state; and, finally, that manorial power is beneficial to the serf estate: the lord is the legally established protector of his serf. . . . The relations of pomeshchik and serf are based upon patriarchal principles, which are inherent in human nature and make a kind of family of the master and his dependents. The pomeshchik is a father, the serfs are his children.[98]

The behavior of the nobility in 1858 indicates that this widely held interpretation is wrong, and that by mid-century there was scarcely any sentimental or patriarchal element in serfdom. Once they had recovered from their initial shock and anguish, nobles hastened to renounce their arbitrary power over "their own kind" and to seek economic advantage in the new situation. Iakushkin described this evolution among his pomeshchik neighbors:

"How can they take away what is mine?," I heard soon after the promulgation of the rescript. . . . "I do own the man, after all, and my Van'ka brings me an obrok of fifty a year. If they take away Van'ka, who will pay for him, who will assess him at his value?"
 Even before two months had passed after the first reactions, the same people were saying, "It is immoral, and no one will dispute it, to own a man like some kind of thing! We won't make a stand on men, the peasants should be freed, but for Christ's sake tell me why they should take my land away and give it to someone else?"[99]

The pattern Iakushkin described was nearly universal. When the initial shock had passed, and nobles began to respond to the rescripts in writing, they invariably seized upon the economic provisions. If the early comments on the rescripts were the only surviving sources, historians would suppose that the estates of the pomeshchiki were simply commercial enterprises, and that by 1858 serfdom utterly lacked any basis in sentiment, pride, or sense of responsibility. Unsophisticated nobles did refer to their paternal solicitude for the peasants and their efficiency as guardians of order and censors of morals, but merely as eulogy, without any attempt to cling to serfdom as a personal relationship. The force of this eulogy was diminished by the reiterated complaint that the peasants were immoral, backward, and utterly unprepared for freedom, despite centuries of tutelage by their pomeshchiki. The contradiction passed unnoticed because both elements were rhetorical ornaments to economic demands.

The nobles did not disclaim all power over persons, but they sought to preserve only those forms of arbitrary power that promised economic benefit. The form varied with the area and the character of the estate; here, the nobles wanted ascribed labor, there a monopoly of land; some would convert obrok into a perpetual charge on the peasants, others would maintain barshchina as before, while many would be content with a capital sum from the treasury. In general, they sought a permanent shelter from the harsh world of the market. As the Third Section reported to the tsar, "Although almost all the nobles are dissatisfied . . . all their grumbling derives from their apprehensions that their income will diminish or in many cases even disappear."[100] With their income at stake, nobles did not cling to their power to buy and sell serfs, turn them into lackeys, control their marriages, or even improve their morality and industry.

Barstvo, then, unexpectedly turned out to be of little account. The nobles abandoned quixotic intransigeance in order to secure economic benefits in the reform settlement. Their notion of economic benefits had been formed by serfdom, and so had their idea that these benefits were to be had from their traditional benefactor, the tsar. There is no reason to doubt the effusive loyalty to the tsar expressed in most of the nobility's petitions in 1858. Monarchist sentiment alone was not enough to make the nobility renounce what it believed to be its interest, although some petitions were meant to give that impression. Yet in the balance of hopes and fears, faith in the tsar had great weight. Nobles came to realize that they were more likely to enjoy the favor that Alexander and his predecessors had lavished upon them if they acquiesced than if they negotiated in an adversary posture.

As this tendency gained ground and official pressure for compliance became stronger, the flow of argument reversed: excuses for temporizing became forces for assent. These excuses most frequently concerned the danger of peasant discontent and the nobles' debts. In December and January, pomeshchiki warned the government that the mere attempt to reform serfdom could provoke a peasant rebellion; by the springtime of 1858, officials were warning laggard pomeshchiki of the danger of violent retribution if they did not renounce serfdom. Similarly, nobles initially argued that they could not accept the terms of the rescript because their estates were mortgaged, but subsequently found it prudent to conciliate their principal creditor, the government. In both instances, the initial response was probably sounder. Debts to the state and the danger of rebellion were by no means political liabilities for a resolute and united class; the government could not tolerate anarchy in the countryside simply to spite the squires, and a massive default on mortgages would have jeopardized the fiscal and administrative aspects of the impeding reform. But the pomeshchik reacted as an individual, fearing that *his* peasants might get out of hand or *his* estate be foreclosed, and turned compliant. Because of the nobility's long-standing lack of cohesion, its traditional leaders could play upon these fears.

As regards leadership, there is no doubt that the provincial marshals and governors maintained their influence over the nobility, despite their abrupt conversion from upholders of serfdom to agents of its destruction. It was hard for the nobility to find alternative leadership under the pressure of time and events, for prestige in mid-century Russia generally derived from rank, and high rank in the government entailed the obligation to make a show of assent to the tsar's wishes. The sanovniki in the Secret Committee, many of whom had resisted the reform of serfdom for a generation, set an example of compliance and did not encourage provincial nobles to resist the pressure for assent. Most dignitaries followed their lead.

There were, of course, magnates in the provinces who were not bound by official position, but they rarely stepped in to provide leadership for the nobility at large. Some, bearing such distinguished names as Iusupov, Sheremetev, and Vorontsov, responded to the rescripts with a burst of humanitarian sentiment: they decided to avail themselves at long last of the laws on manumission of 1803 and 1842 and write their own emancipation statutes for their estates. These selfless gestures foundered on the caution of bureaucrats and the skepticism of serfs.[101]

One man to whom the nobility looked for unofficial leadership in 1858 was Prince A. S. Menshikov. Menshikov could not be seduced by official favor, for he was rich beyond dreams of avarice and already had all the decorations a grateful emperor could bestow. He was not wholly free of official ties, being a member of the Council of State, adjutant-general in the suite of the Grand Duke Konstantin and at the Naval Ministry, a general in a guards regiment, and an honorary member of the Academy of Sciences. These were merely the distinctions appropriate for a distinguished retired admiral, emphasizing his rank without entailing any administrative responsibility. Menshikov had fought in the councils of Nicholas I against far milder measures than the rescripts to Nazimov and Ignat'ev; under Alexander he continued to oppose emancipation with land and to speak up for the pomeshchiki. At a New Year's ball in 1858, when Alexander congratulated him on a generous grant of land to some of his serfs, Menshikov pointedly reminded the tsar that his lesser neighbors could not be expected to make a comparable sacrifice.[102]

Emancipators feared Menshikov, while provincial nobles looked to him with hope; marshals and other officials flocked to his house. A memorandum attributed to him circulated in many manuscript copies. Attacking the idea of "expropriation," the memorandum argued that peasants would follow the state's example and take to arbitrary seizure, while the dispossessed petty squires, loyal servants of the state turned out of their homes, would become seditious city-dwellers. The epigrams attributed to Menshikov were in the same spirit; he was supposed to have said of the tsar, "He wants to be Alexander the Great, but since that is very hard to do, he has begun by turning Russia into Macedonia." And who could doubt the significance of his constant trips between Moscow and St. Petersburg? The lion of Nicholas's council-chamber seemed ideally placed and naturally disposed to lead the recalcitrant nobility.[103]

By 1858, however, Menshikov was a very old lion. He was so harassed by importunate children and rebellious bowels, so distracted by constant trips between the capitals to fulfill his ceremonial obligations, that he had little energy left for public questions.[104] More important, he was no more inclined than Alexander's ministers to carry opposition into the public domain. The memorandum in circulation was indeed his, but it had been written before the rescript to Nazimov (as any but the most uncritically friendly or hostile reader should have seen). He lamented that its circulation might seem a breech of official secrecy, though he now was bound to secrecy not by position but by habit. As for the anecdote, it was surely a calumny, for Menshikov was linked to the tsar by personal ties that could be renewed by no more than a nod or a vague remark from Alexander. Although officials on active government service were encouraged to participate in the provincial committees established by the rescripts, Menshikov felt he must ask the tsar before accepting election to the Moscow Committee; Alexander gravely gave his permission.

Finally, like most of the nobility, from Zakrevskii to the pomeshchiki in the "bears' corners," Menshikov was optimistically confident that the rescripts would not be applied in all their supposed rigor to Great Russia. His confidence was bolstered by visits to St. Petersburg. Conversations with Dolgorukov and other high officials convinced him that the "reds" surrounding Lanskoi were being confounded and that the reform might follow the Estonian model—that is, "without encroaching on property and without the reckless haste with which they are now proceeding." Menshikov was not to be bullied by a district marshal or some other ill-informed functionary. He was a man to whom the functionaries deferred, and his informants were the very best. Even when in Moscow, he was visited by such dignitaries as S. G. Stroganov and M. N. Murav'ev, who reported that the tsar was "much more moderate in his demands for the alienation of property" and "inwardly inclined to make concessions on the question of household plots."

Confined as he was by affinity and habit, armed with informal influence and disarmed by credulity, Menshikov would not take a stand on the issue of assent. When his district marshal asked for his signature to the petition from Moscow Province, he gave it, and his diary records no misgivings.[105] His example may have convinced many lesser pomeshchiki that they had little to lose by giving their assent—and much to lose by making a show of opposition—since the old paths of influence were still open.

Indeed, it was not until August 1858 that there was a concrete manifestation of political opposition from the nobility, in the form of a pronunciamento: "We Summon you, Nobility of Russia, Headed by the Muscovites." Dolgorukov, head of the Third Section, pronounced it "extremely harmful." Not satisfied with the efforts of the Moscow police to find the author, he instructed his subordinate in Moscow to set up "secret surveillance" to prevent its further dissemination. The surveillance was effective, for no more copies appeared, but the perpetrators were never discovered.

The appeal begins,

How has the Sovereign Tsar requited you, pomeshchiki of Moscow, for your willingness to be deprived of your ancient rights at His pleasure? Did He not meet you, not with gratitude for your servile submission, but with a sharp reproach and abuse because you did not, at the very hour and minute he wanted, express your readiness to lay a sacrifice on the altar of his hunger for power?

This, as Academician Druzhinin observes, is the language of the krepostniki, or adherents of serfdom, although the grammar and spelling of the original do them little credit. The appeal proceeds to a political conclusion, summoning the nobles to overthrow the "incompetent tribe" of bureaucrats; the support of the Old

Believers and the army officers, who have been "utterly ruined by the constant modifications of their uniforms," is assured. The tone becomes increasingly shrill and weird:

Fear no more to violate your oath and thereby sink to hell. Ha! Ha! Ha! Fear not, Gentlemen, He [the tsar] violated his oath before you and consequently has already annulled yours, by permitting himself to scorn the fundamental laws and take your property away for nothing. This plundering benefits a robber, but not a Tsar.

While the wavering handwriting of the originals recalls Iakushkin's pomeshchik neighbors who, "never before having set pen to paper," undertook to express their views on the emancipation, the painstaking block lettering, marred by the insertion of afterthoughts, bespeaks a lunatic intensity. The impression conveyed by the tone and form is confirmed by the peroration, where the nobility is exhorted to "drive out the plunderers and set at the head of the government the man who, not by birth or size but by intellect, stands above us all. . . . You probably have guessed that the future chief of Russia is—Herzen." It is clear that the object of Dolgorukov's anxiety, the one overt *frondeur* among the Russian nobility, was deranged. And even he did not urge the retention of serfdom, conceding that "by the rights of humanity the peasants should be free from bondage."[106]

Russian serfdom, then, had no articulate advocates in its last hour, and its beneficiaries formally acquiesced to its abolition. Very few nobles positively approved of the terms to which the nobility assented, the rescript and directive to Nazimov. Positive approval was rare not only because most nobles cherished their prerogatives, but also because those nobles who, like Unkovskii, had long favored the abolition of serfdom wanted a more thorough-going reform than the government initially proposed. While the nobility's assent was equivocal, its acquiescence was virtually complete—if silence denotes acquiescence. The petitions from the provinces were backed by doubtful authority or signed by a small proportion of the pomeshchiki, but the pomeshchiki at large did not publicly object. When conditions and reservations, attached to these petitions with the encouragement of the constituted authorities, were ignored, no formal protest was made. Russia's nobles were not used to protesting, nor even to taking an adversary stance to the administration. Their acquiescence, then, can best be explained by the continued operation of long-standing attitudes. By the middle of the nineteenth century, Russian squires were by no means capitalists, but they regarded their estates primarily as sources of income. When pressed, they tolerated a considerable change in their legal relationship to the peasantry in the hope that the flow of income would be maintained. A belligerent defense of prerogatives, putting the noble at odds with the government in St. Petersburg and the peasantry all around, would jeopardize the flow of income. The nobles were accustomed to the "favor" of the authorities as one of the operating conditions of their estates and their very lives. Under challenge, they continued to give their trust and deference to those who traditionally enjoyed them—the marshals, the governors, and the tsar himself—even though they had unexpectedly become the bearers of the challenge. Other considerations, such as indebtedness, dread of a solution imposed by the bureaucracy, and fear of peasant violence, played a role. These considerations inclined the nobility to acquiescence because they operated in a context determined by the pomeshchik's attitude to his estates and to authority.

The Evolution of Policy

4

This chapter follows the regime's misgivings about the commitment to reform and then examines the new commitment to a far-reaching reform made by the Imperial Order of December 4, 1858. With that order the government undertook not merely to abolish the legal status of serf but to construct a postservile system in which the peasant would be economically autonomous and juridically independent of the squire. If there had been a device to measure the extent to which government policy favored the peasants, it would have registered its highest reading in December of 1858. As the principles set forth in the Imperial Order were translated into legislative detail, there would be a marked tendency to cater to the nobility and maintain the ways of serfdom under other forms and names. For the moment, however, the thoroughgoing abolitionists had gained a striking victory in principle.

This victory did not elevate the reformers to power and influence. It was achieved by the traditional methods of court politics, through the agency of a courtier and general who enjoyed the tsar's personal confidence. Reform had triumphed, but the reformers had not; throughout the reform era they were insecure, anxious, and defensive. Their antagonists were correspondingly confident, often mistakenly so. Yet the sanovniki and the spokesmen for the pomeshchiki measured political success in terms of ministerial portfolios and the day-to-day administration of the country and, in these terms, they continued to prevail. In a sense, their program could not prevail because, unlike the abolitionists, they did not have an articulated program. They had the conventional wisdom—an affinity for serfdom and the polity associated with it, a desire to bolster the nobility and cater to its prejudices, and a limited capacity to conceive any worthy successor to the servile order. For most of 1858, the conventional wisdom reigned supreme, although the commitment to reform serfdom could not be renounced, since it had been made from the height of the throne. Then, at the end of the year, the conventional wisdom was repudiated. Yet its exponents were tenacious, and their understanding of politics was not wholly mistaken. The emancipation legislation of 1861 was compounded of the concepts of the reformers and the inclinations of the Nicholaevan sanovniki. While the triumphs of the sanovniki throughout 1858 were ephemeral, their defeat in December was less than conclusive.

From the first, a majority of the Main Committee was at odds with Lanskoi on issues of policy, but all agreed on the necessity of securing the nobility's assent. The majority did not protest when Lanskoi browbeat or misled provincial officials. Sometimes he deceived the committee, too, but the other members in effect permitted the deception. It would have been easy enough for them to establish direct contact with the pomeshchiki in the provinces; indeed, affronted provincials were crowding their anterooms.[1] The committee, however, did not choose to take a stand on wounded feelings. It was a policy-making body, composed of ministers and military men who respected a proper chain of command. Lanskoi, in his dealings with marshals and governors, was not making policy; he was dealing with his subordinates and was entitled to deal with them as he saw fit. Ministerial circulars and general directives, being matters of policy, had to pass through the Main Committee and were permissive. Letters and directives to particular officials, being administrative matters, issued directly from the ministry and tended to be exacting. Lanskoi could hector individual officials on his own authority, which the Main Committee respected. Also, the ministry's correspondence with its subordinates was confidential, while the general directives issued through the Main Committee were not. The committee's overt encouragement and the ministry's covert coercion reflected a diversity of both outlook and function, but the combination did much to secure the nobility's assent.

Furthermore, Lanskoi and the committee agreed from the first that the rescripts were inviolable. None of them (including Lanskoi) had been an outspoken abolitionist, but the rescripts were government policy, issued through a body of which they were members, and so must prevail. Menshikov's diary records that, at a time when the nobility's "grumbling" about the rescripts dismayed the tsar and disheartened reformist officials, "Orlov has no doubts of success" in securing assent and told Menshikov that, "as chairman of the Committee, he will oppose any departure . . . from the rescripts."[2] And so Orlov and the other sanovniki joined Lanskoi in ignoring the provincial nobility's appeals that the rescripts be modified.

While the sanovniki stood with Lanskoi on the issues of acquiescence and adherence to the rescripts, they were inclined to give the nobility as much latitude as the rescripts allowed. They clashed with Lanskoi on this point when Ignat'ev first raised the issue of the provincial committees' competence,[3] and the conflict continued. Lanskoi, for example, used his authority as minister to prevent the convocation of extraordinary assemblies, where the nobles of a province could consider the question of assent. The Main Committee, on the other hand, authorized district conferences where pomeshchiki could set forth their ideas to guide their representatives on the provincial committees. Solov'ev, one of Lanskoi's subordinates, found this authorization to be a subtle attempt to undermine the government program, since a district conference would be a sounding board for the most retrograde views. Solov'ev was right as to the probable character of district conferences, and Lanskoi later managed an amendment to the committee's ruling: district conferences would be held, but in the provincial capitals.[4] This issue, like many greater ones, suggests the futility of applying the terms "liberal" and "conservative" to nineteenth-century Russians, especially bureaucrats. Lanskoi was advancing the "liberal" cause in discouraging the district conferences, where the enemies of emancipation could congregate and speak out. Yet it is a questionable liberalism that denies a forum to potential opponents, then reluctantly sets up a rostrum beside the governor's palace, excluding the petty squires who could not raise the fare to the provincial capital.

The committee's desire to give the nobility as free a hand as the rescript allowed became clearer still when it rejected Lanskoi's program for the provincial committees and substituted its own version. The committee's program was issued on April 21, when it was no longer necessary to make concessions to tempt the nobility into acquiescence. It should be said, however, that the draft program produced by the Ministry of Internal Affairs was unworkable.

The ministry's draft was the work of Iakov Solov'ev, chief of the Civil Division of the Central Statistical Committee of the ministry—more simply, the ministry's emancipation bureau. The draft program was specific on some points where the original rescript and directive had been ambiguous; for example, peasant allotments were to be perpetual, and the pomeshchiki could not exact more than their fair rental value. It asked the committees to spell out the pomeshchik's "manorial police power" and the peasants' rights during the transition period. It raised the possibility of redemption of plowland, which the Main Committee had rejected in March. The draft would determine the size of the allotments according to a mixture of criteria, some taken from Lanskoi's directive to Ignat'ev, others anticipating the statutes of 1861, and would impose on the whole empire the Ukrainian system of categorizing households according to their prosperity. In sum, the draft program was restrictive on some points, vague on others, and merely interrogatory on still others; it could scarcely have elicited a finished draft statute from a body of laymen.

Solov'ev complained that the sanovniki rejected his program because it expressed his zeal for real emancipation. He observed with more justice that he alarmed them with his breach of secrecy; he printed and distributed a hundred copies of his draft. However, one of these copies went to Iurii Samarin, whose credentials as an emancipator were in good order, and his comments were highly adverse. On many issues, Samarin's objections were minor or semantic; on others, he sought more protection for the pomeshchik's economic interests. He would restore the rescript's provision indicating that peasants must redeem their own homes and outbuildings as well as the ground they stood on, and he would spell out the pomeshchik's powers as both employer and police chief. Most important, he complained that Solov'ev's draft was "not so much a program of activities as a decision in advance of many very important questions, or a draft of a general statute for all provinces."[5]

Samarin should have been pleased with the Main Committee's substitute, which was a blank check for the provincial committees.[6] The committees' work was divided into three periods. In the second period, they were authorized to implement the reform, and in the third, to draft a "Rural Code," based on the experience of the reform. Thus they were elevated to semipermanent status, a concession that was quietly forgotten two years later, when the committees were dispersed forever. However, the first period was of immediate importance. In the course of six months, a committee was to collect detailed information about every estate in the province, review and systematize the opinions expressed at the district conferences, and draft a reform statute with various supporting documents. "For more convenient review and considera- tion in the Main Committee," the draft statutes were to have a "common form."

On some points, the form provided in the April Program was a laconic paraphrase of the original rescript and later statements of policy. For example, the committees were instructed, in the second of ten chapters, to indicate "the term appointed for temporary obligation (transitional status), independent of the redemption of household plots." Implicitly, this plank held that the maximum duration of transitional status was twelve years, as the rescript provided; explicitly, it incorporated the Main Committee's subsequent ruling that peasants would pass out of transitional status even if they had not managed to redeem their plots within that time. Like the rescript, the form made no mention of "freedom" or "emancipation," leaving unanswered the question, Transition to what?

Most significant, the form was no more than a form; all questions of definition, quantity, and limitation were left up to the provincial committee. Section II of Chapter IV is an example:

Dues to the pomeshchik

Dues in money (obrok)

Dues in kind (daily labor)

Their extent, based on the value of the household plots, arable land, and the nonagricultural [*promyshlennye*] advantages of the area.

The system for rendering dues.

The determination of labor tasks and their introduction.

The guarantee of full and punctual rendering of dues by the mutual responsibility of the village society and by measures for exacting dues from those in default.

The services of peasants who have, by virtue of the pomeshchik's solicitude, been instructed in various trades and managerial functions.

The extent of their compensation for extra working days; the term of their service.[7]

This section followed the rescript where necessary, as in the provision for mutual responsibility. On a point where the rescript was silent but pomeshchiki were voluble, it suggested that blacksmiths, overseers, and other skilled serfs would have to pay dearly for the privilege of quitting their jobs, if they could do so at all. Otherwise, this section, like the rest of the form, left the committees to demand whatever they thought they could get away with.

The program did disappoint those nobles who, with diverse ends in view, saw the provincial committees as instruments for administrative reform or vessels of political power.[8] The imposition of an obligatory form reinforced the government's insistence that the committees confine their discussion to the emancipation settlement.[9] Most nobles and most committees, however, had an overriding concern for the economic and related provisions of that settlement and, within that perimeter, the April Program gave them a relatively free hand.

The April Program was the handiwork of Rostovtsev's protege M. P. Pozen. According to Solov'ev, it was laconic and unclear in order to deceive the inexperienced Rostovtsev and, through him, the tsar. Rostovtsev's subsequent apology for the program suggests that Solov'ev was right.[10] Solov'ev also maintained that Pozen's program was meant to open the door to landless emancipation; he found the "Rural Code" particularly ominous, since it could strip the peasants of their land or re-enserf them, according to the committee's taste. Here Solov'ev went too far. Many of the supposed portents of landless emancipation were simply restatements of directives issued, sometimes reluctantly, by his own ministry.[11] And his apprehensions make no allowance of the prudence of the autocrat, whom he praised effusively elsewhere; Alexander could always veto a rural code or, for that matter, a draft statute.

Pozen subsequently disclaimed sinister intentions. The April program, he maintained, was a mere form, which could not and did not influence the actions of any committee—though many of the drafts drawn up according to the program were good enough to enact without change. However, the program was premised not on regard, but on contempt for the legislative skills of the nobility; there was no need for detailed regulation of its committees, since their output would be only raw material for a general statute to be drafted by the central government. For, like most of the reputed intriguers in behalf of the nobility, Pozen was no admirer of the nobility or its institutions. To be sure, his memory played him somewhat false as to his original reasoning. He did not begin to advocate a common statute for all provinces until after the April Program was issued; in an early draft, he justified its looseness by explaining that many questions should be postponed and resolved only in the light of experience, during the period of temporary obligation.[12]

However mixed his motives, Pozen achieved a personal triumph in winning the tsar's approval for the April Program. He had not acted in bad faith. He opposed certain provisions of the original rescripts and directive, but he did so explicitly, in letters to Rostovtsev and other members of the Main Committee. If the government accepted a program written by such a man and consistent with his views, the fault lay in the government's own uncertainty. And while the program reflected certain views that would shortly become heretical, its immediate impact was simply to widen the latitude the Main Committee consistently offered the nobility.

A further ground of disagreement between Lanskoi and the committee was the immediate regulation of serfdom. During 1858, the pomeshchik's powers over his serfs were sharply curtailed. Reforms previously rejected as too radical were enacted casually and quietly—so quietly, indeed, that officials responsible for their enforcement were rarely aware of any change. The fact remains that a series of administrative decrees abolished or drastically limited the lord's power to sell serfs apart from land, convert them into household serfs, send them into the army or exile, take over their household plots, and relocate them. In most cases, the initiative was Lanskoi's; the committee cut back on his proposals, preserving the substance but limiting the publicity, and thus the effect, the measures would have. This limitation was a further concession to the nobility and of more practical value than the latitude the committee offered the provincial committees.[13]

The provincial committees' semblance of authority reached its apogee before most of them had convened. In early July of 1858, the Main Committee offered a system for processing the provincial drafts; the rescripts had indicated only that they would be reviewed by the tsar. The committee's proposal, which was confirmed and circulated as an Imperial Order, directed each provincial committee to elect two deputies to assist the government in its review of its draft. The order took pains to avoid constitutional ramifications. The deputies were to present whatever "information and explanation" the central government might think necessary; the Main Committee and its subcommittee *could*, at their discretion, invite deputies to their sessions. Nonetheless, provincial nobles were assured that their elected representatives would participate in the drafting of the reform at every stage except the last, formal one, at which the Council of State could be expected to approve the Main Committee's draft. Then, too, the announced membership of the four-man subcommittee that would review the drafts promised a friendly reception for the deputies; Lanskoi would be overbalanced by three supposed opponents of reform, Count V. N. Panin, M. N. Murav'ev, and Rostovtsev.[14]

It would be Rostovtsev's unexpected apostasy that would signal, if not precipitate, the reversal that would sweep away most of the assurances and concessions given to the nobility and its committees. Some of the policies and institutions that the Main Committee had established would be effectively annulled, others perverted out of recognition, and others simply forgotten. One of the first to slip out of sight would be the four-man subcommittee, which seemed so auspicious for the still-apprehensive pomeshchiki. For the moment, however, the government seemed to have adopted the point of view of the pomeshchik of Pskov Province who had written, "What is most important is that we ourselves should be allowed by the government to arrange this business along the lines we think necessary." The tsar's marginal comment on this dictum was, "How else!"[15]

Censorship and the Press

The first years of Alexander II's reign, "a tumultuous and chaotic period in the history of the Russian censorship,"[16] have given rise to diverse interpretations. One historian finds that in 1858 the government deliberately relaxed the censorship in the interests of the peasant reform, but, for another historian of the censorship, 1858 was a year of reaction.[17] More broadly, prerevolutionary historians tend to emphasize the direct and positive contributions made by public opinion, and the press in particular, to the emancipation legislation.[18] Many of these historians may have hoped to induce the regime to give a freer reign to the journalists of a later era by associating the press with a great achievement of the past; at any rate, Soviet historians have not laid much emphasis on the role of the press, although some of them do attach special importance to the work of radical journalists.[19] The most authoritative opinion on this matter is that of the writers and editors involved; they complained bitterly in private and obliquely in public that restrictive censorship made it impossible for them to make a significant contribution to the government's deliberations.[20] Certainly there was a relaxation of the censorship in comparison with the last years of Nicholas's reign. This striking contrast may obscure the continuity of censorship policy and divert attention from the restrictions that were imposed on the press with regard to the peasant reform. Under Alexander II, editors found it easier than before to get permission to establish new journals, but they also found, in some cases, that the day-to-day operations of the censors made it impracticable to publish these journals. The tsar himself contributed to the eccentricity of the censorship. He took a keen interest in censorship and undertook to resolve difficult cases personally.[21] While he was eager for constructive help from the press, he was fiercely intolerant of criticism, as in his instruction to Nikitenko to use your influence on literature so that it acts in accord with the government for the common good, and not in a contrary spirit. . . . There are aspirations which do not accord with the government's views. They must be stopped. But I do not want any restrictive measures. I very much wish that important questions be reviewed and discussed in a scholarly manner; our scholarship is still weak.[22]

It was hard for a censor to "stop" the wrong sort of articles and books without imposing "restrictive measures," and censors found their work very difficult; it was with a view to easing their own lot that many of them favored a general reform of the censorship. And on no question was their work more difficult in 1858 than on the subject of the peasant reform, because the "government's views," which they were to uphold, were still in flux. Furthermore, many censors were swayed by the assumption that the emancipation of the serfs promised the delivery of the press from bondage to the censorship. When, at the end of 1858, the government's vacillation on the terms of emancipation gave way to a new and clear formulation of policy, the censorship became very rigorous indeed, even for supporters of the new policy. The censorship was somewhat relaxed as a result of the rescripts to Nazimov and Ignat'ev, but the relaxation was not a matter of policy but the product of uncertainty within the regime.

On this matter, as on others, uncertainty was acted out as conflict within the Main Committee. At the committee's meeting on January 3, 1858, Lanskoi argued that the public should be enlightened by periodical articles about the ongoing reform, which embodied such unfamiliar ideas; he offered a model article, subtitled "Thoughts of a Dispassionate Pomeshchik." A majority of the committee found that the article was inadmissible, because its defense of the government program might encourage counterarguments. After all, the tsar had renewed the ban on discussions of government policies on serfdom as recently as last November. The government's views should be made known, but this could best be achieved through a circular urging provincial officials to stop false rumors; the circular might even be made public. Nothing, however, that seemed to challenge the rescripts or set one class against another could be published; only scholarly or historical articles would be acceptable.

Lanskoi and the committee were operating in the familiar Nicholaevan framework. The dread of false rumors aroused by official silence was traditional; so was the view that reasoned defense of policy might admit a counterattack. But Lanskoi's idea of public discussion was an article by a treasury hack, as in the era of

Nicholas I; the "dispassionate pomeshchik" was his deputy, Levshin. Alexander's action on the committee's recommendation was characteristic of his statecraft; he endorsed the commitee's recommendations, but added, in flat contradiction to these recommendations, "for greater clarity, the rules guiding the censor should be supplemented: articles written in a pro-Government spirit are to be passed for publication in all magazines."[23] Thus the question was left up in the air, but the censors, often literary men themselves, gave more weight to Alexander's supplement than to the committee's formula. They believed that times had changed.

Times had not changed that much, however. In the February and April numbers of *The Contemporary*, Chernyshevskii published a two-part article on the peasant question. Cautiously, he took as his point of departure the writings of two officials, Tengoborskii and Kavelin. The censors passed both installments, though passages on the injustice and baneful effects of serfdom were removed. However, certain extracts from Kavelin's memorandum calling for the redemption of both serfs and plowland were apparently critical of the rescripts. This was not Kavelin's intention; he had written the memorandum long before the rescripts were issued. The second installment nonetheless provided the committee with a pretext for reviving and reinforcing its earlier recommendations. It issued, over the signature of the Minister of Education, two circulars to the censors. The first called attention to the inadmissibility of Kavelin's suggestion that serfs redeem their present allotments. The second complained in general of periodical articles that could arouse the serfs against the pomeshchiki and their property rights, and continued,

It has come to the attention of H.I.M., that while the censorship permits the publication of articles written with the advantage of the present estate in mind, it bans all articles written in behalf of the pomeshchiki.

The circular called for rigorous enforcement of the rules laid down (by the Secret Committee) in January, for

It is His Majesty's pleasure . . . that the censorship allow the publication only of purely scholarly, theoretical and statistical articles, where nothing is discussed except matters of agriculture and estate management, articles consistent with the spirit and tendency of the aforementioned [April] Program, without indulging in any judgments on the subject of the eventual arrangements for the peasants in the final period of the reform now undertaken by the government.[24]

Alexander's "pleasure" derived from his resentment at the apparent treachery of Kavelin, a member of his household. He was also inspired by the warnings of one Zubrzycki, whose letter to the Minister of Education he had recently read. Zubrzycki, an Austrian alarmed by the events of 1848 in Galicia, warned of peasant rebellion; benevolent monarchs, like Alexander and Louis XVI, are the preferred victims of the masses. He suggested that the nobles of St. Petersburg and Nizhnii had assented to the reform under the influence of English gold. He argued in particular that the best remedy against revolution was a ban on articles unfavorable to the nobility, including its incidental vices, such as bribetaking. Alexander took this part of the letter to heart, judging by his underlinings.[25]

However, the circulars were also another of the Main Committee's gestures to the nobility. It was not Zubritskii who had alerted the tsar to the distressing ban on articles favoring the nobility; the second circular was a voice from the manor house. D. N. Shidlovskii wrote to Lanskoi from Simbirsk to insist that any public speculation about the emancipation legislation was an inadmissible encroachment on the prerogatives of the provincial committees; citizens with useful suggestions should simply forward them to the appropriate committee, since articles like Chernyshevskii's formented hatred and disrespect for the nobility. And the marshal of the nobility in Usman' complained that articles about the reform in newspapers and magazines had instilled a new spirit of insolence and disobedience among the serfs of his district. According to Iakushkin, "noble gentry, never before having set pen to paper, began to draft proposals" and were astonished when Chernyshevskii's *Contemporary* did not publish them. "If some inveterate scribbler who doesn't even have any pants writes a proposal, they print it. But when our lad writes one, these gentlemen-with-no-pants don't give it a chance."[26]

The Main Committee's effort to restrain the literary sansculottes did not mollify the squires. When Levshin toured the provinces in the summer of 1858, he had to remind them that the government could not compel a journal to print an article contrary to its editorial policy. To this the nobility's rejoinder was, "In a state where there is censorship, it should guide journalism, and if this is impossible, then let the government give the nobles an organ for defense against the onslaughts of the democrats."[27] On this matter, then, as on others, the regime's concessions fell far short of the nobility's desires but, while nobles were quick to complain, their mood was scarcely belligerent.

Reaction

For many Russian officials, the early part of 1858 was a season for second thoughts. The commitment to the abolition of serfdom, which the public had greeted with a mixture of elation and misgivings, precipitated a spirit of reaction within the government; caution and convention reclaimed their own. Nikolai Miliutin, who would be one of the principal architects of the emancipation legislation, described the new mood in a letter to his brother.

Sad to say, a reaction has recently begun to manifest itself and will not, of course, end with a mere beginning. The root of discord is the question of land. Reactionaries of all sorts and conditions have concentrated all their militant efforts upon it. At first, the Sovereign firmly demanded the household plots and suggested that the rest of the land be yielded. Now there is already a marked vacillation. Besides, the idea of providing the pomeshchiki with some kind of *droits seigneuriaux* (which they can't even translate into Russian) has been set in motion. It will be an odd result if the so-called emancipation creates here just what it abolished everywhere else. . . . Which is more surprising, the stupidity or the bad faith? Antipathy to the cause is being openly expressed in the higher ranks of the government—by some, out of self-interest, by others, because it is popular. Most distressing of all, cardsharps [*rober-makhery*] have taken command—[M. N.] Murav'ev, Rostovtsev and even (like the nymph Egeria) Pozen, who appears here on the horizon, twinkles, and always leaves a dark trail behind him.[28]

Prince Cherkasskii visited the capital at this time, called upon high officials, and came to the same conclusion as Miliutin. Nikitenko discerned a reaction, embracing the whole government, but laid the blame on a different set of officials, also members of the Main Committee—Orlov, Dolgorukov, and Panin. Even Levshin and Lebedev, who had been distressed by the original commitment to reform, were now distressed by the apparent retreat from it. Herzen's *The Bell*, perhaps embarrassed by its burst of enthusiasm for the rescripts, declared on July 1 that it was breaking with the government; in the next few issues, correspondents expressed their disillusionment and charted the retreat from reform. The wave of reaction was not quite so apparent to those who were supposed to be riding it—Murav'ev and Pozen, for example. They were optimistic, however, and their optimism was enough to dishearten their opponents.[29]

The onset of reaction was, to some extent, a matter of semblance. The public was not aware of the regime's efforts to win the nobility's assent to reform or of the immediate limitations it was imposing on the pomeshchik's authority. Yet there is evidence of misgivings within the government after the initial commitment to reform. In January, the Main Committee decided that the government should encourage the manumission of serfs since, in those provinces where the nobility had not yet solicited rescripts, "it is still impossible to determine how long the proprietary peasants will remain in their present servile status."[30] In April, the Main Committee assembled at the tsar's order to mull over a pamphlet by Nikolai Bezobrazov and, somewhat later, to consider an anonymous attack on the very idea of emancipation. Neither session was intended to produce an official rejoinder, but the very fact that senior members of the government felt obliged to review these partisan squibs indicates that the spirit of reform was still weak.[31]

In the summer of 1858, M. N. Murav'ev and V. P. Butkov, the Minister of State Properties and the Chief of the State Chancellory, toured the provinces. These two members of the Main Committee are alleged to have told nobles that the government would shortly proclaim a merely nominal reform without consulting the provincial committees. Murav'ev is said to have been reproved by the tsar for his careless talk.[32] The only hard evidence for these allegations is a curious circular issued by Lanskoi attacking a rumor that "the future disposition of the peasant estate has already been finally determined by the Government and that the resolutions of the Provincial Committee are therefore . . . an unnecessary labor."[33] There is no doubt that Levshin's summer tour of the provinces as Deputy Minister of Internal Affairs did encourage the pretensions of the nobility, but, as he subsequently explained, he could not lay down any clear line because the government's policy was so vague and wavering.[34]

Finally, Lanskoi's defeat within the Main Committee on the April Program and on other issues demonstrated the continued authority of the old sanovniki and could be interpreted as rebuffs to the reform impulse. Yet the rescripts and directives were ambiguous; only those who read their own hopes and assumptions into these documents could accuse the Main Committee of violating their spirit. The tsar had endorsed reform and participation by the nobility. Lanskoi emphasized the first element, most sanovniki emphasized the second. Where the original rescript was unequivocal, all members of the Main Committee worked in harmony; where it offered latitude, they interpreted the tsar's wishes in the light of their own well-known views. If the tsar was dissatisfied with their interpretations, even when there was conflict among them, he did not so indicate.

The intensity of the conflict among the tsar's ministers should not be exaggereated, as it is in the memoirs of Lanskoi's subordinates. Lanskoi almost did resign in the middle of 1858, not because he was continually overruled by the Main Committee, but because of a personal rebuke from the tsar.[35] So long as the tsar did not fill in the outline program of 1857, Pozen and Dolgorukov, Lanskoi and the diverse Murav'evs, could all represent themselves, without hypocrisy, as his zealous servants. So long as the tsar did not intervene, government action was compounded from the views and habits of these servants. Most of them were inclined to secrecy and authority, restraint on the press and latitude for the nobility. There was little more to the retreat of 1858.[36]

Because the autocrat's role was decisive, both those who were pleased and those who were dismayed by the apparent trend of affairs adhered to some kind of conspiracy theory. Ardent reformers fixed the blame on the "camarilla" of sanovniki, usually naming various members of the Main Committee as false counselors-in-chief. Nobles saw the sanovniki as their champions, frustrated only by the machinations of the coterie around Konstantin Nikolaevich and Lanskoi. Few if any ventured a direct criticism of the tsar's brother or his most amiable minister; they were being manipulated by radical subordinates. And all factions were convinced that the tsar was ultimately in accord with them. Dmitrii Shidlovskii, who was soon to feel the tsar's wrath for his immoderate claims for the nobility, set forth a commonplace view of the structure of Russian politics:

As regards the support of the nobility as a viable estate, there is no doubt that if the Sovereign Emperor himself could discuss every question and opinion personally, our future would be absolutely assured, but unfortunately His August Mind of necessity hears out and in part believes the suggestions of His intimates, and who will guarantee us a clear and dispassionate view of things and a lack of any selfish consideration in their activities?[37]

Menshikov would subscribe to Shidlovskii's analysis, but so would Cheraksskii, Miliutin, and even Herzen, though they would substitute "the peasantry" for "the nobility." Miliutin's presentation of the situation, written for the benefit of Kiselev in Paris, is the mirror image of Shidlovskii's:

Into whose hands has everything passed? Fine stupidity and confusion! It's distressing to recall how this difficult and important business is being brought to pass. The nobility, though selfish, unprepared, and backward, has been left to its own devices. I cannot imagine what will emerge from all this, without guidance and supervision, given the gross opposition of the senior sanovniki and the intrigues and bad faith of the responsible officials. One can only wonder at the rare firmness of the sovereign, who *alone* restrains the present reaction and resists the force of inertia.[38]

For each of them, as for less sophisticated Russians, a proposal of policy embodied the assumption that the tsar was essentially in favor of that policy—or would be, if one could get through to him. Without this assumption, the alternatives were resignation or revolution; in the late 1850s, with the structure of society at stake, resignation seemed folly, and no one was yet ready for conscious revolutionary activity. For those who were discouraged by the government's actions, the remedy was always "to get through to the tsar with the whole truth"—a recurrent theme of Russian political thought. This basic assumption did not preclude intrigue and dissimulation on behalf of one's policy, since in practice the tsar's favor—or attention—had to be won in combat with ordinary mortals. Similarly, a pious theologian can serve the deity through sophistry. Indeed, the tsar was almost as remote as the deity and, unfortunately, more easily misled. Kavelin, urging Alexander's merits on Herzen early in 1858, conceded that he was "badly prepared for the duties of ruling and unfortunate in his choice of men." When he fell abruptly from the tsar's favor, Kavelin did not blame his own and Russia's misfortunes on Alexander, but on the intrigues of Rostovtsev. Still later, he discovered that Rostovtsev had intervened on his behalf; Kavelin then redirected the blame but clung to the conspiracy theory, for within the given structure of politics, if the tsar was consciously and firmly opposed to a policy, that policy was an idle exercise.[39]

Alexander's conduct gave encouragement to conspiracy theories and diverse assumptions about his real disposition, for he liked to be all things to all men. Menshikov reported a conversation with the tsar about the compulsory redemption of household plots in these terms:

I proposed to him the means to which the St. Petersburg [provincial] committee is inclined. He replied that this idea [dropping compulsory redemption] was unknown to him, and while he did not express his opinion, it seemed to me nonetheless that he is not opposed to . . . the idea, as a means of getting out of the impasse.

Alexander left Menshikov with the impression that he approved of his proposal, but was temporarily constrained from expressing this approval openly. But a few months later, he conveyed a similar impression to Miliutin, who was regarded as Menshikov's polar opposite.[40]

Indeed, Alexander appears to have believed the conspiracy theory himself, and in both its forms. He attached real significance to the charges that Miliutin was a radical democrat and that bureaucrats in key positions were opposed to autocracy.[41] He wrote to Bariatinskii of the "so-called progressives" who would weaken the bond between tsar and people and who "take it as their task to discredit everything that relates to the government. In this matter, Messrs. Slavophiles have done much harm." Yet he also believed he was isolated by the camarilla, complaining to Rostovtsev that he heard nothing but reproaches for undertaking the reform of serfdom.[42] The complaint was a curious one; the tsar, as Alexander would be the first to insist, was freer than most men to choose his associates.

In the summer of 1858, Alexander toured the provinces. His speeches to the nobility were bland enough to offer some comfort to everyone. He emphasized his gratitude for past services and reiterated his hope that the nobility would justify his confidence in regard to the peasant reform. In contrast to the cautious wording of the recent Imperial Order, he assured the nobles that their deputies would play a major role when the provincial drafts were brought to St. Petersburg for review and confirmation. At Tver, he did not acknowledge the existence of any restrictions on the provincial committees except the rescripts and his own hopes. At Nizhnii Novgorod, however, he unexpectedly indicated that the April Program had the same binding force as the rescripts. He made a point of thanking the nobles at Nizhnii for their quick response to the rescripts, at the same time recalling the inglorious mission of Sheremetev and Potemkin. At Vilna, his emotional appeal to the nobility elicited no response, and only Nazimov's tact saved the situation.[43]

At Moscow, Governor-General Zakrevskii greeted him with a memorandum attacking the rescripts. Zakrevskii proposed to deny the peasants both the right to redeem their household plots and the right of perpetual tenure of their allotments, and urged a minimum transition period of twenty-four years. Alexander responded with a relatively forthright speech. He emphasized his devotion to the nobility, as he had elsewhere, but allowed a plaintive note to intrude.

I gave you the principles, and I shall not depart from them in any way. . . . I love the nobility, I consider it the first bastion of the throne. I seek the general welfare, but do not desire to attain it at your expense; I am always ready to stand up for you, but you, for your own advantage, should strive for the peasants' eventual benefit. Remember, all Russia looks to Moscow Province. I am always ready to do what I can for you; make it possible for me to defend you. Do you understand, gentlemen?[44]

He also reproached the Moscow nobles for delay in assenting to reform. He did praise the Moscow Provincial Committee, but criticized it for limiting "household plots" to the peasants' houses. Alexander insisted that the "household plot" subject to redemption included "all the land," a definition that left the Moscow nobility aghast until it was corrected in the published text to read "all the plotland." (An ordinary citizen who stated in a public speech that the peasants should receive "all the land" would have been exiled to Viatka.) Even the corrected definition was badly received by the Moscow nobility, according to a Third Section agent.[45]

Alexander's reassertion of his original commitment presumably allayed any misunderstandings that Murav'ev and Butkov may have aroused. He had clarified the government's program by rejecting a narrow interpretation of the rescript's provision for redemption, but this interpretation had been offered only because the language of the original rescript was woolly. Otherwise, the government program was as vague as ever, while the latitude that Alexander's speeches seemed to offer the provincial committees indicated that he did not have a more precise program.

Zakrevskii and the nobles of Moscow Province were not alone in laying themselves open to reproof. As Koz'ma Prutkov, Chief of the Assay Office, observed, "Malicious opposition has been imputed to many simply because they did not know what opinion would be pleasing to the higher authorities. The situation of these people is inexpressibly grievous." Like many other officials, Prutkov was perplexed by the seeming inconsistency and vagueness of the government's program. Prutkov wondered,

How is one to learn the opinion of the authorities? It will be said that it is apparent from the measures they undertake. True. . . . But no! That is not true! . . . The government frequently conceals its purposes because of lofty considerations of state, which most men cannot understand or appreciate. Frequently it atains a result through a series of indirect measures, which may seem contradictory, as if there was no connection between one and the other. But it only seems so! They are always linked together by the secret hinges of a single state concept, a single state plan, and that plan would boggle the mind with its grandeur and its consequences! The plan does come to light in the ineluctable results of history. But how is a subject to know the opinion of the government before the onset of history?[46]

For the basic issues of the emancipation, the onset of history came abruptly, in late 1858.

Redefinition

The government's revised policy was set forth in a pair of Imperial Orders, dated October 26 and December 4, 1858. The orders were ostensibly journals of the Main Committee, which were not ordinarily made public, reporting on sessions at which the tsar had presided. Presumably, this unique format was meant to emphasize that both the tsar and sanovniki stood behind the new program, for in effect—but only in effect—the two orders overturned everything that had been done so far on the peasant question. The rescripts to Nazimov and Ignat'ev remained in force and the Main Committee continued to function. But the agencies that would actually draft the legislation of February 19, 1861, take their origin from the first of these orders, while the second set forth the principles that would underlie that legislation.

The order of October 26[47] outlined "the system for reviewing, confirming and promulgating the statutes of the Provincial Committees." The new system had been set forth in a series of letters from General Rostovtsev to Alexander, and the imperial order consisted almost entirely of quotations from these letters. The order ceremoniously hailed the rising star of Rostovtsev, and this tribute to a man who was reviled by the partisans of reform may have reassured the apprehensive provincial nobility. The order also made explicit the subjugation of the Ministry of Internal Affairs to the Main Committee.[48]

The order itself seemed innocuous, for most of the innovations it contained were apparently matters of rhetoric or form. All proposals were now to be judged according to a three-point standard:

a) that the peasant feel at once that his way of life has been ameliorated; b) that the pomeshchik be reassured at once that his interests have been protected; 3) that strong authority not waver for a minute in any locality, and hence that public order not be disrupted for a minute.

The criteria concerning the pomeshchiki and the local authorities went without saying, but the government now appeared to be taking the euphemism "amelioration" literally. The provincial committees should "without fail explain in detail wherein the condition of the proprietary peasants will be ameliorated" by their drafts. To be sure, "the Sovereign Emperor is relying entirely on their honor as nobles as to the fidelity of their testimony" on this question.[49] In case their honor might falter, the Ministry of Internal Affairs was directed to subject each draft to preliminary review to determine "whether it departs in any way from the principles and directions confirmed by the Emperor," and "whether it actually does ameliorate the way of life of the proprietary peasants, and precisely how." It remained to be seen whether the government and the committees had the same concept of "amelioration."

The order also empowered the Main Committee and its subcommittee to summon, along with the deputies elected by the provincial committees, "experts" whose "knowledge of agriculture and peasant life might be beneficial." While the draft statutes would be reviewed one by one, the reform would be proclaimed as "one general Statute for all Russia, with the supplements, changes and special statutes necessary for various localities." This was a complete reversal; previously, each provincial committee had been empowered to draw up a separate statute for its province, subject to review in St. Petersburg.[50]

The significance of these changes was not made clear in the order, and it is not certain how great a change the government intended in October. However, the provisions of this order, when put into effect, would drastically reduce the provincial nobility's capacity to influence the reform. The order did not transmit Rostovtsev's observation, in one of the letters to the tsar, that the proposed experts should "not [be] obliged to defend the one-sided interests of the pomeshchiki of their province."[51] In fact, these experts, particularly the most influential, would function as antideputies. Selected for their commitment to landed emancipation, they would bring their "knowledge of agriculture and peasant life" to bear to expose the defects of the provincial drafts and then, their authority enhanced by bureaucratic support, confront the deputies with an alternative reform. The provision for a single statute would mean that a proposal from any committee (or a minority of a committee, even a minority consisting of one member appointed by the government) could be taken up and applied to the other forty-six provinces and Siberia. This procedure, which the order termed "using the best ideas of each province for the benefit of all," had been used in considering the petitions on the formation of provincial committees; Lanskoi had applied the good ideas of some provinces—the absence of any explicit condition or reservation—to benefit other provinces that had not attained such good ideas.[52] This simple device, now elevated to a procedural principle, was consistent with Russian legislative practice; the tsar could adopt and enact the opinion of a minority of the Council of State, or indeed enact a law over the unanimous dissent of the constituted authorities. And the provincial committees were fledgling institutions of uncertain status. The fact remains that the procedure established by the order of October 26 would reduce the provincial committees' draft statutes to the level of petitions, tributary to the course of legislation.

The order of October 26 dealt with legislative procedure and contained no rulings on questions of substance. However, in a curious epilogue, the Main Committee announced that the tsar had also directed it to consider Rostovtsev's proposals on five major aspects of the reform. Discussion was presumably postponed in deference to the majority's radical disagreement with Rostovtsev's recommendations, although they had the tsar's blanket endorsement.

Between the two rounds of the debate, Rostovtsev did make an effort to appease the majority. First of all, he secured from the tsar the further postponement of "secondary questions," which he thought would resolve themselves once the government's general policy was set on a new footing. Rostovtsev also decided in advance not to discuss the machinery for implementing the reform, a question on which his own views were changing but already remote from previously established policy.[53] Then, too, the fourteen-point agenda that he drew up for the session of November 24 was milder than the memorandum, "Extracts from Ad.-Gen. Ia. A. Rostovtsev's Letters to the Sovereign," from which it was derived. It repeated the memorandum's key phrase on manorial authority—"The pomeshchik deals only with the commune and does not have any relationship with individual peasants"—and this phrase was duly reproduced in the Imperial Order of December 4; however, neither the agenda nor the order indicated, as Rostovtsev's memorandum had, that the pomeshchik's title "chief of the village community" would be only a license to do good works in the villages.[54]

Rostovtsev and the tsar deferred to the opinions of the majority, but the majority was not appeased; only Lanskoi and one other member supported Rostovtsev. The others concentrated their fire on the proposals to grant substantial rights to the peasants and the commune and to diminish the pomeshchik's authority correspondingly, but almost every item of the agenda came under attack. Rostovtsev summarized the majority's arguments against his proposals:

Don't give the peasants the rights of free rural inhabitants; keep them under the ferule of the pomeshchik; turn authority [rasprava] within the commune over to bureaucrats; take away the peasants' hope of redeeming land and furthermore compel the peasant to pay annual interest for the household plot, which he and his grandfathers lived on for free. If all these opinions were accepted and brought together in one statute, what . . . would be left of the amelioration of the peasants' way of life, to say nothing of their emancipation?[55]

The majority was able to salvage almost nothing. Of the twelve numbered points in the Imperial Order of December 4, four reproduced the proposals in Rostovtsev's agenda exactly or with insignificant verbal change. Other points, in which his utter inexperience in civil affairs was particularly obvious, were restated in appropriate bureaucratic language. For example, his proposal that the monarch's generosity should be extended to petty proprietors and household serfs was split into two, eliminating the implicit aanalogy between nobles and serfs. Rostovtsev's new conception of the long-range goal of reform, "that the peasants gradually become owners of land," was directly incorporated into the order. This innocuous language expressed the essence of Rostovtsev's system and his most significant advance. The original rescripts and directives would leave the emancipated peasants economically dependent on their pomeshchiki. Rostovtsev insisted that only a landowning peasantry, free of economic dependence, would be truly emancipated. Redemption of allotments (as well as household plots) was his means to this end. However, the order dropped his suggestion that the government's credit apparatus be mobilized to encourage redemption, while his basic proposal on redemption was rephrased in the form of a question:

It is the Sovereign Emperor's Imperial pleasure to order . . . that the [Main Committee's Sub-] Committee reflect whether it is possible to define the termination of the status of temporary obligation thus: the status of temporary obligation terminates for the commune as a whole and for each peasant when they, as a whole society or as individuals, redeem from the pomeshchik that land which will, by virtue of the Imperial rescripts, be set aside for their use.

The new trend of policy was clear, and Rostovtsev, at least, attached little importance to its tentative formulation; six weeks later he declared flatly that the order provided that temporary obligation would terminate with the redemption of allotment land.[56]

The order stated unequivocally that non-nobles would be allowed to purchase estates, in which case the redemption of allotment land would be compulsory, but otherwise, allotments could be redeemed only with the pomeshchik's consent. The majority did insert a promise to "promote the security of large-scale agriculture by all possible means, but without restricting the personal freedom of the peasants." Nonetheless, the order overturned the axiom of Russian statecraft that the nobility's land must be kept in noble hands.

With this axiom fell another: that the peasantry must be kept under control of the nobility. The order held that the peasants would acquire the civil rights of free men upon publication of the reform statute. The pomeshchik was to be stripped of his powers over the individual peasant, which would pass to the commune.[57] The commune would administer the peasant and adjudicate his disputes, while communal officials would judge and punish him and make him meet his obligations to the pomeshchik and the state.

The order did not renounce the Main Committee's policy of giving latitude to the provincial committees. Indeed, it provided that any proposal offered by a provincial committee would be considered on its merits, even though it did not accord with the newly adopted principles. The majority of the committee saved face, but not the policies it had been advocating. It had been flatly opposed to the redemption of allotment land even after the tsar had indicated his enthusiasm for Rostovtsev's plan. At the insistent demand of the Tver nobility, the Main Committee had recently authorized provincial committees to offer redemption schemes as supplements to their draft statutes, which must otherwise conform to the April Program. But when the tsar had asked it to consider a general redemption plan drawn up by Count Bobrinskii, Orlov reported that the committee rejected Bobrinskii's plan as incompatible with the tsar's stated principles. The committee would not even invite Bobrinskii, who was the tsar's adjutant, to testify, for the invitation might become known; the provincial committees would then start to doubt "both the firmness of the basic principles prescribed for [their] work and the confidence with which Your Majesty has favored the nobility."[58]

A month after Orlov reported on this decision, he and all the other members signed the order of December 4. As in 1857, the sanovniki expressed their reservations and objections and then acceded to the tsar's express wishes. None of them was willing to challenge the sovereign's prerogatives, including the prerogative of changing his imperial mind. They had encouraged a reaction against reform in 1858—at least, they had encouraged the belief that there was a reaction. Now the supposed reaction, which had been the product of the ambiguity of the reform program, was dispersed by a commitment to a far-reaching reform. The pomeshchiki in the provinces might have learned a lesson from this second capitulation by their patrons and champions.

In fact, the public took little notice of the government's revision of its policy. The two imperial orders received little publicity. By virtue of the pretext that they were for guidance in reviewing the provincial drafts, they were not thrust upon the provincial committees as the original rescript and directive and the April Program had been.[59] Besides, the sanovniki were still in charge of government policy on peasant reform. They were effectively relieved of this responsibility two months later, when the Editorial Commission was set up.

The pretext for the formation of the Editorial Commission was the impracticality of the four-man subcommittee that was supposed to review the work of the provincial committees. Three of the four members were ministers, and it was impossible for them to go through the mountain of complicated documents turned out by the provincial committees. Accordingly, on February 17, the tsar ordered the formation of an Editorial Commission, composed of "experts" from the provincial nobility and bureaucrats designated by the appropriate ministries. The new commission, which was to review the proceedings of the provincial committees and draft the emancipation statute and other legislation, was ostensibly subordinate to the Main Committee, but in effect replaced it. Hereafter, no question of policy (except certain problems of local administration) would be put before the Main Committee until the new commission had completed its work.[60]

The Editorial Commission was set up according to a proposal by General Rostovtsev, and was further proof, if proof were needed, of his paramount influence. The Ministry of Internal Affairs had offered a plan identical to Rostovtsev's, with one interesting difference: the proposed commission would be subordinate to the ministry. Lanskoi hoped to recover some of the ground he had lost to the Main Committee by interposing his own forces between the pomeshchiki in the provinces and the sanovniki in the committee. The Main Committee did not favor his plan with a reply. Some three months later, however, once Rostovtsev had presented his plan to the tsar, the Main Committee hastened to approve a third plan, drawn up by Lanskoi's subordinate Miliutin. In its Journal of February 4, 1858, the committee proposed a commission under the joint chairmanship of its executive secretary and the chief of Lanskoi's Civil Division. By seeking to establish this condominium of the committee and the ministry, the two agencies closed ranks against the usurper-apostate Rostovtsev. The tsar tactfully endorsed the journal. This was a meager moral victory because the endorsement was conditional upon Rostovtsev's accepting the chairmanship, and the chairman would have authority to determine the membership, procedure, policy, and structure of the new commission. Rostovtsev hesitated, expressed his gratitude for the Sovereign's favor, testified to his prayerful humility, and accepted.[61]

Rostovtsev

Rostovtsev provided the government with a radically new policy on the peasant question and with the machinery to translate that policy into law. He is more responsible than any other man for the Emancipation Statutes of February 19, 1861, issued a year after his death. In the pantheon of Russian liberalism which memoir-writers and prerevolutionary historians labored to build, he is consigned to an anteroom. He has been praised, but the praise has been apologetic, patronizing, and colored by astonishment. In 1884, Kavelin wrote to Dmitrii Miliutin, "Remember that Iashka Rostovtsev emancipated the peasants—Iashka, the thickheaded scoundrel, the shady political cardsharp! Why, that would be the most howling absurdity, if it weren't true!"[62]

Contemporary and retrospective misgivings about Rostovtsev have a common source. He was a career military man, with the appropriate authoritarian temperament and conventional loyalties. Starting without wealth or connections, he had made his career by denouncing the Decembrists and his reputation by stultifying a generation of cadets in the military schools. Herzen's systematic and unwittingly mendacious attacks on Rostovtsev in 1858 were not inspired by his views on emancipation.[63] Neither Herzen nor his informants bothered to inquire very closely into these views, which in fact were still in flux; the views of a betrayer of the Decembrists and a faithful servant of Nicholas I could be taken for granted. Herzen came to appreciate Rostovtsev's services to the cause of emancipation and mourned his death as the death of the cause. But historians have been less indulgent than Herzen. A six-volume set issued in 1911 to celebrate the jubilee of the emancipation contained only a cursory essay on Rostovtsev, largely devoted to a demonstration that his treachery in 1825 had been forthright and his motives honorable.[64]

In 1857, Rostovtsev, like the other sanovniki, conceived emancipation to be a danger to the security of the state and favored modest and tentative measures. By 1859, he would turn the serfs into a landowning peasantry, independent of the pomeshchik in fact as at law. This conversion has generated fantastic explanations, involving the ghosts of the martyred Decembrists, a pledge to his dying son, and his seduction by the Grand Duchess Elena Pavlovna.[65] These explanations are of interest only for the assumptions they embody: that it required a miracle for a Russian statesman to seek to balance the interests of the estates of the realm, that the quasi-serfdom advocated by most officials met the real interests of the nobility, and that the Emancipation Statutes of 1861 were acts of philanthropy, not statecraft. These explanations are more curious still because their exponents were convinced determinists or monarchists, or both. If the legislation of 1861 was the inevitable issue of social and economic conditions, or if the tsar-liberator simply wrested it from his reluctant but submissive servants, Rostovtsev's conversion should be no surprise. It is rather the failure of the other sanovniki to convert that is surprising. In 1857, the members of the Secret Committee pledged to ponder the question of serfdom and study proposals for reform. Rostovtsev alone took the pledge seriously, studied in earnest, went abroad to consider the issues in peace, and arrived at the ideas set forth in his letters to the tsar.

The ideas were not original. He was a novice on peasant affairs, who could tell a hawk from a handsaw, but not, in all likelihood, a *plug* from a *sokha*. Rostovtsev's lack of originality is partly responsible for the patronizing tone in which his contribution is generally discussed. He worked with all the celebrated abolitionists and each of them modestly presents himself, or is presented, as Rostovtsev's preceptor.[66] None of these claims is implausible and none of them is of much importance. Rostovtsev's policies were common coin in a wide circle, whose perimeter ran through the Ministry of Internal Affairs, the Imperial Russian Geographic Society, the court of Elena Pavlovna, and the slavophile salons of Moscow. The leading figures of the circle were Nikolai Miliutin, Solov'ev, Kavelin, Koshelev, Cherkasskii, Iurii Samarin, Petr Semenov, and Zablotskii-Desiatovskii, some of them officials, others pomeshchiki, and all intellectuals who had thought hard about emancipation—since 1856, at least.[67] A historian does not like to minimize the contribution of reformist intellectuals, but no one of these worthy men was certainly and solely responsible for any particular idea in the emancipation legislation. No one of them was indispensable. There was no shortage of ideas about reform in the late 1850s, nor had there been in the century preceding. What was essential, and what Rostovtsev provided, was the will and the ability to overcome opposition and scruples and put these ideas into effect. Perhaps he was not so wise or so well informed as the least of his preceptors, but he had Alexander's confidence, and they did not. Armed with this confidence, he could manipulate, overbear, or ignore the exponents of the conventional wisdom, giving them the short shrift that they usually gave to reformers.

Alexander's confidence was not vested in Rostovtsev's program but in Rostovtsev himself. Ideas that had been dismissed as impractical or radical were adopted when Rostovtsev advocated them; Alexander accepted every major proposal he made in the last eighteen months of his life. The tsar's confidence, derived from his general affinity for military men and personal association with Rostovtsev, was great at his accession, grew as the debate on emancipation proceeded, and reached a maudlin climax as Rostovtsev lay dying. Feeble and in pain, Rostovtsev was pressed to draw up a testament setting forth his views on emancipation. The tsar lingered at the deathbed and cross-questioned Rostovtsev's associates in search of supplementary advice, as if Rostovtsev was the dying autocrat and Alexander his bereaved and unworthy successor.[68]

Their relationship was compounded of the tsar's shortcomings as an autocrat and his ability to recognize these shortcomings. He was malleable and credulous, and particularly credulous when disaster was predicted. Again and again in this period, when expressions of anxiety and alarm crossed his desk, he morosely noted "just" or "businesslike" in the margin.[69] He dreaded controversy and feared opposition, which moved him to indignation even in its insignificant and ridiculous forms. These qualities made the practice of autocracy difficult. Alexander could keep the machinery of government running smoothly, if not harmoniously, and was capable of effective action when a single decision would suffice. The issue of emancipation could not be reduced to routine or resolved with a pen stroke. It required conviction, considered judgment, and steady leadership; Alexander recognized this, and the burden he assumed in undertaking reform seemed like a labor of Hercules, if not an affliction of Job.

Every mind [he wrote in 1857] is extremely preoccupied with the emancipation of the peasants, which is natural enough, for it more or less touches the interests of all classes. But unfortunately, with our mania for babble and fabrication about things that have never been in question [i.e., emancipation], passions are excited, which produces a feverish anxiety; it would be good to see this anxiety subside. However, all that will not stop me from persevering, with God's help, in carrying a measure which I regard as a vital question to a satisfactory conclusion. I swear, I often need a good dose of patience to push forward with the heavy burden which has fallen my lot.[70]

The anxiety did not subside. In Nizhnii Novgorod, for example, it erupted into a scandalous controversy between an abolitionist governor and a recalcitrant provincial committee, which in turn was split into warring factions, one fearing for its obrok revenues, the other for its land. Alexander arrived in Nizhnii and delivered an august reproof to the combatants for indulging in "personalities."[71] Compared with his own heavy burden, land, revenues, and even gubernatorial authority were "babble and fabrication." Despite the tsar's impatience, the burden did not move forward and, indeed, inertia seemed to be carrying it backward. No one in his entourage was pushing in the same direction, and Alexander was not a man to break with the world of magnates and professional soldiers in which he had grown up. His speeches in the summer of 1858 testify to his discomfiture. Small wonder that, in 1858, Alexander began to attend the seances of a medium.[72]

When, late in the year, a trusted military man demonstrated the capacity to take on Alexander's burden and the determination to carry it forward, he became the tsar's plenipotentiary for emancipation. Alexander's relief is evident in his letters to his friend Bariatinskii. Throughout 1858, he wrote of his burden and his discouragement with the slow progress of the cause; he was dismayed that "private interests" found expression in the committees of the nobility. On April 1, 1859, just as Rostovtsev's Editorial Commission was beginning its work, Alexander reported that progress had been so rapid that emancipation of the serfs would be promulgated by the end of the year. He did not mention the issue of emancipation to Bariatinskii again until after Rostovtsev's death.[73]

Alexander showed both insight and modesty in delegating broad responsibility to Rostovtsev. The tsar realized that he was not suited for the role of reformer by temperament or training. He had been schooled to be jealous of his autocratic power, but also to show great personal consideration for his associates and subordinates. This habitual consideration facilitated the ordinary operations of government, but became an impediment when the interests and prejudices of his associates were challenged by the emerging reform. By putting Rostovtsev in the role he might have played himself, Alexander not only deflected the importunities of his associates, he transferred them from the sphere of policy to the sphere of personal loyalty. An attack on the government program was now an attack on the tsar's beloved counsellor and could be rebuffed on that ground.[74]

In embracing Rostovtsev, Alexander took on a program clear in tendency but still evolving in its details. By early 1859 this program was already remote from the rescripts and directives of 1857 and, especially in its semiofficial versions, more generous to the peasantry than the statutes of 1861.[75] Rostovtsev carefully distinguished administrative and juridical reforms from the land settlement. As regards peasant rights and peasant institutions, his program was unequivocal. The pomeshchik's power over his serfs was to be abolished immediately and completely; he would retain only the right to intercede on behalf of his ex-serfs at their request. Real power over individual peasants would pass to the commune and, in the event of dispute, to Arbiters of the Peace—local pomeshchiki elected by the peasants. Rostovtsev rejected a long period of "temporary obligation," as indicated in the government's original program, because it would perpetuate the servile relationship. Barshchina, which was inseparable from serfdom, must be replaced by obrok within three years.

Rostovtsev's proposed land settlement would freeze the existing situation until the ex-serfs began the redemption process. Peasant allotments could not be reduced until they were redeemed, and the allotment to be redeemed must meet a minimum standard close to the existing average. He sympathized with the provincial committees which opposed the redemption of household plots and tried to make it impossible in practice, but his answer to the "difficulties" they adduced was redemption on a broader scale, including allotments as well as household plots. He rejected proposals that the allotments be rented, purchased, or redeemed through "voluntary agreements" between nobles and their ex-serfs. Because of the inequality of the parties, these agreements would be a disguised form of landless emancipation; a pomeshchik could, Rostovtsev complained, drive his peasants out into the cold if they did not agree to unfavorable terms.[76]

Many of thes arguments and proposals could be found on the pages of The Bell, which Rostovtsev read with respect despite the personal attacks on himself.[77] Rostovtsev parted with The Bell in that he would not endorse compulsory, government-backed redemption of the allotment land; he rejected it reluctantly, because it would, according to treasury officials, overstrain the government's finances. Redemption would be by voluntary agreement, but the range of bargaining would be narrow, since the allotments could not be significantly reduced and the redemption payments could not exceed the peasants' dues under serfdom.

In forming his program, Rostovtsev had turned away from the conventional wisdom to the doctrines of avowed reformers. Most of them favored a redemption plan like Rostovtsev's, but this proposal did not have any definite political color; by early 1859, a considerable number of provincial nobles also favored redemption of the allotment land. The derivation of Rostovtsev's other ideas is more certain. For example, his firm commitment to the existing peasant allotments set him apart from the sanovniki and pomeshchiki alike, and linked him to Solov'ev and Kavelin. Nikolai Miliutin and Petr Semenov had, like Solov'ev and Kavelin, advocated a commission very similar to Rostovtsev's Editorial Commission in structure, function, and personnel.[78]

Rostovtsev's relationship to reformist officials is particularly clear with regard to the machinery for implementing the reform statute. In 1858, Rostovtsev and other members of the Main Committee had proposed that, before promulgation, military governors-general must be installed in each province and supplemented by new district chiefs with broad powers. Alexander clung to this idea despite the virulent objections from the Ministry of Internal Affairs and its provincial officials. However, Rostovtsev began to waver, acquiring growing confidence in the regular bureaucracy and the proposed arbitration system. In time, the objections of reformist bureaucrats, rejected at first, prevailed; Rostovtsev had changed his mind and carried Alexander with him.[79] Finally, any doubt about the character of Rostovtsev's counsellors was dispelled by his appointments to the Editorial Commission.

Rostovtsev remained an alien among the reformers, although even Miliutin soon agreed he was by no means an enemy alien.[80] He spoke the new language with difficulty, and his accent revealed his origins; thus parts of his agenda for the Main Committee were nearly unintelligible, while his three-point standard for the reform seemed to emphasize the maintenance of order far more than the substance of the reform. Sometimes, indeed, he lapsed entirely into his native dialect. After carefully circumscribing the pomeshchik's powers over his ex-serfs, Rostovtsev casually provided him with the right to expel "peasants he considers harmful and dangerous" from the village.[81] In outlining his program to a friend, the Decembrist E. P. Obolenskii, Rostovtsev remarked that "if all the pomeshchiki of our good land would immediately transfer their peasants to obrok," the main goal of the reform would be achieved. These lapses were of no significance; they expressed the naivete of a man who had spent his life in another sphere—the same naiveté that moved Rostovtsev to suggest that the reform statute include an article conceding that all the works of man are fallible and soliciting complaints from peasants who could not perceive any amelioration of their lot.[82]

It was not simply inexperience that distinguished Rostovtsev from the bureaucrats and intellectuals with whom he worked. He dealt with most men, including these allies, in the authoritative manner of a commandant of cadets, but he did not share his allies' certitude about the issues, for he was well aware of his own ignorance and inexperience. He observed to Obolenskii, "There is a great deal of fire in me, but little light."[83] While he adopted his reform program sincerely, he kept his mind open and continued to cast about for alternative solutions. According to his original ideal, the Editorial Commission should give serious consideration to all proposals, from whatever quarter. Hence Rostovtsev's attitude to the work of the provincial committees was quite different from the attitude of Lanskoi and Solov'ev, for example. Lanskoi instructed Solov'ev, in commenting on the provincial drafts for the Main Committee's subcommittee, to lavish praise on the drafts wherever possible in order to secure the ministry's position on a few essential points. This was the diplomacy of weakness. The ministry's private attitude is reflected in Solov'ev's complaint that the Main Committee, by giving broad latitude, "confused and impeded the work of the provincial committees, making a correct and successful development of the issues impossible."[84] And so it did, if the yardstick of correctness and success was the property of Solov'ev's ministry, and in the keeping of its Civil Division, which he headed.

Rostovtsev's approach to the first provincial drafts was neither patronizing nor apprehensive. He heaped scorn on the aristocratic pretensions of the St. Petersburg Committee and singled out its reluctance to part with serfdom, but praised the committee for offering a generous allotment and moderate dues. He welcomed the three draft statutes offered by the Simbirsk Committee, the first to come from a purely agricultural province. The Simbirsk majority draft displayed no aristocratic pretensions and "great practical knowledge . . . of local conditions and interests," but since most of the measures proposed "provide security for the noble estate *alone* . . . the greater part of the proposals of the Simbirsk Committee absolutely *cannot be confirmed*." Rostovtsev focused special attention on the alternative draft offered by a minority of five on the Simbirsk Committee, for this was the first real indication that the provincial nobility might favor his redemption plan. A second minority of the Simbirsk Committee also offered a redemption plan, but Rostovtsev ignored this splinter group; since it consisted of Lanskoi's son and Solov'ev's brother, it was presumably not representative of the nobility of Simbirsk.[85]

Rostovtsev, then, was willing to learn from the provincial

committees as from his reformist preceptors. Yet he would not accept any deviation from his basic principles, the necessity of making a clean break with serfdom and of giving the peasants a sure hold on their allotments. Conflict with spokesmen for the nobility on both of these points was on the way.

The Provincial Committees

5

In the course of 1858, during the developments described in Chapter 4, the nobles of forty-six provinces elected committees "on the arrangement of the peasants' way of life." All the committees had begun work by the end of the year. Each had its own history. To deal with them in a general and abstract way would be misleading and would, in particular, make it difficult to go beyond the conception of their history that the reformist bureaucrats put forward in 1858, which has proved enduring. On the other hand, it would scarcely be feasible to follow the evolution of more than a few. Accordingly, the main theme of this chapter is the committees' relationship to the central government. The first section follows the imposition of bureaucratic forms and discipline upon them, with special attention to the role of the members appointed by the government. Each of the next three sections deals with a committee in which a major controversy arose on a question of substance. The last, general section shows, in particular, that many of the shortcomings of the committee drafts were deliberately fostered by the central government. This treatment may put too much emphasis upon discord and too little on accommodation and inertia, but it should provide an understanding of the way the committees operated and the forces that impinged upon them.[1]

The provincial committees consisted of two elected members for each of the ten or more districts in the province, two members appointed by the governor, and the provincial marshal, who was chairman. There is no evidence that the government attempted to rig the elections, except possibly in the Northwest.[2] Since the regular franchise law was applied, only nobles with a hundred serfs were entitled to a full vote in the elections, and all committee members had to have won a rank in civil or military service. However, almost all the members had retired from service, although government agencies were told to grant leaves for participation in the committees.[3] There was, to be sure, a large contingent of district marshals, many of them newly elected to that post. Despite the nobility's supposed mania for rank, the overwhelming majority of the members stood in the middle range of the Table of Ranks—from colonel to first lieutenant in the army or the equivalent in the civil service. A few elected members had local reputations for advanced views; Pozen, who was elected to the Poltava Provincial Committee, seemed almost as radical to his pomeshchik neighbors as he seemed retrograde to the reformist bureaucrats.[4] The nobility did not, however, elect the celebrated abolitionists. Cherkasskii, Koshelev, Iurii Samarin, and a few other men of similar background and views, such as G. P. Galagan of Chernigov and Dmitrii Samarin of Riazan, served on the provincial committees by appointment. The nobility's chosen spokesmen, then, were middling resident squires, without national reputations or influential connections. From their lack of rank, fame, and great wealth, it is safe to infer that they were "practical men," experienced in manorial agriculture and in accord with the views of their noble electors.

The provincial committees were, Solov'ev observed, an "unprecedented phenomenon" for Russia: "For the first time, a question of state, indeed, a question of primary significance, was turned over to elective collegial assemblies for discussion."[5] Because there was no precedant for the committees, opinion on their significance and function was divided. Governor Artsimovich of Kaluga, at the opening of the Kaluga Committee, emphasized that nobles should be grateful to the tsar for allowing them to participate in drawing up the reform and that they must show themselves to be statesmen: "It is necessary to have the welfare of the whole state in mind and to bring it into accord with the interests of individuals and of the estates of the realm."[6] Artsimovich did not suggest how the interests of the state were to be balanced with the interests of the members' constituents. Tradition was no guide. The very concept of constituency did not have any currency in Russia, and the word that most members applied to their electors, "doveriteli," suggested that a member was almost a commercial agent for the nobles of his district. Many members interpreted their role in this sense; one of them, for example, held that the nobility "entrusted [doverilo] its feelings and its property to us. . . . One must take a stricter stand in behalf of one who entrusts property . . . than in behalf of one's own."[7] Others might even have described themselves as "a committee on the amelioration of the pomeshchik's way of life," as a dissident member styled the Simbirsk Provincial Committee.[8]

Some nobles had second thoughts in the source of their service on the committees. N. N. Obninskii, a member of the Kaluga Committee, surprised his colleagues by asserting that pomeshchiki should part from their serfs, as from a betrothed daughter, with "a good dowry." He confessed that he joined the committee determined to defend the nobility's material interests, but he had learned a lot during the sessions and had come to realize that he must uphold the nobility's honor, as well.[9] This attitude was pervasive in the Kaluga Committee, according to the leader of its majority (to which Obninskii adhered); the committee inspired by Christian love, had achieved feats of self-abnegation, to the point where he dreaded an accounting before his noble brethren and posterity. A member of the minority took this remark as a reproof of his faction and retorted that they had been "conscientiously solicitous of the nobility's interests." The minority draft was more generous to the peasants than the majority's, but it was inspired by the program that A. M. Unkovskii had worked out at Tver. Unkovskii and his followers characteristically insisted that, while their opponents hypocritically spoke of sacrifice, they themselves advanced the nobility's real interests.[10]

A candidate member of the Kherson Committee was eventually moved to renounce the nobility and its interests. K. A. Roshchakhovskii had been a district marshal and ardently defended the pomeshchiki in speeches and articles but then, in the privacy of his study, no less ardently repented. He scourged himself for neglecting his own peasants' welfare and for tolerating the unequivocal evil of serfdom. By 1861, he was reconciled to the losses that, he expected, emancipation would entail for many pomeshchiki. The "friend of man," he believed, should lament for the peasants, not their masters, who "have done everything they can to hold back the forward progress of the fatherland. They are barbarians on their estates, and at the critical moment for the state, they do evil without even realizing that it is evil."[11]

Other members of provincial committees, however, were inclined to repent of perfidy to the nobility. In the Tula Committee, where Prince Cherkasskii was trying to hold together a respectable minority in favor of a two-desiatina allotment, one of his followers unexpectedly repudiated him and his faction. A. A. Ushakov announced that he was joining the majority because it respected the sancitity of private property and did not exceed the warrant given to the committee by the nobility. Ushakov confessed he was baffled by the conduct of the minority, which "wants to dispose of the property of the pomeshchiki and otherwise act arbitrarily." He appreciated that Cherkasskii was a government appointee, "but for us, the members elected by the nobility, it would be a sin before God, the nobility and our consciences to follow [his] steps."[12]

Ushakov was equally remote from those who summoned the committees to statecraft and from those who saw them as instrumets of philanthropy or even penitence. Most nobles began with the belief that the committees had a serious legislative function, but some were skeptical even on this point. Petr Dolgorukov, a genealogist and professed aristocrat, rejected appointment to the Tula Provincial Committee on the ground that the government would confine the committees within intolerably narrow limits.[13] A. P. Elagina went further, pronouncing the committees a farce: "*Seemingly* the nobles have been entrusted with this matter, but actually they can only babble a little bit among themselves, and only provided that the babble does not offend the ears of the great." The nobles were incapable of offensive babble, according to yet another pomeshchik of Tula, because they were all bureaucrats themselves.[14]

Since the government had established the committees, the government's view of their role—whether Artsimovich's, Ushakov's, Obninskii's, or Mme. Elagina's—ought to have been decisive. However, the government was slow to express any view. The committees had originally been conceived to provide a way around an impasse within the government. As they began their work, it was difficult to formulate a consistent policy because the Main Committee and the Ministry of Internal Affairs disagreed, as the controversy over the April Program showed, about the character and function of the committees.

At first, the ministry acted as if the committees were simply another corporate agency of the nobility and subject to the usual rules.[15] However, the ministry did not maintain this pose of detachment in its correspondence with provincial officials, who were besieged with inquiries from Lanskoi about the peasants' behavior and the committees' progress.[16] Some governors supervised their committees very closely and appealed regularly to the capital, others did not. The ministry attempted to maintain some control by requiring the governors to file detailed reports every two weeks on the committees' work. This system proved ineffective. The reports were usually belated, and in one case, at least, the governor had the provincial marshal write them. As a rule, the ministry got a bare record of resolutions passed some time previously and probably amended or reversed in the interim.[17]

By the beginning of 1859, with all the committees under way and the government's own program reformulated, the Ministry of Internal Affairs and the Main Committee, settling on a congenial precedent, arrived at a common attitude to the provincial committees. They were declared to be subject to the usual regulations for "state and provincial agencies having a collegial composition," that is, they were bureaucratic. This definition provided the central government with the answer to almost every controversy on the practice and procedure of the committees. The dispute that provoked this definition was typical. Some committees were not allowing their members to enter dissenting opinions in the record. The Main Committee ruled that dissenting opinions must be accepted and passed along to the central government, so that the dissenter could not be held accountable for the majority's decision.[18] It was standard practice to allow members of bureaucratic committees to protect their career interests by filing dissenting opinions when they saw fit (although the members of the Main Committee almost never exercised this right).

It followed naturally that if there was an organized minority on a provincial committee, it should choose one of the committee's deputies. At first, the Ministry of Internal Affairs would simply allow an organized minority to select an additional deputy (it would have liked the provincial governor to designate one, as well).[19] The Main Committee, however, following a suggestion of Rostovtsev's, ruled that if a committee was divided, the majority and the minority should each send a single deputy.[20] This ruling was issued at a time when the provincial committees attached great importance to their right to explain and justify their drafts in St. Petersburg. It encouraged dissidents to band together and draw up a rival draft; by organizing a formal minority faction, they acquired the right to send one of their number as deputy. In several committees, the majority strongly resented having to surrender one of their deputies' places to the minority,[21] for the minority might be very small. The twenty-two-man majority of the Riazan Committee was entitled to send one deputy, while each of the two-man minorities, one of which consisted solely of the government members, was represented by a depty of its own. This system was perfectly fair by the standards of the bureaucracy; numbers mattered little in an "agency of collegial composition." Why should a mere numerical majority have more weight in a provincial committee than in the Council of State?

The rulings on dissenting opinions and the minority deputies did not represent a blind grasping at precedent. Rostovtsev decided, after reading the majority and minority drafts from Simbirsk and Nizhnii Novgorod, that if the minorities were not represented, the deputies would be unanimously hostile to the government program.[22] In general, it suited the government's purposes to apply bureaucratic rubrics to the committees because the minorities were comparatively sympathetic to the government's program. The rubrics were systematically applied. For example, the government instructed the committees to vote openly rather than with black and white balls, as was the custom at assemblies of the nobility. This order derived from the assumption that fewer members would dare to oppose the government program in an open vote.[23]

However, bureaucratic procedures were imposed even against the wishes of the program's advocates, especially in regard to the publicity of the committees' proceedings. In some provinces, local pomeshchiki attended the sessions and attempted to intimidate committee members; in others, pomeshchiki were educated in the merits of emancipation by listening to the debate. The Main Committee resolved the dilemma by barring all spectators, including spectators who had elected the committees.[24]

The committees were also forbidden to print and distribute their proceedings. This ruling overturned the oral permission the tsar had given to the Tver Committee. The resolutions of this committee were printed and widely circulated, until the Main Committee intervened, and they had real influence. The Tver redemption plan may have inspired other committees to favor the redemption of allotment land, which was now a goal of government policy. One device in particular, the so-called gradation system for fixing the peasants' dues, was imitated from Tver by the provincial committees of Tula, Kaluga, Iaroslav, and various others. The gradation system was eventually incorporated into the statutes of 1861.[25] On the other hand, provincial committees might use their printing facilities to circulate attacks on the government program, as one member of the St. Petersburg Committee did. The Main Committee did not try to balance advantages and disadvantages, but simply applied the bureaucratic principle that deliberations on legislative matters should not be made public; it clung to this view despite protests from committees and provincial governors.[26]

The government would keep the proceedings of the committees private or even secret in order to free the members from outside pressure. The right to serene deliberation was extended to the members as to any other part of the bureaucracy. However, when the Tver marshal appealed against the ban on printing, the Main

Committee showed that it valued the principle of secrecy more than its ostensible function. A. M. Unkovskii argued that unless he could publish the journal of the Tver Committee, he would be defenseless against charges that he, as chairman, had silenced dissident members and denied the binding force of the rescript. The Main Committee ruled that publication would only make for a further polemic, which would be "highly inappropriate and awkward for the important question at issue."[27]

Otherwise, the government was zealous in shielding members of the provincial committees from public pressure. The nobility was systematically prevented from calling the committees to account, reviewing their work at the provincial assemblies, or influencing their composition and procedure in any way. For example, the provincial marshal was ex officio chairman of the provincial committee, but he continued to preside even if the nobles voted him out of his *officum*. Similarly, the elected members had to be protected from the wrath of their constituents. In several instances, the terrible figure of a district marshal descended upon a provincial committee, bearing his district's protest against a vote by its representative. The offending marshals received formal reprimands from the Main Committee.[28]

Most members did nothing to arouse the wrath of their constituents and had nothing to gain from the immunities bestowed by St. Petersburg, particularly since bureaucratic discipline was imposed along with bureaucratic privilege. It took some time, however, to find a device for imposing discipline. At first, the supervision of the provincial committees was the task of the Ministry of Internal Affairs, through its subordinates, the provincial marshals and governors. Both of them, as it turned out, sat too far above the cockpit to keep matters in hand; it fell to the government members to carry on the day-to-day struggle against departure from the government's program.

Originally, the two government members (*chleny ot pravitel'stva*) were simply the governor's members, for St. Petersburg made no attempt to influence their selection. They did not necessarily defend the government line, although the diversity of their views reflected the government's uncertainty. While they tended to join the minority, if there was a formally constituted minority on the committee, they frequently opposed one another and the trend of government policy.[29] One of the government members of the Orel Committee began his work determined to emancipate the elected members from subservience to the bureaucracy—of which he himself, as an official of the Ministry of Internal Affairs, was a part.[30] The other government member, N. P. Danilov, who had not served in the bureaucracy, construed his role very differently. In the spring of 1858, Danilov composed a profession of humanitarian sentiments and sent it to Lanskoi, ending, "I shall *honorably* and *punctiliously* carry out whatever may be Your Excellency's pleasure." Honor did not, however, require a statement of his specific views, which were, as he spelled them out for Koshelev, far ahead of the administration's: he favored government redemption of all peasant allotments, with a view to merging the nobility and the peasantry. He was careful not to obtrude this long-range goal in his contributions to *The Landowners' Journal*.

Lanskoi enlisted Danilov to provide confidential reports on the Orel Committee, and very providentially; according to Danilov, the committee's journal was drawn up to conceal its real sense, especially the attempt by professed "moderates" to smuggle in a provision for full manorial authority. Danilov reported that he was unmasking these attempts in his dissenting opinions, not with any hope of influencing his colleagues but for the guidance of the government when the Oral draft was reviewed. He promised to continue his reports but, being a realist, he sent the next one to Rostovtsev, whose star was rising so spectacularly. (Nothing was gained, since Rostovtsev simply turned it over to Lanskoi.) In this report, Danilov described his unequal struggle with the majority and suggested that he ought to have the power to set aside resolutions he found unacceptable or contrary to the government program. Had he been vested with this power, he would have had to quash almost everything that the Orel Committee did, for in his review of the majority and minority drafts Danilov found that both "deviate in *equal measure* from the letter and the spirit of the Government's instructions." So indeed they did, from the perspective that was then emerging from Rostovtsev's Editorial Commission, but Danilov was one of the few provincial nobles deft enough to perceive and adopt this vantage point in early 1859. In his last confidential report, he suggested that appointment to the Editorial Commission would be a suitable recompense for his lone struggle and faithful reflection of the government's views. Rostovtsev did not accept this ingenuous suggestion; indeed, he appointed Apraksin, the Orel provincial marshal, whose obscurantist views Danilov had labored to expose.[31]

Because Danilov's maneuvers, although ineffective, were crudely careerist, his evolution is instructive. During 1858, he spoke out in the press in the nobility's behalf. Although he was an ardent westernizer, hostile to everything "asiatic" in Russian life, he was simply unable to understand Chernyshevskii's arguments about the baneful and pervasive effect of serfdom on the polity and

and society. He maintained that there were two elements in the reform of serfdom, "a purely economic transaction" and "a truly Christian *podvig*", or feat of charity. Prescriptive legislation could only pertain to the transaction, for

whoever is willing and able to "do good," let him do so on his own account, as is appropriate for a good Christian; that is marvellous! Actual examples of private benefaction are, indeed . . . inspiring and can stimulate emulation, but to *recommend* any kind of obligatory sacrifice to everyone else—that is quite another matter.[32]

A year later, he offered up a review of the proposals of the Orel Provincial Committee in which he attempted, with indifferent success, to unmask the committee's attempto to turn the reform into a profitable transaction for the nobility. He had become nobility's scornful critic and the champion of the peasantry. In this metamorphosis, Danilov was trying to make a career for himself by moving with the times. He failed, not because he read the mood of the times wrongly, but because he supposed the government was moving in the same direction and at the same pace. Still, when but 1859 would a Russian on the make have thought of taking on the role of champion of the peasantry?

Few government members were as obsequious as Danilov, and many found easy accord with their fellow pomeshchiki. Among the government members who began with a definite program were the neo-slavophiles, Cherkasskii of Tula, Koshelev of Riazan, and Iurii Samarin of Samara.[33] They proceeded from the assumption that the elected members, being lazy, confused, and ill-educated, would yield to the superior wisdom and energy of dedicated emancipators like themselves; they would use the government's program as mere scaffolding for a more generous and harmonious edifice. After the elections and the first sessions of their committees, all three became still more optimistic; they were surprised and pleased that the elected members did not oppose the abolition of serfdom as such, which was the first item for deliberation according to the April Program. Their despair was all the greater when the committees turned to the economic components of the reform, and it was dedicated emancipators who yielded. Cherkasskii and Koshelev found they had to drop their demand that the peasants retain their existing allotments, for the elected pomeshchiki turned out to be more resolute and capable than expected. Cherkasskii observed with surprise and chagrin that there were only two fools in the majority faction, and Koshelev complained of the cunning and determination of his opponents. The elected members did appreciate the intellect of the government members and sometimes exploited it. It turned out that Samarin was the only member of the Samara Committee with any skill as a legislative draftsman, and he traded his skill for some concessions from the majority. But Samara was a frontier town where the pomeshchiki were not as sophisticated as in Tula or Riazan; they were so unsophisticated that Samarin had an armed bodyguard when he walked the streets. Like Cherkasskii and Koshelev, he found the majority of his committee intensely hostile to himself and unwilling to give ground on the vital issues of dues and land.

All three had seen government service but they were not career bureaucrats and did not believe they were acting as bureaucrats in the provincial committees. Cherkasskii insisted, "It is better *not to enter the administration* . . . but not to withhold one's services as a private person." He indignantly denied that he was bound by any government instructions, but the elected members were not convinced. As Samarin put it,

For three months we have thrashed around trying to domesticate these people and somehow make them forget that we were brought into their circle by the government, to convince them that we are pomeshchiki like them and do not despise them or wish them harm.[34]

They did not, indeed, wish the nobility any harm, but they were not ordinary pomeshchiki and (as is clear from their correspondence) they did despise the elected members. It is scarcely surprising that they failed to "domesticate" their colleagues.

Overborne in the provincial committees, Cherkasskii, Samarin, and Koshelev became bureaucrats in spite of themselves. Their experience is complementary to the imposition of bureaucratic controls from above and helps to explain it. The bureaucratization of the provincial committees was, in part, a sign that the regime was beginning to recover its equilibrium so that old habits could reassert themselves. The procedures and attitudes we call "bureaucratic" are compounded of routine and the distinctive outlook that most officials share, and office holding had its effect on the neo-slavophiles. Subsequently, when Cherkasskii and Samarin sat on the Editorial Commission and he did not, Koshelev was chagrined that his friends' official position had altered their perspective. Yet Koshelev's experience on his provincial committee, like his friends' on theirs, showed that the resort to bureaucratic means was not simply a product of the inertia and arrogance characteristic of functionaries. All three were richly endowed with prestige, zeal, and talent. They discovered that these qualities were not enough to procure practical success; to prevail they had to be linked to power—that is, to bureaucratic authority and, ultimately, to the autocracy. Their zeal for emancipation carried these independent public men into the arms of the bureaucracy and within the perimeter of the government's program.

They entered the provincial committees with their own program of reform and a low opinion of the government's, which had not yet been reworked by Rostovtsev; Koshelev, in particular, was apprehensive that the regime would constrict the committees. All three found, however, that the government's minimum, binding demands would have to serve as a maximum program, for the only check on the committees' pretensions was fear of a veto when the statute came up for confirmation; Cherkasskii warned the majority that their overweening demands would only provoke the bureaucracy to impose its own harsh solution. The majority's hostility was so great that Cherkasskii found he had to invoke the procedures of "deliberative instances"[35] simply to get a hearing for his views.

In other respects, Cherkasskii and his allies echoed or anticipated the government in reaching for bureaucratic precedents. They expected bad results if both of a provincial committee's deputies to St. Petersburg were elected. Believing that the assembly of deputies would have major influence over the final statute, they decided that one deputy from each committee should be appointed by the governor. Somewhat later, all three despaired of acting on the provincial committees through persuasion; they would salvage what they could by compiling rival drafts of their own, in the hope of influencing the government. They argued among themselves only about the extent that concessions should be made to win the support of a few elected members. Here Samarin disagreed with Koshelev and Cherkasskii:

I attribute absolutely no importance to the majority. I am firmly convinced that it will be against us and that it will be necessary to submit two drafts—from the majority and from the minority, however numerically insignificant it may be. I see no harm in this. . . . Either the government will adhere to its position despite the majority, or it will yield to the majority, and then there will be no limit to the concessions. But the latter is not to be expected.

Samarin went on to say that he kept himself under iron restraint during the sessions, but at night he was afflicted with fever, sleeplessness, and nightmare visions of battles. He wondered if Koshelev was showing the same symptons. Koshelev noted, "No! I am much more peaceful. We are beginning to argue less. . . . Everyone—the majority and the minority—knows what to expect and from whom, and so we have dinners and parties and are rather serene."[36]

The serenity did not last. Koshelev was soon driven from the committee. Reinstated by St. Petersburg, he was able to win only one signature for his draft, that of Iurii Samarin's brother Dmitrii, whose appointment to the other government membership Koshelev had made a condition of his return. Iurii Samarin's draft, which he privately stated "went to the outer limit of the concessions which the nobility can make without subjecting itself to final ruin and the state to social bankruptcy,"[37] was signed by four other members. Cherkasskii was able to win over the same proportion—seven out of twenty-four elected members, plus a third Samarin brother who held the other government seat in Tula. And like Iurii Samarin and Koshelev, Cherkasskii was favored with official protection from the wrath of his fellow nobles and committee members.[38]

The central government, prompted first of all by Koshelev's troubles at Riazan, intervened on behalf of the appointed members in two ways. Government members were shielded from censure and abuse, to ensure their continued presence on the committees, and they were elevated above the elected members and given special status. A circular of December 9, 1858, ordered that one of them must sit on the Editorial Subcommission of each committee. These subcommissions had the task of compiling a draft statute out of the committee's resolutions; often they virtually wrote the statute themselves because of the gaps and contradictions in the resolutions. A second circular, issued three weeks later, clarified the government member's role in the full committee. They were said to "have absolutely the same rights and obligations as the other Members," recalling Samarin's plaint that "we are pomeshchiki like them." However, the circular of December 9 went on to endow the government members with new rights. "As representatives of the Government," the appointed members must participate in all the committee's work; any resolution passed in their absence was declared void.[39] This ruling embittered an elected member, who observed that the administration seemed to want to keep the committees in a "bureaucratic rut" and use the government members like common policemen, trusting "his words more than the transactions of the thirty-one [other members]."[40]

Administrative action assured the government members of at least minimum consideration from their colleagues, but this assurance carried an obligation to "develop the principles" the government had adopted and to file a dissenting opinion whenever their committee deviated from these principles; in the event of uncertainty, they were to seek the guidance of the provincial governor.[41] Cherkasskii insisted, even after this circular was issued, that he was not bound by any instructions from St. Petersburg, and his disclaimer was sincere. The circular required him to press the government program on the Tula Committee, but he had been doing this of his own accord.

What was the resort of necessity for Cherkasskii was, in the government's eyes, a means of imposing bureaucratic discipline on the provincial committees. This discipline grew tighter with the passage of time. It turned out that a member of a provincial committee could be dismissed like any other functionary, and in January and February of 1859 the Main Committeed removed ten men from four committees. One was removed for challenging Lanskoi's order on open voting. In the other three instances, it was the prestige of the marshal, the governor, and the government members that was at stake.

Two members were expelled from the Riazan Committee at the suggestion of the provincial governor. He warned that the Riazan marshal, weary of constant abuse from the floor, had asked permission to resign the chairmanship of the committee; the chair would pass into retrograde hands if he did. The governor reminded the Main Committee that Koshelev had already resigned because of the same kind of abuse; the tsar himself had reinstated him, expelled his chief antagonist (the other government member), and reprimanded the rest of the committee. The Main Committee obligingly removed those whom the governor identified as the culprits in this new scandal and urged the marshal to withdraw his resignation, which he did. A month later, the governor of Tambov complained that he was unable to report on the provincial committee's transactions during January because its journal consisted largely of attacks on himself and the marshal. Two brothers named Blank openly questioned the right of governor or minister to dictate the committee's procedure, while their ally Prince Engalychev had accused a government member of being a secret police agent. The Blanks and Engalychev were removed. In Vladimir, too, the government members were under attack; they threatened to resign because twelve members had signed a statement that they were not welcome in the committee. The governor had rejected their resignations because, he confessed, he could not think of anyone to replace them. He proposed that their four most virulent detractors be removed, and the Main Committee agreed.[42]

In each instance, the government moved to support its spokesmen by removing their most outspoken opponents. Yet this was not a matter of political opposition, but rather the same kind of uncertainty about the government's purposes that plagued Levshin and Kuz'ma Prutkov. For the members who were removed responded with chagrin and attempts to ingratiate their way back into official favor, like a bureaucrat seeking to clear a reprimand from his record. With the single exception of Tver, no committee and no committee member sustained opposition in the face of the government's clear disapproval.

Even G. B. Blank of Tambov capitulated at once. He was the author of a paean to serfdom, published shortly before the rescript to Nazimov, in which he attacked those who, "in order to please foreigners, out of a slavish enthusiasm for their ideas, from false philanthropy," found an affinity between serfdom and slavery. He praised the "patriarchal and familial bond which the wise tsar-legislators assiduously established between pomeshchiki and their serfs." Without the pomeshchik's benevolent authority, "idleness and dissipation will consume everything they [the peasants] have," and they would give way to "violence, . . . horse-stealing and, perhaps, outright banditry."[43] Once the reform process was under way, Blank became notorious as an extreme adherent of the pomeshchik's interest. According to the governor of Tambov, Blank maintained that, by virtue of the "respect" to which the Tambov Provincial Committee was entitled, he and his colleagues must be guided only by "their own profound convictions, without submitting to outside influences," such as the governor. When Blank was duly removed from the committee, he responded with a fawning letter to the Minister of Justice, beginning, "The greatest misfortune in life for a faithful subject is the wrath of the beloved Monarch. It has pleased God to visit me with this misfortune." He went on to deny that he had ever questioned the governor's authority and pointed to his many years of government service and his unanimous election to the provincial committee, where he had served "according to oath and conscience, strictly on the basis of the Imperial rescripts and speeches."[44] This seems a craven apology, but Blank was consistent. Traditionalist in his approval of serfdom, he was also traditionalist in his loyalty to the government and fealty to the tsar. The conflict between traditional attitudes was made plain to him only by his removal from the Tambov Committee.

The Tambov Committee petitioned for the reinstatement of Blank and his allies; the other committees also petitioned for the return of their ousted members. The Main Committee granted the request from Riazan, over Lanskoi's objections, and rejected the rest.[45] Yet the petition from twelve members of the Vladimir Committee was most worthy of attention, for it simply asked the government to hear out their side of the case. The Main Committee had lavished expulsions, warnings, and reprimands upon the Vladimir Committee, solely on the basis of the governor's account of the facts. According to D. P. Gavrilov, himself a minority member of the Vladimir Committee, the governor had simply relayed a government member's complaint in the form of a report, without making any inquiry of his own. "All we want," protested Gavrilov, "is that they [the Main Committee] ask for our explanation before the retribution which is presumably appointed for us."[46]

The Main Committee did not, however, ask for explanations before pronouncing sentence; to do so might undermine the prestige of the governor of Vladimir or his counterparts in Tula, Riazan, and Tambov.[47] In each instance, the Main Committee acted in response to an appeal from the governor and in support of his authority. The importance attached to the governor's authority can be seen from yet another minor scandal involving a government member, V. N. Karamzin of Kursk. Karamzin declared that the Kursk majority's demand for compensation for the peasant huts, though it adhered to the letter of the law, was cruel; when an elected member replied that Karamzin was eccentric, confused, and naive, Karamzin took offense and resigned. Governor Bibikov accepted his resignation and replaced him. The struggles in the Kursk Committee were unusual, according to Lanskoi, only because the minority was as bad as the majority; poor Karamzin was beginning to rise above the narrow views and inordinate demands of both factions, but was betrayed by the governor, who was an active partisan of the minority. Although it was too late to reinstate Karamzin, Lanskoi urged that the Main Committee express its disapproval to Bibikov. The Main Committee had no disapproval to express. The governor's actions had been "wholly correct"; he had "the right by law" to dismiss any subordinate. It was not Bibikov, but Karamzin himself, who had appealed to the central authorities, and the prestige and wounded feelings of a government member counted for less than the governor's authority.[48]

The Main Committee made its conception of the governor's authority over the provincial committees particularly clear in resolving a controversy in Vologda. The governor had pointed out to the Vologda Committee that the first chapter of its draft did not conform to the April Program, which held that chapter I of each draft should provide for "the termination of personal serfdom in fact and at law." The governor told the committee to review its

resolutions and produce a more convincing termination of serfdom;
he also ordered it to meet more frequently. The governor was
seconded by K. A. Levashev, one of his appointees, who accused the
committee of betraying the confidence of the Vologda nobility. The
committee replied that its resolutions conformed to the original
rescript and directive, which provided for a transition period and
did not require freedom of movement for the peasants; the
committee would not meet more often, for "on the days when it
does not sit, the Members reflect on the questions subject to its
decision." Finally, the governor was asked to restrain Levashev,
whose accusation would be brought before the next provincial
assembly, "so as to acquit the [other] Members of the Commitee of
this undeserved reproof."

Vologda was the northernmost province with a considerable serf
population; agriculture was haphazard and unrewarding, while
lumbering was a major source of income. The provincial
committee's equivocation about terminating serfdom presumably
derived from the fear that once the peasants could move freely
from place to place, the woodcutters would move off the
pomeshchiks' estates and other peasants would migrate to better-
favored provinces. Formally, the committee's position was strong;
the rescript did not make peasant mobility a necessary element of
the reform, nor did it empower the governors to determine the
length or frequency of committee sessions. However, the Main
Committee decided to construe the rescript and the April Program
so as to subjugate the committees to the program, as interpreted by
the governor. The Vologda Committee "is obliged to carry out the
proposals of the Chief of the Province relating to the hastening of
its work and the establishment of proper order in its proceedings,
or which require the Committee to modify resolutions
incompatible with Imperial instructions." The April Program was
now included among the binding instructions, for "it was compiled
and distributed by the Emperor's order 'for the guidance'
[rukovodstvo] of the Committees, therefore the Committees are
obliged to adhere to the . . . program."[49]

This ruling of January 26, 1859, closed the bureaucratic circle
around the provincial committees; it took a year for the official view
to evolve from the indeterminate to the conventional. The
committees had begun as deliberative bodies of uncertain
authority, bound only to apply the vague injunctions of the rescript
to their provinces; within a year it was established that they were
bureaucratic agencies, under the authority of the governor, and
working according to the direction of his agents to draw up
suggestions for the use of the central government. This was a

modest status, but it had the virtue of tradition and carried with it certain prerogatives, such as the protection of the censorship.

Despite the Main Committee's instructions in the first part of 1858, major issues of the peasant reform were debated in the press. General magazines published articles reflecting their usual editorial tendencies; the *Russian Herald* and *The Economic Indicator* were advocates of economic liberalism, while *The Contemporary* defended the commune and the redemption of undiminished allotments for the peasants. New journals appeared, specially devoted to the issues of the reform; *Rural Welfare*, a biweekly supplement to the slavophile *Russian Colloquy*, soon had a rival, aptly named *The Landowners' Journal*. Both of them modestly promised, in contrast to the regular magazines, to serve as sounding boards for diverse points of view within the nobility, but both found themselves reflecting a relatively limited range of noble opinion. Because of "the inability of our gentle pomeshchiki to write for the censorship,"[50] Koshelev, the editor of *Rural Welfare*, had to fall back on his regular stable of neo-slavophiles; their experience in the committees suggested that they were not representative of the nobility. A. D. Zheltukhin launched *The Landowners' Journal* in April 1858, by reassuring his readers, "It is not emancipation or the abolition of the serf status, as foreign writers and a few Russian litterateurs following their example have stated, that the Imperial will requires."[51] Despite this promising start. Zheltukhin found more and more of his correspondents coming out for the redemption of allotment land and the abolition of manorial power. Apprehensive provincial squires did not find much more comfort in *The Landowners' Journal*, after the first few issues, than in its liberal and slavophile competitors, for it was the more venturesome pomeshchiki who rushed into print. At the elections to the Tula Provincial Committee in the fall of 1858, 105 pomeshchiki, including the novelists Tolstoi and Turgenev, signed a resolution in favor of the redemption of allotment land. The resolution was printed in *The Contemporary*; neither *The Contemporary* nor any other publication broadcast the views of the 310 nobles at the elections who had not signed the resolution.[52]

The officials and members of provincial committees who viewed the coming reform with uneasy caution could find little to their liking in the press; a Kaluga pomeshchik, "unable to give up his ingrained habits and accept the necessity of the impending reform," was so distressed by the journalistic discussion of the reform that he cancelled all his subscriptions to periodicals.[53] He and his kind had scarcely any articulate spokesmen. However, they had a mighty ally in the Main Committee.

The committee's earlier efforts to restrict public discussion having proved less than effective, it addressed the problem once again in January 1859. It disclaimed the intention of suppressing articles favorable to government policies, provided they contained nothing irrelevant, unseemly, or inflammatory. However, the right of government agencies to review all articles dealing with matters in their jurisdiction had not been strictly observed. Therefore, the censors must be instructed to

> submit without exception all articles dealing in any way with the peasant question, before they are passed for publication, to the scrutiny of the functionaries not only of the Ministry of Internal Affairs . . . but also of all those Ministries and Central Agencies to whose jurisdiction the subjects discussed in the article pertain.[54]

If an article chanced to survive its passage through the appropriate departments of, say, the Ministries of Justice, Finance, and State Properties and the Second Section of H.I.M.'s Chancery, the censor (an official of the Ministry of Education) was still personally accountable for every word. And, as the censor Troinitskii observed, the various officials who had to pass on the article could not readily ascertain "the views of the government," which they were supposed to uphold.[55] In practice, most articles emerged from this ordeal only after many months of delay, if they emerged at all. The public debate on the reform was effectively halted; the regular journals had to turn to other matters, while *Rural Welfare* and *The Landowners' Journal* ceased publication.[56] The Main Committee would not deny, as Lanskoi would later argue, that the press had aroused public sentiment in favor of landed emancipation. However, the reform was a matter of state, and the interests of the responsible agencies must be protected. This protection was extended to the provincial committees, whether they wanted it or not.

The Main Committee and the Ministry of Internal Affairs worked out a common attitude to the provincial committees by resolving various questions of procedure, discipline, and order; the government intervened more and more freely with the passage of time and the accumulation of precedent. However, the problems on which it took action did not bear directly on the subject of the committees' deliberations. The regime showed great concern for forms and procedures and very little interest in the provisions of the provincial draft statutes. The standards by which these drafts would be reviewed underwent great change, but the central government made little effort to communicate its revised policy to the provincial committees. The new goals of the reform were not kept secret; indeed, Rostovtsev defied bureaucratic custom by circulating the proceedings of the Editorial Commission. However, the revised policy was not thrust upon the committees as the original rescript, directive, and the April Program had been. There were only three issues of substance on which the central government intruded into the deliberations of the provincial committees: the redemption of the serfs themselves, the definition of "household plot", and the redemption of plowland.

The Redemption of Souls: Nizhnii Novgorod and Smolensk

The Nizhnii Novogord Provincial Committee was the first to rule that the serfs must redeem themselves as well as the household plots. It may not have been the issue involved but the committee's attempt to take the bit in its teeth that prompted the government to intervene, for the committee was in continual and apparently successful conflict with governor A. N. Murav'ev. Murav'ev had inaugurated the committee with an ardent speech (an "inflammatory proclamation" according to a Third Section agent) evoking the hopes of the tsar and the serfs' desire to recover their human rights. The committee responded by dispersing, despite Murav'ev's objections, to gather information about the manorial economy of the province. Murav'ev then decided to speed up the committee's work by presenting it with a finished draft statute, drawn up by himself. St. Petersburg upheld the committee on both points; the newly issued April Program required the committees to collect statistics, while Murav'ev was forbidden to put his own proposals before it. When the committee reconvened and began compiling its draft, it did not at first challenge Murav'ev on questions of principle, and he and his allies within the committee were fairly satisfied. A conflict did arise when A. Kh. Shteven, one of the two government members (he had been the courier who brought the Nizhnii petition to St. Petersburg), protested that the committee's valuation of household plots was unrealistically high; he was censured for "disrespect." Murav'ev made a gesture of conciliation by replacing him.[57]

Murav'ev made his move when he caught the committee in violation of the rescript; it voted that household plots could be redeemed only with the pomeshchik's consent. In passing this resolution, according to Murav'ev, the committee was reneging on the Nizhnii nobility's assent to the reform of serfdom, its "solemn pledge to the sovereign and all Russia." He grandiloquently asked the committee to reflect on the possibility that the reproach for resisting the imperial will may issue from the very estate whose way of life the nobility is laboring to set in order; terrible can be the indignation of the people, and terrible the sentence it pronounces, when it sees itself quite arbitrarily deprived of its rightful hope of acquiring by redemption that which the monarch's word has publicly promised.[58]

The majority of the committee not only clung to its decision, but also, confident of a second vindication, laid the controversy before the Ministry of Internal Affairs, charging that Murav'ev's directive was a "bill of indictment."

Somewhat later, when Murav'ev again raised the issue of the committee's pace of work, the majority took more dramatic action. It had been working slowly and, Murav'ev supposed, in bad faith. He reported to Lanskoi, "The leaders of the . . . majority tried to procrastinate on the peasant question, reducing the significance of their work to nil and circulating rumors that . . . the government has altered its intentions and that everything will remain as before.[59] The majority procrastinated by staying away from the sessions; it was difficult to assemble a quorum of sixteen members. The provincial marshal Boltin, who tried to cooperate with Murav'ev, sponsored a change in the committee's rules so that three members constituted a quorum. Murav'ev continued to find the committee dilatory. In mid-July, he urged it to speed up so that the draft would be finished when the tsar visited Nizhnii in August.

The majority replied in a defiant speech, which thirteen members adopted as a resolution; it circulated as a kind of manifesto by would-be spokesmen for the nobility.[60] This rejoinder declared that the committee's function was to "defend the nobility's rights from constraint." The Nizhnii Committee had defaulted on this obligation and its resolutions were "bitter and unripe fruit." So far the committee had acted "heedlessly," inspired by "*the utterly inexplicable hostility of certain members to their own estate.*" This hostility was the product of "an alien influence"; presumably this was an allusion to the machinations of Murav'ev, who was widely assumed to hate the nobility.[61] The members of the majority, however, had thrown off this influence and, "in our concern for the fate of our noble constituents [*doveriteli*], we are adhering to the saving principle of gradualism." They resolved to start again from the beginning. In setting their points of departure, they reiterated their insistence that household plots could be redeemed only with the pomeshchik's consent and on his terms. More important, adopting a position the committee had previously rejected, they voted that the peasants must redeem themselves apart from the plots.[62]

The minority of the committee—stigmatized as "antinobles, wily slaves,"[63] who would lavish everything on the peasants—simply retreated after this unexpected reversal. Surrendering his chairman's gavel to Ia. I. Piatov, the author of the rejoinder, Boltin resigned, along with three other members. Four more members of the minority walked out, on the ground that they would not recognize Piatov as chairman; they appealed to Murav'ev to restore order in the committee and protect them from the slanders of the majority.[64] Except for one government member, a Decembrist comrade of Murav'ev's, Piatov's supporters had the field to themselves. They carried on under his chairmanship for two weeks. Murav'ev declared these rump sessions to be illegal, and when he was upheld by the central government, the resolutions passed under Piatov's chairmanship were quashed.

Piatov's own views emerge from a speech in one of the committee's first sessions. He proposed that peasants should have the use of their present household plots, and the pomeshchik would, within broad limits, determine the size of their allotments and the amount of their dues. Thus the estates would be operated much as before; indeed, Piatov did not believe the serfs were eager to part from their squires, for "if good-natured pomeshchiki could endure forever, our peasants would not desire freedom." He substantiated this finding with some anthropological observations:

The Russian is a good and naturally intelligent man, but not enterprising; he is more prone to imitate than to acquire, and so he needs the example of others. The pomeshchiki themselves have always been the best model for enhanced effort and labor; the peasants are obligated to them for their literacy and their crafts. . . . I venture to think that there is no dignity in the state more honorable than that of a pomeshchik who lives among his peasants, because he stimulates the people to activity and is the soul of the village commune.[65]

The majority's rejection of its previous enactments recalls the Nizhnii nobility's attempt to withdraw its original assent to reform. The capitulation of the minority is not so easily understood, but it was the first of many retreats by minorities within the provincial committees. This minority was led by men like A. N. Karamzin, the historian's son, who were committed to the principle of landed emancipation and thought of themselves as a saving remnant, at odds with the mass of the provincial nobility. When the provincial committees did not reject emancipation as such (and even Piatov did not), Karamzin, like Koshelev and Cherkasskii, was surprised and pleased. All three were correspondingly dismayed when their committees began working out the practical provisions and violently abused those who dissented from them. In most instances, the saving remnant retreated—both Karamzin and Koshelev resigned under attack.[66]

Murav'ev proposed that the thirteen members who had signed Piatov's rejoinder be removed from the committee and that the remaining eleven members draw up the Nizhnii draft, with Boltin restored to his chairmanship. New elections to fill the thirteen vacancies would be pointless "for in that event it would be impossible to count on success."Lanskoi did not favor a sweeping purge, though he may have sought Piatov's expulsion, but he secured the tsar's approval for a thorough vindication of Murav'ev and the minority. An Imperial Order restored Boltin to the chairmanship, administered a stern reprimand to Piatov and a lesser reproof to the other members of the majority; the eight members who had fled the committee were favored with an expression of the tsar's gratitude for their zeal in behalf of the state and humanity. And the same Imperial Order forbade the committee to make any provision for the redemption of the serfs themselves.[67]

The nobles of Nizhnii Novgorod were dismayed by the government's action. Piatov fell ill upon receipt of the imperial reprimand; his colleagues blamed Boltin for turning the rejoinder—which they had signed—over to Murav'ev. In a formal resolution, the nobles of Gorbatov District complained darkly of certain persons standing between the nobility and the tsar and misrepresenting the nobility's views.[68] Misgivings were expressed by Levshin and others within the government. Even Solov'ev conceded in retrospect that Murav'ev had been overbearing with the Nizhnii Committee, but hastened to explain that he had acted on his own, not under direction from the Ministry of Internal Affairs. By the time Alexander visited Nizhnii a month later, he had apparently adopted Levshin's view that the controversy had been a mere clash of personalities, largely provoked by the careerist ambitions of Murav'ev and Boltin.[69] Nonetheless, the government was now committed to the principle that peasants could not be compelled to redeem themselves.

This was a triumph of principle only, which did not promise much amelioration of the peasants' life. When the chastened committee resumed its work under Boltin, it voted, as directed, for the compulsory redemption of plotland without any redemption of the serfs themselves. However, the majority more than doubled the price of the plotland to 480 rubles per desiatina; they also reduced the allotment they had previously set and, taking heed of Levshin's observation that they were more generous than the St. Petersburg Provincial Committee, they increased the barshchina due for the reduced allotment from 130 days a year to 198.[70] Both the majority and the minority favored large allotments on nonagricultural estates where the land was poor. Otherwise, the minority proceeded from different principles, as its leader Boltin observed.[71] Boltin's faction would have the peasants redeem plot and allotment together at 64 rubles per desiatina. This was not quite the reckless generosity of which the minority was accused, for the allotments it proposed were very small. The serfs of the province lost 18 percent of their allotment land by virtue of the reform legislation of 1861, which reduced the allotments recommended by Rostovtsev's Editorial Commission; the majority draft would have reduced the allotments by 37 percent, but the minority would have taken away more than half the allotment land.[72] While the peasant would be spared the indignity of redeeming his own person, he would, if either the majority or the minority system had been put into effect, have paid a very high price for the abolition of serfdom.

Although the tsar had ruled that the Nizhnii Committee's proposal that the peasants must redeem themselves must be rejected as a "flagrant incitement to a perverted interpretation of the Imperially-confirmed principles," the government did not hasten to communicate the new ruling to the other provinces. They were informed one by one, if the issue arose in the deliberations of a provincial committee.[73] It arose again and again. The first resolution voted by the Simbirsk Provincial Committee held that nobles should be compensated for the loss of their prerogatives.[74] When the Chernigov Committee solemnly voted to renounce the nobleman's power over his serfs, one member was, he confessed, moved almost to tears by this fulfillment of the dreams of his youth; he was correspondingly appalled when the prayerful silence that followed the resolution was shattered by a question from the floor, "Do we have the right to demand compensation for this?"[75]

The administration's answer was no, and it would not tolerate attempts to make the serfs pay for themselves through a different form of words. The Main Committee rejected a petition from the Voronezh Provincial Committee asking "compensation to the pomeshchiki for the loss of serfdom." The government firmly maintained that nobles were entitled to compensation for land, but not for serfs or serfdom as such. However, it raised no objection when committees in Nizhnii Novgorod and elsewhere set such a high price on the land that the peasants would, in effect, be buying themselves as well. Some officials were querulous or skeptical. For example, when the Simbirsk nobility proposed that the household plots, some land, and the pomeshchik's "losses" should all be redeemed, Rostovtsev complained that he could not find "an *accurate* reckoning of *precisely what* . . . is to be subject to redemption."[76] Lanskoi was more sophisticated. When the governor of Smolensk informed him that a member of the provincial committee there had proposed the redemption of serfs, Lanskoi informed him that the proposal was inadmissable. He observed, however,

> If the Committee is apprehensive that the proprietors of obrok estates with little land, where the income is derived from nonagricultural resources and the advantages of the site, will suffer great losses when the peasants are personally free, then the Committee can take this circumstance into account . . . in evaluating the household plots and determining the dues for the plowland.[77]

Lanskoi's suggestion was clear encouragement for a fiction that would compensate nobles for their serfs as well as their land. The nobility of Smolensk disdained the fiction in an affecting petition to the tsar, insisting, "We do not lament the end of servile relations, we do not and cannot desire to retain them for the future; we anticipate a better future for ourselves and our serfs when a free relationship is established." In most parts of Russia compensation for the loss of serf labor was not necessary, but Smolensk was different; because of the "stubborn soil of our area . . . serf labor constitutes the main value of our estates." The indirect compensation suggested by Lanskoi and adopted by most committees was neither just nor prudent. It would not be possible, without the serfholder's power over the peasants, to make the peasants continue to pay their present dues, which the nobles of Smolensk conceded "do not correspond to the quantity and value of the land allotted to the peasants." Furthermore, they observed prophetically,

> To compel the peasants to redeem their labor as serfs and their labor in industry by inflating the prices of the household plots would be unjust to the peasants and a miscalculation for the pomeshchiki, because the peasants would not be able to redeem the plots, and the compensation to the pomeshchiki would be only nominal.

Justice demanded direct compensation for "the loss of a part of one's property [i.e., the serfs] to satisfy the needs of society." Compensation was also a practical necessity, so that Smolensk nobles could pay off their creditors and equip their estates for postservile agriculture. Although they were willing to make any sacrifice of life or property for the good of the fatherland, they were compelled to inform the tsar that without full compensation for land and serfs, "six thousand Smolensk nobles, deprived of the good name acquired in the service of Your predecessors, will be subjected to inevitable destitution."[78]

The petition was rejected, on the ground that the nobility had no right to petition on a matter discussed in the provincial committee, and the committee was instructed to withdraw its resolution in favor of the redemption of serfs. The Smolensk Committee stood firm, insisting, however, that its resolution provided for "compensation not for the peasant's person, but for the loss of property that will ensue upon the abolition of serfdom"; hence the resolution "did not express any incitement to perverse interpretation of the Imperially-approved principles." The Smolensk Committee was formally reprimanded for its stubbornness.[79]

Even then, the committee persisted, though on another tack. In their petition the Smolensk nobles had candidly confessed why they wanted compensation for their serfs: their debts precluded the sacrifice that patriotism required, for "at present our property is largely in the hands of our creditors; the good name of the nobility and our concern for the fate of our children demand an honorable accounting with them." Since the argument had been rejected in this rhetorical form, the Smolensk Committee put it more pointedly in a new petition, addressed to the Main Committee. The petition observed that the government did not give mortgage loans on land, but on land with serfs. Extrapolating from the small premium conceded to borrowers with much land and comparatively few serfs, the Smolensk Committee calculated that the treasury, in lending sixty or seventy rubles per serf, conceived the serfs themselves to be the security for forty rubles of this sum. Would it then be just to make the pomeshchik pay back the loan in full when serfdom was abolished?

This was an awkward question. The Ministry of Internal Affairs responded that it was not the serfs, but the land they were settled on that was security for mortgage loans from the treasury, and since, according to the rescripts all the land on the estate remained the pomeshchik's property, pomeshchiki could not be relieved of any part of their debt. This was a doubly specious argument, and the Main Committee adopted an argument from policy instead. The new petition was to be regarded as one more of the Smolensk nobility's interminable requests for the government's indulgence on their mortgage debts; the emancipation was merely a pretext for another request. Furthermore, no other provincial committee had raised the question, and if Smolensk got relief, other provinces would appeal for the same relief and the state's credit agencies would be in jeopardy. The Smolensk Committee's petition was rejected on these grounds.[80]

After this fourth rebuff, the Smolensk Committee dutifully set aside justice and prudence, as it conceived them. Like the committees in Nizhnii and elsewhere, it set a fabulous value on the household plots, high enough to provide for the nobles, their children, their creditors and their good name.[81] The Smolensk Committee, more candid than most, had been slow to realize that its province offered any real "nonagricultural resources and advantages of the site," and it had been more willing than most committees to make a stand on principle. The principle at stake was a basic one. Many nobles argued that they had acquired their serfs legitimately and held them with the full sanction of the laws. The government, in denying them direct compensation for these serfs, seemed to be taking the position that serfholding was illegitimate. The government did not argue in terms of principle on this matter, but its action was implicitly a total condemnation of serfdom and serfholders. However, these abstract issues were kept in the background. Now that reform was inevitable, the provincial nobility was little disposed to make a quixotic defense of the legitimacy of serfdom and the government was even less inclined to an equally quixotic condemnation of serfholding. The ground of dispute, from the first, was fiscal and economic.

The government was consistent; the fiction Lanskoi urged on the Smolensk Committee had been adopted by the Ministry of Internal Affairs in 1857 and was to be incorporated into the emancipation settlement of 1861. This fiction was founded on two considerations: the government should make the smallest possible commitment of its credit, and nobles should be compensated for the loss of their serfs only to the extent that compensation was practically necessary. The overvaluation of household plots met these considerations. Where the land was poor and the pomeshchik drew his income from obrok, the peasants would be compelled to buy their household plots at a price that would cover the lost obrok revenues. Where the pomeshchiki held rich agricultural land, they should get along just as well after emancipation; there was no reason for an overstrained treasury to underwrite a surrogate compensation on their behalf. The fiction that the peasants would redeem their household plots but not themselves enabled the government, with a semblance of consistency, to guarantee as much compensation for the abolition of serfdom as seemed necessary for the nobility of each area.

The provincial committees were slow to accept this fiction. Although no other committee was as reluctant as Smolensk, the government had to reiterate the ban on the redemption of serfs. Many committees, in accepting the fiction, carried it to absurd lengths. A dissident member of the Simbirsk Committee observed that his colleagues assessed the plotland at a rate higher than the market value of the whole estate; at the last minute the leaders of the committee added a petition for compensation for the loss of serfdom, "lest the majority of the nobility be subjected to utter ruin upon the elimination of the peasants' compulsory labor."[82] Yet Simbirsk was an agricultural province, where the land alone was supposed to secure the pomeshchik's revenues. The petition was, to be sure, brief and diffident, to the dismay of a nobleman of Simbirsk, who was sure that the tsar would respond to a forthright presentation. "No one argues about serfdom or defends it," he insisted, but compensation for lost prerogatives was the nobility's due by right and by necessity, since the state would collapse if the nobility were ruined. The petition was equivocal, he explained, because the younger members of the committee ("the democratic party") opposed it, while the older members had learned under Nicholas I to dread affronting the tsar.[83]

The cautious importunity of Simbirsk, like the stubbornness of Smolensk, was rooted in an inability to imagine the manorial economy operating in the absence of serfdom. The government's policy of differentiated and disguised compensation was narrowly fiscal in its motives but based on a broad assumption about the postreform rural economy. Nobles were slow to accept the policy because they could not share the assumption that the rural economy would continue to function as it had under serfdom. It was hard for the black-soil pomeshchiki to imagine how they could operate their estates when the serfs were converted into tenants and hired laborers; the obrok proprietors feared that the peasants would flee rather than make large redemption payments for plots of relatively little value. Many nobles, indeed, could not conceive of Russian society without serfdom.

Household Plots: Moscow

A few days after the government vetoed the redemption of serfs, it reiterated its policy on household plots. The rescripts to Nazimov and Ignat'ev had seemingly been clear: "The peasants are to remain settled in their household plots, which they are to acquire as property by means of redemption within a definite period." Many nobles had singled out this provision for sharp criticism, and provincial committees often flouted it in their early resolutions. On August 31, 1858, the tsar himself intervened, but he did so in a haphazard and oblique way. His intervention took the form of an oral reproach to the Moscow Provincial Committee for defining "household plot" as "living quarters and outbuildings."[84] The committee had formally adopted this absurd definition three months before. However, in the interim the committee had voted that the plots should include seven-twentieths of a desiatina of land. This new definition was not generous, since the existing plots averaged half a desiatina, but it was not manifestly absurd, being borrowed from the regulations for the appanage estates of the crown. Alexander seized upon the earlier definition when the committee itself had apparently repented, for the issue actually at stake was whether the redemption of the plots would be compulsory for the pomeshchik.

In the Moscow Committee's initial debate on household plots, all speakers favored some alternative to the government's program. They did not make a show of opposition. A representative of Ruza District, for example, reported that his constituents "as loyal subjects are ready to advance the paternal design of their beloved monarch." However, the beloved monarch was actually opposed to the redemption of the plots, for he had stated in the rescript that "the pomeshchik retains his property right to all the land"; others also used this phrase to justify their reluctance to part with the plots.[85] The nobles of Bronnitsy professed a sentimental attachment to the peasants' huts and gardens, which were "improved properties . . . our own inestimable treasure. To alienate them would mean the destruction of cherished family memories, which bind noble families to their ancestral estates." Most speakers advanced more practical objections. N. G. Golovin of Moscow District argued that the peasants would never pay the redemption payments since hereditary tenure of the plots was guaranteed; if they did redeem the plots, the estate would lose most of its value because the core would belong to independent property owners. He and several colleagues observed that the government had never made state peasants redeem their plots.[86]

The Moscow nobles were anxious that they might lose their labor force when the peasants redeemed the plots. Golovin remarked that, in the environs of Moscow, obrok was essentially a payment for the plots alone, for the serfs were "very little involved in the cultivation of grain. . . . They buy baker's bread in Moscow and work at various crafts, thereby gaining their entire livelihood incomparably more easily than by agriculture." When they redeemed their plots, they would sell them to a few rich peasants and move away; the pomeshchik's fields would lie untilled.[87] Other members, whatever the relative importance of demesne agriculture and nonagricultural obrok in their districts, echoed Golovin's fears and opposed separate redemption of the plots.

The members of the Mozhaisk District agreed on the nature of the problem but thought the proposed remedy was foolish. Plainly, the rescript demanded the redemption of the plots, and this demand, "as an expression of the Imperial will, we consider compulsory for the pomeshchiki and for the peasants." The experience of emancipation in other countries showed that cooperation with the government was prudent, for "where the nobility struggled with the government and attempted to avoid cooperation, as in France, for example, the eventual outcome entailed utterly ruinous consequences for the state." More important, the redemption of the household plots would in fact secure a labor force for the pomeshchiki, for it would bind the peasants to the land. The Moscow Committee merely had to require that peasants living on the plots must work a certain quantity of the demesne, rendering obrok or barshchina in return. Rovinskii and Gvozdev, representing Zvenigorod District, would achieve the same end by requiring the commune to redeem two desiatiny (including plotland) per soul. They expected that since they were "acting so sincerely before the government, renouncing all variants of serfdom in the name of conviction," the government would show the same sincerity and guarantee the redemption payments.[88] The chairman proposed a compromise between these two systems: the plots and half the allotment land would be redeemed under government guarantee, and the peasants would be obliged to rent the other half; they would not be able to redeem all the allotment land, since they would be buying themselves ("the pomeshchik's right to their labor") as well as the land.[89]

These diverse proposals reflect a common opposition to the separation of the plots from the fields. This opposition is particularly clear in a statement by the members from Dmitrov District, based—like many of the other speeches in the early sessions—on the resolutions of the conference of the district nobles. The Dmitrov nobility proposed a redemption plan like the one advocated by the representatives of Zvenigorod, but provided that if the government did not approve the redemption of plowland, the peasants would not redeem the plots but would hold them as part of their allotment.[90]

It was not redemption, but the separate redemption of the

household plots that the Moscow nobility opposed, and this opposition was natural. The consequences of separate redemption would depend on the other terms of the reform. On the face of things, however, few peasants and fewer pomeshchiki had anything to gain from the redemption of the plots, which were not big enough to support the families that lived on them and had little market value. The government did not call for separate redemption to meet the economic needs of either peasants or nobles, but to promote internal security. This concern was clear even in the laconic language of the rescript, which held that the peasants would redeem their "*usadebnaia osedlost'.*" This curious and untranslatable* expression indicated that the plots were not regarded as economic units, but rather as so many bulwarks against "vagabondage and deleterious mobility," as the accompanying directive made clear. The directive went on to explain that usadebnaia osedlost' denoted "living quarters and outbuildings, the ground they stand on, and the kitchen garden.

Golovin attempted to exploit the language and form of the rescript and directive to meet the anxieties of the Moscow nobility. The rescript, which was binding, called for the redemption of usadebnaia osedlost'; this term was defined in Lanskoi's directive, but the directive and therefore the definition were not binding. Hence the committee was free to define usadebnaia osedlost' as "buildings alone, but not land." This definition made a show of adhering to the rescript without sacrificing any landed property; the peasants would redeem an abstract concept and some lumber. The committee accepted Golovin's tortuous reasoning by a vote of fifteen to fourteen. At the same time, and by the same vote, the committee decided that the pomeshchik could choose between providing his peasants with plots and allotments in usufruct or having them redeem their plots and a desiatina of plowland.[91] This second decision was unduly restrictive for the substantial minority who favored some variety of redemption, and a later resolution held that the peasants' buildings and an unspecified amount of plotland could be redeemed by free agreement. When one of the government members belatedly protested that the redemption of plowland was, according to the rescript, compulsory for the pomeshchik, the committee voted twenty to seven that it was not. The provincial marshal, who had been putting up a feeble struggle for the government's program, justified this interpretation with sophistry surpassing Golovin's; the redemption of household plots

Osedlost' means settlement in the abstract, the opposite of vagrancy or nomadism, while *usadebnaia* is the adjectival form of the word for household plot.

could not be compulsory for the pomeshchik, since any redeeming would obviously be done by the peasants.[92]

The committee did not seek to drive the peasants off the household plots. It resolved to grant the plotland to the peasants in "hereditary usufruct" and that each plot—not to be confused with usadebnaia osedlost'—should be seven-twentieths of a desiatina; both resolutions passed unanimously. Indeed, the committee was determined to provide the peasant with land whether he wanted it or not. It ruled that a peasant who held a household plot, in usufruct or as property, was obliged to accept an allotment of plowland and remit the dues it bore. The committee would also restrict the use of the plots and plowland in various ways so as to keep as many peasants behind the plow as the pomeshchik might need. Thus the committee sought to provide the pomeshchiki with a guaranteed supply of labor and an unequivocal title to all his land. Indeed, the subcommittee that was to compile a draft statute from the committee's various and somewhat contradictory resolutions was specially instructed to supplement them to ensure "the inviolability of the pomeshchik's property rights."[93]

Underlying the Moscow nobles' attitude towards their peasants as potential laborers and renters were striking assumptions about peasant mobility and compulsory labor. The government had specified that peasants could not move freely from place to place during the transition period, and while their mobility after that period was left an open question, the government made its desire to bind the peasantry to the land reasonably clear. Nonetheless, the Moscow Committee assumed that the government would turn the peasants loose and that the peasants would avail themselves of this permission in massive numbers. Both of these assumptions were widespread. The nobles of Smolensk and Nizhnii Novgorod provinces shared them, and also sought to secure themselves against the coming exodus. Indeed, it is difficult to find a spokesman for the nobility in 1858 who thought that affinity, inertia, or self-interest would keep the peasants in their native villages when the reform was complete. The squires of Smolensk believed their province to be particularly ill-favored by nature, while their counterparts in Moscow spoke ominously of the delights of city life. No one explained how large numbers of peasants would support themselves without working the land; indeed, it was commonly asserted that, without direct compulsion, the peasants would indulge in a kind of inner immigration—sitting on the stove or in the tavern and doing nothing. The noble estate had learned its practical economics in the school of serfdom, where economic rationalism was not part of the curriculum.

The remedy proposed by the nobles of Smolensk, Nizhnii, and other provinces was simple: their peasants were being taken away, they wanted money instead. The Moscow nobles, by contrast, optimistically assumed that compulsory labor could be as serviceable after the reform as before. They would leave the pomeshchik free to make contractual arrangements if he desired, but the tendency of their resolutions was to constrain the peasant to continue as he had under serfdom. After all, it was the tsar's wish, Golovin explained, that the committee's draft "should not disrupt the economic arrangement now prevailing on the proprietary estates." Another member hoped that the reform could be implemented "almost without the peasants' noticing."

The change in their personal relations to the landowner, a change which will, by the abolition of his arbitrary power, constitute one of the foundations of the villager's prosperity, should not entail any of the consequences that might follow upon an overturn in the economic life of the peasants and the pomeshchik.[94]

There was no thought, then, of substituting market forces for the constraints of serfdom in the management of estates. For Prince Menshikov, the dominant figure on the committee, the very idea was ridiculous. He met a member of the Iaroslav Provincial Committee who favored the redemption of plowland in order "to be completely disentangled from the peasants"; the demesne could be worked by free labor, which he himself had already used with success. "Politeness," Menshikov noted in his diary, "prevented me from saying that's not true!" Somewhat later, he attempted to convince a member of the Editorial Commission that free labor inevitably costs more than it produces. He was delighted when the head of the Third Section experimented with free labor on his estate and reported a loss, which Menshikov found "a precious admission for a member of the emanc. com. [the Main Committee]."[95]

The Moscow Committee wanted to perpetuate the prevailing relationship with the peasants, but part of that relationship was the pomeshchik's authority to alter it at will; the committee hoped to preserve this authority along with the pattern of allotment and dues. One of its starkest resolutions held simply, "The pomeshchik is to determine the economic arrangements on his estate at his discretion."[96] Then, too, the pomeshchik was to have broad powers to relocate the peasants' household plots when the reform was being implemented.[97] However, the committee did lay down certain norms, of which the most important provided that a tiaglo allotted with four desiatiny should render ninety days of barshchina per year. This formula was offered by Menshikov, and it carried by virtue of his prestige after the provincial marshals' formula, almost identical to Menshikov's, had been rejected.[98] Menshikov's proposal (based, like his norm for household plots, on the regulations of the crown estates) were not generous; four desiatiny per tiaglo was less that half the average under serfdom, and the reduction of barshchina was comparatively small, since the peasants would render three days a week throughout the growing season. The Emancipation Statute of 1861 offered a much larger allotment for lower dues. Perhaps the committee's formula was a program maximum, which the government was expected to moderate in reviewing the draft statute. It seems more likely, however, that the four-desiatina allotment was conceived as a deliberately unattractive option, which peasants would choose to reject in favor of maintaining their present relationship with their pomeshchik. Menshikov had earlier proposed "to leave with the peasants the lands they presently hold and for which they render [barshchina] dues to the pomeshchik." On obrok estates, he would divide the present allotments into two parts, one of which the peasants would hold in usufruct for fixed dues, with the other rented by contract. This simple system had been rejected "because of the way a few members calculated their interest," according to Menshikov.[99] His subsequent proposal, which the committee adopted, was designed to take these calculations into account, but the purpose was still to perpetuate the forms of tenure, cultivation, and compensation characteristic of serfdom. The committee's definition of the peasants' dues was essentially a description of barshchina under serfdom: "the basis for determining the peasants' dues is the quantity of land they will be obliged to work in return for each desiatina set aside for their use." If the serfs' present dues were significantly higher or lower than their capacity to meet them, they must be modified, but it was desirable, as one member explained, "to retain the present distribution of land and other resources in the peasant economy." This was rough justice and dubious amelioration. However, the alternatives offered by some members, based on specious calculations of the output of the land and the value of the working day, would have been more onerous for the peasants than the status quo favored by the majority.[100]

The Moscow Committee's desire to perpetuate existing relationships was in harmony with the rescript to Ignat'ev, but its attempt to prevent the separate redemption of plotland challenged the rescript on a major and sensitive point. Alexander responded to this challenge obliquly, by rejecting the Moscow definition of the usadebnaia osedlost' that would be subject to compulsory redemption. Perhaps he was trying to be tactful; the definition was a minor element of the committee's challenge, but it was such an affront to common sense that its rejection should be no ground for indignation. Perhaps he was confused by the committee's overlapping and inconsistent resolutions, as reported by the partisan Zakrevskii, and did not see the function that the definition was supposed to serve.[101] At any rate, Alexander's reprimand was enough to make the committee change course.

On September 3, the tsar's speech was read to a session of the Moscow Committee, and "after a few minutes of deep silence, it was decided to annul the previous resolution [*zhurnal*] on household plots and acknowledge the peasants' right to redeem them."[102] However, the committee set even higher values on the plots than the outlandish figures suggested in the prior debate. The peasants' right to redeem the plots would lapse if they did not pay over these large sums (along with substantial dues for small allotments and supplementary payments for the use of unredeemed plots) during the transition period. Finally, the committee reiterated its demand that any peasant who held a household plot, redeemed or not, was obliged to accept an allotment of plowland.[103] While the committee formally submitted to the principle of separate redemption of plotland, it strove, after Alexander's admonition no less than before, to retain compulsory labor and prevent the alienation of any land.

The city of Moscow was the second capital, the heart of Great Russia, and the traditional headquarters for nobles at odds with the bureaucracy. Despite its eventual submission to the government program, the Moscow Provincial Committee acquired a reputation for opposition, a reputation derived from suppositions about the influence and views of Zakrevskii and Menshikov. The suppositions were correct. Zakrevskii tried several times in 1858 to dissuade Alexander from proceeding with the reform, and he promised Menshikov to back the committee against the government; he was removed in 1859, ostensibly because of a scandal unrelated to the peasant question. Menshikov was close to Zakrevskii in his private views, and his influence among the noibility was greater. *The Bell* pilloried him as the leader of the opponents of emancipation, the would-be "butcher of the Russian people," and these charges were faintly but distinctly echoed in the upper bureaucracy. Rumors reached Menshikov that he was in bad odor at court because of his intransigent stance in the Moscow Committee, and his own encounters with old friends among the sanovniki and with the tsar himself confirmed the rumors.[104]

The peripatetic Menshikov seemed an ominous figure. He was in regular contact with the sanovniki and in touch with everyone who won notoriety as an extreme exponent of the pomeshchik's interest: Orlov-Davydov, Blank of Tambov, Apraksin of Orel, Shidlovskii of Simbirsk, Gagarin of Voronezh, and the Bezobrazov family. He read a pamphlet in which Nikolai Bezobrazov tried to forestall the reform with legalistic and semantic arguments and found that it "strongly and sensibly defends the nobles' property right." Menshikov opposed almost every element of the government's original program, while Rostovtsev's reformulation of that program was worse still—"the ravings of ignorance." Indeed, Menshikov was moved by the government's renewed commitment to reform in late 1858 to revise his conspiracy theory; he had believed that Konstantin Nikolaevich was being manipulated by a handful of reds, but now the Grand Duke himself, his reason unhinged by masturbation, was the culprit.[105]

Menshikov voiced his sentiments in conversations with officials and private citizens, and he is usually stigmatized as the leader of the krepostniki, or intransigent adherents of serfdom, in the Moscow Committee. Menshikov is conventionally contrasted to D. A. Rovinskii, an advocate of the redemption of plowland, who is supposed to have been the most progressive member of the Moscow Committee.[106] Circumstances alter cases, and circumstances—the government's program and the pomeshchik's views—changed rapidly in 1858-1859. The redemption of plowland was first advocated by those who were most hostile to serfdom and who sought to balance the interests of the peasants and the nobles, but there was nothing inherently generous about redemption as such. In 1859 and 1860, many of the most intransigent and self-seeking pomeshchiki came out for the redemption of allotments on the ground that the government would not provide them with enough coercive power to make compulsory labor serviceable. Rovinskii's position in 1858 by and large anticipates the demands the so-called krepostniki would make a year or two later. For example, he would leave the peasants under the control of an official elected by the nobility, who would have a combination of manorial and administrative authority, and he would also make the peasants' allotments a matter of free agreement after the transition period; these would be the basic demands of the provincial deputies to the Editorial Commission in 1860.[107] Rovinskii may owe some of his reputation to his conflicts with Menshikov and Zakrevskii, and some to his later activities as a reforming jurist and historian of the arts; a man like that, assume, *must* have held broad and philanthropic views.

The odious Menshikov, on the other hand, was an effective defender of the original government program in the Moscow Provincial Committee. His voting record was consistent. He voted against every attempt to challenge or evade the prescribed elements of the government program, such as Golovin's definition of "household plots." He also opposed various self-seeking schemes even when they were not in conflict with the rescript. He rejected the idea that serfs should redeem themselves, before the government took its stand on the issue; he ridiculed the idea that the nobles should be compensated for training given to their household serfs, which was one of the cherished hopes of provincial squires.[108] Menshikov did not indulge in fulminations against bureaucracy, as Rovinskii did. Nor did he offer a general criticism of the committee's excessive demands, like the government members Tomashevskii and Pavlov.[109] However, antibureaucratic talk was cheap, while the government members' polite and systematic dissent produced nothing except a firm retort, weakly argued but strongly stated, from the majority.[110] Menshikov was able to play an effective practical role. Though he was often in the minority on preliminary votes, the major elements of the Moscow draft statute were his handiwork. His proposals reflected his antipathy for change in the operation of estates; indeed, they expressed his over-all conservatism, for often they were simply quarried from the section of the Code of Laws dealing with crown properties. Where the government program offered latitude, Menshikov was quick to interpret it in the nobility's favor. For example, he hoped that after the reform the determination of peasant dues would be left, within broad limits, to the pomeshchik's discretion. Using his authority as vice-chairman, he simply dismissed Rovinskii's plan to convert the dues into something like rent, ruling that the proposal was in conflict with the rescript.[111] However, where the government program was unequivocal and binding, Menshikov actively and effectively advanced it. He carried on a two-front struggle within the committee, against the die-hard serfholders and against the "reds," who, in his opinion, wanted to destroy the nobility and rouse the peasantry to rebellion. By the standards of Rostovtsev's policy statements or the Statutes of February 19, 1861, Menshikov's proposals and the Moscow draft express fundamental opposition to reform. By the standards of the rescript and directive of 1857, which provide the true measure of his intent, it is clear that Menshikov pressed the government's minimum program upon the reluctant committee.

On December 22, with Menshikov in the chair, the Moscow Committee held its eighty-seventh and last session; all members signed the draft statute, although even this formality entailed "uproar and altercation." Afterwards, some of the members approached the old prince to thank him for "support against the reds in the committee." "But I acted," Menshikov noted afterwards, " . . . in defense of my opinions, not theirs."[112] He did not think of himself as the government's man. He confided to his diary that he was "extremely indifferent" to his standing at court, but he scrupulously recorded each of his encounters with members of the imperial family and wrote down their casual remarks. He had served so long that he could not see how much his reflexes as a courtier and functionary prevailed over his prejudices as a pomeshchik.

Menshikov's labors in the government cause went unrewarded and unnoticed. During the star's visit to Moscow, Zakrevskii defended Menshikov's efforts in the provincial committee, but the tsar insisted that "Menshikov is preventing the committee from making progress."[113] Apparently the advocacy of a man like Zakrevskii lent substance to the insinuations against Menshikov. Then, too, Menshikov enhanced his reputation for opposition by using his celebrated sarcasm on behalf of his prejudices; he expressed his contempt for the very idea of reform by proposing that the emancipated peasants be provided with pocket watches to ensure fulfillment of their statutory obligations to the pomeshchik.[114] Finally, by the time his labors in the Moscow Committee were finished, government policy had drastically changed. Socialism and democracy, as Menshikov conceived them, had triumphed, and they claimed him among their first victims. In April 1859, Lanskoi informed him that he had been removed from the Moscow Provincial Committee.[115] The committee had closed down, and the government had already decided not to revive the committees for the second and third periods indicated in the April Program. Menshikov's removal was a gratuitous and purely formal rebuke. Yet Menshikov had served the tsar faithfully, if suppression of one's own inclinations can serve as a measure of fidelity.

The Redemption of Allotments: Tver

When the government overruled basic decisions by the provincial committees of Nizhnii Novgorod, Smolensk, and Moscow, the committees submitted in principle and sought to achieve their previous objectives by other means. The government intervened in the same fashion on a third question of substance, the compulsory redemption of allotments proposed by the Tver Committee. Tver did not yield. The committee reiterated its proposal insistently, and it prevailed; the government accepted the Tver principle and incorporated it—as an option, to be sure—in the statutes of 1861. Many nobles, as individuals or in organized groups, challenged government policy in the period 1857-1860, but when the challenge elicited a refusal or a rebuke, they retreated and often sought forgiveness for their presumption. Only the Tver Committee held its ground.

The Tver Committee's policy was prefigured in a plan offered by A. M. Unkovskii, provincial marshal of the nobility, in reaction to the rescript and directive of 1857. He argued that the government program would perpetuate old relationships under new names and did not offer real emancipation. Like Golovin of Moscow, he fastened on the word "*osedlost'*," but interpreted it broadly; it could not, he argued, be construed merely as ascription to a fixed place of residence, but must include the concept of economic security. The redemption of household plots would not provide economic security, for a plot would not provide a peasant household with even a bare subsistence. He urged that the whole nation should redeem the plots, the allotments, and the serfs themselves (since they were legally acquired property) at a rate of 150 rubles per male soul. Only by means of general and compulsory redemption could the government's purposes be attained; the peasant would be truly free, for all traces of dependency upon the pomeshchik would be gone, and the peasantry would have osedlost', being assured of a place to live and enough land for the necessities of life.[116]

Unkovskii sent his memorandum to the central government and circulated it among the Tver nobility in early 1858. The nobles of Novyi Torg District seized upon this deliverance from ruin and paid effusive tribute to its author, announcing,

Now, for our part, the realization of the generous vision of our monarch is only to be desired. Then and forever after, our descendants will pronounce the name of A. M. Unkovskii with respect, while we . . . are proud to be your contemporaries and to see that the representative of our estate is a man who fully appreciates his lofty role as defender not only of our rights, but also of our property.[117]

The nobility of Novyi Torg and of three other districts around the provincial capital endorsed Unkovskii's system in petitioning for the formation of a provincial committee, but the eight outlying districts did not. More important, the Main Committee directed the Tver Provincial Committee to proceed, like the others, on the basis of the system of redemption and usufruct set forth in the rescript to

Ignat'ev. However, the Main Committee always rejected conditions and proposals attached to expressions of assent, and Lanskoi informed Unkovskii privately that the government was not in principle opposed to the redemption of allotment land.[118]

Unkovskii pressed his case when the tsar and his suite made a ceremonial visit to Tver just as the provincial committee was beginning its work. Before he could speak to the tsar, he was waylaid by V. A. Dolgorukov, head of the Third Section and member of the Main Committee, who explained that the tsar was especially anxious that the peasants should retain their hempfields. Unkovskii replied, as he recalled,

We have not so far given a thought to the hempfields, we are thinking of bigger things. . . . We want to call "household plot" more than the Program provides, but we do not know how to proceed. If the draft is written according to the [April] Program, it will come out balderdash. We want simply to call the whole allotment, except for remote tracts, the "household plot."

Dolgorukov was skeptical at first, but he became enthusiastic when Unkovskii calculated the sum he would receive through the redemption of the allotments on his own estate in Tver Province. The tsar himself was reportedly delighted with the idea.[119]

Encouraged by this informal permission, Unkovskii pressed his plan upon the Tver Committee, using his authority and prestige as chairman. He set up a steering committee packed with his supporters; his prestige in the full committee was enough to overwhelm those who protested or tried to temporize.[120] The steering committee produced three propositions as points of departure for the draft statute. The first, which held that barshchina was incompatible with civil rights for the peasants and must be abolished, passed twenty-one to five. The second held that the peasants, inseparably linked to the land by tradition, would remain a dependent class if their land was burdened with obligations to the nobles. They would be really free only if they were guaranteed "*substantial osedlost'* . . . *in full property,*" which could be achieved, according to the third proposition, if the osedlost' subject to redemption was defined as "*the entire amount of land necessary to secure the peasants' way of life.*" These two points carried by a majority of one.[121]

Unkovskii's party did not deny that their system contradicted the April Program, but they emphasized, as their counterparts in Nizhnii and Moscow did on other issues, that nothing was obligatory except the rescript; if the government accepted the principle of redemption of plowland, the committee would scarcely be penalized for its departure from the program. However, it was not simply departure from the program that bothered the minority members. They argued that Unkovskii's plan was financially impracticable, and indeed, it was premised on a confidence about the economic benefits of landed emancipation that neither the treasury nor most of the nobility could share. They also objected that if the peasants owned an adequate amount of land, there would be no laborers or renters for the pomeshchik's land. Finally, the minority thought that compelling the peasants to redeem plowland, whether they wanted it or not, was a grievous limitation on the peasants' freedom.[122] Advocates of compulsory redemption usually replied to this last point with rhetoric about the peasants' age-old attachment to the land, sliding over the fact that nonagricultural peasants, who were numerous in Tver and other northern provinces, were not attached to very much land.

The factions in Tver and in several other committees of the North were divided by a fundamental difference in attitude. Pomeshchiki usually began to favor the redemption of plowland when they concluded, either before or after the emancipation, that barshchina was unworkable without serfdom. However, many pomeshchiki of the so-called central industrial zone opposed its redemption. In part, they were simply unable to imagine a workable alternative to serf agriculture; they seized upon the April Program's provision that the draft statutes should cover only the quasi-serfdom of the period of "temporary obligation." The Tver minority produced a draft of its own, but did not venture to express in view of the final terms of the reform after the transition period. It may be, as Unkovskii later maintained, that most of the minority members were simply too unsophisticated to appreciate the workings of his system. He recalled,

Most of them simply feared an overly abrupt overturn in the economy and did not believe that immediate redemption was possible because of the enormous scale of the financial operation; that is, they were our opponents because they were short-sighted, the same kind of opponents, in a word, as the members of the Editorial Commission.[123]

The minority sought to invoke the authorities on its behalf, proposing that the committee should request official sanction for Unkovskii's definition of osedlost'. Outvoted fourteen to ten on this point, the minority secretly sent its own emissary to Lanskoi. Lanskoi responded by ordering the Tver majority to adopt the definition of "household plot" set forth in his directive to Ignat'ev.

In effect, he was forbidding the committee to include redemption of allotments in its draft, just as the tsar, in rejecting Moscow's narrow definition, was requiring a provision for the redemption of household plots; the government would not tolerate any semantic device that would expand or constrict the provisions of the rescript, which all parties understood to be binding. The Moscow Committee responded by setting prices on the household plots that were probably meant to be prohibitive; this option was not open to the Tver majority, since its semantic device was not meant to preclude the transfer of land, but to require it. More important, the Tver majority was more venturesome and better led than their counterparts in Moscow. By a vote of eleven to nine, the committee approved a petition appealing Lanskoi's ruling. The petition was submissive in tone and based upon the technicality that only the rescript was obligatory.[124] A three-man deputation, intending to reinforce the petition with forceful oral argument, set out for St. Petersburg to inform Lanskoi (as Unkovskii later recalled), that

we all agree that we will not compile a draft reform except according to those principles that *we ourselves consider appropriate*; if that kind of draft is not wanted, we ask that functionaries, who will write everything that is ordered, be appointed in our stead.[125]

Unkovskii subsequently pictured Lanskoi as flabbergasted by the threat. Historians have gone further and maintained that the defiance of the Tver Committee induced the government to capitulate on a cardinal point.[126] It is true that the Main Committee had previously rejected various proposals for the redemption of allotment land, including one offered earlier by four districts of Tver Province. The Nizhnii Novgorod Provincial Committee began advocating the redemption of serfs only after the Main Committee had indicated that the government would not assist in the redemption of plowland, and the Main Committee subsequently refused to consider other redemption plans. Golovachev, who wrote the Tver majority's appeal, was convinced that it would be rejected, since bureaucrats never admit they are wrong.[127]

Nonetheless, by the time the Tver deputation arrived in St. Petersburg, the government was already adopting redemption of plowland as a major element of its policy. The Tver Committee was showing genuine independence of spirit; it did not understand that Lanskoi could not accept the semantic evasion by which they would include redemption in the Tver draft, because the tsar himself had just forbidden evasions of this kind in his speech at Moscow.[128] However, Rostovtsev's letters to the tsar had already been distributed in official circles with the tsar's endorsement, and it was to Rostovtsev that Lanskoi sent the deputation. He received Unkovskii and his colleagues warmly and expressed enthusiasm for the compulsory redemption of allotments. The Tver appeal was put before the Main Committee the day after it had, by issuing its Journal of October 26, acceded to Rostovtsev's reformulation of the government's policy. The Tver deputation was beating on an opening door.

Lanskoi presented Tver's case to the Main Committee, singling out those views that Tver held in common with many other committees. He reported Tver's insistence that ministerial directives, including the definition of usadebnaia osedlost', were not binding. He raised the conventional objection that separate redemption was impractical because estates would thereby lose most of their value, for,

When the household plots are carved out of the very center of the tract and become the property of another, the pomeshchiki must set a very high value on them, while the peasants, obliged to make a separate payment for the plots apart from their obrok for the fields, will never be in a position to redeem them, so that the Imperial will cannot be fulfilled.

Finally, Lanskoi reported, the Tver majority represented the government's insistence on separate redemption to be dangerous.

The peasants will never consider this measure as an amelioration of their way of life, and, given their boundless faith in the Government, they will conclude that the Nobility has perversely interpreted the Sovereign's will to suit themselves; the consequences of this conclusion could be dreadful.

Lanskoi did not challenge the security argument, but he rejected the others. He recalled the tsar's conclusive definition of usadebnaia osedlost' and suggested (as the Main Committee would insist only subsequently) that provincial committees were obliged to adhere to the April Program. Nonetheless, he endorsed the Tver Committee's idea of substituting "a general redemption of peasant resources for the redemption of plots." The idea was faithful to the spirit, if not the letter of the tsar's rescript. He insisted, moreover, as bureaucratic advocates of redemption often did,[129] that the idea was philanthropic in its motives. "The nobility" he found, "in its praiseworthy zeal for the common weal, is going further" than the government could fairly require. It remained for the government to decide whether fiscal considerations would permit it to underwrite the nobility's generosity. In the meantime, the Tver Committee should be encouraged to develop its plan, provided that it followed the April Program by treating plots and plowland in separate chapters.[130]

The Main Committee adopted Lanskoi's recommendations, although the tsar's support of Rostovtsev's redemption plan was more telling than Lanskoi's arguments. At that, the committee members might not have acquiesced so readily if they had been aware of the line Unkovskii and his colleagues were taking, for Lanskoi's presentation was systematically misleading. Lanskoi did not directly indicate that the Tver majority would make the redemption of allotments compulsory for both lord and peasant. He made no mention of the Tver deputation and its threat, and even suggested that the arrival of a deputation from Tver could be forestalled by yielding along the lines he proposed. Finally, he misrepresented the Tver position; his presentation raised arguments that were being advanced in numerous provincial committees but had found little if any advocacy in Tver, while making no mention of the basic premises and goals of the Tver system.

Unkovskii and his allies did represent their plan as a dutiful fulfillment of the rescript and justified their course with the argument that only the rescript was binding. They argued that redemption of allotments would at once compensate nobles for the loss of their prerogatives and ensure prosperity for the peasants. Other committees rang these changes on behalf of their proposals, but Tver rang them in a different key. What set the spokesmen of the Tver majority apart from other provincial committees—and from the Main Committee—was an essential confidence about their own role and about the consequences of thoroughgoing emancipation. They defended their right of independent judgment, contrasting themselves with mere functionaries; unlike many other committees, they did not draw up outlandish demands, but offered a system based on considered judgment and seriously intended for enactment. As Lanskoi suggested, they made much of the peasant concept of land ownership, but not in the somber colors of the minister's presentation. Unkovskii and his associate N. A. Bakunin were among the very few nobles who maintained that the peasants had a positive right to their allotments. At the same time, they did not play at philanthropy, but insisted that redemption was in the nobility's interest. Bakunin, for example, observed that since the allotment land was in effect alienated by the rescript's provision for usufruct, nobles would be better off with compensation in a lump sum.[131]

Most important, the Tver majority actively desired to eliminate every trace of serfdom as soon as feasible; they would go beyond juridical emancipation and make the peasant self-sufficient, neither economically dependent on his old master nor under the control of a bureaucrat. The desire for a complete break runs from Unkovskii's original memorandum and the report of the steering committee through the majority draft and Unkovskii's declarations as a deputy to the Editorial Commission. The emphasis in the draft on reform of the courts, the censorship, and local government flowed from the idea of a complete break. As Unkovskii later put it, the majority of the Tver nobility "was ready for significant losses, as individuals and as an estate, *but only under the condition of the abolition of serfdom for all the people, not just for the peasants.*"[132]

Lack of nostalgia for the ways of serfdom was essential to the celebrated liberalism of Tver. The Tver program was rooted in sentiments widespread among the nobility—hostility to the bureaucracy and the desire to become disentagled from the serfs without financial loss. Many elements of that program, including thoroughgoing administrative reform and something close to civil equality, had advocates in many provincial committees. Although redemption of allotments was the cornerstone of the program, redemption as such was neither liberal nor conservative, but simply a form of compensation for the loss of the serfholder's prerogative; even in 1858, the nobles of Mozhaisk and other districts advocated the redemption of some plowland. In Tver, these sentiments and proposals were brought together in a coherent system; more important, the system's partisans took a self-reliant stance and pressed for their views in the face of official disapproval.

This combination of optimism, coherence, and persistence was unique to the Tver nobility, and it was fortuitous. It can be explained only by chance circumstances of leadership. Tver was not significantly different in its social and economic structure from provinces where the nobility was apprehensive, confused, and timid. Unkovskii and Golovachev had recently ridden into office on a wave a antibureaucratic feeling that was, however, quite unrelated to the issue of serfdom. They exploited their position in behalf of ideas they shared with many members of the intelligentsia[133] but with few members of the nobility's corporate officialdom. To rally the nobility behind their program, they continued to play upon the nobles' hostility to the bureaucracy, which was augmented, in Tver as elsewhere, by the drafting process. An explanation of the unique career of the Tver nobility between 1858 and 1862 that does not rest upon this complex of circumstances would be forced and specious.[134]

The nobles of Tver were not, of course, unanimously liberal or unanimously amenable to the redemption of plowland. When the government gave its blessing to the idea of redemption, opposition within the Tver Committee dwindled, but nine of the thirteen members who had voted against Unkovskii's plan when it was first proposed signed a counterdraft, which would retain the pomeshchik's property right to the allotments. Furthermore, Unkovskii's party was beset by guerilla raids from the nobility at large.

The first of these raids, a protest by the nobles of Novyi Torg district against the redemption of peasant allotments, was turned aside with irony and eloquence by Bakunin. They complained that the majority was threatening the nobility's status as an aristocracy of birth, to which Bakunin replied that "perpetual service to the nation is the constant and essential condition of noble status." Furthermore, the noble estate of Novyi Torg played the aristocrat badly, for the protest proceeded

purely from the point of view of the despised moneyed aristocracy. The government saw the necessity of emancipating the peasants and providing them with a solid osedlost', and all the hereditary nobility and the nobility of talent and intellect responded joyfully. But suddenly we are presented with a bill—500 silver rubles per desiatina or else no consent [to reform].[135]

However, the Novyi Torg protest was only the first of many, and they became more intense and threatening. At first Unkovskii and his allies replied with reasoned explanations, but the protest of the Kaliazin nobility was so abusive that Unkovskii interrupted it and broke off the session.

All the protests raised an issue that arises under any system of elected representation, the representative's relationship to his constituents' views. This was a new issue for Russians, since the corporate officials of the nobility and the other estates of the realm did not have significant powers of decision. For the Main Committee, the problem was simple. It had already ruled that members of the provincial committees were not restricted by the resolutions of the district conferences at which they were elected; these resolutions were to be conveyed to the central government, where they could be given the consideration they deserved—in practice, no consideration at all. When the spokesmen for Kaliazin District, denied access to the full committee, warned a member for Kaliazin that he must either leave Unkovskii's faction or resign from the committee, the Main Committee ruled that this member should be "invited to continue his useful labors in the Committee, without being inhibited in this work by the opinion of the nobles who signed . . . the letter" posing the alternatives.[136] A member for Vyshnii Volochek dismissed a protest from his electors just as the Main Committee might wish; he maintained that, by advocating the compulsory redemption of allotments,

I am thereby fulfilling my obligation to my constituents by defending their material interests and those of their children against all, even against some of the constituents themselves; though I merit their temporary indignation, in this instance I run this risk.[137]

Unkovskii's view, delivered in reply to a protest from Rzhev District, was more complex. He did not deny that the majority was at odds with the mass of the nobility, but defended the committee's authority, asking,

If we were to make our decisions not on the basis of justice, but according to the quantity of signatures, what would be the significance of the Committee? Would not the matter at hand simply pass to the whole mass of the nobility for a one-sided decision?

The committee could not be moved by complaints from electors because it was a "mediator between the two parties, for whom the protection of the rights of both estates is a holy duty." At the same time, the majority was advancing the nobility's economic interests by providing "a guarantee of compensation."

No one can say to us that we are not concerned about the nobility's interests, or that we exceed our mandate. On the contrary the land is alienated from the pomeshchiki on the basis of the Imperial rescript; to yield it in return for a guaranteed redemption is much more profitable for the nobility than to yield it for an uncertain obrok.[138]

Unkovskii's contradictory justifications of the committee's role suggest that he was uneasy about the protests from the nobility at large, which were apparently organized by dissident members of the committee.[139] In retrospect, Unkovskii insisted that most of these dissidents were no less zealous for landed emancipation than Golovachev or himself, and merely had a different point of view. He singled out three members as real antagonists, Verevkin, Kudriavtsev, and Miliukov. These were the members who went beyond debate on the provisions of the reform and denounced Unkovskii and his party, openly and secretly, for political offenses.[140]

Here, indeed was the ground on which Unkovskii was threatened. He was surrounded by men who were politically suspect; of his close associates, Evropeus and Murav'ev-Apostol were amnestied political criminals, N. A. Bakunin was the revolutionary's brother, and Golovachev was suspected of collaboration with Herzen.[141] It took no great imagination to interpret Unkovskii's forthright liberalism as constitutionalist opposition to autocracy. The government protected Unkovskii and the Tver majority, like other committees and their members, from the wrath of their constituents, but it could be expected to give attention to the political charges, as it eventually did.

By comparison, the protests against redemption of allotments, a principle that the government had approved, were merely vexing. Indeed, Unkovskii explained to the tsar, they expressed the folly of ignorance. The protests were the product of a "misunderstanding," which in turn was

a result of a lack of publicity and of false rumors, which were deliberately circulated by a few inveterate opponents of reform. I can say this positively, and say it before your Imperial Majesty, because I received irrefutable proof in the letters and public confessions of many pomeshchiki who signed the protests and [then] became convinced of their misapprehension.

If the government had not imposed bureaucratic secrecy on the provincial committees, "the truth would long since have prevailed over misapprehensions and the whole mass of the Russian nobility would be in favor of complete and immediate emancipation of the peasants with a full property right."[142]

Unkovskii's faith in publicity (glasnost') in political affairs was very great. His own experience should have convinced him, however, that "the truth"—the merits of the redemption of plowland—had more to cope with than secrecy, for many of those who protested against Unkovskii's proposals were converts who unaccountably lapsed. Novyi Torg District, which produced a paean to Unkovskii's genius in early 1858, was the first district to protest against him, and members of the Tver District Assembly who had endorsed Unkovskii's original plan joined the protest against his faction in the committee. P. I. Snazin-Tormasov was so eager for the redemption of allotments that he resigned his post as government member of the Tver Committee in protest at Lanskoi's initial ruling against redemption; presumably he was too well informed about the majority's plan to be deceived by malicious rumors, but he subsequently joined other pomeshchiki of Vyshnii Volochek District in protesting against the majority's redemption scheme and its apostacy from the nobility.[143] Finally, eight of the twelve district marshals of Tver Province, men who had heard Unkovskii's explanations and arguments from his own lips, formally protested against the majority's draft statute.[144]

There was more than ignorance and gullibility behind the opposition to redemption of allotment land. A reform of serfdom, even the limited reform outlined in the rescripts and directives of 1857, threatened many pomeshchiki in the ring of provinces around Moscow. The climate and soil in this area were poorer than farther south, and many estates, it seemed, could show a profit only because barshchina labor was cheap or because serfs paid obrok from their earnings in trade and industry. While Unkovskii's plan was advanced as a means to promote liberty and economic development, many nobles saw the redemption of plowland as a means of cashing in their chips—liquidating their estates as a form of enterprise with minimal financial loss. To those who wanted to restructure their operations and exploit the demesne with their own equipment and hired labor, redemption promised the necessary capital. Redemption offered little to those pomeshchiki who, wisely or not, wanted to continue agricultural production as before. If the opponents of redemption continued to put their hopes in traditional forms—bureaucracy, manorial power, and barshchina—perhaps they were more closely bound to manorial agriculture as a way of life than were the advocates of redemption, and so more reluctant to part with land. Kadro-Sysoev, for example, who represented the Tver minority before the Editorial Commission, was an enterprising and innovating proprietor of a barshchina estate. Unkovskii, by contrast, had a small obrok estate, while Golovachev had lost almost all his land through speculation.[145] After the emancipation both of them abandoned the countryside for journalism and other nonagricultural pursuits. They were articulate, venturesome, and optimistic about the postservile order; these qualities distinguished them from most of the nobility but also indicate that they were remote from the routine of the village and the attitudes that routine imparted to the squire.

The General Pattern

The Tver Committee was more willing than any other to take a long, affirmative stride from serfdom to a wholly different system and to challenge the cautious government standing in its way. The Nizhnii Committee was unusual for its vacillation, if not for its cupidity. Few committees labored as diligently as the Moscow majority to reconstruct serfdom under another name. All of these tendencies were present, however, in a large number of committees. Their positions lie along a spectrum with a complete surrogate for serfdom at one end and complete reimbursement for real or supposed losses at the other. Each committee made its own estimate of the feasibility of a surrogate and the likelihood of reimbursement. Since the times were uncertain, their estimate was affected by chance factors of timing or leadership, as provided by the government members, the marshal, or the governor. Often, members of one committee arrived at radically different estimates and became embroiled in the conflicts and scandals that were so vexing to the Ministry of Internal Affairs and the Main Committee.

Scandals tended to flare up and the committees to be divided in the territory of old Muscovy—the provinces in the central industrial zone and those on the divide between black soil and clay. In this area, social and economic life was comparatively diverse. This diversity quickened the nobility's political consciousness, or its anxieties, so that members of the provincial committees were more prone to challenge the authorities and one another. In the provinces beyond the Volga, in the steppe, and in New and Little Russia, the socioeconomic character of serfdom was fairly uniform, since barshchina was almost universal; the provincial committees were correspondingly harmonious. On the periphery and in the West, gubernatorial authority was traditionally strong and readily able to maintain its sway during the deliberations on the reform. The provincial committees of the West appear to have been particularly appreciative of the importance of presenting a united front. The nobles of this area, most of them Polish, knew from experience that the wind from St. Petersburg could blow harsh; the committees imposed discipline upon themselves rather than provoke, by giving way to disputes, the imposition of a stricter discipline from without.

The Ministry of Internal Affairs and the Main Committee joined in imposing bureaucratic constraints on the provincial committees. Neither of them showed any desire, however, to determine the provisions of the committees' drafts. The government intervened on three issues: the redemption of serfs, the definition of "household plot," and the redemption of plowland; neither the ministry nor the committee took the initiative on any of them. Once the policy decision was made, it was simply communicated to the committee that had provoked it. The other provinces were informed only belatedly, and at first only if the committee or the provincial governor raised the question in correspondence with the ministry. The ban on the redemption of serfs was made in August and imparted to provincial committees in November and December.[146] The ruling on the Tver committee's appeal reached a few committees in November and December in an oddly crabbed directive. Ostensibly, the directive informed the committees that the administration would not tolerate any perverse definitions of "household plot," a question the tsar had decided three of four months before, only discerning readers could interpret it as a general permission to submit redemption plans. The government did not provide a clear authority to compile redemption plans until March 1859, when all but seven of the provincial committees ought to have finished their deliberations.[147] Later still, the Main Committee discouraged redemption by indicating that the government would not be involved in the financial operation, although the tsar had already ordered that funds be set aside for this purpose.[148] There is a striking contrast between the government's imposition of bureaucratic discipline and its casual attitude to the product of the committees' deliberations.

The position of the Main Committee is comprehensible. At no time did it seek to impose official views on the provincial committees, to which it offered as much latitude as the rescripts allowed. At the same time, bureaucratic discipline on matter of form and procedures was second nature for the sanovniki; they would not tolerate a challenge to gubernatorial authority or to the rescripts, which had the tsar's sanction. More important, if most members of the committee opposed Rostovtsev's program as deeply as the reformers claimed they did, imposing discipline was a more effective form of support for the committees than offering latitude. Once Rostovtsev's program was government policy, the provincial committees were the most likely source of an alternative with a chance of enactment. And if the committees were to salvage their role and their proposals, it would be prudent for them to fulfill their promises of "loyal and dutiful" cooperation by conforming to all the guidelines and submitting to all the authorities in sight. That is what the Main Committee instructed the Vologda Committee to do. These guidelines and authorities—the directives to Ignat'ev, the April Program, the governors and marshals—were much more accommodating to the nobility's anxieties and wishes than Rostovtsev's program was likely to be. No source emanating from the sanovniki indicates that they hoped that submissive committees might generate an acceptable alternative to this emerging program. Nonetheless, they began bureaucratizing the provincial committees in earnest only after they had capitulated to Rostovtsev and been shorn of their policy-making function.

The position of the Ministry of Internal Affairs in regard to the provincial committees is harder to understand. The leading figures of the ministry may have resented Rostovtsev's role, but they agreed with the main lines of the new program. Their desire to impose bureaucratic discipline on the provincial committees followed from the consideration that the bearers of discipline were the ministry's own agents. Yet they did not impose policies along with forms and procedures; not only were they laggard about informing other committees about the rulings elicited by the committees at Nizhnii Novgorod, Moscow, and Tver, they also virtually suppressed the Imperial Order of December 4, 1858. This order was the cornerstone of the reorientation of the government's reform plan. It was omitted from a compendium of official pronouncements on the reform published by the Ministry of Internal Affairs.[149] It was not published or discussed in the ministry's journal or in the leading privately-owned journals (*The Russian Herald, The Contemporary, The Landowner's Journal, Rural Welfare*), all of which had special departments devoted to the reform. It was even omitted from a register of government edicts on the reform which the ministry distributed in July 1859.[150] Yet a provincial committee that drew up a draft statute in ignorance of the Imperial Order would be bound to contradict this authoritative formulation of policy. The reason for the ministry's reluctance to keep the committees informed on major questions of substance, while flooding them with rulings on minor matters, can be elicted from the survey of the committees' work that the ministry composed for the tsar.

Lanskoi presented the survey to Alexander in Augest 1859, when almost all the provincial committees had submitted their drafts.[151] "One must acknowledge with regret," Lanskoi reported, "that the committees's statutes do not decide the peasant question." Mastering his regret, he analyzed the committees' failings. The nobility's opinions, he found, fell into three categories. Nobles in the first category "have shown little sympathy for the emancipation of the peasants, for they are moved by the private material advantages of the pomeshchik." The minister refused to condemn these benighted squires: "Born and reared in the concepts of serfdom, they are impervious to the insistent necessity of a transformation and expect inevitable losses from it." Hence they temporized, "seeking to frighten the government with prophecies of [peasant] rebellion" and representing emancipation as a "calculated plan of democratic revolution." However, they had recovered expeditiously from their initial panic. "Finally persuaded of the impossibility of resisting the emancipation of the peasants, they now are concerned only to turn the abolition of serfdom into a profitable operation for themselves." Their means to this end were diverse or even contradictory; some would retain barshchina while others favored landless emancipation.

Nobles in the second of Lanskoi's categories were less acquisitive and emphasized the interests of the nobility as an estate. This tendency "found its adherents largely among our titled and wealthy pomeshchiki." Lanskoi ventured to press the accusation, observing that "several dignitaries in attendance upon Yourself, My Sovereign, and several members of the Main Committee" belonged in this category. These adherents of a "landed aristocracy like the English" followed the St. Petersburg Provincial Committee in striving for " 'manorial rights,' special rights which have heretofore been alien to our legislation." But their "real goal . . . quite consciously and insistently, is the emancipation of the peasants without land."

Official commentators castigated the St. Petersburg Provincial Committee for its aristocratic pretensions,[152] and historians have followed their lead. In making the insinuation, Lanskoi and his colleagues may have been responding to the manner of life or perhaps to unarticulated and private sentiments of the magnates of St. Petersburg Province, whom they had ample opportunity to observe. They were apprehensive about the influence of the St. Petersburg Provincial Committee on nobles elsewhere, who did seek landless emancipation and use the St. Petersburg Committee's terminology.[153] Deliberately or not, Lanskoi misrepresented the committee's position. It did not seek a landless emancipation; it offered the peasants permanent use of their allotments for fixed dues.[154] Its draft statute did provide for manorial authority, but the provision was eminently consistent with the rescript's "manorial police power" and may even represent an attempt to conform to the Imperial Order of December 4, 1858.[155] The notorious "manorial land rights," through which the committee was supposedly conniving at introducing feudalism into Russia, actually represented a commonplace aspiration for entrepreneurial advantage; under this heading the nobles of St. Petersburg Province sought the exclusive right, within the perimeters of their estates, to engage in such aristocratic pursuits as distilling, tavern-keeping, and conducting bazaars—but not hunting; pretentious or not, they were not eager to ride to hounds.[156] They did seek to shore up the nobility's status through a variety of entail, a matter not covered by the rescripts and not directly related to the abolition of serfdom. The problem the St. Petersburg draft statute presented to the reformers was the gap between the initial rescript and directive, to which the committee tried to adhere, and the policies the regime was now pursuing. The sovereign had changed course, but he did not like to be reminded that he had. More important, it was essential to maintain before the public that his will was unshakable. By pretending that all official edicts concerning the reform were still in force and that the tsar had not changed course, the reformers forestalled pressure upon him to change course again and abandon their program and themselves. Their expressions of outrage at the aristocratic proclivities of the St. Petersburg Provincial Committee were part of this strategy. Thus the second of Lanskoi's categories met his strategic requirements nicely; it may have corresponded to the private sentiments of influential nobles and it did anticipate the political demands that some of them would advance subsequently. As represented in his survey of provincial committees, however, the second category did not exist.

The third of Lanskoi's categories, in which he placed the Tver Committee and factions of several others, favored the "complete abolition of the pomeshchik's authority" and the redemption, on moderate terms, of some or all of the allotment land. These opinions were "the fruit of independent convictions, arduously acquired through a long and many-sided study of the subject." Naturally, then, nobles in the third category were "sympathetic to the views of the government . . . although they disagree among themselves on many particular questions." The other two groups were accused of trying to mobilize "what they call *public opinion*, in order to alter the government's policy," but Lanskoi was careful to exclude the third category from this political charge. He did not mention the demands for reform of the administration, the courts, and the censorship that often came attached to their drafts. He conceded that the advocates of the redemption of plowland represented "the most contradictory tendencies, some defending the pomeshchik's interest exclusively, others devoted to the peasant cause." Nonetheless, the "maturity of formulation, dispassion, and correctness of opinion" characteristic of the redemption plans consisted entirely, by Lanskoi's reckoning, in the generosity of their concessions to the peasants.

Lanskoi's analysis, then, was a partisan statement in behalf of the committee members who favored the redemption of plowland. More important, it was a bill of indictment against the committees that did not. Lanskoi sought to convict them, without much justice, of two unequivocal heresies: seeking landless emancipation and injecting public opinion into a questionof state. However, the indictment went further. The committees suffered from a "lack of rational knowledge of economic life and local conditions, and hence

[from] vagueness in their understanding of the matter." They were prey to "conflicting rumors from the capitals." They descended to trivial details or wandered outside their sphere, for "they did not have any firmly established plan." Finally, "in most of the drafts submitted by the Committees one cannot find a dispassionate regard for the interests of both estates, nor even a clear understanding of the pomeshchik's own advantage."

The only restraint on the retrograde and greedy nobles had been "the firm will of Your Imperial Highness," as expressed to the committees of Nizhnii and Moscow. The tsar's rebuff to these committees had been especially salutary because it brought some committees around to the redemption of plowland. Here Lanskoi was correct; the realization that there would be no compensation for the serfs themselves and that the household plots must be redeemed provided great impetus for redemption plans. Subsequent events would show, if there was any doubt, that the nobles' demands were largely determined by their sense of what the government would and would not accept. This is clear from the committees' predilection for barshchina and manorial power, which, Lanskoi maintained, proved their hostility to reform. Barshchina and manorial power were explicitly sanctioned by the initial rescripts and directives and by the April Program; Lanskoi's ministry had pressed these documents ever more insistently on the provincial committees after they had been effectively superseded by the Imperial Order of December 4. By emphasizing these elements in his survey, Lanskoi was able to produce the "statistical fact," as Cherkasskii put it, that most committees had acted "at odds or in conflict with the government's views." M. P. Pozen replied to Cherkasskii's accusation, "If that was so, it was because the government's views, as set forth for the committees, were not the views the government now holds."[157]

Indeed, most committees had not realized that His Highness's firm will had changed and hence (unless it should change again) that most elements of their draft statutes must be summarily rejected. Just before the opening of the Riazan Committee, the tsar himself had spoken of his "unalterable will" to the committee's chairman, who duly informed the members; the chairman was given to understand that the tsar's will did not extend beyond the irrevocability of allotments and the redemption of household plots. Beyond that, the tsar said, "Do whatever is best in the committee. I will agree to everything."[158] No one attempted thereafter to disabuse the chairman and the committee of the idea that they had a very broad patent.

The committees' failings had been tolerated, and therefore

encouraged, until they submitted their drafts to St. Petersburg "for confirmation." Then these failings were subjected to withering criticism by the ministry and the Editorial Commission in light of the government's revised views. Then, too, the committees were not disabused of the assumption that each was drafting a separate statute for its own province. Hence the drafts were readily indicted on another count: they "diverge in those parts that should be the same for all Russia," Lanskoi lamented, " . . . and, conversely, converge just where local differences ought to be reflected, in allotments and dues."

Most of the deficiencies that the ministry's survey found to be common in the committee drafts concerned matters on which the ministry itself and its subordinates had deliberately failed to inform the provinces. The ministry gave the committees a free hand on questions of substance in order to reduce their legislative significance to a minimum. The further the committees departed from the government's revised program, the more squarely the choice was posed between indulging the nobility and defending the autocrat's chosen policy. Hence the committees' failings were so many cards in the hand of Lanskoi and the reforming bureaucrats, who themselves set up the situation that Lanskoi reported to his sovereign with such regret.

The committees did indeed display the qualities of which Lanskoi complained: confusion, vacillation, gullibility, and cupidity. These are abstract qualities, however; a practical standard is necessary in order to assess the committees' performance, particularly on the crucial points of land and dues. N. A. Tsagolov offers a standard that divides emancipation plans into two groups; those that would make each peasant community economically independent and viable, and those that would not.[159] Tsagolov's standard casts light on the limits of the government's and the nobility's ambitions, for all the successive variants of the government's program and all the provincial committees would bind the peasants, as laborers or as renters, to the nobles' estates. Some relied on ascription or other forms of compulsion, others on carefully crafted economic pressures. The Economic Section of the Editorial Commission reproached provincial committees for offering "a quantity of land that is deliberately inadequate for the peasants' security, so as to deprive them of the means of maintaining an independent economic unit of their own in its former extent."[160] The commission's own final recommendations, however, were open to the same reproach. Tsagolov's standard, then, is little help in differentiating among the plans that were current within the government and the nobility. The same may be said of Ianson's standard, which has been used by some historians.[161] Ianson calculated the minimum allotment necesssary to support a peasant household in the postreform period in different areas of Russia. Unfortunately, few peasant households ever held Ianson's minimum either before or after the abolition of serfdom, which vitiates the utility, if not the accuracy, of his norms.

Kornilov, in his study of the provincial committees, uses a flexible standard. He compares the proposals of the committees with the proposals of the Editorial Commission for the province in question. This is not an ahistorical or speculative standard, but it produces the same result as Tsagolov's and Ianson's: all the committees offered less land for higher dues than the Editorial Commission. Kornilov concluded that the committees, including most minorities, were myopic and greedy. This conclusion recalls the accusations made in Lanskoi's survey, and indeed, many of Kornilov's judgments are borrowed from this survey.[162] The affinity is natural because, despite Kornilov's explicit criticism of the survey, the standard is essentially the same.[163]. Both Lanskoi and Kornilov judged the provincial committees in the light of the government's policy as of mid-1859. This standard was not available to the committees. When men make decisions, they must find their parameters in the past and present. For the members of the provincial committees, the parameters were their own experience of serfdom; their expectations about the economy, the society, and the peasantry; their interpretation of various orders and directives; and their sense of the character of the government. It is little wonder, then, that the confusion and apprehension evoked by the government's commitment to reform was not dispelled. As the Penza Provincial Committee confessed, "Amidst the fog of situations and conflicts yet to come, it is difficult to determine in advance precisely where and just when this great transition can be accomplished safely and with impunity."[164]

Even for a committee with a clear and optimistic view of the great transition, neither experience nor official edicts provided a certain answer to the simple question of the committees' function. When they set a figure for dues and allotments, were they legislating, petitioning, or negotiating? The norms for dues and allotments set by the Moscow Committee were meant to be so onerous as to permit the pomeshchik to retain his present arrangements by agreement with the peasantry. Many committees assumed, as the April Program seemed to indicate, that their drafts would apply only to the transitional period of temporary obligation. And apart from all considerations about the meaning of the committee's norms, the adequacy of any level of obrok or barshchina depended on a variety of unknowns—the pomeshchik's own authority, the structure and attitude of local authorities, and the reaction of the peasants. To cite an extreme example, the Pskov Committee voted that civil rights were granted to the peasants contigent upon their rendering barshchina to the same extent as under serfdom. Even this resolution was too much for one member, who complained that "the nobility had not provided him with the authority to renounce their right to the serf's person."[165]

Fearful of the hostility of the government and the peasantry, uncertain of the future and the very ground they stood on, the committees were prone to vacillation and contradiction, as Lanskoi and later commentators observed. The Samara Committee, for example, began its deliberations with a general resolution in behalf of civil liberties for the peasantry, but then rejected a series of specific proposals that necessarily followed from the general resolution.[166] Nor was the Nizhnii Committee the only one to reverse its course in mid-passage. The Khar'kov Committee began with the intention of forestalling change. A few months later it turned around and came out for a short period of temporary obligation, the abolition of barshchina, and the compulsory redemption of a small allotment. The exponents of caution were reduced to complaining of their mistreatment by the new majority and by the governor, who compelled them to sign the majority draft, which they opposed.[167]

In the neighboring province of Chernigov, the provincial committee attempted a similar reversal of field, but there the governor intervened *against* the advocates of redemption of allotments, procuring their defeat and preventing the reversal from taking effect. When the Chernigov Provincial Committee assembled in a final, formal session to endorse the text of the draft statute, the advocates of redemption managed to convert enough waverers to stage a coup; the committee now rejected the completed draft and replaced its chairman and Editorial Subcommittee. At this point, the governor called the committee out of its meeting room and crushed the coup with a mixture of official pressure and avuncular advice. After threatening to shut the committee down and inform the tsar that it had engaged in "rebellion," he then, speaking "as a nobleman of your province," exhorted the members, "Bethink yourselves, and do not let a matter of personalities besmirch the nobility's cause." The members duly endorsed the draft statute they had just rejected.

To Pokorskii-Zhoravko, a member of the briefly ousted Editorial Subcommittee, this "indescribable farce" disgraced the Chernigov nobility before Russia and all Europe. The Chernigov Committee had behaved like a "mob," which gladly goes to watch the convulsions of an innocent man being hanged. [A] mob, and what is worse still, a mob of nobles. A holy and vital question was scorned for the sake of stupid interests, to suit the momentary caprices of idiots.[168]

Pokorskii-Zhoravko was stern in his judgment, but he, too, was prey to the kind of vacillation and uncertainty that produced the inglorious finale. He held that the redemption of allotment land—the issue on which the Chernigov and Khar'kov committees had divided—was "perhaps the only possible means of reconciling various incongruities and avoiding losses" for the peasantry and the nobility. His provincial committee, however, had no warrant to incorporate the concept into its draft statute because it was "a measure of state"; if the government intended the permission it had given to the Tver Committee to apply to other provinces, it would have stated so plainly.[169] Notwithstanding, Pokorskii-Zhoravko was well pleased with the Chernigov draft; as he finished drawing up the last chapter, just before the final session, he was moved to apostrophize his handiwork, a labor of love for a million of his countrymen. They, blinded by petty material interests, would not see it for the grand design of truth and justice it was; indeed, they would "throw stones of condemnation at me." But, having functioned as the "instrument of Providence," he could deliver the draft to posterity in prayerful serenity. He was prepared to defend his creation by any means, "not halting before the play of passions, and exploiting even . . . the pitiful vanity of those who do not understand thee [the draft] aright." When the play of passions broke out in earnest, however, and it was his fellow members who reached for the stones of condemnation, Pokorskii-Zhoravko explained his role more succinctly and quite differently: "I will salvage, if not the nobility's honor, then at least its profits and its existence."[170] Under challenge, the instrument of Providence became the nobility's trustee in bankruptcy. Pokorskii-Zhoravko was a conscientious member of his committee and regarded himself as the leader of the practical abolitionists on it, standing betwween the self-seeking extremes, the die-hards and the windy liberals. For all his rhetorical excesses, his experience was common; many committees and many of their members underwent wild swings of exultation, alarm, frustration, uncertainty and dismay. Under the circumstances, their vacillation and inconsistency are perfectly understandable.

There remains the matter of selfishness, or, as Lanskoi put it, the lack of "a dispassionate regard for the interests of both estates"; apparently the committees did not, after all, behave like "deliberative agencies of a collegial composition." The problem lies not in the committee's selfishness but in the minister's expressed surprise. It is taken for granted in most societies that the elected members of a deliberative body will reflect the prejudices and defend the interests of the electorate. As the deliberative body acquires tradition, the expression of interest becomess less blatant; rhetoric becomes smoother and the members learn to keep their demands within the range of the possible. A Scottish M.P. will emphasize his concern that the workers of the Midlands be warmly and fashionably dressed, he will speak persuasively of the national economy as a whole; he will not demand a prohibitive tariff on woolen imports, and he may indicate his approval of the principle of free trade; but he will defend the interests of his sheep-raising constituents as best he can.

The members of the provincial committees tried to defend their constituents' interests, but in a very different context. There was no tradition at all for their institution, and the issues before them were new. In most committees, no voice was raised in behalf of a contrary interest, unless the state's interest should be so conceived. The times were uncertain, the future was more so. Only serfdom itself provided any guidelines, and the government was pledged to destroy it. There was no check on the nobility's demands, and they were usually extravagant; the expression of interest was as raw as the institution in which it was expressed.

Whether the nobles were stupid as well, and lacked "a clear understanding of the pomeshchik's own advantage," is a different question. Events would show, even before emancipation was proclaimed, that under many circumstances barshchina and manorial power would be unworkable. If nobles were foolish in seeking to preserve them, this was a folly from which the government had only recently and partially recovered. If they were foolish in setting high prices on small quantities of land, the Statutes of February 19, 1861 display the same folly, to a lesser degree, but without the excuse that the figures might be modified by a higher and unsympathetic agency. The statutes are the ancestor of the famine of 1891 and the manifesto of 1905 by which the state wrote off two-thirds of the redemption payments, uncollected and uncollectable. Finally, while the statutes of 1861 were far from the demands and the desires of most pomeshchiki, it is doubtful that the provincial committees would have had more influence if they had expressed their interests with more sophistication and moderation. The committees' position was radically changed by the adoption of Rostovtsev's program, even though it was enacted with imperfect consistency. Armed with a program of its own and a wealth of data and supplementary proposals, the autocracy recovered its equilibrium. It did not and would not cease to patronize the nobility, but it was quick to curtail the principle embodied in the committees, which were an anomaly in the political structure. The tsarist regime would never adopt Nikolai Miliutin's maxim, "Everything for the people, nothing by the people," but if "nobility" is substituted for "people," the maxim expresses the regime's attitude towards the noble estate.[171]

The deputies elected by the provincial committees (whose arrival in St. Petersburg was the pretext for Lanskoi's survey) saw the regime's attitude in another light. They did not think the emerging reform legislation met the nobility's interests, and they were dismayed that the government was not relying on the nobility, as represented by themselves, to compile the legislation. Before discussing the deputies, however, it is necessary to follow the progress of the Editorial Commission, which was the target of their outrage and the agency that was compiling the emancipation legislation.

The Editorial Commission

6

The policies and procedures of the Editorial Commission were largely determined by its chairman, General Rostovtsev. By early 1859, Rostovtsev was determined to cut all the ties that bound serf to lord, and had worked out a systematic program to that end. He proposed to eliminate the pomeshchik's administrative authority over the peasants by substituting village self-administration for manorial authority. He would curtail the peasants' economic dependence on the pomeshchik by having them redeem their present allotments; the improvement of their situation would be assured by setting the redemption payments no higher than their present dues. According to this system, squire and ex-serf would meet as fellow citizens—as employer and employee, perhaps, or lessor and tenant—but without any obligatory element in the relationship. The policy statements Rostovtsev had produced in the previous six months, in which he outlined this system, consisted of general principles. The primary task before the commission was the refinement and application of these principles, through an infinite number of practical decisions, so as to transform them into statutes. By virtue of the opposition of most officials and most nobles to these principles, the commission had a further task. The citadel of reform had to be defended while it was under construction, and there were Trojan horses within the citadel itself. Indeed, it was not at first clear who the devious Greeks were, and who the Trojan soldiers, for Rostovtsev made both errors of judgment and concessions in his appointments to the commission. The struggle for his program had to begin within his own commission, or so he believed; this struggle against opposition, to which the latter part of this chapter is devoted, was the commission's other primary task.

The Editorial Commission had thirty-eight members, of whom fewer than thirty took an active part in its work.[1] Half the members represented ministries and departments. Rostovtsev himself, assisted by his young confidant Petr Semenov, chose many of these departmental members. He recruited all the prominent abolitionists serving in the bureaucracy. Apart from Ia. A. Solov'ev, head of the Civil Division, and S. M. Zhukovskii, Chief of the Chancellory of the Main Committee, who both served ex officio, Rostovtsev secured the appointment of Nikolai Miliutin, acting Deputy Minister of Internal Affairs; A. D. Zablotskii-Desiatovskii, Kiselev's leading disciple; and less prominent officials who shared their views: Lamanskii, Kachalov, Liuboshchinskii, and A. K. Giers. However, some of the departmental members, such as V. I. Bulygin of the Ministry of State Properties and N. P. Semenov of the Ministry of Justice, were appointed out of deference to their superiors. They could be expected to follow Rostovtsev's lead, but only so long as their superiors thought it prudent to do so.

The so-called expert members, who comprised the balance of the membership, were not accountable to official superiors, and would have to be won around to Rostovtsev's program, if they did not already favor it. The experts were selected to provide balanced representation for the major economic regions, with the obvious purpose of stealing a march on the elected deputies. Some, like Bunge, an economist and future Minister of Finance, Zheltukhin, editor of the *Landowners' Journal*, and the financial wizard Pozen,[2] were chosen for their position or specialized knowledge. A. P. Bulgakov was chosen because the presence of the chief of the army commissariat ought to discourage the widespread notion that landed emancipation would leave the cities and the military forces without bread.

Rostovtsev also appointed seven expert members from the provincial committees, recommended by Petr Semenov.[3] Among these were Prince Cherkaskii and Iurii Samarin, who would, with Miliutin and Petr Semenov, be the most influential members. The other members appointed from provincial committees proved passive and acquiescent in the bureaucratic setting; one of them recalled that he kept quiet and "always submitted to the *vozhaki*," or bosses.[4] A. N. Tatarinov of the Simbirsk Committee did turn out to be an amiable and unsystematic dissident; he was persuaded to leave the commission for the sake of his health. He had the distinction, unique among these seven members, of having been elected to a provincial committee.[5] The others had been government members and all seven, including Tatarinov, had been minority members of their committees. The experts from the provinces were scarcely representative of the nobility at large.

Rostovtsev wanted cooperative expert members, and rejected three of Semenov's nominees because he thought they would be disruptive. He rejected the provincial marshals of St. Petersburg and Tver, for P. P. Shuvalov was an influential opponent of redemption while Unkovskii was an "ardent and immoderate political agitator." Koshelev was also turned down, to his bitter disappointment, because a man who had made a fortune in the liquor trade did not have the spotless reputation Rostovtsev demanded.[6]

Four additional experts were to be appointed from the western provinces. They proved to be systematically dissident, but they did not join the Editorial Commission until the General Commissions in Kiev and Vilna had finished their work. It would be three Great Russian members, appointed at the tsar's suggestion, who took the lead in dissent. Encountering Rostovtsev at a ball, the tsar complained that none of the expert members was a great landed proprietor. Rostovtsev replied that magnates were not usually rich in expertise, but after an impromptu consultation with Miliutin, he suggested three great proprietors present at the ball—Shuvalov, V. V. Apraksin, and Prince Paskevich. Alexander demurred at Paskevich:

Of course, he is a great landowner and a good pomeshchik but I don't know of any kind of work at which he would be useful to you. It would be better if you took another of my former adjutants, Prince Golitsyn . . . I think he will be more capable at the work that lies ahead of you.

Confusion followed. Rostovtsev picked the wrong Prince Golitsyn, Sergei Pavlovich, author of a curious homily to the peasants on the impending emancipation. No damage was done, since the capable Golitsyn, who was duly appointed when the error came to light, never attended a session of the commission. Also, the tsar, fearing that Paskevich would hear of his sovereign's opinion and take offense, decided to spare his feelings by appointing him, too, saying, "I hope he won't do you any harm."[7] Decked out with his titles, Adjutant-General Count F. I. Paskevich of Erivan, Prince of Warsaw, sounded bellicose. However, it was his father who had conquered Erivan and Warsaw, and the son did not, indeed, do any

harm on his own account. He was content to play esquire to the
nobility's champion, Shuvalov.

As marshal of the nobility of St. Petersburg Province, Count Petr
Pavlovich Shuvalov was the nobility's natural leader in the present
crisis. He duly took up this role, and established an active
correspondence with marshals all over Russia.[8] His house in St.
Petersburg would be the gathering place for both convocations of
deputies from the provincial committees. He himself had been
elected a deputy; now, thanks to the tsar's intervention, he could
exploit a combined role as deputy and member of the commission.
Rostovtsev's initial refusal to appoint him is understandable, for
the draft statute of the St. Petersburg Committee, over which
Shuvalov presided, had little in common with Rostovtsev's
program. Apart from his double role in the commission, Shuvalov
was in an ideal position to coordinate the opposition to that
program among the Poles, the Russian nobility, and the sanovniki.
He had estates in both Great Russian and western provinces, an
influential position at the tsar's court, and close ties with the upper
bureaucracy. Semenov suggested, many years later, that Shuvalov
was thrust into the leadership of the opposition by a band of highly
placed conspirators.[9] No covert conspiracy has come to light, but
the theory that Shuvalov was a reluctant leader does explain his
ineptitude.

The Development of Rostovtsev's Program

The Editorial Commission began its work in March of 1859.
After attending his first session, Tatarinov reported that the
proceedings were informal and friendly, but he felt "a certain sense
of oppression before the authority of the chairman."[10] Tatarinov
guessed that everything would be done as Rostovtsev wished, and
indeed the chairman soon made it plain that he would determine
the commission's line of march. He thoughtfully provided each
member with a collection of his writings and began the first
working session by reading the latest formulation of his views, a
twelve-point memorandum. When these points elicited no
objections, Rostovtsev formally instructed every member "to state
his convictions frankly, even if they diverged in any respect from
his [Rostovtsev's] ideas."[11] However, the members who did state
divergent opinions in the early sessions did not find the chairman
sympathetic. When he was reproached for pushing the commission
outside its proper jurisdiction, Rostovtsev replied that he was
acting with the authorization of the tsar, who had read the
commission's first journals with enthusiasm. Two sessions later
when the commission examined the first of its own preliminary

reports, Rostovtsev found that it did not incorporate certain of his own ideas. The author of the report, A. K. Giers, was one of Lanskoi's subordinates and no opponent of Rostovtsev's, but he ventured to suggest that Rostovtsev's writings were merely expressions of opinion. Rostovtsev explained, "I propose that the Sections [of the commission] should reflect on the most suitable means for incorporating my ideas into the reports, so that these ideas lie at the basis of the work of the Section."[12]

The matter could not rest there. Rostovtsev convened a special meeting of the most influential members and read aloud yet another memorandum, which should serve "to bring the activities of the Sections of the Commission into accord, so that they will have one common program." He would not, of course, impose any "*a priori*, that is, theoretical" restrictions on the sections, nor would he simply cast aside the rescripts and other early statements of official policy. "I would like," he said, "to uphold all past actions concerning the peasantry, simply supplementing and altering them where necessary, but without annulling them. If mistakes have been made, I would like to correct them imperceptibly . . . so that we can remain faithful to the government's word." This process of imperceptible correction was well under way. The tsar had read Rostovtsev's latest memorandum, the supplement to "The Course and Outcome of the Peasant Question," and noted, "The main principles are in complete accord with my thinking." Since the tsar had also approved Rostovtsev's latest pronouncement on "temporary obligation," or the transition from serfdom, this pronouncement would be entered in the Journal of the Editorial Commission even over the objections of the members. "In such instances I shall act like a despot," the chairman acknowledged, for the commission must defer to the tsar's wishes.[13] It was easy for Rostovtsev to take an attitude of loyal submission, since the tsar's wishes were apparently at his disposal. Henceforward, none of the key members offered a direct challenge to the thoughts of chairman Iakov Ivanovich.

Since the commission must adhere to Rostovtsev's ideas and also maintain a semblance of conformity to "all past actions," such as the rescripts and the April Program, the draft statutes composed by the provincial committees had to be consigned to a sorry third place. The commission's ostensible function, however, was simply the collation and codification of these drafts; to ignore them entirely would be tactless and foolhardy, for Rostovtsev explained that the tsar "wishes to remain faithful to his original idea [that] the peasants' freedom must proceed from the pomeshchiki, as specified in the rescripts."[14]

It was the subdivisions of the Editorial Commission that had to cope with the provincial drafts in the first instance, and they discovered a suitable procedure. The commission was divided into the Economic, Legal, and Administrative sections and the Financial Commission (which dealt with the fiscal aspects of redemption). The sections, sitting separately, produced a series of reports covering the major aspects of the reform, such as the pomeshchik's property rights, the responsibilities of village officials, and the maximum size of allotments. Each report began with a survey of the proposals of the provincial committees that were relevant to the subject of the report. The survey would be followed by a summary of the comments, almost invariably devastating, that provincial governors, officials of the Ministry of Internal Affairs, or Rostovtsev himself might have made on these proposals. The report would then dismiss certain proposals as incompatible with one of the government's obligatory criteria and show the rest to be incompatible with one another. Having established the hopeless diversity of opinion among the nobility, the report would offer a solution, in the form of a series of numbered conclusions, to the problem at issue. Rostovtsev cleared each report before it was printed and brought before a full session of the commission. Here the conclusions would be read aloud, discussed, and usually ratified with minor changes or with none.

The Economic Section was particularly caustic about the proposals of the provincial committees, while the Administrative Section treated them with some respect, but all the reports from all the sections emphasized the diversity among the committees, for this diversity was the pretext for the commission to make its own disposition. For example, the report on manorial authority fragmented the committees' proposals, presenting separately each grant or limitation of power and singling out those committees that would deny the pomeschik the role of "chief of the village community" (nachal'nik obshchestva).[15] The fact remains that thirty-five majorities and nine minorities proclaimed the pomeshchik "chief of the village community" and endowed him with broad police power.[16] Indeed, all committees were obliged to do so by the rescript and the April Program; only in the Imperial Order of December 4 did the government maintain that the pomeshchik should have no power over the individual peasant.

The members of the commission had few misgivings about ignoring the provincial drafts. Pozen was the only member who seriously sought to defend the legislative prerogatives of the provincial committees, and he took this position belatedly, once he saw he could no longer influence Rostovtsev. When Panin, in the later stages of the commission's work, complained that it would be dangerous to release household serfs from compulsory service only two years after emancipation was proclaimed, Miliutin defended the commission's two-year limit, saying, "After all, we didn't invent this [term], for two committees voted for it."[17] Miliutin had no qualms about the other sixty drafts that provided for a longer term. Miliutin, to be sure, was a life-long bureaucrat, but the expert members, who were not bureaucrats, generally shared his point of view. Prince Cherkasskii, for example, in defending the commission's proposal that pomeshchiki must provide their ex-serfs with fuel, conceded that no majority of any committee had made such a proposal. However, he argued that the commission must be attentive to the unspoken thoughts of the provincial committees; as a member of the Tula Committee, he had suppressed his private inclinations and assented to a niggardly allotment "to achieve accord" with other members. Zheltukhin then reproached him for neglecting "the general spirit and tendency" of the separate drafts, which "in some cases, perhaps, are not clearly expressed, but they by no means want what you attribute to them." Cherkasskii replied, "I set forth what is explicit, but I cannot sort out the premises of ideas."[18]

The commission followed Cherkasskii in being solicitious of unspoken thoughts and causal about the general tendency of the committees' proposals. Rostovtsev himself restrained his subordinates, complaining that some reports were ostentatiously contemptuous of the provincial drafts. Overruling the majority, he held that the drafts must be collated in three separate compilations, each according to a different system, so that no idea emanating from any committee could slip by without consideration. He also ordered that specific proposals to be found in Russian and foreign journals, including The Bell, and in memoranda submitted to the government, should be studied and collated.[19] Finally, he privately canvassed various pomeshchiki of his acquaintance, sending them the proceedings of his commission and asking for their comments.[20]

To most members of the commission, Rostovtsev's solicitude was rather silly.[21] Indeed, he was casting a wide net while jealously guarding his own catch, which was an awkward but appropriate stance. He was used to imposing discipline, but he did not have the self-assurance on questions of substance that came naturally to most of his colleagues on the commission, who were bureaucrats or intellectual pomeshchiki. He had recently adopted a definite program of reform, but he knew that the solutions he favored entailed many difficulties and provoked much opposition; while he moved aggressively against opponents, he was receptive to suggestions that might minimize difficulties and opposition. In his combination of rigidity and receptivity, Rostovtsev retained something of the spirit in which the government had undertaken the reform two years before, for he continued, even while imposing his program on others, to hope for a magic formula that would reconcile irreconcilable conflicts of principles and interests.

Rostovtsev was steadfast on matters of principle and would tolerate no opposition, but he observed a nice distinction between principles and their application. In the forty-fourth General Session of the Editorial Commission, Solov'ev presented the fifteenth report of the Economic Section, which prescribed the maximum and minimum statutory allotment for each district. Rostovtsev praised the report as "marvellously and very conscientiously drawn up," but he was not yet prepared to take on the responsibility of determining allotments or to allow his commission to do so: "I frankly admit that I do not understand this and cannot judge. This is entirely a matter for the deputies." At length he permitted discussion of the report, but despite the objections of Solov'ev and others, he would not allow the commission to confirm it. Instead, "having given it preliminary approval," the commission undertook to hear out the opinions of both groups of deputies "before giving it final confirmation."[22] Yet, unless all the government's promises from the rescripts onward were to be forgotten, the size of the allotments was the most important part of the reform. Rostovtsev and the commission upheld the principle that the peasants should receive their present allotments, provided they fell within a statutory maximum and minimum for each area. This principle could be entirely vitiated by the reduction of the maximum. And while the commission, despite Rostovtsev's remark, did not leave it to the deputies to set the figures, it was vitiated for many villages by the statutes of 1861.

The application of Rostovtsev's principles was a considerable task. The men who undertook it were reviled as socialists and rabid enemies of the nobility. Even Nikolai Semenov, a member of the commission whose brother was Rostovtsev's closest collaborator, was prone to grumble about the cabal of Cherkasskii, Samarin, and Miliutin. In the midst of a debate on a minor point, the pomeshchik's right to sand and stone on allotment land, he burst out,

Why is it that you always think so ill of the pomeshchiki? Whence this hatred for them? . . . Is there any basis whatsoever for supposing that the pomeshchik will . . . but himself in a hostile relationship with [the peasants] at the very time when the peasants will be absolutely independent of him, and when, all the same, he will not be able to get along without them?[23]

The accusation of prejudice against the nobility, directed first of all against Cherkasskii, was unjust. Cherkasskii was trying to adhere to what he conceived to be the golden mean. After the first session of the Economic Section, he wrote to Samarin urging him to hurry and take his place in the commission, for

it will be too hard for me to cope by myself, for here I am obliged to argue very, very much. It will be hard to keep to the golden mean. On some questions, it seems, they want to go too far, on others, especially redemption, they want to renounce absolutely everything that has been said so far.

Two weeks later he wrote again: "Your presence is *essential*; at present, the heaviest and most thankless burden falls to me alone—now to defend sensible advantages for the nobility against one side, now to argue about allotments with the other."[24]

In time, Cherkasskii came to realize that his colleagues from the bureaucracy were not systematically opposed to "sensible advantages for the nobility," but they had criteria of their own—centralization, regulation, consistency, and caution. Soon they reached an understanding with Cherkasskii and other expert members, and together they developed Rostovtsev's principles. Both sides, the pomeshchiki and the bureaucrats, cut into the original program, and it is clear that Rostvtsev yielded to his erudite collaborators as he would not to his supposed antagonists.

This process of development and practical application emerges from a comparison of two texts: the twelve-point formulation that Rostovtsev read to the second general session of the commission and the nine-point revision published in the commission's Journal for that session.[25] Miliutin and Rostovtsev's other collaborators labored over the revision for some time. First of all, they smoothed out the forthright language of the original and described the objectives of the reform more guardedly. Rostovtsev had written that pomeshchiki should be compensated for redeemed land "justly, insofar as possible, without losses and without ruination"; in the official version, the equivocation and the equally alarming allusion to the nobility's fear of ruin were removed, but so was the assurance that the pomeshchiki would suffer no losses. Similarly, the official version toned down Rostovtsev's promise of government participation in the redemption process and did not commit the government's credit. Rostovtsev's rejection of the separate redemption of household plots was reworked into a bland observation that separate redemption "no longer presents the essential importance" it had before the Imperial Order of December

4. After all, separate redemption was one of the compulsory elements of the original rescripts. It could not simply be dismissed as Rostovtsev had done, as "a dangerous . . . half-measure, which will not achieve its purpose," espeically since "the peasant . . . will not understand what he is paying for."

Finally, Rostovtsev's text held, "Simultaneously with personal emancipation, the peasants should receive a full option to acquire as property an amount of land adequate to secure their way of life and osedlost'; otherwise, amelioration of their way of life would be only a word, not a fact." Rostovtsev had been made to understand that compulsory redemption of allotment land was not considered feasible, but all he had done was avoid the word "compulsory." His collaborators reworked this passage to bring it into line with official policy; the peasants should be able to acquire land from the pomeshchiki "by free agreement with them." However, the revision did provide for a truly free agreement: the peasants could not be compelled to redeem their allotments. (Later on, the commission inserted a provision for redemption at the unilateral demand of the pomeshchik, on the ground that he was entitled to a capital sum since he could not increase the peasants' statutory dues.)[26]

These revisions were dictated by bureaucratic caution, but the practical knowledge of Rostovtsev's pomeshchik collaborators also penetrated the revised text. For example, where Rostovtsev's original held that the peasants should receive "an adequate . . . amount of land," the official text was more specific, adding that this land "should consist of a *consolidated tract of both household plots and fields, with other necessary resources*"—presumably hayfields, pasture, watering places, and woodlots. This was an important addition. The statutes of 1861 would leave many peasants at the mercy of the pomeshchik because he retained his full title to these "other resources," which were absolutely necessary to the peasants since they were bound to their plots and allotments.[27] On other points, a practical accommodation to the imperfect world of the village corresponded to the prejudices, if not the interests, of the nobility. Rostovtsev's text condemned barshchina unequivocally as "incompatible with the generous intentions of the Sovereign" and "still more unbearable for the peasant" after the reform since then it would be "serfdom clothed in legal forms"; he held out the hope that the commission could "do without it altogether." The official text conceded, that

compulsory barshchina dues even during temporary obligation, will all the same constitute an aspect of serfdom, but serfdom subjected to legal regulation. Therefore they cannot but be onerous for the peasants, while they can become a source of serious difficulties for the pomeshchiki and the Government. . . . If the Commission can manage to shorten [their] term or moderate [their] effect, then amelioration can be consolidated even during the period of temporary obligation.

Since barshchina could not be eliminated at once, it should not be unequivocally condemned.

Both versions express the same general goal for the reform, the redemption of land by the peasants, with government assistance, at a rate close to the present level of obrok. However, the official version was more accommodating to the traditions of the bureaucracy and the village, especially the needs of the pomeshchik. This accommodation went so far as to encroach on the domain of principle.

As the commission worked out the details of the reform the pattern of accomodation continued. Barshchina, for example, could not be abolished at once, and, it was thought to be unworkable without manorial power. Nonetheless, the first report of the Legal Section provided for the abolition of "the right to subject [the peasants[to exactions and punishments." Iurii Samarin objected when the report was brought to the floor, arguing that the barshchina proprietor, like an employer of labor, should have this right. Samarin was seconded by Pozen, who would extend the right to obrok proprietors as well. Rostovtsev recalled that, according to the Imperial Order he had sponsored, the pomeshchik could not deal with the peasants except through the commune. Samarin did not challenge this dictum, but argued for a "close and direct relationship to the pomeshchik." Rostovtsev stilled the controversy by offering a verbal change, but the issue was unresolved.[28] Samarin raised it again later, when Rostovtsev was no longer well enough to preside. He reminded the commission that barshchina peasants would be free to shift to obrok; they would be encouraged to make this desirable change by the pomeshchik's use, within legal norms, of summary punishment. Also, it was necessary to provide some recourse for the pomeshchik, since the allotments constituted payment in advance for his barshchina laborers.

It is not our concern that the peasants be reassured that they don't have to render their dues, and that there will not be any constraint to this end; the result would be the ruin of the pomeshchik, while the peasants, reluctant to abandon their carefree existence, would serenely continue to remain on barshchina.

Cherkasskii sided with Samarin, arguing that corporal punishment would be effective even when entire villages were malingering. "Today you order that Ivan be punished, tomorrow it's Peter's turn, then the others, and so you run through them all, if that is necessary. It's impossible to work against them all in any other way."

Solov'ev continued to oppose "unlimited punishment without trial." He argued that "we cannot enact just what the nobles themselves renounce," for only eight provincial drafts had provided the pomeshchik with the power of punishment and exaction Samarin demanded. It was unusual for Solov'ev to fall back on the committee drafts, and Tatarinov correctly observed that the power in question was subsumed in most drafts under the title "chief of the village community." Solov'ev himself made it clear he was not quibbling about the rights of the provincial committees, for,

I am saying, all this with a view to protecting the peasants. . . . Many *pomeshchiki*, in their annoyance at emancipation, will send them to be punished every day; the cantonal administration or the police, if they are obliged to punish with the birch, must become butchers, carrying out the lawless fantasies of the pomeshchik.

Clearly, the chief of the Civil Division had a lower opinion of the noble estate than did Samarin and other expert members from the provinces. He also had problems of bureaucratic personnel in mind. "What decent man," he asked, "would consent to undertake the function of dispenser of punishments?" The pomeshchik's right to impose punishments and exactions was put to a vote, which ended in a tie, broken in Samarin's favor by the acting chairman, Bulgakov. Only one expert member sided with Solov'ev; Miliutin and two other departmental members joined Samarin, Cherkasskii, and the rest of the experts in favor of giving the pomeshchik the "sensible advantage" of summary punishment.[29]

G. P. Galagan was somewhat confused by the debate, announcing at one point, "I entirely agree with Iurii Fedorovich [Samarin] and Iakov Aleksandrovich [Solov'ev]," but he voted with Samarin and the other expert members. Three days later, he wrote with a mixture of pleasure and dismay about the commission's recent reaction in favor of the pomeshchik, citing the vote on barshchina punishments as an example. In the early sessions, he recalled, Cherkasskii and Samarin had swept all before them with their theory of the peasant's right to his land; the commission had gone to extremes and so given arms to its enemies. But now, Galagan reported, Cherkasskii and Samarin had split with Solov'ev and the other *biurokraty* who indiscriminately defended the peasant interest. Galagan was pleased that "we have won a victory over the theoreticians," but still wondered if summary corporal punishment was compatible with freedom.[30]

There was a real basis for Galagan's misgivings, but once the commission accepted barshchina, however reluctantly, barshchina began to claim its own. At least it was possible to keep it within decent limits. In its twelfth report, the Economic Section proposed to limit barshchina to two days in each week, and the commission endorsed this proposal, eighteen to seven. Only a few habitual dissidents, unexpectedly joined by Petr Semenov, opposed this ceiling.[31] Six months later, however, when the twelfth report was brought back to the General Session for final consideration, the ceiling had been quietly dropped. The Economic Section substituted a provision that no more than three-fifths of the annual total of barshchina days could be exacted in the summer.[32] The revised report prompted Solov'ev to observe that "according to our formulations, barshchina will be worse than before." Even Nikolai Milliutin complained that the report permitted barshchina beyond the present legal limit of three days a week. Galagan conceded the point: "Yes, we simply stated frankly what was not stated before, that is, that they [the pomeshchiki] never took three days, but much more than we now propose." Miliutin replied that an illegal abuse was of no account in setting statutory norms. Galagan defended the new norm on the ground that it was linked to a statutory norm for allotments, which was absent from the existing law. Since the existing law was unenforceable, he added (speaking not as a legislator but as a pomeshchik), "I did as I liked." Hence "our statutes significantly alleviate the peasants' lot compared to what it was in reality."[33]

Petr Semenov agreed. Since the barshchina maximum to which Miliutin objected would correspond to a maximum allotment, and since the commission would abolish various supplementary dues, amelioration was assured. Miliutin clung to his objections and to the necessity of reducing three-day barshchina. He was not moved by Galagan's confession that he gave as little land as he liked, for "it's irrelevant for us how much land the pomeshchik gave. Where he gave little, that was inhuman, and it was an abuse of the proprietary authority." Semenov professed amazement, asking, "How can what was not forbidden by law be considered an abuse?"

Semenov's position was hard; the report under challenge was the result of a hard-won compromise within the Economic Section, and Miliutin's attack was unexpected. Usually, Miliutin joined Cherkasskii, Samarin, and Semenov himself in establishing the line

of policy from which the "theoreticians," like Solov'ev and
Zablotskii-Desiatovskii, and the avowed spokesmen for the
pomeshchiki, like Aprasksin and Pozen, dissented in vain.
Rostovtsev had acknowledged Miliutin's crucial role, saying, "I do
not want to hamper you, you are like the nymph Egeria for us."[34]
This time, however, Miliutin dissented, even when Semenov,
trying to forestall a vote, stated that Rostovtsev favored the report,
whatever the majority might think. The majority, by a vote of
thirteen to six, agreed with the absent chairman. Miliutin and four
"theoreticians" were unexpectedly joined in the minority by
Shuvalov, who explained that he continued to oppose the
commission's entire system and voted against the new barshchina
norm as a "mistake within a mistake."[35]

The new barshchina norm, like the provision for summary
punishment, was added during the period when, as Galagan
correctly noted, the commission underwent a reaction in favor of
the nobility. This period, beginning with the departure of the first
group of deputies and the illness of Rostovtsev, and ending with
Rostovtsev's death and the chairmanship of Panin, does stand
apart. Samarin and Cherkasskii and the other expert members
advocated the nobility's interests more intently and frankly than
they would before or after; the reforming bureaucrats, temporarily
isolated, faced personal attacks. However, this period was simply
the most dramatic phase of the commission's general tendency,
which emerges from its basic decisions on allotments and dues.

The retention of the existing allotments was a crucial element of
Rostovtsev's program; allotments could be reduced only as part of a
mutual agreement on the terms of redemption, and reduced only to
the level of a statutory norm. This was a generous or even radical
premise. The emancipation settlement has been criticized for
perpetuating the economic characteristics of serfdom, including
the peasants' poverty.[36] However, most provincial committees and
other participants in the debate over the emancipation legislation
advocated giving the peasants much less than their present
allotments.

Not even the Economic Section of the Editorial Commission
would go as far as Rostovtsev. In its first report, it accepted the
existing allotment as a criterion, but added qualifications. The
peasants would receive their present allotments provided they fell
within a statutory maximum and minimum for each area. In the
abstract, this was simply a levelling device, which would give land
to the poorest peasants and take land from the richest. However,
few peasants held less than the minimum, which was everywhere
one-third of the maximum. When the system was put into practice,

it was not necessary to make much use of the minimum, but "cutouts" (*otrezki*) from allotments that exceeded the statutory maximum were widespread.[37]

The cutouts were first debated and accepted in principle during a discussion of another qualification of the peasants' right to their holdings, a provision that no more than two-thirds of an estate could be allotted to the peasants. At first, Rostovtsev reiterated his stand that allotments could not be modified at the time of emancipation. Then he suggested that if the pomeshchik was to recover any allotment land, he should do so gradually; "that way we shall avoid riots, gentlemen!" In the third day of debate, he admitted the possibility of cutouts under the two-thirds rule if the resulting allotments would not fall below the minimum. He was still opposed to cutouts in principle, for

we destroy the peasant with a cutout, and that means a riot. All legal theories are beautiful, but it's a piece of bread that is at stake here. We are taking away that piece of break out of consideration for the pomeshchik, for the sake of popularity among the nobility. The Sovereign has ordered us to ameliorate; what kind of amelioration is that?[38]

Samarin picked up this thought and insisted that the commission was bound to ameliorate the lot of rich peasants as well as poor, therefore there could be no maximum allotment or cutouts. But the weight of opinion was overwhelmingly in favor of cutouts. The Economic Section did accept the existing allotment in principle, and Cherkasskii, the editor of its first report, explained that the maxima would be set high enough to make cutouts a rare exception. Eventually, Rostovtsev yielded. He observed, in despite of the findings of the commission's Legal Section, that under serfdom the pomeshchik had an unqualified title to the peasant allotments; the reform would qualify this property right, and "in this new situation, it is impossible to leave the peasants with everything he gave them under different conditions. That would be very unjust." The cutout principle was put to a vote and carried almost unanimously.[39]

Rostovtsev was still impressed with the danger of taking land away from peasants, but he was increasingly moved by the importance of fairness to those pomeshchiki who had assigned large allotments to their serfs. Accordingly, six months later, in one of his last actions as chairman, he laid down two rules for the commission: the allotment maxima should be adjusted so that "*the most limited possible number of peasants* will be subject to cutouts," and "in so far as possible not [to] change the income the pomeshchik presently receives from his landed property."[40]

The commission was already adhering, at least implicitly, to this second rule. The Financial Commission had conceded that the statutory dues (and hence the redemption payments derived from them) would in many instances "surpass the actual value of the [allotment] land and property, since, in determining the amount of peasant obrok, the Editorial Commission has taken as its point of departure not rental rates but the present dues, which were established under the influence of serfdom."[41] With dues, then, as with allotments, the commission proceeded from the existing situation in refining and applying Rostovtsev's program, and once again this procedure produced "sensible advantages for the nobility."

Peasant dues were treated in the ninth report of the Economic Section, first presented to the full commission on August 13, 1859. The report provided that the dues established by the reform statutes would be unalterable. The amount of cash or labor days was determined according to the relation between the peasants' present allotments and the statutory maximum allotment for his area. Once established, this amount could not be raised, a provision that favored the peasants, since the value of land was expected to rise and the value of money to fall. Unalterable dues had the further advantage of impelling the pomeshchik to agree to the redemption of the allotments; since he could not increase his revenues from this land, he would prefer to receive a capital sum instead of semiannual payments. Only Apraksin, Tatarinov, and Paskevich voted for periodic reassessment of dues (pereobrochka) when the issue was first put to a vote.[42]

Furthermore, in the interests of amelioration, the peasants' statutory dues could in no event exceed the dues they presently rendered. Tatarinov agreed tht this rule would penalize the kind pomeshchik who, whether he was generous or simply lax, granted his peasants adequate allotments for modest dues. After the emancipation, he would presumably not want to raise the dues when they were being reduced on neighboring estates, but his generosity should be a matter of magnanimity, not compulsion. The deputies would also bemoan the kind pomeshchik. To be sure, no one identified himself as one of these amiable squires, whose plight was generally evoked in behalf of schemes with a negligible element of kindness. Rostovtsev would not acknowledge the existence of the kind pomeshchik and excluded him from the proceedings of the commission.[43]

However, the ninth report was mindful of the pomeshchik who, through poverty or cupidity, was not kind. He was the beneficiary of the so-called gradation of dues, which the report explained as follows:

The maximum of dues established for a maximum allotment . . . is allocated . . . unequally, according to descending progression, beginning with the first desiatina. The first desiatina is everywhere levied with not less than 3.50 silver rubles and not more than 4, or with a number of labor days corresponding to these sums. In the zone where regular artificial fertilizing of peasant fields is practiced, the second desiatina is levied with less than the first but more than the rest.

Otherwise, each desiatina after the first would bear an equal proportion of the dues.[44] In other words, in an area where the statutory maximum allotment would be five desiatiny and the obrok for that alloment would be eight rubles, a household that presently held two desiatiny would retain that allotment and pay an obrok of five or six rubles. The smaller the allotment, the higher the rate per desiatina.

Gradation had been proposed by three committees from the obrok provinces of the North and taken up by Petr Semenov, the editor of the ninth report, who later claimed to have conceived the idea.[45] To Semenov, gradation was a matter of simple justice, for the household plot, which would be included in the first desiatina,[46] was everywhere more valuable than ordinary plowland. In the North, manure might be generously applied to the land around the house while often the farther reaches of the allotment were not cultivated and not even arable. Semenov did not explain why peasants must, in effect, ransom the manure of their own animals, but he insisted that gradation was in the peasants' interest. The gradation system

has the enormous advantage of entirely eliminating the separate redemption of the peasants' household plots, which could, in essence, turn into the redemption of the person and eventually deprive the peasants of their land. Separate redemption, by exhausting the means of the peasants and the government . . . would postpone the redemption of the allotment land or push it into the background.[47]

Semenov did not admit that the separate redemption of household plots might be advantageous for some peasants. Traders and craftsmen might exhaust their resources renting or redeeming

uncultivated and unarable allotment land, although this land was a
pretext for the gradation system. In any event, separate
redemption could be discouraged, but not eliminated, since the
rescripts of 1857 required it. Semenov's argument in terms of the
peasants' interest was specious.

The pomeshchik, however, would derive solid advantages from
the gradation system. Semenov argued, as was usual in the
Editorial Commission, from the existing situation. There were
many estates with small allotments where the peasants were as
prosperous and paid the same obrok as neighboring peasants with
large allotments. It would be unfair, he maintained, to deprive the
owners of these estates of three-quarters of their obrok. The
gradation system came to their rescue.

The Economic Section [Semenov explained] has no thought of
undertaking the defense of the extremes of the obrok system,
which often turns into a personal levy, but it supposes that an
absolutely equal allocation of dues on all the desiatiny of the
peasant allotment and the lowering of these dues proportional to
the decrease in the quantity of land would not correspond to the
peasants' actual means, while the pomeshchiki would be subjected
to extremely unequal losses.

"A peasant's means," he had just pointed out, "depend on the
relationship between the allotment and the working capital, time,
and labor power at the peasant's disposal."[48] Gradation, then, was a
way of giving the pomeshchik a return on the peasants' working
capital, time, and labor power, as well as on last year's manure; it
was, in fact, a complicated form of the "personal levy" and
"redemption of the person" that Semenov magisterially rejected.

Nonetheless, the commission was determined to pursue
Rostovtsev's primary goal and make amelioration a reality, rather
than a euphemism for emancipation. It was not concessions of
principle, but practical application of Rostovtsev's program, that
contracted the scope of amelioration. Rostovtsev's collaborators
gently explained the process to him when he asked why
supplementary dues (watchman's service, produce, and so on) were
being left out of account. Cherkasskii, Miliutin, Solov'ev, and Petr
Semenov candidly replied that "it is primarily the abolition of these
supplementary dues that will make amelioration of their way of life
obvious to the peasants."[49]

A year later, Petr Semenov was more candid still in defending the
revised obrok rates recommended by the Economic Section. He
conceded that these rates far surpassed the rental value of the
peasant allotments, "but all this was done to protect the

pomeshchiki from ruin; also, there is a corrective in our system, for nowhere do we allow the existing obrok to be increased, but simply leave the existing fact, regulating and moderating it for the peasants' benefit." In some areas, to be sure, obrok was almost unknown and there was no fact to modify. Semenov justified the application of an eight-ruble maximum to certain northern districts of this kind:

We know that this eight-ruble obrok is too high in relation to the cost of the land and the benefits their allotments offer to the peasants. But we allow this because the pretensions of the Provincial Committees were incomparably higher; we are compelled to make concessions, for we are burdened with the accusation of ruining the [noble] estate to which we all belong.[50]

Rostovtsev had privately maintained that the commission must keep "possible concession . . . in reserve" so that outraged pomeshchiki could be mollified without sacrificing the vital interests of the peasantry.[51] His collaborators were drawing freely on that reserve now that he was dead.

Still more concessions came to seem necessary. The commission stood by the eight-ruble obrok Semenov defended, but redefined the zone where it would obtain, thus increasing the rate to nine rubles in some areas. Nikolai Miliutin agreed to this change, although he judged that nine rubles was more than most peasants could pay; nine rubles would not be a burden for very long, he argued, because Russia's finances were so badly administered that the ruble would soon lose half its value.[52]

Miliutin's colleague Cherkasskii preferred to argue in positive terms, changing the terms to suit the occasion. When the cautious and gloomy Nikolai Semenov raised a minor point, Cherkasskii rejoined, "Our primary obligation is to protect the peasants; that is why we were summoned here. They have no delegates or advocates in our midst." Challenged by an ardent reformer like Solov'ev, Cherkasskii laid a new obligation before the commission: preventing the starvation of nobles. Solov'ev suggested that the commission's resolutions on the exaction of obrok arrears should make some allowance for fires and other natural disasters. "That is absolutely inadmissible," Cherkasskii replied. "I, for example, should receive 1000 silver rubles on January 1, 1859. If there has been a fire, and if I have no other means of existence, I will die of hunger while the police confer with the governor." While the government could aid peasants afflicted by fire or famine, "it has no right to make free in a private citizen's pocket." If an allowance were made for natural disasters, "sometimes the pomeshchik himself would have nothing to eat. After all, the two estates have equal rights." In the spirit of this new equality, Cherkasskii and Samarin insisted that if the pomeshchik did not receive his obrok punctually and in full, the police must collect the arrears, selling the movable property of the offending peasant. Solov'ev found little support for his protest, and the issue was not even put to a vote.[53]

The process of refining and applying Rostovtsev's system extended over nineteen months, beginning when some provincial committees were still sitting, and ending, after the dispersal of the second convocation of deputies, with the delivery of finished statutes to the Main Committee. Rostovtsev's collaborators were harmonious and united in the first phase of the Editorial Commission's existence and again after Rostovtsev's death, when they had to confront a new chairman and other perils. During the middle phase, when Rostovtsev was too ill to exercise much authority over his collaborators and they felt secure against their opponents, pomeshchiki disputed with bureaucrats about the accommodations the commission should make to the attitudes of rural nobles. These nobles believed that a high degree of personal authority was necessary for the functioning of manorial agriculture. The commission was erecting an edifice of fiscal and contractual relations among free men, in which there was little room for arbitrary authority derived from caste. It regarded compensation in kind as backward and demoralizing, but it did admit barshchina as a temporary expedient. And under barshchina, the commission acknowledged, "the proprietor will all the same be a pomeshchik for them [the peasants]."[54] To what extent should the proprietor be allowed to behave as a pomeshchik always had? On such matters as exactions against peasants in arrears and authority over barshchina laborers, the commission made accommodations to the habits and views that serfdom had imparted to the nobility. Indeed, a distinction can be made between this kind of accommodation and the commission's concessions, on such matters as the size of allotments and the rate of obrok, to the nobility's interests. The concessions, largely in quantitative terms, were ostensibly made in response to pressure from without; the accommodations were prompted by misgivings voiced by members of the commission and by second thoughts among its leaders. The commission did not cater to the full range of the nobility's prejudices and anxieties, and the dues and allotments it proposed were much more generous to the peasantry than what the provincial committees had offered. Yet it is fair to say that the commission did not introduce any detail into Rostovtsev's system that was more favorable to the peasant than the principles he had laid down. The refinement and practical application of that program consisted, very largely, of accommodations and concessions to the nobility.

Opposition within the Commission

Solov'ev, now and again, would castigate an article of the emerging statute. Galagan objected to granting the peasants their present allotments, the commission's basic principle. Miliutin Cherkasskii, and Samarin sometimes fell out among themselves. Such controversies were not manifestations of opposition, for all these men conceived themselves to be part of the commission's shifting consensus and usually moved with it. They embraced the commission's basic principles as their own and would not, when defeated in a particular issue, carry the dispute outside the commission. Opposition was a different phenomenon, and Rostovtsev was apprehensive about it. He handled his opponents within the commission with consummate skill.

Paradoxically, Rostovtsev's main weapon against opposition was publicity. Against all custom, Rostovtsev had the proceedings of the commission printed and distributed in a large edition. The departmental members objected, Miliutin remarking that "we should not appear in public with our hair down."[55] Rostovtsev prevailed, explaining that the commission's proceedings were "the business of all Russia." So far, all Russia had remained calm while vital interests were weighed in the balance. "Experience has shown," he held, " . . . that this calm can partly be attributed to a certain degree of publicity with which this business has, by the Emperor's order, been conducted from the very first." And he insisted that the commission "owes all Russia an honorable accounting of its actions." This perverse idea led to another. The commission, continued Rostovtsev, "despite the experience of its Members, will scarcely avoid errors." Consequently, it was necessary "to deliver oneself over to the court of public opinion, appealing to everyone for aid and collaboration." Drawing on this collaboration, the commission would be able to resolve its problems and correct its errors.[56]

Rostovtsev did not, however, intend simply to put the commission in the dock. The court of public opinion was initially composed of governors, provincial marshals, and some of Rostovtsev's friends, but not the deputies from the provincial committees; they would receive the commission's proceedings "when appropriate".[57] In the event, they did not see the commission's work until they were summoned to discuss it.

Rostovtsev ordered the most important of the commission's
working papers, the "Register of Conclusions," to be kept strictly
secret from all "outsiders," especially members of the Main
Committee. Furthermore, the material that was distributed, the
journals and the confirmed reports of the sections, was sometimes
censored. The unequivocal decision not to permit any increase in
peasant dues upon promulgation of the emancipation legislation
was removed from the published report lest pomeshchiki raise their
serfs' dues prior to promulgation. Then, too, the published *Journal*
was composed to conceal from the public the controversies within
the sections, which were the real arena of combat. Here
Rostovtsev, like Miliutin, would not "make the public a witness to
the household activities, so to speak, of the commission."[58] A show
of unanimity, then, was a corollary of the principle of publicity. The
corollary was as important as the principle, and perhaps the source
of the principle. Since the *Journal* could not reflect controversies
within the commission, dissidents must either keep silence or
withdraw. Manipulating these options and the polemical skills of
his collaborators, Rostovtsev induced his major adversaries to
purge themselves, one by one, from the commission.

The first of these adversaries was Shuvalov. After sparring with
Rostovtsev in the early sessions, he launched an attack on his major
weakness, the formula for temporary obligation. The weakness
was not a matter of lack of authoritative support. Rostovtsev had
written out his views on temporary obligation, and the tsar had
read and approved the outline. Armed with this approval,
Rostovtsev had also secured the assent of the leaders of the
commission, modestly explaining that he would despotically
enforce any idea that the tsar had approved. However, Shuvalov
and most other members heard the outline for the first time at the
twelfth session.

The outline was directed against the basic dilemma of
Rostovtsev's system. According to that system, the redemption of
allotments was the royal road from serfdom. Peasants could not, as
a rule, dispose of their allotments or evade the dues these
allotments bore.[59] The redemption of allotments, therefore,
promised the optimal combination of freedom and security.
However, the immediate and compulsory redemption of allotments
was rejected on fiscal grounds; Rostovtsev's Financial Commission
argued against compulsory redemption in terms of equity and
efficiency, as well, but only the fiscal arguments held water.[60] It
was correspondingly necessary to insert temporary obligation
between serfdom and the onset of the redemption process. Since
redemption was optional, however, temporary obligation might

continue indefinitely for many peasants; and temporary obligation was much like serfdom, as Rostovtsev himself conceded. His system, then, did not terminate serfdom "in fact and at law" for all peasants, since the termination was a private arrangement.

Rostovtsev resolved the dilemma by declaring that

it is necessary to set a single general term (for example, no more than twelve years), at the expiration of which the Government, to bring the period of temporary obligation to an end, will take measures consonant with the circumstances and demands *of that time*.[61]

Rostovtsev, who ordinarily used the printing press with such abandon, would not allow any copies to be made of the outline. Although he was willing to read it aloud again, he did not want to waste valuable time discussing it or, worse still, considering written dissenting opinions. Tatarinov protested that "if we are going to be ordered around and there's no freedom of opinion, then there's nothing to discuss"; Shuvalov went further, stating that if he was not allowed to disagree with the chairman, he would resign.[62]

Tatarinov swallowed his objections for the moment. Shuvalov, joined by Paskevich, offered a written dissent two sessions later.[63] In the interim, most members had attended a special conference set up to reconcile the two dissidents and realized that Shuvalov's position was not far from Rostovtsev's. The chairman, however, accepted the first dissenting opinion in the commission's short history with bad grace. He refused to append it to the published *Journal*, accusing Shuvalov of rejecting the rescripts of 1857 and the very idea of redemption. "If you use the expression 'apart from redemption,'" Rostovtsev insisted, "that means you positively reject any redemption." If Shuvalov was dissatisfied, he could appeal to the tsar.[64]

Shuvalov disclaimed any challenge to the binding statements of government policy but he reemphasized that Rostovtsev's opinions were not binding. He would, however, withdraw his dissent in deference to the chairman's finding that it was in conflict with the tsar's principles. Rostovtsev praised this generous gesture. In the next session, however, he announced that he had submitted Shuvalov's dissent to the tsar after all, so that he could dictate a procedure for dealing with these awkward documents. The tsar's order, handed down a week later, turned out to coincide with the formula Rostovtsev wanted.[65]

The tsar ordered that dissenting opinions could be passed along to the Main Committee, either immediately or together with the commission's draft. However, "in order to avoid any open manifestation of disagreement within the commission, as a governmental agency," dissenting opinions could not be inserted into the proceedings, which "are printed and distributed for all to read."[66] Paskevich and Shuvalov promptly submitted their resignations.

However, Rostovtsev pressed his counterattack, seeking a victory on principle as well as on procedure. He insisted on the compilation of a secret journal, provided for in another article of the tsar's order on dissent, setting forth the lines of disagreement. The departure of the two dissidents would be regrettable, he maintained, but he could do nothing to prevent it, for their views were unacceptable: they desired to recreate western feudalism in Russia and "to give the peasants the freedom of birds." Cherkasskii, who observed that the commission would give the birds no more than their nests and would make them pay for them, tried to restrain Rostovtsev, and so did Miliutin, but he was adamant. A secret journal was duly composed in accord with Rostovtsev's remarks.[67]

The secret journal noted that nothing in the muddled dissenting opinion of Shuvalov and Paskevich explained their emphatic rejection of the commission's system. Consequently, they must be opposed to the commission's major objective, emancipation with land. If the dissidents did seek landless emancipation, perhaps without clearly perceiving the goal they were pursuing, then they were indeed in radical disagreement with the rest of the commission; if not, then the controversy they had provoked was inexplicable. In other words, Shuvalov and Paskevich could either admit to heresy, if not worse, or else resume their places on the commission and keep silent.[68]

Cherkasskii and Miliutin, who overcame their misgivings and helped compose this secret journal, did very well. They did not directly accuse Shuvalov and Paskevich of opposing the tsar's wishes or advocating landless emancipation. Indeed, once they were defeated, the commission dropped the imputation of heresy and replaced it with a new series of reproaches and ad hominem arguments. For example:

It is only rich landowners who can remain more or less indifferent to the success of the redemption operation. They can . . . convert the very failure of this enterprise to their own advantage. There is no doubt that their extensive lands, with the aid of capital, will have both settled peasants and an adequate amount of homeless laborers.[69]

Shuvalov and Paskevich may have looked to their own private advantage, as other members of the commission did. While they did not oppose the redemption of plowland as a principle, they preferred that the pomeshchik retain his property right to the allotments; the peasants would then pay dues either according to a contract or on a prescriptive schedule, periodically revised by the state.[70] In short, the two magnates wanted what the government had demanded in 1857 and still proclaimed as binding policy.

The dissenting opinion submitted by Shuvalov and Paskevich was, as the secret journal suggested, less than clear, but it did not advocate landless emancipation. It stated that the peasants' economic security would be assured by their "right to perpetual usufruct" of their allotments. They could renounce their allotments and leave, but they could not be expelled. They could redeem the allotments, but redemption must be, just as government policy and the other members of the commission maintained, "a free bargain." The government could assist the redemption process, but it ought not to impose or even encourage it.

The great defect of Rostovtsev's system, they charged, was that it did not provide any effective escape from serfdom apart from redemption. Peasants must be provided with a certain term to their temporary obligation, for "it is necessary that the civil rights granted to them *not be restricted by property relations, imposed by compulsion.*[71] Shuvalov may have been "playing the liberal as strongly as he can," as Cherkasskii put it,[72] but he had a point. Rostovtsev's formula, which tied civil rights to redemption and threatened further action in twelve years, meant either that compulsory redemption would be imposed at that time[73] or that semi-serfdom would continue still longer. Both alternatives were contrary to government policy, Shuvalov observed, while the vague threat of further action would impede the orderly implementation of the reform by causing uncertainty.

Shuvalov and Paskevich took their stand squarely on the rescripts of 1857. While Shuvalov and Rostovtsev accused each other of violating the rescripts, Rostovtsev was more nearly in the wrong. For example, the rescripts, as Shuvalov pointed out, gave the pomeshchik police power and made him "chief of the village community," but Rostovtsev would abolish his authority over the individual peasants.[74] To be sure, Rostovtsev had secured official sanction for his view in the Imperial Order of December 4, but the order did not have the same binding force as the rescripts. The struggle was waged in terms of fidelity to the rescripts and, as such, it was a sham, which is probably why everyone except the protagonist and the antagonist tried to make peace. Shuvalov pretended to be oblivious to the reorientation of government policy in hopes of securing a retrenchment to the policy of 1857. Rostovtsev wanted to establish that reorientation more firmly with a victory over highly placed, influential, but maladroit opponents. He won his victory by tempting them into tactical errors and more or less wilfully misrepresenting their views. Shuvalov and Paskevich had access to the tsar and could explain their own views; it is a measure of Rostovtsev's influence with the tsar that he was the final authority on Shuvalov's views.[75]

The controversy ran on fitfully for two months while Shuvalov and Paskevich awaited the tsar's action on their resignations. The tsar eventually endorsed the two secret journals, adding, "I desire that the two Members will remain in the Commission, hoping that they, sacrificing their personal opinion, will participate with their former zeal."[76] They must, then, let the proceedings of the commission go all over Russia with their signatures and seeming assent appended to proposals that they opposed. They did not resign, but simply stayed away from the commission.[77] This was a political victory for Rostovtsev.

Eventually, to be sure, Shuvalov would win a moral victory on the immediate points in dispute. The threat of further action after twelve years was not included in the Emancipation Statute of 1861, many peasants did languish on temporary obligation, and compulsory redemption was eventually imposed in 1881. Shuvalov was vindiated as both legislator and prophet.

Shuvalov had been outmaneuvered, but he could fight another day as a deputy. Pozen, who joined the commission in the middle of the Shuvalov affair, was more tenacious, but he also had to fall back on his position as deputy, that is, as adversary; within the commission he soon found himself isolated. Shuvalov may or may not have been the involuntary champion of the magnates and would-be oligarchs, but there is evidence that the commission's enemies within the government were putting their hopes on Pozen.[78]

Pozen was no aristocrat, but a practical functionary and pomeshchik. His was a volatile practicality, for he readily changed his views to suit the circumstances. Within the Editorial Commission, he sponsored the view that under serfdom the pomeshchik had only a conditional property right to the land on his estate, since he was obliged by law to allot some land to his peasants.[79] The commission took this position to anticipate the objection that the statutory allotments it proposed would violate property rights. A few days later, however, Pozen himself made that objection, arguing that the pomeshchik enjoyed an unconditional property right to his estate and therefore the statutory allotments must lapse after the transitional period.[80] Concerning the statutory allotments in his native province, he took five diverse positions in the course of eighteen months.[81]

His views on the Editorial Commission's relationship to the provincial committees also fluctuated. When he realized that Rostovtsev had undergone a conversion and foisted his new faith on the government, Pozen took a stand for the provincial committees, maintaining that "it is necessary to set very strict limits on the influence of the bureaucrats." In the months that followed, however, he concluded that while Rostovtsev would direct the drafting of the reform, he was still susceptible to the flattery and impressed by the expertise of his old friend. Pozen accordingly told him that the committee drafts could serve only as raw material; the allotments, for example, must be determined by experts.[82] In his first days as a member of the commission, Pozen assumed from Rostovtsev's show of respect that he himself would be chief among these experts.

He soon realized, however, that Rostovtsev had taken on a phalanx of new counsellors; all of them were hostile to Pozen, whatever his position of the moment might be, and there is some justice in Pozen's bitter accusation that they poisoned the chairman's mind against his old friend.[83] Consequently, Pozen resumed his partisanship of the provincial committees. Petr Semenov blandly assured him that the committees' proposals were given careful consideration in the Economic Section, but Miliutin, the section's chairman, responded with more passion and candor. He assailed "some members" who "are making accusations against us outside the walls of the Commission; or rather they lay charges against the Economic Section, alleging that its members do not take the opinions of the Provincial Committees into account." In fact, the section was giving them all the consideration they deserved, which was not very much; since the drafts were mendacious and contradictory, the commission had to find its own solutions to the problems of the reform. But it was "paralyzed" by the circulation of false accusations, which aroused the public against the commission and impeded "the acceptance of our proposals in higher spheres." He therefore protested in the name of the Economic Section against malicious rumormongers.

Pozen identified himself as the target of Miliutin's protest, and did not directly deny it, saying, "I am not obliged to give you any account of my activities." He went on the complain that the Economic Section, of which Miliutin was chairman, tyrannized over the commission. In the general sessions, its members constituted an automatic majority and "they do not even let the rest of us speak against its opinions."[84]

Pozen's complaint was a confession of his complete loss of influence within the commission;[85] until he took his place among the deputies, he continued to attend the general sessions and to vote, but he spoke only two or three more times. The leaders of the commission regarded him as a hostile outsider, and henceforward any proposal he had favored was suspect on that ground alone. He was too deft to be hamstrung as quickly as Shuvalov had been, but he, too, thought it better to withdraw and regroup; in the event, he would find it impossible to return to the commission as a member.

There was an inncer consistency to Pozen's diverse views, from first to last; he took his position according to his estimate of his influence on the outcome. When his influence seemed to be on the wane, he stressed the practical wisdom of the provincial committees, but a bureaucratic solution was perfectly acceptable when it seemed he would be the principal author. His vacillations as a member of the Editorial Commission represented attempted alliances. At first he did not commit himself on the Shuvalov-Paskevich affair, but then came cautiously to their defense, circulating an explanation that they did not hold the heretical views imputed to them.[86] Shuvalov and Paskevich, however, gave no indication that they regarded Pozen as a suitable ally.[87] He embraced the view that the peasants' right to their allotments lapsed after twelve years, to achieve a rapproachement with Apraksin, another dissident magnate on the commission.[88]

Apraksin never made enough of an impression on his fellow members to become an object of controversy, though his position was very far from the consensus of the commission. He was too prudent to embrace the cause of Shuvalov and Paskevich, though the views they were supposed to hold were very close to his own. He submitted two dissenting opinions and occasionally interjected an objection during the early debates in the commission, but apparently he thought his stock in trade was his influence on the tsar; far from collaborating with the deputies, he was off on a hunting trip with the tsar when they were confronting the commission. However, since Apraksin really did hold some of the heretical views that were being promiscuously attributed to the nobility, his plight is of interest; Lanskoi and Rostovtsev disposed of him neatly, by way of rehearsal for the encounter with the deputies.

In August 1859, Apraksin wrote to the tsar to explain that in all his official statements (the Orel Committee's minority draft and his dissenting opinions as a member of the Editorial Commission),[89] he had muted his views.[90] He proceeded to expound these views frankly, in three parts. He began by tracing the inconsistencies, omissions, and abrupt reversals in the government's program; he attributed the divisions within the committees and the shortcomings of their draft statutes to the government's ambiguous policies on manorial power and redemption. Apraksin went on to spell out his own views on the reform. Although he preferred the rescript of 1857, which did not use the word "emancipation," to the April Program and later policy statements, he would not turn the clock back; rather, he insisted that the government make a clear choice between a limited, very gradual reform and "instant emancipation" with immediate compensation for the allotments, which would be subject to compulsory redemption. The decision, he argued, was purely fiscal. However, the Editorial Commission was framing an unworkable compromise between the two alternatives, relying on communal self-administration, land tenure, and mutual responsibility to make temporary obligation work. The commune was retrograde, unreliable, and hateful to the peasantry, for the rich peasants turned usurers in self-defense; furthermore, it was an arbitrary institution that was compatible only with "the general servile state in which our Fatherland now finds itself." To emancipate the Fatherland from serfdom, Apraksin concluded with a ten-point program, including administrative and judicial reforms, but emphasizing the devolution of political power from the bureaucracy to the nobility.[91]

Judging by his comments on the margins of the original, the tsar was primarily interested in Apraksin's views on the reform of serfdom. The complaints of inconsistencies in the past were valid, and so was the warning against perpetuating elements of serfdom in the reform statutes. Lanskoi, however, concentrated on the ten-point program of political reforms. Analyzing Apraksin's memorandum at the tsar's request, he linked this program to various manifestations of an oligarchic tendency among the nobility. With one or two exceptions, all the manifestations Lanskoi cited were the handiwork of the Bezobrazov brothers,[92] but he pronounced the tendency "intolerable" and reported that it embraced both anglophiles in the capitals and provincial "squireens," resentful at the impending emancipation of the serfs.

My dealings, both official and private, convince me that the mass of the nobility cannot and should not dream about representative government as it is utterly contrary to our customs, our level of education, and the basic interests of the state.

As a rule, sound Russian sense perceived this. At the moment, however, Apraksin and other ordinarily reliable noblemen and courtiers had been unhinged by slanderous charges about the reform and the Editorial Commission. While these magnates protested their loyalty to the tsar, their criminal conspiracy "threatens to shake the peace of the state."

Lanskoi proceeded to refute the slanders, which were indeed circulating, but had almost nothing in common with the main part of Apraksin's note, which he ignored.[93] He ended by resuming his attack on Apraksin's political program, remarking that a devolution of power from the bureaucracy to the nobility was unthinkable because the worst bureaucrats were nobles, while the corporate organization of the nobility executed its limited functions very badly. Besides, the bureaucracy was undergoing reform; private proposals "do not deserve attention," especially since any form of opposition or factionalism would jeopardize the "holy cause" of emancipation.[94]

Lanskoi's warning against factionalism and constitutionalism struck a responsive chord in the tsar, who raised no objection to the one-sided treatment of Apraksin's note; he returned Lanskoi's commentary with an effusive expression of gratitude and complete accord. Alexander did not like to be reminded of the government's waverings on emancipation and he was apprehensive of opposition. He certainly did not want to yield any of his authority to the nobility, but he was solicitous of its welfare. It was to this solicitude that Rostovtsev directed his answer to Apraksin.

Apraksin, according to Rostovtsev, would hold in abeyance any decision that would exact sacrifices from the nobility. "God only grant that these sacrifices be few!" Rostovtsev exclaimed, but they were inevitable. To avoid them entirely would mean arresting the reform process. Furthermore, whatever the commission might propose, the pomeshchiki would be dissatisfied and demand concessions. Therefore

the Commission should draw up the draft Statute so that possible concessions are left in reserve. . . . Let them lavish its work with reproaches, lamentation, and even slander; let them say that the Commission's work was imperfect and even bad, and that they corrected it.[95]

Rostovtsev, then, took the line that the commission was overly generous to the peasants so that concessions could subsequently be made in order to give the nobility an illusory victory. Concessions were indeed made, most of them when Rostovtsev was no longer able to preside. As presented by Rostovtsev, Apraksin appears rigid and a little stupid, since he was unable to perceive this tactical scheme, but is not the dangerous figure (or sympton) evoked by Lanskoi.

In dealing with Apraksin, Rostovtsev and Lanskoi played complementary roles. Lanskoi was the watchful guardian of state interests who told the truth and shamed the devil; Rostovtsev was a genial greybeard, less austere and more practical, who hated to speak ill of any man; yet his sense of duty and his forthright, soldierly nature might bring him close to Lanskoi's interpretation of events. They would assume these complementary roles once again to turn back the first convocation of deputies.[96] Against Apraksin, they were an effective combination; he was rarely seen in the Editorial Commission after they delivered their judgments.

Petr Semenov later maintained that if the opposition within the commission had been united, it would have prevailed.[97] The opposition was so far from unity that the outspoken opponents were, in effect, purged one by one; they were not removed, they resigned or simply stopped coming to the sessions. None of the other members took a stand on their behalf; they were too prudent to embrace a hopeless cause, and this prudence meant that the cause was, indeed, hopeless. The first cluster of opponents was dispersed before another cluster, the experts from the western provinces, arrived in St. Petersburg. Shuvalov flirted briefly with them, but other members did not want to link their own fortunes with the Poles. Some of the bureaucratic members of the commission, notably Bulygin, voiced reservations along the way but did not express fundamental opposition until the commission's labors were almost over.[98] Nor was there any coordination among the skeptical bureaucrats—between Nikolai Semenov, for example, whose objections were legalistic and abstract, and Bulgakov, who took the position, "I am a pomeshchik myself and cannot deprive myself of everything."[99] Even Zheltukhin, the ex-publisher of the Landowners' Journal,[100] proved a relatively accommodating member. He did compose an appeal to the deputies, urging them to expose the commission's basic fallacies, but this appeal had little impact and provoked no retribution.[101] Only in the fourth from the last general session, seizing a minor pretext, did Zheltukhin himself denounce the commission's system. He maintained that it would produce "the ruin of the pomeshchiki, which is not one of the conditions of the Imperial rescript." To Solov'ev's remark that he should have made his objections earlier, the unhappy Zheltukhin replied,

It's easy to say that, but we never reviewed everything as a whole here. Formerly we were not allowed to protest against the system. If you begin to speak, they reply, you have no right, that's already settled, why didn't you speak then? If you say something else, they say, that is still to come, you can object to that later, at the right time and place.[102]

Pozen was the only member who made any real attempt to organize a rival faction. These attempts were tentative; he seems to have been seeking an influential patron to replace Rostovtsev, not a ground of opposition. Certainly, he did not articulate any national pomeshchik program.

The tyranny of Miliutin's Economic Section, of which Pozen and others complained, was a matter of organization, tenacity, and mastery of the bureaucratic skills.[103] Rostovtsev's counsellors may not have been wiser than their detractors, but they were more diligent and more prolific. Opposition to the commission was simply overwhelmed with a flood of paper. Within the commission, however, it was the successive isolation and neutralization of opponents that was crucial. Barely half of the commission's original members thought well enough of the commission's end product, the draft statutes, to sign them; several of those who signed had recently expressed major reservations. The malcontents, however, simply drifted away or acquiesced, for there was no alternative to which they could rally.

The Deputies

7

This chapter deals with the first convocation of deputies from the provincial committees. In the summer and early autumn of 1859 they ventured an ill-coordinated sortie against the Editorial Commission, which the commission anticipated and beat back; as a result, the deputies had little direct influence on the emancipation legislation. The commission's triumph was a personal defeat for deputies who have figured in other capacities in earlier chapters: Koshelev, Unkovskii, Shuvalov, and Pozen. More important, the confrontation between the deputies and the commission provided an occasion for articulating and developing antibureaucratic sentiment. It is primarily for this reason that historians have devoted so much attention to these deputies. Their addresses to the tsar, in particular, are thought to prefigure the major political tendencies of the postreform nobility,[1] but here they will be examined in their immediate context, as bench marks of disunity and uncertainty. The transactions of the deputies also reveal a great deal about Russian nobles in the last days of serfdom—their attitude towards politics, economics, and bondage, and their conceptions of the peasantry and the noble estate. Finally, analysis of the evolution of the deputies' thinking about the impending reform reveals significant and largely unrecognized affinities between these spokesmen for the nobility and their bureaucratic antagonists.

The deputies elected by the provincial committees were divided into two convocations or "summonses" (*prizyvy*). The thirty-six deputies of the first convocation represented the first nineteen provinces to submit draft statutes.[2] Only five of these provinces lay in the agricultural heartland—the central black-soil zone, the Transvolga and the steppe. Almost half of the thirty-six deputies came from the central industrial zone and the provinces around St. Petersburg. Consequently, proprietors of obrok estates were disproportionately represented.[3]

Ten deputies from eight provinces represented minority factions; of these ten, four were government members, as were the single deputies from Astrakhan and Viatka. Five deputies were provincial marshals, all representing united committees or majority factions. Two or three of the marshals were great magnates, as were several of the minority deputies; Koshelev of Riazan and Petrovo-Solovovo of Tambov had more than 2000 serfs, and M. S. Lanskoi of Simbirsk had more than 1000.[4] However, the provincial committees usually chose middling pomeshchiki as their representatives. Apart from the marshals, the only magnate among the majority deputies was Pozen. Of the others, five are not listed among the owners of estates of 100 or more souls; eleven are credited with from 100 to 300 male serfs, and five with between 300 and 600. Several more apparently lived on estates belonging to relatives and falling in the middling range.[5]

By comparison with the nobility at large, then obrok proprietors, government members, and committee minorities were overrepresented in the first convocation. Otherwise, the deputies were representative of the nobility as a corporate entity, in which only holders of 100 or more serfs had a full franchise. I. V. Gagarin of Voronezh, Shuvalov of St. Petersburg, and Shcherbatov of Saratov, all provincial marshals, bore aristocratic names. Pozen and Koshelev had attained some celebrity. By and large, however, the first group was a cross section of the provincial nobility. Iruii Samarin, following Gogol's example, divided them into the fat and the skinny.

Among the fat, two types predominate: the retired soldier with a red moustache, the order of St. Anne around his neck, and frogs on his collar; and the pomeshchik, purple-faced and bursting with fat. . . . The skinny generally belong to the category of consumptive youths with long, hempen hair and a certain expression of lassitude on their faces.[6]

By the end of August 1859, the Editorial Commission had solved the main problems of the reform to its satisfaction and was ready to face the deputies. Most of the commission's solutions would be incorporated into the emancipation legislation, issued eighteen months later. Like this legislation, the commission's proposals were by no means hostile to the nobility's practical interests. At the same time, they were very far from the draft statutes presented by the provincial committees; they might be similar in their purposes, but not in their means. For example, most committees favored uniform norms for dues and allotments; the commission proposed lower dues and larger allotments, which was only to be expected, but also rejected norms as such. The commission concluded that even if the committees' norms had been acceptable, any norms entailed insuperable problems of assessment and land measurement. The commission took existing dues and allotment as its point of departure, and the disparity between this system and any system based on norms was a natural ground of conflict with the deputies.

Furthermore, the commission offered simple proposals in the peasants' interest, while its devices to favor the nobles were complicated. Many deputies were slow to appreciate that the gradation system, for example, was a concession to the nobility, for most of them arrived in St. Petersburg ignorant of the commission's system and convinced that the commission was antagonistic.[7] The events of the last two years had increased the nobility's conventional hostility to the bureaucracy many times over, and the deputies bore this accumulated hostility with them. They were not mollified by assurances that the Editorial Commission was largely composed of pomeshchiki. "Although the members [of the commission] disguised themselves with the title of pomeshchiki," one deputy observed, "this fooled no one."[8] The deputies were manipulated, divided, and deceived by this overbearing commission, just as the nobility at large had been by the regular bureaucracy. Naturally enough, the deputies reflected and augmented the provincial nobles' animosity to the functionaries of St. Petersburg.

These functionaries greeted the deputies with certain stratagems of crowd control, although Lanskoi all but indicated that counterinsurgency techniques were called for. His survey of the provincial committees ended with a warning about the deputies. (In official terminology, they were no longer "deputies" but "the members elected by the provincial committees.") The tsar was told that their present views were diverse, but there was no doubt they would strive for mutual accord "in their attempt to achieve changes in the principles adopted by the government." By his own order, the tsar was reminded, the deputies were simply to provide whatever information the government might request. This request should be limited to questions about the application of the

Editorial Commission's draft to the deputy's own province. The deputies should not be consulted about "basic principles, which are acknowledged to be unalterable, nor about the development of these principles." It was for the government itself to develop its principles, Lanskoi insisted, forgetting that the provincial committees had been charged in 1857 with the "development of [the rescript's] fundamental principles and their application to local conditions."[9] A lapse of memory is natural in a time of peril, and the deputies, according to Lanskoi, threatened the abolitionist cause and the state itself. It was essential to put an end to the deputies' "dreams" that they

are summoned to resolve any legislative questions or to change the structure of the state. The abolition of serfdom is already settled. . . . The word of the tsar is unshakable. It is for subjects to carry out this holy word with the same elation and love with which You pronounced it.[10]

The instructions that were drawn up for the deputies reflected Lanskoi's anxiety;[11] they may have awakened the deputies from grandiose dreams, but they produced no elation. The deputies were informed, as Iurii Samarin put it, "You are nothing more than walking reference books; when you are asked about something, answer the question, but you are relieved from participation in the discussions."[12]

Rostovtsev expressed disapproval and even embarrassment about the instructions, but insisted that the commission must accept them to maintain solidarity with the Ministry of Internal Affairs, where they had been drawn up. He softened their rigor in applying them and assumed the role of intercessor for the outraged deputies. Rostovtsev was disingenuous, for the instructions did not arrive like snow on his head. He himself had arranged for Miliutin to compile the instructions, and Miliutin had been determined from the first that the deputies would have no influence on the reform.[13]

According to the instructions,[14] the deputies were to answer certain ancillary questions that had arisen during the drafting process. They concerned the prevention of forest fires, the recruitment of surveyors, and other weighty problems; to solve these problems, the deputies complained, "there would be no necessity of summoning deputies, nor would it even be worthwhile to disturb the district marshals at their posts."[15] Rostovtsev could put further questions of his own choosing pertaining to the reports of the sections of his commission. The deputies were to reply in writing to both sets of questions, as individual or jointly for a single province, within one month; these responses would be submitted to the Main Committee along with the Editorial Commission's draft. Rostovtsev could also, "at his discretion and insofar as necessary," invite the deputies from one or several provinces to testify in a general session of the commission. When Rostovtsev's hunger for "local information and explanations" from a particular province was satisfied, he was to inform the Minister of Internal Affairs, who would tell the deputies that they had discharged their function and could go home. Finally, the instructions allowed the deputies to supplement their responses to the questions with "special considerations" relating to "the application of the [commission's] general rules to local circumstances." Under this rubric, the deputies could write whatever they pleased. The instructions, then, did not serve to silence the deputies, but to show them that they had no necessary function and no collective status, indeed, no status at all except as Rostovtsev chose to confer it. The purpose was humiliation, not constraint.

On August 25, the first convocation was summoned to a general session of the Editorial Commission to hear the instructions. The members faced the deputies across an enormous table, each side drawn up in serried ranks. As the instructions were read, Samarin observed that Rostovtsev was flushed and uneasy, while the deputies' faces registered various forms of dismay and Pozen's expression was a wry admission that his enemies had won the first round of this new engagement. After the reading of the instructions and the questions, Rostovtsev said a few flustered words and the deputies were dismissed without a word on their part, "and thank God," Samarin wrote.

If one of them uttered so much as a word, raised even one question, then, to judge from the ill-concealed anxiety on our part, the ensuing discussion might have led to a whole series of unexpected concessions. It is fortunate that they are still more afraid of us than we are of them.[16]

Samarin predicted that the deputies would not be able to unite and act together. D. N. Shidlovskii, the deputy from the Simbirsk majority, who tried to mobilize the deputies, observed their disunity with dismay. He appealed for help to Count Orlov-Davydov, a great landowner of Simbirsk and a leading figure on the Simbirsk Committee. Orlov-Davydov had just published an anonymous attack on Rostovtsev, and Shidlovskii assured him that he was "the hero of the hour."

Come then, Count, to enjoy your triumph and to give a little courage to our unfortunate deputies, for my energy is exhausted and I am getting nowhere, the opinions of the deputies are so divided. They all condemn the proceedings of the Editorial Commission, but . . . go no further. It is a very well-plotted plan of battle that our antagonist[s] have drawn up, for discord is sown in our army before it is formed.[17]

The Count's triumph was purely literary, for he had suffered a series of practical reverses. He and Shidlovskii had been elected as the deputies from the Simbirsk Provincial Committee. He had prepared for his duties by having two anonymous pamphlets *"par un deputé de comité provincial"* published in Paris; unfortunately, by virtue of the ruling that committee minorities must be represented, he had to yield his place as *deputé* to M. S. Lanskoi, son of the Minister of Internal Affairs and spokesman for a two-man minority on the Simbirsk Committee. He did not learn of this reversal until he came to St. Petersburg to serve as a deputy. Angry and disappointed, he labored to unite the deputies against the Editorial Commission.[18] The commission's recommendations, he argued, not only jeopardized the nobility's property, they also undercut its political role as the bastion of the throne. It was the deputies' positive duty to close ranks and form His Majesty's Loyal Opposition, on the English Model.[19]

Orlov-Davydov's appeal failed. He was introduced to Volkonskii, one of the Riazan deputies, by the Voronezh provincial marshal, who warned him that "the count is not so wild as he seems." Orlov-Davydov gave Volkonskii one of his pamphlets and raged against Rostovtsev, but Volkonskii, who was no admirer of the Editorial Commission, found the Count even wilder than he seemed and otherwise remarkable only for his enormous nose.[20] After such inconclusive consultations as these, Orlov-Davydov retreated to his estate and apparently did not respond to Shidlovskii's appeal to return and galvanize the deputies.

Not even their indignation at their frigid reception and subsequent affronts could unite the deputies. Yet the rationale of the reception and the affronts was the danger that they would unite to overwhelm the commission. This assumption underlay the Editorial Commission's strategy, which was worked out by a select group of six members just before the confrontation with the deputies.

According to Petr Semenov, these strategists and the tsar himself conceived the confrontation with the deputies to be "decisive" for the reform.

We all knew very well [he recalled] that the most resolute opponents of the emancipation of the serfs, putting all their hopes on the deputies, were importuning vigorously for the co-option of the arriving deputies to the membership of the Editorial Commission [so that] the deputies would have an equal right to speak and vote with the members of the commission.

These opponents were pressing this plan on Rostovtsev and the tsar. Miliutin, who presided over the strategy meeting, gravely put the plan to a vote; the participants unanimously decided not to co-opt the deputies, who would outnumber the regular members several times over. However, a dispute arose between the departmental and expert members about the restrictions to be placed on the deputies. Samarin and Petr Semenov argued that the deputies, as representatives of the estate that had taken the initiative for emancipation, should be able to speak freely. They predicted that, although the deputies would be hostile, their views would diverge and could not be worked into "a coherent counterdraft to rival the consistent draft of the commission." Besides, "the government will have the last word."

To this Miliutin, Solov'ev, and Zhukovskii replied that most deputies were so hostile to the Editorial Commission that they "will make all possible compromises among themselves, if only they can overturn the draft legislation they dislike." More important, there were officials in the highest ranks of the government who would exploit this hostility to forestall emancipation, as in the reign of Nicholas I. These officials would use all their power to replace the Editorial Commission's proposals with "general and vague rules," so that the peasants would be emancipated only on paper; the basic economic issues of Russian life would remain unresolved if these dignitaries had their way.[21]

The planners of the commission's strategy all agreed that they were threatened by a conspiracy of oligarchs and dignitaries and disagreed only on the measures to be taken in response. Unfortunately, the conspirators are not mentioned by name. Occasional mention is made of the hostility of the Main Committee, and indeed, most of the sanovniki on the committee were very far from Miliutin or Samarin in their private views. However, the sanovniki had capitulated several times over on the basic issues of emancipation and there was no clear reason to suppose they would put up a struggle at this point. The deputies hopefully called upon Count Orlov, chief among the sanovniki, and he would not even receive them.[22] There were many other high officials, like Orlov, who had not welcomed the original rescripts and disliked almost everything the Editorial Commission had done. But they voiced their opposition in private letters, or confided it to their diaries, or expressed it in drawing-room aphorisms. M. N. Murav'ev told a subordinate, "If the conclusions of the Editorial Commission pass, I will keep silence, *mais nous avons la revolution.*"[23] Neither Murav'ev nor any other high official ventured any concrete act of opposition to the commission in 1859. Nonetheless, there is no doubt that the leading emancipators believed they were threatened by a conspiracy. It was easy enough to retaliate against overt, though hesitant, opponents like Shuvalov, but the conspirators stubbornly refused to declare themselves; preemptive retaliation had to be visited upon the unfortunate deputies.

Samarin and Petr Semenov, the expert members[24] on the commission's strategy board, agreed on the danger but disagreed with the departmental members about the measures to be taken. However, they yielded to Miliutin's view that the deputies should be rigorously isolated one from another and restricted in the subjects they could discuss. Within two weeks, however, the strictures would be relaxed, for Samarin and Semenov were quite right in predicting that the deputies would be hopelessly divided.

The day after the deputies received their instructions, they assembled at Shuvalov's house. Their "inexpressible woe" and rage at the bureaucracy was distilled into an address to Alexander II. The deputies recalled that the tsar had summoned the deputies "to sit in the Main Committee and jointly review the draft statutes." This decision had aroused universal joy, but "the bureaucracy has been sowing weeds."

Having misrepresented the deeds of the Tsar and the people in the Provincial Committees, having perverted all the best ideas of the tsars for so many years . . . , could the bureaucracy complacently allow this rapprochement to take place, whereby the Tsar would hear the voice of his people otherwise than through its lying lips?

The question answered itself. The bureaucracy, "contrary to the most elementary concepts about the arrangement of consultative assemblies," had provided for the minority deputies and divided the deputies into two random groups. Finally, the tsar's orders had been unceremoniously set aside and the instructions had been substituted. The tsar's will was commonly perverted in the depths of the provinces, but the deputies had not supposed it could be openly flouted in the capital.

They went on to insist that, like the tsar and the whole nation, they desired to secure prosperity and civil rights for the peasantry, but

not only are we halted at our first step, we are overwhelmed at the very root of our hopes. . . . The Journals of the Editorial Commission and all the actions of the administration are full of harmful, fatal principles; we see them and are deprived of the possibility of exposing them.

However, the deputies did not despair, for they were confident that the tsar, now that his faithless servants had been exposed, would see to it that his "commandment, ceremonially proclaimed to the nobility, would be fulfilled." The address ended by reminding the tsar just what his commandment had been:

Great Sovereign! Permit all the deputies [including those in the second group and the minority deputies] to assemble in session with the Main Committee and there proceed to a general and faithful review, reconciliation and correction of the statutes of the Provincial Committees.

The tsar or some member of his family should preside, "for illegal and unscrupulous actions have taken away all our faith in persons who act in the name of the government in the matter now under discussion."

Rostovtsev turned this intemperate document over to the tsar. Alexander made no comment on the bulk of the address—the broadside against the bureaucracy and the Editorial Commission, the arrogation of privileges and of the title "deputy." All this only confirmed Lanskoi's warnings about the deputies' sinister intentions. The tsar did underline the statement that he had promised that the deputies would review the provincial drafts together with the Main Committee; he noted "never" in the margin.[25] Formally, Alexander was right, for the Imperial Order on the election of deputies did not guarantee them any hearing at all. However, the instructions and the attitude they reflected were very far from the assurances Alexander had given the previous summer in his speeches to the provincial nobility.[26]

The autocrat was not grateful for a reminder that he had exercised his sovereign prerogative to break a promise; the deputies' appeal was impolitic as well as intemperate. Indeed, cooler heads had prevailed. The address, written under the immediate impact of the instructions, had been withdrawn, and the cooler heads—Unkovskii, Pozen, and Shuvalov—had been delegated to compose something more suitable. The deputies did not intend that the version they had repudiated should reach the tsar, even unofficially, and did not realize that it had. It is not clear how Rostovtsev got a copy of the draft address, but he did not do the deputies any service in passing it on to the tsar.[27]

The three deputies who were to draft a new appeal could not agree; each offered his own version and other deputies produced versions of their own. A new subcommittee—Unkovskii, Koshelev, Pozen, and Gagarin—was appointed to draw up a letter to Rostovtsev. Their text was modified and adopted by twenty-nine deputies on August 29. The letter was far milder than the address to the tsar, although the deputies were by no means reconciled to the instructions or the commission itself. According to Unkovskii, who was unhappy with the final version, most of the deputies were "scoundrels, ignoramuses and rabid 'planters,'" but they were "terrible cowards."[28] Volkonskii was equally dismayed by the turn of events.

Nothing could be uglier than the last two sessions at Shuvalov's; no noble feelings or high aspiration, nothing harmonious, correct, or logical was expressed at these general meetings of the deputies. The same petty vanity, the same narrowness of views, the same vagueness of purpose and the same servility which have always characterized Assemblies of the Nobility and prevailed in the Committees. . . . This is especially sad as it gives the bureaucracy a powerful weapon against us.

Because the deputies were hesitant and divided, Volkonskii believed, they were only playing into the bureaucracy's hands by seeking to meet as a body, for nothing but pointless arguments would emerge from the meetings. "Then the bureaucrats will be right [in maintaining] that the nobility is not capable of anything."[29]

The twenty-nine deputies' letter to Rostovtsev, apart from the mildness of its tone and the modesty of its request, represented a retreat simply because it was addressed to Rostovtsev instead of the tsar. Reproaches for broken promises, charges of bureaucratic malfeasance, and indictments of the Editorial Commission's "fatal" tendencies were forgotten. Instead, the deputies apologized for the diversity and incompleteness of the drafts of the provincial committees, explaining that the committees had worked rapidly and in isolation one from another; "besides, the views of the government itself progressively clarified with the course of time and became better known to us." The Editorial Commission, despite its intentions and diligent work, could not embrace the requirements of all localities. . . . The slightest error can have the most fatal consequences for the state and all the estates of the realm. More than anyone else, we, coming as we do from various localities, are in a position to know the applicability of general statutes in this matter; besides, obscurities and omissions, which are inevitable in any human undertaking, will be more apparent to us, standing at a remove.

In short, the deputies accepted the official verdict on the provincial drafts and the official view of their own role as consultants on the applicability of the commission's decisions to their home provinces. Lest their helpful comments contradict and duplicate one another, as the provincial drafts had, the deputies asked Rostovtsev to intercede "for permission for us to confer together,"[30] in whatever form the tsar might be pleased to indicate.

This was an easy enough concession for Rostovtsev to make, for the deputies could no longer be imagined to represent a threat to the Editorial Commission. Their address to the tsar had confirmed the warnings of Lanskoi and Miliutin. By withdrawing that address and quarreling about a substitute, the deputies had shown themselves to be irresolute and divided. The eventual substitute, the letter to Rostovtsev, constituted a submission on institutional grounds: the deputies would work in the unfavorable framework set up by Miliutin and Rostovtsev. They were discredited for seeking to make a major challenge and doubly discredited because they could not mount one.

Rostovtsev could afford to be generous. He prevailed upon the tsar to let the deputies meet unofficially among themselves; otherwise, the original instructions were still in force.[31] Rostovtsev showed the same generosity in using the broad discretion that the instructions gave him. He now solicited the deputies' comments on a wide range of the commission's decisions, including the most important and controversial, such as the size of allotments, the terms of barshchina, and village institutions.[32] Finally, Rostovtsev decided that any deputy who wanted to testify before the commission could do so. Now that the deputies had submitted, and submitted first of all to Rostovtsev himself, the adept courtier gave way to the earnest seeker after opinions and information. "For God's sake," Rostovtsev exclaimed later, when the first deputies testified, "don't think we distrust you. And don't, for God's sake, think that there is any desire here to cause you distress!"[33]

After Rostovtsev secured permission for the deputies to meet together and laid the commission's work open to their comments, the deputies were further mollified by an audience with the tsar. Alexander gave a short speech, expressing his confidence

that My faithful nobility, which is always devoted to the throne, will zealously collaborate with Me. . . . I have not ceased to consider Myself a member of your estate. I undertook [the emancipation] with complete confidence in you, and, with the same confidence, summoned you here.

The tsar understood that the instructions, compiled at his order, had caused some misunderstanding and hoped that this misunderstanding was cleared up. He reiterated the assurance that the deputies' responses, insofar as they were not adopted by the commission, would reach the Main Committee and himself. (In the event, these responses ran to more than four thousand printed pages, but they did, in the simple physical sense, reach the committee and the tsar.) In conclusion, Alexander admitted that sacrifices were inevitable, but he hoped that the nobles' losses through emancipation would not be too painful. At this, the Voronezh deputy Gagarin declared that the nobility was willing to sacrifice a third of its fortune, but Alexander replied, "No, I do not ask such major sacrifices, I want the great enterprise to be accomplished satisfactorily for all, so that none will suffer."[34]

The satisfaction created by Rostovtsev's indulgences and the tsar's speech did not last long. The deputies discovered that their views were so much at odds that they could accomplish nothing meeting together. The general meetings split into caucuses, and the caucuses proved incohesive and ephemeral.[35] There was a certain amount of interchange among the deputies, for they plagiarized from one another in compiling their responses; on most matters, however, they had to work individually or in pairs, a procedure that had seemed so onerous and offensive when imposed by the instructions.

Furthermore, the government indicated, from the height of the throne, that the indulgence shown to the deputies did not mean that any importance was attached to their work. This was made plain by a special expression of the sovereign's gratitude to M. S. Lanskoi, the minority deputy from Simbirsk. The younger Lanskoi had never been an enthusiastic collaborator with his fellow nobles. Appointed to the provincial committee by the governor of Simbirsk, he made common cause with N. A. Solov'ev, whose brother was chief of the Civil Division. The two came under attack from the rest of the committee; in time they withdrew, composed a draft on their own, and submitted it to St. Petersburg. Reportedly, they did not even show it to the rest of the committee, although they quietly borrowed some elements from the majority's draft.[36] By submitting this draft, Solov'ev and Lanskoi constituted themselves a minority, entitled to be represented by a deputy on a par with the majority and the five-man minority of the committee.

As a deputy, Lanskoi did not join the others in their meetings, statements, and caucuses. He also distinguished himself by the brevity and promptness of his response. His cursory answers to the questions posed, often coupled with pleas of ignorance, made no pretence of seeking advantages for the nobility.[37] He did not ask to testify before the commission, nor did he respond to the invitation to comment in writing on the reports of the sections; presumably he scarcely read them, since major reports of the Economic and Legal sections were delivered to the deputies on September 10 and Lanskoi's response is dated September 12. The same day, Lanskoi was favored with the tsar's thanks (which Rostovtsev secured by telegraph as the tsar was on a hunt) for his "exemplary zeal." Having acquitted himself of his responsibilities, Lanskoi got permission from his father (in his capacity as minister) to leave the capital. In case the point might be lost on the other deputies, since Lanskoi had not cut much of a figure among them, the tsar's thanks to Lanskoi were lithographed and distributed to them.[38] The government's model deputy did not burden the Editorial Commission by commenting on its work and was studiously indifferent to his noble brethren, both the other deputies and the pomeshchiki of his province.

Finding a Role

The deputies were indignant at the tribute to Lanskoi. Gagarin and Shidlovskii registered their protest, the latter with an ironic expression of gratitude for this official guidance on the performance of his duties.[39] Rejecting the government's model was easy enough, but did not provide the deputies with a positive concept of their own role. They had to decide, quite simply, what they were. Tradition was no guide; the government was trying to reimpose the traditions of bureaucratic absolutism, which had no place for the deputies as an institution. As they proceeded with their work of composing responses and testifying before the commission, the deputies were defining their role. Here, as elsewhere, they were divided.

Lanskoi defined his role in a bureaucratic sense. Four other deputies followed his example, to one extent or another. N. I. Zheleznov was, like Lanskoi, a government member of his provincial committee (Novgorod) and a minority deputy. However, he had been appointed to the Editorial Commission. He rarely spoke in the commission and had little influence, although he endeared himself to the other members by sketching their portraits during the sessions.[40] Unlike Pozen and Shuvalov, who were also expert members as well as deputies, he was reasonably satisfied with the commission's decisions; he did not choose to abandon his seat on the commission to join the deputies, and the Novgorod minority had no spokesman.

The single deputies from Viatka and Astrakhan were also government members with strong bureaucratic ties; they proved self-effacing deputies. Both represented peripheral provinces, where there was no corporate organization for the few resident pomeshchiki and gubernatorial authority was correspondingly strong. The governor of Astrakhan set aside the two deputies elected by the committee and sent one of his own subordinates in their stead.[41] This deputy, N. N. Kishenskii, was brief and conciliatory in his written responses. He found that the commission had violated the rescripts and the April Program by stripping the pomeshchik of manorial power, but noted this without apparent dismay, for he was candid enough to admit a complete lack of concern for the emancipated peasants. With the abolition of the "patriarchal tie" of serfdom, he asserted, "the pomeshchik becomes alien to his peasants and their interest." Consequently, he withheld comment on the commission's decisions that affected the peasants alone, and on most other matters he simply expressed his accord with the commission. He did find that the Astrakhan Committee's system of allotment and dues was simpler and more suitable than the commission's; in other words, he objected, mildly but systematically, to the basic economic components of the commission's plan. Unlike Lanskoi, he sought to defend the economic interests of his pomeshchik neighbors, but the defense was tentative and maladroit. All his attention, if not loyalty, ordinarily went to his work in the provincial administration, as became clear when he pressed his case in testimony before the commission. Under interrogation, he was unable to provide data about Enotaevsk District, though one of the two proprietary estates in the district belonged to him.[42] The Viatka deputy, aptly named Tikhovidov, was even milder and more conciliatory than Kishenskii; he, too, testified in the hope of gaining a few concessions on economic matters and cut an inglorious figure.

D. P. Gavrilov reflected his bureaucratic allegiance in a different way, for he belonged to a different part of the bureaucracy. He owed his place as one of two minority deputies from Vladimir to the intervention of the Ministry of Internal Affairs, and in March of 1859 he had become an employee of that ministry, working under Miliutin.[43] Gavrilov had absorbed the views of the commission's leaders. In his response, he singled out various provisions that his friends on the commission had opposed or reluctantly accepted, as if he were the commission's conscience. He would reduce or eliminate the quasi-servile elements of the commission's recommendations—the harsh exaction of arrears, corporal punishment, cartage obligations, and the compulsory service of household serfs. Like many expert members, he spoke out strongly in favor of peasant custom; like many departmental members, he would eliminate any trace of manorial authority; hence he would do more than either to make the peasant independent of the pomeshchiki and the functionaries alike. Like Samarin, Gavrilov believed that the peasants had a positive right to their allotments. While many deputies argued that pomeshchiki must have a broad power to relocate allotments and that the commission's restrictions on relocation would impair the efficiency of the estates, Gavrilov alone found that these restriction were too weak. The commission's restrictions did not, he argued, entirely preclude the exercise of arbitrary power, and this failure "means the destruction of any guarantee that the peasants will retain their land, which they have worked from of old."[44]

As a deputy, Gavrilov was not bound by the government's decision that compulsory redemption of allotment land was not feasible. He made compulsory redemption the cornerstone of his response, bringing it up in various contexts and summarizing his arguments in a separate memorandum. Many members of the commission privately favored compulsory redemption, but so did many deputies from northern provinces like Vladimir. Gavrilov set forth one of their principal motives, the fear that the peasants would renounce their allotments when and if they could. He sought to protect the interests of the Vladimir nobles in this way and in others, as in his attempts to secure an increase in dues or a reduction of the maximum allotment for some areas. Being an insider, Gavrilov made his case within the framework of the commission's system and in terms, backed by supporting evidence, that the members would appreciate.[45] He got most of the specific concessions he sought for the Vladimir nobles, but had little success in the role of the commission's conscience.

Gavrilov and the other four deputies with strong ties to the bureaucracy criticized the Editorial Commission on particulars, some very important, but in a cooperative spirit. At the other end of the spectrum stood the deputies who challenged the commission as an institution, questioning its legitimacy as well as its wisdom. The most thoroughgoing intransigents were I. V. Gagarin of Voronezh (who, because their views were similar, is easily confused with P. P. Gagarin of the Main Committee) and D. N. Shidlovskii of Simbirsk.

Shidlovskii had entered the Simbirsk Provincial Committee *"con amore"* as he put it, because he had "the blood of a real Russian nobleman." His noble blood ran hot, and he distinguished himself by the extravagance of his demands and his eagerness to challenge the provincial governor's attempts to keep these demands within the limits of the rescript. The other members would not go far, but they admired Shidlovskii's courage, for he topped the poll when the committee elected its deputies.[46]

Shidlovskii was no less courageous as a deputy. He would not even respond to the compulsory questions distributed with the instructions, turning them aside with questions of his own. Nor would he comment on the recommendations of the Administrative Section. The section had flouted the monarch's will and introduced a new constitutional principle by abolishing manorial authority and providing for peasant self-rule; he would be an accessory to this political crime if he did more than refer the commission to the Simbirsk majority draft for a proper solution of administrative problems. In discussing both juridical and economic issues, Shidlovskii took his stand on the sanctity of private property, as he understood it, maintaining that the state could not unilaterally alienate a desiatina of noble land. Pozen and several other deputies called for an affirmation of the nobility's *pozemel'nye prava*, or "land rights," but they were reticent about the meaning of the term. Shidlovskii was not. He argued that

it would be appropriate to reaffirm the pomeshchiks' land rights, in accord with the Imperial rescripts, so that *the peasants will see from the very beginning that they have no rights to the land and that they can become landowners only by acquiring this property through purchase . . . according to a free agreement with the pomeshchik.*

No one, he held, has the right to alter or violate the right to property. The proposals of the Editorial Commission consistently did so, and must be rejected root and branch. The commission's attempt to justify spoliation in the name of "higher morality" revealed the tainted source of its inspiration.

The division of morality into degrees and the expression "higher principles" are often encountered in works with a communist and socialist tendency; consequently, it is somehow strange to find the same expression amidst the reflections of modern legislators.

The works of the commission were illegitimate and must perish. At the same time, the tsar was tolerating these modern legislators, if only for the moment. Shidlovskii was not wholly impractical. Having denied the commission's authority, he could not refrain from offering various modifications and amendments to its system. He found that the commission's ruling that the pomeshchik must provide his ex-serfs with fuel was immoral and impractical, but, he added, no district of Simbirsk Province corresponded to the commission's definition of the "forest zone," where this ruling would be most onerous for the nobles. The commission had illegally arrogated the provincial committee's rights to define allotments, but Shidlovskii went on to complain of its provisions covering fishing rights and sandy soil.[47] These attempts to have Simbirsk relieved from certain articles after rejecting the whole system introduced a note of uncertainty. The works of the commission were ephemeral and ridiculous, but if they should be enacted, against all probability and the tsar's real wishes, Shidlovskii wanted to salvage something for the despoiled pomeshchiki of Simbirsk. By seeking particular advantages, he sacrificed the consistency of his position.

Shidlovskii initially refused to testify before the commission, but then made a further sacrifice of consistency and took the stand, giving the commission de facto recognition. Gagarin also testified after refusing,[48] but his appearance was very brief. After hearing out Gagarin's denunciation of the commission and the concept of landed emancipation, Miliutin declared that there was no basis for any discussion with Gagarin and called the other Voronezh deputy to the stand.[49]

There was not, indeed, much to talk about. Like Shidlovskii, Gagarin proclaimed the sanctity of private property, but he did not waver in his intransigence by dickering with the commission. He complained that the commission treated the nobility's land like "conquered property" and spoke of the nobles themselves as if they were the government's agents. Fortunately, they were hereditary proprietors and, as such, the nobility had been *"summoned by virtue of the Emperor's trust simply to ameliorate the status of its peasants, not to alienate or transfer its landed property."* Therefore allotments must be small and granted for a short term, after which free agreements would obtain. Any greater generosity would be an error, even if the nobility should consent; the peasants would be secure because they would retain their household plots and the free labor market would favor them, but agricultural enterprise was too risky for any but great landowners. The state must have the courage to defend the rights of property against the expectations of the peasants; it would not be necessary to use force against them unless the government aroused their hopes by imprudent actions.[50]

None of the other intransigents, such as Kosagovskii of Novgorod and Podvysotskii of Chernigov, went so far as Gagarin in challenging the Editorial Commission. Yet Gagarin was not so rigid as he seemed, for he had moved towards the commission's position during his service as deputy. Before his arrival, he composed a speech to deliver to the other deputies in the name of "the nobles of a majority of the Provinces." These nobles, observing that the Editorial Commission "deviates both from the real sense of the Imperial Rescripts and from the drafts submitted by the Provincial Committees, look to the immediate future with terror." However, Gagarin struck out this forthright passage and substituted a mild complaint that the commission did not seem to offer "adequate . . . guarantees for the immediate future."[51] This was a prudent change. It was well enough to reproach the commission, as many deputies did, for neglecting the provincial drafts. Accusations of contradicting the tsar's will were another, more delicate, matter. Officially, the rescripts of 1857 were still the only statement of "Imperially-confirmed principles," binding on the commission the committees alike. The commission paid lip service to some elements of the rescripts and quietly ignored the rest. Its members were aware that their system had no more formal sanction than the provincial drafts.[52] However, the deputies knew that, as Rostovtsev never ceased to point out, the commission had the tacit approval of the tsar. This informal sanction had far more value in practice than literal adherence to a document that the government had abandoned but would not renounce. Gagarin and other deputies wanted to persuade the tsar to withdraw that approval. Vigorous complaints that the commission had flouted the rescripts might elicit a new and binding expression of the tsar's will. A paper victory on this ground held the danger of utter defeat so long as the tsar's will—the real entity, not the polemical device—inclined to the commission and its system.

Consequently, Gagarin's accusations were guarded. He drew up a list of the commission's departures from the rescripts, but did not use it in his response.[53] Instead, he tried to make his point ironically and obliquely. For example, he broke off his tirade against the commission's arguments for maintaining existing allotments, stating that it was "superfluous" to proceed, for "we simply turn our gaze reverently to the solemn acts which represent the Emperor's will that the rights of the pomeshchiki are inviolate."[54]

Clearly, Gagarin came to realize that it was sounder to offer an alternative to the commission's system than to indulge in vain reproaches, however valid. Even in his draft speech to the deputies, he offered an alternative, "a remedy which promises to avert the

terribly calamity which threatens universal destruction because of
the Mistakes of a few persons." The deputies must unite around
this remedy, for,

guided by devotion to the throne and the fatherland, we consider it
our obligation to remind the worthy deputies . . . that it is now up
to them, their wisdom and united efforts, to arrest the inevitable
danger which threatens the whole fatherland.[55]

Gagarin's remedy, set forth in seven "considerations," was
simple. Emancipation, he conceded, was "a settled question," but
the nobles were legally entitled to full compensation for the loss of
servile labor. They were willing to waive some compensation, but
the balance must be paid by the emancipated peasants and the state.
The state's contribution would take the form of bonds, which
would bear no interest for the first ten years. Gagarin was
solicitous of the treasury's anxieties, and also ingenious in
alleviating the burden of redeeming oneself. Under his system,
some peasants would choose to pay the whole sum due from them
at once. They would continue to use their household plot and
allotments, paying dues set by the provincial committee; after three
years, however, their rights to this land would lapse. They would
retain a right to their old houses and outbuildings and so, while
they would be free to contract as they liked, they might well choose
to become renters or laborers on their former pomeshchik's land. A
second group would choose to buy their freedom in installments; in
the meantime, they would be "ascribed to the lands of their former
pomeshchiki, and although they are emancipated from personal
dependency on them, they do not have the other rights of the free
categories of the population." The peasants in this second group
would also pay dues set by the provincial committees, but
otherwise, despite the absence of "personal dependency," their
status would seem close to serfdom. Peasants in the third category
would be closer still. These, whom Gagarin called "*subject* or
proprietary peasants" (*pomeshchich'i krest'iane*, the official term for
"serfs") must submit to undiminished manorial authority until
their villages chose to enter the first or second group; individual
peasants could not make this transition without the pomeshchik's
consent. Gagarin conceded that "malevolent persons" had
persuaded the peasants to expect complete freedom and the
nobility's land. His remedy would therefore evoke "more of less
overt resistance." However, if the government was firm and
unequivocal, it could "destroy any hope in the possibility of
successful resistance."[56]

The deputies did not unite behind Gagarin's simple remedy. One of them wrote a point-by-point commentary, explaining why "the memorandum . . . is scarcely deserving of any consideration whatsoever." He found some elements unjust, others impractical. He observed that the third of Gagarin's categories was serfdom pure and simple, and therefore unacceptable. And if the pomeshchiki were to fix the price the peasants must pay for their freedom, Gagarin's talk of sacrifice was meaningless.[57] Most important, Gagarin gave so much weight to existing legislation on property and other matters that he left no initiative to the legislative power. Autocracy had established serfdom and could abolish it; given the autocrat's commitment to abolition, the haphazard legislation arising from serfdom was irrelevant.[58]

The commentator was more forthright and more sensible than many deputies in acknowledging the positive function of legislative power. On other matters, he expressed the rough consensus of the deputies of the first group. He did not object in principle to Gagarin's ultimate goals, landless emancipation plus compensation for the loss of serfs. Other deputies were jealous of their land or insistent on compensation, though none combined these two sentiments as Gagarin did. But Gagarin would keep the peasants in bondage until they paid for themselves. To judge by their responses to the Editorial Commission, the other deputies did not think it was possible or even desirable to retain serfdom in the forms Gagarin favored. As a body, the deputies set comparatively little store by manorial power and displayed almost no nostalgia for the arbitrary authority of the serfholder.

Gagarin yielded, perhaps to the weight of opinion, perhaps to common sense. He may have decided that the government would never accept gradual, state-assisted self-redemption, the gist of his original plan, for that would be even less than the rescripts of 1857 had promised. In his response to the commission, he clung to landless emancipation as an ultimate goal, but made an attempt to conform to the rescripts and to subsequent rulings banning compensation for serfs and requiring the redemption of household plots. Although it was by no means apparent from the haughty irony of his response, the most intransigent of deputies made many concessions.

Gagarin and Gavrilov stood at opposite poles. However, the conventional global metaphor does not provide enough poles to accommodate the diverse positions of the deputies. For example, Unkovskii, the Tver majority deputy, agreed with Gavrilov on many points of substance but almost matched Gagarin in the intensity of his attack on the commission.[59] Unlike Gavrilov, he did not suppose he was addressing his pleas for administrative reform and compulsory redemption of allotments to a friendly audience. His hostility to the commission was bolstered by his fear of a conspiracy of retrograde oligarchs—the same fear that underlay the commission's hostility to the deputies. He observed that "the commission is visibly uneasy about the party of 'planters' at court"[60] and he expected it to surrender to them on the main issues of the reform. His response to the Editorial Commission has some of the venom of his later attacks on the turncoats, trimmers, and doctrinaire bureaucrats who "emancipated the peasants more stupidly than could have been imagined."[61]

Like Shidlovskii and Gagarin, Unkovskii even turned the compulsory questions into an occasion for raising broad issues. Regulations on fire prevention, grain reserves, and other practical matters raised in these questions would be meaningless, he argued, without a general political reform. The arbiters of the peace who would implement the reform must be independent of the bureaucracy, like the English justices of the peace. All officials must be accountable before the courts, and the courts themselves must be transformed—provided with independent judges and public trials by jury.[62]

A great part of Unkovskii's response is simply an essay on the state of Russia's government. Staffed by pomeshchiki who ran their departments as they ran their estates, the administration was permeated by serfdom. Its officials cherished the arbitrary power enjoyed by the serfholder. The administration was also notable for its red tape, corruption, and constraint of private life; it was "a system of abuses elevated to the level of a system of government," which "leaves no real place for a free and rational life." The necessity of administrative and judicial reform derived from the emancipation and must be simultaneous with it; these reforms should be drawn up by political scientists and representatives of the people, presumably elected; otherwise, the devious bureaucrats would introduce "minor" modifications that would spoil everything. The beneficiaries of the present abuses, Unkovskii observed, charged advocates of reform with opposition to autocracy, but they launched these slanders in the hope of clinging to "their own autocracy."[63]

Unkovskii descended from these general considerations to particular criticisms of the commission on such matters as the force of customary law and the composition of the canton (volost'). He also offered comments on economic matters, particularly allotments and dues. The Tver majority draft was closer than most to the commission's sytem. It also offered the peasants their present allotments within a maximum and minimum, and the maximum was not far from the commission's. But the Tver majority favored a uniform maximum of four desiatiny for the whole province, while the commission's maxima for Tver ranged between four and six desiatiny.[64] Like most other deputies, Unkovskii argued for a single maximum for each province and defended his committee's position on most other points on which the commission disagreed. He also hotly refuted the commission's insinuation that the composition of the allotment advanced by the Tver majority was a cunning attempt at extortion. Finally, Unkovskii showed considerable foresight on the subject of barshchina, arguing that no statute or code could make it function effectively, but that it would persist through inertia and mutual agreement, however the commission attempted to discourage it.[65]

On economic as on administrative matters, Unkovskii's response was essentially a polemical essay. This essay argued that redemption by ostensibly free agreement, as proposed by the commission, was a craven half measure; intended to mollify both the friends and the enemies of emancipation, it would satisfy no one. The government saw the necessity of redemption, but sought to achieve it by enacting an onerous and unworkable alternative; Unkovskii found this tactic unworthy of a strong government. The commission maintained that compulsory redemption would be expropriation, and therefore unacceptable, but compulsory allotment of plowland would be expropriation to the same degree, without bringing the same benefits. Compulsory redemption was doubly necessary because contractual redemption would be a slow process; at first, the peasants would not consent because they believed the allotment land to be their property, while the pomeshchiki would hesitate because of their poor understanding of economics and their growing distrust of the government's fiscal policies. Finally, it was essential not only to maintain the nobles' revenues, as the commission argued, but also to maintain the productive capacity of the demesne. If the pomeshchiki did not, through compulsory redemption, get capital to reconstruct their estates, the grain trade and the economy would collapse.

Unkovskii's essays were carefully prepared in advance,[66] and the whole response was a polished performance. Deputies who did not share his literary skills or many of his views paid him the tribute of selective plagiarism. However, borrowed eloquence made for discord. The Riazan deputies Ofrosimov and Volkonskii took over the program of Koshelev, with whom they had fought so hard in the Riazan Provincial Committee, and decked it out in the language of Unkovskii. The result was expressive, but somewhat contradictory.[67] Unkovskii's views were not unique; Koshelev, at least, expressly shared his faith that emancipation would be a boon to the nobility and to Russia. Many deputies agreed with Unkovskii on the necessity of compulsory redemption, but they would considerably reduce the present allotments. Even more advocated administrative reform and some form of local self-government, but they would guarantee the hegemony of the nobility within the new institutions as a matter of right, while Unkovskii assumed that the nobility's wealth and education were guarantee enough.[68] Resentment of bureaucratic tutelage was commonplace, but Unkovskii coupled distrust of bureaucracy with a distrust of privilege and a faith in market forces. This consistent liberalism was too heady for the other deputies; under its influence, his closest allies staggered in an unseemly fashion.

The two Khar'kov deputies, D. A. Khrushchov and A. G. Shreter, caucused with Unkovskii, copied parts of his response into their own,[69] and followed him on other points. They, too, argued for compulsory redemption, reform of the courts, and the amalgamation of nobles and peasants in elective agencies of local government. They took pride in their advanced views, but they vacillated between Unkovskii's vigorous self-confidence and querulous pettifogging. They wanted compulsory redemption, but if it should not be enacted, the government must understand that peat was a precious commodity and give the Khar'kov pomeshchiki the right to cut it on the peasants' allotment land. They maintained that the pomeshchiki who thought barshchina could work after emancipation were naive; Unkovskii voiced the same idea, but the Khar'kov deputies arrived at it on their own, for they later insisted, like the most hidebound black-soil pomeshchiki, that a proprietor would be helpless without complete manorial authority over the labor force on his demesne. Like Shidlovskii, they accused the Editorial Commission of reckless philanthropy and irrational prejudice against the deputies. Finally, on the main points at issue, the size of the allotments and the dues they would bear, they argued in the same terms as the other Little Russian deputies, who had no aspirations to advanced views. Unlike Podvysotskii, the gloomy spokesman for the Chernigov majority, they would consent to a somewhat larger allotment than their committee had proposed, but their revised figure was far lower than the commission's or the existing allotments. They maintained, among other things, that after emancipation the peasants would not have the capacity and resources to cultivate their present allotments, an argument that is hard to follow despite its reiteration by the Little Russian deputies.[70]

The Khar'kov deputies concluded their remarks on allotments and dues by returning to more congenial ground and warning that the peasants would be ruined by the emancipation, however generous its terms, if it was implemented by the bureaucracy. The force of these brave words was undercut by the two obsequious letters to Rostovtsev, which they appended to their original responses.

In his letter, Shreter complained that the dues the commission proposed for Khar'kov Province were premised on the fallacy that land values varied in different parts of the province. He dropped the role of forthright public man, which he had assumed in his response, and was transformed into an incoherent suppliant. Apart from a very abstract benevolence, he was consistent only in his antipathy to the bureaucracy and his fervent monarchism; it may have been Rostovtsev's proximity to the throne that induced Shreter to unbend as he did. His vacillation was the product of the unsettled times and the pressures upon him; his own views evolved so rapidly that he could scarcly assimilate them.

Shreter had opposed the government's initial commitment to reform on the ground that the tsar's counsellors (except for a few veterans like Orlov and Dolgorukov) were impractical functionaries, ignorant of the realities of rural life; Butkov, for example, the "product of an ordinary grammar school, has never been the proprietor of even a chicken." In the early sessions of the Khar'kov Provincial Committee, Shreter opposed the redemption of household plots, since the reform must not *"empieter sur la sainteté du droit de propriété des propriétaires"*; it should *"conceder des droits aux paysans en limitant a l'infini la possibilité de quitter leurs terres."* Yet even then he was annoyed at the *"soi-disant noblesse"* who would not understand that labor must be recompensed and that *"la corvée obligitaire, très profitable et pas dispenseuse, est une anomalie dans la civilization."* In time, like many colleagues on the Khar'kov Committee, he became a convert to the redemption of allotments and, as a deputy, he fell under the spell of Unkovskii. Yet he was mindful that his anxious constituents would not be satisfied with merely literary triumph over the bureaucrats, and it may have been the imminence of his return to Khar'kov that moved him to appeal to Rostovtsev. If Shreter's performance was inglorious, his experience was painful. He was humiliated by his treatment as a deputy and dismayed that Unkovskii was not disposed to pursue their collaboration. Many deputies were lionized on their return home, but Shreter and Khrushchov were isolated. Officials shunned them because they had signed the inadmissible address to the tsar, but so did their fellow nobles; Shreter castigated them as slavish, selfish, and lacking the courage of their convictions, little supposing that his reproaches might be applied to himself and, more particularly, to Khrushchov.[71]

While Khrushchov did continue to advocate compulsory redemption and administrative reform, his letter to Rostovtsev was an abject plea for intercession in the pomeshchik's behalf before the tsar. He conceded that "it is impossible to observe the interest of all, so that no one loses," but if the Editorial Commission's system was enacted, the Khar'kov nobility would lose 45,033,562 silver rubles. This impressive figure included the entire hypothetical value of the serfs' barshchina, since Khrushchov valued the barshchina proposed by the commission at zero. An indulgent accountant who accepted this reasoning might complain that he had added together the capital value of the peasants themselves and a year's return on this capital to arrive at his interesting total. Nonetheless, Khrushchov was inspired by his calculation to reduce the allotment figure proposed in his original response and retract some of his other concessions on economic matters.[72]

It was a season for second throughts. The young representative of the Nizhnii Novgorod minority also recanted after submitting his response. Originally, G. N. Nesterov gave unstinting praise to the Editorial Commission's plan, including its schedule of dues and allotments for Nizhnii.[73] Then he received a packet of letters from home attacking the commission's land settlement. M. N. Sushchov wrote that these lavish allotments would grossly violate the pomeshchik's property rights and leave him nothing but patches of weeds for a demesne; yet they would not benefit the peasants, who would be better secured by their own "capital"—their physical strength and free time. N. I. Rusinov wrote in similar terms, noting that small allotments would be progressive because the amount of land engrossed in the archaic system of communal tenure would be kept to a minimum. He also invoked the kind pomeshchik, who had attempted to "redeem" the evil of serfdom by giving his serfs large allotments, and would now be penalized for his generosity.

These objections were commonplace among the deputies, but Sushchov and Rusinov were Nesterov's colleagues on the minority of the Nizhnii Committee. Furthermore, the Nizhnii nobles had reacted to the commission's system by healing their schism. A letter from still another minority member, the provincial marshal Boltin, informed Nesterov that the minority's plan for the redemption of a small allotment now represented the "general desire" of the Nizhnii nobility; Sushchov and Rusinov were writing in the name of all the marshals and the resident pomeshchiki. [74] Nesterov was moved by the plaints of his friends to submit a second response attacking the commission's system of allotment and dues. He took many of his new arguments from his recent antagonist, the majority deputy from Nizhnii;[75] this was a wise course, as he still did not understand the commission's system very well.

The single deputy from Moscow, S. S. Volkov, took the trouble to understand the commission's system and he commented on it in the light of his experience, without making a display of either hostility or deference to the commission. When he insisted that statutory barshchina would be unworkable, he was not raising a principle but reporting an observation that the productivity of barshchina had notably declined since the peasants had learned they would be emancipated. Volkov had thought hard about the implementation of the reform and the problems it posed for commercial agriculture. He realized the importance of making the legislation comprehensible to the peasants and urged formation of effective agencies, composed of peasants as well as pomeshchiki, to explain the reform and mediate between the parties.[76] The disruption, bloodshed, and disillusionment that followed the promulgation of the legislation in 1861 would have been diminished if Volkov's advice had been intelligenty applied.

Volkov was an acute observer, but he was first of all the advocate of his pomeshchik electors, and his deliberate assumption of this role limited the range of his insight. In his attempt to secure smaller allotments, he was obliged to assert that the allotments recommended by the commission were more than adequate for the peasant's subsistence, taxes, and other obligations; this questionable judgment led him to the assumption, which many deputies shared, that emancipation would not reduce the cost of hired labor. Similarly, he criticized the principle that dues could not be increased at the time of emancipation, arguing that the peasants whose dues were high at present would not understand why they must pay more than the ex-serfs on a neighboring estate; however, he gave no thought to the resentment of the peasants on that neighboring estate, where dues would be raised by the alternative he proposed.[77] As a rule, he was reluctant to offer positive alternatives. He was the only deputy from a committee full of magnates and dignitaries, which had been almost evenly divided on redemption and other basic issues of the reform;[78] Volkov himself was a petty proprietor and newly elected marshal in Prince Menshikov's home district. He did not think he had the authority to depart from the Moscow draft, despite the overturn in government policy since it had been drawn up.[79] He could do little more than criticize the commission from afar, since the Moscow draft was barely tangential to the commission's. The most conscientious of the deputies was one of the most guarded and constrained.

Acquiescence, intransigence, liberalism, vacillation, caution—these were only some of the tactical lines the deputies followed. The Pskov deputies struck a pose of humility and deference, though they did not pretend to like the commission's proposals; they appear to have thought they could gain more by arousing the commission's compassion than by making controversy. The deputies from Kostroma used naiveté as a weapon, innocently offering various amendments and amplifications that would render the commission's system meaningless. The Iaroslav deputies and the majority deputies from Vladimir and Nizhnii Novogorod struck a pose that was tightfisted, if not hardheaded; they made it plain that they wanted to maintain the nobles' revenues, and everything else was secondary. They were as apprehensive as Gagarin and Shidlovskii, but not quite so rude, for they did not insist on any principle, such as landless emancipation, that was obviously unacceptable to the government and the commission. The Vladimir majority deputy Parnachev candidly explained to the commission,

In defense of our material interests, we are now raising all kinds of accusations against you in our responses; we are accusing you of revolutionary tendencies and comparing you with the terrible social democrats, such as we conceive Proudhon, for example, to be; in colloquial language, we are calling you "reds." . . . And yet, you have only to raise the obrok rate by one paltry ruble and lower the maximum allotment by half a desiatina in some districts, by only a quarter desiatina in others, and we will stop challenging your figures.[80]

Semenov's rendition of Parnachev's view may be more nearly a travesty than a transcription, but these words convey what the deputies had in common: animosity to the bureaucracy and a concern for particular economic advantages.

The Limited Consensus

Few deputies refrained from making jibes at the bureaucracy. Frequently they turned abruptly from points of substance to this more agreeable occupation. They knew whereof they spoke; twenty-nine of the deputies had served in the civil service, most of them long enough to achieve a fairly high rank.[81] Despite the dominant role of the nobility within the administration and the favor that the government traditionally lavished on the pomeshchiki, they assumed that bureaucrats were hostile to nobles and would continue to be. Only Unkovskii foresaw that the officials who carried out the reform would favor the pomeshchiki, and this prediction was really a thrust at the commission: if its recommendations were enacted, the wretched plight of the pomeshchiki would sway the most dispassionate official in their favor.[82]

Various motives lay behind these protests against bureaucracy as a principle and the bureaucrats as a class. The protests were often raised in behalf of political concessions to the nobility; many deputies argued for the designation of a pomeshchik as "guardian of the canton" [*volostnoi popechitel'*] and for the administration of districts and even provinces by noble-dominated assemblies. Then, too, the deputies were staunch monarchists; the Nizhnii Novgorod deputy Stremoukhov privately remarked that there was no hope now that the tsar was a red,[83] but this despairing view does not appear in the responses or testimony of any deputy. The reformist bureaucrats represented the deputies as a threat to the autocracy, but some deputies entertained the same suspicion about the Editorial Commission.[84] Certainly none of them ventured direct criticism of the tsar; the devoted subject of an autocrat, dissatisfied with the policies the autocracy is pursuing, must direct his reproaches at the autocrat's servants.

Finally, the protests against bureaucracy expressed the hostility of many nobles to the very idea of the proposed reform. It would have been pointless to voice this hostility directly, and the deputies did not even find it prudent to speak well of serfdom—except as an institution that sheltered the peasantry from predatory bureaucrats. No deputy even ventured to echo Orlov-Davydov's vague complaint about the methods used to secure the nobility's assent to the reform.[85] The deputies accepted accomplished facts in the hope of securing favor in the future. Nonetheless, they resented the manipulation to which the nobility and they themselves had recently been subjected, and this resentment gave new intensity traditional laments about the formalism and corruption of provincial officials.

The deputies' criticism of the bureaucracy reflected the events of the past two year, but also exposed the nobles' conception of themselves. No deputy acknowledged that the noble estate enjoyed any favor or privilege apart from the right to hold serfs. Even the nobility's right of petition was of no practical value, according to the deputies Ofrosimov and Volkonskii:

Complaints of oppression by the local administration were turned over to the judgment of those against whom they were lodged; the nobility's representations about the eradication of abuses were considered interference into matters outside its competence; even recently, proposals for the emancipation of the peasants were considered inflammatory documents; and at the present time, the drafts of the Provincial Committees have not even been favored with attentive discussion.[86]

Perfect fairness would have required some mention of the bureaucracy's support of individual nobles—that is, of serfholders—but the description was generally true. Other deputies complained of the nobility's plight in similar terms. Taken together, the responses suggest how the plight came about, for they indicate that the deputies, like the nobility at large, attached little importance to institutional forms and prerogatives.

In withdrawing their appeal to the tsar, the deputies as a group decided to work upon those who presently enjoyed influence rather than raise issues of form and procedure. Almost every deputy went on to retrace this path by himself, in that he did not seek to defend the institution he represented, the provincial committee. At most, the deputies defended the specific positions their committee had taken. One of them reported to his provincial marshal that "duty and conviction" compelled him to conform to his committee's draft, since it constituted "the will and solemn resolve of the nobility concerning the surrender or alteration of certain rights belonging to it"; where the draft was so remote from the Editorial Commission's principles that it contained nothing to offer in their stead, he had simply tried to preserve the pomeshchik's position and protect his interests.[87] Most deputies chose to argue for their committee's proposals on their supposed merits. They did not make an issue of the authority and responsibility that had been vested in the committees and then withdrawn. The rescripts instructed the committees to work out the particulars of the reform; the April Program had divided this work into three periods, of which only the first was so far complete. Only two responses made any mention of the committees' duties during the second and third periods, duties that the Editorial Commission had quietly assumed. Pozen urged that the economic settlement be left to the provincial committees but not even he, the author of the April Program, insisted that its provisions be strictly followed.[88] As a rule, the deputies did not evoke the warrant given to the committees in order to reclaim lost authority, but by way of apology, explaining that many committee drafts were defective because, in accord with the April Program, they covered only the period of temporary obligation.

Of all the duties of the first group, only Shidlovskii and Gagarin spoke up emphatically for the committees' prerogatives, but their advocacy was inept. Shidlovskii's argument assumed that the property rights in land and serfs were vested in the nobility of each province as a body, an idea that would have been more of a juridical innovation than the cautious formulations of the Editorial Commission. Shidlovskii was perhaps the only deputy who sought to defend the authority of the committees as such; the Simbirsk Committee waived compensation for the peasants' buildings, but Shidlovskii argued that the commission must impose payments for these buildings in any province where the committee had not renounced them.[89] The example of Shidlovskii and Gagarin did not invite imitation; most deputies prudently accepted accomplished facts. Habitual deference to accomplished facts, however, must leave an institution like an assembly of the nobility or a provincial committee without any force of its own.

The deputies preferred a pragmatic, if not practical, course. Their responses show very little sense of cohesion or caste pride. They are almost free of conventional rhetoric about the nobility's past services and traditional devotion to the throne, and the only deputies who claimed any credit for the nobility's initiative in the emancipation were those who, judging from the tenor of their responses, most deeply regretted that initiative. One deputy weakly suggested that the nobility might take revenge upon the government, stating that "I do not believe I have the right to conceal from the Government that *granting the peasants a perpetual right to the use of the pomeshchik's resources may be interpreted by the nobility as coercion."*[90] This was something less than an intimation of a Fronde, but the other deputies did not go so far. In their attempt to avert spoliation and ruin they represented their electors as victims, abused by the bureaucrats and cheated by the peasants—a category of men to be pitied or indulged but not, surely, to be feared.[91]

The deputies also made it plain that they valued commercial advantages more than the cohesion and privileged position of the nobility as a whole. One of the compulsory questions accompanying the instructions asked whether nonnobles should be allowed to buy estates settled with temporarily obligated peasants. Some deputies argued that this right should be extended only to certain categories of the population, but others were so eager for an expanded market and a consequent rise in the sale value of their estates that they did not understand that a question of status was being raised.[92] Only eight responses argued for the retention of the nobility's last exclusive privilege, the ownership of "populated estates."[93]

The image of the peasantry that emerges from the responses is consistent with the image of the nobility. The peasant, as throughout the consideration of the peasant question, does not make an appearance except as part of a mass. The salient features of this mass are malingering, thieving, and evasion of responsibilities. Implicitly, the serfs enjoyed almost luxurious ease, since most deputies argued that they could render their present dues or more while holding much less than the commission's reckoning of their present allotments.[94] A few deputies upheld the merits of peasant custom in such areas as family law and the procedure of village assemblies. Only the Kostroma deputy Lopukhin would trust peasant custom where the pomeshchik's interests were at stake; he argued that dues should be fixed in terms of yield and sown area rather than days of barshchina; since the peasant "obeys the law of necessity first of all . . . he will never refuse to work in the fields" if there is useful work to be done.[95] Not even Koshelev, who delivered several effusive tributes to the peasants, argued that they were naturally industrious in the pomeshchik's behalf. In most responses, the peasants figure only as desultory barshchina laborers and reluctant payers of obrok.

It was not the deputies' intention to paint a panorama of serfdom in its last days, and the incomplete picture that does emerge from their responses is naturally colored by their belief that their property and incomes were in grave jeopardy. Nonetheless, nowhere did they indicate any sentimental element in the relationship between pomeshchik and serf. The Saratov deputies raised the issue indirectly, in commenting on the Economic Section's apprehensions of conflict between the peasantry and the nobility. They recalled, as spokesmen for the nobility were fond of doing, that serfdom had been established by law as a "necessity of state at that time," and insisted that "no right-thinking pomeshchik regrets" that the state was now abolishing it. Serfdom was onerous for the serfs, and they were now impatient for emancipation.

Some, doubtless, are angry at the pomeshchiki, and this feeling is disruptive to the state, but do they all foster this feeling? . . . Serfdom is so dintinct from slavery [nevol'nichestvo[that we do not suppose that this anger is an absolutely inevitable attribute of the former.

This was cautious language, but the rest of their response indicated that they were prepared for unremitting hostility between nobles and emancipated peasants. They expected a massive exodus of peasants from the lands of the pomeshchiki, who would be subjected to an extortionist conspiracy by those who remained; the statute must be drawn up to exclude these possibilities. In particular, it must convince the peasants that they had no rights at all to their allotments, although they were obliged to accept them. Since the peasants were too immature to run their own affairs, the "legal and moral authority of the pomeshchik should not . . . be shaken." However, moral obligations were not mutual, to judge from arguments of the Saratov deputies against the immutability of peasant dues. They observed that

the poor craftsman in St. Petersburg does not now buy his meat according to the prices fixed in 1800, although, on the other hand, his work is not paid for at the rates prevailing then.* It seems to us that the same rules should be applied to the peasant in regard to the land.[96]

The other deputies were no more sentimental about their serfs.

The Editorial Commission was aware that the peasants might react to the coming reform with violent disillusionment. Rostovtsev, who had almost no experience with peasants, was more explicitly apprehensive of riots and disorders than the other members,[97] but this danger was more or less obliquely mentioned in the reports of the sections. The Economic Section concluded its justification of granting the peasants their present allotments by predicting that

given a universal disruption of all the economic conditions of rural life and a simultaneous, more or less general, reduction of the peasant allotments, it would, beyond any doubt, be impossible for the government to answer for the maintenance of domestic tranquility, or, at least, to achieve this purpose otherwise than by using means which the most elementary wisdom would enjoin it to avoid assiduously.[98]

Passages like this in the publications and debates of the commission provide support for the view that fear of the peasantry was the mainspring of the government's peasant policy, but these passages are so rare that the support is weak. Furthermore, judging by the deputies' responses, this fear increased directly with one's remoteness from the peasants. The deputies emphasized that the government's apprehensions about the peasants' reaction to the emancipation was a further example of bureaucratic myopia and caution; while they were not free of these apprehensions, they would not be guided by them.

Several deputies did assert that the reform would produce a

---

*This concessive clause is a veiled admission that the analogy was specious, since, unlike the craftsman, the peasant would not be able to seek better terms elsewhere, and his compensation—that is, his allotment—could not increase.

major social upheaval—unless the program of the Editorial Commission was modified as they suggested.[99] More often they simply argued that it was the government's responsibility to suppress any disturbances provoked by the reform. Gagarin made the point with his usual heavy irony. The Economic Section, by guaranteeing the peasants their present household plots,

can only provide justification for the groundless supposition that it acknowledges what is lawful but fears to provoke grumbling among the masses. But if, in the reform of estate relations now under way, a consideration with such dangerous consequences is taken as a premise; if it is admitted in advance that law has lost its holy inviolability and the Government has lost the force to compel respect for the sanctity of law, then it would be better not to begin the great enterprise of reform.[100]

The Chernigov deputy Markovich was more moderate.

Of course, there is not one nobleman who would not sacrifice everything, so that domestic tranquility will not be disrupted, or so that the Government will not be compelled to maintain order by using those grievous means which wisdom and humanity enjoin it to avoid. . . . However, who can foresee the consequences [of the reform]? Under any circumstances, it is possible to be apprehensive even about the reform itself.[101]

The Tambov deputies were less apprehensive than Markovich, maintaining that it was incompatible with the spirit and purpose of the reform

to do what is unjust and harmful out of an apprehension of future disorders; they probably will not happen, because the peasant himself will understand and appreciate the time, freedom, and civil rights, which are being given to him and which he awaits with such joy.[102]

The Khar'kov deputies, however, denied that the peasants would be satisfied with free time and civil rights and articulated a kind of pomeshchik populism.[103] They declared

In Khar'kov province, the peasants are very hopeful that they will immediately receive freedom and all the proprietary land as their property without any obligations to the pomeshchiki, who, upon receiving compensation from the Government, will depart forever from their estates. This hope . . . has become a dogma, embracing the whole people, from small to great.[104]

The people's hopes must not be affronted, for the peasantry would patiently suffer oppression, but not disillusionment; "in an instant [the people] will pass from stolid patience to desperate rebellion and will present its affronted dogma with blood sacrifices." The peasants' expectations were boundless, but only because they were traditionally hopeless; they should be "strictly and dispassionately weighed . . . eliminating everything that is excessive and childish and satisfying, in conformity with law, justice and honor, the people's basic demand, which in essence is always just."

Strictness and dispassion subtly transmuted the popular dogma. Because of their inherent sense of justice, the peasants acknowledged the pomeshchik's title to all his land; they wanted not "property" but "freedom of property" for themselves and they resented their ascription to the land. In short, "the dogma of the whole people" corresponded to the Khar'kov deputies' program: compulsory, government-assisted redemption of a small allotment.[105] Like most members of the first group, the Khar'kov deputies were willing to waive direct authority over the individual peasant; even the Saratov deputies, who spoke up for the "legal and moral authority of the pomeshchik," suggested ways to avoid direct confrontations between the pomeshchik and his ex-serfs. The deputies were not, however, willing to yield a kopek or a desiatina of land simply to forestall or diminish the danger of a disillusioned peasantry.

Because the deputies and the members of the Editorial Commission were in overt conflict concerning the economic provisions of the reform, neither party could see the extent to which their views were converging. For the deputies, quite unaware, echoed the debates that had gone on in the closed sessions of the commission; the objections they made most frequently had already been raised within the commission, and many deputies were evolving in the same general direction as most members of the commission.

The conflict between the deputies and the commission was a product of the deputies' defense of the allotments proposed by their provincial committees. The intransigent deputies did not advance detailed arguments; they considered their committees' endorsement to be argument enough. Gagarin, for example, parried the commission's complaint that the committees had not offered data in support of their allotment figures, by asserting that the figures themselves were data, since they constituted an expert judgment.[106] Few deputies disdained argument as Gagarin did, although most were inclined to criticize the commission's recommendations rather than justify their own. Volkov of

Moscow, for example, calculated that the owners of eighty estates in his home district would lose almost one-third of their obrok incomes according to the commission's system; on the other twenty estates, the peasants would suffer correspondingly, for they would lose a substantial part of their allotment while paying nine rubles per soul as before. According to the computations of the deputy Stremoukhov, the nobles of Nizhnii Novgorod would lose from 17 to 35 percent of their incomes and therefore, being unable to keep up their mortgage payments, lose their estates as well. Neither Stremoukhov nor Volkov offered similar computations on the allotments and dues they advocated.[107] The Poltava and Khar'kov deputies did propose a modest increase in the allotments their committees had voted, but most deputies did not offer any compromise.

The range of argument was wide, because the contending parties did not simply differ about quantities of land and dues, they proceeded from different systems. Various parts of the commission's system, such as the use of a maximum and minimum and a differentiated allotment for districts or parts of districts, could be found in one or more committee drafts, but the whole system could not be found in any. Some committees had voted a single normative allotment, with a few attendant conditions, for the entire province; others had followed the April Program and fixed the allotment according to the density of population on the estate. The deputies tended to uphold these alternatives, particularly the use of norms instead of the existing-allotment principle, and attacked the commission's system as well as the results it produced.

To a limited extent, the deputies divided along regional lines in singling out objects of attack. The deputies from the black-soil, barshchina provinces complained that the commission did not offer the pomeshchik enough discretion in the relocation of the peasants' plots; clearly, they had given some thought to the problems of postreform agriculture and wanted to consolidate the best land in the demesne. Deputies from the North showed little interest in reallocating land; they tended to isolate the subject of dues and call for a flat increase of the commission's figures. The deputies from Riazan, a province on the edge of the black-soil zone, attacked the commission on both counts.

There were some issues, however, on which almost all the deputies attacked the commission. Few could refrain from attacking the harsh measures the commission proposed to apply to peasants in arrears, including what amounted to the sale of the defaulting peasants.[108] The deputies enjoyed denouncing the commission for adopting a brutal and retrograde policy; Pozen claimed that a pomeshchik who applied the commission's exactions under serfdom could have his estate sequestered for abuse of manorial power.[109] Most deputies urged a simple and humanitarian alternative: if a peasant fell into arrears, his allotment would revert to the pomeshchik. Clearly, then, they understood the rationale of the commission's Draconian exactions: to keep the land in the hands of the peasant community, whatver the cost in terms of dignity, humanitarian principle, or justice to the individual peasant.[110]

The deputies argued with equal ardor against the immutability of dues, usually proposing that they should be periodically redetermined in accord with the going price of grain, which was Pozen's formula. Several deputies also followed Pozen in urging that the pomeshchik not be required to allot more than half of his estate; the commission guaranteed him unencumbered tenure of only one-third of his land.

The most popular target of all was the commission's requirement that the pomeshchik provide peasants with fuel, either including a woodlot in the allotment or supplying the wood himself. Even the most cooperative deputies, such as Tikhovidov and Lanskoi, joined in the protest. Volkov of Moscow bluntly asserted that if the peasants had any allotment land within the squire's forest, they would steal his wood without restraint. Many deputies shared Volkov's dread of the peasants' axes, judging by their comments on the proposed forest code.[111] So did Unkovskii, who explained that the peasantry had a "weak concept of property rights in forest lands," which they thought belonged to God, and hence to everyone, since they are "not a work of human hands." Other deputies made this point, but Unkovskii's anthropological studies embraced the nobility, as well, and his elucidation of the nobles' attitude to the forest explains the deputies' unanimous aversion to the commission's proposal. "The sale of forest," he pointed out, "usually takes place because the owner happens to have a pressing need for money, in large quantity and in a short time." No pomeshchik, then, wanted an encumberance on what he conceived to be his capital reserve. Unkonskii himself opposed the idea, and effectively criticized the commission's complicated system. The pomeshchik's obligation to provide fuel or an allotment of woodland depended upon the character of the area and the estate, being greater where wood was more plentiful; thus the peasants, Unkovskii argued, were promised fuel where wood was cheap, and left to their own devices where it was scarce and expensive.[112]

The objects of attack reveal an unexpected affinity between the deputies and the members of the commission. The deputies singled out the provisions that had aroused the most intense debate within the commission. For example, the requirement that the pomeshchik provide fuel to the peasants, which, like most of the commission's economic proposals, was justified as a continuation of present practices, had carried in the General Session of the Editorial Commission by a single vote. Among the deputies' favorite targets, only the immutability of dues had been adopted without much controversy. The decision came up for review after the deputies departed, and the commission reversed itself, adding a provision that the Minister of Internal Affairs could alter the dues of peasants on temporary obligation after twenty years. Some members of the commission believed, quite rightly, that they were making an empty gesture, since the minister would not dare to increase the dues at that time.[113]

The deputies and the members of the commission were similar in their preoccupations because they themselves were similar. There were no Miliutins among the deputies, there were no Gagarins or Unkovskiis on the commission; on the whole, however, the deputies were pomeshchiki with bureaucratic experience while the members were bureaucrats with pomeshchik backgrounds. The two sides fell so quickly and easily into antagonistic roles that neither could see its affinity with the other.[114]

The affinity between Cherkasskii and Koshelev had been very strong. Neither was a professional bureaucrat. They had collaborated as government members of the Tula and Riazan provincial committees and on the magazine *Rural Welfare*. However, Cherkasskii was appointed to the Editorial Commission, while Koshelev was elected minority deputy from Riazan. Cherkasskii urged his friend to assume this office and resist the anticipated "cabal" between the deputies and the commission's enemies. Koshelev yielded to Cherkasskii's plea, but he took up his role as deputy as ardently as Cherkasskii labored on the commission; the accord between them disappeared, to Koshelev's dismay. "Have we parted, then," he wrote to Cherkasskii, "so that we no longer understand one another?" The rupture came about because Cherkasskii had dismissed Koshelev's response as "a malicious pamphlet" and derided him for making common cause with the other deputies, so that "our enemies are exploiting you with particular pleasure." Koshelev had, according to Cherkasskii, "submitted to a general law, applicable to us all, and proved that it is hard to stand up against the influence of the surrounding milieu."

Cherkasskii's wife was appalled by Koshelev's transformation, but she might have given some thought to her husband's. The enlightened pomeshchik who, a year previously, would not condescend to enter the bureaucracy, now identified himself with the institution he served and equated criticism of that institution with an attack on his ideal. He was at one, in his loyalties and attitudes, with the cold-eyed functionaries of the capital. He had made concessions to reach an accord with his fellow nobles on the Tula Provincial Committee; now he complained to his wife of the necessity of even listening to the deputies, whom he found "very dull; it is necessary to hear out such nonsense, and the nobles traffic so shamefully!"

Iurii Samarin was abroad on sick leave during the confrontation with the first group of deputies, but he, too, had submitted to Cherkasskii's "general law." When Koshelev ventured to air his grievances against the Editorial Commission publicly, in a pamphlet published in Leipzig, Samarin wrote to him,

You do not want to understand that the present [April 1860] mood is such that every word said against the Editorial Commission is seized with joy and immeidately turned into a weapon against the emancipation of the peasants with land, while all the advice with which these attacks on us are bolstered, though it were wiser than the book of Sirach, is *wasted*, goes by the boards. . . . Shidlovskii bows at the mention of your name, Gagarin has gone out of his mind about you. Rejoice![115]

Koshelev was, to be sure, embarrased by his situation. He was now allied with Ofrosimov and Volkonskii, who had been his bitterest enemies in the Riazan Committee, but in most respects they had simply come around to his position. However, Koshelev insisted on drawing up a separate response in his own name because of the embarrassment at his role of spokesman for the pomeshchiki. He inserted several rhapsodies on the peasantry as "Russia's strength," and at the end of his criticism of the Economic Section there was an apologetic note, which Ofrosimov and Volkonskii did not think of striking.

It is painful to raise my voice against land allotments that are too large, dues that are too low in several area, and excessive favors granted to the peasants, but justice comes before all. As formerly I did not fear to attract the indignation of many by defending the interests of the peasants, so it is now; though my heart grieves, I cannot permit myself to be carried away even for the sake of the long-suffering.[116]

Koshelev was, perhaps, carried away by the excitement of combat with the commission. He took the lead, which several deputies followed, in scoring points off the commission to no clear purpose. The commission, like many provincial committees, modestly veiled its legislative function by citing existing laws,[117] some of them irrevelant or inapplicable; the arguments it advanced to justify certain concessions to the pomeshchiki were inconsistent with the basic principles it proclaimed. It was easy enough to point out, as Koshelev and other deputies did, that if the commission's minimum allotments conformed to the terms of the rescripts, as the commission pretended, then the maximum allotments were obviously excessive. It is doubtful that anyone thought the commission's minimum allotments, which were everywhere one-third of the maximum and always less than the provincial committee had set as a norm, were adequate to sustain the peasants. All that might be achieved by exposing the commission on this point was an increase in the minimum, which was set low for the sake of a few poor pomeshchiki with little land. But Koshelev and many other deputies took it as their task to embarass the commission by any means at hand.

Not all the deputies appreciated the steps the commission had taken in the pomeshchik's favor. Many critized the gradation of dues, and the criticisms were often persuasive since the rationale for gradation in the reports of the Economic Section was disingenuous, or, at least, incomplete. However, Cherkasskii and Petr Semenov explained candidly to the deputies that gradation could only work to the pomeshchik's advantage.[118] Most deputies, presuming the commission to be antagonistic, were deaf to these explanations. Some of them simply did not understand the workings of the gradation system, the maximum and minimum, and other complex provisions. This was another unrecognized affinity with the members of the commission, some of whom had the same difficulty.[119]

The commission and the deputies treated one another as adversaries. They were bound to do so, given the structure the commission had imparted to the relationship, its neglect of the committee drafts, and, finally, the deputies' conception of their own role. Ofrosimov and Volkonskii explained, "*The nobility did not empower us to make any concessions or sacrifices; it elected us simply to defend its interests.*"[120] Defense without concessions usually meant insisting on the recommendations of the provincial committees, and where they were specific or quantitative, the deputies allowed themselves little latitude. The redemption of allotment land, however, could be represented as a further stage rather than a concession; many drafts, as the Editorial Commission pointed out, were more or less complete before the committee realized that redemption was possible.[121] At any rate, the deputies did allow themselves latitude

on the subject of redemption, and there was a strong flow of
sentiment to the commission's view that redemption was the only
satisfactory issue from serfdom and temporary obligation.

Eleven deputies represented committees or factions that had
advocated redemption. Almost all of them now went further and
favored compulsory redemption, and other deputies were
converted to their view—both deputies from Iaroslav Province, the
majority deputy from Riazan, and even Gagarin's fellow deputy
from Voronezh. Parnachev and Kadro-Sysoev, representing
factions of divided committees, did not follow the other deputies
from Vladimir and Tver in favoring compulsory redemption, but
they were amenable to government-backed redemption as on
option. No deputy flatly opposed redemption as a solution, though
it followed from Gagarin's remarks that he did not like the idea,
while Shidlovskii implied that it would not be suitable in Simbirsk.
The Kostroma deputy Lopukhin offered what he called a
redemption scheme, though it could scarcely be recognized as such.
Otherwise, the deputies who did not advocate redemption of
allotments were ostentatiously silent on the subject; several simply
observed that they were not authorized to comment on anything
except the regulations for temporary obligation. The consensus of
the deputies was overwhelmingly in favor of the commission's view
of the merits of redemption.

This consensus did not represent a reconciliation between the
two sides. The commission was bound by the government's
insistence that redemption must be gradual and voluntary, so that
Unkovskii's demands were as far from its formal position as
Gagarin's.[122] Most of the ardent partisans of compulsory
redemption were as explicitly uncompromising in defense of the
pomeshchik's interests as Gagarin and Shidlovskii. Like them, the
deputies from Riazan, Iaroslav, and Khar'kov imputed malice to the
commission and were unequivocal in their defense of private
property. They argued that the state could not require the
pomeshchik to allot land to free peasants, but could only seize the
land by eminent domain. In and of itself, then, advocacy of
redemption was not a concession to the peasantry or the
commission;[123] everything depended on the size of the allotment to
be redeemed and the price to be paid, and on these matters most
deputies clung to the norms proposed by their provincial
committees. Support of redemption simply expressed a judgment
that temporary obligation, or state-regulated quasi-serfdom, would
not work. Unkovskii and Gavrilov opposed this alternative because
it was too much like serfdom, but other deputies appear to have
opposed it because it was not enough like serfdom; they were not so
much troubled by the constraints on the peasants as by the

constraints on the pomeshchik—the limitation of the peasants' obligations, the determination of their allotments by statute, the certainty, as they conceived it, that the peasants would prevaricate and solicit official interference while the crops rotted in the fields. The deputies' enthusiasm for redemption was another expression of their attitude to the peasantry and the bureaucracy, and represented an intuitive judgment that estates could not be run under the constraints proposed by the commission. The deputies of the second convocation would make the same judgment, but they drew the opposite conclusion and sought to have the constraints reduced or eliminated.

There was a degree of economic calculation in this conclusion. Most deputies of the first convocation represented provinces where serfdom was essential to the pomeshchik's revenues. If an estate was overpopulated, or the land was poor, or there was plenty of arable land available in the neighborhood, it was the pomeshchik's personal power over his serfs that kept them working in his behalf. Without that personal power, he would probably be better off with a capital sum, based on the dues under serfdom; hence it was the provincial committees of the North, where the peasants' dues least resembled rental payments for land, that first came out for redemption. Redemption was most obviously in the interests of the owners of obrok serfs who supported themselves and paid their dues by wage labor or crafts. They were not a large proportion of the serf population, but they were concentrated north and east of Moscow, and many deputies in the first convocation represented this area.

Deputies from other areas, however, also supported redemption, for this was a political as well as an economic judgment. The Editorial Commission attempted to meet the needs of obrok proprietors, owners of estates with little land, and the pomeshchiki of the underpopulated Southeast. If a deputy suspected that these provisions would be ineffective or temporary, if he assumed that the bureaucracy was adamantly hostile to the nobility, he would favor redemption.[124] By and large, the first convocation despaired of swaying the commission or the government, and this despair inclined them to redemption, as Koshelev explained in answering: "Why have many, including the undersigned, shifted so decisively to compulsory redemption, when formerly, and even quite recently, we affirmed that it was unfeasible, unprofitable, and even all but impossible?" The answer, which most deputies were not candid enough to provide, was that they had not known how confining the government's alternative would be. When he had favored redemption as an option, Koshlev continued, at that time, neither the peasants' perpetual usufruct of the land, nor the immutability of dues, still less the peasants' right, at the expiration of a certain term, to depart as a whole community to other places—none of these had been articulated and proclaimed for all to hear.

Koshelev correctly noted that the government had not committed itself on the subject of free movement and still might enact some form of ascription, but the peasants' perpetual right to their allotments for fixed dues had been broadcast in the proceedings of the Editorial Commission; it was impossible to withdraw that promise, and compulsory redemption was the only satisfactory solution consistent with it. Or, as the Riazan deputies baldly explained to the nobility of their province,

In the present period of struggle between the bureaucracy and the nobility, a struggle which threatens the latter with destruction, it seems to us that the essential and only possible [course] for the nobility is yielding part of its land to the peasants for an acceptable price, with the government guaranteeing full and punctual payment, and then . . . asserting our own rights to participate in the administrative and economic governance of the area; for, so long as even a shadow of manorial authority remains, the interference of the bureaucracy . . . is inevitable and will lead to the enslavement of all classes of the people to the all-powerful functionaries.[125]

Most deputies of the first convocation were explicitly hostile to the bureaucracy, held similar views of the peasantry and the nobility, and were inclined to redemption as the best way out of the present dilemma. These common sentiments could not either unite the deputies or reconcile them to the Editorial Commission. They were divided in their concept of their own role, and in so far as they had a common attitude, it was divisive. Each deputy defended the interests of his own province; they could not find a formula to meet the needs of the nobility as a whole.[126]

A Final Effort

The deputies pursued their duties with a growing sense of futility. Consultations among themselves and testimony before the Editorial Commission proved equally unproductive. The time allotted was too short, several deputies complained, to compile a proper critique of the commission's voluminous proceedings.[127] Yet they spun their responses out to such length that the Main Committee and the Council of State would not be able to give them serious consideration. Koshelev predicted that the responses would be rolled into cigarettes,[128] but his own was longest of all. The deputies began to drift away. The Tver deputy Kadro-Sysoev departed with bravado, assuring Rostovtsev that the commission's system had been devastated.[129]

The other deputies were not content to whistle in the dark. They reassembled, now somewhat reduced in numbers, and resolved on a course of action: they would appeal to the tsar. If this decision did not produce a sense of *déjà vu*, surely the wrangle that followed did. Again there was a preliminary accord on a text, again second thoughts prevailed and a new version was substituted, again the deputies divided.[130]

Both versions of the new address to the tsar recapitulated elements of the address the deputies had drafted and rejected earlier, but nonetheless they differed significantly one from the other in their tenor. The first, signed in draft by twenty-one deputies, acknowledged that the disagreement between the commission and the deputies was "significant, even basic." The emphasis, however, was on practical difficulties; the deputies had not been able to discuss certain questions on which the commission had not yet come to a decision. Seeking to fulfill their obligations before the tsar and the nobility, the deputies asked permission to review the commission's final proposals and to testify before the Main Committee "in support of the opinions we set forth."

This was the same request, warmed over in a bland sauce, that the deputies had made and withdrawn three weeks before. It may be that Pozen, who was not among the twenty-one signers, won the deputies around to a substitute once again. The address he did sign, which was submitted to the tsar a day or two later, did not raise any ominous demands. The eighteen signers simply asked permission to "present our comments on the final proceedings of the Editorial Commission before they are presented to the Main Committee." On the other hand, the address of the eighteen deputies was harsher towards the Editorial Commission, whose proposals "do not correspond to the general requirements and do not carry out the basic principles which the nobility reverently and willingly accepted for direction on the peasant question."[131] This criticism was a milder form of the other main element of the deputies' initial reaction to the instructions: the commission was pursuing a fatal course, in conflict with the rescripts. This, the only one of the three collective addresses that was actually submitted to the tsar, was reasonable in tone and substance, but it suffered by association with unruly neighbors. Two rivals, one written by Khrushchov, the other by Shidlovskii, were presented to the tsar independently, after they had been rejected in a general gathering of the deputies.[132]

Khrushchov's address bore the signatures of five deputies—Khrushchov and Shreter from Khar'kov, both Iaroslav deputies, and Unkovskii. It expressed gratitude for the "inexpressible favor" the tsar had shown in inviting them to participate in the reform and apologized in advance for their presumptuous appeal, which was prompted by their love of tsar and country and their conviction that

the pomeshchiki will be ruined by the increase of the peasants' allotment of land and the extreme decrease of the dues, while in general, the peasants' way of life will not be ameliorated, because the provisions that the peasants administer themselves will be suppressed and destroyed by the influence of the functionaries.

Presumably, the five deputies meant that the commission had increased the allotments proposed by the committees, not those the peasants held under serfdom.[133] Even so, wild alarm on this count was not to Unkovskii's taste,[134] although it was in keeping with the responses and testimony of the other four. He had no misgivings about the reform program with which the address ended.

The five called for compulsory redemption (avoiding the word "compulsory") "on terms that will not be ruinous for the pomeshchiki." They also sought three major administrative reforms: the establishment of what would soon be known as the zemstvo; the creation of public, independent courts with juries; and a relaxation of censorship. The antibureaucratic sentiment characteristic of the deputies is apparent in this brief program; government officials were to be accountable to the reformed courts, while restraint on the censors would mean that "the shortcomings and abuses in local administration [can] come to the attention of the sovereign power."[135]

The other addresses presented to the tsar simply requested a further hearing in more congenial circumstances; only the address of the five deputies was specific in its requests. To this extent, it was more venturesome. It contained nothing on either economic or administrative matters, however, that was not set forth more pointedly and in greater detail in the responses of various deputies, including some who did not sign the text.[136] Nor were these ideas manifestly subversive. The Ministry of Internal Affairs conceded that each of the four proposed reforms was under active consideration,[137] and in the next few years, the government would act, though more cautiously than these five deputies might have liked, in the sense of all four. Even when representing the nobles' behavior in the blackest terms, Lanskoi urged the tsar to compensate them for the loss of their powers over their serfs by granting them a dominant role in local affairs.[138] Finally, the Editorial Commission did modify its proposals on allotments and dues in the nobility's favor.

From the offical point of view, however, the address of the five deputies was far from innocuous, for it challenged the government's attempts to limit the deputies' competence to a minimum. The Riazan deputy Ofrosimov, who refused to sign this address though it corresponded in many respects to his response, pronounced it "terribly untimely; there is a great danger that we shall all be dispersed from Petersburg."

Shidlovskii submitted his own address, "in which," according to Ofrosimov, "he demands a constitution, neither more nor less. That is very stupid, and he does not even look us in the eye."[139] Shidlovskii's address did not demand a constitution, but Ofrosimov's evaluation was correct. Not even Gagarin would sign it. The only specific request Shidlovskii made was this: "Deign, O Sovereign, to summon especially elected plenipotentiaries from the nobility to the steps of Thy throne and conclude under Thy personal direction, O Sovereign, the undertaking that will be the glory of Thy reign." This direct relationship was necessary because "the nobility has been debased and slandered before Your Majesty, for it has been represented as a backward estate which desires to retain serfdom, and which thought only of its own interests in composing the draft Statutes." But the nobility was the natural guardian of the throne and the fatherland; to meet the perils of the moment, and stem the subversive influx of western ideas, the autocrat must cleave to it.

Apart from his request for the tsar's personal intervention, Shidlovskii had little to communicate except his alarm. He revived many of the complaints of noble malcontents, such as the baneful influence of "persons from the government" and "the promptings of outsiders" on the provincial committees. Where his insinuations tended towards the concrete, there was some justice in them, as when he reproached the Editorial Commission for casting aside the committees' drafts and substituting principles "unknown to the nobility." On the whole, however, Shidlovskii's florid appeal was at once vague and alarmist; he held that the commission's system was founded "on an apparent desire to destroy the significance of the nobility as an estate and as property-holders," while the dissemination of its proceedings was a clear threat to the maintenance of order.[140]

All the addresses expressed dismay about the Editorial Commission, a sentiment that was universal among the deputies. All the deputies who had not left the capital and who were not under bureaucratic discipline signed one of them, according to Koshelev, who explained that the addresses were necessary simply because the responses were too long to be effective.[141] Indeed, in their substance, they were as innocuous as the responses but, unlike the responses, they were specifically addressed to the tsar. All the addresses constituted an attempt by the deputies to bypass the Editorial Commission and hence, despite their submissive tone and guarded requests, they held a political challenge.

It was easier to represent the addresses of the deputies as a political challenge because they went before the tsar in compromising company. M. A. Bezobrazov, despairing of resolute action by the deputies, submitted a memorandum of his own simultaneously with their appeals. The Bezobrazov brothers had been trying to stiffen the nobility's backbone for two years. Nikolai published a series of pamphlets in Germany defending the sanctity of the nobility's rights. Mikhail, an official of the Ministry of Internal Affairs who also had a post at court, produced a series of manuscript articles of his own, criticizing the provincial committees of Moscow and St. Petersburg for their suicidal self-abnegation.[142]

More recently, Mikhail Bezobrazov had composed a protest against administrative abuses concerning emancipation. Because the bureaucracy had harried, coerced, and purged the provincial committees (after rigging the elections and perverting the tsar's will),

the renunciations, allocations of land, concessions of property and so on that have been expressed in various instances in this matter were the consequence of ignorance, indiscretion and even coercion; they can have no significance before Your Majesty and no obligatory force for the Nobility.

Bezobrazov warned that the reform, as conceived and now being imposed by the bureaucracy, promised economic collapse, anarchy, and famine. Nonetheless, matters could be set right by submitting the emancipation legislation for review to an elected assembly of two nobles from each province. Bezobrazov predicted that some hypocrites would find an affinity between this Assembly of the Nobility and the Estates General and would warn the tsar of a "revolutionary tendency" in the nobility, although they themselves

consciously or unconsciously, have assumed a revolutionary tendency, covered over with administrative forms, and fear those who can expose them.

In the heart of the Russian Tsar, a dread of seeing a revolutionary tendency in the Russian Nobility is impossible, and we are convinced, O Sovereign, that Thou trusteth in us as firmly as we place our hopes in Thee.[143]

This document was circulated under the title, "Materials to Convey to the Tsar in an Address from the Nobility . . ."; however, the address was not conveyed to the tsar after all, because Bezobrazov could not find enough nobles willing to sign it. Prince Menshikov would not endorse it, despite his admiration for the pamphlets of Bezobrazov's brother. By October of 1859, Bezobrazov's only visible success had been the insertion of one of his memoranda into the proceedings of the St. Petersburg Provincial Committee; however, the Ministry of Internal Affairs refused to accept it even as a dissenting opinion appended to the committee's draft.[144]

Bezobrazov's machinations did have one unintended result, of which he was unaware: he had succeeded in rousing the tsar's anxieties about the nobility's political ambitions to a still higher pitch. The Third Section secured a copy of the stillborn "Materials to Convey to the Tsar" and turned it over to Alexander. He commented, "I am afraid that revolutionary or at least oppositionist ideas are concealed here, under a mask of loyalty."[145] Bezobrazov was well aware of the tsar's jealousy of his autocratic prerogatives, and had sought to appease it by invoking the tradition of mutual trust between the autocrat and the nobility; it was out of deference to the tsar's sensitivity in this sphere that discontented nobles had refused to sign Bezobrazob's draft address and that he had abandoned the project. As Bezobrazov and others would discover, however, to recognize the tsar's jealousy of his prerogatives and to cater to it, even with professions of devotion to autocracy, was not enough. Alexander perceived almost any appeal for his intervention into the legislative process, or simply for a hearing, as an illegitimate challenge. Officials were able to discredit their critics by diverting the tsar's attention from questions of substance to the presumption entailed in making (in some cases, of considering) a direct appeal to the tsar.

Bezobrazov persisted, however, and was moved by the plight of the deputies to a desperate effort. He finally did submit an appeal to the tsar, through the Third Section, the day before the address of the five deputies. This appeal was more extreme than his previous effort. He charged that, because officials had interfered in the election of deputies and minority representatives had been substituted for duly elected deputies, the members of the first convocation were merely emissaries "from the local authorities to suit the central authorities." Although he did not acknowledge the deputies to be legitimate, he reiterated, in exaggerated form, their complaints about their reception and treatment. The tsar was not sympathetic; opposite the complaint that the deputies had been "broken into fragments" by the instructions, he noted, "So it should have been"; to the accusation that the bureaucracy had broken the tsar's promise to co-opt the deputies to the Main Committee, Alexander responded "Never" and "Nonsense."[146]

Clearly, Bezobrazov was incorrect in his assertion that Rostovtsev, Lanskoi, and their associates were acting against Alexander's wishes, but this assertion was merely a necessary fiction, as Bezobrazov himself all but conceded.[147] His other assertions were exaggerated, but by no means groundless. For example, at least two deputies were arbitrarily designated by provincial governors.[148] There was some justice to the charge, which Shidlovskii and Koshelev also made, that the Editorial Commission was publishing its proceedings in order to bind the government to its ostensibly provisional formulations: the main lines of its system could not be altered because the commission, and therefore the government, was publicly committed to them.

However, Bezobrazov proceeded from the exaggerated to the outlandish. He argued that all the government's actions on the emancipation since the original rescripts were the work of a conspiracy of constitutionalists, domestic traitors, and foreign enemies, coordinated by Herzen. Going far beyond laments about baneful foreign influences, Bezobrazov found that "the greatness and might of our Sovereign has long aroused envy" in Europe; the conspirators had learned that autocracy could not be brought down from without, and now sought to undermine it from within. They had fastened upon serfdom, not because it was the worst aspect of Russian life, but because, "despite its shortcomings, the pomeshchik's authority is the best and strongest underpinning of the state." Now the secret constitutionalists—"Who are they?" Alexander inquired in the margin—were defaming the deputies and the nobility because they feared exposure. The only way to restrain the Ministry of Internal Affairs and the Editorial Commission was to "convene *real* elected representatives from the Committees, not the pawns of factions, together with the Main Committee." This was "a direct, broad and clear path, on which factions and intrigues cannot appear without being immediately exposed." To this Alexander replied, "The Provincial Committees themselves serve as the best example to the contrary." Nor was he impressed by Bezobrazov's assurances that "an elective assembly is a natural component of autocracy," which otherwise is merely arbitrary rule. And he could only respond with exclamation marks to Bezobrazov's evocation of the traditional "right of the Russian land to have elected representatives to advise the supreme power."[149]

The three addresses submitted by the deputies were cautious, although cautious in different ways; caution was alien to Bezobrazov. There was a direct relationship between the moderation of an address and its support among the deputies. The majority appealed for no more than permission to submit their reflections; no other deputy would underwrite Shidlovskii's accusations; Bezobrazov was specific and provocative where Shidlovskii had been vague, but Bezobrazov was not a deputy at all. To make these distinctions required no great discrimination or sympathy for the deputies. However, if these distinctions were blurred, the appeals confirmed all the dire warnings about oligarchic strivings and opposition to emancipation among the nobility.

In the event, it was easy for Lanskoi and Rostovtsev to convert the addresses into political assets, for they were playing to an audience of one, which they understood very well. Alexander's sympathies were broad, if mild, but his apprehension of opposition and his jealousy of his prerogatives were intense; he abruptly withdrew his sympathy when these sentiments were aroused. The deputies were aware of these traits and tried to accommodate them; even Bezobrazov professed his devotion to autocracy and framed his appeal as a warning against covert opposition. The constituted authorities had every advantage in this kind of contest, however, because Alexander's personal loyalty and commitment to emancipation favored them. As Alexander wrote to Rostovtsev upon receiving the addresses from the deputies,

I am so convinced of the justice of the holy cause we have undertaken that no one can prevent me from accomplishing it. But the main question remains how to accomplish it?
    In this, as always, I count on God and on the aid of those who, like you, sincerely desire this as ardently as I do and see in it the salvation of Russia and a boon for its future.[15]

The letter was characteristic of Alexander, expressing support for his subordinates coupled with hesitancy about issues—the means of accomplishing the holy cause.
Although Lanskoi and Rostovtsev labored to interpret the addresses to their own advantage, Alexander was more than half-convinced of their interpretation before they began. Opposite the

five deputies' request that he "form an agency for the management of economic affairs for all the estates [of the realm] together, based on the elective principle," Alexander noted, "i.e., a constitution."[151] His verdict on Bezobrazov's appeal was, "he has entirely convinced me that his ilk desire to establish oligarchic rule in this country." And his immediate reaction to the three addresses from the deputies was, "If these gentlemen think they are frightening Me, . . . they are very much mistaken."[152] Frightening Alexander was just what the deputies had tried to avoid.

When they were subjected to official review, the addresses were considered in what might seem reverse order, beginning with Bezobrazov's. Alexander convened the Main Committee for the first time in five months, "so that it can judge whether this kind of insolence can and should pass unnoticed and unpunished." Count Orlov, picking up this broad hint, disqualified himself since he was Bezobrazov's uncle, "although for a long time now ["about two years," Orlov added in his own hand] I have not had any relations with the members of Bezobrazov's family and absolutely do not approve of his present action." Prince Dolgorukov hastened to explain that he had turned the address over to the tsar without reading it carefully. The rest of the committee followed their lead and condemned Bezobrazov for "perverse interpretation" of the tsar's orders, "false accusations, . . . insolent and unseemly judgments about the actions of his superiors," and proposing measures "contrary to the spirit of autocracy." The committee judged that a criminal trial would cause harmful publicity, but ordered that Bezobrazov be dismissed from his post at the Ministry of Internal Affairs, barred from both capitals, put under police surveillance, and warned that he would be prosecuted if he wrote or otherwise spread his perverse views.[153]

While Bezobrazov found no avowed supporters among the sanovniki, he had very few among the pomeshchiki; his appeal might reasonably have been dismissed as ridiculous, were it not for its putative association with the addresses of the deputies, which the committee considered a week later.

In the meantime, Lanskoi produced an interpretation of the three addresses. He began by lumping them together and insinuating a relationship between all three and Bezobrazov's "Materials for Conveying an Address to the Tsar," which in turn he related to the intemperate appeal that the deputies had drafted in late September. The two earlier addresses did have certain traits in common, notably their authors' decision not to submit them. However, Lanskoi remembered them, although imperfectly, since he confused the deputies' stillborn address with their letter to

Rostovtsev in order to demonstrate that the regime's "trust" in the deputies had been misplaced. This chain of evidence brought Lanskoi

to the sorrowful conclusion that the unconditional condemnation of the editorial commission does not concern its work (which is not yet known to everyone) so much as the basic and fundamental principles which have been adopted by the government at the highest level and which the commission has followed.

After recalling once again that the provincial committees and the deputies were so divided in their views that the Editorial Commission could not follow their "one-sided and unsatisfactory" recommendations, Lanskoi turned to the "essential aspect of this matter . . . the importunity that the peasant question be resolved by an assembly of representatives elected by estates." The importunity was Shidlovskii's, but

the same aspiration, although in a substantially muted tone, is expressed in the address of the eighteen members, and also appears, in a more covert form, in the address of the five members.

In fact, neither of these addresses mentioned any elected national assembly, but Lanskoi brushed aside

secondary nuances, arising from personal views. What is important is the general tendency which has just recently begun to spread. [The] general welfare of the state requires that these illegal aspirations be kept within bounds, to protect even these by and large irrational zealots for the nobility's interest.

The nobility had had three chances to state its views on the peasant question, but the final decision must be made in the highest spheres of government; Lanskoi was fond of this formula, but no one had publicly argued the contrary. The legislative procedure for the reform was settled, he insisted; "Any vacillation [presumably meaning any further vacillation] . . . would be incompatible with the dignity of the governmental authority and truly fatal for the peasant question."[154]

The other twenty-four deputies might just as well have signed Shidlovskii's address, from Lanskoi's point of view; they had been "summoned only to present necessary information and explanations," and all had trespassed outside their competence. He did not suggest any distinction to be made in reprimanding them.

The Main Committee, which discussed the addresses with the tsar in the chair, did make distinctions. The committee was divided on the form of reprimand, if not on the essence of the matter.[155] It ruled that the five deputies be reprimanded for "incorrect and unsuitable importunities," a diplomatic rendition of the tsar's view that the address was "extremely insolent."[156] The eighteen were given a lesser reproof for "troubling His Majesty with a petition" on a matter about which his will had been clearly expressed. As an afterthought, it was explained to the deputies that they had no right to petition in common.[157] Lanskoi had exploited their division by reproaching them for importunities that all but Shidlovskii had avoided, but, officially, it was their limited degree of solidarity that was culpable.

The Eclipse of Shuvalov and Pozen

The deputies' confrontation with the Editorial Commission, one of them recalled, was a dialogue between the chickens and the cook.[158] It was Miliutin, Lanskoi, and the Main Committee that finally put the deputies in the soup—the same soup in which Pozen and Shuvalov had found themselves as members of the Editorial Commission. They were among the eighteen deputies who received the mildest form of reprimand,[159] but the reprimand meant that they had been bested once more. They had not profited from their previous encounters, for the deputies, under their leadership, had committed the tactical error Shuvalov and Paskevich had made before and Pozen had sedulously avoided: they had been provoked into making a challenge. In each instance, the challenge was cautious, but it was nonetheless unacceptable in form and served to discredit the challenger. Yet the range of tactics open to the deputies was narrow. None of them considered desperate action, and vigorous exploitation of one's position invoked the wrath of the autocrat who had provided the position.

Apart from the rebuff to the deputies as a group, Shuvalov had to absorb a private defeat. He was the last deputy to appear before the Editorial Commission. He testified after the tsar had written to Rostovtsev of his indignation at the deputies' appeals, although no formal action had yet been taken. The commission responded to Alexander's private gesture of support by interrogating the deputies more severely than before.[160]

Cherkasskii was designated to cross-examine Shuvalov and he took the trouble to study the response of the St. Petersburg deputies beforehand. The response raised many points of detail, but offered few alternatives; instead, the authors simply advised against excessive regulation or else cited the draft of the St. Petersburg Provincial Committee. The response was also meager in data, which it was the deputies' ostensible function to provide. Concerning the size of allotments, the response stated:

Assuming that local conditions in St. Petersburg Province are fairly well known to anyone who lives in the capital, the undersigned refrain from more detailed considerations . . . and confine themselves to stating the idea that arbitrarily depriving the pomeshchik of the proper income from his land—a deprivation which will frequently surpass half his income—is utterly unjustifiable.[161]

Cherkasskii derived his line of questioning from the response and began by confronting Shuvalov with contradictions in it. Shuvalov admitted to the errors and conceded, "I will not undertake to defend every article" of the St. Petersburg Provincial Committee's draft.

Cherkasskii: But at the end of your response you praise it and direct us to it?
Shuvalov: Yes, but only on the main principles.
Cherkasskii: On what, then, is your proposed allotment based. . . . On real data or simply guesswork?
Shuvalov: I can explain that to you now—our figures there are somwhat arbitrary.

Cherkasskii then inquired whether he really favored the allotment size he had endorsed as chairman of the St. Petersburg Committee or the allotments set by the commission and "adopted with your participation and your consent?" Actually, Shuvalov had not formally consented to the commission's allotments,[162] but he forgot that, and further revealed that he did not understand the difference between normative allotment and the commission's system. When Cherkasskii asked why he opposed gradation, which was designed to favor the pomeshchiki of the North and had been sponsored by several northern committees, Shuvalov replied, "I do not know these provinces and their needs, but in my province I cannot consent to the imposition of their system, when all of us do not want it and ask to be left with ours."
    Shuvalov then tried to counterattack, complaining that the commission had grouped St. Petersburg Province with Viatka (notorious as a place of exile).

Cherkasskii: These are all questions which it would be not at all hard to settle if all the local circumstances of these provinces were exactly known to us. We simply ask you to indicate to us what system you would be pleased to adopt for Petersburg Province, and precisely wherein and why it should be different from the system for Viatka?

Recalling Shuvalov's treble role as provincial marshal, member of the commission, and deputy, Cherkasskii insisted, "We simply ask this of you as an expert. Tell us where we are mistaken." Shuvalov replied, "If you want, for example, to set us the problem of determining a line, to the right of which the peasant should be alloted three desiatiny, and to the left, two , then that will be a very hard problem to solve."

Despairing of eliciting information from Shuvalov himself about his native province, Cherkasskii asked where it might be had and how it might be collected.

Shuvalov: I do not really know.
Cherkasskii: Then your norm of nine desiatiny [per tiaglo] does not offer us anything?
Shuvalov: It goes without saying that it demands the same degree of trust as one can have in the persons and bureaucrats who produced it.

The other members of the commission intervened to end Shuvalov's discomfiture. His parting words were, "I must admit that I find myself in a very arduous position without my colleague [Count Levashev, a courtier and army officer], who did not come."[163] Everyone laughed, though Shuvalov's laughter may have been forced.

Shuvalov surpassed most deputies and marshals in his ignorance of the economic life of his province. His inglorious finale to the appearance of the first group of deputies nonetheless illustrates one of the nobility's major problems in coping with the emerging reform. Unless the government was to accept the advice of Shuvalov and other deputies and confine its actions to a few general guidelines, drafting the emancipation was an enormous bureaucratic undertaking. Serfdom was premised on mutual confidence between the government and the serfholders; the laws governing serfdom were simple, haphazard, and rarely enforced. Shuvalov supposed, as he indicated in his testimony, that this trust would continue. In his response, justifying the retention of manorial power, he disarmingly admitted that some might anticipate abuse of this power, but "one can positively say that apprehensions of this kind simply derive from a one-sided and not entirely impartial view."[164]

The government had succumbed to this one-sided view, and intended to encumber the Russian countryside with prescriptions and regulations. To do so required a plethora of citations, statistics, and other forms of data, to say nothing of forensic and legal skill. The spokesmen for the nobility could not match the reformers on this ground. If they had successfully undertaken a coup or some other form of resolute action, the situation would have been different. Since they did not consider any such action, bureaucratic expertise was a powerful political weapon.[165] If the nobility wanted to prevail on more than isolated articles of the reform, it had to produce an alternative that conformed to the bureaucratic norms of the state. This its spokesmen could not do. They had acquired the jargon of the bureaucracy, as the deputies' responses show, but few of the concomitant skills. They were able to set forth their opinions with more or less force, but until they could produce a consistent body of alternative legislation which formally met the government's standards, they were at the mercy of agencies controlled by their antagonists and could only secure alterations within the system they opposed. For all the nobility's attacks on the Editorial Commission, only one rival draft was actually drawn up. This rival, called the "Adjutants' Draft," was a meager list of vague rules, following the rubrics of the April Program; it would retain most of the pomeshchik's manorial power and apply the land settlements of each provincial committee. While it used the language of a legislative act, it was really no more than another memorandum.[166]

The Adjutants' Draft followed Pozen's recommendations, but he had no hand in it; by the fall of 1859, he was discredited. Like Shuvalov, he was one of the leaders of the first group of deputies who had advised moderation; he, too, had signed the appeal of the eighteen and submitted a response that was mild in its language but thoroughly adverse. Shuvalov emerged from the experience battered but intact and kept his posts as marshal, on the commission, and at court; Pozen was driven back to his estates in Poltava. He was not removed from the commission, but his position there became untenable.[167] Since Pozen was more tenacious and more vulnerable than Shuvalov, his opponents on the commission risked less in attacking him and had more to gain.

Pozen attributed his disgrace to two accusations: that he had opposed giving the peasants a perpetual right to their allotments, and that he had denounced the members of the Editorial Commission to the political police. He denied both accusations, citing the documents in which he had advocated perpetual tenure and insisting that no denunciation had ever come to light.[168]

The matter hangs upon the definition of advocacy and denunciation. As a member of the Poltava Provincial Committee, he assured his fellows that they were deluding themselves if they thought the allotments could revert to the pomeshchik. As a deputy, he held that the peasants should have a right to their household plot and allotment until they chose to redeem them or move away; the value of this right was limited, since the peasants' dues would be subject to free agreement after the transitional period.[169] As a member of the Editorial Commission, however, he had several times insisted that the peasants' allotments must revert to the pomeshchik's complete control. He took this line during his attempted rapprochement with Apraksin, and never committed himself to it in writing. When Apraksin proved a weak reed, Pozen resumed his previous position. Rostovtsev remembered this lapse, however, and included it in his bill of particulars against Pozen.[170]

Perpetual tenure of allotment land was one of the commission's dogmas, but Apraksin had opposed it without dire consequences for himself. Pozen's alleged denunciations were a more serious matter. The allegations were not conjured up retrospectively to justify Pozen's disgrace; Pozen's antagonists believed them at the time.[171] Apparently their informant was Rostovtsev, who related that the tsar himself told him of reports that he presided over the commission "despotically," that he was under the sway of "demagogues," and that the commission's decisions were permeated by "a purely anarchistic tendency." "All this," Rostovtsev quoted Alexander as saying, "has come to my attention officially, and it is your friend Pozen who says all this about you."[172]

This is a circumstantial account, written soon after the event and drawn from an august source. However, Pozen's parting letter to Dolgorukov, his ostensible imtermediary with the tsar, does not substantiate Rostovtsev's charges.[173] In this letter, Pozen emphasized that his views had been misrepresented. "Neither orally nor in writing did I ever utter a word against perpetual usufruct," he insisted. He also denied willfully misconstruing the commission's rulings in order to incite the deputies. These calumnies were the commission's "maneuvers" to justify ignoring the deputies as the provincial drafts had been ignored. However, the deputies had perceived that the commission's basic system was worthless, and the second convocation would make the same judgment. "That is what the Commission ought to pay attention to," he insisted.

The deputies can be derided and accused of this or that, but their voice is all the same the voice of the entire Nobility. Can one even admit the wild idea that the reform can be carried out without the participation of the Nobility?

Pozen wrote in the accents of outrage, but other deputies and members of the commission had made the same points. Much of the letter was false; Pozen had advocated temporary allotments and he had misconstrued the commission's rulings, if not wilfully.[174] Nowhere in this letter, however, is there any hint of the kind of political denunciation Pozen is supposed to have passed on to Dolgorukov.[175]

Pozen bitterly realized that he had been manipulated and outflanked, just as Shuvalov and Apraksin had. The charges against him, he explained to Dolgorukov, were "a strange trick, but this is not the first time it has been used by the leading members of the commission against their enemies." Later, he insisted that he had never denounced the members of the commission to Dolgorukov, but merely given him a memorandum explaining that Shuvalov and Paskevich were not actually at odds with the commission's position.[176] Rostovtsev, replying to Pozen's final plea for vindication, laid particular emphasis upon this memorandum. It had, he conceded, simply argued that the controversy with Shuvalov and Paskevich could easily be resolved, but this argument made the tsar wonder whether Rostovtsev was willing and able to resolve the controversy, and, "for the first time since the beginning of the enterprise, I was aggrieved by the Sovereign." Since Pozen must have known the memorandum would reach the tsar, Rostovtsev maintained, it constituted a "devious" attempt to do him harm. Indeed, "if the Sovereign did not have an enormous store of favor for me," it would have been necessary to resign as chairman of the Editorial Commission.[177]

Rostovtsev went on to complain of Pozen's other activities, but it was the perfidious memorandum on the Shuvalov affair that he emphasized. Apparently, then, this modest document was not merely simultaneous with the slanderous denunciations but identical to them. Since the tsar's favor for Rostovtsev was indeed enormous, the memorandum eventually served to discredit Pozen as thoroughly as the imputed slanders would have.[178]

Scarcely any of Pozen's contemporaries spoke well of him. He was an apostate and suspected embezzler who truckled to the mighty and turned too good a profit on his serf estates. None of his successive reform plans was generous to the peasantry. He vaunted himself as an abolitionist, however, and had, in fact, advocated the abolition of serfdom sooner than most of his adversaries; in his last formal statement on the reform, he plaintively rehearsed his credentials as an emancipator.[179] He shared with Levshin, Unkovskii, and Koshelev the special bitterness of men shunted aside by the miscarried fulfillment of their own hopes, but Pozen acquired an infamous reputation in the bargain. He was, in a sense, caught in his own web; he was so given to flattery and maneuver that discreditable stories about him seemed plausible. On the whole, the stories were false. They contained elements of truth, but the sum of these elements does not make much of a blackguard of Pozen, for calumny and conspiracy were not a significant part of his strategy.

The reformers in the Editorial Commission and the Ministry of Internal Affairs liked to maintain that their opponents were devious courtiers who relied on flattery, conspiracy, and false insinuation. Historians have accepted this verdict and, going further, have assumed that because the reformers labored in a good cause, their tactics were forthright. In fact, they drew heavily upon the arsenal of bureaucratic chicanery (just as one might expect) and the most adept courtier in the reform era was their patron Rostovtsev. It was because of his success in the arts of the courtier that their manipulations, denunciations, and misrepresentations were effective. Their opponents, on the other hand, were doggedly and astonishingly aboveboard. They conferred together, but cannot be said to have engaged in conspiracy. They availed themselves of the high offices they enjoyed, but did not abuse them. They took their stand on the promises and solemn policy statements the regime had made and sought to prevail by using the prerogatives the regime had conferred upon them. They entertained the worst suspicions about the reformers, but, while some of the hangers-on descended to hysterical accusations, the recriminations they formally made against the reformers had a solid basis in fact; certainly, they did not engage in misrepresentation as systematically—or successfully—as the reformers. The most cunning and devious of them, who was probably Pozen, was astonishingly forthright in his tactics, compared with his enemies.

Pozen and Shuvalov were well placed to act for the mass of pomeshchiki opposed to the emerging reform. They were unable to exploit their advantages. Like Shuvalov's ineptitude, Pozen's diffidence in intrigue and slander was an expression of the general inhibition upon the deputies and other spokesmen for the nobility. They were restrained from making a forceful and sustained challenge by their hopes for a renewal of the tsar's traditional favor. The deputies' maneuvres followed a pattern of challenge and submission that was characteristic of the nobility and its leaders; Piatov, Blank, the nobles of Smolensk and Moscow, and even the members of the Main Committee were prone to the same kind of vacillation. Political inexperience and lack of cohesion played a certain role, but it was primarily the hope for favor that prevented the nobility's alarm from taking a political form that the reformers and the regime would have to accommodate.

Towards Enactment

8

By the fall of 1859, the political fate of the emancipation legislation was settled. The Editorial Commission had met a series of challenges from within and without, and all the challengers had been rebuffed or neutralized. With each challenge, the tsar had to make a choice; each time he conceived the choice as the reformers interpreted it for him. Accordingly, he turned away from his friends Apraksin and Shuvalov, his own previous commitments, and the nobility at large, as represented by the deputies. He continued to cherish them all and placated them with some skill.[1] The choices he made, however, left the Editorial Commission alone in the field. Details were still open to change; the commission at this very time was making the concessions Rostovtsev called for once the challenges had been met. But these were concessions to the commission's own misgivings or second thoughts; it could draw up the emancipation legislation without sharing its function with outsiders or having to defer to their point of view.

The members of the commission, however, were not convinced of the strength of their position. They carried on with their defensive and counteroffensive maneuvers. For example, at Lanskoi's request, Cherkasskii wrote an apologia for the commission, which was then translated into French. The purpose was to ward off an oblique attack by the magnates at court; they were thought to be working upon the empress, who was more accessible in French than in Russian. Cherkasskii explained that the commission's critics were inspired by greed and suggested that the real target of their criticisms was the empress's husband.[2] Thus the commission secured the gynaeceum as well as the palace. Yet the leading members were not confident of their position; some months later, they privately expressed the fear that they would be unceremoniously dismissed before they completed their work.[3]

The best proof of the commission's institutional victory in late 1859 is the way its system survived the perils that followed. In the fifteen months before the emancipation was proclaimed, the commission saw all the worst eventualities, short of a palace coup or a peasant rebellion, come to pass. Rostovtsev died, and was succeeded by an archsanovnik who did not conceal his disapproval of the commission's system. The second convocation of deputies proved capable of unity and was more consistently opposed to the commission than the first. Finally, the sanovniki roused themselves at last to make a stand against the commission's finished draft. This sustained but uncoordinated offensive captured almost nothing. There were some further reductions in the statutory allotments, of the kind the commission had been making on its own. The language of the statute was modified in ways that a hard-driving pomeshchik could turn to his advantage.[4] Down through the last day of the Council of State's deliberations on the emancipation legislation, however, no major change was made in the commission's system. On that day, the "beggarly allotment" was introduced as an option. Otherwise, the commission prevailed against all the perils of 1860 and 1861.

By mid-November 1859, Rostovtsev was no longer able to preside over the general sessions of the Editorial Commission. As his health declined, he strained to draw up his testament, an exposition of the commission's decisions so far, indicating what could be modified and what should be sacrosanct.[5] This document was turned over to the tsar upon Rostovtsev's death, February 6, 1860. Rostovtsev had not proposed a successor, but the tsar elicited the late chairman's views from Petr Semenov. According to Semenov, Rostovtsev found all the leading figures in the government too weak, too senile, or too hostile to the commission's policies. The least undesirable would be Count Panin, Minister of Justice, who was so rich that he would not seek advantages for himself as a pomeshchik; while he might privately oppose the commission's policies, Rostovtsev judged he could be counted on to carry out the tsar's wishes faithfully.[6]

Panin

Rostovtsev's image of Panin was Panin's own. As he explained to the Grand Duke Konstantin,

I do have convictions, strong ones. Those who think I do not are wrong. But I consider myself obliged to learn the views of the sovereign emperor first of all, as is my duty according to my oath of fidelity and submission. If I establish by some means, direct or indirect, that the sovereign's attitude to something is different from mine, I consider it my duty to abandon my convictions and even work against them, with as much or even more energy than if I were guided by my own private opinions.[7]

This was the creed of the Nicholaevan bureaucrat who, Polievktov observes, lacked any sense of aristocratic liberty and "remained a functionary even on the highest rungs of his official career."[8] As chairman of the Editorial Commission, however, Panin did not conform to this creed. He did decline the proffered chairmanship, out of regard for his strong convictions, but the tsar insisted he accept and imposed three conditions upon him: he must adhere to Rostovtsev's testament, maintain the present membership of the commission, and let majority rule prevail within it.

It was awkward to be chairman on parole, and Panin showed his discomfiture in his first days in the chair.[9] His appointment aroused the dissidents within the commission from their passivity, but at first Panin rebuffed them. He expressed his personal opposition to many of the commission's decisions as they came up for review, but made no attempt to alter them. He complained that the members were wasting time replying to his objections, which were only for their information.[10] Drawing on his legal experience, he helpfully corrected the wording of various decisions, to make them more precise.

In the third general session of his chairmanship, Panin volunteered a correction that was not regarded as helpful. He proposed to excise the word "perpetual" from an article on the charter defining the peasants' allotments and dues. "That's not right," he said. "According to the law, I think, there are no perpetual contracts, and it would be rather odd to admit perpetual contracts for usufruct." Cherkasskii proposed to exclude the word "contract," but Panin's objections were not simply legalistic.[11] "Presumably, it was not part of the government's plans to bind the landowner and peasant together forever." To this, Cherkasskii replied that the omission of the word "perpetual" would undermine the commission's whole system. Panin insisted he was merely warning the members that the word "perpetual" "decides the question in advance, and it is very imprudent. . . . However, if you think it necessary to reaffirm your position, do as you like, I will certainly not compel you." He was not swayed by a lengthy speech in his support by Nikolai Semenov, who was his subordinate in the Ministry of Justice.[12]

Panin raised the issue again in subsequent sessions. He observed, disclaiming any attempt to persuade the members, that permanent ascription and perpetual allotment were inadmissible for reasons of state, since the productive forces of the nation would be constricted. Later, he contended that neither the rescripts nor any other statement by the tsar promised their allotments in perpetuity.[13]

More than a month after becoming chairman, Panin made his move. He proposed (anticipating the strategem of his English counterpart, the Lord Chancellor, in *Iolanthe*) to modify the provision for perpetual usufruct by omitting the word "perpetual." The government would reserve the right to further action on the allotments after nine years. Objections were raised and Panin in effect reversed his position. "The Sovereign," he pointed out, "does not want the land taken away from the peasants after the transitional period," and he hotly denied that the Main Committee desired temporary allotments. In effect, Panin narrowed his objections to the earlier legalistic ground, suggesting the formula "usufruct continues" even if the peasants did not begin redemption within nine years.

The leading members of the commission were firm and would no longer accept any equivilant for "perpetual" (*bezsrochnyi*—literally, "without term," a word the Economic Section had chosen in preference to *vechnyi*, or "eternal," in order to encourage peasants to redeem their allotments).[14] Cherkasskii had earlier suggested a semantic compromise. Now he observed that the government's commitment to reform had provoked a "crisis of impressions" among the nobility, including himself. Any major verbal change would renew this crisis. More important, it would evoke pressure for more significant changes. Here, in effect, he admitted that the commission, by broadcasting its proceedings, hoped to commit the government to its ostensibly tentative solutions. He held that the commission's provision for perpetual usufruct had put the government "in a most advantageous relationship to the pomeshchiki and the peasants," but, he predicted, "if the government retreats from what it has proclaimed, then society will be very much demoralized by the hope that it will retreat from another one of its principles." And despite the complaint of a Polish expert member that perpetual usufruct was a Communist principle, Cherkasskii's view prevailed.[15]

Panin tried a final, pathetic, gambit against perpetual usufruct. Drafting the journal of the session at which the issue had most recently been debated, he stated that the members could not agree. He was reminded that, by the tsar's order, the commission could not air its controversies in its published *Journal*. Panin replied that it was not a dissenting opinion that was involved but "the disagreement of the chairman . . . with a resolution of the Editorial Commission." He reminded the members that he realized that the allotment would be "irrevocable," but, pursuing a tortuous line of argument, he held that perpetual usufruct nonetheless "remains *une question pendante* among us." The advantage of his draft journal was that it did not "decide the question in advance," but "simply says that it is not yet decided." The members of the commission, he complained, imperiously "want it decided absolutely according to your definition." Clearly, the chairman found it hard to adapt to majority rule.

Furthermore, while Panin's convictions were admittedly malleable, his scruples were delicate. He insisted, in a thinly veiled threat to sabotage the commission later on, that he did not want to commit himself to perpetual usufruct until he was completely convinced of its merits. "I am an honorable man. I do not want to say one thing here and then do the opposite. To sign a journal in one sense and then defend my own opinion in different tendency in the Main Committee—I would consider that dishonorable." The controversy over the journal was settled according to a tried formula; final confirmation was deferred until the second convocation of deputies had been heard.[16] This was an appropriate way to paper over Panin's defeat, since he had proposed the excision of the word "perpetual" to placate these deputies, who were already gathered in St. Petersburg.

The tsar, however, turned Panin's defeat into a standoff. Before the compromise on the journal text, nineteen members of the commission submitted a memorandum on permanent usufruct to the tsar; after the compromise, Panin submitted a rebuttal. Both memoranda summarized the arguments made during the commission's debates. The nineteen members emphasized the importance Rostovtsev had placed on perpetual usufruct and the failure of the first convocation of deputies to object to it.[17] To be sure, thirty-four deputies of the second convocation had already joined in a statement against perpetual usufruct, but many of them represented committees that had adopted the principle. The implication was that Panin's stand within the commission encouraged this kind of backsliding. The nineteen members warned,

Under these circumstances, the omission of the two controversial words from the final version will give a pretext for the argument that the government has deliberately retreated from its original principles, and that stubborn resistance to its views can actually lead to the landless emancipation of the peasants.

This belief, which has been gradually growing in the course of several years, will engender new opposition in society, much stronger and more deliberate opposition. . . . While at present it is hard for the government to utter a decisive word, that word, once it is conclusively uttered, will at least eliminate any further agitation. . . . Only a complete and frank expression of the government's intentions as to the peasants' perpetual usufruct of the land provides a guarantee of a favorable outcome for the peasant question.[18]

Lanskoi and Rostovtsev had worked upon Alexander with great success using this kind of argument. Now, however, the immediate target of the argument had direct and regular access to the tsar, and the tsar was impressed with his counterarguments. In writing as in speaking, Panin wavered between objections merely to the words "constant" and "perpetual" and to the policy they expressed. He began by recalling that Alexander had told him personally that "after the transitional period, the land cannot be taken away from the peasants." The tsar underlined this phrase and wrote in the margin, "not under any pretext." Panin went on to explain that it was nonetheless undesirable to use the words "constant and perpetual" with reference to the allotments. They were in direct contradiction to the tsar's original rescript and would discourage peasants from undertaking redemption, since they would know their tenure of the allotments was secure. Finally, the Editorial Commission's version

will irrevocably ruin all the landowners by virtue of the preservation, in so far as possible, of the existing allotments; on this basis, the best land in the very center of the manor will be taken away forever and given into the eternal disposition of the peasants; the manor will be reduced to scattered patches of land, the greater part of them uncultivated or inadequate to provide a meager income for the owner. There is no necessity of indicating the consequences from this for the nobility and for the state.[19]

This was no verbal or legalistic objection, but a concise summary of the protests of the most intransigent pomeshchiki against the principle that "the land cannot be taken away from the peasants." Panin's jeremiad rested on three premises: that the present allotments were the best land on the estate, that the statutory allotments would provide the peasants with everything they needed, and that the peasants would not remit any dues for these allotments, so that the pomeshchik's entire income must come from his beggarly bits of demesne. These premises repudiated the government's policy from the rescripts onward, and they were utterly and deliberately false. There was a possibility of arrears under perpetual usufruct, as under serfdom, although deputies were quick to point out that the exactions the commission proposed were ferocious; there were some obrok estates where the peasants did hold the best land and might keep most of it as statutory allotments; there might even be some peasants who would be able to take care of their subsistence, taxes, and dues simply by working their statutory allotments. This series of possibilities was very far from the final ruin of all landowners.

Nonetheless, the tsar was impressed. He underlined Panin's hint at the dire consequences of perpetual usufruct for the nobility and the state and inquired in the margin, "How to escape from this difficulty?" And he endorsed Panin's recommendation that the issue be left unresolved until it was reviewed by the Main Committee, although Alexander emphasized that he himself would decide it at that time. This reservation was formally as meaningless as Panin's recommendation, since every article of the commission's draft was subject to review by the Main Committee and by the tsar. The tsar's action simply indicated that he was impressed by Panin's vision of the spoliation of the noble estate. For the first time, he refused to be moved by representations about the necessity of firmness with dissidents. Rostovtsev and Lanskoi had moved the tsar by inflating or inventing signs of opposition among the nobility; the modest prophecy of the nineteen members was not so effective, although more valid: the government's hesitation on perpetual usufruct did encourage protest against other elements of the Editorial Commission's system.

Most important, the member of the commission got a vivid reminder that the tsar represented the one serious threat to the enactment of their system. They were reluctant to acknowledge this threat, even privately or in retrospect, but all their strategy was ultimately designed to meet it. Now some of the most specious and self-serving arguments to emerge from the nobility, arguments that had been raised and ignored before, had reached the tsar and impressed him. If this kind of argument should move him to action, that action could only be the repudiation of all that the Editorial Commission had done and the dismissal of its leading members, for the implications of Panin's memorandum went far beyond the immediate issue of perpetual usufruct. It may be that neither Panin nor the tsar perceived these implications, but the reformers did, and this perception made them anxious and insecure throughout the year 1860.

The tsar's endorsement of Panin's position also underlined his dual role as chairman of the Editorial Commission and member of the Main Committee and so gave encouragement to Panin's tactics within the commission. Panin attempted to trade on his influence in the Main Committee and, after the tsar's intervention, Miliutin, Cherkasskii, and Samarin offered a verbal change with the explicit purpose of winning Panin's support there. Accordingly, the commission's draft statute held that the allotments would be "in the constant usufruct of the village society, without term or limit of time." Panin was mollified by this change, which did not affect the substance. Even the omission of "without term or limit of time," which brought the Great Russian Statute as enacted into line with Panin's original idea, did not have any practical effect.[20]

Despite the tsar's intervention and the ensuing semantic concession, Panin's influence on the commission was very limited. He pursued an erratic course, making and withdrawing objections, alternatively rebuffing and courting the deputies and the dissidents within the commission. Throughout his chairmanship, he cast about for a means of imposing himself upon the commission, but he never found one. The deputies might be enlisted in a frontal assault upon the emerging reform legislation, but they were so remote from the commission in their views that they did not offer Panin a vantage point for exerting influence upon it. The dissident members who still attended the sessions of the commission were few. Panin's very presence in the chair galvanized the leaders of the commission, who had descended to rancorous disputes before his arrival, into renewed solidarity. They could counter Panin's sorties with a dependable majority. In time, he could exert his authority only by convening the commission at long intervals.

Despite his professed subservience to the tsar's wishes and refined sense of honor, Panin systematically ignored the conditions under which he had assumed the chairmanship. Rostovtsev had emphatically called for perpetual usufruct of the allotments in his testament; the gambit with the journal was an attempt to evade majority rule; Panin even tried to introduce his own nominee into the commission.[21] Many of his objections to the commission's recommendations were formal. On major issues, however, his views were those of the second convocation of deputies. He favored temporary allotments and broad manorial power, although he was evasive or inconsistent on these and many other issues. He was not, however, a conscious spokesman for the pomeshchiki at large. Very few pomeshchiki, for example, felt as he did that minute and precise regulation of rural life was one of the goals of the reform statutes. Like many practical pomeshchiki, Panin would continue the peasants' cartage obligation after emancipation. But a *praktik* would not seek to establish the distance a peasant could be made to walk to render barshchina by extrapolating from his walking tours in Switzerland.[22] Panin, then, was a sanovnik, haughtier, richer, and more diligent than most. Unlike Menshikov and Shuvalov, he did not cultivate the acquaintance of provincial nobles. His aristocratic pride was so elevated that he ordinarily refused to deal directly with his social inferiors, including members of the Senate and his subordinates in the Ministry of Justice. Judging by his abortive attempts at debate within the commission, he was simply passing along objections gathered in casual conversation with his tiny group of peers. These titled magnates and dignitaries found little to their liking in the commission's work, but Panin could not make the commission reverse itself on any major point.

The Second Convocation of Deputies

The controversy over perpetual usufruct indicated, as Cherkasskii put it, that the honeymoon was over and the relationship between Panin and the members of the commission was a marriage of convenience.[23] Cherkasskii, Miliutin, and the other leaders were reasonably satisfied with this arrangement. Koshelev was appalled. "There is not much good news here," he wrote to Ivan Aksakov from St. Petersburg. "The appointment of Panin has dismayed us all. Cherkasskii and Samarin are satisfied; think of it! He puffs them up and, incredible but true, they submit to the deception." Two weeks later, he reported the "anomaly" that while the Editorial Commission was pleased with Panin, so were the deputies of the second convocation, confident that the commission was "interred at last" and that their program would prevail in the Main Committee.[24]

Many provincial pomeshchiki believed, as the deputies did, that Panin would secure what they wanted; relief and elation were widespread. Iurii Samarin received a letter from Kazan reporting that the avowed conservatives were confident and their ranks were growing; "There is no possibility of convincing them that the serfholder's power will not be restored again in its former magnitude."[25] A Third Section agent in Pskov reported.

With the appointment . . . of Count Panin, minds are noticeably calmer; instead of their previous distrust for the government, the greater part of the nobility is manifestly confident that the Count will not follow in the footsteps of General Rostovtsev and, as the owner of several thousand serfs, will defend the interests of the pomeshchiki.[26]

Those closer to the scene were not so sure.

All the high and mighty [according to a letter from St. Petersburg] are indignant with Panin, and the krepostniki long for Rostovtsev. What they forgive in the latter, an owner of forty-five souls, they do not forgive in a grandee and owner of 14,000, especially one in whom they placed all their hopes.[27]

As a rule, however, Panin's appointment gave new encouragement to the expectation, which was widespread despite repeated disappointment, that the sanovniki would come to the rescue of the lesser pomeshchiki. The second convocation of deputies, who were assembling in St. Petersburg when Panin was appointed, shared this expectation and it largely determined their attitude. Panin himself gave the deputies little encouragement. In his speech of welcome, one of his first acts as chairman, he began by calling for "familial" collaboration between the deputies and the commission, but he assumed the role of minatory father for himself. He warned the deputies to avoid the baneful influences to be found at Shuvalov's house and urged them not to indulge in petty and groundless reproaches of the commission, as the earlier deputies had.

My doors are open to whomever may need to see me; but at the present time, I cannot receive you. . . . Each of you may have convictions which do not always accord with my own, consequently, in these clashes of diverse views of things, much time would be wasted without any benefit.
   Furthermore, outsiders might suppose that I shared one of those convictions and that I am under its exclusive influence.[28]

For Panin, it was unthinkable to be influenced by a miscellaneous group of provincial pomeshchiki. He confidentially explained to the Editorial Commission that the deputies had been invited to the capital simply to satisfy their desire to speak out,[29] and later he was embarrassed by the second convocation's coordinated expression of support for his stand on perpetual usufruct.[30] He did, in fact, agree with the deputies on many issues, but he made no public gesture of solidarity with them. During their testimony before the commission, Panin was sometimes hectoring and impatient, sometimes utterly silent, and the deputies were surprised at his failure to support them. When Zommer, the last deputy to testify, realized he was being dismissed, he turned to Panin, who had said nothing during his interrogation, and said, "I appeal to Your Excellency to direct his attention to the allotments. They are very onerous for us." To this Cherkasskii rejoined, "What do you mean, your land [in Olonets Province] is worth nothing." Even then, Panin did not intercede, favoring Zommer with no more than a grave parting handshake.[31]

The deputies were disappointed by their reception, but not discouraged, for Panin's aloofness and formality were notorious. They were more impressed by his stand for short-time allotments and manorial power and by the private assurances they received from well-informed sources. M. N. Murav'ev, the Minister of State Properties, assured three of them that "the whole matter will straighten itself out easily" since it was the tsar's will that "rights will not be violated." Panin's position as Minister of Justice, according to Murav'ev, meant that he had to proceed cautiously but it also assured a favorable final outcome.[32]

The appointment of a supposedly sympathetic chairman encouraged the second convocation to take a more intransigent stand than the first, despite the chairman's explicit advice. At first, more than half the deputies reportedly favored redemption; only two advocated it in their formal responses to the commission.[33] This emphatic turning away from redemption contrasts sharply with the first convocation's growing inclination towards a reform based upon redemption. Underlying this contrast, however, there is an affinity. In 1860, as in 1859, attitudes towards redemption derived from estimates of the government's intentions and of its sympathy for the nobility. The about-face of the second convocation represented the deputies' political judgment that they could get better terms from the government than a complete break with the serfs and more or less generous compensation for allotment land.

To be sure, these deputies arrived at this judgment more readily because most of them came from areas where commercial agriculture after the emancipation looked promising.[34] The first convocation had been dominated by representatives of the provinces around the capitals, where nonagricultural activities were important to the manorial economy. This area had no representatives in the second convocation except for the marginal and impoverished province of Smolensk. There were five deputies from the thinly populated provinces of the extreme North, where mining and lumbering were important. All the other deputies came from areas were demesne cereal production through barshchina was dominant.[35]

Compared with the first convocation, the new deputies were richer, more obscure, and more representative of the provincial nobility—or at least, of the committees they spoke for. Nine of them, including five from the western provinces, were provincial marshals of the nobility. Except for these holders of corporate office, the deputies were not closely identified with the administration. Most of them had been in the civil service, as before, but only four of the new group had risen as high as the fifth rank, and only five had served on their provincial committees by appointment.[36] All but seven deputies represented majorities or unanimous committees. While none of them had acquired a national reputation in government service or outside it, many must have enjoyed provincial celebrity as great proprietors. Of the thirty-nine deputies from provinces where registers of estates were compiled, eleven had more than five hundred souls; only six do not appear in the register and presumably had fewer than one hundred.[37] Almost all the deputies kept some or all of their serfs on barshchina, and many had a large complement of household serfs.[38] All the information indicates that, as a group, the deputies were rich, hard-driving, resident squires.

Apart from the regions they represented and the chairman they confronted, the second convocation was in a more favorable situation than the first. The new deputies were forewarned and forearmed. They received the instructions, which had surprised and appalled the first convocation, well in advance.[39] Before he came to St. Petersburg, each deputy had ample time to become familiar with the Editorial Commission's system, if not with its quantitative recommendations for his own province. Finally, he could benefit from the advice of Shuvalov, Shidlovskii, and Koshelev, veterans of the first convocation who volunteered their help.[40] The second convocation was not hampered, as the first had been, by disorientation and shock.

Furthermore, the provincial nobility's indignation at the government's reform plans reached its crest in the winter of 1859-1860, between the departure of the first deputies and the arrival of the second convocation in the capital. The affronted deputies had told of their unhappy experiences in St. Petersburg; the provincial assemblies of the nobility, which were held in many provinces around the turn of the year, provided a natural forum. Koshelev correctly predicted that the reprimands laid upon the deputies would be interpreted in the provinces as tokens of zeal.[41] The deputy Stremoukhov, for example, was elevated to the office of provincial marshal.

The government anticipated manifestations of discontent at the assemblies of the nobility, and Lanskoi acted to contain them. He instructed the provincial governors that the peasant reform could not be discussed at the assemblies, since the nobility had had three chances to express its views—in the district conferences, in the provincial committees and through the deputies.[42] The same rule had been imposed a year earlier without arousing much resentment; since the nobles were now convinced that the government was ignoring the conferences, committees, and deputies, Lanskoi's circular added insult to injury.

Only the Riazan Provincial Assembly ventured to violate Lanskoi's circular directly; after paying tribute to the returning deputies, the assembly voted for a petition endorsing the Riazan deputies' demand for compulsory redemption.[43] To this extent, the ban was effective. The ban itself, however, provided a target on which nobles could focus their indignation, since Lanskoi's circular violated the assembly's right, proclaimed in the Charter of the Nobility, to discuss the needs of the province and to explain them to the crown. The assemblies of the nobility at Tver and Orel accordingly sent petitions to the tsar protesting the circular.[44] The nobles of Vladimir went further; their petition fulminated against the bureaucracy and reiterated in greater detail the appeal of the five deputies for administrative reforms. Since the nobility of an entire province had never before endorsed a reform program of this kind, this was a remarkable gesture.[45] The Iaroslav Provincial Assembly drew up a similar petition, but then resolved on a more prudent means of expressing its zeal for reform; it instructed the outgoing provincial marshal to submit the petition in his own name, and elected the returning deputies Vasil'ev and Dubrovin, both of whom had signed the address of the five deputies, as marshal and vice-marshal of the province.[46]

The nobility's indignation was great, but there was some question whether it was wise to register a formal protest. Apraksin, the provincial marshal of Orel, consented to a mild protest against the ban on discussion only as an alternative to a tirade against the Editorial Commission, which fell one vote short of passage in the Orel Assembly. A similar tirade drawn up by Mikhail Bezobrazov gained a majority in the St. Petersburg Provincial Assembly, but Shuvalov used his powers as marshal to ensure that the petition eventually submitted was a mild plea for continued participation in local administration.[47]

Apraksin and Shuvalov conceived themselves to be spokesmen for the nobility, but they were inhibited by their official position as marshals. Apraksin was no admirer of the Editorial Commission, but, he wrote to his uncle, it was his duty to uphold the government's position before the assembly.[48] Orlov-Davydov, however, was not constrained by official position and he was well known as a staunch advocate of the nobility's interest; Apraksin summoned him to Orel to bolster his cause. Orlov-Davydov told the assembly that it had a right to keep silent as well as to make representations, and silence was the proper rejoinder to the follies of the Editorial Commission. An open attack on the commission would imply that there was a choice to be made between the government and the nobility, but "in my opinion, Government and Nobility are synonymous."[49]

In the St. Petersburg Assembly, Orlov-Davydov also argued for dignified silence. The assembly should not, he said, insist on its "right to discuss a subject I do not even name." Instead of "ranting about mistrust," the assembly should confound the "preachers of perverse theories" by setting an example of "calm confidence." This gesture would express the "corporate spirit of the nobility," which was "our strength" and consisted primarily of loyalty to the throne.[50]

Orlov-Davydov, then, believed that the polity that had sustained serfdom was still intact. He had encouraged the first group of deputies to undertake "loyal opposition," but he would not, even when Rostovtsev still ran the Editorial Commission, undertake political action outside the channels set up by the government. A show of compliance, coupled with behind-the-scenes influence, still seemed to promise more than unruly protest; politics was still the pursuit of favor.[51] Orlov-Davydov's restraint suggests that it was calculated as much as official obligations that inhibited Apraksin and Shuvalov.

The government's reaction to the petitions from the provincial assemblies indicated that this calculation was correct. The Riazan petition, which flatly violated Lanskoi's ruling, was brought before the Main Committee and simply dismissed, without any action against the petitioners.[52] The Tver petition, which questioned the legality of the ruling, evoked official retaliation; Unkovskii was removed as provincial marshal for passing the petition along. A few weeks later, Unkovskii and his friend Evropeus, whose oratory had dissuaded the Tver Assembly from violating the minister's ruling, were sent into exile. There was no formal investigation and no official explanation of this action, which was inspired by the denunciations of Unkovskii's political enemies and the judgment that Unkovskii and his friends were an upsetting influence in Tver.[53] Consistency would dictate that Apraksin suffer along with Unkovskii. However, the tsar found that Apraksin, "for all his stupidity," had done better than would have been expected; he had secured the substitution of a protest against the circular for a protest against the government's emancipation plans. The sponsor of that more offensive petition, a courtier and magnate named S. I.

Mal'tsev, was confined to his estates by the tsar's orders; this was not as onerous as exile to Viatka nor even very restrictive, since Mal'tsev's estates covered a good part of Kaluga and Orel provinces. He was also favored with an explanation, as Unkovskii was not. Dolgorukov, the chief of the Third Section, wrote to Mal'tsev explaining that if he objected to government policy, he should explain the matter forthrightly to the tsar instead of dragging it before a public forum.[54]

There were two lessons to be drawn from the government's actions on the petitions. The first was that expounding a program of judicial and administrative reforms was culpable; the Vladimir marshal was given a strict reprimand for his assembly's petition, although it was taken almost word for word from the response officially submitted by a Vladimir minority deputy.[55] The second lesson was that overt political action was culpable, even within the framework of prerogatives provided for the noble estate. It was not outrageous views that brought the tsar's wrath down on Mal'tsev; his petition was similar in its tenor and narrower in its range than the memorandum Apraksin had submitted a few months earlier. Apraksin had not suffered anything worse than scorn, but he had expressed his views in a memorandum privately submitted to the tsar. It was wrong to solicit public support for these views. For a man of Mal'tsev's standing, it was also foolish, as Dolgorukov took pains to point out; the sanovniki still ruled in St. Petersburg, the traditional channels of influence were still open.[56]

The deputies of the second group drew the appropriate conclusion from the events of the preceding few months. It was inconceivable that ministers like Panin, Murav'ev, and Dolgorukov and dignitaries like Apraksin and Shuvalov should be manipulating levers of power that no longer worked. If these levers did work, the Editorial Commission was doomed (as its members sometimes feared); there was no need of making concessions to the commission and little point in showing it much consideration. Scarcely half the deputies sought to testify before the commission.

All the deputies responded to the apparent trend of events, which served, along with their common economic interests, to close their ranks. Koshelev wrote an epistle to the second convocation urging unity as a basic tactic;[57] the deputies followed Koshelev's advice slavishly, to his dismay, since he opposed the demands on which they united. The deputies received permission, reportedly thanks to Dolgorukov,[58] to submit a collective response to the reports of the Administrative Section. This permission was another sign of a favorable political climate; for the first convocation, signing a collection statement was in itself a ground for a formal reprimand.

Thirty-nine deputies endorsed this general response; most of them went on to sign four collective responses to the reports of the Economic Section, a brief response to the Legal Section, and finally, a general statement of their position, their "Concluding Opinion."[59]

These seven documents constituted a full-scale attack on the commission and a rejection of all its works. Of all the responses from the first convocation, perhaps only Shidlovskii's was so hostile, and none was so outspoken. The solidarity of the group exerted a powerful influence on all its members. The deputies from provinces under the inventory system stood aloof from some or all of the collective statements,[60] as did one of the deputies from Kherson, but they expressed the same views in their separate responses. Some deputies supplemented the collective responses with pleas for consideration of the "local peculiarities" of their area, others with answers to the compulsory questions, which many disdainfully ignored.

Even the two deputies who were expected to be most friendly to the commission responded to the pressures for solidarity with the other deputies. A. V. Obolenskii, representing the Kaluga minority, prefaced his separate response by stating that he endorsed the collective responses to the extent that they were compatible with compulsory redemption of allotments.[61] This was the logical equivalent of endorsing prohibition to the extent that it would not interfere with the sale and consumption of alcohol. For I. A. Pushkin, who represented Cherkasskii's faction of the Tula Committee, the conflicting pressures were too much to bear. Unable to take a stand against the other deputies, he signed the collective responses, but then, unwilling to confront his former chief as a hostile deponent, he ignominiously fled the capital and his responsibilities.[62]

The Concluding Opinion of the second convocation was, by and large, the most coherent and powerful of all the attacks on the Editorial Commission. The commission's recommendations, it declared,

unquestionably destroy the basic principle of the inviolability of property, excessively and arbitrarily reducing the agricultural incomes of the pomeshchiki and making it impossible to carry on work in the pomeshchik's fields. . . . Having renounced the rights it has under serfdom, the nobility does not think it possible to undertake in addition any sacrifice whatsoever of land. . . . With the abolition of the previous relationship between pomeshchiki and peasants, the previous tie between the peasant and the pomeshchik's land is terminated.

This was a familiar argument in an extreme form. The deputies went on, however, to protest restrictions on the freedom of the ex-serfs, particularly through the perpetuation of ascription and compulsory labor. They argued with some justice that "the emancipation of the peasants has been converted into a mere regulation of the servile relationship." The servile elements of which the deputies complained—ascription and barshchina, in particular—were intended as concessions to the pomeshchiki, but these concessions did not divert the deputies from their primary goal. What they most wanted was a clear title to the allotment land, for the doctrine of laissez faire had secured a belated but over-whelming triumph. Indeed, the deputies emphasized theoretical rigor more than practical wisdom.

Theory teaches that freedom is a man's best security, which no administrative tutelage will provide. Why, then, are these complex and restrictive measures, supervised by outsiders, proposed to meet the requirements of free men?
Theory shows that it is equally harmful to a man's energies if he fears that he will not get the fruits of his labors or if he hopes he can be supported by another's labor or another's property. . . . Theory teaches and practice confirms that it is wrong to interfere with property rights or relations between private persons.

"Theory," of course, was harsh and hard to assimilate; accordingly, the deputies proposed a three-year transition, after which the allotments would revert to the pomeshchik and all further relations between lord and peasant would be by free agreement.[63] Peasants would be allowed to move where they liked, and rent land or work for hire wherever they could find the best terms.[64] They would not suffer, since the law of supply and demand would ensure that "no one can take more for his property than it is worth"; indeed, demesne cultivation would be reduced and the peasants would hold more land than under serfdom.
The deputies were self-seeking, as exponents of laissez faire sometimes are. However, in the West European conceptual framework of rich pomeshchiki and senior officials, their arguments were persuasive. To sophisticated Europeans of the mid-nineteenth century, the merits of laissez faire were as self-evident in economics as they are in child rearing today. For the authors of the reform statutes, it was embarrassing that their system was utterly at odds with the doctrines of the leading economists of the day—with what the deputies called "theory."[65] The deputies were also correct in substance. The Editorial

Commission did perpetuate serfdom in many ways, largely in order
to perpetuate and consolidate the peasants' hold on their land. If
arguments alone had any force in the combat between the nobility
and the bureaucracy, the deputies had seized the commanding
heights.

They could not hold out there, however, for their conversion from
the practices of serfdom to the theory of laissez faire was too
abrupt. In particular, the deputies were undone by their concern for
the pomeshchiki whose land was poor or underpopulated—that is,
by their attempt to represent the interests of all the nobles. After
their strictures against government interference and constraints
on labor and property, they undercut their own position with their
recommendations on redemption. Within the three-year
transition, they proposed, the pomeshchik could decide to have the
allotments on his estate redeemed. This was compulsory
redemption of a kind—compulsory for the peasants and for the
government, which would pay the pomeshchik at once with five-
percent negotiable bonds and recover the sum at leisure from the
peasants. The price of the allotments would be determined by local
assessing commissions, but it would not be left to supply and
demand, for in no case would it be less than a capitalization of the
peasants' average dues under serfdom.[66] The sovereign theory of
laissez faire, then, would have no more than condominium in areas
where the pomeshchiki might find it oppressive.

The six collective responses, the consensus of the second
convocation, display the same qualities as the Concluding
Opinion—vigorous defense of the nobility's interests, rigorous
adherence to laissez faire, and striking inconsistency whenever
these two tendencies came into conflict. To be sure, in these six
responses, and in the supplementary responses submitted by
individual deputies, many objections raised during the first
convocation were made again. Like their predecessors, the new
deputies opposed immutable dues, gradation of dues, and the
requirement that the pomeshchik provide his ex-serfs with fuel;
they, too, maintained that the Editorial Commission condemned its
own system by proposing Draconian exactions to make it work.
They argued that the allotments and dues proposed in the
provincial drafts were solidly based upon local data, but they were
no better able than the first convocation to indicate the character of
the data. They were even more prone than their predecessors to
make elaborate calculations of the financial losses the commission's
system would entail for the nobility.

The reiteration of these familiar points should not obscure the
fundamental difference between the two convocations. More

important than the second group's relative indifference to the reform of the central administration and to the redemption of allotments, more important even than its virtual unanimity, was its boldness. Each of the collective responses was more outspoken than anything submitted from the first convocation. In their first joint effort, the deputies of the second convocation accused the commission outright of violating the rescripts of 1857. The "communist principles" they found in the reports of the Legal Section were balanced by the anarchist and democratic tendencies of the Administrative Section.[67] Where the first convocation had been reticent, the second was outspoken, insisting, for example, that the serfs were simply the property of the pomeshchik.[68]

The deputies were free of sentimentality about serfdom. To the commission's contention that the pomeshchik's losses through the reform would be compensated by his release from obligations to his serfs, the deputies plausibly replied that these obligations "were not very onerous, as is apparent from the fact that money was paid to acquire these [serfholders'] rights and the concomitant obligations."[69] They refused to waver before the specter of peasant rebellion, which the Editorial Commission evoked in arguing against cutouts from the peasants' allotments. They insisted,

The nobility knows the conditions of rural life well and could not propose a dangerous measure, especially since that danger would affect the pomeshchiki themselves first of all. Also, a government does not renounce its obligation to maintain and defend the rights of property, even though attempts may be made to persuade it that this defense is dangerous to domestic tranquility; on the contrary, domestic tranquility is founded upon the maintenance of private rights.[70]

A peasant allotment was analogous to an apartment; there was no reason to compel the rightful owner to rent it.

The simplest conception of justice does not permit one estate, with the aid of the law and the patronage of the government, to benefit at the expense of another; it does not permit that a property holder be compelled, ostensibly by free agreement, to yield his property for a price that does not correspond to [its value],—nor does it, finally, permit that in a matter of property, all the profits and advantages should be on one side only.[71]

It did not occur to the deputies that this Manchestrian rhapsody was a devastating condemnation of themselves as serfholders.

On legal and economic matters, then, pomeshchiki were simply property holders, neither more nor less, and entitled to the protection that justice and economic theory alike demanded. On administrative matters, however, pomeshchiki were still the noble estate, vested by birth and status with rights and obligations. Here nostalgia for serfdom, or the outlook formed under its influence, was too strong for even superficial consistency with the exigencies of "theory." The Administrative Section, the deputies explained, erroneously supposed that the nobility was reluctant to reassume the burden of its "eternal vocation" of administration, supervision, and adjudication in the village. The section's proposals betrayed a "distrust for the upper class" and, "leaving the lower strata of society without any control or direction" they could *"bring in their wake a disruption of the entire internal administration."*

Do the peasants, the deputies rhetorically inquired of the Economic Section, require "perpetual tutelage?" The answer (to be found in their response to the Administrative Section) was yes. The peasants could not get along "without the aid, without the direction, and without the defense of the landowning class."[73] The commune was not an adequate substitute, particularly since it would impose restrictions on the inalienable rights of the peasants; nonetheless, communal tenure could not be abolished without the pomeshchik's consent, since his rights as property holder prevailed over all.[74] Basically, the communal structure proposed by the commission amounted to a "permanent trade union," directed against the pomeshchik. Consequently, local authority must be vested in the pomeshchik as "chief of the canton."[75]

Despite their intransigence, twenty-six deputies extended to the commission the courtesy of testifying before it. In most instances, this was demonstrative diplomacy; they were not bargaining with the commission, but exposing it for the benefit of the lofty patrons on whom they were counting. Their testimony had the same tenor as their responses and displayed further inconsistencies. Although they vaunted "theory," most deputies did not see any major disadvantages to barshchina cultivation. The Orel deputy Khliustin was unmoved by arguments about the low productivity of compulsory labor, while the Kiev deputy steadfastly maintained that if the peasants could choose to transfer to obrok, no one would cultivate the pomeshchik's fields and he would starve. The benevolent workings of supply and demand were forgotten. When Samarin complained that the Orenburg deputy Kartashevskii was carrying gradation too far in demanding the same dues for two desiatiny as for eight, Kartashevskii innocently replied, "What is in question here is dues, not the value of the land."[76]

There were exceptions. Like the deputies from the periphery in the first convocation, the Don Cossack deputies proved "the nicest of folk" in a face-to-face encounter. The Penza deputy Gorskin, playing the role of canny graybeard, argued hotly and effectively with the members, but he unexpectedly concluded, "I am afraid I have gone too far. Everyone told me all kinds of things about you, but you are forward-looking men." This was a rare admission. The members of the commission had little more success in eliciting data from the second group than they had had with Shuvalov, while their insistence that they, too, were pomeshchiki was skeptically received. When Cherkasskii suggested to the Kursk deputy Iz"edinov that he verify the commission's data, Iz"edinov thanked him but declined; there was no point in reviewing data since "we have the views of diverse parties."[77]

Iz"edinov's party was consistent in its tactics, if not always in its arguments; the second convocation displayed the solidarity and intransigence that the reformers had feared and expected to encounter with the first. The second group of deputies made less of an impression on public opinion than the first had, but it did not thereby have any greater influence on the course of the reform. The deputies' hopes for influence hung upon the sole premise of their strategy, the assumption that the Editorial Commission and all its works were doomed. The condescension most of them displayed to the members of the commission was quite sincere and appropriate, since the nobility's champions now seemed to be recovering their old sway. As Gorskin genially explained, pointing to the commission's published proceedings,

Here are your books; Russia has read them and they circulate everywhere. If the indignation of the nobility has not turned into a single rising groan, into one general, shattering howl, that is only because they still think that it will not happen. The Government can't do that. It has no reason to ruin us.[78]

All the tactics of the second convocation, then, were based on the expectation that the sanovniki would intervene at last to overthrow the reformers and rescue the nobility.

The Sanovniki

In January 1861, the Prussian ambassador informed his government that most members of the Council of State opposed the emancipation legislation they were then reviewing, but they would suppress their economic interests and their convictions and defer to the tsar's wishes. "Except, perhaps, for a few members—the Germans—there is scarcely anyone on the Council of State who desires to share with Prince [P. P.] Gagarin the glory of an independent view."[79] The Prussian ambassador, Otto von Bismarck, was badly informed. It was in the Main Committee and especially in the Council of State that the sanovniki finally took their stand. Miliutin and Cherkasskii feared their opposition, Lanskoi had warned the tsar about them, and thousands of squires were counting on their intervention. Everyone assumed that the sanovniki were intriguing to subvert the reform. It turned out that they were waiting until the Editorial Commission's draft, which they did indeed oppose, came into their purview through the proper legislative channels. The sanovniki were bureaucrats before they were pomeshchiki, and so their intervention came too late to make any great difference.

For Valuev, who was pressed into the service of the sanovniki on this occasion, their opposition was disgraceful.

Two things are clear [he wrote in his diary]. First, the timidity of our worthy ministers and Co. when Rostovtsev was alive gives them no right to their present opposition. The other is that the camp of N. A. Miliutin and Co. has forehandedly taken advantage of this timidity to secure, under a cloak of bureaucratic secrecy, the emperor's sanction for all their main principles.[80]

However, the cloak of bureaucratic secrecy was not lifted even for Miliutin's benefit. Bismark was probably correct in supposing that the sanovniki would not directly oppose the tsar's will, but Alexander showed great restraint in making his will known. He had blazoned his unequivocal support for Rostovtsev, but had never extended this support to the commission as a whole. More precisely, he consistently upheld the chairman and continued to do so, as in the controversy over perpetual usufruct, when the chairmanship passed to Panin; in that instance, he supported the chairman in a challenge to one of the commission's basic premises. He had, to be sure, instructed Panin that the peasant allotments could never be taken away; similarly, he had praised the commission's work to Rostovtsev. Private, oral statements gave little assurance to the commission, considering the policies that had been quietly forgotten after they had been ceremoniously proclaimed to the public.

Even when the commission's work was complete, the tsar refrained from any expression of support. In dismissing the members, Alexander thanked them for their arduous labor. "Of course, all the works of man have their imperfections. You know this; I know it too, very well. Perhaps it will be necessary to change *much* but in any event, the honor of the first effort belongs to you, and Russia will be grateful to you."[81] This was faint praise. If Alexander did not encourage opposition to the statutes drawn up by the Editorial Commission, he did not discourage it, and this was enough for the sanovniki.

The tsar's role was crucial. There were no avowed opponents of autocracy involved in the debate. Ostensibly, the struggle over the terms of the reform was a series of disagreements as to who was correctly interpreting and implementing the autocrat's will, as set forth in the rescripts and certain Imperial Orders. Shuvalov, Apraksin, Panin, the deputies, the Editorial Commission, even Bezobrazov—all of the combatants pretended they were simply carrying out the tsar's wishes, hampered by perverse or imperceptive rivals. They did not admit that they were trying to persuade Alexander to change his mind, or dissuade him from doing so. All the implements of struggle—conspiracy theories, fidelity to the rescripts, accusations of political disloyalty—derived from the fiction that the tsar's will was clear and unchanging. It was a fiction nonetheless; the struggle over the reform was a struggle for Alexander.

In discussing a successor to Rostovtsev, Petr Semenov told the tsar that it made little difference who presided so long as the commission's system had Alexander's support. Cherkasskii privately took the same view. Rostovtsev's dying words were, "Don't be afraid, my Sovereign."[82] The sovereign was not afraid. He had little to fear so long as the contending parties maintained they were trying to outdo one another in zealous service to himself. Alexander did not like any other kind of controversy. "How good it would be," he remarked to Galagan of the Editorial Commission, "if it was all done so that everyone was satisfied and there were no complaints and reproaches."[83] In the meantime, Alexander deflected complaints and reproaches from himself by taking the line that nothing had been finally decided. He would not tolerate attacks on the institutions and individuals that served him, but this patronage was extended to Orlov and the Main Committee as well as Rostovtsev and the Editorial Commission. And, between October of 1858 and February of 1861, he did not commit himself on any point of controversy concerning the terms of emancipation.

Because the autocrat did not commit himself, the struggle continued in the same form to the very end. Pomeshchiki and even high officials volunteered alternate reform plans until the statutes were enacted.[84] Bulygin and Apraksin, two dissident members of the Editorial Commission, proposed to collect six thousand signatures on a petition against the commission's draft when it was already under review in the Main Committee. And when M. N. Murav'ev organized the opposition to that draft within the committee, he did so in hopes of currying favor with the tsar. Murav'ev cleaved to Dolgorukov, the head of the political police, who reported in person to the tsar every day. Surely Dolgorukov would not oppose the Editorial Commission's draft if it had the tsar's support?[85]

Initially, the Editorial Commission had only three supporters on the Main Committee—Lanskoi, Chevkin, the Chief Administrator of the transport system, and the Grant Duke Konstantin, who had replaced Orlov as chairman. The commission's supporters set about to recruit a majority, beginning with Panin. Panin had not signed the Editorial Commission's final draft; he was assumed to be holding his fire until the draft came before the Main Committee.[86] Petr Semenov recalled that "because of the delicacy of his nature, [the tsar] did not want to coerce the curious and often surprising convictions of Count Panin." However, Panin agreed to parley with the Semenov brothers, and Valuev correctly observed that he would not have agreed unless he was prepared to capitulate. It turned out that Panin's reservations were purely formal; he withdrew his objections on three basic issues after listening to Petr Semenov's explanations, with which he was perfectly familiar already. Panin then insisted that he and Semenov go over the statutory allotments for every district in Russia. They reduced a few, and Panin's assent to almost every article of the reform was secured.[87] He simply wanted a show of deference to himself before he would give his *nihil obstat*.

It took another month for Adlerberg,[88] the Minister of the Court, and Secretary of State Butkov to follow Panin's example. According to Semenov, Butkov simply wanted to be on the winning side.[89] So did Kniazhevich, the Minister of Finance, but he chose the other side. Despite Kniazhevich's defection, the Editorial Commission's drafts had a majority of five or six on every vote; five was enough, since the opposition, as always, was divided.

P. P. Gagarin constituted a minority of one, as he had in 1857, for his opposition was so unrestrained that, as Semenov recalled, "he did not know how to win reliable and steady allies to his side."[90] Like most officials in the capital, and unlike most spokesmen for the nobility, Gagarin professed anxiety about the danger of peasant rebellion. Accordingly, he wanted to retain much of the pomeshchik's manorial authority until there was a "strong authority" in the countryside to replace it. He held that the proposed communal and arbitrative institutions, being perpetually embroiled in litigation, would not be able to restrain the peasant's self-will, while the retention of cherished prerogatives would "reconcile the nobility to the abrupt and unexpected deprivation of its rights."[91]

Concerning the economic settlement, Gagarin offered a trenchant criticism of the Editorial Commission's system and an alternative to it. In his criticism, he avoided the overheated accusations and recriminations to which many deputies and other spokesmen for the nobility were inclined. Instead, he elicited six essential conditions from the rescripts and other authoritative policy statements and showed that the commission's system satisfied none of them: the peasants would not be satisfied, the pomeshchiki would not be reassured, the flow of tax revenue would not be secure, and so on.[92] Gagarin was able to make a forceful case by fastening on inequities and inconsistencies, most of which derived from the commission's taking the existing situation as its point of departure and then inserting various reservations in the pomeshchik's favor. Other critics had pointed out, for example, that the system of maxima and minima could produce drastically different allotments in two adjacent and virtually identical villages, but Gagarin's criticism was unusual for its brevity, lucidity, and thoroughness. His alternative system was taken from a dissenting opinion of Zheltukhin's, which the Editorial Commission had simply ignored.[93] It provided for free agreements on allotments and dues within a framework derived from the law on three-day barshchina. Indeed, it was tailor-made for those barshchina proprietors who intended to continue cultivating the demesne in much the same way; peasants who wanted to shift to obrok would have to pay the wages of the hired laborers who replaced them, and Gagarin sought to make sure that there would be plenty of peasants available for hire.[94] He denied the contention that pomeshchiki would coerce their ex-serfs to accept unfavorable terms and insisted that if the two sides came to an agreement, with the aid of an arbiter of the peace, "then the question is already decided and there is not, it seems, any necessity of knowing how it was decided."[95]

Gagarin was close to the position of the second convocation and he referred to the deputies with respect. M. N. Murav'ev was also impressed with the deputies' criticisms of the Editorial Commission,[96] but he could agree with Gagarin on little else, for he and his allies kept their proposals within the framework set up by the Editorial Commission.

Murav'ev entered the contest with his vanity doubly wounded; he had hoped to succeed to Rostovtsev's chairmanship and he assumed that the Ministry of State Properties, which he headed, would be given a major role in the emancipation. By July of 1860, he was convinced that the members of the Editorial Commission were ignorant and possibly subversive, but found its system could not survive "sound discussion and practical analysis."[97] Thus reassured, Murav'ev did not begin work on an alternative until the commission's draft was brought before the Main Committee. He told Valuev that he could draw up a rival body of legislation, on the Baltic model, in two weeks. After one week, he had made little progress, having adopted another model, but later he swung back to the Baltic. "It is strange," Valuev observed, "since he now is busying himself so energetically with all kinds of questions like these, that he did not undertake this work earlier." As the difficulties mounted, Murav'ev recruited Valuev, who had been Shuvalov's ghost-writer in his conflict with Rostovtsev, to "recompile" parts of the Editorial Commission's system. Throughout October and November, Murav'ev and his allies thrashed about trying to work out an alternative. Dolgorukov inclined for a while to a refinement of the April Program; he also considered exploiting his office and informing the tsar that he could not be responsible for maintaining order if the commission's system was enacted, but repented of this tactic. Murav'ev insisted that he was unshakable, but, Valuev found, "as soon as he is simply reminded of the sovereign, or objections are raised to his plan, all his former arguments are consigned to oblivion. He is beginning to deal with allotment figures even more unceremoniously than the Editorial Commission did."[98]

Eventually, Murav'ev finished dealing with allotment figures and offered a plan, supported by Dolgorukov and Kniazhevich. The three of them explicitly rejected the Editorial Commission's system of zones, maxima and minima, and the principle of granting the existing allotment. Instead, they proposed that the Provincial Boards should establish a single statutory allotment for each area, to be applied if the pomeshchik and his peasants did not reach agreement. These statutory norms should, in most cases, be two-thirds of the figures set forth in a separate schedule. The three-man minority framed their proposal in this curious way because the attached schedule was simply a copy of the Editorial Commission's maxima;[99] they had not worked out any norms of their own. Similarly, the Great Russian Statute they offered was the commission's, modified here and there to conform with the plan. Like so many of the commission's opponents, they came to grief because they lacked the tenacity, information, and skill to draw up a coherent alternative. Semenov supposed that the tsar might have accepted an alternative system "if proposals, emanating from the entire Russian nobility, were vested in the form of an acceptable (according to His convictions) counterdraft . . . but no such counterdraft was presented to the Soverign.[100]

The Main Committee rejected all the proposals of Murav'ev's faction, and approved the Editorial Commission's draft statutes with only two changes, both consistent with the commission's general tendency. For Valeuv, the commission's victory in the committee was a foregone conclusion.[101] He was critical of the commission's work on many points, but his private criticism of Murav'ev's faction was scathing. He appreciated the effort and expertise that underlay the commission's draft, and it went againt his grain, as á professional bureaucrat, to see this careful construct challenged by an impromptu and amateurish rival. Since he had to draw up this rival system himself, on behalf of the three-man minority, his position was "intolerable."[102] Yet he took on this unwelcome burden, obviously assuming that it would help his career to accommodate Murav'ev and Dolgorukov. This assumption was correct. Days after the promulgation of emancipation, Valuev replaced Lanskoi as Minister of Internal Affairs. The author of the major rival to the new legislation was placed in charge of its implementation.

Opposition to the emancipation legislation was no bar to a successful bureaucratic career. Even when the Main Committee's version passed to the Council of State, Gagarin pressed for his views; he shortly became chairman of the council. Panin, Dolgorukov, and Murav'ev also continued to advocate proposals that the Main Committee had rejected, for even at this late date, the tsar would not commit himself.

The deliberations of the Council of State opened with an improvised speech by Alexander. He expressed surprise and pleasure at the patience with which the serfs had awaited their fate, and praised the nobility, more equivocally, in the same terms. He wanted the nobles' sacrifices kept to a minimum and would consider any change "for the protection of the interests of the pomeshchiki." Furthermore, he invoked the rescripts of 1857 as the basis of the reform and revived the rescripts' contradictory stand on property rights. However, he explicitly rejected landless emancipation and the example of Russia's Baltic provinces. As for the Editorial Commission, many of the reproaches against it might well be just, Alexander conceded, but it had been conscientious and punctual. He expected the same from the councillors; they must put aside their private interests and deliberate as "Sanovniki of the state."[103]

Golovnin, Konstantin Nikolaevich's secretary, rejoiced at this speech. He found that it set Alexander "infinitely higher than all his ministers and members of the Council. He has grown immeasurably, while they have fallen behind."[104] The councillors had fallen so far behind that they did not interpret Alexander's speech as an endorsement of the legislation under review. This legislation had won a bare majority in the Editorial Commission and in the Main Committee. The major articles were rejected by a large majority in the council. Some contemporaries thought Alexander put pressure on individual councillors to vote for the statutes as proposed, but there is no sign of this pressure in the voting record.[105] The legislation of February 19 did not even carry the imperial family, three members of which sat in the council.

The council showed its temper immediately. On its first division, sixteen members came out for unrestricted free agreements. They argued, despite what the tsar had just said, that a grant of personal rights to the peasants was amelioration enough. A system of unconstrained agreements would uphold the sanctity of private property and would provide a salutary continuity, for "the ties uniting the two estates will not be abruptly sundered by the interference of outside authority, and the indestructible preservation of these ties will serve as the best guarantee of the preservation of tranquility."[106] Thus these sixteen members repudiated the very idea of a reform of serfdom by rejecting the interference of the state between squire and serf. To these arguments, a twenty-nine man majority replied that pomeshchiki and peasants would not conclude agreements unless there was a statutory alternative: at best, nobles would compel their former serfs to accept unfavorable terms. Twenty-nine to sixteen represented a comfortable majority for the bare concept of reform, but subsequent votes revealed that the council was not disposed to go much further than that.

The crucial economic provisions of the reform concerned allotments. Since the establishment of the provincial committees, debates had raged over two issues: the size of the allotments and the terms under which peasants might or must redeem them. A majority of the Council of State proved oblivious to nearly three years of controversy and regressed to the level of discussion that had preceded the initial rescripts of 1857. On the second division, nineteen councillors maintained that the statutes should not contain any allotment figures at all; they should be determined, as Murav'ev had proposed, by Provincial Boards. Only seventeen members voted that the statutes must make a quantitative determination of the size of the allotments, since the Provincial

Boards would be "under the influence of local interests."[107] In essence, a slight majority of the council would let the nobility of each province dictate the economic content of the reform.

The council was an unembarrassed partisan of "local interests," which obviously meant the nobility's interests. Fifteen members even dredged up the "guardian of the canton"; both the Editorial Commission and the Main Committee had rejected this device to reconstitute manorial authority on an official footing.[108] Indeed, the attitudes of legislative agencies towards the new officialdom form a neat sequence. The Editorial Commission rejected the idea, set forth in the Imperial Order of March 25, 1859, that one of the three members of each District Arbitration Board should be a peasant, but it decided, after heated debate, that the arbiters of the peace who would sit on that board should be elected from the nobility by the ex-serfs.[109] The Main Committee, making a rare departure from the commission's proposals (and adopting the view of the Ministry of Internal Affairs) ruled that, for the first three-year term, provincial governors should appoint the arbiters, since it would take some time to set up the village institutions that would elect them.[110] The Council of State voted thirty-one to thirteen that the arbiters should be nominated by the nobility.[111]

Many of the other alternatives offered by the majority had been raised before by spokesmen for the nobility. Pozen had proposed that allotments be set by provincial agencies and he incorporated this idea into the April Program. A large majority of councillors voted for a redetermination of dues in fourteen years; they were not satisfied with the commission's concession to the deputies on this point, *pereobrochka* after twenty years. A similar majority endorsed Panin's plan for continuing barshchina, at the pomeshchik's option, for as long as nine years.[112] Even the old misunderstandings cropped up again; the councillors seem to have thought that the gradation of dues would give the pomeshchik proportionately less for an allotment smaller than the maximum.[113]

The councillors voted like sanovniki, as Alexander had asked, but a sanovnik was a variety of pomeshchik. It was not the same thing. On vote after vote, the council rejected the recommendations of the Editorial Commission in favor of proposals advanced by spokesmen for the pomeshchiki in the provincial committees and in the two convocations. The council did not, however, share the squire's characteristic distrust of officialdom. Pomeshchiki generally assumed that obrok would be uncollectable and barshchina unworkable when imposed by statute instead of manorial power. They had no confidence in the capacity of officials to enforce this part of the reform, particularly as regards barshchina. Hence they had been inclined to one of two extremes: either the retention of broad arbitrary power over their peasants or a complete end to the relationship (with generous compensation for lost land and revenues). The councillors were not so skeptical about the force of law and the efficiency of the bureaucracy, or perhaps they were not so aware of the stringency of the agricultural cycle. At any rate, their votes did not reflect the provincial nobles' anxiety that they would be ruined by delays arising from the arbitration and adjudication of disputes.

Although it rejected most elements of the legislation before it, the spirit of the Council of State was not defiant or even disputatious. The sanovniki were no more disposed than the pomeshchiki were to challenge the autocrat and flout his cherished wishes. Like the provincial committees and the deputies, they believed they should take their mandated responsibilities seriously, for they were under the impression that very little had been conclusively decided. This impression, which often took the form of hope for the autocrat's favor, persisted from the issuance of the rescripts through the discussions in the Council of State. While vital interests and deep-seated prejudices hung in the balance, it had served to allay anxieties and stifle challenges. It had enabled the legislative process to go forward with remarkable serenity. Now this impression had to be dispelled.

In response to the tsar's invitation, the Council of State had produced a great many changes "for the protection of the interests of the pomeshchiki." Alexander considered these changes, as he had promised, and rejected all but two departures from the statutes proposed by the Editorial Commission and the Main Committee.[114] To do so, he had to endorse the minority opinion on sixteen of the thirty-two issues, most of them major, on which the Council of State was divided.[115] This was not the time for ceremonial courtesy to subordinates—what Semenov called Alexander's delicacy. The tsar turned away from the sanovniki and at last openly committed himself to the emancipators' point of view.

There was one exception, the so-called beggarly allotment. Under this option, ex-serfs could, by mutual agreement with their pomeshchik, acquire a full title to one-quarter of the statutory maximum and a release from temporary obligation; the peasants would not be required to fulfill any obligations to the pomeshchik and he would not be obliged to provide any more land. This amendment was not necessarily against the peasant's interests, but it was intended as a concession to the pomeshchiki of the Southeast; the peasants were expected to be eager to escape the statutory dues, which were very high but would soon be outstripped by rising land values in this underpopulated area.[116]

The beggarly allotment was in conflict with the basic principles underlying the reform statutes. The Editorial Commission had argued forcefully that peasants must be prevented from exercising their "still immature will" and renouncing their allotments. The commission acknowledged that, despite its own best efforts and those of the provincial committees, the statutory dues

will by no means correspond everywhere and always to the actual value of the peasant allotment and, representing a transitional stage from arbitrarily determined dues to a just rent, will often work to the temporary disadvantage of the peasant estate. Under these conditions, which it is beyond anyone's power to avoid entirely, any temporary relief from the peasant dues established by law . . . would almost inevitably lead in a multitude of instances to a heedless renunciation by the peasants of their precious right [to their allotment], which constitutes the best guarantee of their security and prosperity in the future. . . . The inferior estate, set by the force of things in an unequal relationship to the landowning class, is more than ever in need of the sovereign tutelage of the Government.[117]

This was a rare admission of the defects inherent in the emerging statutes; the legislative power was unable to protect the peasant from the inequities of legislation but it could, by binding him to his allotment, protect him from himself.

This line of reasoning had prevailed at every step of the legislative process. A majority of the Council of State had resorted to it in rejecting free agreements as an alternative to allotments determined by the regime.[118] And quite recently, the tsar himself had dismissed a proposal similar to the beggarly allotments as "a pasquille," which indicated that its author (D. A. Tolstoi) was neither loyal nor well informed.[119] Yet, at the end of its deliberations, the Council of State adopted the beggarly allotment, unanimously and apparently without debate.[120] Perhaps the reformers and the tsar himself (who gave the amendment his sanction) were worn down by forty months of recriminations. At any rate, the beggarly allotment was the only contribution of the sanovniki to the emancipation settlement.

The sanovniki did not oppose the abolition of serfdom as such, as N. M. Kolmakov, a subordinate of Panin's, subsequently pointed out in their defense, and they tried to submit to the will of the tsar. However, while

the will of the Sovereign Emperor shone radiantly in the zenith like a guiding star, the actual ground of the path by which it was necessary to proceed was still dark, and therefore, the idea of emancipating the peasants in the form that is embodied and set forth in the Statute of February 19, 1861, did not emerge at once, but gradually, with more or less effort and delay.

As it emerged, Kolmakov observed, the sanovniki communicated their misgivings about timing, procedure, and other terms of the reform. They did so openly and through the institutional forms the tsar provided. Consequently, there was not, as Solov'ev and other reformers charged in retrospect, a conflict of parties. The combatants were simply

men in service, with varying degrees of influence and intimacy with the tsar, who reflected on how best to arrange this matter, how to conclude it without convulsing the state, and how to prevent the tsar from being misled; they should not be condemned for this, but given due praise. It goes without saying that these men grew up under the system of serfdom and hence they could not look upon the system that must emerge with the emancipation of the peasants without alarm. . . . But there was no *sage* who, from the very outset of these proceedings, embraced the whole matter at once, so to speak, and in general had a clear idea . . . of how to emancipate the peasants.[121]

Valuev, on the other hand, held that the sanovniki had behaved ignobly; for statesmen, acting by legitimate means and in good faith was no excuse for ineptitude. Hence the sanovniki were to blame for the defects of the legislative process and the reform statutes. The statutes did not, according to Valuev, display adequate concern for the nobility's economic interests; by summoning the nobility to deliberate on the reform and then ignoring their advice, the regime created political problems with which he, on becoming Minister of Internal Affairs, had to cope. "But," he argued,

the chief culprits responsible for these errors were precisely those who lamented them most, those who blamed them on the Editorial Commission, Gen. Rostovtsev, Count Panin and the Sovereign himself. Everything happened as it did only because the Sovereign did not find aid where he first sought it and ought to have found it. The very men who ought to have given him this aid and brought the matter to its culmination let it slip through their hands. Not only did they do nothing better than the Editorial Commission, as a rule they did not know how to do anything, and only contradicted, opposed and delayed.

The few sanovniki who did come to the tsar's aid prevailed only because of the incapacity of their rivals—Orlov, Murav'ev, and the rest. Lanskoi simply knew enough to rely on clever subordinates; Rostovtsev won the tsar's complete confidence, despite his meager endowments, because of his strength of will. The combination was sufficient, for,

From the day the Editorial Commission was established, the question was essentially decided; all the myopic or ambiguous *cunctatore*, the ranking sanovniki of high estate, represented a lost cause. It remained only to concentrate all efforts on guaranteeing, so far as possible, the correct resolution of various secondary but all the same important questions. It was especially desirable to prove to the sovereign that the arguments and aspirations of the opposition did not concern the essence of the reform, but particulars. . . . This they did not know how to do. The main representatives of the interests of the nobility and of the so-called aristocratic interests complained, howled, tried to frighten the sovereign, and only succeeded in strengthening his confidence in their opponents.[122]

This was Valuev's retrospective view, but at the time his opinion of the sanovniki was no higher, and in the main, he was correct. To be sure, he himself realized that the question was "essentially decided" only in November of 1860, nineteen months after the establishment of the Editorial Commission, but he reached this conclusion sooner than sanovniki in regular contact with the tsar. He might, however, have been kinder to them in retrospect, since he was the only beneficiary of their belated and misconceived counterattack. The misgivings voiced by sanovniki scarcely penetrated the reform legislation. Almost as soon as the legislation was promulgated, they found expression in the dismissal of Lanskoi and Miliutin, a principal sponsor and the principal author of the legislation. Valuev was installed as Minister of Internal Afffairs, charged with the implementation of the statutes he had, in behalf of the sanovniki, unsuccessfully opposed.

The regime also expressed its misgivings in the promulgation of the reform. February 19, 1861, was the sixth anniversary of the tsar's accession. Since the debate in the Council of State was over by the middle of the month, it was widely expected that the emancipation of the serfs would be proclaimed on that day. So great was the tension and expectancy that the governor-general of St. Petersburg announced in the newspapers that "No governmental dispositions on the peasant question will be promulgated on February 19." On the fateful day, army units patrolled the streets of the capital; concierges were instructed to report loose talk about emancipation and any gathering of more than three persons.[123] The 19th passed uneventfully, but the widespread expectation had been essentially correct. The tsar signed the reform into law on February 19, but the legislation was not made public until March 5. The delay was intended to meet the danger of peasant disillusionment. March 5 was the first day of Lent, and the regime hoped that the penitential season would put the peasants in a compliant and grateful mood. Furthermore, during the forty-day fast, the faithful were supposed to abstain from alcohol, the great fuel of riot and disorder.

The reform was promulgated in the form of a ceremonious manifesto outlining the history and terms of the legislation; a "General Statute on Peasants Formerly in Servile Dependency"; supplementary statutes on household serfs, the redemption of household plots and allotments, and the implementation of the reform; four local statutes tailored to the peculiarities of the major regions where serfdom was widespread (Great Russia, the Left-Bank Ukraine, the Right-Bank Ukraine, and Lithuanian and Belorussian territories); and seven collections of Supplementary Rules applicable to special categories of serfs.

This mass of enactments reflected the successive stages of the legislative process, but in varying degrees. The rescripts and directives of 1857, which had inaugurated the process, exerted a lingering influence on the language of the statutes but very little on their substance. There was, however, a vestige of the regime's original program in the provision for the separate redemption of household plots. The provincial committees had produced thousands of pages of statutory material, of which there were only a few traces—the most significant being the gradation system—in the enacted legislation. Two convocations of deputies had filled four folio volumes with comments, complaints, and suggestions. Not one provision was inserted into the statutes at their behest. However, the pressure exerted by the deputies and the sentiment they represented did find some indirect expression through the mediation of the sanovniki. The Main Committee and the Council of State did not contribute any principle to the legislation, apart from the beggarly allotment. However, allotments were diminished in some zones and dues increased in others out of deference to the sanovniki or in response to their specific request. The pomeshchik mentality was characteristically crass and unsentimental, much more concerned about revenues than about status or esteem; the sanovniki served, sometimes unwittingly, as the embodiment of this mentality. Yet the reformers often anticipated the wishes of the sanovniki because they themselves were by no means free of the pomeshchik's concerns and anxieties. While the pomeshchiki were excluded, in despite of solemn assurances, from the legislative process, the pomeshchik mentality exerted a powerful inertial force.

It was Rostovtsev and his collaborators who provided the structure and rationale of the reform. In general, the statutes represented an inconsistent enactment of Rostovtsev's system. His wish to abolish the pomeshchik's arbitrary authority over the peasants on his estate was, indeed, enacted. The peasants passed out of the control of their ex-master, but came under the authority of a hierarchy of officials, most of them drawn from the landowning nobility. The legislation did not succeed in ending the peasants' economic dependence on the pomeshchik, as Rostovtsev had wished, because redemption of allotments was the only significant means to that end. The regime was willing to sponsor and underwrite the redemption process, but not to impose it.

Because redemption was left as an option, the legislative edifice rested upon an equivocation. Yet that edifice represented a momentous transformation. Article 1 of the General Statute did, in crabbed, legalistic language, proclaim the abolition of "the law of bondage," which is the Russian term for serfdom. Bondage had been the basis of Russia's social and economic life for more than three centuries. The significance of the change is best expressed in the physical form in which the new statutes were issued. The statutes were bound and distributed as bulky books. They were full of compromises and inconsistencies, but they were nonetheless books. For a millenium, Russia had been a nation of villages ruled from cities. The city-based regime had not, however, ruled in the villages. It had delivered the villagers into the hands of its agents; under serfdom, these agents were private persons, vested with almost unlimited arbitrary authority. Now, the regime ceased to devolve its authority to individuals, for henceforth it would seek to administer peasants by the book. In the spring of 1861, the book was duly delivered to the countryside.

Conclusion

Russian serfdom was durable. Many elements of serfdom, such as barshchina and the relegation of the peasantry to a separate status, survived the emancipation. With the collectivization of Russian agriculture, the peasants were once again ascribed to their villages and their compensation was determined by fiat; household plots became a vexed question, as in the 1850s. Nonetheless, *krepostnoe pravo*, serfdom as an institution, expired in 1861. It had been fatally stricken three and a half years earlier, and within a few months its beneficiaries had accepted fate with moderately good grace. They began haggling over the legacy, with no thought of preventing the death of the testator.

The explanation of their behavior lies in the peculiar character of serfdom in its last stage. Serfdom was not simply a system of commodity production and exploitation of labor, but most nobles perceived it as neither more nor less than a reliable device for providing them with income. Under pressure, they surrendered most of the privileges that law and usage conferred upon them, in hopes of retaining the practical advantages these privileges had brought. The rest of the population was no more sentimental. Even though few Russians clearly conceived an alternative, serfdom had no positive support in popular tradition. It persisted because of systematic support by the state, of which the use of police power and credit facilities were conspicuous examples. Serfdom was so dependent upon political agencies that when the state diffidently proposed to withdraw its support, serfdom had little or no momentum to carry on. Yet it was, until the very end, the basis of the Russian polity, and determined or influenced every social and economic relationship. Prereform Russia, then, was an anomaly—a society where the fundamental institution enjoyed almost no sanction apart from the patronage of the state.

Many nobles, whether in praise or blame, presented the reform as an attempt to bring Russia into conformity with Western Europe, but the nobles themselves were so westernized that they could not defend serfdom in principle. Imported ideas were not so important in precipitating the decision to emancipate as in disarming resistance to that decision, for nobles were incapable of finding arguments for serfdom except temporizing and prudential ones. Even for them, serfdom had no vitality or moral validity of its own.

Serfdom expired without a shot fired in its defense, but many shots were fired in defense of advantages for the pomeshchiki. This was ragged fire, with many wide shots and misfires, for the defense was uncoordinated; the terms the pomeshchiki sought varied according to the area they lived in, their appraisal of the political climate, and chance circumstances of leadership. More important, the defense operated under a major inhibition. From the sanovniki to the petty proprietors, the nobility was schooled in submission to the autocracy, and the reform was a political matter, initiated and enacted by the autocracy. There was no leader who was willing, when challenged, to pass from objecting to the draft legislation to political opposition. Since the reform was being drawn up under the aegis of the autocracy, it was easy to discredit and inhibit criticism of ostensibly tentative decisions by representing it as opposition to the autocrat and the holy cause of emancipation. The autocrat was, indeed, tentative and irresolute, but the shibboleths of autocratic authority and unswerving will were powerful weapons in the political culture of Imperial Russia.

The nobles were culturally remote from the peasants, but lived in one country under the same institutions, and common situations produced common myths. The nobility, like the peasantry, was susceptible to the myth of the benevolent tsar. For both groups, the myth did not produce positive support for government action, but it diffused and weakened resistance.

The peasantry's immediate response to the reform shows how the monarchist myth functioned. Despite its fear of a peasant rebellion, the regime managed the promulgation of the reform badly, in that its preparations were largely military. The emancipation manifesto was obscure, and the major statutes were long and complex; neither in form nor in substance could they meet the peasants' expectations. Furthermore, the institutions that were to explain and implement the reform were not yet in being. Apart from a special complement of the tsar's adjutants, the government had no agents in the countryside except for officials and squires, for whom serfdom was a way of life. Disillusionment and willful and innocent misinterpretations were widespread; some peasant lives were sacrificed to the nervousness of the officials, but there was no jacquerie. The greater the peasants' disappointment, the more readily they persuaded themselves that the legislation of February 19 was not the tsar's true and final dispensation. Real freedom would come in two years or else "at the hour which has been foretold." There was discontent and resistance, but the discontent was abated and the resistance diffused by the monarchist myth. At no one time did a substantial body of peasants acknowledge the emancipation legislation as a final settlement and make a stand on that basis. They continued to hope for a manifestation of the tsar's authentic, benevolent will in the near future.

"Monarchist illusions," as Soviet historians call them, were the counsel of prudence. Abandonment of these illusions led either to despair or to resistance, punishment, and suffering, for the tsar was remote and the authorities at hand were powerful. It may be that the myth of the benevolent tsar was half-deliberately adopted as an anodyne against reality.[1] Reality was harsh for the emancipated or "temporarily obligated" peasant. Nonetheless, the legislation of 1861 was a radical solution, given the political and social structure of nineteenth-century Russia. Certainly it was more generous to the peasantry than anyone in authority had thought possible in 1857, and most officials in 1860 and 1861 thought it was too generous. At the same time, it did not threaten the pomeshchiki with ruin, as they feared. There were exceptions; Lanskoi's estate was destined to be sold to merchants, with the woodlots plundered and the manorhouse in ruins. But even Shidlovskii, who protested the statutes of 1861 by moving to France, returned to Simbirsk and conceded in 1870 that his revenues were higher than under serfdom.[2] Objectively, the reform was more favorable to both parties than either believed it to be at the time. The decision to resist or acquiesce, however, depends upon a subjective assessment of one's interests. Just as most peasants were disappointed by the eventual reform, so most nobles were opposed to the government's plan at each stage of its spasmodic evolution. Their opposition, like the peasants', never developed into resistance because it was mollified and diffused by faith and hope in the autocrat.

The nobles' faith was more of a deliberate fiction than the peasants', although it was better supported by past evidence. The absolute distinction between the tsar and his officials, which was the ostensible premise of every expression of opposition, required the willful suspension of disbelief. As with the peasantry, monarchist illusions were a force for prudence, and prudence severely constricted the nobility's room for maneuver; Unkovskii and Mikhail Bezobrazov were dismissed and exiled for submitting unseemly petitions, couched in deferential language. Without imprudence, however, political change is impossible.

Most nobles did not want political change, or did not acknowledge that they did. They wanted the tsar's favor, which the noble estate had enjoyed for so long. At each stage in the development of the government's program, the nobility swallowed its objections or stated them obliquely, in the expectation that the aberration of the moment, issued in the tsar's name, would soon give way to some further expression of the tsar's favor. This process was repeated with each new formulation of policy, none of which corresponded to the nobility's conception of royal favor.

The nobility was by no means passive during the drafting process because there were few points on which the tsar's will was clear. The more radical a formulation of official policy, the more equivocally it was set forth for the public. There were many legitimate occasions for pressing for advantage. Again and again, groups of nobles exploited these occasions and were rebuffed and rebuked. The attachment of conditions to the petitions of 1858, the attempts of the provincial committees to legislate according to their own lights, the addresses of the deputies, and the votes in the Council of State all fall into this pattern. Indeed, apart from the original rescripts and certain proposals of Rostovtsev's, the limits of government policy and the authority of legislative institutions were defined by a series of responses to challenges from the nobility. Each challenge, except for those from Tver Province, was withdrawn as soon as it was rebuffed; to sustain the challenge would have been an act of conscious dissent from the autocrat's will, and hence both distasteful and self-defeating. Besides, there were always new occasions for challenge on a different aspect of policy. Because the tsar expressed his will so rarely, and expressed it publicly more rarely still, everyone involved could persist in his monarchist illusions until the reform was enacted. New policies were officially adopted, but the old policies were never renounced; the sanovniki were made to accept these new policies, but they continued to enjoy their offices and, apparently, the tsar's confidence. Until the very end, the tsar never made what had to be taken as an irrevocable commitment to a particular policy. The nobles persisted in their illusions, and there was no Fronde or conspiracy of oligarchs.

Yet the reformers believed that their cause was threatened by opposition from the nobility, and their representations of this threat were convincing to the tsar. These representations were false. They were not, however, manufactured out of nothing; the opinions, inclinations, and associations of high officials and prominent spokesmen for the nobility provided abundant material. In all legislative instances, the consensus of the nobility was very far from the reform that was eventually enacted. There was articulate discontent from the first, limited statements of reform policies. Dissident views were expressed in pamphlets published beyond the reach of censorship—the nobility's counterpart to the Free Russian Press. The writings of Bezobrazov had many admirers, and even Valuev, the quintessential Alexandrine bureaucrat, was impressed by Orlov-Davydov's attacks on the Editorial Commission. Opposition was voiced in salons and manor houses, and in various kinds of appeal to the tsar.

It was scarcely to be expected, however, that the whole of educated society should sincerely renounce the old order and its ways overnight. Menshikov and many other prominent magnates were privately well disposed to serfdom. To Orlov-Davydov, it seemed self-evident that the nobility be the exclusive beneficiaries of governmental largesse, as under serfdom. And all the leading exponents of opposition, within the government and without, were in touch with one another. Orlov-Davydov can be linked to Dolgorukov, Menshikov to Orlov, even Panin to Pozen.

This was no sinister conspiracy to subvert the reform, but the natural relationship for men of wealth and position and similar views. Conspiracy is not merely a matter of association and sentiment, it requires an intention to undertake illegitimate action—in this instance, to carry opposition to the emerging reform outside the framework the autocracy provided. The supposed conspirators had no such intention; the insinuations of their detractors about the very existence of the conspiracy are not confirmed by independent evidence. At most, there was a loose association of men who could not resolve on a course of action. In political terms, this is the same as no conspiracy at all, since the sentiments that linked these men were generally known.

The nobility's spokesmen, self-designated and otherwise, represented traditional loyalties and they used traditional methods: attempts to influence high officials, to work upon the bureaucracy's anxieties, to play upon the tsar's sympathies—in short, the pursuit of favor. Opposition that operated in traditional channels could be contained, because all the channels flowed to the tsar. Those who opposed the emancipation settlement in conversation with the tsar and his ministers, in the resolutions of provincial committees, or in voting in the Council of State may have been myopic and selfish, but their activities were neither covert nor dangerous.

The reformers maintained that their opponents were adamant, united, devious, and powerful. It was perfectly natural that they should take this position. Until the reform was enacted, they operated under the same uncertainty as their antagonists, and they inflated the opposition of these antagonists in order to bind the tsar to their own program. To serve immediate political purposes, Lanskoi, Miliutin, and Rostovtsev portrayed the nobility's opposition in garish colors. This picture passed almost unmodified into the memoirs and biographies of the reformers. The only false note in the retrospective accounts of the struggle is the conventional paean to the tsar-liberator; if the tsar was firm in his devotion to the abolitionist cause, the whole struggle was of no more account than the adverse votes in the Council of State.

The picture of a resolute, conspiratorial opposition persisted when the rationale had disappeared, because it satisfied subjective a well as practical political needs. To compile a complicated body of legislation is a fine thing, but to prevail against overwhelming odds in a noble cause is heroic. In fact, the emancipation legislation was a compromise between serfdom and the legislators' ideals of liberty and general welfare. As Iurii Samarin, the wisest of the leading emancipators, put it to Cherkasskii, "Legislation should never be regarded as a Credo [simvol very], for it always has the character of a bargain between the longed-for future and all the circumstances of the present."[3] The Editorial Commission understood this bargain, which in practice meant that it went to considerable lengths to meet the pomeshchik's immediate needs and desires.

This bargain between the past and the future was repugnant to men like Ogarev and Serno-Solovevich, and it precipitated the emergence of the radical intelligentsia as a distinct group, at odds with educated society. It was not easy, however, for the artificers of the bargain to justify it to themselves, for they came from the same social and intellectual environment as Ogarev and Serno. The abolition of serfdom had enjoyed a long and healthy life as an ideal, and the ideal made no provision for the compromises entailed in putting it on a practical footing. Consequently, the reformers were pleased to believe they had wrested each article of the reform from the legions of darkness; the legislation was a victory, not a sordid bargain and certainly not an expression of their own misgivings.

The subjective importance of having cunning and powerful opponents is clear in the memoirs of Petr Semenov. He wrote decades after the event, when passions were cooled, if not spent, and he found it hard to speak ill of any man, except for Poles. Yet he continued to emphasize the perils he and his associates had faced and the power of hostile dignitaries. In describing the confrontation with the deputies, Semenov repeatedly pointed out that the Editorial Commission made no concessions of principle, but attempted to placate these irate opponents on points of detail; here the statutory dues were increased by a ruble; there a desiatina, or only half a desiatina, was cut from the maximum allotment. These concessions were not so trivial as they seem, since dues and allotments were expressed in small numbers. For example, the commission originally proposed a maximum allotment of four desiatiny for Serpukhov District, then lowered it; in the Great Russian Statute it was lowered again to three desiatiny, reducing the original figure by 25 percent. Similarly, to expand the zone where the maximum allotment carried an obrok of nine rubles meant to increase the dues of thousands of households, many of them close to the margin of subsistence, by more than 10 percent. The concessions were major, and they were gratuitous. The commission had no authority to surrender the principles to which it was proudly steadfast, and there was no necessity of doing so. It traded land and cash for a security that the deputies could not provide or withhold, since principles were beyond their reach. Unless, as Semenov continued to maintain, the commission and its whole system were in constant jeopardy, disputing with the deputies over principles was an idle exercise.

The leading members of the commission were forward-looking men, as they believed and the deputy Gorskin conceded, but they had been formed by a servile and stratified society. Most were pomeshchiki, and they professed their concern for the pomeshchiki at large; the more naive members discussed some questions in terms of the future of their own estates. Even those who were career bureaucrats with few serfs or none had matured in the service of a state that was, as Unkovskii and Bezobrazov agreed, based upon serfdom and permeated by it. The members welcomed the reform and approved of the statutes they drafted, as most of the nobility did not, but they, too, were encumbered by loyalties and attitudes formed under serfdom. They could not leap into an uncertain future without misgivings and backward glances. It is not certain where the nobility's material interests lay, since the reform of 1861 did not prevent (or reverse) a gradual deterioration of its economic position. It is clear, however, that the leading members of the Editorial Commission secured many immediate advantages for the nobility, as the advocates for the nobility could not. Although krepostniki came into use as an abusive epithet, no real krepostniki participated in the legislative process, for there were no avowed and articulate defenders of the institution of serfdom. By the same token, there was a touch of the krepostnik in the reformer. For who could, blithely and without misgivings, break all links to the old order, renounce all affinity for the noble estate, and eliminate all the habits of mind that serfdom had imposed? The apprehensions that the commission allayed were within the commission itself and within its members.

The opposition without, of which the reformers made so much, was inhibited and ultimately neutralized by its persistent monarchism. The government did not deliberately divert opposition into safe channels by sustaining false hopes. It may have dreaded a Fronde as it did a jacquerie, but these calamities were averted by circumstances, not statecraft. The monarchist illusions that proved so useful were not of the monarch's making, and the equivocation that nourished these illusions derived from the government's own ambiguity and uncertainty. Evidence to the contrary may come to light, as it may concerning a resolute and concerted conspiracy against the reform. For the present, there is ample evidence about ambiguity and uncertainty—which were perfectly natural, considering the scale of the undertaking—and no evidence indicating Machiavellian cunning. Given the nobility's disposition to count on the tsar's favor, equivocation did the work of cunning.

It would not seem that either cunning or a substitute was necessary, for no disappointment could provoke the nobles and their leaders into vigorous protest. As Herzen had predicted, the Muscovite boyars confined themselves to grumbling. In some hypothetical circumstance, they might have done more. If, in January of 1859, Alexander had publicly renounced the rescripts and other outmoded policy statements, dismissed his ministers, informed the provincial committees and the Council of State that their views would be of no account, and outlined the reform that was eventually enacted—then opposition to the reform and the autocracy might have been as serious as the reformers maintained. This hypothesis is entirely fanciful. Alexander's notions about institutions, prerogatives, and persons were firm, but on matters of policy he was tentative as long as he could be and still maintain his role. The concept of autocracy he shared with his contemporaries made it impossible to admit that the binding, "Imperially-confirmed principles" had been supplanted. The contradiction on property rights in the original rescripts was incorporated, without any practical consequence, into the Emancipation Manifesto.

Furthermore, the tsar-liberator was bound by affinity to the old order and the world of the magnates and sanovniki, as he showed by dismissing Lanskoi and Miliutin as soon as the reform was safely enacted. Apart from his private uncertainties, Alexander was eager to have the sanovniki and the entire nobility stand sponsor to the new order. To set up this tableau, it was necessary that institutions and policies should keep the semblance of authority, and individuals the illusion of influence, as long as possible. The dissimulation that served to mollify the nobility was practiced so that the Emancipation Manifesto could ceremonially declare:

We began this undertaking with a formal expression of Our confidence in the Russian Nobility, in its proven loyalty to the throne, testified by great deeds, and in its willingness to sacrifice for the Fatherland. At the Nobility's own initiative, We charged it to compile proposals for a new disposition of the peasants' way of life. . . . Our confidence was justified. . . . These proposals were diverse, as was to be expected in a matter of this kind; they were collated, brought into accord, put in proper form, corrected and supplemented by a Main Committee dealing with this matter; the new statutes on the proprietary peasants and household people, compiled in this fashion, were reviewed in the Council of State.

Having invoked God's aid, We resolved to carry them into execution.[4]

This was not a faithful account of the drafting process. Yet the Editorial Commission's version of the first article of the General Statute had gone further by saying that serfdom was abolished "according to the desire of the nobility of the whole Empire." This phrase was removed by the Main Committee, in response to Adlerberg's complaint: "It's a lie from the first article, there's no point in reading the rest."[5] Nonetheless, it seemed necessary to emphasize the nobility's initiative and participation, out of regard for the nobles' self-esteem and, in particular, to dissuade the peasants from celebrating their emancipation by taking revenge on their masters. The fiction of nobiliary participation, like the fiction of the autocrat's unswerving will, had a function, even though it was equally transparent. Much ink was spilled during the drafting process and many false hopes were sustained, so that a police official in Iakushkin's neighborhood could tell the peasants, "The pomeshchiki knew it would be better for you to be free, and so they asked the Sovereign to give you freedom; your squire took the lead."[6]

Note on Abbreviations

For archival material

ORGBL   Gosudarstvennaia biblioteka imeni V. I. Lenina
                (Moscow), otdel rukopisei.

f. 327   Archive of V. A. and E. A. Cherkasskii.
f. 219   Archive of Count V. P. Orlov-Davydov.

TsGAOR   Tsentral'nyi gosudarstvennyi arkhiv Oktia-
                brskoi revoliutsii i sotsialisticheskogo
                stroitel'stva (Moscow).

f. 109   Archive of the Third Section.
f. 647   Archive of the Grand Duchess Elena Pavlov-
                na.
f. 722   Archive of Grand Duke Konstantin Nikolae-
                vich.
f. 728   Archive of the Winter Palace.
f. 945   Archive of V. A. Dolgorukov.

TsGIAL   Tsentral'nyi gosudarstvennyi istoricheskii
                arkhiv v Leningrade.

f. 982   Archive of S. S. Lanskoi.
f. 1092   Archive of Count Petr Pavlovich Shuvalov.
f. 1180   Archive of the Secret and Main Committees,
                including the papers of the Editorial Com-
                mission. This archive is still arranged
                according to the published inventory (*Opis'*

del arkhiva Gosudarstvennogo soveta, vol. XV),
which provides a detailed register of the
contents.

f. 1291   Archive of the Civil Divison (Zemskii otdel).

PD   Pushkinskii dom, Leningrad.

f. 616   Archive of A. D. Zheltukhin.

The usual Russian abbreviations are used in citations.

f.   fond (collection).
op.   opis' (inventory—subdivision of fond).
d.   delo (item).
l., ll.   list, listy (leaf, leaves).
ob.   obratnaia (verso).

                          For published material

GM   Golos minuvshego.

MIA   Ministry of Internal Affairs (Ministerstvo
                          vnutrennikh del).

MRK, I, II, etc.   Pervoe izdanie materialov Redaktsionnykh kom-
                          missii dlia sostavleniia polozhenii o krest'ianakh,
                          vykhodiashchikh iz krepostnoi zavisimosti (St.
                          Petersburg, 1859-1860), part (i.e., vol.)
                          I, II, etc., through XVIII. Since each item
                          is separately paginated, the following
                          abbreviations are used for the com-
                          ponent parts of the volumes:

ZhOP   Zhurnal obshchego prisutstviia Redaktsion-
                          nykh kommissii.

DKhO   Doklad Khoziaistvennogo otdeleniia.

DIuO   Doklad Iuridicheskogo otdeleniia.

DAO   Doklad Administrativnogo otdeleniia.
                          Supplementary volumes, Prilozheniia k trudam
                          Redaktsionnykh   kommissii   dlia   sostavleniia
                          polozheniia. . . .

MRK, Otzyvy   Otzyvy chlenov, vyzvannykh iz gubernskikh komite-
                          tov, 4 vols. in 6.

MRK,   Otdel'nye mneniia chlenov Redaktsionnykh kom-
Mneniia chlenov   missii, 2 unnumbered vols.

MRK, *Svedeniia*	*Svedeniia o pomeshchich'ikh imeniiakh . . . po velikorusskim guberniiam*, 8 vols. in 6.
(2-oe) *PSZ*	*Polnoe sobranie zakonov Rossiiskoi imperii. Sobranie 2-oe* (for 1825-1855), 55 vols. (St. Petersburg, 1830-1884).
RA	*Russkii arkhiv.*
RS	*Russkaia starina.*
Rev. Sit.	M. V. Nechkina et al., eds., *Revoliutsionnaia situatsiia v Rossii v 1859-1861 gg.* [fasc. I-VI] (Moscow, 1960-1974).
SbIRIO	*Sbornik Imperatorskogo russkogo istoricheskogo obshchestva.*
SbPR	Ministerstvo vnutrennikh del, *Zemskii otdel: Sbornik pravitel'stvennykh rasporiazhenii po ustroistvu byta krest'ian . . .* , vol. I, third ed., (St. Petersburg, 1869).
SZA	*Krest'ianskaia reforma v Rossii 1861 g.: Sbornik zakonodatel'nykh aktov*, K. A. Sofronenko, ed. (Moscow, 1954).
TGK	*Trudy gubernskikh komitetov.* A compilation of the draft statutes and supporting documents produced by the various provincial committees. Most of the material is printed, but some is in manuscript. As a rule, each item produced by each committee is separately paginated, and some items have no page numbers at all. Most citations are made from a microfilm of the materials of the Orel, St. Petersburg, Simbirsk, and Khar'kov provincial committees, kindly provided by the Lenin Library, Moscow, which now holds this apparently unique compilation.
Velikaia reforma	A. K. Dzhivelegov, S. P. Mel'gunov, and V. I. Picheta, eds., *Velikaia reforma. Russkoe obshchestvo i krest'ianskii vopros v proshlom i nastoiashchem*, 6 vols. (Moscow, 1911).
ZhMVD	*Zhurnal Ministerstva vnutrennikh del.*

ZhSGK

Arkhiv Gosudarstvennogo soveta, *Zhurnal Sekretnogo i Glavnogo komiteta po krest'ianskomu delu*, vol. I (Petrograd, 1915).

ZOR, X

E. A. Morokhovets, ed., *Krest'ianskaia reforma 1861 g.:* Gosudarstvennaia biblioteka im. V. I. Lenina, *Zapiski otdela rukopisei*, fasc. X (Moscow, 1941).

Notes

Introduction

1. A. I. Gertsen, *Byloe i dumy*, chap. XXV, in his *Sobranie sochinenii v tridtsati tomakh* (Moscow, 1954-1965), IX, p. 38.
2. George F. Kennan, *The Marquis de Custine and His RUSSIA IN 1839* (Princeton, N.J., 1971), p. 112.

1. Servile Russia

1. M. M. Speranskii, "O korennykh zakonov gosudarstva" (1802), in his *Proekty i zapiski*, ed. S. N. Valk (Moscow-Leningrad, 1961), p. 24. Speranskii later softened "idlers" to "people." The best monograph on the prereform nobility is still A. Romanovich-Slavatinskii, *Dvorianstvo v Rossii ot nachala XVIII veka do otmeny krepostnogo prava* (2nd ed., Kiev, 1912). See also S. A. Korf, *Dvorianstvo i ego soslovnoe upravlenie za stoletie, 1762-1855 godov* (St. Petersburg, 1906) and M. Iablochkov, *Istoriia dvorianskogo sosloviia v Rossii* (St. Petersburg, 1876). There is also useful information in A. P. Korelin's study of the postreform nobility, "Dvorianstvo v poreformennoi Rossii (1861-1904 gg.)," *Istoricheskie zapiski*, no. 87 (1971), pp. 91-173, and M. A. Polievktov, *Nikolai I: Biografiia i obzor tsarstvovaniia* (Moscow, 1918), pp. 290-320. Marc Raeff's *Origins of the Russian Intelligentsia: The Eighteenth-Century Nobility* (New York, 1966) is better characterized by its title than by its subtitle, but many of the preliminary studies that Raeff made for this work and cites in his footnotes are important for an understanding of the nobility at large.
2. V. P. Botkin to I. I. Panaev, January 29, 1858, in N. L. Brodskii, ed., *Turgenev i krug "Sovremennika"* (Moscow-Leningrad, 1930), pp. 435-436.
3. Korelin, "Dvorianstvo v poreformennoi Rossii," p. 122, and V. M. Kabuzan and S. M. Troitskii, "Izmeneniia v chislennosti, udel'nom vese i

razmeshchenii dvorianstva v Rossii v 1782-1858 gg.," *Istoriia SSSR*, 1971, no. 4, pp. 164-165, 167. The authors find that the nobility more than quadrupled between 1782 and 1858, but do not establish how much of this growth was due to natural increase, and how much to ennoblement and the assimilation of non-Russian elites.

4. In his Table of Ranks, Peter the Great divided the bureaucracy and officer corps into fourteen parallel ranks and provided that anyone who attained the eighth rank automatically acquired hereditary nobility. The requirement was raised in 1845 and again by the law of December 9, 1856, by which those who reached the fourth rank in the civil service and the sixth in the military became hereditary nobles. Through the table of ranks an officer or official could also attain "personal nobility," which did not entail the right to hold serfs.

5. R. E. Pipes, *Karamzin's Memoir on Ancient and Modern Russia: A Translation and an Analysis* (Cambridge, Mass., 1959), p. 201.

6. S. F. Starr, *Decentralization and Self-Government in Russia, 1830-1870* (Princeton, N.J., 1972), p. 47-50.

7. On the nobility's emphatic expression of hostility to the bureaucracy in response to Speranskii's attempt to favor nonnobles in the civil service by means of competitive examinations for promotion, see M. Raeff, *Michael Speransky, Statesman of Imperial Russia*, 2nd ed. (The Hague, 1969), pp. 64-65, 177.

8. Of a sample of 174 officials in the top five grades of the table of ranks, all of whom were automatically ennobled even if they were of nonnoble birth, 42.5 percent had no serfs; W. M. Pintner, "The Social Characteristics of the Early Nineteenth-Century Russian Bureaucracy," *Slavic Review*, XXXIX, 3 (September 1970), p. 437.

9. The number 1700 corresponds to more than 40 percent of the male hereditary nobles registered in the province in 1857. See A. D. Povalishin, *Riazanskie pomeshchiki i ikh krepostnye* (Riazan', 1903), p. 10; A. Troinitskii, *Krepostnoe naselenie v Rossii po 10-i narodnoi perepisi* (St. Petersburg, 1861), p. 45; Kabuzan and Troitskii, "Izmeneniia v chislennosti . . . dvorianstva," p. 166.

10. The deputy Naryshkin at Catherine II's Codification Commission, quoted in V. O. Kliuchevskii, *Sochineniia*, vol. V, p. 97. Compare Ford's observation that "the taille privilege not infrequently appeard to be the irreducible core of noblesse, as seen by the noble himself." Franklin Ford, *Robe and Sword: The Regrouping of the French Aristocracy after Louis XIV* (Cambridge, Mass., 1962), p. 27.

11. Quoted in A. V. Predtechenskii, *Ocherki obshchestvenno-politicheskoi istorii Rossii v pervoi chetverti XIX veka* (Moscow-Leningrad, 1957), pp. 76-77. Pushkin agreed with his contemporary Chichagov, to judge from the fragments reproduced in his *Sobranie sochinenii*, 10 vols. (Moscow, 1962), vol. VI, p. 407.

12. In eighteenth-century France, the crown had established the doctrine that a specific royal grant was required for noble status, and there was a marked rapprochement between the *noblesse de la robe* and *de l'épée*—in Russian terms, the *sluzhiloe* and *rodovoe dvorianstvo*; Ford, *Robe and Sword*, pp.

23, 201, and chap. XI. On the generally successful attempts of eighteenth-century monarchs to bind the nobility to officialdom, see the studies in A. Goodwin, ed., *The European Nobility in the Eighteenth Century* (London, 1953).

13. *Arkhiv kniazei Vorontsovykh*, vol. XI, p. 391, cited by Predtechenskii, *Ocherki*, p. 56.

14. A. I. Gertsen, "Iur'ev den'! Iur'ev den'! Russkomu dvorianstvu" (1853), in his *Sobranie sochinennii*, 30 vols. (Moscow, 1954-1965), vol. XII, p. 81.

15. "The Eighteenth Brumaire of Louis Bonaparte," in Karl Marx and Frederick Engels, *Selected Works*, 2 vols. (Moscow, 1962), vol. I, p. 334.

16. V. M. Kabuzan, *Izmeneniia v razmeshchenii naseleniia Rossii v XVIII—pervoi polovine XIX v. (po materialam revizii)* (Moscow, 1971), pp. 167-178.

17. Troinitskii, *Krepostnoe naselenie*, pp. 65-66. Troinitskii's totals of serfholders are approximate because the *reviziia* materials from which he worked did not reckon nobles, but estates with serfs; he did not indicate by what alchemy he produced his figures for "proprietors." The reviziia figures tend, as several authors have pointed out, to inflate the number of serfholders and minimize the concentration of serfs because a proprietor holding twenty serfs in each of five provinces would appear in the total as five petty proprietors. On the other hand, if an estate was held in common by the heirs of a previous owner (a common practice), the heirs would appear in the reviziia totals as a single proprietor. Finally, historians who have studied the raw material of the tenth reviziia for Moscow and Riazan provinces produce figures that are close to Troinitskii's totals but wildly different in the subcategories. See Povalishin, *Riazanskie pomeshchiki*, pp. 23-24, and N. M. Druzhinin, "Moskovskoe dvorianstvo i reforma 1861 g.," *Izvestiia AN SSSR. Seriia istorii i filosofii*, vol. V, no. 1 (1948), p. 63.

18. Cited in [A. I. Levshin], "Istoricheskaia zapiska o raznykh predpolozheniiakh po predmetu osvobozhdeniia krest'ian," in P. Bartenev, ed., *Deviatnadtsatyi vek. Istoricheskii sbornik* (Moscow, 1872), vol. II, p. 159. Romanovich-Slavatinskii provides the best systematic summary of the nobles' powers over their serfs.

19. 2-oe *PSZ*, vol. II (1827), pp. 183-184.

20. See S. B. Okun' and E. S. Paina, "Ukaz ot 5 aprelia 1797 g. i ego evoliutsiia," *Issledovaniia po otechestvennomu istochnikovedeniiu* (Leningrad, 1964), pp. 283-299.

21. See I. I. Ignatovich, *Pomeshchich'i krest'iane nakanune ikh osvobozhdeniia*, 3rd ed. (Leningrad, 1925), p. 45.

22. Quoted by V. N. Bochkarev in "Byt pomeshchich'ikh krest'ian," in A. K. Dzhivelegov et al., eds., *Velikaia reforma*, 6 vols. (Moscow, 1911), vol. III, p. 22.

23. V. V. Golubtsov, ed., "Imperator Nikolai Pavlovich v ego rechi k deputatam Sanktpeterburgskogo dvorianstva 21 marta 1848 g.," *RS*, vol. XXXIX (September 1883), p. 595.

24. On the administrative practices of the 1850s on petitions from serfs, see Ignatovich, *Pomeshchich'i krest'iane*, pp. 46-50; N. P. Semenov, *Osvobozhdenie krest'ian v tsarstvovanie Imperatora Aleksandra II*, 3 vols. in 4 (St.

Petersburg, 1889-1892), II, pp. 371-372; and Povalishin, *Riazanskie pomeshchiki*, p. 142. On the origins of the prohibition, see Isabel de Madariaga, "Catherine II and the Serfs," *Slavonic Review*, LII, no. 126 (January 1974), pp. 48-54.

25. See Aksakov's account of a provincial assembly in Ekaterinoslav, in *Ivan Sergeevich Aksakov v ego pis'makh*, 4 vols. (Moscow-St. Petersburg, 1888-96), vol. III, pp. 292-293.

26. *Ukazy* of January 1, 1832, and May 13, 1843, in Iablochkov, *Istoriia dvorianskogo sosloviia*, p. 646.

27. See Robert E. Jones, *The Emancipation of the Russian Nobility, 1762-1785* (Princeton, N.J., 1973), p. 286.

28. S. M. Seredonin, *Istorichesskii obzor deiatel'nosti Komiteta ministrov*, 3 vols. in 5 (St. Petersburg, 1902), vol. I., p. 277.

29. This complex law did provide a full franchise to nobles with fewer than a hundred serfs who could meet certain other rank, education, and property qualifications; very few provincial squires could meet these alternate qualifications. As a result of this law, only 635 of the 3926 nobles of Riazan Province had the franchise for the assembly of 1858; the corresponding figures for Chernigov Province were 476 of 6268; for Kaluga, 463 of 3406. These figures, collected by officers of the general staff, are reproduced in Jerome Blum, *Lord and Peasant in Russia from the Ninth to the Nineteenth Century* (Princeton, N.J., 1961), p. 354.

30. S. B. Okun', *Ocherki istorii SSSR: vtoraia chetvert' XIX veka* (Leningrad, 1957), p. 185.

31. See. N. S. Kiniapina, "Promyshlennaia politika russkogo samoderzhaviia v gody kriziza feodal'noi sistemy," *Voprosy istorii*, 1965, no. 6, pp. 61-75; and W. M. Pintner, *Russian Economic Policy Under Nicholas I* (Ithaca, N.Y., 1967), pp. 43, 183, passim.

32. Quoted in Karl-Hans Ruffman, "Russicher Adel als Sondertypus der europäischen Adelswelt," *Jahrbücher für Geschichte Osteuropas*, N.S., vol. 9 (1961), no. 2, p. 177.

33. A. I. Gertsen, "Kreshchennaia sobstvennost'" (1856), in his *Sobranie sochinenii v tridtsati tomakh*, vol. XII, p. 105.

34. Protocols (in French) of the Unofficial Committee, as given in Velikii Knaiz' Nikolai Mikhailovich, *Graf Pavel Aleksandrovich Stroganov (1774-1814)* (St. Petersburg, 1903), vol. II, pp. 111-112. On Stroganov's views on reform at this time, see Predtechenskii, *Ocherki*, especially pp. 150-151 (where the passage here quoted is cited) and 102.

35. The most important descriptive study of the nineteenth-century manorial economy is Ignatovich's *Pomeshchich'i krest'iane;* the best analytical study is that of I. D. Koval'chenko, *Russkoe krepostnoe krest'ianstvo v pervoi polovine XIX veka* (Moscow, 1967). See also Arcadius Kahan, "Notes on Serfdom in Eastern and Western Europe," *Journal of Economic History* XXXIII, 1 (March 1973), pp. 86-99. Koval'chenko's *Krest'iane i krepostnoe khoziaistvo Riazanskoi i Tambovskoi gubernii v pervoi polovine XIX veka* (Moscow, 1959) is the best regional study. Michael Confino's *Systèmes agraires et progrès agricole. L'assolement triennal en Russie aux XVIII-XIX siècles. Etude d'economie et de sociologie rurales* (Etudes sur l'histoire, l'economie et al sociologie des pays slaves, XIV)

(Paris-The Hague, 1969) is much broader in its implications than the lengthy title indicates and is of special value for the economic attitudes of the nobility. The monographs on the holdings of particular noble families by Indova, Sivkov, Bakounine and others are generally disappointing, but Nasonov's articles on the Iusupovs are a glittering exception. Of the general studies, Liashchenko's *History of the National Economy of Russia* (New York, 1949) is valuable because nineteenth-century agriculture was Liaschenko's specialty; Blum's *Lord and Peasant* concentrates on this same period, with results that are often more original and more controversial than Blum's bland tone suggests. V. A. Fedorov, *Pomeshchich'i krest'iane tsentral' no–promyshlennogo raiona Rossii kontsa XVIII—pervoi poloviny XIX v.* (Moscow, 1974) appeared too late for use here.

36. The Vorontsovs even hired a senator to carry out a *reviziia*, or formal senatorial review, of their operations; E. I. Indova, *Krepostnoe khoziaistvo v nachale XIX veka* (Moscow, 1955), pp. 51-53.

37. Diary of P. D. Kiselev, quoted in N. M. Druzhinin, *Gosudarstvennye krest'iane i reformy P. D. Kiseleva*, 2 vols. (Moscow-Leningrad, 1946-1958), vol. I, p. 251.

38. "Proshenie krest'ian P. D. Kiselevu . . . ," in S. B. Okun', ed., *Krest'ianskoe dvizhenie v Rossii v 1850-1856 gg. Sbornik dokumentov* (Moscow, 1962) pp. 135-137.

39. See Prince Volkonskii's instructions to his steward quoted by Povalishin, *Riazanskie pomeshchiki*, p. 46, passim. Picheta finds that the instructions of Volkonskii and other magnates testify to a "petty regulation" of agriculture, but even the examples he cites show that the pettiness concerned revenues, not the working of the land. V. I. Picheta, "Pomeshchich'e khoziaistvo nakanune reformy," in *Velikaia reforma*, vol. III, p. 134.

40. Confino, *Systèmes agraires*, p. 359.

41. Both Confino and Blum emphasize the orientation to consumption, and Koval'chenko (*Krepostnoe krest'ianstvo*, pp. 95, 338) provides confirmation; he estimates that 21 percent of the harvest from all proprietary estates reached the market; for harvests from the demesne, his estimate is 50 percent, an incredibly low figure, given the average size of estates.

42. Tolstoi's "Utro pomeshchika" portrays the pomeshchik's inability to realize on his authority, even to benefit his serfs.

43. Quoted by Confino, *Systèmes agraires*, p. 149.

44. In *Systemes agraires*, Confino offers a fascinating discussion of the campaign to modernize manorial agriculture and the resistance to it. He does seem, however, to overestimate the number of innovating pomeshchiki on the eve of emancipation (pp. 215-216); for example, neither his presentation nor other evidence indicates that between 10 and 25 percent of the estates in Tula Province had abandoned the three-field system.

45. Confino, *Systèmes agraires*, p. 256.

46. "For a majority of pomeshchiki, enthusiasm for the new technology ended in complete ruin," according to Picheta, "Pomeshchich'e

khoziaistvo," p. 115. Liashchenko (*History*, p. 319) detects a reaction against innovation and a reversion to "indigenous" methods beginning in the 1840s. Compare P. B. Struve, *Krepostnoe khoziaistvo* (n.p., 1913), pp. 62-72.

47. In many cases, of course, he was an absentee proprietor. Fedorov finds that, in the 1850s, the pomeshchik was in regular residence on 822 of the 1960 estates of Tver Province. In the black-soil provinces where barshchina prevailed, the proportion would presumably be higher. V. A. Fedorov, "Mezhevye opisaniia' 50-kh godov XIX v. kak istochnik po istorii krest'ianskogo khoziaistva v Rossii (po materialam Tverskoi gub.)," *Materialy po istorii sel'skogo khoziaistva i krest'ianstva SSSR*, vol. VI (Moscow, 1965), p. 227.

48. Ignatovich, *Pomeshchich'i krest'iane*, p. 385. In these figures, peasants paying more than half the normal obrok for the area are classified as *obrochnye*. Koval'chenko, taking data from estates of a hundred souls or more in Great Russia, found that only on 18.5 percent of the estates did all the peasants render obrok alone. Since barshchina was almost universal outside Great Russia, it prevailed by almost three to one for the nation as a whole. Koval'chenko, *Krepostnoe krest'ianstvo*, pp. 67 and 61.

49. See Koval'chenko, *Riazanskaia i Tambovskaia*, pp. 5, 153-154; and Michael Confino, *Domaines et seigneurs en Russie vers la fin du XVIII siècle* (Paris, 1963), p. 110.

50. For some remarks on the *urochnaia* system, see Koval'chenko, *Krepostnoe krest'ianstvo*, pp. 106, 278.

51. Of the forty-two obrok estates in central Russia studied by Koval'chenko, twenty-nine were essentially agricultural, while on the other thirteen *promysly* (handicrafts and agricultural labor off the estate) played a dominant role. I. D. Koval'chenko and L. V. Milov, "Ob intensivnosti obrochnoi formy ekspluatatsii krest'ian tsentral'noi Rossii v kontse XVIII—pervoi polovine XIX v.," *Istoriia SSSR*, 1966, no. 4, p. 57.

52. Liashchenko (*History*, p. 314) estimates that the cartage obligation consumed up to 30 percent of the barshchina peasant's working time in the winter and 8 percent in the summer. His estimate of the cash value of this service, fourteen to sixteen rubles per serf, seems very high. Excessive use of the cartage obligation was self-defeating, because the peasants' household economy would deteriorate to the point where they no longer had draft animals adequate to fulfill the obligation as before, and the pomeshchik would be obliged to market his crop locally. See Koval'chenko, *Riazanskaia i Tambovskaia*, pp. 95-96.

53. E. K. Rozov, "O sushchnosti 'smeshannoi' formy ekspluatatsii v Tverskoi guvernii nakunune reformy 1861 g.," *Nauchnye doklady vysshei shkoly: Istoricheskie nauki*, 1958, no. 1, p. 28.

54. Koval'chenko asserts that most of these exactions were abolished or converted into cash by the 1830s (*Krepostnoe krest'ianstvo*, p. 60), but this assertion is at most valid only for the large estates he studied. In the discussions of the impending reform in 1858-1860, nobles attached great importance to the supplementary services rendered by serfs.

55. Povalishin estimates that 1.74 percent of the serfs in Riazan Province were *mesiachniki*, mostly on the very smallest estates; *Riazanskie*

pomeshchiki, pp. 32 and 43. Research on the regulatory charters compiled after the emancipation indicates that the proportion elsewhere was even smaller; see B. G. Litvak, *Russkaia derevnia v reforme 1861 goda. Chernonzemnyi tsentr, 1861-1895 gg.* (Moscow, 1972), p. 61. Confino reports (*Systèmes agraires*, pp. 310-311) that he is unable to find any instance where mesiachina was imposed to facilitate agrarian innovation, and only one where mixed dues were used to that end.

56. See Indova, *Krepostnoe khoziaistvo*, pp. 63-64.

57. Confino, *Domaines et seigneurs*, p. 176.

58. Confino takes the nobility to task for failing to reckon with "costs of production," *Domaines et seigneurs*, pp. 146, 176.

59. Koval'chenko finds that, on barshchina estates, the lords usually made these outlays themselves, but on obrok estates they tried to shift the burden onto the commune (*Krepostnoe krest'ianstvo*, pp. 113-114, 170).

60. Every study of obrok estates indicates that arrears were high and increasing. See Koval'chenko, *Krepostnoe krest'ianstvo*, pp. 145-147, 163, 212; Indova, *Krepostnoe khoziaistvo*, p. 91; K. S. Sivkov, "Biudzhet krupnogo sobstvennika-krepostnika v pervoi treti XIX v.," *Istoricheskie zapiski*, no. 9 (1940), pp. 128, 135. Zak cites the instance of a rich serf who rented a mill from his pomeshchik but still fell into arrears on his obrok; I. Zak, "K istorii krepostnogo khoziaistva," *Istorik-marksist*, no. 17 (1930), p. 58. For a contemporary satire on the inevitability of obrok arrears, see Zhukov as quoted by Liashchenko (*History*, p. 322). Like most other pomeshchiki, Zhukov believed that barshchina was more profitable than obrok, but he based his argument largely on the impossibility of arrears under barshchina; see the passage quoted by Picheta in "Pomeshchich'e khoziaistvo," p. 119.

61. An example is the decline in the sowing of wheat, which was an export crop, in the first half of the nineteenth century in the black-soil provinces of Simbirk and Riazan; Koval'chenko, *Krepostnoe krest'ianstvo*, p. 70.

62. Blum, *Lord and Peasant*, p. 323.

63. Blum, *Lord and Peasant*, p. 370.

64. For a table indicating increase or decline by provinces, see Koval'chenko, *Krepostnoe krest'ianstvo*, pp. 387-388.

65. See D. Field, review of *Russkoe krepostnoe krest'ianstvo*, *Kritika*, vol. V, no. 2 (1969), pp. 31-45.

66. Koval'chenko, *Krepostnoe krest'ianstvo*, pp. 327-328. On the decline of the serf economy and the serf population, Koval'chenko has a severe but not very acute critic in P. G. Ryndziunskii, "Vymeralo li krepostnoe krest'ianstvo pered reformoi 1861 g.?" *Voprosy istorii*, 1967, no. 7, pp. 54-70; and "Ob opredelenii intensivnosti obrochnoi ekspluatatsii . . . ," *Istoria SSSR*, 1966, no. 6, pp. 44-64.

67. Compare Koval'chenko's findings in *Riazanskaia i Tambovskaia*, pp. 30-31, and his discussion of tendencies in Great Russia as a whole in *Krepostnoe krest'ianstvo*, especially pp. 73-86, 298, and 346. See also Confino, *Systèmes agraires*, pp. 135-142, passim.

68. Recently Litvak has doubted that there was significant

380   Notes to Pages 30-33

encroachment on the allotment land of barshchina peasants in the nineteenth century; *Russkaia derevnia*, p. 73.

69. These data are most conveniently presented in Koval'chenko and Milov, "Ob intensivnosti," p. 67, table 4, and page 72, table 5.

70. "Ob intensivenosti," p. 73. See also R. M. Vvedenskii, "Kharakter pomeshchich'ei ekspluatatsii i biudzhety obrochnykh krest'ian v 20—40-e gody XIX v.," *Istoriia SSSR*, 1971, no. 3, pp. 48, 54.

71. See the data on obrok in thirty-three districts in Koval'chenko, *Krepostnoe krest'ianstvo*, p. 290.

72. S. Ia. Borovoi, *Kredit i banki Rossii (serediny XVII-1861 g.)* (Moscow, 1958), p. 197. By 1859, when the government stopped accepting serfs as security for loans, the proportion of serfs mortgaged to the state had reached 66 percent. For a breakdown by provinces and regions in 1842 and 1859, see I. D. Koval'chenko, "K voprosu o sostoiannii pomeshchich'ego khoziaistva pered otmenoi krepostnogo prava v Rossii," *Ezhegodnik po agrarnoi istorii Vostochnoi Evropy 1959 g.* (Moscow, 1961), pp. 203-205.

73. See Sivkov, "Biudzhet," p. 141, passim.

74. Borovoi, *Kredit i banki*, pp. 187-188; but see Koval'chenko, *Riazanskaia i Tambovskaia*, p. 133.

75. For examples, see Koval'chenko, *Riazanskaia i Tambovskaia*, p. 186, and Zak, "K istorii," pp. 59-60.

76. Studies of differentiation (*rassloenie*) in serf villages show that the larger households were more prosperous and therefore less exploited, even when the per capita distribution of tiagla was more or less uniform.

77. But see Litvak, *Russkaia derevnia*, pp. 71-72.

78. Cited in Ignatovich, *Pomeshchich'i krest'iane*, p. 93.

79. Koval'chenko, *Riazanskaia i Tambovskaia*, p. 128. For similar patterns on other estates, see A. N. Nasonov, "Iz istorii krepostnoi votchiny XIX veka v Rossii," *Izvestiia AN SSSR*, seriia VI, 1926, no. 7/8, pp. 519n., 526; and G. T. Riabkov, "Posevy i urozhai v pomeshchich'em i krest'ianskom khoziaistvakh v Smolenskoi gubernii v pervoi polovine XIX v.," *Ezhegodnik po agrarnoi istorii Vostochnoi Evropy, 1962* (Minsk, 1964), p. 384; but compare K. V. Sivkov, *Ocherki po istorii krepostnogo khoziaistva v Rossii v pervoi polovine XIX veka* (Moscow, 1951), pp. 84, 97. Milov finds that in the first half of the nineteenth century, price levels for rye were higher than for equivalent quantities of rye flour, and lower than the cost of production; L. V. Milov, "Paradoks khlebnykh tsen i kharakter agrarnogo rynka Rossii v XIX veke," *Istoriia SSSR*, 1974, no. 1, pp. 51-55. Most probably this "paradox" came about because peasants had to market their grain when prices were lowest, while demesne output was withheld until the price rose.

80. N. Semenov, *Osvobozhdenie*, III, part 2, p. 626.

81. Alexander Gershenkron's analysis of the economic ideas of the nineteenth-century intelligentsia can be applied to conservatives and officials as well, though their goals, of course, were different. See A. Gerschenkron, "The Problem of Economic Development in Russian Intellectual History of the Nineteenth Century," in E. J. Simmons, ed., *Continuity and Change in Russian and Soviet Thought* (Cambridge, Mass., 1955), pp. 11-39, and compare Pintner, *Russian Economic Policy*, especially p. 183.

82. Struve's *Krepostnoe khoziaistvo* was written at the turn of the century but appeared in book form in 1913; for a summary of his arguments and a defense of his position, see Richard Pipes, *Struve: Liberal on the Left, 1870-1905* (Cambridge, Mass., 1970), pp. 200-207.

83. See Koval'chenko (*Riazanskaia i Tambovskaia*, p. 115), who finds that the region of his study was not economically ready for capitalism in 1861. If the central black-soil provinces were not ready, which provinces were? But Kornilov, in his review of Struve's book, makes the good point that barshchina survived emancipation largely because of the elements of serfdom that were retained in the emancipation settlement. A. A. Kornilov, "Iz istorii krepostnogo khoziaistva v Rossii," *Nauchnyi istoricheskii zhurnal*, 1914, no. 5, p. 51.

84. Notably Indova in her *Krepostnoe khoziaistvo*. She attacks Struve in the preface, describes the systematic shift of the Shermetevs' landholdings to the South, and breaks off her discussion at the time of a general shift to barshchina on the Sheremetev estates.

85. Andrei Iatsevich, *Krepostnoi Peterburg pushkinskogo vremini* (Leningrad, 1937) includes a discussion (pp. 53-64) of the traffic in serfs, but it is made up of the same kind of unsystematic data adduced by Romanovich-Slavatinskii sixty years earlier. In what may have been analogous situation, Conrad and Meyer found that the export of slaves was crucial to the servile economy of the upper South in the decades before the American Civil War.

86. See Iu. F. Samarin, "O krepostnom sostoianii i o perekhode iz nego k grazhdanskoi svobode," *Sochineniia*, 8 vols. (Moscow, 1878-1911), vol. II, pp. 51-53.

87. These examples are from a circular distributed with the ukaz of April 2, 1842, on "obligated peasants," cited in V. I. Semevskii, *Krest'ianskii vopros v Rossii v XVIII i pervoi polovine XIX veka*, 2 vols. (St. Petersburg, 1888), vol. II, p. 66; this section of Chapter I is largely based on Semevskii's still-unsurpassed study.

88. A. V. Predtechenskii, ed., *Krest'ianskoe dvizhenie v Rossii v 1826-1849 gg.: Sbornik dokumentov* (Moscow, 1961), p. 817, and Ignatovich, *Pomeshchich'i krest'iane*, p. 343; Miss Ignatovich's figures on resistance to troops cover the period 1826-1854.

89. Of the twenty-five estates sequestered for abuse of manorial authority in 1857, the corporate organs of the nobility sequestered six; see the extract from the report of the Department of Police to the tsar in S. B. Okun' and K. V. Sivkov, eds., *Krest'ianskoe dvizhenie v Rossii v 1857—mae 1861 gg.: Sbornik dokumentov* (Moscow, 1963), p. 119; and, for a further discussion of peasant discontent as a security problem, see D. Field's review of this book in *Kritika*, vol. III, no. 3 (1967), pp. 34-55.

90. According to the annual report of the Ministry of Internal Affairs for 1856, of the 109,110 estates in Russia, 38,976 were mortgaged; of these, 4,131 had been inventoried for foreclosure and 402 sold at auction for arrears; *Russkii vestnik*, vol. XIII, bk. 1 (January 1858), "Sovremennaia letopis'," p. 53. Judging from the lists of estates sold for mortgage arrears published from time to time in *ZhMVD*, only very small estates were actually foreclosed and sold.

91. Pintner (*Russian Economic Policy*, pp. 37-39) concludes that these mortgage loans were a deliberate subsidy, made on political grounds, to the nobility as a class.

92. I. I. Ignatovich, "Prodovol'stvennyi vopros v pomeshchich'ikh imeniiakh nakanune osvobozhdeniia," *GM*, 1913, no. 9, pp. 29-64 and no. 10, pp. 73-107. However, the pomeshchik's obligation to feed his serfs in time of famine was also one source of indebtedness, as Ignatovich points out.

93. Through a law of 1834, soldiers with good records could spend their last ten years of service in the reserves. Although the proportion of troops released to the reserves was very small, Adjutant-General Kutuzov was moved to complain that they constituted "the greatest revolutionary danger." J. S. Curtiss, *The Russian Army Under Nicholas I, 1825-1855* (Durham, N.C., 1965), pp. 252-253.

94. 2-oe *PSZ*, vol. XII, part 1 (1837), pp. 304-305.

95. *Sbornik postanovlenii i rasporiazhenii po tsenzure s 1720 po 1862 g.* (St. Petersburg, 1862), p. 265.

96. V. I. Mezhov, in his painstaking bibliography *Krest'ianskii vopros v Rossii* . . . (St. Petersburg, 1865), has almost nothing on serfdom for the period from the accession of Catherine II to 1858. To be sure, he omits most exhortative literature favorable to serfdom, of which Gogol's *Vybrannye mesta iz perepiski s druz'iami* is a well-known example. See also Semevskii, *Krest'ianskii vopros*, vol. II, p. 325.

97. See Norman Yettman, ed., *Life Under the Peculiar Institution* (New York, 1970), a collection of narratives of ex-slaves in the 1930s.

98. Genovese, in his *Political Economy of Slavery* (New York, 1967) argues that the extravagant consumption that produces these debts is a functional component of servile systems, because it provides visible tokens of superiority and distinction that help the ruling class to maintain its authority. Arcadius Kahan represents the eighteenth-century Russian nobility's consumption of imported and western-style goods as a fulfillment of the government's westernizing policy. See A. Kahan, "The Cost of 'Westernization' in Russia: The Gentry and the Economy in the Eighteenth Century," *Slavic Review*, XXV, no. 1 (March 1966), pp. 40-46. Both of these arguments offer insight, but neither can be pushed very far.

99. Nicholas Riasanovsky, *Nicholas I and Official Nationality in Russia, 1825-1855* (Berkeley, Calif., 1961), especially pp. 124, 140-141, 208-211.

100. I. S. Turgenev, "Dva pomeshchika," in *Polnoe sobranie sochinenii i pisem*, 28 vols. (Moscow, 1960-1968), vol. IV, p. 30.

101. See Louis Hartz, *The Liberal Tradition in America* (New York, 1955), pp. 142-200; Eugene Genovese, *The World the Slaveholders Made* (New York, 1970), and, for a sampling of the writings of antebellum defenders of slavery, E. L. McKitrick, ed., *Slavery Defended* (Englewood Cliffs, N.J., 1963).

102. Semevskii lists the members at the beginning of his discussion of each committee. Count Kiselev served on six of the eight committees, Prince I. V. Vasil'chikov on five on the first six, Count Orlov on four of the last six.

103. A case for entail is argued in these terms in "Zapiska kn.

Bariatinskogo o dvorianstve i maiorate," *TsGAOR, f. 728, op. 1, d. 2316, l.6* (for the key to this and other archival references, see list of abbreviations preceding the bibliography). However, only seventeen noble families availed themselves of a law of 1845 that sanctioned the entailing of certain large estates; Okun', *Ocherki istorii SSSR: vtoraia chetvert' XIX veka,* p. 186.

104. Semevskii, *Krest'ianskii vopros,* vol. II, p. 30.

105. Apart from Semevskii's account, see Druzhinin, *Gosudarstvennye krest'iane,* vol. I, pp. 611-628 and A. P. Zablotskii-Desiatovskii, *Graf P.D. Kiselev i ego vremia,* 4 vols. (St. Petersburg, 1882), vol. II, pp. 242-259, and vol. IV, pp. 200-216.

106. Semevskii, *Krest'ianskii vopros,* vol. II, p. 50.

107. The Minister of Finance, Count Kankrin, rejected the marshal's suggestion with thanks, claiming that he was too ignorant of conditions in Skvira District to draw up an adequate contract; Semevskii, *Krest'ianskii vopros,* vol. II, pp. 104n-105n.

108. V. A. Cherkasskii, "O luchshikh sredstvakh k postepennomu iskhodu iz krepostnogo sostoianiia" (1856), in O. Trubetskaia, comp., *Materialy dlia biografii kn. V. A. Cherkasskogo,* in two books (Moscow, 1901-1904), bk. 1, appendix, p. 44 (cited hereinafter as *Materialy Cherkasskogo*).

109. A peculiarity of the Baltic reform was the so-called *Bauerland.* Ex-serfs did not have any rights to their former allotments, but part of the land on each estate had to be rented out to peasants of the province and could not be incorporated into the demesne. However, the *Bauerland* provision was very rarely mentioned either by admirers or detractors of the Baltic system in the provinces where serfdom was still in full sway.

110. Semevskii, *Krest'ianskii vopros,* vol. II, pp. 22-23.

111. A. S. Menshikov, "Mneniia kniazia Menshikova ob osnovaniiakh osvobozhdeniia . . . ," in Zablotskii-Desiatovskii, *Kiselev i ego vremia,* vol. IV, p. 204.

112. Semevskii, *Krest'ianskii vopros,* vol. II, p. 37.

113. See Bludov's memorandum as cited by Semevskii, *Krest'ianskii vopros,* vol. II, pp. 110-111.

114. Semevskii, *Krest'ianskii vopros,* vol. II, pp. 128-129.

115. The nobles of the western provinces took advantage of the reform to arrogate some lands which their serfs had always held; Koval'chenko, *Krepostnoe krest'ianstvo,* pp. 81-82.

116. For an example, see the documents in Okun' and Sivkov, *Krest'ianskoe dvizhenie,* pp. 129-134. On the inventory reform, see Ignatovich, *Pomeshchich'i krest'iane,* pp. 191-223; Iu. F. Samarin, "Zamechaniia ob inventariakh vvedennykh v 1847 g. i 1848 g. v pomeshchich'ikh imeniiakh Kievskoi, Volynskoi i Podol'skoi gubernii i o krepostnom prave v Malorossii," in his *Sochineniia,* vol. II, pp. 1-16; and, for the Northwest, the studies by Ulashchik cited below in chap. 2.

117. The serfs' "monarchist illusions" (in the terminology of Soviet historians) were particularly disruptive in wartime, when peasants believed that the tsar must reward his faithful subjects. During the Crimean War thousands of peasants, on the flimsiest pretext, left their estates illegally to join the militia; they hoped that they would be freed

upon demobilization, as ordinary soldiers were upon discharge. Others journeyed south, where the tsar was supposed to be dispensing land and liberty to all comers. See Ia. I. Linkov, *Ocherki istorii krest'ianskogo dvizheniia v Rossii v 1825-1861 gg.* (Moscow, 1952), chaps. V and VI.

118. Semevskii, *Krest'ianskii vopros*, vol. II, p. 163.

119. For a sample of official indignation at the abuse of serfs by petty proprietors, see Povalishin, *Riazanskie pomeshchiki*, pp. 32-33.

120. Semevskii, *Krest'ianskii vopros*, vol. II, p. 62.

121. A. A. Kizevetter, "Vnutrenniaia politika v tsarstvovanie Nikolaia Pavlovicha," in *Istoriia Rossii v XIX veka*, 9 vols. (St. Petersburg), n.d. vol. I, p. 169.

122. Semevskii, *Krest'ianskii vopros*, vol. II, p. 176.

123. In 1844, nine Tula pomeshchiki had offered to release their serfs with a desiatina (2.7 acres) of land apiece, provided that the bulk of the mortgage debt on the estates was shifted to the peasants; they also asked for a ten-year grace period on the mortgage payments for which they would still be liable. The government expressed its provisional assent, provided the proprietors could get the consent of the peasants, as the laws of 1803 and 1842 required, for the allotment proposed was manifestly inadequate. After this response, nothing more was heard of the plan. Semevskii, *Krest'ianskii vopros*, vol. II, pp. 238-242. Trubetskaia finds Semevskii's account misleading; she asserts that the major obstacle to the implementation of the plans of 1844 and 1847 was not the peasant's reluctance but the government's unwillingness to see land pass out of noble hands. She also maintains that the role Semevskii assigns to Miasnov belongs to her subject, Prince Cherkasskii, *Materialy Cherkasskogo*, bk. 1, pp. 23n, 30.

124. *TsGAOR, f.* 109, *op.* 3, *d.* 2149, *l.* 3ob.

125. Semevskii, *Krest'ianskii vopros*, vol. II, pp. 136, 138. Perovskii exaggerated the nobility's amenability to reform on economic grounds in order to put more weight on the security argument against reform.

126. Semevskii, *Krest'ianskii vopros*, vol. II, p. 251.

127. Semevskii, *Krest'ianskii vopros*, vol. II, pp. 168-169.

128. Semevskii, *Krest'ianskii vopros*, vol. II, p. 144.

129. N. B. Iusupov's letter of January 1, 1857, quoted in A. N. Nasonov, "Khoziaistvo krupnoi votchiny nakanune osvobozhdeniia krest'ian v Rossii," *Izvestiia Akademii nauk SSSR*, series VII, *otdelenie gumanitarnykh nauk*, no. 4/7 (1928), p. 352n.

130. Quoted in M. A. Korf, "Imperator Nikolai v soveshchatel'nykh sobraniiakh," *SbIRIO*, vol. XCVIII (1896), p. 216.

131. For this argument in its extreme form, see W. R. Dodge, *Abolitionist Sentiment in Russia, 1762-1855*, unpub. diss., University of Wisconsin, 1950.

2. The Commitment to Reform

1. See, for example, N. M. Druzhinin's youthful folly "Zhurnal zemlevladeltsev, 1858-1860 gg.," part I, in *Trudy Instituta istorii*, fasc. 1 (1926), pp. 463-507.

2. N. M. Druzhinin, "Krest'ianskoe dvizhenie 1857-1861 gg. po dokumentam tsentral'nykh istoricheskikh arkhivov SSSR," *Voprosy istochnikovedeniia*, 1961, no. 1, p. 17. A variant of this view is an explanation in terms of a "revolutionary situation" that some historians detect in the period 1859-1861. See, for example, M. V. Nechkina, "Reforma 1861 goda kak pobochnyi produkt revoliutsionnoi bor'by," *Revoliutsionnaia situatsiia v Rossii v 1859-1861 gg.,* [II] (Moscow, 1962), pp. 7-17; this series is cited hereinafter as *Rev. Sit.*

3. But only Monas points out that the Chief of Gendarmes stopped warning Nicholas I about serfdom as a danger to security when it became clear that the tsar had decided to leave serfdom intact. Sidney Monas, *The Third Section* (Cambridge, Mass., 1961), p. 277.

4. Apart from the forebodings of Nicholas I, Kiselev, and Rostovstev, quoted below, see P. A. Zaionchkovskii, ed., "O pravitel'stvennykh merakh dlia podavleniia narodnykh volnenii v period otmeny krepostnogo prava," *Istoricheskii arkhiv*, 1957, no. 1, pp. 151-193; and A. E. Presniakov, "Samoderzhavie Aleksandra II," *Russkoe proshloe*, 1923, no. 3, p. 13.

5. M. A. Korf, "Imperator Nikolai v soveshchatel'nykh sobraniiakh," p. 236.

6. For an example, see N. Volkonskii, "Nekotorye dannye o kniaze Sergee Vasil'eviche Volkonskom i ego otnoshenii k krest'ianskoi reforme," *Trudy Riazanskoi uchenoi arkhivnoi komissii*, vol. XX, fasc. 2, p. 137.

7. N. I. Pavlenko et al., "Perekhod Rossii ot feodalizma k kapitalizmu," in V. I. Shunkov et al., eds. *Perekhod ot feodalizma k kapitalizmu v Rossii. Materialy vsesoiuznoi diskussii* (Moscow, 1969), p. 93.

8. See A. S. Nifontov, "Statistika krest'ianskogo dvizheniia v Rossii 50-kh gg. XIX veka . . . ," *Voprosy istorii sel' skogo khoziaistva, krest'ianstva i revoliutsionnogo dvizheniia v Rossii* (Moscow, 1961), p. 186; and Okun's preface to S. B. Okun' and K. V. Sivkov, eds., *Krest'ianskoe dvizhenie v Rossii v 1857-mae 1861 gg.* (Moscow, 1963), p. 13.

9. A. Gerschenkron, "Russia: Agrarian Policies and Industrialization, 1861-1917," in *Continuity in History and Other Essays* (Cambridge, Mass., 1968), p. 142.

10. Genovese's strictures against those who would explain the outbreak of the American Civil War in terms of the profitability of slavery are applicable here; see Eugene Genovese, *The Political Economy of Slavery* (New York, 1967), pp. 281-282.

11. See Iu. A. Gagemeister, "O finansakh Rossii," *Istoricheskii arkhiv*, 1956, no. 2, p. 125; the editor, A. P. Pogrebinskii, dates it "no earlier than December, 1855." Gagemeister, who headed the Credit Chancellory of the Ministry of Finance, held that the government could do no more than encourage serfs to purchase their own freedom. A subordinate described Gagemeister, who later served on the Editorial Commission, as very learned and very influential, but extremely pessimistic about Russia's economic prospects; F. G. Terner, *Vospominaniia zhizni*, 2 vols. (St. Petersburg, 1910-1911), vol. I, p. 186.

12. But see Nifontov's recent study of the year-to year fluctuations of the national economy. Nifontov points out a correspondence between

these fluctuations and the government's thinking on the peasant question in the years 1855-1861, but is cautious about offering causal explanations. A. S. Nifontov, "Kroziaistvennaia kon "iunktura v Rossii vo vtoroi polovine XIX veka," *Istoriia SSSR*, 1972, no. 3, pp. 52-54.

13. See Gerschenkron, "Russia: Agrarian Policies and Industrialization," pp. 140-147.

14. A. J. Rieber gives the military explanation in its most extended form, yet the only source he cites linking the abolition of serfdom to military requirements is a memorandum by D. A. Miliutin, written in 1856 for a special commission "for improvements in the armed forces." See A. J. Rieber, *The Politics of Autocracy: Letters of Alexander II to Prince A. I. Bariatinskii, 1857-64* (Etudes sur l'historie, l'économie et le sociologie des pays slaves, XII) (Paris-The Hague, 1966), p. 25.

15. In a letter of January 30, 1856, K. D. Kavelin told M. P. Pogodin that A. D. Gorchakov, who had commanded Russian forces in the Crimean campaign, had told the tsar to take advantage of the end of the war and attend to internal affairs, and first of all to the abolition of serfdom, "because here is the nexus of all evils." In these letters to Pogodin, however, Kavelin shows himself to be an unreliable reporter, much swayed by rumors and his own mood of the moment. In his next letter, he informed Pogodin that Russia's government was dominated by "the dregs of the human race," with only the elderly Kiselev and Bludov to restrain their villainy, whereas the rank-and-file nobility was fairly well disposed towards emancipation, N. P. Barsukov, *Zhizn' i trudy M. P. Pogodina*, 22 vols. (Moscow, 1888-1910), vol. XIV, pp. 201-219, especially pp. 207, 211-212.

16. See, for example, Valuev's "Thoughts of a Russian" in reaction to the defeat at Sevastopol, which is often cited to show the impact of the war. Valuev calls for moral and political renewal but makes no direct mention of serfdom. P. A. Valuev, "Duma russkogo . . . ," *RS*, vol. LXX (May 1891), pp. 349-360. Similarly, there is no emphasis on the problem of serfdom in Pogodin's celebrated "Historical-Political Letters," reprinted as his *Sochineniia*, vol. IV (Moscow, 1874), or in Mel' gunov's incisive "Mysli ob istekshem tridtsatiletii Rossii," *Golosa iz Rossii*, fasc. 1, (1856), pp. 62-151.

17. A. J. Rieber, "Alexander II: A Revisionist View," *Journal of Modern History*, XLIII, 1 (1971), p. 45.

18. Quoted in V. A. Kokorev, "Vospominaniia davnoproshedshego," *RA*, 1885, no. 10, p. 266.

19. Konstantin Nikolaevich to A. I. Bariatinskii, *RBS*, vol. [IX]: Knappe-Kiukhel'beker (1903), p. 124.

20. Blum, *Lord and Peasant in Russia*, p. 617.

21. According to the director of the Third Section under Nicholas I, Alexander "inherited" the idea of emancipation from his father, who "throughout his reign had the abolition of serfdom constantly in mind"; furthermore, Alexander was inspired to undertake abolition by his father's deathbed warning that serfdom was better abolished from above than from below. A. E. Timashev, "K istorii raskreposhcheniia pomeshchich'ikh krest'ian," *RA*, 1887, no. 6, p. 260.

22. Pavlenko, "Perekhod Rossii ot feodalizma," p. 81; P. A.

Zaionchkovskii, *Otmena krepostnogo prava v Rossii*, 3rd ed. (Moscow, 1968), pp. 61-63.

23. Speech of March 30, 1842, in *SbIRIO*, vol. XCVIII (1896), pp. 114-117.

24. As in V. V. Golubtsov, ed., "Imperator Nikolai Pavlovich v ego rechi k deputatam Sanktpeterburgskogo dvorianskogo obshchestva, 21 marta 1848 g.," *RS*, vol. XXXIX (September 1883), pp. 593-596.

25. In his excellent discussion of prereform local administration, Starr loses sight of this consideration. See Starr, *Decentralization and Self-Government in Russia*, p. 49.

26. Although Pintner finds that "lack of serfs was not a barrier to bureaucratic success in the mid-nineteenth century," 35.6 percent of his sample of officials in the first five civil service ranks owned a hundred or more male serfs. And of fifty-five members of the Council of State in 1855, thirty-four were magnates with more than a thousand male serfs apiece. Pintner, "Social Characteristics," pp. 437-438; P. A. Zaionchkovskii, "Vysshaia biurokratiia nakanune Krymskoi voiny," *Istoriia SSSR*, 1974, no. 4, pp. 156-157.

27. According to Khromov, a law of 1714 (*PSZ*, vol. V, no. 2789) gave the nobleman a full property right to his *pomest'e;* Jones maintains that the Charter to the Nobility of 1785 had this effect. No scholar, however, has demonstrated when the idea that private landed property is the cornerstone of state and society took hold in Russia. See P. A. Khromov, *Ocherki ekonomiki feodalizma v Rossii* (Moscow, 1957), p. 39; Jones, *Emancipation of the Russian Nobility*, p. 282; and the monographs on landed property by El'iashevich and Got'e.

28. For example, I. I. Ivaniukov, *Padenie krepostnogo prava v Rossii*, 2nd ed. (St. Petersburg, 1900), pp. 32-33. Moore quite properly doubts that this sentiment, widely attributed to Russian serfs, represents "actual peasant thinking," but it does bespeak a distinctive concept of landed property. Barrington Moore, *Social Origins of Dictatorship and Democracy: Lord and Peasant in the Making of the Modern World* (Boston, 1966), p. 503n.

29. As Konstantin Aksakov observed, "So long as the question of property has not been decided, the pomeshchik can consider the land his, and so can the peasant, and in practice they can live peaceably, each holding his own opinion and using the land jointly (*vziaimno*). But so soon as the decisive question, whose is the land? is raised, the peasant will say, mine." *Zamechaniia na novoe administrativnoe ustroistvo krest'ian*, p. 4, quoted in A. Popel'nitskii, "Kak priniato bylo Polozhenie 19 fevralia 1861 goda osvobozhdennymi krest'ianiami," *Sovremennyi mir*, 1911, no. 2, p. 213.

30. As suggested by the widespread tendency to speak of a "proletariat"—not *batraki, bobyli*, or another Russian term. On Russian fears of a "proletariat" *avant le fait*, see Reginald E. Zelnik, *Labor and Society in Tsarist Russia: The Factory Workers of St. Petersburg, 1855-1870*. (Stanford, Calif., 1971), chaps. I-II.

31. On the persistence of this hope into the nineteenth century, see Semevskii, *Krest'ianskii vopros*, vol. II, pp. 22, 125; Iurii Samarin complained in 1857 that the new Secret Committee wanted emancipation "accomplished

388 Notes to Pages 59-63

so quietly, that neither the pomeshchiki nor the peasants talk about it." Quoted in B. Nol'de, *Iurii Samarin i ego vremia* (Paris, 1926), p. 77.

32. "K. P. P." to A. M. Turgenev, n.d., in "R.," "Na zare krepostnoi svobody. Materialy dlia kharakteristiki obshchestva (1857-61 gg.)," in seven parts, *RS*, vol. XCII-XCIV (1896-1898); vol. XCII, p. 227. Cited hereinafter as "Na zare" with the appropriate volume number of *RS*.

33. Text in Barsukov, *Zhizn' Pogodina*, vol. XIV, p. 5.

34. For example, "Our gracious sovereign has ordered me to preserve inviolate the rights granted to the nobility by his laureled predecessors." Text in [D. P. Khrushchov, comp.?] *Materialy dlia istorii uprazdneniia krepostnogo sostoianiia pomeshchich'ikh krest'ian v Rossii v tsarstvovanie Imperatora Aleksandra II*, 3 vols. (Berlin, 1860-1862), vol. I, p. 103. Hereinafter cited as *Materialy*.

35. Druzhinin, *Gosudarstvennye krest'iane*, vol. II, p. 542. For a characteristic example of Alexander's tact, compare Zablotskii-Desiatovskii, *Kiselev*, vol. III, p. 31. Yaney aptly remarks that Kiselev's reforms of the administration of the state peasantry "laid the administrative groundwork for the Liberation [of the serfs], yet it seems to have bred a general lack of confidence in the central government's capacity to act in the countryside and a corresponding inclination to trust in the serfowning gentry to reform serfdom on their own." George L. Yaney, *The Systematization of Russian Government: Social Evolution in the Domestic Administration of Imperial Russia, 1711-1905* (Urbana, Ill., 1973), p. 167.

36. This manifesto, dated March 19, 1856, also contained exhortations to piety and morality; text in S. S. Tatishchev, *Imperator Aleksandr II, ego zhizn' i tsarstvovanie*, 2 vols. (St. Petersburg, 1903), vol. I, p. 205.

37. N. Ia. Eidel'man, *Gertsen protiv samoderzhaviia* . . . (Moscow, 1973), p. 43.

38. P. Kh. Grabbe, *Zapisnaia knizhka* (Moscow, 1888), pp. 666, 670, 696, 699.

39. As Emmons emphasizes; T. L. Emmons, *The Russian Landed Gentry and the Peasant Emancipation of 1861* (Cambridge, England, 1968), pp. 40-41. The most influential and widely circulated of the reform proposals composed prior to the government's commitment to reform were: [B. N. Chicherin], "O krepostnom sostoianii," *Golosa iz Rossii*, fasc. 2 (London, 1856), pp. 139-250; A. I. Koshelev, "Zapiski po unichtozhenii krepostnogo sostoianiia v Rossii," *Zapiski A. I. Kosheleva* (Berlin, 1884), appendix, pp. 57-92; Iu. F. Samarin, "O krepostnom sostoianii i o perekhode iz nego k grazhdanskoi svobode," *Sochineniia*, vol. II, pp. 17-136; V. A. Cherkasskii, "O luchshikh sredstvakh k postepennomu iskhodu iz krepostnogo sostoianiia," *Materialy Cherkasskogo*, bk. 1, appendix, pp. 7-67; K. D. Kavelin, "Zapiska ob osvobozhdenii krest-ian v Rossii," *Sobranie sochinenii*, 4 vols. (St. Petersburg, 1897-1900), vol. II, pp. 5-87; and M. P. Pozen, "Pervaia zapiska o merakh osvobozhdeniia krepostnykh krest'ian," *Bumagi po krest'ianskomu delu* (Dresden, 1864), pp. 2-28.

40. Barsukov, *Zhizn' Pogodina*, vol. XIV, p. 211.

41. D. Field, "Kavelin and Russian Liberalism," *Slavic Review*, XXXII, 1 (March 1973), pp. 67-68.

42. Quoted in Jones, *Emancipation of the Russian Nobility*, p. 137.

43. In this version, the tsar continued: "I ask you to reflect on how all this can be most conveniently brought to fulfillment. Convey my words to the nobility for its consideration." Zakrevskii's letter and both texts are given in A. Popel'nitskii, "Rech' Aleksandra II moskovskomu dvorianstvu 30 marta 1856,' *GM*, 1916, no. 5/6, pp. 392-393, 396.

44. Alexander to Elena Pavlovna, October 26, 1856, in A. I. Levshin, "Dostopamiatnye minuty v moei zhizni. Zapiska Alekseia Iraklievicha Levshina," *RA*, 1885, no. 8, p. 489. Levshin's "Zapiska" contains the full texts of the most important documents relating to emancipation that passed through the Ministry of Internal Affairs in 1856-1857. On the Grand Duchess's plan, see W. B. Lincoln, "The Karlovka Reform," *Slavic Review*, XXVIII, 3 (September 1969), pp. 463-470.

45. "Na zare," vol. XCII, p. 24.

46. On the increase of demesne land at the expense of allotments in the period preceding emancipation, see P. A. Zaionchkovskii, *Provedenie v zhizn' krest'ianskoi reformy 1861 g* (Moscow, 1958), p. 301, passim; on the increase of household serfs from 4.79 percent of the serf population in 1850 to 6.79 percent in 1858, see Troinitskii, *Krepostnoe naselenie*, p. 58.

47. As M. N. Pokrovskii emphasizes in his stimulating "Krest'ianskaia reforma," *Istoriia Rossii v XIX veke*, vol. III, p. 94.

48. Report of the MIA to the tsar, December 29, 1856, in Levshin, "Zapiska," p. 495.

49. From January to November of 1857, the only remnant of the old policy was Alexander's remark, in a confidential conversation with A. M. Unkovskii in April, that he wanted the "cooperation of the nobility" in the abolition of serfdom. Unkovskii, the newly elected marshal of the nobility of Tver and the only provincial marshal who was a zealous abolitionist, replied that the government had only to indicate the basic principles on which it intended to proceed. A. M. Unkovskii, "Zapiski," *Russkaia mysl'*, 1906, no. 6, pp. 192-193.

50. For a very different view of the origins and significance of the Secret Committee, see Emmons, *Russian Landed Gentry*, pp. 51-52 and 61-62. Ruud suggests that it was "a means by which Alexander could involve high-ranking bureaucrats in a project he knew they did not favor." C. A. Ruud, "Censorship and the Peasant Question: The Contingencies of Reform under Alexander II (1855-1859)," *California Slavic Studies*, V (1970), p. 151.

51. Report of the MIA to the tsar, December 20, 1856, in Levshin, "Zapiska," pp. 490-492.

52. The original members were Prince A. F. Orlov, who took the chair in the tsar's absence, Counts V. F. Adlerberg and D. N. Bludov, Princes V. A. Dolgorukov and P. P. Gagarin, Baron M. A. Korf, Adjutant-Generals K. V. Chevkin and Ia. I. Rostovtsev and, ex officio, the Ministers of Internal Affairs and Finance. M. N. Murav'ev was added, at Orlov's request, in April of 1857 and the Grand Duke Konstantin Nikolaevich joined the committee in July of the same year upon his return from a tour of the courts of Europe. Count V. P. Panin was appointed in January, 1858, in effect replacing Korf. Thereafter, the membership remained the same except for A. M. Kniazhevich's replacement of his predecessor as Minister of Finance and

Konstantin Nikolaevich's succeeding to the chairmanship upon Orlov's withdrawal in late 1860. *ZhSGK*, pp. 1-2 of preface; *ZhSGK*, II, p. 2; *TsGIAL*, f. 1291, *op.* 1, *d.* 4, *l.* 26; *RBS*, vol. [IX], pp. 124, 127 (see Note on Abbreviations).

53. *ZhSGK*, pp. 1-2, 3. Apart from these formal journals, the tsar requested the executive secretary of the Secret Committee to report to him on each session, but these reports apparently have not survived. *TsGIAL*, f. 1291, *op.* 1, *d.* 4, *l.* 35.

54. *ZhSGK*, p. 6.

55. *ZhSGK*, pp. 7-8.

56. *ZhSGK*, pp. 10-16; seven members favored the ukaz, written by Rostovtsev, which is appended, pp. 17-18.

57. A. Popel'nitskii, "Sekretnyi komitet v dele osvobozhdeniia krest'ian ot krepostnoi zavisimosti," *Vestnik Evropy*, February, 1911, p. 56. These articles (a second part was published in the March number, pp. 127-153) provide extracts from various working papers not available in *ZhSGK*. Hereinafter cited as "Sekretnyi komitet."

58. Zaionchkovskii, *Otmena*, pp. 69-71, and "Sekretnyi komitet," pp. 56-58.

59. According to a scheme devised by Rostovtsev's friend Pozen; see Pozen, *Bumagi*, pp. 2-28.

60. Zaionchkovskii, *Otmena*, pp. 72-73 and "Sekretnyi komitet," pp. 58-59.

61. The nobility was to be instructed to avoid "any abrupt or coercive remedies, . . . all measures of such a kind that the advantages for one side will directly or indirectly work to the detriment of the other [and] everything that might demand sacrifices on the part of the state treasury." On Korf's memorandum see Zaionchkovskii, *Otmena*, p. 73, and "Sekretnyi komitet," pp. 59-60.

62. P. I. Liashchenko, *Poslednii sekretnyi komitet po krest'ianskomu delu. 3 ianvaria 1857 g.-16 fevralia 1858 g. (po materialam Arkhiva Gosudarstvennogo Soveta)* (St. Petersburg, 1911), p. 26.

63. For example, Orlov is reported to have said that he was not prepared to break with the nobility in his declining years; *Materialy*, vol. I, p. 134.

64. "Vsepodanneishaia zapiska kn. Orlova ot 21 iiunia 1857 g.," *TsGIAL*, f. 1180, *op.* XV, *d.* 9, *ll.* 370-378; see also "Sekretnyi komitet," pp. 62-64.

65. Zaionchkovskii, *Otmena*, p. 77. Alexander continued, "Haxthausen has discerned my main anxiety, *that the matter being of itself, from below.*"

66. "Sekretnyi komitet," pp. 67-70. Popel'nitskii here provides the members' answers to four questions. For the text of the eight questions, see Levshin, "Zapiska," pp. 520-521. The fourteen questions he quotes on pp. 519-520 did not precede the Journal of August 18, as he supposes; they were circulated with a view to implementing it.

67. "Sekretnyi komitet," p. 66.

68. Levshin, "Zapiska," p. 492.

69. Report of MIA to Alexander, December 29, 1856, in Levshin, "Zapiska," pp. 494-497.

70. Lanskoi's comment and Report of MIA of December 30, 1856, in Levshin, "Zapiska," pp. 497-498.

71. The lapse is all the more striking because the Ministry of Internal Affairs was then embroiled in a controversy on district and provincial administration, on which see Starr, *Decentralization and Self-Government,* especially pp. 138-145.

72. MIA to Alexander, May 17, 1857, *TsGIAL, f.* 1291, *op.* 33, *d.* 2, *l.* 131.

73. Comment of MIA dated June 14, 1857, in Levshin, "Zapiska," pp. 499-503.

74. Memorandum of MIA for the Secret Committee, July 29, 1857, in Levshin, "Zapiska," pp. 518-519.

75. Memorandum of MIA for the Secret Committee, July 26, 1857, in Levshin, "Zapiska," pp. 503-509.

76. Journal of August 18 with the tsar's resolution, *ZhSGK,* pp. 18-26.

77. S. F. Starr, Introduction to August von Haxthausen, *Studies on the Interior of Russia* (Chicago, 1972), pp. xxxv-xl. Starr here summarizes the memoranda Haxthausen presented to the tsar and to Foreign Minister Gorchakov and the Grand Duchess Elena Pavlovna. (Prof. Starr has kindly provided me with photocopies of these memoranda, and Bettina Beer, who is preparing them for publication, has shown equal kindness in providing me with translations.) Starr correctly attaches great importance to Haxthausen's suasions, but exaggerates the novelty of his specific proposals and his role in procuring the commitment to reform, for there is nothing in these memoranda that cannot be found in the reform plans then circulating in Russia.

78. Diary entry of June 25 and Memorandum for Alexander II of July 9, 1857, quoted in Zaionchkovskii, *Otmena,* pp. 76-77. Kiselev's biographer explains that Kiselev rejected immediate emancipation in behalf of his ideal—emancipation with the redemption of plowland—which seemed unattainable at that time; a letter of Kiselev's supports this interpretation, but elsewhere he held that if redemption was impossible, Gagarin's plan for landless emancipation was the best solution. Zablotskii-Desiatovskii, *Kiselev,* vol. II, pp. 332, 339; vol. IV, p. 264.

79. Kavelin, "Iz dnevnika," *Sobranie sochinenii,* vol. II, p. 1169.

80. Most historians agree on both counts; Zaionchkovskii, *Otmena,* p. 78.

81. Letter of October 1856 to the Grand Duchess Elena Pavlovna, quoted in N. P. Pavlov-Sil'vanskii, "Velikii kniaz' Konstantin Nikolaevich," S. A. Vengerov, ed., *Glavnye deiateli osvobozhdeniia krest'ian* (St. Petersburg, 1903), p. 8. Pavlov-Sil'vanskii holds that the Grand Duke was "in the minority" on the Journal of August 18, but cites no evidence.

82. Golovnin's "Zapiska," quoted in Ruud, "Censorship and the Peasant Question," pp. 152-153.

83. The Journal of August 18 did assign a major role to the Ministry of Internal Affairs; however, Orlov was quite willing, once the abolition of serfdom had been forestalled, to shut down the Secret Committee and let the ministry resume its responsibility for serfs and serfdom; see the letter (probably also by Golovnin) quoted in Zablotskii-Desiatovskii, *Kiselev,* vol. II. p. 336.

84. For example, the Journal of August 18 acknowledged the failure of the law of 1842 on "obligated peasants" and held that pomeshchiki should be given further encouragement to free their serfs; the experience of these transactions would form the basis of prescriptive legislation in the "second period." The law of 1842 had been justified, with reference to the law of 1803, in just the same way.

85. "Vsepodanneishaia zapiska kn. Orlova ot 21 iiunia 1857 g.," *TsGIAL*, f. 1180, *op.* XV, *d.* 9, *l.* 376*ob*; "Sekretnyi komitet," p. 63.

86. "Svod zamechanii na proekty polozhenii dlia pomeshchich'ikh krest'ian Iamburgskogo i Petergofskogo uezdov i Sanktpeterburgskoi gubernii voobshche," *TsGIAL*, f. 1180, *op.* XV, *d.* 10, *l.* 23*ob.*; "Sekretnyi komitet," p. 143.

87. "Svod zamechanii", *l.* 18*ob.*

88. Report of MIA, October 26, 1856, in Levshin, "Zapiska," p. 485.

89. One source holds that Nazimov began working on the nobility even before the coronation, and credits him with persuading the tsar to attempt a policy of appealing to the nobility; anon., "Vladimir Ivanovich Nazimov," *RS*, vol. XLV (March, 1885), pp. 576-578.

90. Quoted in "Sekretnyi komitet," part two, p. 137.

91. Levshin, "Zapiska," p. 486.

92. V. Neupokoev, "Resheniia dvorianskikh komitetov 1857 goda v Litve o lichnom 'osvobozhdenii' krest'ian," *Uchenye zapiski Vil'niusskogo gos. universiteta*, vol. I (1955), pp. 61-62.

93. N. N. Ulashchik, "Iz istorii reskripta 20 noiabria 1857 g.," *Istoricheskie zapiski*, vol. 28 (1949), p. 166.

94. Neupokoev, "Resheniia," p. 67.

95. Note of the Chief of Staff of the Third Section for the Secret Committee, August 24, 1857, *TsGIAL*, f. 1180, *op.* XV, *d.* 10, *l.* 71*ob*. This source holds, as does Neupokoev, that Domeiko's group was the majority, Ulashchik ("Iz istorii . . . , p. 171) that it was the minority, while a member recalls a three-way split. K. K. Gelling, "K voprosu o nachale krest'ianskogo dela," *RS*, vol. LII (December 1886), p. 549. See also M. B. Fridman, *Otmena krepostnogo prava v Belorussii* (Minsk, 1958), p. 69.

96. N. N. Ulashchik, *Predposylki krest'ianskoi reformy 1861 g. v Litve i Zapadnoi Belorussii* (Moscow, 1965), p. 457.

97. Neupokoev, "Resheniia," p. 75.

98. Neupokoev, "Resheniia," p. 68.

99. N. N. Ulashchik, "Vvedenie obiazatel'nykh inventarei v Belorussii i Litve," *Ezhegodnik po agrarnoi istorii Vostochnoi Evropy: 1958 g.* (Tallin, 1959), pp. 261-262.

100. Levshin, "Zapiska," p. 527.

101. Secret dispatch of Nazimov to Lanskoi, September 25, 1857, *TsGIAL, f.* 1180, *op.* XV, *d.* 10, 11. 80-93. In a vituperative letter to Domeiko, Nazimov had criticized him for delaying and for submitting an "absolutely inappropriate opinion" (Ulashchik, "Iz istorii," p. 172). But in his dispatch, Nazimov implied that Domeiko had only one supporter and that they avoided "a direct expression of their ideas," *l.* 86.

102. Report of MIA to Alexander, October 18, 1857, in Levshin, "Zapiska," p. 525.

103. The reports of Timashev and Nazimov cited above were turned over to the Secret Committee along with Lanskoi's report.

104. "Sekretnyi komitet," part II, p. 138.

105. Perhaps the presence of Nazimov was decisive. The central government had abandoned the policy of appealing to the nobility, but Nazimov had expended much time and effort pursuing it in the Northwest, and arrived in St. Petersburg in October bearing the fruits of his labors. I would be understandable if his pride and self-esteem were invested in them. He may have pressed that policy on Alexander more vigorously and candidly than other officials felt able to do, since their close personal relationship was of long standing. In time, however, Nazimov was overwhelmed by second thoughts. In 1860, he warned the central government that the local statute covering the northwestern provinces, which was then under final review, would produce "the destruction of the pomeshchik class." Fridman, *Otmena*, p. 99.

106. Levshin, "Zapiska," p. 528.

107. "Obzor osnovanii," dated November 6, 1857, in Levshin, "Zapiska," pp. 529-533.

108. "Obshchie nachala dlia ustroistvu byta krest'ian" (on which see Zaionchkovskii, *Otmena*, pp. 83-84), "O sostave . . . and "O zaniatiiakh Gubernskikh Komitetov i Tsentral'noi Komissii," and "Po proektu reskripta," TsGIAL, f. 1180, op. XV, d. 10, ll. 95-107. Two of these documents are dated November 8, 1857; the *reestr* to this file attributes all four to Lanskoi and Murav'ev.

109. Text in *Sbornik pravitel'stvennykh rasporiazhenii po ustroistvu byta krest'ian, vyshedshikh iz krepostnoi zavisimosti*, vol. I (for 1857-1860), third ed. (St. Petersburg, 1869), pp. 2-4. Hereinafter cited as *SbPR*. In the Northwest, committees were to meet in each of the three provinces and forward their proposals to a General Commission composed of their members. The General Commission would draft a statute for the Governor-Generalship as a whole. This two-stage procedure would later be applied to the Southwest (Kiev, Podolia, Volynia).

110. The expression "amelioration of the way of life" (*uluchshenie byta*) had been used as a euphemism for emancipation during the drafting of the reform for the Baltic provinces. Zaionchkovskii, *Otmena*, p. 59, citing an ukaz of May 11, 1803.

111. "*Krest'ianam ostaetsia ikh usadebnaia osedlost . . .* "; on the controversy over the meaning of this phrase, see above, pp. 202, 206, 210-213.

112. Lanskoi complained of the presence of these conflicting principles in the proposals of the St. Petersburg nobility ["Svod zamechanii . . . ," cited in note 86 above], but was now reconciled. The rescript did not go so far as the earlier draft, which affirmed that "all the land is the pomeshchik's inviolable property." Levshin, "Zapiska," p. 531.

113. Directive of the MIA, November 21, 1857, SbPR, pp. 71-76.

114. In 1859, the Editorial Commission used the expression to denote the manorial authority of Estonian landlords; Doklad Aministrativnogo otdeleniia, no. 8, p. 48 (appended to Zhurnal Obshchego prisutstviia Kommissii dlia sostavleniia polozhenii o krest'ianakh . . . , no. 47, August 29, 1859), *Pervoe izdanie materialov Redaktsionnykh kommissii dlia*

sostavleniia polozhenii o krest'ianakh vykhodiashchikh iz krepostnoi zavisimosti (St. Petersburg, 1859-60), 18 vols. plus appendices, vol. III. Cited hereinafter as DAO (or DIuO, DKhO for the Juridical and Economic sections, respectively), ZhOP no. 00, and *MRK*.

115. "O soobshchenii mestnym Nachal'nikam i predvoditeliam Dvorianstva soderzhaniia Vysoch. reskripta [*sic*] Gen.-ad"iutantu Nazimovu," November 22, 1857, and "Dokladnaia zapiska kn. Orlova," November 23, 1857, TsGIAL, *f.* 1180, *op.* XV, *d.* 10, *ll.* 149-150, 153-153*ob*; see also "Sekretnyi komitet," p. 142.

116. *ZhSGK*, p. 32. The committee chose that vehicle because material from the official section of *ZhMVD* could not be reprinted or discussed in print without special permission; hence the rescript would be published but it would not be *glasnyi*. On the other hand, it would scarcely be secret, despite the fond hopes of the Chief of Gendarmes, who sent copies to his provincial staff officers on November 26 with strict instructions to convey it "to absolutely no one, neither senior officials nor subordinates nor friends," for it "applies *only* to the three northwestern provinces." "Po proektu reskripta," TsGIAL, *f.* 1180, *op.* XV, *d.* 10, *l*, 106*ob.*, and Zaionchkovskii, *Otmena*, p. 85.

117. "Dokladnaia zapiska" of November 23, as quoted in Zaionchkovskii, *Otmena*, p. 85. The Secret Committee had a different disclaimer in mind; it would reassure the Great Russian nobles that the government would take no action on emancipation except through them and with full regard for their property rights; *ZhSGK*, p. 32.

118. *SbPR*, p. 120.

110. The dynasty begins with Herzen who (writing when he had only French translations of the documents to go on) described how "the senior sanovniki in St. Petersburg took fright and tried to persuade the sovereign not to distribute the circular." Khrushchov, the first chronicler of the reform and one of the least discriminating, fleshed out the anecdote: "It is said that Prince Orlov and the other members [of the Secret Committee] wanted to block the distribution of this circular, but it was too late; the airy-winged post had already carried the great news across the broad expanse of the vast empire. *Alea jacta est!*" So far, the anecdote is plausible, although inconsistent with the report, which Khrushchov appended to it, that the Secret Committee itself compiled the circular. (In the committee's journal and archive there is no trace of its involvement with it). Levshin incorporated both the anecdote and the appendage into his memoirs, heightening the inconsistency by asserting that Lanskoi, who had supposedly ordered the circular printed and dispatched in one night, had not intended to put any pressure on the nobility. While the anecdote is plausible, it is probably false, even in its original version. It would have taken rare courage for the sanovniki to block a circular that bore the tsar's explicit endorsement. And the day before the date of the circular, the Secret Committee began discussing the terms of reform for St. Petersburg Province. With the passage of time, however, Khrushchov's version came to seem pallid. Others began to retell the anecdote, substituting the rescript and directive of November 20-21 for the circular. Historians, in

turn, gave credit to this new version. Only the October Rolution, which dried up the demand for this kind of anecdote, prevented its further dissemination and embroidery. *Kolokol*, no. 7 (January 1, 1858), p. 52; *Materialy*, I, p. 156; Levshin, "Zapiska," pp. 534-535 (and Bartenev's note on p. 533); Timashev, "K istorii," pp. 261-262; Ia. A. Solov'ev, "Zapiski senatora Ia. A. Solov'eva," *RS*, vol. XXX (March 1881), p. 726; "Sekretnyi komitet," p. 143; A. Leroi-Beaulieu, *Un homme d'etat russe (Nicholas Miliutine)* . . . (Paris, 1882), p. 15n; A. A. Kornilov, "Gubernskie komitety 1858-1859 gg.," *Ocherki po istorii obshchestvennogo dvizheniia i krest'ianskogo dela v Rossii* (St. Petersburg, 1905), p. 176n. A congruent anecdote, related by Khrushchov and Solov'ev, holds that on November 22, Alexander announced to the governor of Voronezh Province, "I have resolved to carry this matter through to the end and hope that you will persuade your nobles to help me in this." There is no mention of this memorable interview in the governor's memoirs. *Materialy*, I, p. 154; N. P. Sinel'nikov, "Zapiski," *Istoricheskii vestnik*, vol. LIX (1895), especially pp. 731-734.

120. "Dokladnaia zapiska kn. Orlova," November 23, 1857, *TsGIAL, f.* 1180, *op.* XV, *d.* 10, *ll.* 154-155.

121. "Dokladnaia zapiska kn. Orlova," November 25, 1857, *TsGIAL, f.* 1180, *op.* XV, *d.* 10, *ll.* 160-161. According to Solov'ev, P. P. Shuvalov, Marshal of the Nobility of St. Petersburg Province, and A. F. Veimarn were also involved. Solov'ev, "Zapiski," *RS*, vol. XXX, p. 729.

122. The tsar wrote on Orlov's report of November 30, "I hope that it will be finished on Wednesday [i.e., December 4] and do not understand how you can be encountering difficulties again." *TsGIAL, f.* 1180, *op.* XV, *d.* 10, *l.* 174.

123. *ZhSGK*, pp. 42-43.

124. An early draft (*TsGIAL, f.* 1180, *op.* XV, *d.* 10, *ll.* 163-166) credited the St. Petersburg nobility with expressing a desire for the abolition of serfdom, but this was dropped in the final version.

125. Text in *SbPR*, pp. 76-81.

126. Levshin, "Zapiska," pp. 535, 539n, 544-545, 548.

127. Letters of November 20, 1857, "Pis'ma (grafa) D. A. Miliutina k kniaziu A. I. Bariatinskomu," A. L. Zisserman, ed., *RA*, 1889, no. 2, p. 318.

128. The MIA remedied the oversight with a circular of March 4, 1858, *SbPR*, pp. 127-128.

129. "Sekretnyi Komitet," part II, p. 135.

130. Murav'ev's position has caused controversy. Starr remarks that he did not "belong to the 'planter' faction" and that his "primary concern . . . was with the problem of domestic security rather than with emancipation *per se*." But this priority, substantiated with the kind of arguments Murav'ev used and often accompanied by an endorsement of emancipation in principle, had served in the past to justify an indefinite postponement of emancipation. Furthermore, from his attempts to reverse Kiselev's reforms in the Ministry of State Property through his opposition to the Editorial Commission in 1860, Murav'ev was at odds with the ardent abolitionists within the bureaucracy. See Starr, *Decentralization and Self-Government*, p. 142; Liashchenko, *Poslednii sekretnyi komitet*, p. 48; and

Popel'nitskii's review of that book (where he takes a position like Starr's) in *Sovremennyi mir*, 1911, no. 4, p. 361; Solov'ev, "Zapiski," vol. XXX, pp. 729, 737.

131. Levshin identifies article 21 of the Survey of Basic Premises in which the provision for *votchinnaia politsiia* first appears, as the product of the conference of Lanskoi, Murav'ev, and their three assistants. Levshin, "Zapiska," p. 532.

132. See the excerpts from annual reports of the Third Section published by E. A. Morokhovets as *Krest'ianskoe dvizhenie 1827-1869* (Moscow, 1931).

133. In July, when they had only palliative legislation in view, some members of the Secret Committee were willing to give the nobility only a minor, consultative role in the drafting process, others would give none at all. Popel'nitskii, "Sekretnyi komitet," p. 70.

134. D. A. Obolenskii, "Moi vospominanii o Velikoi kniagine Elene Pavlovne," *RS*, vol. CXXXVIII (April, 1909), p. 62.

135. Diary of P. D. Kiselev, quoted in Zablotskii-Desiatovskii, *Kiselev*, vol. III, p. 32.

136. Diary of D. A. Obolenskii, quoted in Nol'de, *Iurii Samarin i ego vremia*, p. 75.

137. Iu. I. Gerasimova, "Krizis pravitel'stvennoi politiki v gody revoliutsionnoi situatsii i Aleksandr II," *Rev. Sit.* [fasc. II], pp. 93-106.

138. Rieber, *The Politics of Autocracy*.

139. Rieber observes that "political alignments constantly shifted on different issues, but all of them revolved around the person of the autocrat." Rieber, "Alexander II," p. 44.

140. See M. Raeff, "L'état, le gouvernement et la tradition politique en Russie imperiale avant 1861," *Revue d'Histoire moderne et contemporaine*, October-December, 1962, pp. 295-307.

141. P. N. Miliukov, *Ocherki po istorii russkoi kul'tury*, 3 vols. in 4 (Paris, 1930-1937), vol. III, especially p. 157 ff. See also Hans Rogger, *National Consciousness in Eighteenth-Century Russia* (Cambridge, Mass., 1960).

142. See Pipes, *Karamzin's Memoir*, pp. 162-167 and compare chapters XI-XII of Catherine's *Nakaz;* also note that, beginning in chapter XV, she surveys the estates of the realm in descending order, but never descends as far as the serfs.

143. Riasanovsky, *Nicholas I and Official Nationality*, passim.

144. Anthony Netting, "Russian Liberalism: The Years of Promise, 1842-55" (unpub. diss., Columbia University, 1967), especially pp. 12, 194-195, 613-659. Kitaev makes much the same point in different language when he maintains that the "westernism of the liberal nobility [was] inconsistent and contradictory." V. A. Kitaev, *Ot frondy k okhranitel'stvu. Iz istorii russkoi liberal'noi mysli 50-60kh godov XIX veka* (Moscow, 1972), p. 163.

3. The Engineering of Assent

1. A. A. Zakrevskii, "O slukhakh i tolkakh . . . ," December 24, 1857, quoted in Popel'nitskii, "Sekretnyi komitet," p. 147; "Zapiski Solov'eva," vol. XXX, pp. 743, 752.

2. "Sekretnyi komitet," p. 148; A. N. Murav'ev quoted in V. I. Snezhnevskii, "Krepostnye krest'iane i pomeshchiki nizhegorodskoi gubernii nakanune reformy 19 fevralia . . . ," *Deistviia Nizhegorodskoi gubernskoi uchenoi arkhivnoi komissii: Sbornik*, vol. III, p. 59; V. N. Murav'ev to Lanskoi, February 15, 1858, quoted in G. M. Deich, *Krest'ianstvo Pskovskoi gubernii vo vtoroi polovine XIX i nachale XX vv.* Unpub. diss., n.p. [Novogorod?], 1960, vol. I, p. 279.

3. S. V. Volkonskii, "Nekotorye zamechaniia otnositel'no uluchsheniia byta pomeshchich'ikh krest'ian," *Trudy Riazanskoi uchenoi arkhivnoi komissii*, vol. VI (1891), no. 3, p. 34; "Pis'ma . . . Aksakovykh k I. S. Turgenevu," in L. Maikov, ed., *Russkoe obozrenie*, December 1894, p. 595.

4. Kavelin, *Sobranie sochinenii*, vol. II, p. 1182; A. Popel'nitskii, "Zapreshchennyi po vysochaishemu poveleniiu banket v Moskve 19 fevralia 1858 g.," *GM*, 1914, no. 2, p. 202.

5. *Kolokol*, no. 7 (January 1, 1858), pp. 51, 53; [N. I. Turgenev], *O sile i deistvii reskripta 20 noiabria 1857 g.: Russkii zagranichnyi sbornik*, chast' 2, tetrad' 1, (Leipzig, 1859), pp. 21-22; N. A. Bezobrazov, *Ob usovershenii uzakonenii kasaiushchikhsia do votchinnykh prav dvorianstva* (Berlin, 1858, edition of 100 numbered copies), preface and p. 7.

6. [V. P. Orlov-Davydov], "O darovanii krest'ianam prava vykupit' v svoiu sobstvennost' ikh usadebnuiu osedlost' i o predostavlenii v ikh pol'zovanie kolichestvom zemli za obrok ili rabotu, otbyvaemuiu pomeshchiku" [dated 1857], *ORGBL, f.* 219, *karton* 80, *d.* 7, *l.* 9ob-10.

7. In the Editorial Commission's register of estates, Orlov-Davydov is credited with at least nine estates, including three in Samara Province and two in Simbirsk. Despite his vast holdings, he was an unusually aggressive and exploitative pomeshchik; see N. A. Bogoroditskaia, "Vnutrennii stroi krupnoi krepostnoi votchiny . . . ," *Uchenye zapiski Gor'kovskogo gos. universiteta (Seriia istoricheskaia)*, fasc. 151 (1971), pp. 3-21.

8. [Orlov-Davydov], "O darovanii," *l.* 11.

9. Volkonskii, "Nekotorye dannye," pp. 138-139.

10. "Proekt Unkovskogo," *Kolokol*, no. 39 (April 1, 1858), pp. 316-321. On the first part of this memorandum, written by Unkovskii's collaborator A. A. Golovachev, see Emmons, *Russian Landed Gentry*, pp. 90-95 and 427-443.

11. *TsGAOR, f.* 1291, *op.* 33, *d.* 1, *ll.* 298-304, unsigned and undated but presumably submitted in early 1858. A pencil note on the ms. attributes it to the marshal of the nobility of Moscow Province.

12. V. P. Orlov-Davydov, "Zamechaniia na reskript Aleksandra II Nazimovu ot 20/XI/1857 g." (November, 1857—title supplied by archivist), *ORGBL, f.* 219, *karton* 80, *d.* 6, *ll.* 1, 3ob.

13. This generalization applies to the forty or more letters and memoranda dating from the period just after the rescripts preserved in the

files of the Civil Division (*Zemskii otdel*) of the MIA. "O proektakh po voprosu ob osvobozhdenii krest'ian," *TsGIAL, f.* 1291, *op.* 33, *d.* 1.

14. Dispatch of A. N. Murav'ev to Lanskoi, March 14, 1858, in Okun' and Sivkov, *Krest'ianskoe divzhenie*, p. 139; Ushakov's letter to Lanskoi, December 13, 1857, is in *TsGIAL, f.* 1291, *op.* 33, *d.* 1, *ll.*-2*ob.* The governor forwarded the letter to Lanskoi, but wrote to Ushakov urging him to calm down and put his faith in God and the tsar, both of whom were anxious to maintain order.

15. "Na zare," vol. XCIII, p. 81.

16. M. E. Saltykov (N. Shchedrin), "Gospozha Padeikova," *Sobranie sochinenii v dvadtsati tomakh* (Moscow, 1965 *ff*), vol. III, p. 295.

17. P. I. Iakushkin, "Velik bog zemli russkoi," in *Russkie ocherki*, vol. II (Moscow, 1956), p. 119 (originally in *Sovremennik*, 1863, no. 1).

18. Reports to Panin, Dolgorukov, and Lanskoi during 1858 as published in Okun' and Sivkov, *Krest'ianskoe dvizhenie*, pp. 129, 144, 173, 147 and 155; letter of P. Novokshchenov to P. I. Mel'nikov, September 23, 1858, *TsGAOR, f.* 109, *op.* 3, *d.* 2001, *ll.* 1-1*ob.*

19. See the excerpts from the report of the Department of Executive Police in Okun' and Sivkov, *Krest'ianskoe dvizhenie*, pp. 180-184; the report of the MIA, "Zapiski Solov'eva," vol. XXXIV, pp. 136-141; and the summary of the Minister of Justice's report to the Main Committee, *ZhSGK*, p. 265.

20. Quoted in "Zapiski Solov'eva," vol. XXX, p. 755.

21. *TsGIAL, f.* 1291, *op.* 33, *d.* 1, *ll.* 33-34*ob.*, 41-52. Zakrevskii reported that pomeshchiki supposed that the reform had been imposed on Russia by her "secret enemies" at the Peace Conference of 1856; "Sekretnyi komitet," part two, p. 148.

22. Hence it was frequently argued that peasants holding household plots must be obliged to work an allotment; an example is Baron Fitnigof's memorandum, *TsGIAL, f.* 1291, *op.* 33, *d.* 1, *ll.* 53-54.

23. *TsGIAL, f.* 1291, *op.* 33, *d.* 1, *ll.* 29-30*ob.*

24. "Mnenie bol'shinstva dvorian, nakhodiashchikhsia v g. Ekaterinoslave po predmetu uluchsheniia i uprochneniia byta pomeshchich'ikh krest'ian," n.d., *TsGAOR, f.* 722, *op.* 1, *d.* 298, *l.* 2.

25. I. V. Likhachev, "Mnenie otnositel'no darovaniia lichnosti i sobstvennosti krest'ianam krepostnogo sostoianiia," January, 1858, *TsGIAL, f.* 1291, *op.* 33, *d.* 1, *ll.* 362-383.

26. "Dokladnaia zapiska st. sov. Kishkina . . . ," January 10, 1858, *TsGIAL, f.* 1291, *op.* 33, *d.* 1, *ll.* 22-28.

27. "Sekretnyi komitet," part two, pp. 148-149. No provincial committee was "already open" when Zakrevskii wrote; presumably he was referring to the four provinces covered by the rescripts to Nazimov and Ignat'ev, since he would not have known of the rescript, which bears the same date as his report, on the establishment of a provincial committee in Nizhnii Novgorod.

28. "Postanovlenie sobraniia dvorian Poltavskogo uezda . . . ," January 21, 1858, in A. Z. Baraboi et al., eds., *Otmena krespostnogo prava na Ukraine: Sbornik dokumentov i materialov* (Kiev, 1961), pp. 98-100.

29. On Kazan, see "Ottisk ot otnosheniia . . . k kazanskomu

gubernatoru," January 13, 1858, *TsGIAL*, *f*. 1291, *op*. 1, *d*. 7, *l*. 1: for Samara and Orenburg, I. P. Krechetovich, *Krest'ianskaia reforma v Orenburgskom krae*, vol. I (Moscow, 1911), pp. 9, 82; on Tambov, the letter from the provincial marshal to Lanskoi published as appendix 2 to Krechetovich's work, p. 582; on Pskov, Deich, *Krest'ianstvo Pskovskoi gubernii*, p. 290.

30. Liashchenko, *Poselednii sekretnyi komitet*, p. 55; [A. A. Kornilov], *Obshchestvennoe dvizhenie v Rossii pri Aleksandre II* (Paris, 1905), p. 35.

31. [N. B.] G[ersevano]v, quoted in "Na zare," vol. XCVII, p. 470; N. Shishkov to A. I. Levshin, March 6, 1858, *TsGIAL*, *f*. 1291, *op*. 33, *d*. 1, *l*. 388 *ob*.

32. A. I. Gertsen, "Cherez tri goda," *Kolokol*, no. 9 (February 15, 1858), p. 67; see also Blum, *Lord and Peasant*, pp. 580-581, and Emmons, *Russian Landed Gentry*, p. 62.

33. Zaionchkovskii, *Otmena*, p. 87.

34. "Postanovlenie Dvorianstva Nizhegorodskoi gubernii," *ZhMVD*, *chast'* 27 (1857, *kn*. 12), "Ofitsial'naia chast'," p. 65.

35. Murav'ev had been a Decembrist, and the nobles of Nizhnii did not find him completely rehabilitated. A local satirist wrote,

> Working in secret ways
> With a mason's hammer
> You wanted to butcher
> The nobility and the throne.

Cited in A. A. Savel'ev, "Neskol'ko slov o byvshem Nizhegorodskom gubernatore A. N. Murav'eve," *RS*, vol. XCIV (June, 1898), p. 613.

36. Murav'ev to Lanskoi, December 18, 1857, quoted in Savel'ev, "Neskol'ko slov," p. 616.

37. See "Na zare," vol. XCIII, p. 75.

38. Savel'ev, "Neskol'ko slov," p. 617. A questionable source reports that the resolution was unexpectedly presented to the nobles at the banquet that concluded their assembly, when they were well in their cups and in a benevolent mood; V. I. Gloriantov, "Nizhnii Novgorod bylogo vremeni," *RA*, 1907, no. 2, pp. 287-288.

39. Despite his wealth, title, and celebrated philanthropies, Sheremetev was a hard taskmaster; in 1859 his estates were sequestered because of his oppression of his serfs. Snezhnevskii, "Krepostnye krest'iane," pp. 68-74; Seredonin, *Istoricheskii obzor*, vol. III, part 1, pp. 340-342.

40. Savel'ev, "Neskol'ko slov," pp. 619-620; F. Chebaevskii, "Nizhegorodskii dvorianskii komitet 1858 g.," *Voprosy istorii*, 1947, no. 6, p. 87. For a different and in some respects demonstrably inaccurate version, see Levshin, "Zapiska," p. 537.

41. The announcement of the award "for special labors attested to by the Minister of Internal Affairs" was published together with the text of the resolution of the Nizhnii nobility; *Russkii vestnik*, tom XIII, *kn*. 1 (January 1858), "Sovremennaia letopis'," p. 47.

42. *ZhSGK*, pp. 50-52.

43. Ignat'ev's inquiry, which makes clear that he is writing on behalf of the provincial marshal of the nobility, and Lanskoi's draft reply are in *TsGIAL, f.* 1291, *op.* 1, *d.* 1, *ll.* 103-106*ob.*

44. *ZhSGK*, pp. 52-53.

45. "Zapiski Solov'eva," vol. XXXI, p. 12n.

46. See for example, Kokorev, "Vospominaniia davnoproshedshego," no. 9, and especially no. 10, p. 266. One account holds that initially Zakrevskii categorically forbade the provincial marshal of Moscow to assemble the nobility and propose acquiescence to the reform, but this anecdote includes chronological confusions that make it suspect; I. V. Selivanov, "Zapiski dvorianina-pomeshchika," *RS*, vol. XXVII (August, 1880), p. 735, and vol. XXXI (August, 1881), pp. 543-544.

47. "Zapiski Solov'eva," vol. XXXI, p. 12; N. M. Druzhinin, "Moskva i reforma 1861 g.," AN SSSR, *Istoriia Moskvy*, 8 vols. (Moscow-Leningrad, 1952-1967), vol. IV, p. 26. The Secret Committee had already decided in December that "the principles set forth in the rescript . . . are essential and unalterable and equally applicable to all provinces of Russia." See *ZhSGK*, pp. 42-43 and, on the *adresa* from Moscow, pp. 74-79.

48. V. N. Shiriaev, "Iaroslavskii gubernskii komitet 1858-59 gg . . . ," *Trudy Iaroslavskoi uchenoi arkhivnoi komissii*, bk. 6, fasc. 2 (1912), p. 17. Compare "Zapiski Solov'eva," vol. XXXI, p. 2.

49. *ZhSGK*, p. 76.

50. *SbPR*, pp. 125-126.

51. Letter from V. P. Butkov, executive secretary of the Secret Committee, to Lanskoi, February 16, 1858, *TsGIAL, f.* 1291, *op.* 1, *d.* 1, *ll.* 123-123*ob.* Butkov sent Lanskoi the text of the directive along with this letter, but the workings of the upper bureaucracy were so formal that this does not mean Lanskoi was not present when the directive was drawn up. However, Lanskoi's subordinates indicate that it was imposed on him by the Secret Committee, and so does Popel'nitskii. See "Zapiski Solov'eva," vol. XXXIII, p. 242; and Popel'nitskii's review of Liashchenko in *Sovremennyi mir*, 1911, no. 4, p. 363.

52. A letter by one Kindiakov reported that the advocates of oligarchic government and landless emancipation were making great strides, and pointed to their power in the Secret Committee as an example: they had compelled Lanskoi to sign the directive of February 17, which (Kindiakov believed) in effect annulled the peasant's right to his household plot. The conspiracy of oligarchs cannot have been so far advanced as Kindiakov optimistically imagined, since one of the supposed conspirators intercepted the letter and, in his capacity as head of the political police, turned it over to the tsar. *TsGAOR, f.* 945 *op.* 1, *d.* 85, *ll.* 20-21.

53. "Zimmerman" to A. V. Surovshchik, June 2, 1858 (in French), *TsGAOR, f.* 109, *op.* 3, *d.* 2018, *l.* 3.

54. V. N. Bochkarev, "Iz istorii pomeshchich'ego khoziaistva v Rossii serediny XIX v.," RANIION, Institut istorii, *Uchenye zapiski*, vol. IV (1929), p. 210. The prophecy of this marshal, M. A. Stakhovich, was perversely fulfilled. Stakhovich, although a collector of folk songs and "a well-known liberal and philanthropist" was not able to keep his lust for serf girls under decent restraint. He was killed by a vengeful overseer a few months later.

Unsigned letter from Orel, November 3, 1858, *TsGAOR, f.* 109, *op.* 3, *d.* 2018, *l.* 12*ob.* See also M. Gorodetskii, "Ubiistvo M. A. Stakhovicha," *Istoricheskii vestnik,* vol. XV, pp. 594-599, and "Postel'naia barshchina prodolzhaetsia," *Kolokol,* no. 38 (March 15, 1859), p. 314.

55. Quoted in Bochkarev, "Iz istorii," p. 207.

56. *TsGIAL, f.* 1291, *op.* 1, *d.* 6, *ll.* 1-2*ob.*

57. Confidential circular of December 10, 1857, in *SbPR,* pp. 122-123.

58. *TsGIAL, f.* 1291, *op.* 1, *d.* 6, *ll.* 4-6*ob.*; "Zapiski Solov'eva," vol. XXX, p. 748.

59. *TsGIAL, f.* 1291, *op.* 1, *d.* 6, *ll.* 7-8*ob*; the resolution and the list of names are reproduced in *ZhMVD, chast'* 29 (1858, *kn.* 3), "Ustroistvo pomeshchich'ikh krest'ian," pp. 51-70.

60. *TsGIAL, f.* 1291, *op.* 1, *d.* 6, *ll.* 54-63.

61. See the derisive summary of the resolution of Volkhov district, quoted in Bochkarev, "Iz istorii," p. 207.

62. E. Markov, "Nikolai Karlovich Ruttsen, † 6-ogo dek. 1880 g.," *RS,* vol. XXXIII (March 1882), p. 609.

63. *TsGIAL, f.* 1291, *op.* 1, *d.* 6, *ll.* 64-65.

64. *ZhSGK,* pp. 116-118. The text of Lanskoi's report to the Secret Committee (*TsGIAL, f.* 1291, *op.* 1, *d.* 6, *l.* 52) confirms, as the journal indicates, that he did not pass along Apraksin's "Supplementary Report."

65. *TsGIAL, f.* 1291, *op.* 1, *d.* 6, *ll.* 76-76*ob.*

66. *ZhSGK,* pp. 108-113; letters to Lanskoi from the governor and provincial marshal of Saratov, *TsGIAL, f.* 1291, *op.* 1, *d.* 8, *ll.* 1-3*ob.*; Krechetovich, *Krest'ianskaia reforma,* especially pp. 7-13 and 70-80.

67. *ZhSGK,* pp. 117-118. In a text of the Tver protocol, as published and corrected by Emmons, the breakdown by districts is somewhat different and Vyshnii Volochek District is not accounted for; *Russian Landed Gentry,* pp. 96-97.

68. This and the other quotations from responses by Riazan pomeshchiki are taken from Povalishin, *Riazanskie pomeshchiki,* pp. 305-309.

69. *ZhSGK,* p. 129.

70. Directive from Lanskoi to the governor of Kazan, January 13, 1858, *TsGIAL, f.* 1291, *op.* 1, *d.* 7, *ll.* 1-1*ob.* This directive was routinely sent to governors and marshals who took literally Lanskoi's instruction not to use "insistence or persuasion"; see "Zapiski Solov'eva," vol. XXX, p. 753, and vol. XXXI, p. 4.

71. Letters to Lanskoi from the marshal (January 20, 1858) and governor (March 17) in Kazan and Lanskoi's reply to the former (February 5), *TsGIAL, f.* 1291, *op.* 1, *d.* 7, *ll.* 4-5*ob.*, 9.

72. Levshin, "Zapiska," pp. 548-549.

73. Of the Kostroma serfs, 87.5 percent were on obrok, the highest proportion of any province; as of 1859, 62.3 percent of them were mortgaged, which was slightly above the national average. Ignatovich, *Pomeshchich'i krest'iane,* p. 75; Borovoi, *Kredit i banki Rossii,* p. 201.

74. Report of Mironov to Lanskoi (January 25, 1858); undated reply from the ministry with covering letter by Lanskoi; letter from Lanskoi to Mironov (March 4, 1858); *TsGIAL, f.* 1291, *op.* 33, *d.* 1, *ll.* 79-90*ob.*

75. *ZhSGK,* pp. 126-128.

76. Resolution published as "Proekt kniazia Gagarina," *Kolokol,* no. 35 (February 15, 1859), pp. 285-287; *ZhSGK,* p. 146. See also "Zapiski Solov'eva," vol. XXX, p. 747; vol. XXXI, p. 7; and Governor Sinel'nikov's report to Lanskoi of February 21, 1859, in P. P. Suvorov, "Dva senatora," *Istoricheskii vestnik,* vol. LXXXIX (1900), p. 626.

77. *Russkii vestnik,* 1858, *tom* III, *kn.* 1, p. 392.

78. "Zapiski Solov'eva," vol. XXXI, pp. 23-24.

79. Letters to Lanskoi from the Penza Marshal Arapov (December 18, 1857) and Governor Panchulidzev (January 2, 1858) with a note in an unknown hand on the latter; Lanskoi's replies to them (both January 7); Panchulidzev's letters to Lanskoi (January 11 and February 15); and Arapov's letter to Lanskoi with Popov's petition; *TsGIAL, f.* 1291, *op.* 1, *d.* 5, *ll.* 1-13, 22-26*ob.* See also "Zapiski Solov'eva," vol. XXXI, p. 4. When the Penza Provincial Committee convened and voted a ritual renunciation of serfdom "in accord with its [the nobility's] desire," Arapov protested, arguing "the nobility did not desire it in the least, but is acting according to order." N. V. Zagoskin to V. V. Saburov, November 22, 1858, *TsGAOR, f.* 109, *op.* 3, *d.* 2020, *l.* 13*ob.*

80. "Postanovlenie sobraniia dvorian Poltavskogo u. . . ." (January 21, 1858) and "Donosenie poltavskogo gubernatora . . ." (February 19, 1858), in Baraboi, *Otmena,* pp. 98-101.

81. Liashchenko, *Poslednii sekretnyi komitet,* p. 14; *Ivan Sergeevich Aksakov v ego pis'makh,* vol. III, p. 249, and appendix, p. 40; "Na zare," vol. XCII, pp. 27-38; Pozen, *Bumagi,* p. 40.

82. Pozen, *Bumagi,* p. 192.

83. "Donosenie poltavskogo gubernatora . . . ," Baraboi, *Otmena,* p. 101.

84. "Predstavlenie ministra vnutrennikh del . . ." (April 2, 1858), in Baraboi, *Otmena,* pp. 109-112; *ZhSGK,* p. 96, and Circular of March 20, 1858, in *SbPR,* p. 130. The Main Committee's journal on the petition from Poltava is not given in *ZhSGK.* However, the committee's disposition of a similar plea from the adjacent province of Chernigov corresponds to Lanskoi's recommendations for Poltava, Lanskoi having informed the committee that "local circumstances" in the two provinces were identical. See *ZhSGK,* pp. 157-158 and Baraboi, *Otmena,* pp. 113-115. Subsequently, the Editorial Commission would invoke the Main Committee's ruling that a survey should not delay the allotting of land to justify the principle that peasants must be granted their existing allotments; *MRK,* II, DKhO no. 6, p. 17.

85. V. N. Murav'ev to Lanskoi, February 11 and 15, 1858, quoted in Deich, *Krest'ianstvo Pskovskoi gubernii,* pp. 278-280.

86. Shiriaev, "Iaroslavskii gubernskii komitet," pp. 11-15.

87. "Planter" (*plantator*) was an opprobrious term for a pomeshchik unsympathetic to the reform. Letter of D. I. Gavrilov to Solov'ev, quoted in "Zapiski Solov'eva," vol. XXXI, pp. 8-9; see also vol. XXX, p. 748, and Zaionchkovskii, *Otmena,* p. 88.

88. L. Zagoskin, "Kiubopytnyi statisticheskii fakt," *Zhurnal zemlevladel'tsev,* 1858, no. 11, vol. VII, p. 43.

89. Listed in *ZhMVD, chast'* 28 (1858, *kn.* 2), pp. 105-121.

90. The official positions of the signers were determined from the *Adres-Kalandar, ili Obshchaia rospis' vsekh chinvovnykh osob v gosudarstve; 1857* (St. Petersburg, 1857).

91. The estates in Moscow Province with a hundred or more serfs are listed in MRK, *Svedeniia*, vol. II. For three districts, only the last name of the owner is given, and initials are also missing from some names on the list cited in note 89; consequently, the results of a comparison must be approximate.

92. See, for example, "Pis'mo Kazanskogo gubernatora P. Kozlialinova . . . S. S. Lanskomu," April 22, 1861, in E. Chernyshev, ed., "Materialy po istorii klassovoi bor'by v 60-kh godakh XIX veka," *Izvestiia Obshchestva arkheologii, istorii i etnografii* (Kazan), vol. XXXII, fasc. 4 (1927), p. 79.

93. Levshin, "Zapiska," p. 537; "Zapiski Solov'eva," vol. XXXI, p. 17.

94. "Na zare," vol. XCIII, p. 80; D. [I.] Nikiforov, *Moskva v tsarstvovanie Imperatora Aleksandra II* (Moscow, 1904), p. 79. See also Berg's letters from Tambov in Barsukov, *Zhizn' Pogodina*, vol. XVI, pp. 36-55.

95. M. E. Saltykov-Shchedrin, "Soglashenie," *Sobranie sochinenii v dvadtsati tomakh*, vol. III, pp. 324-325, 328; suspension marks in the original.

96. G. P. Galagan, who was later to serve on the Editorial Commission, wrote from Kiev to Iurii Samarin, "There are people among us, and perhaps more of them than there are thought to be, who are ready for this noble cause, but cannot bring themselves to make a beginning, neither in practice nor even on paper." "Na zare," vol. XCIII, p. 77.

97. A. V. Nikitenko, *Dnevnik*, vol. II (Leningrad, 1955), p. 8. *"Barstvo"* is formed from the word *barin*, or "squire."

98. Diary entry for February 26, 1858, S. P. Trubetskoi, *Zapiski* (St. Petersburg, 1906), pp. 104-105. According to Trubetskoi, the nobles of Kiev Province assented to the reform because of direct pressure from the tsar himself upon the provincial marshal.

99. Iakushkin, Velik bog russkoi zemli," p. 120.

100. Quoted in N. G. Sladkevich, *Ocherki istorii obshchestvennoi mysli Rossii v kontse 50-kh—nachale 60-kh godov XIX veka* (Leningrad, 1962), pp. 90-91.

101. Koval'chenko, *Krest'iane i krepostnoe khoziaistvo Riazanskoi i Tambovskoi gubernii*, p. 189; Snezhnevskii, "Krepostnye krest'iane," p. 70; *ZhSGK*, pp. 141-143.

102. *Dnevnik kniazia A. S. Men'shikova, 1858-65 gg.* (a copy), entry for January 1, 1858, *TsGAOR*, f. 728, *op.* 1, *d.* 2538a, *l.* 2.

103. "Otzyv kniazia Men'shikova," *Kolokol*, no. 27 (November 1, 1858), pp. 223-224; a contemporary ms. copy is in the Orlov-Davydov archive, *ORGBL*, f. 219, *karton* 81, *d.* 8; see also *ZhSGK*, p. 132. The epigram is from a letter from Menshikov's nemesis A. V. Golovnin to D. A. Miliutin, quoted in M. Liadov," Arkhiv D. A. Miliutina i krest'ianskaia reforma," *ZOR*, X, p. 92.

104. Also, in 1855-1861 Menshikov was much preoccupied with answering the critics of his performance as commander in the Crimea; A. A. Panaev, "Kniaz' A. S. Menshikov v rasskazakh byvshego ego ad-"iutanta . . . ," *RS*, vol. XIX (1877), p. 640.

105. *Dnevnik Menshikova*, January 4 to March 29, 1858, especially *ll*. 9*ob*., 7, 5, 30*ob*., 12*ob*., and 2*ob*.

106. A. A. Zakrevskii to V. A. Dolgorukov, November 8, 1858; "K vam vyzyvaem my, dvorianstvo russkoe, i v glave ego Moskovskoe" (two copies); comments by Dolgorukov; exchange of letters between Dolgorukov and Lieutenant General Perfilev, November 8 and December 3, 1858; *TsGAOR, f.* 109, 1-*aia eks.*, 1858 *g., d.* 372, *ll.* 1-5, 10-11*ob*; Druzhinin, "Moskva i reforma," p. 46.

4. The Evolution of Policy

1. "Zapiski Solov'eva," vol. XXX, p. 754.

2. *Dnevnik Menshikova, l.* 3.

3. See correspondence cited in notes 43 and 44, chap. 3.

4. For the original ruling, see *ZhSGK*, p. 55; for Lanskoi's reinterpretation, Baraboi, *Otmena*, p. 111. Solov'ev complained that most participants were "backward petty nobles, extremely hostile to the peasant cause," but conceded that the conferences were not much more than drinking parties at the district marshal's house. "Zapiski Solov'eva," vol. XXXI, pp. 11 and 26.

5. Iu. F. Samarin, "Zamechaniia na 'Proekt plana rabot, predstoiashchikh dvorianskim gubernskim komitetam po ustroistvu krest'ianskogo byta,'" *Sochineniia*, vol. III (Moscow, 1878), pp. 56-71. The quotation is from an undated covering letter to Levshin, p. 57n. The text of Solov'ev's program is given here, pp. 58n-71n. For his comments, see "Zapiski Solov'eva," vol. XXXIII, pp. 247-249.

6. In the event, he complained that it was vague and contradictory; M. A. Miliutina, "Iz zapisok Marii Aggeevny Miliutinoi," *RS*, vol. XCVII (February 1899), p. 283.

7. "Programma zaniatii Gubernskikh Dvorianskikh Komitetov ob Uluchshenii byta pomeshchich'ikh krest'ian," *SbPR*, pp. 137-149. Passages quoted from pp. 141, 142, and 144-145. Signed by the Main Committee and "compiled at H.I.M.'s order."

8. Thus A. P. Platonov, an exponent of the sanctity of private property and the personal freedom of the peasantry—in short, of landless emancipation—found the April Program restrictive, and so did P. V. Dolgorukov, who favored a comprehensive scheme of reform. *TsGIAL, f.* 1291, *op.* 1., *d.* 1, *ll.* 146-146*ob*.; D. Field, "P. V. Dolgorukov's Emigration from Russia," *Slavonic Review*, XLVIII, no. 111 (1970), pp. 262-263.

9. Emmons also emphasizes that a provincial committee's deliberations during the first of the three periods were to cover only a transition stage, and concludes, "The primary purpose of the [April] program was to restrict severely the field of initiative open to the provincial committees." *Russian Landed Gentry*, p. 67.

10. See "Zapiski Solov'eva," vol. XXXIII, p. 251, and Ia. A. Rostovtsev, "Dva dokumenta iz bumag . . . ," ed. F. P. Elenev, *RA*, 1873, no. 1, pp. 502-503.

11. Compare "Zapiski Solov'eva," vol. XXXIII, pp. 251-256, and *SbPR*, pp. 126-127.

12. Compare his early outline of the program and his letter to Rostovtsev of October 3, 1858, with his retrospective remarks; Pozen, *Bumagi*, pp. 52-53, 98, 56-58. See also his remarks about the nobility on pp. 60-61 and 70; however, like Levshin, Pozen thought the regime must not offend the nobles, who, "for the time being, constitute the most effective instruments of governmental power" (p. 68).

13. *ZhSGK*, pp. 80-83, 87-90, 116, 118-120, 180-183, 277-281. The corresponding instructions to local officials can be found under the appropriate dates in *SbPR*. The actual force of these rulings is suggested by the absence of any reference to them in the 83 documents on serf discontent in 1858-1860 published by Okun' and Sivkov. A particular effort was made to prevent the manumission of individual serfs without land and without their consent. The officials responsible for registering documents of manumission were instructed to make sure of the serf's consent; in April, 1858, 3,246 such documents were accepted, and 85 rejected because of lack of consent.

14. *SbPR*, pp. 27-29; *ZhSGK*, pp. 197-199.

15. "Na zare," vol. XCIV, pp. 50-51.

16. A. M. Skabichevskii, *Ocherki istorii russkoi tsenzury (1700-1865 g.)*, St. Petersburg, 1892), p. 389.

17. Ruud, "Censorship and the Peasant Question," p. 167; N. Engel'gardt, "Tsenzura v epokhu velikikh reform," *Istoricheskii vestnik*, vol. XC, p. 141. The best study of this matter is now Iu. I. Gerasimova, "Otnoshenie pravitel'stva k uchastiiu pechati v obsuzhdenii krest'ianskogo voprosa . . . ," *Rev. sit.* [VI], pp. 81-105.

18. For example, Ivaniukov, *Padenia krepostnogo prava*, especially chap. IV; G. Dzhanshiev, *Epokha velikikh reform*, 7th ed. (Moscow, 1898).

19. Hence Nechkina's unconvincing attack on Zaionchkovskii for neglecting the role of the "revolutionary democrats," in "Reforma 1861 goda kak pobochnyi produkt revoliutsionnoi bor'by," *Rev. sit.* [II], pp. 13-14.

20. See, for example, M. N. Katkov's letter to Rostovtsev of March 21, 1859, *RS*, vol. LXI (January 1889), pp. 191-93; N. A. Dobroliubov, "Literaturnye melochi proshlogo goda," *Sobranie sochinenii*, 9 vols. (Moscow-Leningrad, 1961-1964), vol. IV, p. 88; and Koshelev's plaint quoted in Skabichevskii, *Ocherki*, p. 425.

21. For two examples, see M. K. Lemke, *Ocherki po istorii russkoi tsenzury i zhurnalistiki XIX stoletiia* (St. Petersburg, 1904), pp. 316-317.

22. Nikitenko, *Dnevnik*, vol. II, p. 71.

23. *ZhSGK*, pp. 57-62; Levshin, "Zapiska," p. 539. Subsequently, however, Lanskoi did move to give the press considerable latitude in discussing the reform, but was overruled by the Main Committee; Gerasimova," Otnoshenie pravitel'stva," pp. 91, 94.

24. Texts of the circulars of April 15 and 22 from *Kolokol*, no. 20 (August 1, 1858), pp. 162-163. On the Main Committee's responsibility for these circulars and the Kavelin affair, see also "Zapiski Solov'eva," vol. XXXIV, p. 126; Levshin, "Zapiska," pp. 540-543; Nikitenko, *Dnevnik*, vol. II, pp. 19-20. The precensorship of Chernyshevskii's text is detailed in his *Polnoe sobranie sochinenii*, 15 vols. (Moscow, 1939-1953), vol. V, pp. 65-136.

25. "Na zare," vol. XCIII, pp. 486-490.

26. D. N. Shidlovskii (later celebrated as deputy from the Simbirsk Provincial Committee), "Zapiska . . . ministru vnutrennikh del S. S. Lanskomu," July 5, 1858, in N. K. Piksanov and O. V. Tsekhnovitser, eds., *Shestidesiatye gody* (Moscow-Leningrad, 1940), pp. 383-385; Okun' and Sivkov, *Krest'ianskoe dvizhenie*, pp. 156-157; Iakushkin, "Velik bog." pp. 122-123.

27. Levshin, "Zapiska," p. 542.

28. Letter of April 19, 1858, quoted in Liadov, "Arkhiv D. A. Miliutina," *ZOR*, X, p. 91.

29. *Materialy Cherkasskogo*, vol. I, p. 104; Nikitenko, *Dnevnik*, vol. II, p. 20; Levshin, "Zapiska," pp. 542-543; K. N. Lebedev, "Iz zapisok," *RA*, 1893, no. 4, pp. 373-374; Pozen to Rostovtsev, May 9, 1858, in Pozen, *Bumagi*, pp. 62-63.

30. *ZhSGK*, p. 66.

31. Neither session is registered in *ZhSGK*, Bezobrazov's *Ob usovershenii* was discussed at a session on April 21, 1858; *TsGIAL, f.* 1291, *op.* 1, *d.* 4, *ll.* 89-90; on the discussion of the "Zapiska pod lit. A", see "Zapiski Solov'eva," vol. XXXIV, pp. 389-99, and *Otchet Zemskogo otdela MVD za 1858 g.*, *TsGIAL, f.* 1291, *op.* 123. *d.* 21, *ll.* 34-36.

32. "Zapiski Solov'eva," vol. XXXVI, pp. 134 and 139; F. P. Elenev, "Pervye shagi osvobozhdeniia krest'ian," *RA*, 1886, no. 7, p. 385. The accusations, like many others in memoirs of the period, may be derived from Khrushchov's *Materialy* rather than from the writer's memory; see *Materialy*, vol. I, pp. 361-365. A functionary of the MIA who was conversant with the Main Committee at this time classified only two of its members (Konstantin Nikolaevich and Chevkin) as unequivocally in favor of emancipation, and listed Butkov and Murav'ev among the waverers; A. Popel'nitskii, ed., "Fed. Lavr. Barykov o chlenakh Glavnogo komiteta po krest'ianskomy delu," *GM*, 1916, no. 11, p. 208.

33. Circular of August 29, 1858, *SbPR*, pp. 173-174; see also Lanskoi's retrospective explanation in N. Semenov, *Osvobozhdenie*, vol. I, appendix, p. 828. Menshikov, at any rate, derived no encouragement from his meetings with Butkov and Murav'ev in June of 1858; Butkov, he found, "does not understand what it means to disrupt the provincial administration and the enjoyment of property." *Dnevnik Menshikova*, June 18, 21, and 25, *ll.* 19ob-20.

34. Levshin, "Zapiska," pp. 546-551; on Levshin's visit to Tula see I. Iashunskii, "Iz perepiski N. A. Elagina," *ZOR*, X, p. 66, and *Materialy Cherkasskogo*, bk. 1, p. 172.

35. M. A. Miliutina, "Iz zapisok," vol. XCVII, p. 281; "Zapiski Solov'eva," vol. XXXIII, p. 594; Starr, *Decentralization and Self-Government*, pp. 145-149.

36. Rieber remarks on Alexander's habit of "unconsciously exploiting rather than reconciling the conflicting interests within the government and throughout the country. . . . Where he felt himself uncertain, he . . . waited to be convinced by the strongest or most clever" of his ministers." Alexander II: A Revisionist View," p. 44.

37. Letter from D. N. Shidlovskii in Simbirsk to M. N. Shidlovskii in St. Petersburg, July 8, 1858, *TsGAOR, f.* 109, *op.* 3, *d.* 2029, *ll.* 1ob.-2.

38. Undated letter (1858), quoted in Miliutina, "Iz zapisok," vol. XCVII, p. 271.

39. Kavelin to Herzen, letter of early 1858, ed. N. N. Zakhar'in, *Literaturnoe nasledstvo*, vol. 62 (1955), p. 386; P. P. Semenov-Tian-Shanskii, *Epokha osvobozhdeniia krest'ian v Rossii (1857-1861 gg.)*, vol. I (St. Petersburg, 1911), pp. 65-66; Kavelin to M. I. Semevskii in 1885, published in *RS*, vol. XLIX (January 1886), p. 132. Semenov-Tian-Shanskii's memoirs will be cited hereinafter as P. Semenov, *Epokha*.

40. *Dnevnik Menshikova*, February 7, 1858, *l.* 7; Miliutina, "Iz zapisok," vol. XCVII, p. 51.

41. See Miliutina, "Iz zapisok," vol. XCVII, pp. 59-63, and Alexander's marginal notation on [Artsimovich's] memorandum, pp. 280-281.

42. Alexander to Bariatinskii, July 7, 1858, in Rieber, *Politics of Autocracy*, pp. 120-121; Elenev, "Pervye shagi," p. 379; see also Alexander's remark to Kiselev, quoted in Zaionchkovskii, *Otmena*, p. 76.

43. Texts of the speeches of August 11, 16, and 19 in Tatishchev, *Imperator Aleksandr II*, vol. I, pp. 335-337; I. A. Nikotin, "Iz zapisok," *RS*, vol. CIX (February 1902), p. 361.

44. Druzhinin, "Moskva i reforma 1861 g.," pp. 39-41 and 44-45.

45. "Zapiski Solov'eva," vol. XXXIV, p. 420; report of the chief of the second *okrug*, Corps of Gendarmes, September 2, 1858, TsGAOR, f. 109, 1-aia eksp., 1858 g., d. 372, ll. 8-9; and Druzhinin, "Moskva i reforma 1861 g.," p. 45. The tsar's speech at Moscow is also discussed on pp. 200 and 206 above.

46. A. M., V. M., and A. M. Zhemchuzhnikov and A. K. Tolstoi, "Proekt: O vvedenii edinomysliia v Rossii" (dated 1859), in *Sochineniia Koz'my Prutkova* (Moscow, 1965), pp. 163-164. Suspension marks in original. Prutkov would resolve the dilemma of the dutiful subject by having the government publish a periodical "which would give guidance and direction on all subjects." Many high officials expressed identical views and proposals at this time, as can be seen from I. V. Porokh, "Iz istorii bor'by tsarizma protiv Gertsena (Popytka sozdaniia anti-'Kolokola' v 1857-59 gg.," *Iz istorii obshchestvennoi mysli i obshchestvennogo dvizheniia v Rossii* (Saratov, 1964), pp. 119-146.

47. *SbPR*, pp. 30-35.

48. The injunctions to the ministry were complemented by the Imperial Order of October 19, 1858, which held that any matter relating to serfdom or its reform was to be turned over to the Main Committee, *SbPR*, p. 30.

49. In a subsequent session, the Main Committee decided that the appeal to honor was a mistake. The allusion might suggest that the government was skeptical about the nobility's honesty, while on the other hand it might embarrass and confine the government if the nobility did prove dishonest. Accordingly, the committee directed Lanskoi to solicit information on amelioration without any mention of honor. *ZhSGK*, p. 291.

50. See, for example, P. Semenov, *Epokha*, vol. I, p. 72; Rostovtsev still assumed that each province would have a separate statute when he wrote the letters to Alexander on which the Imperial Order is based; see "Izvlechenie iz vsepodanneishikh pisem general-ad"iutanta Rostovtseva," in *MRK*, I, appendix to ZhOP no. 2, p. 8.

51. Rostovtsev, "Izvlechenie," p. 2.

52. For a striking example, see *ZhSGK*, pp. 108-112.

53. Rostovtsev explains his tactics in an undated letter to the tsar, published as an appendix to Elenev, "Pervye shagi," pp. 400-401.

54. Compare the point of departure, the "Izvlechenie" cited above, with the agenda Rostovtsev drew up ("Voprosy po krest'ianskomu delu," Elenev, pp. 399-400) and the text of the Imperial Order of December 4, 1858, *SbPR*, pp. 36-39.

55. "Pamiatnaia zapiska Ia. I. Rostovtseva 24 noiabria 1858 g.," Elenev, "Pervye shagi," pp. 398-399. This is one of the very few surviving records of a debate within the Main Committee.

56. Ia. I. Rostovtsev, "O proekte Polozheniia Komiteta Simbirskoi gubernii," *MRK*, I, appendix to ZhOP no. 2, p. 48.

57. Rostovtsev represented the passage of authority as a direct substitution. "Now, at the present moment, the communal system is necessary for Russia; the common people still need a strong authority, which would replace the authority of the pomeshchik." "Izvlechenie," p. 23.

58. Orlov to Alexander, November 1, 1858, *TsGIAL, f.* 1180, *op.* XV, *d.* 31, *l.* 109ob.

59. Kornilov ("Gubernskie komitety," p. 285) remarks that the Imperial Order of December 4 was not communicated to the provincial committees and cites this consideration as one reason for the committees' tendency to retain manorial authority.

60. The formation of the Editorial Commission was made public in an ukaz of March 30, 1859, after it had already begun to work. The ukaz provided for two commissions, one on general matters, the other on local; while this division was never put into effect, the commission was formally styled the "Editorial Commissions."

61. "Zapiski Solov'eva," vol. XXXVII, pp. 260-265 and 607-610; *SbPR*, pp. 41-44; the Journal of February 4, 1859, is not given in *ZhSGK*; N. Semenov, *Osvobozhdenie*, I, pp. 14 and 48-49; P. Semenov, *Epokha*, vol. I, pp. 122-126.

62. Letter of April 13, 1884, quoted in part by Zaionchkovskii, *Otmena*, p. 110; see also "Iz pisem K. D. Kavelina k grafu D. A. Miliutinu, 1882-1884 gg.," *Vestnik Evropy*, 1909, no. 1, p. 26.

63. In *Kolokol* for 1858, see especially pp. 157, 161, and 201; on misinformation about Rostovtsev supplied by Herzen's correspondents in Russia, see Lemke's edition of Herzen's works, vol. IX, pp. 284-285.

64. V. Bogucharskii [V. Ia. Iakovlev], "Iakov Ivanovich Rostovtsev," *Velikaia reforma*, vol. V, pp. 62-67. See also Ivaniukov, *Padenia krepostnogo prava*, p. 43.

65. Unkovskii, "Zapiska," pp. 98-99; S. V. Bakhrushin, "Velikaia kniagina Elena Pavlovna," *Osvobozhdenie krest'ian: deiateli reformy* (Moscow, 1911), pp. 146-147; "Zapiski Solov'eva," vol. XXXVII, pp. 265-269 is an intelligent discussion of Rostovtsev's "conversion."

66. The claims of Miliutin, Solov'ev, and Petr Semenov are advanced, respectively, in Miliutina, "Iz zapisok," *RS*, vol. XCVII, pp. 575-576; "Zapiski Solov'eva," vol. XXXVII, pp. 279-281; P. Semenov, *Epokha*, vol. I, pp. 69-70 and 120.

67. Emmons rightly emphasizes the extent of the accord among "enlightened citizens", but exaggerates their numbers; *Russian Landed Gentry*, pp. 39-46 and passim. For a wooden discussion that does bring out the relationship among diverse reform-minded Russians, see V. N. Rozental', "Ideinye tsentry liberal'nogo dvizheniia v Rossii . . . ," *Rev. Sit.* [3] pp. 372-398. See also P. Semenov, *Epokha*, vol. I, chap. I, and W. B. Lincoln, "The Circle of the Grand Duchess Yelena Pavlovna, 1847-61," *Slavonic Review*, XLVIII, no. 112 (1970), pp. 373-388.

68. P. Semenov, *Epokha*, vol. I, p. 418-439.

69. Alexander was prone to make these remarks on letters intercepted by the Third Section and presented for his information; they are now preserved in *TsGAOR, f.* 109.

70. Alexander to Bariatinskii, November 2, 1857, Rieber, *Politics of Autocracy*, p. 109.

71. Levshin, "Zapiska," p. 549.

72. A. F. Tiutcheva, *Pri dvore dvukh imperatorov* [vol. II] (Moscow, 1929), pp. 173, 175. It was also at this time that Alexander banned the word "progress" from government documents; A. Popel'nitskii, " 'Progress'—slovo zapreshcheno," *GM*; 1916, no. 11, p. 207.

73. Rieber, *Politics of Autocracy*, pp. 128, 136.

74. Menshikov, who thought well of Rostovtsev until his conversion, complained that the tsar dismissed all criticism of Rostovtsev as intrigue. *Dnevnik Menshikova*, l. 77.

75. The following discussion of Rostovtsev's views is based primarily on the "Izvlechenie" and "Khod i iskhod krest'ianskogo voprosa" (February 14, 1859, with supplement dated April 8), *MRK*, I, appendix to ZhOP, no. 2, pp. 54-62.

76. Rostovtsev, "O proekte . . . Simbirskoi gubernii," *MRK*, I, supplement to ZhOP no. 2, p. 47.

77. As is clear from his correspondence with Obolenskii, notably his letter of November 18, 1858, where he claimed: "Of course, the Main Committee will make use of *all* of Herzen's practical suggestions." Ia. I. Rostovtsev, "Dva dokumenta iz bumag. . .," ed. F. P. Elenev, *RA*, 1873, no. 1, p. 504. See also L. B. Dobrinskaia, "Dekabrist Evgenii Obolenskii posle Sibirskoi ssylki," *Osvoboditel' noe dvizhenie v Rossii*, fasc. 2 (Saratov, 1971), p. 42.

78. See "Zapiski Solov'eva," vol. XXXVII, pp. 279-281 and 587; Kavelin, "Zapiska ob osvobozhdenii krest'ian v Rossii," *Sobranie sochinenii*, vol. II, p. 83; P. Semenov, *Epokha*, vol. I, pp. 121-122; and Kavelin, "Mnenie o luchshom sposobe razrabotki voprosa ob osvobozhdenii krest'ian," *Sobraine sochinenii*, vol. II, pp. 103-106; see also note 61 to this chapter.

79. "Zapiski Solov'eva," vol. XXXIII, pp. 566-596, and vol. XLI, pp. 599-605.

80. See his letter to Iurii Samarin of March 9, 1859, "Tri pis'ma N. A. Miliutina," *RS*, vol. XXVII (1880), p. 388.

81. Rostovtsev, "Izvlechenie," p. 17.

82. Rostovtsev to E. P. Obolenskii, January 25, 1859, "K istorii osvobozhdeniia krest'ian," *RS*, vol. CIV (1900), p. 372; "Izvlechenie," p. 7.

83. Letter of February 24, 1859, *RS*, vol. CIV (1900), p. 373.

84. "Zapiski Solov'eva," vol. XXXVII, pp. 587, 263. It is not clear

whether Solov'ev's complaint is retrospective or a paraphrase of the memorandum he is summarizing.

85. "O proekte . . . Simbirskoi gubernii," pp. 44, 48, 50. Rostovtsev's criticisms of the St. Petersburg draft and of the Simbirsk minority drafts are also to be found in the supplement to ZhOP no. 2 in *MRK*, I. See also P. Semenov, *Epokha*, vol. I, p. 118.

5. The Provincial Committees

1. Emmons chooses to treat the provincial committees by focusing "primary attention on the fortunes of the liberal reform program" and offers five persuasive reasons for his choice, in *Russian Landed Gentry*, pp. 71-72. Even though Emmons is alert to the discords and divisions among the advocates of that program, his approach does seem to exaggerate the support the program enjoyed among the provincial nobility—just as this chapter (which deals with some of the same committees) may seem to exaggerate the conflict between the nobility and the administration.

2. Ulashchik, "Podgotovka krest'ianskoi reformy," p. 69. For M. A. Bezobrasov's obscure and unsupported charge of interference in the elections in Great Russia, see *Materialy*, vol. II, p. 97, and compare Kornilov, "Gubernskie komitety," p. 203.

3. These remarks about rank and office-holding are based on the membership lists of the provincial committees in N. Semenov, *Osvobozhdenie*, I, appendix 2. For six sample committees, only eighteen of the 142 elected members stood in the first five grades of the Table of Ranks; for the two committees (Orel and Nizhnii Novgorod) checked against the *Adres kalendar'* for 1857, only three members were on active service; of these one resigned from the committee while another presumably resigned his post in Orenburg prior to his election. Studies of four separate committees show that most members were middling pomeshchiki, holding at least 100 and never more than 800 souls; see Emmons, *Russian Landed Gentry*, pp. 148-149; E. I. Chernyshev, "Krest'ianskaia reforma v Kazanskoi gubernii," *Materialy po istorii Tatarii*, fasc. 1 (Kazan', 1948), pp. 378-379; N. Tikhonov, "K kharakteristike dvorianskoi ideologii nakanune padeniia krepostnogo stroia (Iz istorii Khar'kovskogo Gubernskogo Komiteta)," *Naukovi zapiski ukrains'koi kul'turi*, no. 6 (1926), p. 239; and A. E. Kil'miashkin, "Podgotovka krest'ianskoi reformy v gubernskikh komitetakh (Penzenskoi, Simbirskoi, Tambovskoi gubernii)," *Issledovaniia po istorii Mordovskoi ASSR* (Nauchno-issledovatel'skii institut iazyka, literatury, istorii i ekonomiki pri Sovete ministrov Mordovskoi ASSR, *Trudy*, fasc. 40) (Saransk, 1971), pp. 187-188.

4. Pozen's retrospective account (*Bugami*, especially p. 192) is confirmed by his letters at the time and those of other members of the Poltava Provincial Committee in *TsGAOR, f. 109, op. 3, d. 2023, ll. 5-9 ob.*, 13-15.

5. "Zapiski Solov'eva," vol. XXXVI, pp. 131-132.

6. Quoted in A. A. Kornilov, "Krest'ianskaia reforma v Kaluzhskoi gubernii pri V. A. Artsimoviche," *Viktor Antonovich Artsimovich. Vospominaniia—kharakteristiki* (St. Petersburg, 1904), pp. 170-171; the MIA may,

as Kornilov states (p. 169) have forbidden the *Kaluzhskie gubernskie vedomosti* to print the speech, but it did publish the speech in its own journal. See *ZhMVD, chast'* 34 (1859), *chast' ofitsial'naia*, pp. 109-111.

7. Speech of July 23, 1858, and *mnenie* of March 11, 1859, by V. O. Podvysotskii (subsequently a deputy in the first convocation), "Izvlecheniia iz zhurnalov Chernigovskogo Dvorianskogo Gubernskogo Komiteta . . . ," *Trudy Chernigovskoi arkhivnoi komissii*, fasc. 9 (1912), pp. 389, 121.

8. N. A. Solov'ev in a letter to his brother Ia. A., "Zapiski Solov'eva," vol. XXXVI, pp. 146.

9. Rostovtsev, "K istorii osvobozhdeniia krest'ian," p. 368.

10. Kornilov, "Kaluzhskaia gubernia," pp. 242-243. Dzhanshiev emphasizes that Unkovskii always spoke in terms of "advantage," not sacrifice, and compares him to Chernyshevskii's utilitarian hero Lopukhov; Dzhanshiev, *A. M. Unkovskii*, p. 87.

11. K. A. Roshchakhovskii, "Memuary . . . vremini osvobozhdeniia krest'ian," *Kievskaia starina*, 1887, no. 6/7, pp. 411, 414.

12. Quoted in *Materialy Cherkasskogo*, bk. 1, p. 297n. Compare *ZhSGK*, p. 429.

13. Field, "P. V. Dolgorukov's Emigration from Russia," pp. 262-263.

14. A. P. Elagina to O. F. Kosheleva, August 11, 1858, and F. P. Svechin [member of the Tula Committee] to E. P. Gorchakov, December 12, 1858, *TsGAOR, f.* 109, *op.* 3, *d.* 2037, *ll.* 5 and 34.

15. Directive of March 20, 1858, *SbPR*, p. 129. However, the MIA did yield to a request from one district of Smolensk Province that all nobles have an equal vote; *TsGIAL, f.* 1291, *op.* 1, *d.* 2, *ll.* 51-53.

16. Unkovskii, "Zapiski," p. 195.

17. Governor-General Ignat'ev simply forwarded the reports submitted to him by the St. Petersburg Provincial Marshal, P. P. Shuvalov, *TsGIAL, f.* 1291, *op.* 1., *d.* 1, *ll.* 147 ff. The governors' reports are preserved in *TsGIAL, f.* 1180, *op.* XV, *dd.* 150-157.

18. Circular of the MIA, December 29, 1858, *SbPR*, pp. 191-192. See "Zapiski Solov'eva," vol. XXXVI, p. 146.

19. "Predstavlenie MVD," January 10, 1859, and Lanskoi to A. N. Murav'ev, October 17, 1858, *TsGIAL, f.* 1291, *op.* 123, *d.* 4, *ll.* 14-15 and 2.

20. The Main Committee justified the formula that was adopted on the ground that the tsar's original order had provided for only two deputies per committee; *ZhSGK*, pp. 414-415 and circular of the MIA, May 9, 1859, *SbPR*, p. 217. Rostovtsev proposed that a minority should elect one of a committee's two deputies, but later believed that each minority had been instructed to send a deputy in addition to the majority deputies; Ia. A. Rostovtsev, "O proekte Polozheniia men'shinstva Komiteta Simbirskoi gubernii," MRK, I, supplement to ZhOP no. 2, p. 53; Rostovtsev to Lanskoi, April 17, 1859, *TsGIAL, f.* 1180, *op.* XV, *d.* 113, *ll.* 1-1ob.

21. Kornilov, "Kaluzhskaia guberniia," p. 237; "Dnevnik Menshikova," *l.* 36; A. I. Pokorskii-Zhoravko, "Pis'ma . . . k zhene . . . ," *Trudy Chernigovskoi uchenoi arkhivnoi komissii*, fasc. 11 (1915), p. 84.

22. "Zapiski Solov'eva," vol. XXXVII, pp. 602-603; compare P. Semenov, *Epokha*, vol. I, p. 122.

23. Directive of the MIA, October 20, 1858, and Imperial Order of February 22, 1859, *SbPR*, pp. 101, 45. "Zapiski Solov'eva," vol. XXXVI, pp. 226-227. A. N. Karamzin detected a dramatic reversal in the Nizhnii Novgorod Committee when secret balloting was temporarily introduced; *TsGAOR, f.* 109, *op.* 3, *d.* 2016, *l.* 4.

24. Kornilov, "Kaluzhskaia guberniia," pp. 217, 222-223; the Kaluga Committee complained that the imposition of secrecy was a "sign of complete mistrust for itself and for the whole noble estate."

25. The gradation system is perhaps the only element of the statutes of 1861 that can definitely be attributed to a single man, M. E. Vorob'ev of the Tver Committee. See Emmons, *Russian Landed Gentry*, pp. 133-134 and, on the circulation of the Tver Committee's journal, *Materialy Cherkasskogo*, bk. 1, p. 177, and Dzhanshiev, *A. M. Unkovskii*, pp. 117-118.

26. *ZhSGK*, pp. 352, 362-363. On A. P. Platonov's use of the facilities of the St. Petersburg Provincial Committee to circulate an article by M. A. Bezobrazov, see *TsGIAL, f.* 1291, *op.* 1, *d.* 1, *l.* 227; *f.* 1092, *op.* 1, *d.* 178, *ll.* 9-11 *ob.*; text in *TsGAOR, f.* 728, *op.* 1, *d.* 2574.

27. Unkovskii had previously sought this permission on other grounds and had even arranged to publish the resolutions of the Tver Provincial Committee in *Russkii vestnik;* the Main Committee was probably correct in suspecting that he wanted to circulate his views on administrative and judicial reform and other subjects which "certainly were not submitted to the [Tver] Committee for discussion." *ZhSGK*, pp. 420-421; V. Pokrovskii, *Istoriko-statisticheskoe opisanie Tverskoi gubernii* (Tver, 1879), part one, p. 234.

28. *ZhSGK*, pp. 402-403, 424.

29. Sixteen provincial committees divided into factions, each of which produced its own draft statute. On eight of these committees the two government members signed a minority draft and on one they both joined the majority; on the other eight they were divided. Membership in factions is indicated, with some inaccuracy, in A. I. Skrebitskii, *Krest'ianskoe delo v tsarstvovanie Imperatora Aleksandra II . . .*, 4 vols. in 5 (Bonn/R, 1862-1868), vol. I, pp. 886-908.

30. V. K. Rzhevskii to I. S. Turgenev, November 16, 1858, in M. P. Alekseev, et al., eds. *Turgenevskii sbornik*, vol. IV (Moscow, 1968), pp. 232-233.

31. N. P. Danilov to Lanskoi, May 28, 1858, *TsGIAL, f.* 1291, *op.* 33, *d.* 1, *l.* 579; to A. I. Koshelev, July 17, 1858, *TsGAOR, f.* 109, *op.* 3, *d.* 2018, *ll.* 4-4 *ob.*; to Lanskoi (December 28, 1858), Rostovtsev (January 18, 1858), and Lanskoi (April 18, 1859), *TsGIAL, f.* 1291, *op.* 1, *d.* 6, *ll.* 85-86*ob.*, 89-90*ob.*, and 102-103*ob.*; "Mnenie chlena ot pravitel'stva Danilova o dvukh proektakh polozheniia," p. 1, in *TGK* (Orel).

32. N. P. Danilov, letter to the editor, April 10, 1858, *Sel'skoe blagoustroistvo*, no. 4 (1858), p. 38; see also his *zametki* in section III of *Zhurnal zemlevladel'tsev*, nos. 7-11 (1858).

33. The following discussion is based on their three-cornered correspondence, reproduced in *Materialy Cherkasskogo*, bk. 1, pp. 104-331. Their account of the facts is substantiated by Povalishin and Krechetovich, whose monographs are based on the archives of the Riazan and Samara committees. However, Krutikov in his *Otmena krepostnogo prava v Tul'skoi*

gubernii (Tula, 1956) takes the same view of Cherkasskii as Lev Tolstoi, whom he quotes (p. 54): "Cherkasskii and Co. are the same rubbish as their opponents, only rubbish with a French accent."

34. *Materialy Cherkasskogo*, bk. 1, pp. 210, 249.

35. *"Prisutstvennye mesta"*; speech of November 4, 1858, in *Materialy Cherkasskogo*, bk. 1, appendix 10, pp. 115-117.

36. *Materialy Cherkasskogo*, bk. 1, pp. 184-185.

37. Samarin continued: "Let it be said between ourselves: our losses will be enormous (the majority does not even understand this), but will the people be satisfied with our sacrifices? Will the sacrifices even approach their hopes?" Letter to A. F. Smirnova, in *Materialy Cherkasskogo*, bk. 1, p. 314.

38. At the Tula provincial elections of 1858, a campaign to censure Cherkasskii and petition for his removal was quashed by the governor on the ground that the assembly of the nobility could not discuss the work of the provincial committee. However, six of the twelve districts indicated their support for Cherkasskii before the governor's intervention. *Materialy Cherkasskogo*, bk. 1, pp. 266-271; *ZhSGK*, pp. 357-358.

39. Circulars of the MIA, December 9 and 29, 1858, *SbPR*, pp. 186-187, 190-191. Compare the instructions issued to the appointed members of the General Commissions at Vilna and Kiev, who were avowed functionaries of the MIA, *SbPR*, pp. 103-105.

40. (In fact, there were thirty elected members and two government members on the Chernigov Committee.) Pokorskii-Zhoravko, "Pis'ma," p. 80. Characteristically, Pokorskii-Zhoravko directed his recriminations at the bureaucracy only, proceeding directly from the passage just quoted: *"Nu, bog s nimi.* A just cause remains just. May the lord preserve Russia and our good monarch from all attempts to infringe on peace and the people's happiness."

41. *SbPR*, p. 191.

42. *ZhSGK*, pp. 326-328, 360-361, 399-402; Povalishin, *Riazanskie pomeshchiki*, pp. 314-322. On the removal of other members for various reasons, see *ZhSGK*, pp. 365, 463-465; "Zapiski Solov'eva," vol. XXXVI, p. 153 and notes 67 and 115 to this chapter.

43. G. [B] Blank, "Russkii pomeshchichii [*sic*] krest'ianin," *Trudy Imperatorskogo volnogo ekonomicheskogo obshchestva*, June, 1856 (vol. II, no. 6), pp. 124, 123, and 128.

44. "Spravka po delu St. Sov. Blanka 1-ogo" and letter from Blank to Panin, March 14, 1859, *TsGIAL, f.* 1180, *op.* XV, *d.* 35, *ll.* 210 *ob.*, 212-213*ob.*

45. "Predstavlenie MVD . . . ," March 11, 1859, *TsGIAL, f.* 1180, *op.* XV, *d.* 31, *l.* 192*ob.* Compare *ZhSGK*, p. 403, which holds Lanskoi did not object to the ousted members' return. Perhaps the Main Committee tacitly confessed it had failed to remove the chief culprit who was, according to Koshelev, F. S. Ofrosimov. A. I. Koshelev, *Zapiski* (Berlin, 1884), p. 97.

46. Quoted in "Zapiski Solov'eva," vol. XXXVI, p. 145. Once before the government members had walked out in indignation and the governor had induced them to return; *TsGIAL, f.* 1180, *op.* XV. *d.* 35, *l.* 163.

47. See *ZhSGK*, pp. 424-429 for the appeals from Vladimir, Tambov, and Tula.

48. *ZhSGK*, pp. 422-424, makes it clear that Bibikov did not take the

initiative, and Karamzin denounced Bibikov to Lanskoi at least once for his retrograde views and support of the minority. If Karamzin's judgments of his fellow members were as harsh in his speeches as in his private letters, he got off lightly. Letter of V. N. Karamzin to D. A. Obolenskii, December 19, 1858, TsGAOR, f. 109, op. 3, d. 2012, ll. 18-22, and other letters, ll. 2, 6, and 12-13.

49. ZhSGK, pp. 349-351; it went without saying that Levashev could not be hailed before the provincial assembly.

50. Materialy Cherkasskogo, bk. 1, p. 122.

51. "Ot izdatelia," Zhurnal zemlevladel'tsev, no. 1 (April, 1858), p. 2.

52. Krutikov, Otmena krepostnogo prava v Tul'skoi gubernii, p. 53; "Mnenie 105 tul'skikh dvorian o nadele krest'ian zemleiu," Sovremennik, December, 1858, pp. 300-302.

53. Kornilov, "Kaluzhskaia guberniia," p. 148.

54. ZhSGK, p. 322; the publication of the Tula resolution was one of the pretexts for this ruling, which was based upon a decree of January 1858, which had not been strictly observed; see Seredonin, Istoricheskii obzor, vol. III, part 2, p. 196.

55. "Iz bumag A. G. Troinitskogo. Zapiska ego ob uchastii periodicheskoi literatury v obsuzhdenii i razreshenii krest'ianskogo voprosa," dated May 9, 1859, RA, 1896, no. 7, p. 421. See also Gerasimova, "Otnoshenie pravitel'stva," pp. 92-96.

56. On the rise and fall of Rural Welfare and The Landowners' Journal, see S. S. Dmitriev, "Arkhiv redaktsii 'Sel'skogo blagoustroistva' (1858-59)," ZOR, X, pp. 33-43, and N. M. Druzhinin, "Zhurnal zemlevladel'tsev 1858-60 gg.," Trudy instituta istorii (RANIION), fasc. 1 (1926), pp. 463-507; Institut istorii (RANIION), Uchenye zapiski, vol. II (1927), pp. 251-310; N. A. Tsagolov, Ocherki russkoi ekonomicheskoi mysli perioda padeniia krepostnogo prava (Moscow, 1956).

57. Savel'ev, "Neskol'ko slov," RS, vol. XCV, pp. 70-71; Chebaevskii, "Nizhegorodskii dvorianskii komitet," pp. 87-90; I. P. Popov. "Liberal'noe dvizhenie provintsial'nogo dvorianstva v period podgotovki i provedeniia reformy 1861 goda, "Voprosy istorii, March 1973, p. 39n.

58. Otnoshenie of July 8, 1858, quoted in part in Chebaevskii (p. 90) and in part by Savel'ev (p. 76).

59. Murav'ev to Lanskoi, September 25, 1858, quoted by Savel'ev, p. 72.

60. Dnevnik Menshikova, l. 25ob.

61. For two letters sent from Nizhnii Novogord in 1858 reflecting this assumption, see TsGAOR, f. 109, op. 3, d. 2016, ll. 9, 16.

62. Snezhnevskii, "Krepostnye krest'iane i pomeshchiki Nizhe-gorodskoi gubernii," p. 77; Chebaevskii, p. 91.

63. These epithets were omitted when the speech was adopted as a resolution by the thirteen-man majority; Savel'ev, p. 73.

64. It was assumed in the capital that all eight members of the minority withdrew because the committee's resolution on household plots was an intolerable violation of the imperial rescript, but in fact it was the insults of the majority that drove them out. See Boltin's remarks quoted in

Snezhenvskii, p. 78, and A. I. Eshman's letter to Samarin, in *Materialy Cherkasskago*, bk. 1, appendix, pp. 104-105.

65. Extracts from Piatov's speech of February 26, 1858, in Savel'ev, "Neskol'ko slov," *RS*, vol. XCIV, pp. 623-624. It was Piatov's views rather than his position that elevated him to temporary leadership, for he held the modest post of secretary to the corporate organization of the nobility; his father had been a merchant who acquired noble status through service as mayor of Nizhnii Novgorod.

66. After a favorable initial impression, Karamzin became so despondent about the course the committee was taking that he considered resigning even before the scandal erupted. Compare his letters in Miliutina, "Iz zapisok," *RS*, vol. XCVII, p. 282, and in *TsGAOR, f.* 102, *op.* 3, *d.* 2016, *l.* 4.

67. Savel'ev, vol. XCV, p. 74; compare Snezhnevskii, p. 81, and Chebaevskii, p. 91. The measures taken correspond by and large to Solov'ev's recommendations to Lanskoi. Solov'ev recalled that the Main Committee confirmed his recommendations after Lanskoi had, with great trepidation, secured the tsar's advance approval. However, there is no record of any action by the committee in *ZhSGK* or in the committee's file on this matter. (*TsGIAL, f.* 1180, *op.* XV, *d.* 31, *ll.* 114-137). Solov'ev urged that Piatov be removed, and erroneously believed that he was and that the other members of the majority were given a strict reprimand; Tatishchev's account is a fanciful embroidery on Solov'ev's version. It seems most probable that the tsar accepted Lanskoi's recommendations in principle but softened the disciplinary action proposed. "Zapiski Solov'eva," vol. XXXIV, pp. 400-402; Tatishchev, *Imperator Aleksandr II*, vol. I, p. 329.

68. Eshman to Samarin, in *Materialy Cherkasskogo*, bk. 1, appendix, p. 105; Snezhnevskii, pp. 80-82.

69. "Zapiski Solov'eva," vol. XXXIV, pp. 402-405; Levshin, "Zapiska," pp. 546, 547, 550. Levshin was sent to Nizhnii only after the government had acted and did not, as he reported he did, forestall an imperial reprimand for the Nizhnii nobility. Compare his letter as quoted by Solov'ev, p. 402.

70. Levshin complained that he did not, as his many enemies charged, encourage the Nizhnii Committee to increase the barshchina obligation, but rather congratulated it for its generosity. Compare Levshin, "Zapiska," p. 548, and Eshman's letter, p. 106.

71. Boltin's comment is quoted by Snezhnevskii, p. 82. Boltin was replaced at the next election by an antagonist of Murav'ev's, P. D. Stremoukhov, the deputy elected to represent the majority before the Editorial Commission. Stremoukhov found that the majority's resentment of Murav'ev's interference and his patronage of the minority was the main source of conflict within the committee. Chebaevskii indicates that the conflict represented a struggle between the small-scale agricultural estates of the South and the large, nonagricultural estates in the northern part of the province. However, two of the six elected members of the minority represented the northern district of Vasil'. See Chebaevskii, p. 89, and P. D. Stremoukhov, "Nizhegorodskii gubernator A. N. Murav'ev," *RS*, vol. CVI (May, 1901), p. 354.

72. Chebaevskii, pp. 93-94.
73. The directive (SbPR, p. 109) sent in November and December of 1858 to the governors of unspecified provinces communicated the tsar's ruling on the Nizhnii resolution.
74. "Otchetnye vedomosti . . . ," TsGIAL, f. 1180, op. XV, d. 155, l. 91.
75. Pokorskii-Zhoravko, "Pis'ma," p. 60.
76. Rostovtsev, "O proekte . . . Simbirskoi gubernii," MRK, 1, supplement to ZhOP no. 2, p. 50; on the Voronezh petition see ZhSGK, p. 305.
77. Lanskoi to Governor Akhverdov of Smolensk, November 28, 1858, in TsGIAL, f. 1291, op. 1, d. 2, l. 84ob.
78. Text in Kornilov, "Kaluzhskaia guberniia," pp. 211n-212n.
79. ZhSGK, pp. 322-323, 359; TsGIAL, f. 1291, op. 1, d. 2, l. 98.
80. TsGIAL, f. 1291, op. 1, d. 2, ll. 147-151. This is a spravka prepared for Lanskoi as a result of consultations with the Komitet po delam bankovykh ustanovlenii and intended for presentation to the Main Committee. Lanskoi rejected these arguments and took the line set forth in ZhSGK, p. 451.
81. Kornilov, "Gubernskie komitety," p. 239n.
82. Letter of N. A. to Ia. A. Solov'ev, quoted in "Zapiski Solov'eva," vol. XXXVI, p. 146; "Zapiska Simbirskogo dvorianskogo komiteta o voznagrazhdenii poter', kotorye mogut ponesti pomeshchiki pri unichtozhenii krepostnogo prava," appendix to the majority proekt in TGK.
83. Unsigned letter from Simbirsk, December 26 [1858], TsGAOR, f. 109, op. 3, d. 2031, ll. 8-8ob.
84. This speech is also discussed above, pp. 157-158.
85. Statement by [A. A. Valitskii (Ruza)] in N. P. Ogarev, ed., "Moskovskii komitet: Glavnye osnovaniia priniatye Moskovskim komitetom po krest'ianskomu delu, nachavshim zasedaniia svoi s 26 aprelia 1858," Kolokol, No. 30/31, pp. 242-249; no. 32/33, pp. 265-271; no. 34, pp. 276-279; no. 35, pp. 281-285; p. 244.
86. Statements by Maksimov and Aznachevskii (Bronnitsy) and by Golovin (Moscow), "Moskovskii komitet," pp. 245, 242-244.
87. "Moskovskii komitet," p. 243; Golovin did not explain how craftsmen who lived on baker's bread would be induced to till the demesne.
88. Statements by Krapotkin and Zamiatin (Moshaisk) and by Rovinskii and Gvozdev (Zvenigorod), "Moskovskii komitet," pp. 245-247.
89. Statement by Voeikov, "Moskovskii komitet," pp. 248-249. This debate and vote took place in May, 1858, before the government had annulled the Nizhnii resolution on the redemption of serfs.
90. On Pal'chikov and Danilov's statement, see V. I. Picheta, "Vopros ob usadebnoi osedlosti v Moskovskom gubernskom komitete," Institut istorii (RANIION), Uchenye zapiski, vol. V (1929), pp. 438-439. In "Moskovskii komitet," Valitskii's statement cited above is wrongly attributed to Pal'chikov and Danilov.
91. Resolution of May 27, "Moskovskii komitet," p. 249; compare Golovin's argument, pp. 243-244; Picheta, "Vopros ob usadebnoi osedlosti," pp. 444-445.
92. "Moskovskii komitet," pp. 265, 267.

93. "Moskovskii komitet," pp. 265-269 (resolutions IX, XXV, XXIV and XV); Picheta, "Vopros ob usadebnoi osedlosti," pp. 445-447; Druzhinin, "Moskovskoe dvorianstvo," pp. 67-68.

94. Statements by Golovin and Karepin (Moscow) and by Vysotskii (Bogorodsk), "Moskovskii komitet," pp. 268, 247.

95. *Dnevnik Menshikova,* September 21, 1858; May 31, August 18, 1859; *ll.* 30, 55*ob.*, 63.

96. Ogarev, who was no admirer of the Moscow Committee, assumed that this resolution applied only to the demesne lands, but it is clear from the speeches and other resolutions that most members hoped their "discretion" would be enforceable on the allotments and even on the plotland. See resolution XVI and Ogarev's note, "Moskovskii komitet," p. 266.

97. On May 13, the committee voted unanimously to forbid the pomeshchik to relocate the peasants' houses and plots once the transitional period of "temporary obligation" had begun. Later, presumably as part of the committee's reaction against the tsar's speech, a proposal to allow the pomeshchik to relocate the plots even *after* temporary obligation was defeated by a single vote. V. I. Picheta, "Vopros o perenesenii usadeb v Moskovskom gubernskom komitete . . . ," Institut istorii (RANIION), *Uchenye zapiski,* vol. IV (1929), pp. 198-202.

98. Voeikov proposed to set certain tasks in return for four desiatiny, while Menshikov's proposal determined the dues in labor-days (which the committee subsequently reduced from ninety to sixty-four). However, the tasks that Menshikov assumed would take up ninety days correspond closely to Voeikov's norm. See "Moskovskii komitet," pp. 279, 281-282.

99. *Dnevnik Menshikova* for July 8, 1858, *l.* 21*ob.*; Menshikov's proposal, "Ob osnovakh osvobhdeniia pomeshchich'ikh krest'ian," is quoted from N. S. Bargamian, "Pomeshchich'i proekty . . . ," *Rev. Sit.* [II], p. 31, where it is misdated July 8, 1859. This proposal made special provisions for estates where the peasants were traders, artisans, or truck-farmers.

100. "Moskovskii komitet," p. 277 (resolution LXVII and statement by Vysotskii); compare the proposals on pp. 270, 277-278. For example, Urusov and Polivanov estimated the income (earnings plus the value of crops grown for consumption) of an agricultural tiaglo at seventy-five rubles. According to calculations of Koval'chenko and Milov it was less than fifty; "Ob intensivnosti," p. 75.

101. There is no evidence that Alexander saw the texts of the committee's resolutions; he was moved to intervene when Zakrevskii reported the Moscow Committee's definition of *usadebnaia osedlost'.* Alexander noted on the report, "That is wrong; 'and the land on which they are settled' should be added." *ZhSGK,* p. 273.

102. *Dnevnik Menshikova,* September 3, 1858, *l.* 27*ob.*

103. Picheta, "Vopros ob usadebnoi osedlost'," pp. 447-454.

104. "Moskovskii komitet," p. 281n; *Dnevnik Menshikova, ll.* 9*ob.,* 28*ob.* 30*ob.,* 41.

105. *Dnevnik Menshikova, ll.* 25*ob.,* 48*ob.,* 10, 86*ob.,* 72*ob.,* 53*ob.,* 14*ob.,* 47*ob.,* 54.

106. Druzhinin, "Moskovskoe dvorianstvo," p. 68, See also Dzhanshiev, *Epokha velikikh reform*, p. 735, and Ogarev's notes to "Moskovskii komitet," especially p. 281n.

107. "Moskovskii komitet," pp. 247, 268, 270.

108. *Dnevnik Menshikova*, April 13 and July 25, 1858, *ll.* 16ob. and 23.

109. They were appointed after the original government members, one of them Menshikov's son, had resigned. Pavlov recalled that Zakrevskii stood by him even though he took a position in the committee very far from Zakrevskii's own views and those of his original appointees. N. N. Pavlov, "Redaktsionnye komissii 1858-60 godov," *Istoricheskii vestnik*, vol. LXXXVI (November, 1901), p. 517.

110. For their criticism of the majority and a reply on behalf of the majority, see "Moskovskii komitet ob uluchshenii byta krest'ian," *Kolokol*, nos. 47 and 48 (July 1 and 15, 1859), pp. 383-386 and 391-395.

111. *Dnevnik Menshikova*, August 25, 1858, *l.* 25.

112. *Dnevnik Menshikova*, *l.* 38ob.

113. *Dnevnik Menshikova*, *l.* 26.

114. "Moskovskii komitet," p. 283.

115. *Dnevnik Menshikova*, *ll.* 110 and 49ob. Menshikov records his removal without comment, and it attracted no attention at the time. *ZhSGK* contains no reference to it; however, all lists of the members of provincial committees (*SbPR*, Skrebitskii, and N. Semenov) indicate that Menshikov left the Moscow Committee. The suggestion ("Zapiski Solov'eva," vol. XXXIV, p. 419) that Menshikov and Count S. G. Stroganov resigned in indignation after the tsar's speech at Moscow is groundless.

116. "Proekt Unkovskogo," *Kolokol*, no. 39 (April 1, 1859), pp. 316-321.

117. Resolution of the Novyi Torg nobility, in Dzhanshiev, *A. M. Unkovskii*, pp. 76-77.

118. *ZhSGK*, pp. 117-118; Unkovskii to A. I. Koshelev, September 18, 1858, in *Materialy Cherkasskogo*, bk. 1, appendix, p. 111.

119. Unkovskii, "Zapiski," *Russiaia mysl'*, 1906, no. 6, pp. 195-196.

120. Emmons, *Russian Landed Gentry*, p. 147. Unkovskii later wrote to his comrade-in-arms Golovachev that they had prevailed in the Tver Committee only because of his authority as marshal and ex officio chairman; letter of May 28, 1860, *TsGAOR*, *f.* 109. *op.* 3, *d.* 2034, *l.* 36.

121. Texts in Dzhanshiev, *A. M. Unkovskii*, pp. 84-85; voting results in M. A. Rozum, "Podgotovka krest'ianskoi reformy v Tverskom komitete . . . ," *Uchenye zapiski Kalininskogo pedagogicheskogo instituta im. M. I. Kalinina*, vol. X, vyp. 1 (1945), pp. 11, 13.

122. Rozum, "Podgotovka," p. 12; Pokrovskii, *Istoriko-statisticheskoe opisanie*, p. 178.

123. Letter to Dzhanshiev of May 31, 1894, quoted in Dzhanshiev, *A. M. Unkovskii*, p. 95; Rozum (p. 28) agrees with Unkovskii's diagnosis.

124. Emmons, *Russian Landed Gentry*, pp. 124-126.

125. Letter to Dzhanshiev, quoted in his *A. M. Unkovskii*, p. 95; in a letter to Cherkasskii sent just before the deputation's departure, Unkovskii stated that they would seek an audience with the tsar himself and that fourteen members would resign from the Tver Committee if the appeal

was denied; *Materialy Cherkasskogo*, bk. 1, appendix, p. 114.

126. Unkovskii, "Zapiski," *Russkaia mysl'*, 1906, no. 7, p. 88; Dzhanshiev, *A. M. Unkovskii*, pp. 96-97; Rozum, "Podgotovka," pp. 20 and 36. Compare "Zapiski Solov'eva," vol. XXXVI, p. 245: "The whole deputation was received there in the most cordial fashion."

127. *ZhSGK*, pp. 138-140; letter of A. A. Golovachev to Dzhanshiev, in Dzhanshiev, *Epokha velikikh reform*, p. 169n.

128. The speech of August 31 had not yet been published; when Unkovskii had conferred with Lanskoi, just before the tsar's Moscow speech, the minister had specifically approved the contorted definition of "household plot" as a device to include compulsory redemption in the draft; see Unkovskii's letter to Koshelev in *Materialy Cherkasskogo*, bk. 1, appendix, p. 111.

129. For example, the governor of Kaluga Province confessed that he could not help favoring the minority of the Kaluga Provincial Committee, which favored the redemption of plowland, for it was "guided by more elevated and selfless considerations" than the majority; *zapiska* of V. A. Artsimovich for A. Kh. Kapger, October 18, 1861 in *V. A. Artsimovich. Vospominaniia—kharakteristiki*, p. 522.

130. *ZhSGK*, pp. 271-274.

131. Rozum, "Podgotovka," pp. 15-16; Emmons emphasizes the extent to which Unkovskii and his associates at Tver appealed to the nobility's self-interest, *Russian Landed Gentry*, pp. 110, 113, passim.

132. Letter of January 24, 1893, quoted in Dzhanshiev, *A. M. Unkovskii*, p. 133n.

133. As Emmons puts it, "they were applying to local conditions . . . the liberal reform program which was the common property of most 'educated opinion' in Russia." He does indicate that the administration confirmed Unkovskii's irregular election as marshal because of his abolitionist views, but offers no evidence on this count. *Russian Landed Gentry*, pp. 149, 87-88.

134. Emmons and Starr quite rightly resist the temptation to contrive such an explanation; *Russian Landed Gentry*, p. 148, passim; *Decentralization and Self-Government*, pp. 203, 207. Several historians have recently pointed out that Unkovskii's private views were more radical and more generous to the peasantry than were the policies he sponsored as marshal. See, for example, E. K. Rozov, "Oppozitsionnoe dvizhenie tverskogo dvorianstva . . . ," A. A. Kondrashenkov et al., eds., *Voprosy agrarnoi istorii tsentra i severo-zapada RSFSR* (Smolensk, 1972), p. 197.

135. Quoted in Dzhanshiev, *A. M. Unkovskii*, pp. 114n-115n.

136. *ZhSGK*, p. 349.

137. Dzhanshiev, *A. M. Unkovskii*, p. 112n.

138. Quoted in Dzhanshiev, *A. M. Unkovskii*, pp. 113, 112.

139. Emmons suggests (*Russian Landed Gentry*, p. 138) that they "probably provoked the whole campaign." Eleven dissidents (the nine who would sign the minority draft plus Miliukov and Rakovskii) cited protests received from six districts of Tver Province in a belated appeal to the Ministry of Internal Affairs against the principle of redemption; *TsGIAL, f.* 1291, *op.* 123, *d.* 4, *ll.* 11-12*ob*.

140. On these accusations, see Unkovskii, "Zapiski," *Russkaia mysl'*, 1906, no. 7, pp. 89-91; Dzhanshiev, *A. M. Unkovskii*, pp. 95, 113-116; *ZhSGK*, p. 420.

141. Historians at Kalinin (as Tver is now called) are beginning to investigate the radical involvements of Unkovskii and his associates, with no striking results as yet; see E. V. Kartashov, "Iz istorii obshchestvennogo dvizheniia v Tverskoi gubernii v period revoliutsionnoi situatsii kontsa 50-kh—nachala 60-kh godov XIX v.," Kh. D. Sorina et al., eds., *Iz proshlogo i nastoiashchego Kalininskoi oblasti (Istoriko-kraevedcheskii sbornik)* (Moscow, 1965), pp. 125-152.

142. Unkovskii (writing from exile in Viatka, 1860) to Alexander II, in M. K. Lemke, *Ocherki osvoboditel'nogo dvizheniia "shestidesiatykh godov"* (St. Petersburg, 1908), appendix, p. 451. In a private letter, Unkovskii maintained that three-quarters of the Tver nobles at the elections held in December, 1859, favored the redemption of allotments; letter to N. F. Shcherbatskii, May 5, 1860, *TsGAOR, f.* 109, *op.* 3, *d.* 2034, *l.* 19ob.

143. Rozum, "Podgotovka," p. 35; Emmons, *Russian Landed Gentry*, p. 138.

144. *ZhSGK*, p. 469.

145. Emmons, *Russian Landed Gentry*, pp. 81, 83, 119; Dzhanshiev, *A. M. Unkovskii*, pp. 16-17.

146. Directive of the MIA, *SbPR*, p. 108, sent to unspecified governors in November and December of 1858. The governor of Tambov received a copy dated December 3, 1858, but did not find it applied to the Tambov Committee's resolution that "pomeshchiki retain the right to compensation for losses deriving from the status of temporary obligation." At least, neither he nor the MIA moved to quash the resolution, despite a complaint from the committee's minority. *MRK*, I: "Sistematicheskie svody po proektam polozhenii 21-i gubernii," p. 3.

147. Directives of the MIA, *SbPR*, pp. 107-108, and 111. Appendix III to *SbPR* indicates the dates on which each provincial committee opened and presented its draft for review. The committees were supposed to finish in six months, but many were granted extensions or submitted their drafts well after they had closed.

148. *ZhSGK*, pp. 448-449; compare pp. 298-299.

149. See *Sbornik postanovlenii po ustroistvu byta pomeshchich'ikh krest'ian za 1857 i 1858 gody* (St. Petersburg, 1859), which was (according to *SbPR*, p. 196) distributed to provincial governors and marshals on January 28, 1859.

150. "Perechen' pravitel'stvennikh rasporiazhenii po ustroistvu pomeshchich'ikh krest'ian," *ZhMVD, chast'* 37 (July 1859), *chast' ofitsial'naia*, p. 77ff.

151. "Vzgliad na polozhenie krest'ianskogo voprosa v nastoiashchee vremia (August, 1859)," text in N. Semenov, *Osvobozhdenie*, II, appendix, pp. 826-834. N. A. Miliutin is generally regarded as the principal author of this survey. Zaionchkovskii attributes it to P. A. Valuev because there is a copy in his archive, although he notes that it is strikingly at odds with Valuev's activities and expressed views. The survey may, however, have found its way into Valuev's archive by virtue of his subsequent service as Minister of Internal Affairs. Furthermore, although Valuev was a consummate opportunist, it is difficult to see why Lanskoi would have entrusted the

composition of so important a document to the hostile subordinate of a rival minister. *Dnevnik P. A. Valueva, Ministra vnutrennikh del*, 2 vols., P. A. Zaionchkovskii, ed. (Moscow, 1961), vol. I, pp. 26-27.

152. S. S. Lanskoi and Ia. A. Solov'ev ["Otzyv Ministra Vnutrennikh Del"], January 26, 1859, p. 5, and MVD, Zemskii otdel, "Zamechaniia na proekt Polozheniia S-Peterburgskogo Gubernskogo Komiteta po ustroistvu byta pomeshchich'ikh krest'ian," p. 5, both appended to the St. Petersburg draft in *TGK*; see also Rostovtsev's critique of the St. Petersburg draft in *MRK*, I, appendix to ZhOP no. 2.

153. See, for example, *MRK, Otzyvy*, II, p. 479.

154. The committee did not deny that it discouraged peasants from purchasing their allotments, but maintained that granting the peasants a legal right to their allotments without an obligation to accept them guaranteed both amelioration and *"osedlost' "*; "Obzor osnovanii," pp. 3, 4, 11, in *TGK* (St. Petersburg). The Civil Division of the MIA held, however, that the dues prescribed in the St. Petersburg draft were more burdensome than the dues under serfdom; *MRK*, III, DKhO no. 17, p. 75.

155. The rescript provided for *votchinnaia politsiia*, the St. Petersburg draft statute (article 29) for *pravo votchinnogo nachal'stva . . . nad sel'skim obshchestvom*.

156. Valuev's "Riad myslei po povodu krest'ianskogo voprosa," which may have been a prototype for the St. Petersburg Committee's draft, provided for various *pozemel'nye votchinnye prava* set forth in article 30 of that draft and for *pravo okhoty* as well; *Dnevnik Valueva*, p. 25.

157. Exchange between Cherkasskii and Pozen in the Editorial Commission, N. Semenov, *Osovbozhdenie*, I, p. 220.

158. To be sure, the tsar took advantage of the Russian language's indulgence of ellipsis; his words, as the chairman reported them to the committee, were: *"Delaite v Komitete tak, kak luchshe. Ia na vse soglasen. Moia nepremennaia voila, chtoby . . . etc.* Povalishin, *Riazanskie pomeshchiki*, p. 310.

159. Tsagolov, *Ocherki russkoi ekonomicheskoi mysli perioda padeniia krepostnogo prava*, p. 216, passim.

160. *MRK*, II, DKhO no. 1, p. 20.

161. For example, Ignatovich, *Pomeshchich'i krest'iane*, pp. 100-102; on Ianson's *Opyt statisticheskogo issledovaniia o krest'ianskikh nadelakh i platezhakh* (St. Petersburg, 1877), see Zaionchkovskii, *Provedenie v zhizn'*, pp. 10-12.

162. For example, he stated that the Astrakhan Provincial Committee "imitated its allotment norms without any further reflection from the draft of the Petersburg Committee, although, it goes without saying, the conditions in Petersburg and Astrakhan provinces had nothing in common." Lanskoi made the same point, presumably taking it from the first report of the Economic Section of the Editorial Commission. However, the norms of the Astrakhan and Petersburg committees were not, in fact, the same. Kornilov, "Gubernskie komitety," p. 253; Lanskoi's "Vzgliad," p. 829; *MRK*, II, DKhO no. 1, p. 5; *MRK*, III, appendix to DKhO no. 15, pp. 3, 11.

163. Compare "Gubernskie komitety," pp. 179-181 with pp. 238, 282, and the three tendencies outlined on p. 193 passim.

164. "Obzor osnovanii," [I, 1], in *TGK* (Penza).

165. Deich, *Krest'ianstvo Pskovskoi gubernii*, p. 288.

166. Krechetovich, *Krest'ianskaia reforma*, pp. 152-154.

167. On the Kharkov Committee, see N. Tikhonov, "K kharakteristike dvorianskoi ideologii," pp. 225-46. The minority's complaints to Lanskoi and V. A. Dolgorukov (*TsGIAL, f.* 982, *op.* 1, *d.* 49, *ll.* 136-155 and 202-203) are obliquely reiterated in a statement five of them appended to the committee's draft in *TGK*.

168. Pokorskii-Zhoravko, "Pis'ma," pp. 88-90.

169. Speech of January 12, 1859, "Izvlecheniia iz zhurnalov Chernigovskogo Dvorianskogo Gubernskogo Komiteta," pp. 184-185.

170. Pokorskii-Zhoravko, "Pis'ma," pp. 85-86, 90.

171. Miliutin himself put the matter in the same terms in explaining the abolition of serfdom to a French journalist: "Since the Russian government had the French example before it, it had the good sense to make intelligent use of that example in order to safeguard the future of that same nobility which is now howling and complaining." Quoted in L. G. Zakharova, "Dvorianstvo i pravitel'stvennaia programma otmeny krepostnogo prava v Rossii," *Voprosy istorii*, 1973, no. 9, p. 48.

6. The Editorial Commission

1. The members are listed in N. Semenov, *Osvobozhdenie*, I, appendix I. Petr Semenov provides a detailed account of the selection process and a biographical sketch of each member, *Epokha*, vol. I, pp. 132-205. For an excellent study of the Editorial Commission, see L. G. Zakharova, "Pravitel'stevennaia programma otmeny krepostnogo prava v Rossii," *Istoriia SSSR*, 1975, no. 2, pp. 22-47.

2. It was Rostovtsev, not the tsar, who insisted on Pozen's appointment to the Financial Commission, a branch of the Editorial Commission. Compare Rostovtsev's memorandum on his break with Pozen, Elenev, "Pervye shagi," p. 402, and P. Semenov, *Epokha*, vol. I, pp. 169, 197.

3. One of these seven nominees, N. N. Pavlov of the Moscow Provincial Committee, was designated a departmental member from the Ministry of State Property.

4. Pavlov, "Redaktsionnye komissii 1859-60 godov," p. 519.

5. V. V. Tarnovskii expected to be elected to the Chernigov Committee and was appointed to it after he campaigned and lost; "Na zare," vol. XCIV, p. 52.

6. P. Semenov, *Epokha*, vol. I, p. 167. At the time, Koshelev assumed that he was excluded, after Rostovtsev had promised him a place, because of the inexplicable enmity of the Semenovs. Later he decided it was his role as journalist and "head of the slavophiles" that was responsible. See his letter to Cherkasskii, *Materialy Cherkasskogo*, bk. 2, p. 11, and his *Zapiski*, p. 105.

7. P. Semenov, *Epokha*, vol. I, pp. 194-195.

8. For example, with Prince Shcherbatov, the Saratov marshal;

TsGAOR, f. 109, *op.* 3, *d.* 2027, *l.* 4. Shuvalov's archive (*TsGIAL, f.* 1092) contains miscellaneous papers from a number of provincial committees.

9. P. Semenov, *Epokha*, vol. I, p. 212; compare pp. 193-194.

10. Letter of May 1, 1859, to his wife, in "Iz perepiski deiatelei osvobozhdeniia krest'ian," *Russkaia mysl'*, 1911, no. 3, p. 108.

11. *MRK*, I, ZhOP, no. 2, p. 5.

12. N. Semenov, *Osvobozhdenie*, I, pp. 123, 137-138.

13. N. Semenov, *Osvobozhdenie*, I, pp. 144-147.

14. N. Semenov, *Osvobozhdenie*, I, p. 146.

15. *MRK*, III, DAO no. 8, pp. 3-10, 51-52; see Apraksin's dissenting opinion in N. Semenov, *Osobozhdenie*, I, appendix, pp. 837-840.

16. According to the Administrative Section, however, subsequent "clarification" of the government's program made these provisions "an anachronism"; *MRK*, III, DAO no. 8, pp. 2, 54.

17. N. Semenov, *Osvobozhdenie*, II, p. 805.

18. "*Podkladki mnenii*"; N. Semenov, *Osvobozhdenie*, I, pp. 408-409.

19. N. Semenov, *Osvobozhdenie*, I, pp. 119, 121, 114, 130.

20. Among others, Koshelev and E. P. Obolenskii; see Koshelev's *Zapiski*, p. 105, and A. A. Kizevetter, ed., "K istorii osvobozhdeniia krest'ian," *RS*, vol. CIV (November 1900), pp. 376-377.

21. N. Semenov, *Osvobozhdenie*, I, pp. 91, 112, 119, passim.

22. N. Semenov, *Osvobozhdenie*, I, p. 636; *MRK*, III, ZhOP no. 48, p. 1.

23. N. Semenov, *Osvobozhdenie*, I, p. 481.

24. Letters of April 22 and May 6, in *Materialy Cherkasskogo*, bk. 2, pp. 7-8.

25. *MRK*, I, ZhOP no. 2, pp. 3-5. For Rostòvtsev's original, see N. Semenov, *Osvobozhdenie*, I, pp. 86-87.

26. *MRK*, II, ZhOP no. 39, p. 2. The commission left this provision intact when, later still, it ruled that the peasants' dues could be raised after twenty years.

27. G. T. Robinson, *Rural Russia Under the Old Regime* (New York, 1932), pp. 82, 99.

28. N. Semenov, *Osvobozhdenie*, I, pp. 243-246. Semenov wrongly states that Rostovtsev's verbal change was incorporated into the report; see *MRK*, II, DIu O no. 1, p. 9.

29. N. Semenov, *Osvobozhdenie*, II, pp. 549, 551, 547; *MRK*, V, Dop. DKhO no. 16, pp. 105-107, 111.

30. N. Semenov, *Osvobozhdenie*, II, p. 551; G. P. Galagan to F. V. Chizhov, January 29, 1860, *TsGAOR, f.* 109, *op.* 3, *d.* 1959, *ll.* 6-9. Galagan had impressed his colleagues on the Chernigov Provincial Committee as a muddleheaded radical philanthropist, but within the Editorial Commission he took the role of pragmatic advocate of the pomeshchik's interest. He himself was proud of his struggle against "inveterate conservatives" in Chernigov but, so soon has he joined the Editorial Commission, he appreciated that his antagonists there were to the left and that he must now struggle "against the illegal demands of theory." Letter to A. M. Markovich, April 20, 1859, "Dva pis'ma G. P. Galagana 1859 g.," *Kievskaia starina*, September, 1895, p. 70.

31. N. Semenov, *Osvobozhdenie*, I, p. 594.

32. Compare *MRK*, III, DkhO no. 12, p. 50, and *MRK*, V, Dop. DKhO no. 12, p. 73.

33. N. Semenov, *Osvobozhdenie*, II, pp. 506, 503-504.

34. This was a particularly appropriate compliment for a man who a year ago had privately lamented that Pozen was Rostovtsev's tutelary nymph. N. Semenov, *Osvobozhdenie*, I, p. 245; compare Miliutin's letter cited above, in note 28 to chap. 4.

35. N. Semenov, *Osvobozhdenie*, II, pp. 505, 507-508.

36. Notably by Robinson in *Rural Russia under the Old Regime*, and M. N. Pokrovskii in "Krest'ianskaia reforma," pp. 173-179.

37. Zaionchkovskii, *Provedenie v zhizn'*, chap. III.

38. N. Semenov, *Osvobozhdenie*, I, pp. 292, 300, 315, 316.

39. N. Semenov, *Osvobozhdenie*, I, pp. 293, 317-319, 322.

40. *MRK*, IV, ZhOP, no. 72, pp. 2-3.

41. *MRK*, III, "Predvaritel'nye soobrazheniia o vykupe . . . ," p. 19.

42. N. Semenov, *Osvobozhdenie*, I, p. 565. Shuvalov and Samarin did not vote, and Pozen was absent. So was N. P. Semenov, hence he provides no record of the debate and his text of the motion that was voted, providing for "immutability of dues with compulsory redemption of land," is corrupt.

43. N. Semenov, *Osvobozhdenie*, I, pp. 569, 287; Tatarinov, "Otdel'noe mnenie . . . ," *MRK*, *Mneniia chlenov* [I], pp. 1-3.

44. *MRK*, II, DKhO no. 9, pp. 40-41. In the statute of 1861, the report's maximum of four rubles for the first desiatina became a minimum, while the progression descended more sharply; half the dues levied on the maximum allotment fell on the first desiatina and a quarter fell on the second. See article 169 of the Great Russian Statute, *SZA*, p. 219.

45. *MRK*, II, DKhO, no. 9, p. 10; P. Semenov, *Epokha*, vol. I, p. 235.

46. Despite the implications of the report's conclusion; compare DKhO no. 9, pp. 41-42 and 33.

47. N. Semenov, *Osvobozhdenie*, I, p. 567.

48. *MRK*, II, DKhO no. 9, pp. 27, 26.

49. N. Semenov, *Osvobozhdenie*, I, p. 684; the point at issue was the exclusion of supplementary dues in calculating the average obrok.

50. N. Semenov, *Osvobozhdenie*, III, 2, pp. 551-552.

51. See N. Semenov, *Osvobozhdenie*, II, appendix, p. 913.

52. P. Semenov, *Epokha*, vol. I, p. 149.

53. N. Semenov, *Osvobozhdenie*, I, p. 467; II, pp. 439-441.

54. *MRK*, II, DIuO no. 6, p. 29.

55. Miliutin continued for some time to object to the distribution of the proceedings; N. Semenov, *Osvobozhdenie*, I, pp. 127, 201.

56. *MRK*, I ZhOP no. 8, pp. 22-23.

57. *MRK*, I, ZhOP no. 2, p. 9. Miliutin explained that the deputies did not want to receive the proceedings in advance; N. Semenov, *Osvobozhdenie*, I, p. 170. After the first convocation of deputies had departed, however, Rostovtsev attempted to have the commission's proceedings distributed with the *Journal of the Ministry of Internal Affairs*; ZhSGK, pp. 476-477.

58. N. Semenov, *Osvobozhdenie*, I, pp. 164, 569, 142.

59. Peasants who owned an adequate amount of land elsewhere could,

with the pomeshchik's permission, leave the estate and end their temporary obligation; temporary obligation could also end through a change of status from the peasantry to one of the urban categories. No one expected much use would be made of these alternatives, and the effective ascription of the peasants to their allotments underlay the rationale of the redemption system, particularly the provision for redemption at the pomeshchik's demand. See *MRK*, III, "Predvaritel'nye soobrazheniia o vykupe . . . ," p. 15.

60. "Predvaritel'nye soobrazheniia . . . ," pp. 13-15.

61. *MRK*, I, ZhOP no. 13-15, p. 43.

62. N. Semenov, *Osvobozhdenie*, I, pp. 151-153.

63. P. A. Valuev, Deputy Minister of State Properties, assisted Shuvalov and Paskevich in writing this and subsequent statements of their position. Valuev, "Dnevnik," *RS*, August and September, 1891 (vol. LXXXI), pp. 278, 547, 550-553. For the text of one of these later statements and an admittedly inadequate account of the debate on another, see N. Semenov, *Osvobozhdenie*, I, pp. 262-266 and 257-260.

64. N. Semenov, *Osobozhdenie*, I, pp. 156, 161-163.

65. N. Semenov, *Osvobozhdenie*, I, pp. 162, 168.

66. Text of the order in N. Semenov, *Osvobozhdenie*, I, pp. 176-177.

67. N. Semenov, *Osvobozhdenie*, I, p. 181; Paskevich and Shuvalov were absent from this session, having submitted their resignations on learning of the tsar's order.

68. "Dopolnitel'nye zhurnaly Obshchikh Prisutstvii Redaktsionnykh Komisii v pervom periode ikh zaniatii," no. 2, May 27, 1859, in N. Semenov, *Osvobozhdenie*, I, pp. 790-794.

69. "Dopolnitel'nye zhurnaly Obshchikh Prisutstvii . . ." no. 4, June 15, 1859, p. 800.

70. N. Semenov, *Osvobozhdenie*, I, p. 258.

71. "Osoboe mnenie Kniazia Paskevicha i Grafa Shuvalova . . . ," May 13, 1859, in N. Semenov, *Osvobozhdenie*, I, pp. 787-789.

72. *Materialy Cherkasskogo*, bk. 2, p. 8.

73. Despite his disclaimers, this is what Rostovtsev assumed would happen; compare N. Semenov, *Osvobozhdenie*, I, pp. 293 and 791.

74. N. Semenov, *Osvobozhdenie*, I, p. 158.

75. As an unhappy sympathizer of Shuvalov's, who thought it absurd to stigmatize him as an "oligarch," observed with dismay; V. A. Mukhanov, "Iz dnevnykh zapisok . . . ," *RA*, 1896, no. 11, p. 332.

76. "Dopolnitel'nye zhurnaly Obshchikh Prisutstvii . . . ," no. 5, July 15, 1859, p. 802.

77. N. Semenov, *Osvobozhdenie*, I, p. 518.

78. When Pozen joined the commission, M. N. Murav'ev told Valuev "*Il donnera un coup de poignard à Rostowtzeff.*" Valuev, "Dnevnik," *RS*, vol. LXXXI, p. 278.

79. However, he opposed the use of the term "*nepolnaia sobstvennost*" in this context, as it was open to legalistic and common-sense objections. N. Semenov, *Osvobozhdenie*, I, pp. 248-251. The commission clung to the concept of the pomeshchik's limited property right in an attempt to

reconcile the rescript's reaffirmation of this right and its own determination to give the peasants their allotments in perpetuity. However, the existing legislation requiring the pomeshchik to allot land was very limited in its application and did not, in any event, affect his tenure of the land; if he was unable to satisfy the law's requirements, he was theoretically obliged to dispose of the extra peasants, but kept the land.

80. N. Semenov, *Osvobozhdenie*, I, pp. 276-276, 542.

81. Pozen, *Bumagi*, p. 168; N. Semenov, *Osvobozhdenie*, I, pp. 282, 290, 656; *MRK, Otzyvy*, I, pp. 844-845.

82. Pozen to Rostovtsev, November 29, 1858, and February 28, 1859, in Pozen, *Bumagi*, pp. 133, 141-142.

83. Pozen, *Bumagi*, p. xvi.

84. N. Semenov, *Osvobozhdenie*, I, pp. 479-480.

85. It was also a reasonably accurate representation of the Economic Section's methods and its sway over the rest of the commission; See P. Semenov, *Epokha*, vol. I, p. 219.

86. Pozen, "Raznoglasie v Redaktsionnykh Kommissiiakh," and headnote, *Bumagi*, pp. 258-263.

87. See, for example, N. Semenov, *Osvobozhdenie*, I, p. 544.

88. Apraksin argued for the reversion of the allotments in a dissenting opinion on DluO no. 2; text in N. Semenov, *Osvobozhdenie*, I, appendix, p. 808.

89. According to Petr Semenov (*Epokha*, vol. I, pp. 299-301), Apraksin appealed to the tsar because the commission was ignoring his dissenting opinions, at least one of which, Semenov reports, was written by Pozen.

90. Apraksin to Alexander II, received August 9, 1859, *TsGIAL, f.* 982, *op.* 1, *d.* 57, *l.* 1.

91. Untitled memorandum by Apraksin, *TsGIAL, f.* 982, *op.* 1, *d.* 57, *ll.* 9ob.-10, 12, 23-23ob., 20-22ob., 24-27.

92. If Cherkasskii's statement (*Materialy Cherkasskogo*, bk. 2, p. 93) that Mikhail Bezobrazov was largely responsible for Orlov-Davydov's pamphlets is correct, then the only exception would be the *Etudes* of Schedo-Ferroti.

93. The slanders that Lanskoi refutes are to be found in M. A. Bezobrazov's "Materialy," cited in chap. 7, note 143; concerning the emancipation as such, the only point of contact with Apraksin's note is on the issue of property rights.

94. "Sekretnoe mnenie Ministra Vnutrennikh Del po povodu vruchennoi emu gosudarem zapiski V. Apraksina," August 31, 1859, text in Miliutina "Iz zapisok," vol. XCVIII, pp. 106, 107-108, 110, 112. N. A. Miliutin was the principal author of this and of many similar documents that went to the tsar over Lanskoi's signature.

95. Rostovtsev to Alexander II, November 26, 1859, in N. Semenov, *Osvobozhdenie*, II, appendix, p. 913.

96. Compare N. Semenov, *Osvobozhdenie*, II, appendix, pp. 928-932 (Rostovtsev's letter on the first group of deputies), and Lanskoi's report on their appeals, in Miliutina, "Iz zapisok," vol. XCVIII, pp. 113-117.

97. P. Semenov, *Epokha*, vol. I, p. 198.

98. In one of the last general sessions, Bulygin proposed that the economic settlement be negotiated between the ex-serfs and their pomeshchik, who would be adequately restrained by the force of public opinion and his own sense of shame; N. Semenov, *Osvobozhdenie*, III, 2, pp. 394-395.

99. N. Semenov, *Osvobozhdenie*, II, p. 514.

100. The censorship regulations imposed by the Main Committee made it impossible to publish a journal devoted to the problems of emancipation, and *The Landowners' Journal* ceased publication. In its death throes, however, it received 8,000 rubles from the so-called Bureau de la presse, on the ground that it was "the most irreproachable" of the journals on the peasant question and the most popular among the nobility. Zheltukhin applied the subsidy to his estates, which were heavily mortgaged. Note in Gertsen, *Polnoe sobranie sochinenii i pisem*, ed. Lemke, vol. IX, pp. 564-571; Nikitenko, *Dnevnik*, vol. II, p. 78.

101. A. D. Zheltukhin, "O sisteme nasil'no doborovol'nykh soglashenii," n.d., but obviously 1859, *PD, f.* 616, *d.* 1. There is no evidence that this appeal actually was distributed to the deputies, but three were among the collaborators of *The Landowners' Journal.*

102. N. Semenov, *Osvobozhdenie*, III, 2, p. 621.

103. A minor member of the Editorial Commission, in general accord with Miliutin, found him a quintessential bureaucrat, not very well educated or cultivated, but endowed with the knack of forming and uniting factions; E. I. Lamanskii, "Iz vospominanii," *RS*, vol. CLXI (March 1915), p. 586.

7. The Deputies

1. Kornilov, for example, finds that the deputies' struggle with the "bureaucratic principle" prefigured the zemstvo liberalism of the early twentieth century; "Gubernskie komitety," p. 297. For a good study of the first convocation, see Zakharova, "Dvorianstvo i pravitel'stvennaia programma," pp. 37-47.

2. The deputies are listed in N. Semenov, *Osvobozhdenie*, II, appendix, pp. 909-910. Of the original forty-four, the five deputies from Minsk and Vitebsk were shifted to the second group, and three duly elected deputies did not participate.

3. The provinces are ranked according to their percentage of obrok serfs in Ignatovich, *Pomeshchich'i krest'iane*, pp. 86-87.

4. In this paragraph, deputies are categorized according to *MRK, Svedeniia*, which is a somewhat incomplete register of estates with a hundred or more serfs. The figures apply to the district or, with government members and marshals, the province, which the deputy represented.

5. For example, the Simbirsk deputy Shidlovskii had more than three hundred serfs in Voronezh Province, but apparently was elected to the Simbirsk Provincial Committee by virtue of his wife's estate of 260 souls in Simbirsk District, which he represented.

6. Samarin to E. A. Cherkasskaia, August 26, 1859, in *Materialy Cherkasskogo*, bk. 2, p. 83.

7. At the first confrontation between the deputies and the commission, the Moscow deputy came up to Samarin and shook his hand, saying, "I hope you appreciate the act of courage I have accomplished in approaching you under the eyes of all my colleagues." *Materialy Cherkasskogo*, bk. 2, p. 82.

8. [A. I. Koshelev], *Deputaty i Redaktsionnye kommissii po krest'ianskomu delu* (Leipzig, 1860), p. 42.

9. Rescripts to Nazimov and Ignat'ev, *SbPR*, pp. 1, 6. The wording of the rescripts is *"razvitie . . . osnovanii,"* Lanskoi's is *"razvitie . . . korennykh nachal."*

10. "Vzgliad na polozhenie krest'ianskogo voprosa . . . ," in N. Semenov, *Osvobozhdenie*, I, pp. 833-834.

11. A deputy stole a copy of the unflattering survey and circulated it, and the deputies recognized it as the inspiration of the instructions. Miliutina, "Iz zapisok," vol. XCVII, p. 585; N. Semenov, *Osvobozhdenie*, I, p. 607n.

12. Letter to Cherkasskaia, in *Materialy Cherkasskogo*, bk. 2, p. 84.

13. P. Semenov, *Epokha*, vol. I, pp. 282, 286-287. Five months previously, Miliutin had written to Samarin urging him to join the Editorial Commission. "The deputies . . . will probably have only a consultative voice. I can absolutely assure you that the bases for work are broad and rational." Quoted in Miliutina, "Iz zapisok," vol. XCVII, p. 285. See also *Materialy Cherkasskogo*, bk. 2, p. 88.

14. On August 7, the MIA submitted the instructions to the tsar, who gave his formal approval on the 9th; they were issued to Rostovtsev two days later, in the form of a directive from Secretary of State Butkov. Both Semenovs state that the Main Committee, of which Butkov was executive secretary, approved the instructions; however, the committee's archive does not indicate that the instructions were brought before it, and *ZhSGK* does not record a meeting of the committee between May and October of 1859. *TsGIAL*, *f.* 1180, *op.* XV, *d.* 31, *ll.* 33-70, and, for the text of the instructions, *MRK*, III, appendix to ZhOP no. 45.

15. Draft of an appeal to the tsar, August 26, N. Semenov, *Osvobozhdenie*, I, p. 616.

16. Samarin to Cherkasskaia, *Materialy Cherkasskogo*, bk. 2, p. 84.

17. Shidlovskii to Orlov-Davydov, October 4, 1859, *ORGBL, f.* 219, *karton* 67, *d.* 50, *l.* 1ob. Original in French.

18. Cherkasskii's wife reported that because of the disappointment, "V[ladimir] P[etrovich] . . . was so upset that his position has become ridiculous," but "he now gives dinners for the deputies and intrigues with them." Cherkasskaia to Countess Baranova, August 20, 1859, in *Materialy Cherkasskogo*, bk. 2, p. 82.

19. P. D. Stremoukhov, "Zametka odnogo iz deputatov pervogo prizyva," *RS*, April 1900 (vol. CII), p. 141.

20. N. Volkonskii, "Nekotorye dannye . . . ," pp. 146-148.

21. P. Semenov, *Epokha*, vol. I, pp. 283-286. Semenov states that the

conference, which took place on August 20, reviewed the instructions for deputies. However, the instructions were issued on August 9, and it is clear from the correspondence among Rostovtsev and various participants (*Materialy Cherkasskogo*, bk. 2, pp. 80-81) that the conference reviewed the questions to be put to the deputies, not the instructions. Nikolai Semenov describes the conference in the same terms as Petr and makes the same error; Nikolai was not present, and obviously here, as elsewhere, he worked from Petr's notes, later incorporated into *Epokha*. Nolde follows the Semenovs, but dates the conference August 10; Nol'de, *Iurii Samarin*, p. 120.

22. [Koshelev], *Deputaty i Redaktsionnye kommissii*, p. 46.

23. Valuev, "Dnevnik," *RS*, September 1891 (vol. LXXI), p. 562. See also the diary of another of Murav'ev's subordinates and his private letter to a third; Lebedev, "Iz zapisok," *RA*, 1897, no. 8, pp. 634, 638; M. N. Murav'ev, "Pis'ma k A. A. Zelenomu, 1857-62," *GM*, 1914, no. 11, p. 222.

24. Semenov does not indicate the position taken by Cherkasskii, the sixth member of the strategy board, but it would appear from his letters that he agreed with the departmental members. *Materialy Cherkasskogo*, bk. 2, pp. 85-86.

25. The text of the address and the tsar's marginal comment are in N. Semenov, *Osvobozhdenie*, I, pp. 615-617.

26. Cited above in note 43 to chap. 4. In their letter to Rostovtsev, substituted for this address, the deputies acknowledged that the instructions had the tsar's sanction, and simply alluded to the broad promises held out in his speeches. N. Semenov, *Obvobzhdenie*, I, appendix, p. 834.

27. N. Semenov (I, p. 614), states that the address was "the result" of a conference at Shuvalov's on August 26, and that it was submitted to Rostovtsev "by them"—presumably by the deputies. The accounts by the deputies themselves all agree that this address was rejected—by a vote of twenty-two to six, one of them suggests—on August 26. Of these accounts, Volkonskii's is the most detailed and closest to the events. When the others are read in the light of Volkonskii's diary, it appears that the retrospective accounts somewhat telescope the confused events of the 26th and the next few days. Nikolai Semenov, ordinarily so lavish with personalia, failed to mention that he conferred with the deputies on their response to the instructions (as did Bulgakov, another member of the commission). It seems probable that Semenov acquired a copy of the address and that through his brother Petr it reached Rostovtsev and the tsar. N. Volkonskii, "Nekotorye dannye . . . ," pp. 152-154; [Koshelev], *Deputaty i Redaktsionnye kommissii*, p. 5; Pozen, *Bumagi*, pp. 229-230; Unkovskii, "Zapiski," *Russkaia mysl'*, 1906, no. 7, p. 97; and his letter to N. F. Shcherbatskii, May 12, 1860, *TsGAOR, f.* 109, *op.* 3, *d.* 2034, *ll.* 14-16ob.; V. Podvysotskii, "Otchet deputata bol'shinstva Chernigovskogo komiteta po krest'ianskomu delu o deistviiakh po vozlozhennym obiazannostiiam v S. Peterburge," *Trudy Chernigovskoi arkhivnoi komissii*, fasc. 9 (1912), p. 402.

28. Letter to Shcherbatskii just cited, *ll.* 15ob-16; in his memoirs, Unkovskii laid particular blame on Shuvalov's "accommodating nature." "Zapiski," p. 97.

29. Volkonskii attributed the deputies' retreat and capitulation to Pozen, who he suspected was secretly working in the commission's interest; Volkonskii, "Nekotorye dannye," pp. 153-154, 150, 152.

30. *"Imet' obshchie soveshchaniia."* "Pis'mo deputatov pervogo prizyva k Rostovtsevu," August 29, 1859, N. Semenov, *Osvobozhdenie*, I, appendix, pp. 834-836.

31. N. Semenov, *Osvobozhdenie*, I, p. 618, and Rostovtsev's reply to the deputies, appendix, pp. 836-837.

32. The questions Rostovtsev put to the deputies and the decisions on which their comments were invited are appended to ZhOP nos. 49 and 52 (September 2 and 5, 1859), *MRK*, III.

33. N. Semenov, *Osvobozhdenie*, II, p. 41.

34, Alexander's speech of September 4 and the exchange with Gagarin are in N. Semenov, *Osvobozhdenie*, I, p. 726.

35. [Koshelev], *Deputaty i Redaktsionnye komissii*, pp. 12-13. Pozen denied the existence of the short-lived caucus with which Koshelev identified him; *Bumagi*, p. 231. However, Unkovskii reported that the general meetings broke down because the most retrograde deputies began meeting secretly, apart from the rest; letter to N. F. Shcherbatskii, May 12, 1861, *TsGAOR, f.* 109, *op.* 3, *d.* 2034, *l.* 16*ob.*

36. "Otchetnye vedomosti [gubernatorov] o zaniatiiakh Gubernskikh Komitetov . . . ," *TsGIAL, f.* 1180, *op.* XV, *d.* 155, *ll.* 134-138; Aleksandr Kindiakov to A. V. Pashkov, December 20, 1858, *TsGAOR, f.* 109, *op.* 3, *d.* 2029, *ll.* 10-10*ob.*: see also their "Obzory osnovanii" in *TGK* (Simbirsk).

37. The younger Lanskoi was, however, an enterprising enough pomeshchik to forestall the inconvenient provisions of the emancipation legislation by relocating the peasant allotments on his own estate; N. A. Krylov, "Nakanune velikikh reform," *Istoricheskii vestnik*, vol. XCIII (September 1903), p. 814.

38. *MRK, Otzyvy*, II, pp. 545-564; [Koshelev]. *Deputaty i Redaktsionnye komissii*, p. 14.

39. *TsGIAL, f.* 1180, *op.* XV, *d.* 133, *ll.* 41-42.

40. *Materialy Cherkasskogo*, bk. 2, p. 86.

41. *ZhSGK*, place 406; P. Semenov, *Epokha*, vol. I, p. 389; *MRK, Otzyvy*, I, pp. 37, 33, 54.

42. N. Semenov, *Osvobozhdenie*, II, pp. 145-146.

43. Lanskoi upheld Gavrilov's election by a rump session of the Vladimir Committee and then presented the case, in a rather misleading light, to the Main Committee for its formal sanction; *TsGIAL, f.* 1180, *op.* XV, *d.* 31, *l.* 20; *ZhSGK*, pp. 416-417. In the meantime, Gavrilov had been transferred from Vladimir to head the chancellory of the Commission on Provincial and District Institutions, but he also "directly took part in the work of the Editorial Commission"; P. Semenov, *Epokha*, vol. I, p. 312.

44. *MRK, Otzyvy*, I, p. 174; original in italics.

45. Gavrilov wrote out a summary of his oral testimony and appended it to his response; this summary does not, however, indicate the half-desiatina reduction he sought, on which see N. Semenov, *Osvobozhdenie*, II, p. 45-46. According to Semenov, Solov'ev was overwhelmed by Gavrilov's

forceful presentation; Semenov was apparently unaware that the witness and his interrogator were friends.

46. D. N. to M. N. Shidlovskii, July 8, 1858, *TsGAOR*, f. 109, *op.* 3, *d.* 2029, *ll.* 2-2*ob.*; four dissenting opinions submitted to the Simbirsk Provincial Committee, *ORGBL*, f. 219, *karton* 81, *d.* 20; "Otchetnye vedomosti . . . ," *TsGIAL*, f. 1180, *op.* XV, *d.* 155, *ll.* 87*ob.*, 99*ob.*-102, 162*ob.*; Krylov, "Nakanune velikikh reform," p. 803.

47. *MRK, Otzyvy*, II, pp. 481-482, 479, 485, 491, 498.

48. Shidlovskii and Gagarin explained their refusal in the same words, and apparently agreed between themselves to boycott the sessions. Letters to Rostovtsev of September 24 and 25, 1859, *TsGIAL*, f. 1180, *op.* XV, *d.* 133, *ll.* 63-64, 66-67.

49. The journals of the Editorial Commission provide no details on the debates with the deputies, simply listing the names of those who testified on a particular day. Nikolai Semenov was absent from all of these sessions except the first and the last; his accounts of the debates were compiled from the notes of his brother Petr, later incorporated into Petr's memoirs. Petr recorded a few remarks and striking incidents; otherwise, his accounts seem to be digests of the deputies' written responses and the commission's written replies, as published in *MRK*. The accounts of Shidlovskii's and Gagarin's testimony are of this kind; the purported summary of Shidlovskii's testimony runs to three pages and every element of it can be found in his written response. Yet Rostovtsev made a point of informing Lanskoi that Shidlovskii attended the session of October 28 but "refused to make any such [oral] explanations." Similarly, the Semenov brothers make no mention of exchange between Rostovtsev and the deputy Nesterov, described in an unpublished letter from the latter to the former. It seems likely that Petr Semenov made his notes well after the fact, relying primarily on the published proceedings of the commission to reconstruct the debates. In any event, the Semenov brothers do not, as a rule, offer any independent evidence on the deputies of the first convocation. On Nikolai's use of Petr's notes, see N. Semenov, *Osvobozhdenie*, II, p. 43n; on the testimony of Gagarin and Shidlovskii, see his pp. 120-121 and 135-137, and the corresponding sections of his brother's *Epokha*, vol. I, pp. 370-371, 376-377; Rostovtsev's letter of October 30 to Lanskoi (which departed from the standard form for such letters) and Nesterov's letter of October 13 to Rostovtsev are in *TsGIAL*, f. 1180, *op.* XV, *d.* 133, *ll.* 174, 124.

50. *MRK, Otzyvy*, I, pp. 273, 288, 274-277.

51. I. V. Gagarin, "Adres Gg. Deputatam gubernskikh komitetov," signed and corrected in the author's hand; *ORGBL*, f. 219, *karton* 81, *d.* 1. The reference to "nobles from a majority of the provinces, assembled in St. Petersburg and Moscow," for whom Gagarin speaks, suggests that it was written just before he began his service as deputy. The five short mss. in this *delo*, of which this is the first, are not dated, but their present sequence appears from their contents to be chronological.

52. See P. Semenov, *Epokha*, vol. I, p. 284. Various agencies and individuals imputed binding force to various directives and imperial orders, but no other document had been given parity with the rescripts

publicly and officially.

53. I. V. Gagarin, "Sblizheniia i raznoglasiia," *ORGBL, f.* 219, *karton* 81, *d.* 1 [document III].

54. *MRK, Otzyvy,* I, p. 278. Garagin is here using the editorial we, whereas in his speech he is speaking for a group of nobles.

55. Gagarin, "Adres Gg. Deputatam," *l.* 1.

56. I. V. Gagarin, "Obshchie soobrazheniia," *ORGBL, f.* 219, *karton* 81, *d.* 1 [document II, in two copies], *ll.* 1, 5-7.

57. This allusion to Gagarin's remark to the tsar (see note 34 above) indicates that the commentary was written after September 4. Very likely Ofrosimov, the majority deputy from Riazan, was the author, because certain points recur in the responses of the Riazan deputies.

58. "Vozrazheniia na mnenie Gagarina, I. V." (title supplied by archivist), *ORGBL, f.* 219, *karton* 81, *d.* 1 [document V], *ll.* 1-2. Orlov-Davydov wrote in the margin beside the last point, "*Admission importante.*"

59. Unlike Gagarin, he stuck by his decision not to testify before the commission; he was willing to appear in response to a special invitation, which was not forthcoming; *TsGIAL, f.* 1180, *op.* XV, *d.* 133, *ll.* 96-96*ob.*

60. Unkovskii to N. F. Shcherbatskii, May 5, 1860. A month earlier, he wrote to F. S. Ofrosimov, who had been the majority deputy from Riazan, predicting that the peasants would be emancipated without any land apart from their plots. Unkovskii had not been so pessimistic as a deputy; he wrote these letters from exile in Viatka and blamed his troubles on the emancipators in St. Petersburg, notably Miliutin, "a most vicious bureaucrat and the enemy of all proper reforms in the administration." *TsGAOR, f.* 109, *op.* 1, *d.* 2034, *ll.* 8, 14*ob.*, 16*ob.*

61. Unkovskii, "Zapiski," no. 7, p. 100.

62. *MRK, Otzyvy,* II, pp. 636-637; this section was submitted jointly by Unkovskii and Kadro-Sysoev, the Tver minority deputy.

63. *MRK, Otzyvy,* II, pp. 664, 668, 682-684, 678.

64. The commission originally proposed a maximum of four desiatiny for five districts of Tver, four and one-half for four districts, five for two districts, and six desiatiny for Ostashkov district; *MRK,* III, DKhO no. 15, pp. 31-33. The statute of 1861 was closer to the Tver majority's figure, providing a maximum of five *desiatiny* in Ostashkov and four or four and one-half in the other nine districts.

65. *MRK, Otzyvy,* II, pp. 701-702, 710, 726, 722.

66. Indeed, in composing his response, Unkovskii drew on his "Zamechaniia o neobkhodimosti i pol'ze vykupa," which had been published in *Russkii vestnik,* vol. XIX, no. 2 (January, 1859), pp. 112-125.

67. On their rapprochement with Koshelev, see Koshelev, *Zapiski,* p. 118; on their use of Unkovskii's response, compare *MRK, Otzyvy,* II, pp. 101-102 and 680-681; 115 and 693.

68. However, he did not go so far as the resolution of the Tver nobility in 1861 and renounce all privileges for the noble estate.

69. Compare *MRK, Otzyvy,* II, pp. 780-781 and 637-638.

70. *MRK, Otzyvy,* II, pp. 841, 821 (cf. 864), 808, 831, 862-863, 828.

71. Five letters from Shreter to various correspondents, May 15, 1858-

June 6, 1860, in *TsGAOR, f.* 109, *op.* 3, *d.* 2039, especially *ll.* 1*ob.*-2, 10-11, 15-16, 21*ob.*; letters of October 8, 1859, and January 12 [1860], A. A. Kizevetter, ed., "K istorii krest'ianskoi reformy 1861 g.," *GM*, 1915, no. 2, pp. 226-228.

72. Shreter to Rostovtsev, October 9, 1858, and Khrushchov to Rostovtsev, October 14, 1859, *MRK, Otzyvy,* II, pp. 875-885.

73. *MRK, Otzyvy,* I, p. 703. He praised the commission's perception that redemption was the only adequate solution and its restraint in not imposing it. The compromise he suggested—a provision for redemption at the pomeshchik's demand—was incorporated into the statute of 1861.

74. *MRK, Otzyvy,* I, appendix, "Prilozhenie k otzyvu . . . Nesterova," pp. 5-6, 8-10, 3. This appendix consists of Sushchov's and Rusinov's "Zamechaniia" on DKhO no. 1, both dated June 9, and a covering letter from Boltin to Nesterov dated September 26, 1859.

75. Compare, for example, *MRK, Otzyvy,* I, p. 712 (Nesterov) and 656 (Stremoukhov). Nesterov's original response is dated September 12, his supplement (pp. 709-719), October 6.

76. *MRK, Otzyvy,* I, pp. 609-610, 601, 635-36: Petr Semenov, who edited the deputies' responses for publication, took the trouble to point out in a footnote on p. 596 that Volkov had misunderstood the commission on one point.

77. *MRK, Otzyvy,* I, pp. 610-614, 617.

78. Fourteen members of the Moscow Committee belatedly submitted a redemption plan which the commission reviewed with those from other committees; the Main Committee, out of deference to Governor-General Zakrevskii, ruled that this plan had no official status, so that the fourteen members were not represented by a deputy. *ZhSGK,* pp. 358-359, 404.

79. *MRK, Otzyvy,* I, p. 648-649; compare P. Semenov, *Epokha,* vol. I, p. 319.

80. P. Semenov, *Epokha,* vol. II, p. 171.

81. Only one of the nine deputies with military rank had risen as high as colonel; of the 29 with civil ranks, twelve had risen at least to the sixth grade, the civilian equivalent of a colonel's rank.

82. *MRK, Otzyvy,* II, p. 729. Addressing the Tver Committee, however, Unkovskii had predicted that both self-interest and a sense of common interests would induce the officials implementing the reform to favor the nobility; quoted in Pokrovskii, *Istoriko-statisticheskoe opisanie,* part I, p. 195.

83. Tiutcheva, *Pri dvore dvukh imperatorov* [vol. 2], p. 157.

84. N. Volkonskii, "Nekotorye dannye . . . ," p. 150.

85. V. P. Orlov-Davydov, *Réflexions préalables sur les bases proposées au mode de l'emancipation des serfs en Russie, par un deputé d'un comité provincial* (Paris, 1859), p. 6.

86. *MRK, Otzyvy,* II, p. 98.

87. Podvysotskii, "Otchet deputata," p. 408.

88. *MRK, Otzyvy,* II, pp. 339-341 (Shuvalov and Levashev); p. 471 (Shidlovskii); I, pp. 887-888 (Pozen).

89. *MRK, Otzyvy,* II, p. 502.

90. *MRK, Otzyvy,* I, p. 750 (Kosagovskii of Novgorod).

91. Jones finds much the same qualities in the nobility's *nakazy* to the

Codification Commission, composed almost a century previously: they "gave no indication that the *dvorianstvo* viewed itself as an ascendant class or that it believed that the state was being run in the interests of all the nobles." *Emancipation of the Russian Nobility,* p. 89.

92. *MRK, Otzyvy,* I, p. 447.

93. Compare the attitude of a self-styled defender of the nobility's aristocratic qualities, D. K. Schedo-Ferroti [Theodor, Baron von Fircks], *Etudes sur l'avenir de la Russie,* IV: *La noblesse,* 2nd ed. (Berlin, 1859), pp. 6, 115.

94. Several deputies contended that the commission's figures on these allotments were inflated because they were taken only from estates with more than a hundred serfs. The commission replied that allotments were about the same on smaller estates (N. Semenov, *Osovobozhdenie,* II, p. 33). However, since less than one-fifth of all the serfs lived on these smaller estates, their allotments would have had to be very small indeed to make a significant difference in the averages from which the commission proceeded.

95. *MRK, Otzyvy,* I, p. 547.

96. *MRK, Otzyvy,* II, pp. 443, 435, 455, 414, 437, 420, 442.

97. N. Semenov, *Osvobozhdenie,* I, pp. 285, passim.

98. *MRK,* II, DKhO no. 1, p. 23. Markovich and the Tambov deputies, quoted below, were commenting on this passage.

99. For example, *MRK, Otzyvy,* II, p. 99 (Koshelev).

100. *MRK, Otzyvy,* I, p. 262; the original is in bold face and italics, which Gagarin used freely.

101. *MRK, Otzyvy,* II, pp. 998-999.

102. *MRK, Otzyvy,* II, p. 609.

103. In eulogozing Rostovtsev, Shreter observed that for him, as for Shreter himself and his fellow-deputy Krushchov, the "transcendent word, the people!" was always uppermost in his mind. Letter to N. A. Vedemeir, February 23, 1860, TsGAOR, f. 109, *op.* 3, *d.* 1959, *l.* 27.

104. *MRK, Otzyvy,* II, p. 850; original in bold face italics. Many peasants, reportedly expected that the pomeshchiki would go off to live in the cities as the tsar's pensioners. In Khar'kov Province, however, according to a parody statute circulating in 1861, their lot would not be so easy; they would receive an allotment of stony or swampy ground and cultivate it themselves, and if they could not manage a plow, their ex-serfs should show them how, "without laughing." V. A. Fedorov, "Lozungi krest'ianskoi bor'by v 1861-1863 gg.," *Rev. Sit.* [III], pp. 241, 243; Okun' and Sivkov, *Krest'ianskoe dvizhenie,* p. 498.

105. *MRK, Otzyvy,* II, pp. 850-851.

106. *MRK, Otzyvy,* I, p. 282.

107. *MRK, Otzyvy,* I, pp. 619, 658.

108. The commune, being accountable for the dues of its members through mutual responsibility, could send a defaulting peasant to the army out of turn; it would receive a certificate which would be sold to another commune for submission in lieu of a recruit. The proceeds would be applied to the arrears, and the new soldier would get any money that might be left over. *MRK,* III, DKhO no. 11, p. 45.

109. *MRK, Otzyvy,* I, p. 884.

110. See Cherkasskii's explanation to Stremoukhov, N. Semenov, *Osvobozhdenie,* II, pp. 88-90 but compare the extreme instance cited in *MRK,* III, DKhO no. 11, p. 44.

11. *MRK, Otzyvy,* I, p. 608; see also the deputies' replies to the special question "O merakh k okhraneniiu vladel'cheskikh lesov," to be found at the beginning of most responses.

112. *MRK, Ozyvy,* II, pp. 714-715. On October 6, the commission held a special conference with the deputies on this requirement, which was relaxed in article 49 of the Great Russian Statute; *MRK,* IV, DKhO no. 3, p. 32, and *SZA,* pp. 193-194.

113. After the departure of the first group of deputies, the commission rejected *pereobrochka* again, by a vote of fourteen to nine. However, the Economic Section, following Rostovtsev's testament, adopted it in its final report, noting that although *pereobrochka* would be a "new levy on his [the peasant's] own labor," only two deputies favored unalterable dues. Miliutin and Samarin argued against the reversal, but only Samarin and four other members voted against it. N. Semenov, *Osvobozhdenie,* II, pp. 576, 977; and III, 2, pp. 487-489; *MRK,* XIII, *DKhO po otzyvam chlenov Gubernskikh Komitetov* [III], pp. 20, 32.

114. Starr makes this point with regard to local government in his treatment of the deputies, which is somewhat misleading on points of detail; *Decentralization and Self-Government,* p. 215.

115. *Materialy Cherkasskogo,* bk. 2, pp. 50, 94-95, 98, 160-161. See also Koshelev's letter of February 1, 1860, pp. 140-143.

116. *MRK, Otzyvy,* II, pp. 278-279. Later Koshelev explained his refusal to submit a response together with Ofrosimov and Volkonskii: "How could I sign my name to something with which I do not entirely agree, in a form which I do not wholly approve?" *Deputaty i Redaktsionnye kommissii,* p. 50.

117. Many of these were drawn from the statutes and regulations for state peasants and crown serfs. There is no doubt that Kiselev's reforms had great influence on the commission and on the emancipation legislation of 1861. In many instances, however, statutes were cited and terminology was borrowed simply to justify a decision, or rather to minimize the fact that a decision was being made. Similarly, in the Moscow Provincial Committee Menshikov cited the regulations on crown serfs, but it is doubtful that there was any flow of influence. Druzhinin does not take this consideration into account and so exaggerates the connection between Kiselev's reform and the emancipation of the serfs; *Gosudarstvennye krest'iane,* vol. II, pp. 559-565.

118. N. Semenov, *Osvobozhdenie,* II, pp. 40, 76.

119. Count Panin, who became chairman upon Rostovtsev's death, did not understand gradation even at the end of the commission's deliberations. See N. Semenov, *Osvobozhdenie,* III, 2, p. 498.

120. *MRK, Otzyvy,* II, p. 4. They reiterated this point in a report on their activities as deputies, which they circulated among the nobles of Riazan Province upon their return from St. Petersburg; Povalishin, *Riazanskie pomeshchiki,* p. 377.

121. Of the committees and factions represented by the first group of deputies, the Saratov and Kharkov committees, the Tver and Novgorod majorities, and one or more minorities of the Vladimir, Riazan, and Simbirsk committees are credited with redemption plans; *MRK*, III [third appendix to ZhOP no. 45], "Predvaritel'nye soobrazheniia o vykupe pozemel'nykh ugodii krest'ianami . . . ," pp. 4-5.

122. Privately, Rostovtsev still favored compulsory redemption. Describing the deputies in unflattering terms to the tsar, he observed that some of them favored compulsory redemption, "seeing in it, perhaps very justly, the simplest and most convenient issue from the problem." Rostovtsev to Alexander II, October 23, 1859, in N. Semenov, *Osvobozhdenie*, II, appendix, p. 930. The tsar continued to believe that compulsory redemption was unjust and unfeasible; see his comments on [A. I. Koshelev], "Pis'mo deputata pervogo prizyva," A. I. Popel'nitskii, ed., *RS*, vol. CXLV (February, 1911), pp. 352-353 and also *ZhSGK*, p. 491.

123. As Zakharova emphasizes, pointing out that all but three deputies advocating compulsory redemption would diminish the peasants' allotments; "Dvorianstvo i pravitel'stvennaia programma," p. 43.

124. Emmons takes just the opposite view, holding that nobles came to favor redemption as they realized "that the government was steadfast in its intentions . . . and that the reform was not going to be a wildly radical departure in which gentry interests would be neglected." *Russian Landed Gentry*, p. 245.

125. *MRK, Otzyvy*, II, pp. 293-294; Povalishin, *Riazanskie pomeshchiki*, p. 377.

126. Emmons imputes a high degree of accord and unity to the first convocation. In his exposition he concentrates on those deputies whose views were closest to Unkovskii's and then adduces the "fact . . . that the majority of the deputies were advocates of the *liberal gentry program*, and their chief spokesman was . . . A. M. Unkovskii." *Russian Landed Gentry*, p. 264.

127. *TsGIAL*, *f*. 1180, *op*. XV, *d*. 133, *ll*. 53-56.

128. [Koshelev], *Deputaty i Redaktsionnye kommissii*, p. 33.

129. Kadro-Sysoev to Rostovtsev, September 23, 1859, *TsGIAL*, *f*. 1180, *op*. XV, *d*. 133, *l*. 58ob.

130. The only consecutive account of these deliberations is in Koshelev's *Deputaty i Redaktsionnye kommissii*, pp. 17-20, 24-25.

131. Texts of both versions in N. Semenov, *Osvobozhdenie*, II, appendix, pp. 933-935.

132. [Koshelev], *Deputaty i Redaktsionnye kommissii*, p. 18.

133. However, the MIA's report on the appeal interpreted it in the latter sense, which made refutation very easy; *TsGIAL*, *f*. 982, *op*. 1, *d*. 62, *l*. 2.

134. "Concerning the economic side . . . I had nothing to argue about with the Commission, and therefore could not complain about them concerning allotments and obrok." Unkovskii to Dzhanshiev, January 24, 1893, in the latter's *A. M. Unkovskii*, p. 132n.; compare *MRK, Otzyvy*, II, p. 718, passim.

135. Text in N. Semenov, *Osvobozhdenie*, II, appendix, pp. 935-937, dated

October 16. The other appeals are not dated, but Shidlovskii's appeal must have been written on or before the 16th, while it was submitted on the 23rd; *Materialy*, vol. II, p. 180. The originals of the other two appeals have resolutions in the tsar's hand dated October 23; *TsGIAL*, f. 982, *op.* 1, *d.* 62, *l.* 1; *d.* 63, *l.* 2.

136. Notably the Vladimir deputy I. S. Bezobrazov; see *MRK, Otzyvy*, I, 246-247; Emmons's suggestion (*Russian Landed Gentry*, p. 238n) that six more deputies would have signed this address if they had not left St. Petersburg before it was compiled does not follow from the sources he cites and is difficult to infer from the positions they took.

137. *TsGIAL*, f. 982, *op.* 1, *d.* 62, *ll.* 2-4.

138. "Vzgliad na polozhenie krest'ianskogo voprosa . . . ," in N. Semenov, *Osvobozhdenie*, I, appendix, p. 833.

139. F. S. to M. Ofrosimov, October 19, 1859, *TsGAOR*, f. 109, *op.* 3, *d.* 1959, *ll.* 1-1*ob.*

140. Text in N. Semenov, *Osvobozhdenie*, II, appendix, pp. 937-939.

141. [Koshelev], *Deputaty i Redaktsionnye kommissii*, pp. 24, 17.

142. *TsGAOR*, f. 728, *op.* 1. *d.* 2574 (October 29, 1858); *ORGBL*, f. 219, *karton* 80, *d.* 33 (March 14, 1859); see bibliography.

143. "Materialy dlia dostavleniia adresa ot dvorianstva gosudariu sobrannye v mae 1859," *Materialy*, II, pp. 105, 107.

144. *Dnevnik Menshikova*, April 4, 1859, *l.* 50, and note 26 to chap. 5.

145. Popov, "Liberal'noe dvizhenie," p. 47n. There is not much doubt that the address on which the tsar made this comment was Bezobrazov's "Materials," although Popov does not identify it.

146. "Zapiska kamergera Mikhaila Aleksandrovicha Bezobrazova o znachenii Russkogo dvorianstva i polozhenii, kakoe ono dolzhno zanimat' na poprishche gosudarstvennoi deiatel'nosti," with covering letter to A. E. Timashev, October 15, 1859, in N. Semenov, *Osvobozhdenie*, II, appendix, pp. 940-942.

147. Presumably alluding to Rostovtsev, Bezobrazov complained of authorities who have "Imperial orders in reserve, ready to annul those preceding. There are even persons who scarcely speak except in the name of the Sovereign Emperor." "Zapiska kamergera . . . Bezobrazova," p. 944.

148. The governor of Chernigov ordered A. M. Markovich to serve as deputy from the minority on the provincial committee, although he belonged to the majority; the minority was bereft with the appointment of its two leading members, Galagan and Tarnovskii, to the Editorial Commission. Markovich was unhappy in this role, but the governor's choice was felicitous in that Markovich proved a much more effective spokesman for the Chernigov majority than the deputy it had chosen, Podvysotskii. See N. Volkonskii, "Nekotorye dannye . . . ," p. 148.

149. "Zapiska kamergera . . . Bezobrazova," pp. 945-950.

150. Alexander to Rostovtsev, October 25, 1859; N. Semenov, *Osvobozhdenie*, vol. II, p. 128.

151. Marginal note on original of "Adres piati chlenov gubernskikh komitetov," *TsGIAL*, f. 982, *op.* 1, *d.* 62, *l.* 7; it should be said in Alexander's behalf that the appeal of the five did not make clear, as their responses did,

that the zemstvo they proposed would be a purely local agency.

152. Note on "Zapiska kamergera . . . Bezobrazova," and letter to Rostovtsev of October 25, in N. Semenov, *Osvobozhdenie*, II, pp. 128, 952.

153. "Dokladnaia gr. Orlova," October 23, 1859, *TsGIAL, f.* 1180, *op.* XV, *d.* 40, *l.* 114*ob.*; *ZhSGK*, pp. 471-472; N. Semenov, *Osvobozhdenie*, II, p. 953.

154. "Zapiska ministra vnutrennikh del s predstavleniem trekh vsepodanneishikh adresov chlenov gubernskikh komitetov," November 4, 1858, quoted from the version published by Miliutina, "Iz zapisok," *RS*, vol. XCVIII, pp. 113-117.

155. Orlov's report to the tsar of November 8 reveals that the committee was divided, but does not indicate what the disagreement was or how the committee was divided: *TsGIAL, f.* 1180, *op.* XV, *d.* 40, *l.* 146.

156. Resolution on the original, dated October 23, 1859, *TsGIAL, f.* 982, *op.* 1, *d.* 62, *l.* 1.

157. This count was added to the original draft by Chevkin, who also struck out an order that Shidlovskii be kept under surveillance and specified that the surveillance of Unkovskii should be secret; "Proekt otnosheniia Gosudarstvennogo Sekretaria k Ministru Vnutrennikh Del," TsGIAL *f.* 1180, *op.* XV, *d.* 40, *ll.* 144-145. See also [Koshelev] *Deputaty i Redaktsionnye kommissii*, pp. 26-27.

158. Stremoukhov, "Zametka odnogo iz deputatov pervogo prizyva," p. 143.

159. Shuvalov's copy is preserved in his archive, *TsGIAL, f.* 1092, *op.* 1, *d.* 182.

160. Formal action on the addresses was postponed until Rostovtsev's health permitted him to deliberate with the Main Committee. However, it appears that the deputies were more roughly handled in the last two days of testimony, when Alexander's initial verdict was in hand. Both Petr and Nikolai Semenov held that the commission took the initiative against the deputies from the fifth of the ten days of testimony, by which time the members had received and scanned the deputies' written responses; N. Semenov, *Osvobozhdenie*, II, p. 82, and appendix, p. 1001.

161. *MRK, Otzyvy*, II, p. 391.

162. Shuvalov was present in the commission when DKhO no. 15 was discussed (N. Semenov, *Osvobozhdenie*, I, p. 635), but did not sign ZhOP no. 49, which gave the commission's provisional approval to the allotment figures.

163. N. Semenov, *Osvobozhdenie*, II, pp. 154-161.

164. *MRK, Otzyvy*, II, p. 347.

165. Wortman makes this point with respect to the reform of the courts, showing that trained jurists were able to exploit their near-monopoly of legal expertise to gain decisive influence on questions of policy; Richard Wortman, "Judicial Personnel and the Court Reform of 1864," *Canadian Slavic Studies*, III, 2 (1969), pp. 231-234.

166. Text in N. Semenov, *Osvobozhdenie*, II, appendix, pp. 954-959. The principal author was A. P. Bobrinskii. According to Petr Semenov, the draft was sponsored by Andrei Pavlovich Shuvalov (but not P. P. Shuvalov, the

St. Petersburg marshal of the nobility) and Paskevich, but Semenov may have confused the draft with a letter Paskevich sent to the tsar in the fall of 1859. See Valuev, "Dnevnik," *RS*, vol. LXXII, pp. 145-146 and P. Semenov, *Epokha*, vol. I, p. 393.

167. Informing Rostovtsev of Pozen's dismissal as deputy, Lanskoi emphasized that he was still a member of the Editorial Commission; Lanskoi to Rostovtsev, October 29, 1859, *TsGIAL, f.* 1180, *op.* XV. *d.* 133, *l.* 170*ob.*; compare *Materialy*, II, pp. 89-92. According to Petr Semenov, the tsar informed Pozen informally, through the head of the Third Section, that he would be dismissed if he did not resign, but this is probably an embroidery on the account in *Materialy*, which is very hostile to Pozen and inaccurate in most respects; *Epokha*, vol. II, p. 303. According to *MRK*, IV, ZhOP no. 68, p. 1, Pozen resigned voluntarily.

168. Letter to Rostovtsev, November 29, 1859, *Bumagi*, pp. 315-316; see also pp. 264-266.

169. "Zapiska o nadele," Pozen, *Bumagi*, p. 161; *MRK, Otzyvy*, 1, p. 932.

170. "Pamiatnaia zapiska Ia I. Rostovtseva o razmolvke s M. P. Pozenom," September 25, 1859, appendix to Elenev, "Pervye shagi," *RA*, 1886, no. 7, p. 403; the incident Rostovtsev describes appears as two separate incidents in N. Semenov, *Osvobozhdenie*, I, pp. 275-276, 311-312.

171. *Materialy Cherkasskogo*, bk. 2, p. 50; Miliutina seems to think the denunciation was made in August, 1859, but she was confused on chronological matters; "Iz zapisok," *RS*, vol. XCVII, p. 583.

172. Pozen tried this expedient, according to Rostovtsev, only after Rostovtsev had ignored his charges that the other members of the commission were "reds" and impractical pedants; "Pamiatnaia zapiska," p. 402.

173. [M. P. Pozen], "Pis'mo neustavlennogo litsa V. A. Dolgorukovu po povodu svoikh raznoglasii s Redaktsionnoi komissiei po podgotovke krest'ianskoi reformy" (title supplied), November 23, 1859, *TsGAOR, f.* 945, *op.* 1, *d.* 86, *ll.* 18-21. The signature is illegible, but the contents establish Pozen's authorship beyond doubt.

174. In the letter to Dolgorukov, Pozen denied that he had misrepresented the commission's ruling that the pomeshchik need not allot more than two-thirds of his land to the peasants to mean that he *must* allot two-thirds; compare *MRK* II, DKhO no. 1, p. 33, and Pozen's comment, *MRK, Otzyvy*, I, p. 810.

175. During 1860, at least three of Pozen's letters to his son were intercepted by the Third Section, copied, and presented to the tsar by Dolgorukov; they are hostile to the Editorial Commission and patronizing to Rostovtsev, but provide no support for the notion that Dolgorukov and Pozen conspired to defame the reformers. M. P. to L. M. Pozen, January 29, 1860, *TsGAOR, f.* 109, *op.* 3, *d.* 1959, *ll.* 15-16*ob.*; February 17 and November 26, 1860, *TsGAOR, f.* 109, *op.* 3, *d.* 2023, *ll.* 17-18, 26-26*ob.*

176. "Raznoglasie v Redaktsionnykh Komissiiakh po zhurnalu No. 13-15," and headnote, *Bumagi*, pp. 258-263.

177. "Pamiatnaia zapiska Rostovtseva," p. 403.

178. Petr Semenov (*Epokha*, vol. I, p. 302) sought to support Rostovtsev's

version but confirmed, apparently unwittingly, Pozen's main point that the infamous *kharakteristika* was simply his memorandum on the Shuvalov affair.

179. "Pis'mo . . . k G. Predsedateliu Redaktsionnykh Kommissii," November 5, 1859, *MRK, Otzyvy*, I, pp. 890-891.

8. Towards Enactment

1. See, for example, his speech to the deputies cited above (N. Semenov, *Osvobozhdenie*, I, p. 726), and, for his speeches at Pskov after the rejection of the deputies' appeals, *Materialy*, vol. II, pp. 218-219.

2. *Materialy Cherkasskogo*, bk. 2, p. 103, and appendix, pp. 36-49.

3. Cherkasskii to Baron Mengden, April 23, 1860, *Materialy Cherkasskogo*, bk. 2, p. 170; Miliutina, "Iz zapisok," vol. XCVIII, p. 120.

4. For example, article 18 of the General Statute and article 9 of the Great Russian Statute, which constituted changes of emphasis but not of substance, were added by the Council of State; *SZA*, pp. 42, 184.

5. "Posledniaia zapiska Rostovtseva o krest'ianskom dele, posle ego smerti priniataia Gosudarem," N. Semenov, *Osvobozhdenie*, II, appendix, pp. 968-993.

6. P. Semenov, *Epokha*, vol. I, pp. 428-432; vol. II, pp. 9-10.

7. Valuev, "Dnevnik," *RS*, vol. LXXII, pp. 149-150.

8. Polievktov, *Nikolai 1*, p. 71.

9. P. Semenov, *Epokha*, vol. I, pp. 438-439; Semenov's account is confirmed by Lanskoi's letter to Miliutin and a remark imputed to the tsar, in Miliutina, "Iz zapisok," vol. XCVIII, pp. 122-123.

10. N. Semenov, *Osvobozhdenie*, II, pp. 724-725, 738.

11. Indeed, he had raised no objection to the St. Petersburg Provincial Committee's provision for perpetual usufruct when, as a member of the ephemeral four-man subcommittee of the Main Committee, he reviewed the Petersburg Committee's draft statute; *MRK*, II, DKhO no. 8, p. 30.

12. N. Semenov, *Osvobozhdenie*, II, pp. 768-769, compare pp. 775-776. The issue kept arising because the commission was reviewing the regional statutes, each of which provided for perpetual usufruct.

13. N. Semenov, *Osvobozhdenie*, II, pp. 819-820, 851. The members noted in reply that the tsar had sanctioned perpetual usufruct by ruling against Shuvalov and Paskevich, and not even they had sought temporary allotment.

14. *MRK*, II, DKhO no. 8, p. 37.

15. N. Semenov, *Osvobozhdenie*, III, 1, pp. 3-6, 11-13.

16. N. Semenov, *Osvobozhdenie*, III, 1, pp. 70-75.

17. This point was supported with a digest of the views of the first group of deputies; text in N. Semenov, *Osvobozhdenie*, III, 2, appendix, pp. 793-796.

18. "Osobaia zapiska 19-ti chlenov Redaktsionnykh Komisii po krest'ianskomu delu o bezrochnom pol'zovanii . . . ," April 14, 1860 (originally submitted to Panin), N. Semenov, *Osvobozhdenie*, III, 1, appendix, pp. 478-479.

19. "Vsepodanneishaia zapiska grafa V. N. Panina o nesoglasii ego s 19-iu chlenami Redaktsionnykh Komisii . . . ," April 19, 1860, with Alexander's comments, in N. Semenov, *Osvobozhdenie*, III, 1, appendix, p. 491. Panin went on to restate his recriminations against the members of the commission, but these did not provoke any comment from the tsar.

20. Two undated notes from Miliutin to Cherkasskii, in *Materialy Cherkasskogo*, bk. 2, pp. 166-168; N. Semenov, *Osvobozhdenie*, III, 2, p. 457; "Proekt mestnogo polozheniia . . . v guberniiakh Velikorossiiskikh, Novorossiskikh i Belorusskikh," *MRK*, XVIII, p. 352 (article 97); compare the corresponding article (98) in *SZA*, p. 204.

21. According to Valuev, Panin proposed Vladimir Bobrinskii, but he refused to join the commission after the tsar explained he must sign the journals whether or not he approved of the contents; Valuev, "Dnevnik," *RS*, vol. LXXII, p. 153.

22. N. Semenov, *Osvobozhdenie*, III, 2, pp. 45 passim; p. 514.

23. Cherkasskii to Baron Mengden, April 23, 1860, in *Materialy Cherkasskogo*, bk. 2, p. 170.

24. Koshelev to Aksakov, March 15 and 30, 1860, *TsGAOR, f.* 109, *op.* 3, *d.* 1959, *l.* 36, 50-50*ob.*; text of second letter also in *GM*, 1918, no. 7/9, p. 182.

25. D. N. Rychkov to Samarin, February 21, 1860, *TsGAOR, f.* 109, *op.* 3, *d.* 1959, *l.* 25*ob.*

26. Khodkevich to Dolgorukov, quoted in Deich, *Krest'ianstvo Pskovskoi gubernii* p. 311. Later, Khodkevich reported that the nobility was disillusioned with Panin; *TsGAOR, f.* 109, *l-aia eksp.*, 1857 *g., d.* 321, *chast'* 34, *ll.* 7-8.

27. N. Shch. from St. Petersburg to V. F. Korsh in Moscow, March 1, 1860, *TsGAOR, f.* 109, *op.* 3, *d.* 1959, *l.* 29.

28. Panin's speech to the deputies, February 22, 1860, in N. Semenov, *Osvobozhdenie*, II, p. 699.

29. N. Semenov, *Osvobozhdenie*, II, 1, p. 22.

30. In the covering letter to their "Concluding Opinion," discussed below, the deputies informed Panin that they put their hopes in him as a "dispassionate sanovnik, a *pomestnyi dvorianin*, and the supreme guardian of the law." N. Semenov, *Osvobozhdenie*, III, 1, appendix, p. 480. On Panin's embarrassment, see P. Semenov, *Epokha*, vol. II, p. 50.

31. N. Semenov, *Osvobozhdenie*, III, 1, p. 250.

32. Valuev, "Dnevnik" (for April 3, 1860), *RS*, vol. LXXII, p. 152-153.

33. *Materialy*, vol. II, p. 427; *MRK, Otzyvy*, III, 1, pp. 133-134 (Obolenskii of Kaluga), and III, 2, p. 294 (Kasinov of Kherson). Other deputies from Kaluga and Kherson and the majority deputy from Samara seemed, in their several responses, to favor redemption; all three, however, signed a collective response in which twenty-nine deputy rejected the commission's redemption plan, without offering any alternative beyond the insistence that ex-serfs be put on the same footing as other prospective purchasers of land. See *MRK, Otzyvy*, III, 1, p. 294, and IV, 2, pp. 22-23, 116, and 189.

34. Emmons also cites this regional consideration and the political climate of the moment as the major determinants of the positions the deputies took; *Russian Landed Gentry*, pp. 204-205.

35. The deputies of the second *prizyv* came from Smolensk, Perm, Olonets, and Vologda; Kazan, Penza, Samara, and Orenburg; the three provinces of New Russia and the Territory of the Don Cossacks; Orel, Kaluga and Kursk; Kiev, Podolia, Volynia, Grodno, Vilna, Kovno, Mogilev and (reassigned from the first group) Vitebsk and Minsk.

36. Including the Perm deputy Vsevolozhskii, the appointed chairman of a committee in a province with no nobiliary institutions. Iurii Samarin, the elected deputy from the Samara minority, had also served by appointment, but since he did not assume any of the duties of a deputy, he is left out of account in this paragraph.

37. Data from *MRK. Svedeniia*, referring to the district (with marshals and appointed members, the province) from which the deputy was elected. Because of discrepancies in spelling or the omission of the pomeshchik's initials, the classification of six deputies, including two great proprietors, is tentative.

38. For example, Gorskin of Penza had 61 *dvorobye*, Obukhov of Samara had 107, Iz″ edinov of Kursk had 205. If these serfs were not household servants or specialized workers, presumably their masters either transferred ordinary peasants to this category to avoid giving them a statutory allotment, or else sent out peasants not needed on the demesne to earn their dues elsewhere.

39. *MRK*, III, ZhOP no. 52, p. 2.

40. In a letter of April 18, 1860, to Orlov-Davydov, Shidlovskii describes his work with the deputies and his enthusiasm for their "concluding opinion," *ORGBL, f.* 219 *karton 67, d.* 50.

41. [Koshelev] *Deputaty i Redaktsionnye komissii*, p. 28.

42. For the text of Lanskoi's circular as read to the assemblies, see *Kolokol*, no. 65/66 (March 15, 1860), p. 547; for his accompanying confidential circular to the governors, see Krechetovich, *Krest'ianskaia reforma*, pp. 427-428.

43. *Materialy*, vol. II, pp. 264-267; Povalishin, *Riazanskie pomeshchiki*, pp. 378-386; Emmons, *Russian Landed Gentry*, pp. 284-286 and appendix II, where the petitions from the assemblies of Tver, Riazan, Iaroslav, Orel, Vladimir, and St. Petersburg provinces are given in translations made (with one exception) from the archival originals.

44. *Kolokol*, no. 65/66 (March 15, 1860), p. 549; *Materialy*, vol. II, pp. 300-302; Emmons, *Russian Landed Gentry*, pp. 268-269 and 288-290.

45. "Adres Vladimirskogo dvorianstva," *Kolokol*, no. 71 (May 15, 1860), pp. 591-592; *Materialy*, vol. II, 303-315; Emmons, *Russian Landed Gentry*, pp. 291-294.

46. Strictly speaking, assemblies of the nobility submitted to the government the names of two candidates for the marshalship; as a rule, the candidate with the most votes was confirmed as provincial marshal, and the other as his deputy. In this instance, however, neither Vasil'ev nor Dubrovin was confirmed. Similarly, the ex-deputy Podvysotskii was confirmed as chairman of the Chernigov *Mezhevaia palata* only through the intervention of the Committee of Ministers, for the MIA and even the tsar himself were anxious that the returned deputies and other troublemakers

not be elected to office by the provincial nobility. *Materialy*, vol. II; pp. 296-300; Seredonin, *Istoricheskii obzor*, vol. III, 1, p. 293; Emmons, *Russian Landed Gentry*, pp. 287-288 and 286, n. 2.

47. *Materialy*, vol. II, pp. 316-325. See also Starr, *Decentralization and Self-Government*, pp. 196-197, 200n.

48. Apraksin's letter of December 20, 1859, followed by the Orel petition, a covering letter from the marshals, and the narrowly defeated alternative sponsored by S. I. Mal'tsev; *TsGAOR, f. 109, op. 3, d. 2019, ll. 5-12ob*.

49. V. P. Orlov-Davydov, "Rech' skazannaia pri postanovlenii Orlovskogo dvorianstva poslat' adres na vysochaishee imia," December 17 (1859), *ORGBL, f. 219, karton 80, d. 19, l. 2*.

50. "Slova . . . v gubernskom sobranii S. Petersburgskogo dvorianstva," March 16 (1860), *ORGBL, f. 219, karton 80, d. 24, ll. 1-3*.

51. See the scathing comments of one of Herzen's correspondents on this attitude, in "Tverskoi komitet i Unkovskii," *Kolokol*, no. 65/66, March 15, 1860, p. 549.

52. *ZhSGK*, pp. 490-491. To be sure, when the Riazan marshal submitted a petition to the tsar in his own name, in which he reiterated the terms of the rejected peition, he was formally reprimanded; *Materialy*, vol. II, p. 267.

53. *Kolokol*, no. 65/66, pp. 549-550; *Materialy*, vol. II, pp. 293-294; Emmons, *Russian Landed Gentry*, pp. 266-281. Unkovskii himself initially thought he was exiled because the regime was misled by a secret and false denunciation, but later he maintained that the regime acted deliberately and in reaction to his real activites. Letters from Viatka to A. V. Vel'iagiev, March 14, 1860, and to N. S. Rzhevskaia, June 20, 1860, *TsGAOR, f. 109, op. 3, d. 2034, ll. 3, 33*.

54. Marginal note on letter from Dolgorukov to Alexander, December 23, 1859; marginal resolution on Mal'tsev's draft petition; Mal'tsev's reply to Dolgorukov, January 7, 1860, *TsGAOR, f. 109, op. 3, d. 2019, ll. 23, 10, 16-18*. Writing in reply to Dolgorukov (in the second person singular), Mal'tsev professed his devotion to the tsar and insisted that his petition was acutally more moderate than Apraksin's; apart from a eulogy to the late tsar Nicholas, it simply consisted of a warning about a universal anxiety among the nobility, and it was the loyal subject's duty to warn the tsar about such phenomena.

55. See *MRK, Otzyvy*, I, pp. 246-247.

56. Mal'tsev disputed this. He reminded Dolgorukov that he had warned the empress, Alexander, Orlov, and Dolgorukov himself about the dangers of precipitate reform. Orally and in writing, both before and after the government's commitment to emancipation, he had indicated the measures necessary "for the salvation of the fatherland," but (he implied) to no avail as yet. *TsGAOR, f. 109, op. 3, d. 2019, ll. 16-18*.

57. [Koshelev], "Pis'mo deputata pervogo prizyva," pp. 344-362.

58. *Materialy*, vol. II, p. 446.

59. The number of signatures varies from twenty-nine to thirty-nine; the Concluding Opinion has thirty-six, and each section of the long

response to the Economic Section bears a different number of signatures. Since all seven collective statements were interrelated and equally offensive, it seems that the discrepancy is due to the haste and confusion of the deputies' deliberations (see *MRK, Otzyvy*, IV, 2, p. 135) rather than selectivity and discretion on their part.

60. Petr Semenov explained that the treacherous Poles seduced the Russian deputies over to their point of view, but then held back from the scandalous Concluding Opinion; he emphasized that the Poles were cowardly as well as retrograde, for they feared removal from their provincial marshalships. P. Semenov, *Epokha*, vol. II, p. 46. However, two of four Polish marshals endorsed three collective responses and a third, Orzhesko, endorsed five.

61. *MRK, Otzyvy*, III, 2, pp. 133-134, and IV, 1, p. 49; on the commission's expectation of support from Obolenskii, see P. Semenov, *Epokha*, vol. II, pp. 112-113, and *Materialy Cherkasskogo*, bk. 2, p. 157.

62. In a letter to Panin dated April 2, 1860, Pushkin explained that he had to return to Tula to see to his estates; in a second letter, bearing the same date, he admitted that the reasons he had just given were spurious but insisted that he must leave anyway; *TsGIAL, f.* 1180, *op.* XV, *d.* 134, *ll.* 50-51ob.

63. "Zakliuchitel'noe mnenie," N. Semenov, *Osvobozhdenie*, III, 1, appendix, pp. 480-483.

64. In practice, the deputies would restrict the contractual freedom of agricultural laborers through the use of labor books, which would replace internal passports; *MRK, Otzyvy*, IV, 2, pp. 207-209.

65. During the confrontation with the second group of deputies, Cherkasskii apologized to a visiting Belgian economist for the commission's departure from laissez-faire. He observed that "highly though the sound principles of science should be prized, all the same, in practical life, it is impossible not to make concessions to the temporary requirements of society." *Materialy Cherkasskogo*, bk. 2, p. 146.

66. "Zakliuchitel'noe mnenie," pp. 486-488. Unlike the *otzyvy*, this document was submitted directly to Panin for transmittal to the tsar and is not found in *MRK, Otzyvy*.

67. *MRK, Otzyvy*, III, 1, pp. 33, 163.

68. "They themselves were the pomeshchik's property"; *MRK, Otzyvy*, III, 1, p. 14. No deputy of the first group went further than the abstruse contention that the pomeshchik had a property right to the peasant's dues.

69. *MRK, Otzyvy*, IV, 2, pp. 62-63.

70. *MRK, Otzyvy*, III, 1, pp. 208-209.

71. *MRK, Otzyvy*, IV, 1, p. 8.

72. *MRK, Otzyvy*, III, 1, pp. 184, 182. The deputies did strive for superficial consistency with their economic doctrine by speaking of "class" and "proprietors" rather than "estate" and "pomeshchiki."

73. *MRK, Otzyvy*, III, 2, p. 74; III, 1, p. 212.

74. *MRK, Otzyvy*, III, 2, p. 85; compare III, 1, p. 164.

75. *MRK, Otzyvy*, III, 1, pp. 162, 185-186. The term *volostnoi popechitel'* or *volostnoi nachal'nik*, was used by the deputies of both groups as a rubric for

the perpetuation of the pomeshchik's personal authority. It was taken from the government's provisional formulation of the postreform local administration, issued May 16, 1858, in a circular to the governors. The deputies were apparently unaware that this formulation had been supplanted by the Imperial Order of March 25, 1859, which provided for an appointed *ispravnik* instead. However, the *ispravnik* system was rejected in its turn in May of 1860, over the objections of Lanskoi and the Grand Duke Konstantin. The majority of the Main Committee found that it would be wrong to deprive the nobles of control of the local police just when economic sacrifices were being exacted from them. The tsar endorsed the majority's view. See *SbPR*, pp. 152, 47-48, and *ZhSGK*, p. 499.

76. N. Semenov, *Osvobozhdenie*, III, 1, pp. 229-231, 103, 169.

77. N. Semenov, *Osvobozhdenie*, III, 1, pp. 148n., 198, 226. Except for Shostakovskii of Kiev, all the deputies quoted or mentioned in the last two paragraphs signed the "concluding Opinion" and most or all of the collective responses.

78. N. Semenov, *Osvobozhdenie*, III, 1, p. 193.

79. Quoted in Boris Nol'de, *Peterburgskaia missiia Bismarka* (Prague, 1925), p. 249.

80. Valuev, "Dnevnik," *RS*, vol. LXXII, p. 397. The published text has *"nadlezhashchii"* enclosed in parentheses, clearly substituted by an editor or censor for *"vysochaishii."*

81. The official text distributed to the members of the commission read "to make changes" instead of "to change much." N. Semenov, *Osvobozhdenie*, III, 2, pp. 753, 810.

82. P. Semenov, *Epokha*, vol. I, p. 433, 424; Cherkasskii to Mengden, April 3, 1860, in *Materialy Cherkasskogo*, bk. 2, p. 157.

83. *Materialy Cherkasskogo*, bk. 2, p. 165.

84. *Materialy*, vol. III, pp. 141-145.

85. Valuev, "Dnevnik," *RS*, vol. LXXII, pp. 412-413, 416-417, 419. In restrospect, Valuev recalled that he put no faith in rumors and little in Murav'ev, but "I had more faith in Pr[ince] Dolgorukov, and, seeing his steadfastness, I thought it was at least possible to suppose that the sovereign had not declared his conclusive opinion and that Pr. Dolgorukov himself had hopes of success." *Dnevnik Valueva*, vol. I, p. 311.

86. Valuev, "Dnevnik," *RS*, vol. LXXII, p. 401; Koshelev to Ivan Aksakov, March 15, 1860, *TsGAOR, f.* 109, *op.* 3, *d.* 1959, *l.* 36.

87. P. Semenov, *Epokha*, vol. II, p. 290; Valuev, "Dnevnik," *RS*, vol. LXXII, p. 424; N. Semenov, *Osvobozhdenie*, III, 2, pp. 763-772. In both the Main Committee and the Council of State, Panin did depart from the Commission's recommendations by proposing a nine-year delay before peasants were free to shift from barshchina to obrok.

88. At first he opposed the Editorial Commission's draft, but after studying the rival proposals of Murav'ev (who was counting on his support) he formally adhered to the Grand Duke's majority. A. Popel'nitskii, "Delo os vobozhdeniia krest'ian v Gosudarstvennom Sovete," *Russkaia mysl'*, 1911, no. 2, p. 159.

89. Butkov's conversion had tactical value; since he was the executive

secretary of the Main Committee, the committee's staff was put at the disposal of those who favored the Editorial Commission's version. P. Semenov, *Epokha*, vol. II, p. 253n.

90. P. Semenov, *Epokha*, vol. II, p. 263. However, Semenov misrepresented Gagarin's position. He did not advocate landless emancipation at this time, but called for a "permanent" (*postoiannyi*) allotment, the word used in the statutes of 1861; "Mnenie Deistvitel'nogo Tainogo Sovetnika kniazia Gagarina," Arkhiv Gosudarstvennogo Soveta, *Prilozheniia k zhurnalu Glavnogo komiteta po krest'ianskomu delu* (Petrograd, 1915), p. 273 (cited hereinafter as *Prilozheniia k ZhGK*).

91. Arkhiv Gosudarstvennogo Soveta, *Zhurnaly Sekretnogo i Glavnogo komitetov po krest'ianskomu delu* (Petrograd, 1915), vol. II, pp. 38, 42 (cited hereinafter as *ZhSGK, II*). See also "Mnenie D. T. S. kn. Gagarina," p. 276.

92. "Mnenie D. T. S. kn. Gagarina," pp. 255-262.

93. He noted that the commission printed it (*MRK, Otdel'nye mneniia* (I), pp. 51-80) "without refutation"; "Mnenie D. T. S. kn. Gagarina," p. 262.

94. A peasant would work a parcel of the demesne that would require two days per week to cultivate; in return, he would receive an allotment half again as large as that parcel, but the pomeshchik would not be required to allot more than half of his arable land to the peasants. Hence in many villages there would be a large number of *zatiaglye* peasants who had no allotments, and their number would gradually increase by virtue of Gagarin's proposed restrictions on the repartition of allotments. "Mnenie D. T. S. kn. Gagarina," pp. 263-265.

95. "Dopol'nitel'noe mnenie D. T. S. kn. Gagarina," *Prilozheniia k ZhGK*, p. 297.

96. He wrote of the deputies' responses, "I regret that many members of the Main Committee will not read them. They explain the matter extremely well." "Pis'ma M. N. Murav'eva k A. A. Zelenomu," *GM*, 1914, no. 11, p. 227.

97. Letter to Zelenyi, June 13, 1860, in *GM*, 1914, no. 11, p. 226.

98. Valuev, "Dnevnik," *RS*, vol. LXXII, pp. 404, 406, 414, 412, 418.

99. "Proekt mestnogo polozheniia . . . sostavlennyi chlenami Glavnogo Komitetom kniazem Dolgorukovym, Murav'evym i Kniazhevichem," p. 168 and appended "Rospisanie norm nadelov," *Prilozheniia k ZhGK*, pp. 219-27; compare *MRK, XVIII*, pp. 440-484. Valuev maliciously stated that Murav'ev settled on the maxima because they came easily to hand, being printed first in the commission's draft.

100. P. Semenov, *Epokha*, vol. II, p. 218; compare p. 302.

101. On November 2 he wrote: "I consider the cause of the Editorial Commission is won." "Dnevnik," *RS*, vol. LXXII, p. 411.

102. Valuev, "Dnevnik," *RS*, vol. LXXII, p. 414. The day before in reaction to an order to revise the commission's draft "according to very flimsy directions," he complained, *"Dura lex sed lex"*; the *lex* in question was the necessity of accommodating Murav'ev and Dolgorukov.

103. Transcript and official text as corrected by Alexander, in Arkhiv Gosudarstvennogo Soveta, *Zhurnaly i memorii obshchego sobraniia Gosudarstvennogo Soveta po krest'ianskomu delu* (Petrograd, 1915), pp. 182-188

(cited hereinafter as *ZhMGS*). Alexander eliminated from the official text a disparaging comparison between the calm and trusting peasantry and the anxious nobility; *ZhMGS*, p. 182.

104. Golovnin to Bariatinskii, February 15, 1861, quoted in Tatishchev, *Aleksandr II*, vol. I, p. 379. Tatishchev quotes a slightly different version of the tsar's speech to the council.

105. *Dnevnik Valueva*, vol. I, pp. 64, 66; compare P. Semenov, *Epokha*, vol. II, p. 448.

106. *ZhMGS*, p. 7.

107. *ZhMGS*, pp. 11-15.

108. *ZhMGS*, pp. 22-24.

109. *MRK*, IX, DAO no. 9, pp. 4-6; compare *SbPR*, pp. 47-53 and p. 46 of "Otchet Kommissii ob uezdnykh uchrezhdeniiakh," also in *MRK*, IX.

110. *ZhSGK*, II, p. 34. Much of the conflict and violence surrounding the implementation of the reform in 1861 occurred because the arbitrative institutions were not yet in being when the reform was promulgated. The delay derived from the consideration that elections could not be held prior to promulgation, but was not eliminated when appointment was substituted for election.

111. *ZhMGS*, pp. 40-43.

112. *ZhMGS*, pp. 69-70, 73-75.

113. "Since the proposed dues decline according to a gradation derived from the maximum allotment, the first consequence . . . will be the ruin of the pomeshchiki and the next—a significant curtailment of demesne agriculture (*ekonomicheskie zapashki*)." *ZhMGS*, p. 101.

114. Apart from the beggarly allotment, Alexander agreed with the majority that the district marshal should preside over the arbitration council. *ZhMGS*, p. 254.

115. Popel'nitskii's reckoning, in his "Delo osvobozhdeniia krest'ian," p. 135n.

116. Zaionchkovskii finds that peasants prospered if they accepted the quarter-size allotment, sold it, and moved away. Most of those who accepted, however, clung to it and became laborers or renters, soon paying high rents, on their ex-master's estate. Zaionchkovskii, *Provedenie v zhizn'*, pp. 298-300.

117. *MRK*, II, DKhO no. 8, pp. 46-47.

118. A few days earlier, sixteen members of the council had held that "an allotment on which peasants cannot exist without renting [land] from the pomeshchiki cannot be deemed adequate to secure their way of life," and the tsar had endorsed their view. *ZhMGS*, p. 312.

119. *Materialy*, vol. III, p. 143.

120. The beggarly allotment was the last matter the council considered, apart from some peripheral issues and the schedule of allotments, in which it reduced the maximum in four more districts. *ZhMGS*, pp. 377-379, 382.

121. N. M. Kolmakov, "Krest'ianskoe delo 1857-60 gg. Zametki k Zapiskam Ia. A. Solov'eva," *RS*, vol. XLVII (September, 1885), p. 470.

122. *Dnevnik Valueva*, vol. I, pp. 312-313; commentary to his own diary, dated April 29, 1868.

123. Zaionchkovskii, *Otemena*, pp. 158-159.

Conclusion

1. On peasant monarchism in 1861, see Daniel Field, *Rebels in the Name of the Tsar* (Boston, 1976), especially chapter 2.

2. Leroy-Beaulieu, *Un homme d'état russe*, p. 46; P. Semenov, *Epokha* vol. I, p. 383.

3. Samarin to Cherkasskii, February 6, 1860, in *Materialy Cherkasskogo*, bk. 2, p. 143.

4. The Manifesto made no mention of the Editorial Commission, but neither did the draft manifesto offered by Samarin and Cherkasskii; compare *SZA*, p. 32, and "Pervonachal'nyi proekt Manifesta ob osvobozhdenii krest'ian," Iu. F. Samarin, *Sochineniia*, vol. IV, pp. 373-376.

5. *Materialy*, vol. III, p. 101; compare *Prilozheniia k ZhSGK*, p. 3, and *MRK*, XVIII, p. 5.

6. Iakushkin, "Velik bog," p. 126.

Bibliography

This bibliography is essentially a list of the published works cited in the footnotes. A few sources, consulted but not cited, and some manuscript items that are congruent to published material are included. Items in the following categories are usually not separately listed:

1. Articles from the following contemporary periodicals: *Kolokol, Sovremennik, Russkii vestnik, Zhurnal Ministerstva vnutrennikh del (ZhMVD), Sel'skoe blagoustroistvo, Zhurnal zemlevladel'tsev.*

2. Book reviews and the like.

3. Secondary articles from three compendia devoted to the reform era, *Velikaia reforma, Rev. Sit.* [fasc. I-VI], and *ZOR*, X.

Primary sources

Adres kalendar', ili Obshchaia rospis' vsekh chinovnykh osob v gosudarstve, 1857, in two parts (St. Petersburg [1857]).

Aksakov, I. S., *Ivan Sergeevich Aksakov v ego pis'makh*, 4 vols. (Moscow-St. Petersburg, 1888-1896).

————, "Pis'ma S. T., K. S. i I. S. Aksakovykh k I. S. Turgenevu (1855-61 gg.)," *Russkoe obozrenie*, December 1894, pp. 571-601.

Anon., "Vladimir Ivanovich Nazimov," *RS*, vol. XLV (February and March 1885) pp. 385-410, 555-580.

Arkhiv Gosudarstvennogo soveta, *Zhurnaly i memorii obshchego sobraniia Gosudarstvennogo soveta po krest'ianskomu delu s 28 ianvaria po 14 marta 1861 g.* (Petrograd, 1915).

————, *Zhurnaly Sekretnogo i Glavnogo komiteta po krest'ianskomu delu*, 2 vols. plus separate vol. of appendices (Petrograd, 1915).

Baraboi, A. Z. et al., eds., *Otmena krepostnogo prava na Ukraine: Sbornik dokumentov i materialov* (Kiev, 1961).

Barsukov, N. P., *Zhizn' i trudy M. P. Pogodina*, 22 vols. (Moscow, 1888-1910).

Bezobrazov, M. A., "Vypiski iz pis'ma deistvitel'nogo Statskogo Sovetnika Mikhaila Bezobrazova k Gen. ad"iut. Ia. I. Rostovtsevu o dopolnenii k stat'e 'Khod i iskhod krest'ianskogo voprosa'," *ORGBL, f.* 219, *karton* 80, *d.* 33.

_____, "Zamechaniia Deistvitel'nogo Statskogo Sovetnika Kamergera M. A. Bezobrazova na proekt polozheniia sostavlennogo [sic] Moskovskim Gubernskim Komitetom," *ORGBL, f.* 219, *karton* 80, *d.* 33.

_____, "Zapiska Deistv. Statsk. Sovetnika, Kamergera Mikhaila Bezobrazova, podannaia S.-Peterburgskomu Komitety (po krest'ianskomu delu) A. P. Platonovym," October 29, 1858. *TsGAOR, f.* 728, *op.* 1, *d.* 2574.

Bezobrazov, N. A., *Dve zapiski po votchinnomu voprosu s predisloviem i obshchim zakliucheniem* (Berlin, 1859). Includes "Ob usovershenii . . . " and "Obsuzhdenie voprosa ob uluchshenii byta pomeshchich'ikh krest'ian."

_____, *Ob usovershenii uzakonenii kasaiushchikhsia do votchinnykh prav dvorianstva* (Berlin, 1858).

_____, *Predlozheniia dvorianstvu* (Berlin, 1862).

Blank, G. [B.], "Russkii pomeshchichii [sic] krest'ianin," *Trudy Imperatorskogo volnogo ekonomicheskogo obshchestva,* June, 1856 (N. S., vol. II, no. 6), pp. 117-129.

Botkin, V. P., "Perepiska V. P. Botkina s I. I. Panaevym," in N. L. Brodskii, ed., *Turgenev i krug "Sovremennika"* (Moscow-Leningrad, 1930), pp. 363-452.

Chernyshev, E., ed., "Materialy po istorii klassovoi bor'by v 60-kh godakh XIX veka," *Izvestiia Obshchestva arkheologii, istorii i etnografii* (Kazan), vol. XXXII, fasc. 4 (1927), pp. 75-97.

Chernyshevskii, N. G., *Polnoe sobranie sochinenii*, 16 vols. (Moscow, 1939-1955).

Chichagov, P. B., *Arkhiv Admirala P. B. Chichagova*, fasc. 1 (St. Petersburg, 1885).

[Chicherin, B. N.], "O krepostnom sostoianii," *Golosa iz Rossii*, fasc. 2 (London, 1856), pp. 139-250.

Dobroliubov, N. A., *Sobranie sochinenii*, 9 vols. (Moscow-Leningrad, 1961-1964).

Dolgorukov, P. V., *Peterburgskie ocherki*, edited with an introduction by S. V. Bakhrushin (Moscow, 1934).

Elenev, F. P., "Pervye shagi osvobozhdeniia krest'ian," *RA*, 1886, no. 7, pp. 353-404.

Fircks, Thedor von (pseud., "D. K. Schedo-Ferroti"), *Etudes sur l'avenir de la Russie: Etude I, La Liberation des paysans* (Berlin, 1858); *Etude IV: La noblesse* (Berlin, 1859).

Gagarin, kn. [I. V.], "Proekt kniazia Gagarina," *Kolokol*, no. 35 (February 1, 1859), pp. 285-287.

Gagemeister, Iu. A., "O finansakh Rossii," *Istoricheskii arkhiv*, 1956, no. 2, pp. 100-125.

Galagan, G. P., "Dva pis'ma G. P. Galagana 1859 g.," *Kievskaia starina*, September, 1895, pp. 68-70.

Geling, K. K., "K voprosu o nachale krest'ianskogo dela," *RS*, vol. LII (December 1886), pp. 545-550.

[Gersevanov, N. B.], *O sotsializme Redaktsionnykh komissii. Pis'ma k predsedateliu ikh Generalu Rostovtsevu pomeshchika E[katerinoslavskoi] gubernii* (Berlin, 1860).

Gertsen, A. I., *Sobranie sochinenii v tridtsati tomakh* (Moscow, 1954-65). The earlier edition of Herzen's works (*Polnoe sobranie sochinenii i pisem*, ed. M. Lemke, Moscow–St. Petersburg-Petrograd, 1919-1925) is still valuable for its annotation.

Gloriantov, V. I., "Nizhnii Novgorod bylogo vremeni," *RA*, 1907, no. 2, pp. 277-289.

Golubtsov, V. V., ed., "Imperator Nikolai Pavlovich v ego rechi k deputatam Sanktpeterburgskogo dvorianstva 21 marta 1848 g.," *RS*, vol. XXXIX (September 1883), pp. 593-596.

Grabbe, P. Kh., *Zapisnaia knizhka grafa P. Kh. Grabbe* (Moscow, 1888).

Haxthausen, August von, *Studies on the Interior of Russia*, ed. S. F. Starr (Chicago, 1972).

Iakushkin, P. I., "Velik bog zemli russkoi," *Russkie ocherki*, vol. II (Moscow, 1956), pp. 118-159.

"Izvlecheniia iz zhurnalov Chernigovskogo Dvorianskogo Gubernskogo komiteta . . . ," *Trudy Chernigovskoi arkhivnoi komissii*, fasc. 9 (1912), pp. 58-399.

Kavelin, K. D., "Iz pis'em K. D. Kavelina k grafu D. A. Miliutinu, 1882-1884 gg.," *Vestnik Evropy*, 1909, no. 1, pp. 5-41.

————, "K. D. Kavelin-Gertsenu" (letter of 1858), N. N. Zakhar'in, ed., *Literaturnoe nasledstvo*, vol. 62 (1955), pp. 385-387.

————, *Sobranie sochinenii*, 4 vols. (St. Petersburg, 1897-1900).

Katkov, M. N., "Pis'mo k Ia. I. Rostovtsevu," *RS*, vol. LXI (January 1889), pp. 191-193.

Kizevetter, A. A., ed., "K istorii krest'ianskoi reformy 1861 g.," *GM*, 1915, no. 2, pp. 217-233.

Kolmakov, N. M., "Krest'ianskoe delo 1857-60 gg. Zametki k Zapiskam Ia. A. Solov'eva," *RS*, vol. XLVII (September 1885), pp. 125-136.

Kokorev, V. [A.], "Vospominaniia davnoproshedshego," *RA*, 1885, no. 9, pp. 154-157; no. 10, pp. 263-272.

Korf, M., "Imperator Nikolai v soveshchatel'nykh sobraniiakh," *SbIRIO*, vol. XCVIII (1896), pp. 101-287.

Koshelev, A. I., *Zapiski Aleksandra Ivanovicha Kosheleva* (Berlin, 1884).

[Koshelev, A. I.], *Deputaty i Redaktsionnye kommissii po krest'ianskomu delu* (Leipzig, 1860).

————, "Pis'mo deputata pervogo prizyva," ed. A. Popel'nitskii, *RS*, vol. CXLV, (February 1911), pp. 344-362.

Krylov, N. A. "Nakanune velikikh reform (lichnye vospominaniia)," *Istoricheskii vestnik*, vol. XCIII (September 1903), pp. 786-821.

Lamanskii, E. I., "Iz vospominanii Evgeniia Ivanovicha Lamanskogo," *RS*, vol. CLXI (January-March 1915), pp. 73-84, 367-375, 576-589.

Lebedev, K. N. "Iz zapisok senatora K. N. Lebedeva," *RA*, 1888, no. 10, pp. 249-270; 1893, no. 4, pp. 337-399; 1897, no. 8, pp. 633-655.

Levshin, A. I., "Dostopamiatnye minuty v moei zhizni. Zapiska . . . ," *RA*, 1885, no. 8, pp. 475-558.

[Levshin, A. I.], "Istoricheskaia zapiska o raznykh predpolozheniiakh po predmetu osvobozhdeniia krest'ian," in P. Bartenev, ed., *Deviatnadtsatyi vek. Istoricheskii sbornik* (Moscow, 1872), vol. II, pp. 145-208.

Kn. D. L. [L'vov?], *Osvobozhdenie krest'ian cherez posredstvo likvidatsionnykh uezdnykh kontor,* Leipzig, n. d. (1859?).

Markov, E., "Nikolai Karlovich Ruttsen, † 6-ogo dek. 1880 g.," *RS*, vol. XXXIII (March 1882), pp. 597-624.

Materialy Cherkasskogo—see O. N. Trubetskaia, ed., *Materialy dlia biografii Materialy dlia istorii uprazdneniia krepostnogo sostoianii pomeshchich'ikh krest'ian v Rossii v tsarstvovanii Imperatora Aleksandra II.* [D. P. Khrushchov, comp.?], 3 vols. (Berlin, 1860-1862).

McKitrick, E. L., ed., *Slavery Defended* (Englewood Cliffs, N.J., 1963).

[Mel'gunov, N. A.], "Mysli vslukh ob istekshem tridtsatiletii Rossii," *Golosa iz Rossii*, fasc. 1 (1856), pp. 62-151.

Menshikov, A. S., *Dnevnik kniazia A. S. Men'shikova, 1858-1865 gg.*, TsGAOR, *f.* 728, *op*, 1, *d.* 2538a.

Miliutin, D. A., "Pis'ma (grafa) D. A. Miliutina k kniaziu A. I. Bariatinskomu," A. L. Zisserman, ed., *RA*, 1889, no. 2, pp. 297-324.

Miliutin, N. A., "Tri pis'ma N. A. Miliutina," *RS*, vol. XXVII (February 1880), pp. 388-392.

Miliutina, M. A., "Iz zapisok Marii Aggeevny Miliutinoi," *RS*, vol. XCVII, pp. 39-65, 265-288, 575-601; vol. XCVIII, pp. 105-27 (January-April, 1889).

Ministerstvo vnutrennikh del, Zemskii otdel, *Sbornik pravitel'stvennikh rasporiazhenii po ustroistvu byta krest'ian, vyshedshikh iz krepostnoi zavisimosti,* vol. I (for 1857-1860), 3rd ed. (St. Petersburg, 1869).

Morokhovets, E. A., ed., *Krest'ianskoe dvizhenie 1827-1869* (Moscow, 1931).

"Moskovskii komitet: Glavnye osnovaniia priniatye Moskovskim komitetom po krest'ianskomu delu, nachavshim zasedaniia svoi s 26 aprelia 1858 g.," N.P. Ogarev, ed., *Kolokol*, no. 30/31, pp. 242-249; no. 32/33, pp. 265-271; no. 34, pp. 276-279; no. 35, pp. 281-285.

Mukhanov, V. A., "Iz dnevnykh zapisok V. A. Mukhanova," *RA*, 1896, nos. 10-12, pp. 161-199, 327-336, 547-568.

Murav'ev, M. N., "Pis'ma k A. A. Zelenomu, 1857-62," *GM*, 1914, no. 11, pp. 212-234.

Nikiforov, D[mitrii Ivanovich?], *Moskva v tsarstvovanie imperatora Aleksandra II. Vospominaniia D. Nikiforova* (Moscow, 1904).

Nikitenko, A. V., *Dnevnik*, 3 vols. (Moscow, 1955).

Nikotin, I. A., "Iz zapisok," *RS*, vol. CIX (January-March, 1902), pp. 71-86, 353-374, 509-527.

Obolenskii, D. A., "Moi vospominaniia o Velikoi Kniagine Elene Pavlovne," part III, *RS*, vol. CXXXVIII (April 1909), pp. 37-62.

Okun', S. B., ed., *Krest'ianskoe dvizhenie v Rossii v 1850-1856 gg. Sbornik dokumentov* (Moscow, 1962).

_____ and K. V. Sivkov, eds., *Krest'ianskoe dvizhenie v Rossii v 1857-mae 1861 gg.: Sbornik dokumentov* (Moscow, 1963).

Orlov-Davydov, V. P. [Otvet na zapisku Gen. Ad' 'iut. Ia. I. Rostovtsev, "O proekte polozheniia komiteta Simbirskoi gub."], *ORGBL, f.* 219, *karton* 80, *d.* 15.

_____ , "Rech' skazannaia pri postanovlenii Orlovskogo dvorianstva poslat' adres na vysochaishee imia," *ORGBL, f.* 219, *karton* 80, *d.* 19.

_____ , "Slova proiznesennye Grafom Orlovym-Davydovym v gubernskom sobranii [Peterburgskoi gubernii] 16 marta [1860]," *ORGBL, f.* 219, *karton* 80, *d.* 24.

_____ , [Zamechaniia na reskript Aleksandra II Nazimovu ot 20/XI/57], *ORGBL, f.* 219, *karton* 80, *d.* 6.

[Orlov-Davydov, V. P.], *Lettre d'un député de comité à monsieur le président de la Commission de Rédaction, Aide de camp général Rostovtzoff* (Paris, 1859).

_____ , "O darovannom krest'ianam prave vykupit' v svoiu sobstvennost' ikh usadebnuiu osedlost' i o predostavlenii v ikh pol'zovanie kolichestva zemli za obrok ili rabotu otbyvaemuiu pomeshchiku," *ORGBL, f.* 219, *karton* 80, *d.* 7.

_____ , *Réflexions prealables sur les bases proposées au mode de l'emancipation des serfs en Russie, par un député d'un comité provincial* (Paris, 1859).

Panaev, A. A., "Kniaz' Aleksandr Sergeevich Menshikov v rasskazakh byvshego ego ad"iutanta Arkadiia Aleksandrovicha Panaeva," *RS,* vol. XIX (August 1877), pp. 617-649.

Pavlov, N. N., "Redaktsionnye komissii 1859-60 godov (Otryvki iz vospominanii)," *Istoricheskii vestnik,* vol. LXXXVI (November 1901), pp. 515-529.

Pipes, R. E., ed. and trans., *Karamzin's Memoir on Ancient and Modern Russia: A Translation and an Analysis* (Cambridge, Mass., 1959).

Podvysotskii, V. O., "Otchet deputata ot bol'shinstva Chernigovskogo Komiteta po krest'ianskomu delu o deistviiakh po vozlozhennym obiazannostiam v S.-Peterburge," *Trudy Chernigovskoi arkhivnoi komissii,* fasc. 9 (1912), pp. 400-411.

Pogodin, M. P., *Istoriko-politicheskie pis'ma: Sochineniia,* vol. IV (Moscow, 1874).

Pokorskii-Zhoravko, A. I., "Pis'ma . . . k zhene . . . ," *Trudy Chernigovskoi uchenoi arkhivnoi komissii,* fasc. 11 (1915), pp. 52-104.

Popel'nitskii, A., ed., "Fed. Lavr. Barykov o chlenakh Glavnogo komiteta po krest'ianskomu delu," *GM,* 1916, no. 11, pp. 207-208.

Pozen, M. P., *Bumagi po krest'ianskomu delu* (Dresden, 1864).

Predtechenskii, A. V., ed., *Krest'ianskoe dvizhenie v Rossii v 1826-1849 gg.: Sbornik dokumentov* (Moscow, 1961).

Pushkin, A. S., *Sobranie sochinenii,* 10 vols. (Moscow, 1962).

"R," ed., "Na zare krepostnoi svobody: Materialy dlia kharakteristiki obshchestva," *RS,* vol. XCII, pp. 5-35, 225-250, 449-476; vol. XCIII, pp. 73-96, 263-280, 465-490; vol. XCIV, pp. 49-71 (October 1897-April 1898). No more published; the remaining installments are not to be found in the archive of *RS* in the Pushkinskii dom.

Redaktsionnye komissii, *Pervoe izdanie materialov . . .* (see list of abbreviations).

[Redaktsionnye komissii . . .], *Sbornik postanovlenii po ustroistvu byta pomeshchich'ikh krest'ian za 1857 i 1858 gody* (St. Petersburg, 1859).

Rieber, Alfred J., ed., *The Politics of Autocracy: Letters of Alexander II to Prince A. I. Bariatinskii, 1857-64* (Etudes sur l'histoire, l'économie et la sociologie des pays slaves, XII) (Paris and The Hague, 1966).

Roshchakhovskii, K. A., "Memuary K. A. Roshchakhovskogo vremeni osvobozhdeniia krest'ian," *Kievskaia starina*, 1887, no. 6/7, pp. 396-450.

Rostovtsev, Ia. I., "Dva dokumenta iz bumag general-ad"iutanta Iakova Ivanovicha Rostovtseva," ed. F. P. Elenev, *RA*, 1873, no. 1, pp. 449-513.

————— , "K istorii osvobozhdeniia krest'ian (Perepiska Ia. I. Rostovtseva s kniazem E. P. Obolenskim), *RS*, vol. CIV (November 1900), pp. 367-378.

Saltykov, M. E. ("N. Shchedrin"), *Sobranie sochinenii v dvadtsati tomakh* (Moscow, 1965-ff.).

Samarin, Iu. F., *Sochineniia Iu. F. Samarina*, 8 vols. (Moscow, 1878-1911).

Sbornik postanovlenii i rasporiazhenii po tsenzure s 1720 po 1862 g. (St. Petersburg, 1862).

Selivanov, I. V., "Zapiski dvorianina-pomeshchika," *RS*, vol. XXVIII, pp. 289-316, 477-484, 725-752; vol. XXIX, pp. 851-882; vol. XXXI, pp. 531-546; vol. XXXIII, pp. 625-636 (June 1880-March 1882).

Semenov, N. P., *Osvobozhdenie krest'ian v tsarstvovanie imperatora Aleksandra II: Khronika deiatel'nosti komisii po krest'ianskomu delu*, 3 vols. in 4 plus index (St. Petersburg, 1889-1893).

Semenov-Tian-Shanskii, P. P., *Epokha osvobozhdeniia krest'ian v Rossii (1857-61) v vospominaniiakh P. P. Semenov-Tian-Shanskogo*, 2 vols. (St. Petersburg, 1911-1916).

Shidlovskii, D. N., "Zapiska . . . ministru vnutrennikh del S. S. Lanskomu," July 5, 1858, in N. K. Piksanov and O. V. Tsekhnovitser, eds., *Shestidesiatye gody* (Moscow-Leningrad, 1940), pp. 383-385.

Sinel'nikov, N. P., "Zapiski senatora N. P. Sinel'nikova," *Istoricheskii vestnik*, vol. LIX (1895), pp. 721-736.

Skrebitskii, A. I., ed., *Krest'ianskoe delo v tsarstvovanie Imperatora Aleksandra II. Materialy dlia istorii osvobozhdeniia krest'ian. Gubernskie komitety, ikh deputaty i Redaktsionnye komissii v krest'ianskom dele*, 4 vols. in 5 (Bonn/R., 1862-1868; all vols. in fact published in 1868).

Sofronenko, K. A., ed., *Krest'ianskaia reforma v Rossii 1861 g.: Sbornik zakonodatel'nykh aktov* (Moscow, 1954).

Solov'ev, Ia. A., "Krest'ianskoe delo v 1856-59 gg.: otryvok iz Zapisok senatora, tainogo sovetnika Ia. A. Solov'eva," *RS*, vol. XXVII (February 1880), pp. 347-360.

————— , "Zapiski senatora Ia. A. Solov'eva," *RS*, vol. XXX, pp. 213-246, 721-756; vol. XXXI, pp. 1-32; vol. XXXIII, pp. 227-258, 561-596; vol. XXXIV, pp. 105-154, 389-426; vol. XXXVI, pp. 131-154, 221-252; vol. XXXVIII, pp. 259-290, 579-614; vol. XLI, pp. 241-276, 575-608 (February 1881-March 1884). A posthumous publication; the concluding chapter or chapters promised by the editors never appeared and are not in the archive of *RS* at the Pushkinskii dom in Leningrad.

For Alexander II's comments, see "Zametki k zapiskam senatora Solov'eva," *RS*, vol. XXX (March 1881), pp. 903-905.

Speranskii, M. M., "O korennykh zakonakh gosudarstva" (1802), *Proekty i zapiski*, S. N. Valk, ed. (Moscow-Leningrad, 1961), pp. 28-55.

Stremoukhov, P. D., "Nizhegorodskii gubernator A. N. Murav'ev," *RS*, vol. CVI (May 1901), pp. 349-361.

————, "Zametka odnogo iz deputatov pervogo prizyva," *RS*, vol. CII (May 1900), pp. 139-144.

Tatarinov, A. N., "Iz perepiski deiatelei epokhi osvobozhdeniia krest'ian," *Russkaia mysl'*, 1911, no. 3, pp. 106-116.

Terner, F. G., *Vospominaniia zhizni*, 2 vols. (St. Petersburg, 1910-1911).

Timashev, A. E., "K istorii raskreposhcheniia pomeshchich'ikh krest'ian," *RA*, 1887, no. 6, pp. 259-262.

Tiutcheva, A. F. *Pri dvore dvukh imperatorov; Dnevnik, 1855-82* (Moscow, 1929).

Troinitskii, A. G., "Iz bumag A. G. Troinitskogo. Zapiski ego ob uchastii periodicheskoi literatury v obsuzhdenii i razreshenii krest'ianskogo voprosa," *RA*, 1896, no. 7, pp. 373-388.

————, *Krepostnoe naselenie v Rossii po 10-oi narodnoi perepisi. Statisticheskoe issledovanie* (St. Petersburg, 1861).

Trubetskaia, O. N., ed., *Materialy dlia biografii kn. V. A. Cherkasskogo*, 2 vols. (Moscow, 1901-1904). Vol. II is entitled *Kn. V. A. Cherkasskii i ego uchastie v razreshenii krest'ianskogo voprosa. Materialy dlia biografii.*

Trubetskoi, S. P., *Zapiski kniazia S. P. Trubetskogo* (St. Petersburg, 1906).

Turgenev, I. S., *Polnoe sobranie sochinenii i pisem*, 28 vols. (Moscow, 1960-1968).

[Turgenev, N. I.], *O sile i deistvii reskripta 20 noiabria 1857 goda (Russkii zagranichnyi sbornik, chast' 2, tetrad' 1)* (Leipzig, 1858).

Unkovskii, A. M., "Proekt Unkovskogo," *Kolokol*, no. 39 (April 1, 1859), pp. 316-321.

————, "Zamechaniia o neobkhodimosti i pol'ze vykupa," *Russkii vestnik*, vol. XIX, no. 2 (January, 1859), pp. 112-125.

————, "Zapiski Alekseia Mikhailovicha Unkovskogo," *Russkaia mysl'*, 1906, no. 6, pp. 184-196; no. 7, pp. 88–116.

Valuev, P. A., "Dnevnik grafa Petra Aleksandrovicha Valueva," *RS*, vol. LXX, pp. 167-182, 339-349, 603-616; vol. LXXI, pp. 71-82, 265-278, 547-602; vol. LXXII, pp. 139-154, 393-459 (May-November, 1891).

————, *Dnevnik P. A. Valueva, ministra vnutrennikh del*, P. A. Zaionchkovskii, ed., 2 vols. (Moscow, 1961).

————, "Duma russkogo vo vtoroi polovine 1855 g.," *RS*, vol. LXX (May 1891), pp. 349-360.

Viktor Antonovich Artsimovich. Vospominaniia—kharakteristiki (St. Petersburg, 1904).

Volkonskii, N., "Nekotorye dannye o kniaze Sergee Vasil'eviche Volkonskom i ego otnoshenii k krest'ianskoi reforme," *Trudy Riazanskoi uchenoi arkhivnoi komissii*, vol. XX (1905), fasc. 2, pp. 123-56.

Volkonskii, S. V., "Nekotorye zamechaniia otnositel'no uluchsheniia byta pomeshchich'ikh krest'ian," *Trudy Riazanskoi uchenoi arkhivnoi komissii*, vol. VI (1891), no. 3, pp. 33-37 and no. 4/5, pp. 47–53.

Yettman, Norman, ed., *Life Under the Peculiar Institution* (New York, 1970).
Zaionchkovskii, P. A., ed., "O pravitel'stvennykh merakh dlia podavleniia narodnykh volnenii v period otmeny krepostnogo prava," *Istoricheskii arkhiv*, 1957, no. 1, pp. 151-193.
[Zhemchuzhnikov, A. M., V. M., and A. M., and Tolstoi, A. K.], "Proekt: O vvedenii edinomysliia v Rossii," *Sochineniia Koz'my Prutkova* (Moscow, 1965), pp. 163-166.

Secondary Material

Alekseev, M. P., et al., eds., *Turgenevskii sbornik*, vol. IV (Moscow, 1968).
Bakhrushin, S. V., "Velikaia kniagina Elena Pavlovna," *Osvobozhdenie krest'ian. Deiateli reformy* (Moscow, 1911), pp. 115-172.
Bakounine, Tatiana, *Le domaine des princes Kourakine dans le gouvernement de Saratov* (Paris, 1929).
Blum, Jerome, *Lord and Peasant in Russia from the Ninth to the Nineteenth Century* (Princeton, N.J., 1961).
Bochkarev, V. N., "Iz istorii pomeshchich'ego khoziaistva v Rossii serediny XIX v.," RANIION, Institut istorii, *Uchenye zapiski*, vol. IV (1929), pp. 206-217.
Bogoroditskaia, N. A. "Vnutrennii stroi krupnoi krepostnoi votchiny v pervoi polovine XIX veka (po materialam Simbirskoi votchiny gr. Orlovykh-Davydovykh)," *Uchenye zapiski Gor'kovskogo gosudarstvennogo universiteta (Seriia istoricheskaia)*, fasc. 151 (1971), pp. 3-21.
Borovoi, S. Ia., *Kredit i banki Rossii (seredina XVII v.-1861 g.)* (Moscow, 1958).
Chebaevskii, F., "Nizhegorodskii dvorianskii komitet 1858 g.," *Voprosy istorii*, 1947, no. 6, pp. 86-94.
Chernyshev, E. I., "Krest'ianskaia reforma v Kazanskoi gubernii," *Materialy po istorii Tatarii*, fasc. 1 (Kazan, 1948), pp. 366-413.
Confino, Michael, *Domaines et seigneurs en Russie vers la fin du XVIIIe siècle* (Paris, 1963).
————, *Systèmes agraires et progrès agricole. L'assolement triennal en Russie aux XVIII-XIX siècles. Etude d'économie et de sociologie rurales* (Etudes sur l'histoire, l'économie et la sociologie des pays slaves, XIV) (Paris-The Hague, 1969).
Conrad, A. H., and Meyer, J. R., *The Economics of Slavery and Other Studies in Econometric History* (Chicago, 1964).
Curtiss, J. S., *The Russian Army Under Nicholas I, 1825-1855* (Durham, N.C., 1965).
Deich, G. M., "Krest'ianstvo Pskovskoi gubernii vo vtoroi polovine XIX i v nachale XX vv.," vol. I (n. p., 1960), unpub. diss. kindly shown to me by the author.
Dobrinskaia, L. B., "Dekabrist Evgenii Obolenskii posle Sibirskoi ssylki," *Osvoboditel'noe dvizhenie v Rossii*, fasc. 2 (Saratov, 1971), pp. 33-55.
Dodge, W. R., "Abolitionist Sentiment in Russia, 1762-1855," Unpub. diss., University of Wisconsin, 1950.
Druzhinin, N. M., *Gosudarstvennye krest'iane i reforma P. D. Kiseleva*, 2 vols. (Moscow-Leningrad, 1946-1958).

_____ , "Krest'ianskoe dvizhenie 1857-61 gg. po dokumentam tsentral'-nykh istoricheskikh arkhivov SSSR," *Voprosy istochnikovedeniia*, 1961, no. 1, pp. 17-26.

_____ , "Moskovskoe dvorianstvo i reforma 1861 g.," *Izvestiia Akademii Nauk SSSR, Seriia istorii i filosofii*, vol. V, no. 1 (1948), pp. 62-78.

_____ , "Moskva i reforma 1861 g.," AN SSSR, *Istoriia Moskvy*, 8 vols. (Moscow-Leningrad, 1952-1967), IV, pp. 13-57.

_____ , "Zhurnal zemlevladeltsev, 1858-60 gg.," *Trudy Instituta istorii* (RANIION), fasc. 1 (1926), pp. 463-507; Institut istorii (RANIION), *Uchenye zapiski*, vol. II (1927), pp. 251-310.

Dzhanshiev, G. A., A. M. *Unkovskii i osvobozhdenie krest'ian* (Moscow, 1894).

_____ , *Epokha velikikh reform*, 7th ed. (Moscow, 1898).

Eidel'man, N. Ia., *Gertsen protiv samoderzhaviia. Sekretnaia politicheskaia istoriia Rossii XVIII-XIX vekov i Vol'naia pechat'* (Moscow, 1973).

El'iashevich, V. B., *Istoriia prava pozemel'noi sobstvennosti v Rossii*, 2 vols. (Paris, 1948-1951).

Emmons, T. L., *The Russian Landed Gentry and the Peasant Emancipation of 1861* (Cambridge, Eng., 1968).

Engel'gardt, N., "Tsenzura v epokhu velikikh reform," *Istoricheskii vestnik*, vol. LXXXIX, pp. 830-853; vol. XC, pp. 133-158, 575-609, 1015-1043 (March-June 1902).

Fedorov, V. A., "'Mezhevye opisaniia' 50-kh godov XIX v. kak istochnik po istorii krest'ianskogo khoziaistva v Rossii (po materialam Tverskoi gub.)," *Materialy po istorii sel'skogo khoziaistva i krest'ianstva SSSR*, VI (Moscow, 1965), pp. 213-248.

_____ , *Pomeschich'i krest'iane tsentral'no-promyshlennogo raiona Rossii kontsa XVIII-pervoi polovine XIX v.* (Moscow, 1974).

Field, D., "Kavelin and Russian Liberalism," *Slavic Review*, vol. XXXII (March 1973), pp. 59-78.

_____ , "P. V. Dolgorukov's Emigration from Russia," *Slavonic Review*, vol. XLVIII, no. 111 (1970), pp. 261-265.

_____ , *Rebels in the Name of the Tsar* (Boston, 1976).

Ford, Franklin, *Robe and Sword: the Regrouping of the French Aristocracy after Louis XIV* (Cambridge, Mass., 1962).

Fridman, M. B., "Podgotovka otmeny krepostnogo prava v Belorussii," *Uchenye zapiski Belorusskogo gosudarstvennogo universiteta*, fasc. 36: *Voprosy istorii B.S.S.R.* (Minsk, 1957), pp. 73-105.

_____ , *Otmena krepostnogo prava v Belorussii* (Minsk, 1958).

Genovese, Eugene, *The Political Economy of Slavery* (New York, 1967).

_____ , *The World the Slaveholders Made* (New York, 1970).

Gerschenkron, Alexander, "Russia: Agrarian Policies and Industrialization, 1861-1917," in *Continuity in History and Other Essays* (Cambridge, Mass., 1968), pp. 140-208.

_____ , "The Problem of Economic Development in Russian Intellectual History of the Nineteenth Century," in E. J. Simmons, ed., *Continuity and Change in Russian and Soviet Thought* (Cambridge, Mass., 1955), pp. 11-39.

Gessen, V. Iu., "Krest'ianskii vopros v pomeshchich'ikh proektakh reformy 1861 g. v Belorussii," *Istoricheskii sbornik AN SSSR*, no. 2 (Leningrad, 1934), pp. 117-168.

Goodwin, A., ed., *The European Nobility in the Eighteenth Century* (London, 1953).

Gorodetskii, M., "Ubiistvo M. A. Stakhovicha," *Istoricheskii vestnik*, vol. XV (1884), pp. 594-599.

Got'e, Iu. V., *Ocherki istorii zemlevladeniia v Rossii* (Sergeev posad, 1915).

Hartz, Louis, *The Liberal Tradition in America* (New York, 1955).

Iablochkov, M., *Istoriia dvorianskogo sosloviia v Rossii* (St. Petersburg, 1876).

Iatsevich, Andrei, *Krepostnoi Peterburg pushkinskogo vremeni* (Leningrad, 1937).

Ignatovich, I. I., "Prodovol'stvennyi vopros v pomeshchich'ikh imeniiakh nakanune osvobozhdeniia krest'ian," *GM*, 1913, no. 9, pp. 29-64; no. 10, pp. 73-107.

————, *Pomeshchich'i krest'iane nakanune ikh osvobozhdeniia*, 3rd ed. (Leningrad, 1925).

Indova, E. I., *Krepostnoe khoziaistvo v nachale XIX veka. Po materialam votchinnogo arkhiva Vorontsovykh* (Moscow, 1955).

Ivaniukov, I. [I.], *Padenie krepostnogo prava v Rossii* 2nd ed. (St. Petersburg, 1903).

Jones, Robert E., *The Emancipation of the Russian Nobility, 1762-1785* (Princeton, N.J., 1973).

Kabuzan, V. M, *Izmeneniia v razmeshchenii naseleniia Rossii v XVIII-pervoi polovine XIX v. (po materialam revizii)* (Moscow, 1971).

————, and S. M. Troitskii, "Izmeneniia v chislennosti, udel'nom vese i razmeshchenii dvorianstva v Rossii v 1782-1858 gg.," *Istoriia SSSR*, 1971, no. 4, pp. 153-169.

Kahan, Arcadius, "The Cost of 'Westernization' in Russia: The Gentry and the Economy in the Eighteenth Century," *Slavic Review*, vol XXV, 1 (March 1966), pp. 40-66.

————, "Notes on Serfdom in Eastern and Western Europe," *Journal of Economic History*, XXXIII, 1 (1973), pp. 86-99.

Kartashov, E. V., "Iz istorii obshchestvennogo dvizheniia v Tverskoi gubernii v period revoliutsionnoi situatsii kontsa 50-kh—nachala 60-kh godov XIX v.," Kh. D. Sorina et al., eds., *Iz proshlogo i nastoiashchego Kalininskoi oblasti (Istoriko-kraevedcheskii sbornik)* (Moscow, 1965), pp. 125-152.

Khromov, P. A., *Ocherki ekonomiki feodalizma v Rossii* (Moscow, 1957).

Kil'miashkin, A. E., "Podgotovka krest'ianskoi reformy v gubernskikh komitetakh (Penzenskoi, Simbirskoi, Tambovskoi gubernii)," *Issledovaniia po istorii Mordovskoi ASSR* (Nauchno-issledovatel'skii institut iazyka, literatury, istorii i ekonomiki pri Sovete ministrov Mordovskoi ASSR, *Trudy*, fasc. 40) (Saransk, 1971), pp. 182-212.

Kiniapina, N. S., "Promyshlennaia politika russkogo samoderzhaviia v gody krizisa feodal'noi sistemy," *Voprosy istorii*, 1965, no. 6, pp. 61-75.

Kitaev, V. A., *Ot frondy k okhranitel'stvu. Iz istorii russkoi liberal'noi mysli 50-60-kh godov XIX veka* (Moscow, 1972).

Kizevetter, A. A., "Vnutrenniaia politika v tsarstvovanie Nikolaia Pavlovicha," in *Istoriia Rossii v XIX veke*, izd. "Granat" (St. Petersburg, n.d.), vol. I, pp. 169-231.

Kliuchevskii, V. O., *Sochineniia*, 8 vols. (Moscow, 1956-1959).

Korelin, A. P., "Dvorianstvo v poreformennoi Rossii," *Istoricheskie zapiski*, no. 87 (1971), pp. 91-173.

Korf, S. A., *Dvorianstvo i ego soslovnoe upravlenie za stoletie, 1762-1855 godov* (St. Petersburg, 1906).

Kornilov, A. A., "Gubernskie komitety 1858-1859 gg.," *Ocherki po istorii obshchestvennogo dvizheniia i krest'ianskogo dela v Rossii* (St. Petersburg, 1905), pp. 119-312.

_____, "Iz istorii krepostnogo khoziaistva v Rossii," *Nauchnyi istoricheskii zhurnal*, no. 5 (1914) (vol. II, no. 3), pp. 30-53.

_____, *Krest'ianskaia reforma* (St. Petersburg, 1905).

_____, "Krest'ianskaia reforma v Kaluzhskoi gubernii pri V. A. Artsimoviche," *Viktor Antonovich Artsimovich. Vospominaniia—kharakteristiki* (St. Petersburg, 1904), pp. 129-404.

_____, *Obshchestvennoe dvizhenie v Rossii pri Aleksandre II* (Paris, 1905).

Koval'chenko, I. D., *Krest'iane i krepostnoe khoziaistvo Riazanskoi i Tambovskoi gubernii v pervoi polovine XIX veka* (Moscow, 1959).

_____, "K voprosu o sostoianii pomeshchich'ego khoziaistva pered otmenoi krepostnogo prava v Rossii," *Ezhegodnik po agrarnoi istorii Vostochnoi Evropy: 1959 g.* (Moscow, 1961), pp. 192-227.

_____, *Russkoe krepostnoe krest'ianstvo v pervoi polovine XIX v.* (Moscow, 1967).

_____, and L. V. Milov, "Ob intensivnosti obrochnoi formy ekspluatatsii krest'ian tsentral'noi Rossii v kontse XVIII—pervoi polovine XIX v.," *Istoriia SSSR*, 1966, no. 4, pp. 55-80.

Krechetovich, I. P., *Krest'ianskaia reforma v Orenburgskom krae (po arkhivnym dannym)*: vol. I, *Podgotovka reformy* (Moscow, 1911).

Krutikov, V. I., *Otmena krepostnogo prava v Tul'skoi gubernii* (Tula, 1956).

Lemke, M. K., *Ocherki osvoboditel'nogo dvizheniia "shestidesiatykh godov"* (St. Petersburg, 1908).

_____, *Ocherki po istorii russkoi tsenzury i zhurnalistiki XIX stoletiia* (St. Petersburg, 1904).

Leroi-Beaulieu, A., *Un homme d'état russe (Nicholas Miliutine) d'après sa correspondence inédite* (Paris, 1882).

Liashchenko, P. I., *History of the National Economy of Russia to the 1917 Revolution*, trans. L. H. Herman (New York, 1949).

_____, *Poslednii sekretnyi komitet po krest'ianskomu delu. 3 ianvaria 1857 g.—16 fevralia 1858 g. (po materialam Arkhiva Gosudarstvennogo soveta)* (St. Petersburg, 1911).

Lincoln, W. B., "The Circle of the Grand Duchess Yelena Pavlovna, 1847-61, *Slavonic Review*, vol. XLVIII, no. 112 (1970), pp. 373-388.

_____, "The Karlovka Reform," *Slavic Review*, vol. XXVII (September 1969), pp. 463-470.

Linkov, Ia. I., *Ocherki istorii krest'ianskogo dvizheniia v Rossii v 1825-1861 gg.* (Moscow, 1952).

Litvak, B. G., *Russkaia derevnia v reforme 1861 goda. Chernozemnyi tsentr 1861-1895 gg.* (Moscow, 1972).

Madariaga, Isabel de, "Catherine II and the Serfs: A Reconsideration of Some Problems," *Slavonic Review*, vol. LII, no. 126 (January 1974), pp. 34-62.

Mezhov, V. I., *Krest'ianskii vopros v Rossii. Polnoe sobranie materialov dlia istorii krest'ianskogo voprosa na iazykakh russkom i inostrannykh, napechatannykh v Rossii i za granitseiu, 1764-1864* (St. Petersburg, 1865).

Milov, L. V., "Paradoks khlebnykh tsen i kharakter agrarnogo rynka Rossii v XIX veke," *Istoriia SSSR*, 1974, no. 1, pp. 48-63.

Miliukov, P. N., *Ocherki po istorii russkoi kul'tury*, 3 vols. in 4 (Paris, 1930-1937).

Monas, Sidney, *The Third Section* (Cambridge, Mass., 1961).

Moore, Barrington, *Social Origins of Dictatorship and Democracy: Lord and Peasant in the Making of the Modern World* (Boston, Mass., 1966).

Morokhovets, E. A., ed., *Krest'ianskaia reforma 1861 g.* (Gosudarstvennaia biblioteka im. V. I. Lenina: *Zapiski otdela rukopisei*, fasc. X) (1941).

Nasonov, A. N., "Iz istorii krepostnoi votchiny XIX veka v Rossii," *Izvestiia AN SSSR*, series VI, 1926, no. 7/8, pp. 499-526.

————, "Khoziaistvo krupnoi votchiny nakanune osvobozhdeniia krest'-ian v Rossii," *Izvestiia AN SSSR*, series VII, no. 4/7, 1928, pp. 343-374.

Nechkina, M. V. et al., eds., *Revoliutsionaia situatsiia v Rossii v 1859-1861 gg.* [fasc. I-VI] (Moscow, 1960-1974).

Netting, Anthony, "Russian Liberalism: The Years of Promise, 1842-55," unpub. diss., Columbia University, 1967.

Neupokoev, V., "Podgotovka 'krest'ianskoi' reformy 1861 g. v Litve (gubernskie komitety 1858 g.), *Uchenye zapiski Vil'niusskogo gosudarstven-nogo universiteta* (Seriia istoriko-filologicheskikh nauk, vyp. II), vol. VI (1955), pp. 169-212.

————, "Resheniia dvorianskikh komitetov 1857 goda v Litve o lichnom 'osvobozhdenii' krest'ian (K voprosu o nachale 'krest'ianskoi' reformy v Litve)," *Uchenye zapiski Vil'niusskogo gosudarstvennogo universiteta*, vol. I (1955), pp. 59-87.

Nikolai Mikhailovich, Velikii kniaz', *Graf Pavel Aleksandrovich Stroganov (1774-1814)*, 2 vols. (St. Petersburg, 1903.

Nifontov, S. A., "Statistika krest'ianskogo dvizheniia v Rossii 50-kh gg. XIX veka po materialam III otdeleniia," in V. K. Iatsunskii, ed., *Voprosy istorii sel'skogo khoziaistva, krest'ianstva i revoliutsionnogo dvizheniia v Rossii* (Moscow, 1961), pp. 181-188.

————, "Khoziaistvennaia kon"iunktura v Rossii vo vtoroi polovine XIX veka," *Istoriia SSSR*, 1972, no. 3, pp. 42-64.

Nol'de B. E., *Iurii Samarin i ego vremia* (Paris, 1926).

————, *Peterburgskaia missiia Bismarka, 1859-62: Rossiia i Evropa v nachale tsarstvovaniia Aleksandra II* (Prague, 1925).

Okun', S. B., *Ocherki istorii SSSR: vtoraia chetvert' XIX veka* (Leningrad, 1957).

————, and E. S. Paina, "Ukaz ot 5 aprelia 1797 i ego evoliutsiia," *Issle-dovaniia po otechestvennomu istochnikovedeniiu* (Leningrad, 1964), pp. 283-299.

Pavlenko, N. I., et al., "Perekhod Rossii ot feodalizma k kapitalizmu," in V. I. Shunkov, et al., eds., *Perekhod ot feodalizma k kapitalizmu v Rossii. Materialy vsesoiuznoi diskussii* (Moscow, 1969), pp. 5-103.

Picheta, V. I., "Vopros o perenesenii usadeb v Moskovskom gubernskom komitete po krest'ianskomu delu v 1858 g.," *Uchenye zapiski Instituta istorii (RANIION)*, vol. V (1929), pp. 195-205.

_____, "Vopros ob usadebnoi osedlosti v Moskovskom gubernskom komitete," Institut istorii (RANIION), *Uchenye zapiski*, vol. V (1929), pp. 430-459.

Pintner, W. M., *Russian Economic Policy under Nicholas I* (Ithaca, N.Y., 1967).

_____, "The Social Characteristics of the Early Nineteenth Century Russian Bureaucracy," *Slavic Review*, XXXIX, 3 (September 1970), pp. 429-443.

Pipes, Richard, *Struve: Liberal on the Left, 1870-1905* (Cambridge, Mass., 1970).

Pokrovskii, V., *Istoriko-statisticheskoe opisanie Tverskoi gubernii*, part 1 (Tver, 1879).

Pokrovskii, M. N., "Krest'ianskaia reforma," *Istoriia Rossii v XIX veke*, izd. "Granat" (St. Petersburg, n.d.), vol. III, pp. 68-179.

Polievktov, M. A., *Nikolai I. Biografiia i obzor tsarstvovaniia* (Moscow, 1918).

Popel'nitskii, A., "Delo osvobozhdeniia krest'ian v Gosudarstvennom Sovete 28 ianvaria-17 fevralia 1861 g." *Russkaia mysl'*, February 1911, pp. 126-160.

_____, "Kak priniato bylo Polozhenie 19 fevralia 1861 goda osvobozhdennymi krest'ianami," *Sovremennyi mir*, 1911, no. 2, pp. 211-234; no. 3, pp. 167-187.

_____, "'Progress'—slovo zapreshcheno," *GM*, 1916, no. 11, p. 207.

_____, "Rech' Aleksandra II moskovskomu dvorianstvu 30 marta 1856," *GM*, 1916, no. 5/6, pp. 392-397.

_____, "Sekretnyi komitet v dele osvobozhdeniia krest'ian ot krepostnoi zavisimosti," *Vestnik Evropy*, February 1911, pp. 48-70, and March 1911, pp. 127-153.

_____, "Zapreshchennyi po vysochaishemu poveleniu banket v Moskve 19 fevralia 1858 g.", *GM*, 1914, no. 2, pp. 202-212.

Popov, I. P., "Liberal'noe dvizhenie provintsial'nogo dvorianstva v period podgotovki i provedeniia reformy 1861 goda," *Voprosy istorii*, March, 1973, pp. 36-50.

Porokh, I. V., "Iz istorii bor'by tsarizma protiv Gertsena (Popytka sozdaniia anti-*Kolokola* v 1857-58 gg.," *Iz istorii obshchestvennoi mysli i obshchestvennogo dvizheniia v Rossii* (Saratov, 1964), pp. 119-146.

Povalishin, A. D., *Riazanskie pomeshchiki i ikh krepostnye. Ocherki iz istorii krepostnogo prava v Riazanskoi gubernii v XIX stoletii* (Riazan', 1903).

Predtechenskii, A. V., *Ocherki obshchestvenno-politicheskoi istorii Rossii v pervoi chetverti XIX veka* (Moscow-Leningrad, 1957).

Presniakov, A. E., "Samoderzhavie Aleksandra II," *Russkoe proshloe*, 1923, no. 3, pp. 3-20.

Raeff, M., "L'etat, le gouvernement et la tradition politique en Russie imperiale avant 1861," *Revue d'Histoirie moderne et contemporaine*, October-December 1962, pp. 295-307.

_____, *Michael Speransky, Statesman of Imperial Russia*, 2nd ed. (The Hague, 1969).

————, *Origins of the Russian Intelligentsia: The Eighteenth-Century Nobility* (New York, 1966).

Riabkov, G. T., "Posevy i urozhai v pomeshchich'em i krest'ianskom khoziaistvakh v Smolenskoi gubernii v pervoi polovine XIX v.," *Ezhegodnik po agrarnoi istorii Vostochnoi Evropy, 1962* (Minsk, 1964), pp. 378-388.

Riasanovsky, Nicholas, *Nicholas I and Official Nationality in Russia, 1825-1855* (Berkeley, Calif., 1961).

Rieber, A. J., "Alexander II: A Revisionist View," *Journal of Modern History*, vol. 43, no 1 (1971), pp. 42-58.

Robinson, G. T., *Rural Russia Under the Old Regime* (New York, 1932).

Rogger, Hans, *National Consciousness in Eighteenth-Century Russia* (Cambridge, Mass., 1960).

Romanovich-Slavatinskii, A. V., *Dvorianstvo v Rossii ot nachala XVIII veka do otmeny krepostnogo prava*, 2nd ed. (Kiev, 1912).

Rozov, E. K., "O sushchnosti 'smeshannoi' formy ekspluatatsii v Tverskoi gubernii nakanune reformy 1861 g.," *Nauchnye doklady vysshei shkoly: Istoricheskie nauki*, 1958, no. 1, pp. 24-34.

————, "Oppozitsionnoe dvizhenie tverskogo liberal'nogo dvorianstva v period podgotovki i provedeniia reformy 1861 g.," A. A. Kondrashenkov, et. al., eds., *Voprosy agrarnoi istorii tsentra i severo-zapada RSFSR* (Smolensk, 1972), pp. 195-204.

Rozum, M. A., "Podgotovka krest'ianskoi reformy v tverskom komitete po uluchshenii byta pomeshchich'ikh krest'ian," *Uchenye zapiski Kalininskogo gosudarstvennogo pedagogicheskogo instituta im. M. I. Kalinina*, vol. X, fasc. 1 (1945), pp. 1-38.

Ruffman, Karl-Heinz, "Russicher Adel als Sondertypus der europäischen Adelswelt," *Jahrbücher für Geschichte Osteuropas*, N.S., vol. 9 (1961), no. 2, pp. 161-178.

Ruud, C. A., "Censorship and the Peasant Question: The Contingencies of Reform under Alexander II (1855-1859)," *California Slavic Studies*, V (1970), pp. 137-167.

Ryndziunskii, P. G., "Vymeralo li krepostnoe krest'ianstvo pered reformoi 1861 g.?" *Voprosy istorii*, 1967, no. 7, pp. 54-70.

————, "Ob opredelenii intensivnosti obrochnoi ekspluatatsii . . . ," *Istoriia SSSR*, 1966, no. 6, pp. 44-64.

Savel'ev, A. A., "Neskol'ko slov o byvshem Nizhegorodskom gubernatore A. N. Murav'eve," *RS*, vol. XCIV, pp. 609-29; vol. XCV, pp. 69-93 (June-July, 1898).

Semevskii, V. I., *Krest'ianskii vopros v Rossii v XVIII i pervoi polovine XIX stoletiia*, 2 vols. (St. Petersburg, 1888).

Seredonin, S. M., *Istoricheskii obzor deiatel'nosti Komiteta ministrov*, 3 vols. in 5 (St. Petersburg, 1902).

Shiriaev, V. N., "Iaroslavskii gubernskii komitet 1858-59 gg. i sostavlennyi im proekt polozheniia ob ustroistve byta pomeshchich'ikh krest'ian," *Trudy Iaroslavskoi uchenoi arkhivnoi komissii*, book 6, fasc. 2 (Iaroslavl', 1912), pp. 3-56.

Sivkov, K. V., "Biudzhet krupnogo sobstvennika-krepostnika pervoi treti XIX v.," *Istoricheskie zapiski*, no. 9 (1940), pp. 124-153.

_____ , *Ocherki po istorii krepostnogo khoziaistva v Rossii v pervoi polovine XIX veka* (Moscow, 1951).

Skabichevskii, A. M., *Ocherki istorii russkoi tsenzury (1700-1865 g.)* (St. Petersburg, 1892).

Sladkevich, N. G., *Ocherki istorii obshchestvennoi mysli Rossii v kontse 50-kh— nachale 60-kh godov XIX veka* (Leningrad, 1962).

Snezhnevskii, V. I., "Krepostnye krest'iane i pomeshchiki Nizhegorodskoi gubernii nakanune reformy 19 fevralia i [sic] pervye gody posle nee," *Deistviia Nizhegorodskoi uchenoi arkhivnoi komissii: Sbornik*, vol. III (St. Petersburg, 1902), pp. 57-86.

Starr, S. F., *Decentralization and Self-Government in Russia, 1830-1870* (Princeton, N.J., 1972).

Struve, P. B., *Krepostnoe khoziaistvo. Issledovaniia po ekonomicheskoi istorii Rossii v XVIII i XIX vv.* (n.p., 1913).

Suvorov, P. P., "Dva senatora," *Istoricheskii vestnik*, vol. LXXIX (1900), pp. 623-630.

Tatishchev, S. S., *Imperator Aleksandr II. Ego zhizn' i tsarstvovanie*, 2 vols. (St. Petersburg, 1903).

Tikhonov, N., "K kharakteristike dvorianskoi ideologii nakanune padeniia krepostnogo stroia (iz istorii Khar'kovskogo gubernskogo komiteta)," *Naukovi zapiski ukrains'koi kulturi*, no. 6 (1927), pp. 225-246.

Tsagolov, N. A., *Ocherki russkoi ekonomicheskoi mysli perioda padeniia krepostnogo prava* (Moscow, 1956).

Ulashchik, N. N., "Iz istorii reskripta 20 noiabria 1857 g.," *Istoricheskie zapiski*, vol. 28 (1949), pp. 164-181.

_____ , "Podgotovka krest'ianskoi reformy 1861 g. v Litve i Zapadnoi Belorossii," *Istoricheskie zapiski*, vol. 33 (1950), pp. 67-91.

_____ , *Predposylki krest'ianskoi reformy 1861 g. v Litve i Zapadnoi Belorussii* (Moscow, 1965).

_____ , "Vvedenie obiazatel'nykh inventarei v Belorussii i Litve," *Ezhegodnik po agrarnoi istorii Vostochnoi Evropy: 1958 g.* (Tallin, 1959) pp. 256-277.

Velikaia reforma. Russkoe obshchestvo i krest'ianskii vopros v proshlom i nastoiashchem, A. K. Dzhivelegov, S. P. Mel'gunov, and V. I. Picheta, eds., 6 vols. (Moscow, 1911).

Vvedenskii, R. M., "Kharakter pomeshchich'ei ekspluatatsii i biudzhety obrochnykh krest'ian v 20-40-e gody XIX v.," *Istoriia SSSR*, 1971, no. 3, pp. 44-57.

Vengerov, S. A., ed., *Glavnye deiateli osvobozhdeniia krest'ian* (St. Petersburg, 1903).

Wortman, Richard, "Judicial Personnel and the Court Reform of 1864," *Canadian Slavic Studies*, III, 2 (1969), pp. 224-234.

Yaney, George L., *The Systematization of Russian Government: Social Evolution in the Domestic Administration of Imperial Russia, 1711-1905* (Urbana, Ill., 1973).

Zaionchkovskii, P. A., *Kriziz samoderzhaviia na rubezhe 1870-1880-kh godov* (Moscow, 1964).

_____ , *Otmena krepostnogo prava v Rossii*, 3rd ed. (Moscow, 1968).

_____ , *Provedenie v zhizn' krest'ianskoi reformy 1861 g.* (Moscow, 1958).

————, "Vysshaia biurokratiia nakanune Krymskoi voiny," *Istoriia SSSR*, 1974, no. 4, pp. 154-164.

Zablotskii-Desiatovskii, A. P., *Graf P. D. Kiselev i ego vremia*, 4 vols. (St. Petersburg, 1882).

Zak, I., "K istorii krepostnogo khoziaistva," *Istorik-Marksist*, no. 17 (1930), pp. 51-68.

Zakharova, L. G., "Dvorianstvo i pravitel'stvennaia programma otmeny krepostnogo prava v Rossii," *Voprosy istorii*, 1973, no. 9, pp. 32-51.

————, "Pravitel'stvennaia programma otmeny krepostnogo prava v Rossii," *Istoriia SSSR*, 1975, no. 2, pp. 22-47.

Zelnik, R. E., *Labor and Society in Tsarist Russia: The Factory Workers of St. Petersburg, 1855-1870* (Stanford, Calif., 1971).

Index

Russian Research Center Studies

*Out of print.
†Publications of the Harvard Project on the Soviet Social System.